SKI
RESORTS
OF
NORTH AMERICA

FODOR'S TRAVEL GUIDES

are compiled, researched, and edited by an international team of travel writers, field correspondents, and editors. The series, which now almost covers the globe, was founded by Eugene Fodor in 1936.

OFFICES
New York & London

Fodor's Ski Resorts of North America:

Editor: Andrew E. Beresky
Coordinating Editor: Guy Thibeadeau
Area Editors: Don Bilodeau, Diana Hunt, Guy Thibeadeau, Sara Widness
Drawings: Diana Huff
Maps: Burmar, Mark Stein Studios, Pictograph

SKI
RESORTS
OF
NORTH AMERICA

FODOR'S TRAVEL GUIDES
New York & London

The following Fodor's Guides are current; most are also available in a British edition published by Hodder & Stoughton.

Country and Area Guides	**City Guides**	
Australia, New Zealand & the South Pacific	Amsterdam	New Mexico
Austria	Beijing, Guangzhou, Shanghai	New York State
Bahamas	Boston	Pacific North Coast
Belgium & Luxembourg	Chicago	South
Bermuda	Dallas & Fort Worth	Texas
Brazil	Greater Miami & the Gold Coast	U.S.A.
Canada	Hong Kong	Virginia
Canada's Maritime Provinces	Houston & Galveston	
Caribbean	Lisbon	**Budget Travel**
Central America	London	
Eastern Europe	Los Angeles	American Cities (30)
Egypt	Madrid	Britain
Europe	Mexico City & Acapulco	Canada
France	Munich	Caribbean
Germany	New Orleans	Europe
Great Britain	New York City	France
Greece	Paris	Germany
Holland	Philadelphia	Hawaii
India, Nepal & Sri Lanka	Rome	Italy
Ireland	San Diego	Japan
Israel	San Francisco	London
Italy	Singapore	Mexico
Japan	Stockholm, Copenhagen, Oslo, Helsinki & Reykjavik	Spain
Jordan & the Holy Land	Sydney	**Fun Guides**
Kenya	Tokyo	
Korea	Toronto	Acapulco
Mexico	Vienna	Bahamas
New Zealand	Washington, D.C.	Las Vegas
North Africa		London
People's Republic of China	**U.S.A. Guides**	Maui
Portugal		Montreal
Province of Quebec	Alaska	New Orleans
Scandinavia	Arizona	New York City
Scotland	California	The Orlando Area
South America	Cape Cod	Paris
South Pacific	Chesapeake	Puerto Rico
Southeast Asia	Colorado	Rio
Soviet Union	Far West	St. Martin/Sint Maarten
Spain	Florida	San Francisco
Sweden	Hawaii	Waikiki
Switzerland	I–95: Maine to Miami	
Turkey	New England	**Special-Interest Guides**
Yugoslavia		
		Selected Hotels of Europe
		Ski Resorts of North America
		Views to Dine by around the World

CONTENTS

FOREWORD

There is nothing that beats the thrill of a skiing vacation, with the possible exception of preparing your trip, planning where to go.

In North America, we are blessed with some of the best skiing in the world. Some of our peaks are up to 12,000 feet high with as much as 4,000 vertical feet of skiable terrain. The powder in Utah and the Bugaboos of British Columbia are legendary. Skiers come from all over the world to experience "Champagne Powder" and "White Smoke," the epitome of snow quality.

The diversity of skiing on this continent is also unmatched elsewhere. There are nearly 1,000 ski areas in the U.S. and Canada, many offering cross-country in addition to alpine skiing. There's something for everyone, and there's skiing almost everywhere. Only nine American states do not have alpine skiing. Even Hawaii has skiing on Mauna Kea in January and February. And in Canada where, contrary to common belief, you can't ski in the summer, all provinces have a good choice of alpine centers.

Skiing in North America also comes with flair, from skiing á la Francaise in Quebec to cowboy skiing in the American West. Après-ski runs the gamut from guitar pickin' in New England to big-time stage productions and international entertainment in the Lake Tahoe region.

Fodor's Ski Resorts of North America is designed to help you plan your own ski trip based on your time, your budget, your energy, and your idea of what the trip should be. Perhaps after having read this guide you'll have some new ideas.

This guide does not claim to list all ski areas in North America. Rather, we have tried to select those areas we feel offer the most attractions for a skiing vacation. The areas were chosen for being among the best destinations or for their importance as day-trip areas near major metropolises. The choices were not easy, and you may not find your favorite local ski area included.

All selections and comments in *Fodor's Ski Resorts of North America* are based on personal experience. some hard choices had to be made about what to include in this guide, since no one book can possibly cover all there is to see and do in all the ski areas on this continent. We feel that our first responsibility is to inform and protect you, the reader.

Errors are bound to creep into any travel guide, however. Much change can and will occur even while the book is on press, and also during the year that this edition is on sale.

We sincerely welcome letters from our readers on these changes, or from those whose opinions differ from ours, and we are ready to revise our entries for next year's edition when the facts warrant it.

Send your letters to the editors at *Fodor's Travel Guides*, 2 Park Avenue, New York, NY 10016. European or British Commonwealth readers may prefer to write to *Fodor's Travel Guides*, 9–10 Market Place, London W1N 7AG, England.

FACTS AT YOUR FINGERTIPS

 **PLANNING YOUR SKI VACATION.** The best favor you can do for yourself when you decide to take a ski vacation is to take the time to plan it well. We all know that if you throw enough money at something it will correct itself, but most of us are not that fortunate and planning is important. Here are some considerations to bear in mind as you make your plans.

Who's Going. Your companions will have a major impact on just about every aspect of your ski vacation. If you go alone or with your friend or mate, you'll probably have a little more money available to spend. You'll probably be more happy in a full service hotel where you will spend the minimum amount of time housekeeping and the most time skiing and having a good time. However if you are planning for a family, and you'll be traveling with children some additional considerations come into play.

Traveling. Traveling may be half the fun of a vacation. However, carrying skis, boots, paraphernalia, and luggage from car to plane to bus while keeping track of young children can make traveling an ordeal if the trip too long or not properly planned. Selecting an area that will require the fewest transfers en route is an important consideration.

Areas relatively close to major airports should be considered first, especially those within a few hours flying time of your home. The more in your group, the simpler your travel arrangements should be. Check for direct flights from your home airport to the gateway city. Excellent ski gateways are Denver, Salt Lake City, Seattle, Portland, Oregon, and Montréal. From each airport you can reach a number of large destination resorts within 2 hours. Resorts such as Jackson Hole, Aspen, and Sun Valley may be great, but they require longer traveling, more transfers, and greater frustrations if you have a group in tow. The same applies to automobile travel. While the logistics are less complex, you should try to avoid those 8–10-hour drives with children. Careful planning and proper mountain selection will avoid the children's version of the Chinese water torture: "When are we going to get there?"

Choice of Mountain. One of the biggest misconceptions is that "the larger the mountain, the greater the fun." Nothing could be farther from the truth, particularly with children. Small children like small things, and while you may think that junior will have the thrill of a lifetime riding the tram at a large mountain, he in fact would quite likely be as happy—probably happier—on the T-bar and the bunny slope at a smaller area. The tremendous success of 620-foot Gray Rocks as a destination resort in the Laurentians north of Montréal is proof that big is not always better.

You may find it as much fun simply driving to Okemo from New York City, to Cannon Mountain from Boston, to Mont Ste Anne from Montréal, or to Alta from Salt Lake City than to go through the tribulations of organizing everyone for a long, sometimes complicated flight to a big-name resort.

Consider skiing skills of those in your party, also. Beginners will do better at a smaller area where they will not be overwhelmed by the mountain's size. The largest areas do cater to beginners, but the more accomplished skier will make better use of the mountain, while the novice will be limited to a certain area, often the lower slopes. And since beginners are almost always in ski school, learning on a smaller mountain can be just as rewarding as doing it on a larger and often colder and windier peak.

As you choose your mountain, take with a grain of salt a ski area's pamphlets which claim "something for everyone." There is no question that all areas have easy and difficult trails, but many areas have more of one than the other. For example, you won't want to initiate your paranoid in-law at Snowbird, Jackson Hole, or even Squaw Valley or Stowe. These mountains have reputations for macho skiing and will eat up unwary skiers. They overwhelm the first-time skier and do not help build the novice's confidence. If the first thing you must tell your group on arrival at the area is that slopes on the other side are easier, you've probably chosen the wrong area.

On the other hand, ski areas such as Winter Park, Park City, Alpine Meadows, Mount Snow, Sutton, and others, while they do have difficult runs for the advanced skier, are better suited to the beginner if only for the fact that easier runs are easily accessible from the base area.

1

Choice of Accommodation. Your choice of accommodations will depend on who's going. Singles or couples will have more leeway; families must be more selective. The larger the group, the more advantageous it is to look at the seemingly pricier condo and slopeside accommodations. Condominiums usually have room for anywhere from 4 to 10 people, and when the cost is split it usually works out quite reasonably. You'll also save a bundle on meals for children in a fully equipped condo. Getting the family organized in the morning is another consideration. Ski-in, ski-out lodging lets you come and go as you please. Depending on buses and shuttles compounds the problem of getting to the slopes and requires better planning on your part. Of course it's no secret that the closer the accommodations are to the hill, the higher the price.

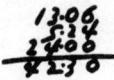 **BUDGET.** This, of course, is not necessarily the final consideration. For most of us it's a part of every aspect of planning. Your budget and availability will affect almost every move you make.

You'll pay more, of course, in high season—Christmas to New Year's as well as mid-February to mid-March, George Washington's Birthday, and in some cases Easter.

Ski packages are always your best bet if you're on a tight budget. The more included in your package price, the fewer the surprises when you get there. Find out if the tour package includes air fare (including your skis), transfer between airport and resort, accommodations, taxes and gratuities, lift tickets, meals, transport from your hotel to the slopes, and lessons.

The farther from the area, generally, the cheaper the accommodations. Condos split several ways are often cheaper than they appear at first view. Good deals can often be had at smaller inns where the overhead is smaller and the smiles often larger.

Length of stay is a direct factor in budgeting, although the longer the stay the cheaper the per-day cost of your vacation. Most resorts now offer a choice of either 2-day weekends, 3–4 day mini-ski weeks, and full-week packages. For European destinations you can often tag on an extra week for a surprisingly small amount. Excellent deals are often available at the large destination resorts for the weekend—staying over Saturday night—since ski-weekers usually leave Saturday with the new guests arriving on Sunday, leaving vacancies on Saturday night.

 **MONEY.** In the Canadian chapters of this guide, all prices are listed in Canadian dollars. The Canadian dollar, like the U.S. dollar, is divided into 100 cents, and coins and bills exist in the same denominations as in the U.S.—i.e., 1¢, 5¢, 10¢, etc.; $1, $2, $5, $10, etc.

Actual exchange rates fluctuate from day to day but the Canadian dollar is usually worth about 83 U.S. cents and about 49 British pence. In order to get the most for your money, convert it before you leave home. Waiting until you get to Canada can create problems. The banks, which are generally open only from 10 A.M. to 3 P.M. Monday through Friday, are sometimes not prepared to exchange foreign currency, and, even if you find one that will, it is not always convenient to go to a bank. Furthermore, hotels, stores, and restaurants may offer something less than the best rate. The best policy is to find the nearest Deak-Perera foreign exchange office. There are Deak bureaus in Vancouver (617 Granville); Toronto (10 King St. E. and 55 Bloor St. W.); and Montréal (1155 Sherbrooke St. W.).

There are no restrictions on the amount of money you may bring into or take out of Canada. Both Canadians and foreign visitors may convert money from Canadian tender to another currency or from a foreign currency to Canadian dollars as often as they want, in amounts as great as they want, either inside or outside Canada.

PACKAGE DEALS. Ski Shows. One of the best places for ski travel information is your local ski show, usually held in most major markets between late September and early December. These are well advertised through the local media and are always listed in the "Coming Events" columns of magazines such as *Ski, Skiing,* and *Powder* as well as in regional publications. Represented at ski shows are most of the main destination resorts accessible from your area as well as the smaller local areas where you will likely do most of your skiing. This is a great opportunity for you to talk to area representatives, people who live and ski there and know the area inside-out. It's the best way to get the inside track and find out what the brochures don't say.

Airlines and tour operators are there as well, along with independent lodges. You can shop around for the best package deal or see if you can do better by making your own arrangements with the independent lodge and tying in with a super-saver fare of some sort. Pick up the literature for the areas which might interest you and take it home for further analysis.

**AIRLINES AND TRAVEL AGENTS.** All major airlines that fly to major ski gateway airports can offer you various package options when you fly with them. Packages are available for just about anywhere in North America. Many airlines offer fly-drive options where a rental car is thrown in; this is something to consider when traveling as a group, and particularly with a family. Other ski vacations are available as ground packages that you can combine with the flight option of your choice. These are not always the cheapest, but are often the most convenient.

Ski resort brochures can give you an excellent idea of what an area is all about, but remember that sales brochures are made to sell and will always make any area look like Shangri-La. If you read between the lines, however, you'll get a good idea of what the area has to offer. A well-presented brochure with color photographs showing the most recent improvements to the area is a sure sign of a first class resort. However, if pictures are out of focus and skiers are depicted in baggie pants, you can probably surmise that the rope tow hasn't been greased in a while and that "quaint" and "rustic" are likely to be the best adjectives to describe the area.

Color trail maps in advertising brochures sometimes project a distorted picture of the area's size and slope difficulty. The use of shadows to accentuate steepness can often make trails seem much more difficult and the mountain higher than they are in reality. Check out the area's vertical rise, number of trails, and number of trails of your skiing ability. Look for a good proportion of top-to-bottom runs of your ability. There's no real sense going to a 3,000-foot mountain if your type of skiing is limited only to part of the top or part of the bottom.

Regional, state or provincial material on skiing vacations in different parts of the world is also available from state, provincial, or national tourist offices or the local chambers of commerce.

Finally, make sure your brochures and price lists are up to date. This is especially important when it comes to foreign destinations where prices are subject to fluctuations in exchange rates. What might have been a bargain two years ago could be out of your range today.

Ski Books and Magazines. Ski travel books such as this one will provide you with a wealth of information on preparing your vacation as well as on the major ski areas. They can be quite enlightening and helpful. Ski magazines such as *Ski, Skiing,* and *Powder,* will feature many destination resorts as well as some smaller, local areas. They can help convey the particular excitement and attraction of the resort with color photographs and the most current developments. They also carry travel guides and advertising with telephone numbers and addresses where you can write for more details. Local ski publications can do the same while adding information on travel opportunities in your region.

Ski Clubs. In areas far away from the mountains, ski clubs are often an excellent source of ski travel information and travel deals. Oddly enough, it seems that the farther from the snow or the mountains, the more and better the ski clubs. Some of the best are found in Miami, Chicago, and London. Here you'll meet skiers who have experienced many different resorts and their advice should help you decide on a package and an area.

You can get in touch with local ski clubs at a ski show, by looking in the Yellow Pages of your telephone book, by contacting your local ski association, through a ski shop in your region, or by asking other skiers.

ACCOMMODATIONS. Lodging can run anywhere from dormitories and bed-and-breakfasts all the way to expensive hotel suites and luxurious condominiums, and the price range is just as wide. Getting a fix on value is not always easy, as per day charges will vary with what's included and with the proximity to the lifts. There are essentially three package options:

European Plan (EP): no meals (except possibly for Continental breakfast) included

American Plan (AP): all meals included

Modified American Plan (MAP): breakfast and dinner included as part of the price (This is the most common and practical option since it is not always possible or desirable to come back from the mountain to the hotel or lodge to grab lunch.)

In some instances a ski-week package will include your lift ticket, so it's important to weigh that cost in the overall price of your stay. Some lodges also have free transportation in the way of a resort bus or hotel shuttle to the lifts and back. This is also a cost saver since it eliminates the need for a rental car.

Some places also provide free accommodations and sometimes free skiing for children under 12 when they stay in the same room as their parents.

There are several types of accommodations at North American resorts to suit all needs.

Small Inns and Lodges are what ski holidays were meant for in the first place and it's a treat to be able to enjoy them again. Don't look for color TV or exercise and video rooms here. What these places lack in modern amenities they more than make up in homey comfort, charm, and warmth. Your dealings are often directly with the owners, who are more sensitive to your needs and to your comfort. They usually serve breakfast and dinner, and in most cases you can have seconds without additional charge, a good thing after a rugged day on the mountain. They're usually quite reasonably priced and are more suited for couples or smaller families. They're not that popular with the singles crowd. However, you must beware—nowadays many so-called inns can turn out to be concrete towers.

Hotels need no particular description, There are now a wider variety of hotels popping up at the resorts, including Hiltons, Sheratons, and Holiday Inns. There is probably a need for these or they wouldn't be there in the first place, but those flashy blocks of concrete and glass always look out of place in a mountain setting. For convenience, however, they can't be beaten: color TV and phone in every room, built-in charge bar, elevators, dining rooms and coffee shops, pools, saunas, exercise and game rooms—the works.

But there are other, more alpine hotels, usually wooden structures with less than 50 rooms, that will give you the feeling of being away from it all. Hotels which have the conveniences of the larger places but not their impersonal traits are good for almost everyone, especially when rooms are equipped with kitchenettes.

Condominiums are offered almost everywhere now and there are so many different versions of condos these days—apartment-hotels, condominiums, condominiumized hotels, time-share units, etc.—that it has become in many resorts the principal form of accommodation. The condo offers you the comforts of home, and while the initial cost may seem high, it can be shared as most condos will accommodate from 4 to 10 people. Condominiums are also ideal for families. You'll save on food as you can inexpensively whip up meals for the children instead of having to pay restaurant prices. In fact, with a condo you can more or less discount your cost of eating; you'd be eating the same amount if you were home.

Reservations and Deposits. Reservations are necessary most of the time, the only exceptions being before December 15 or after the beginning of April. Remember that high season reservations are often booked long in advance with the Christmas–New Year weeks sometimes booked a full year or more ahead at the most popular resorts.

When booking your stay with a lodge, inn, or condo hotel, you'll be expected to send a deposit which will guarantee your reservation. Deposit policy varies with the establishments, but you'll be required to send 25–50 percent of the total cost of your stay when you reserve. The remainder will be payable on arrival. Be sure to find out about the hotel's payment policy: What credit cards are accepted? Will they take your personal check?

FACTS ABOUT THE REGIONS. You will find descriptions of each region and its ski areas in the pages which follow, but as an overview here is some general information to help you understand the differences between them.

EASTERN U.S.

There are well over 100 alpine ski areas in Maine, New Hampshire, Vermont, and New York alone. They range anywhere from a couple of hundred feet vertical to as much as 3,200 ft. at Whiteface, 3,060 ft. at Killington, 2,600 ft. at Sugarloaf and Sugarbush, and 2,350 ft. at Stowe. Ski season has been stretched considerably in the East, thanks to snowmaking systems which allow most areas to open at least a few trails by Thanksgiving. Some centers are out for records; at Killington, they pride themselves on being the first to open and last to close, skiing from October to June (albeit extremely limited at either end). Snowfall, like the weather, is irregular in the East, and temperature is subject to considerable fluctuation. The biggest snowfalls in the East tend to come in February and March, so snowmaking has become a critical element in guaranteeing good skiing, and the number of trails covered with machine-made snow at an area is an important factor to consider.

Early season skiing in the East is often marginal at best despite claims otherwise, but late season skiing is often the best and often when the trails are virtually empty.

Eastern snow is hard snow, but with sophisticated machine grooming trails are resurfaced daily at the major areas. While the "hard stuff" is not yet a thing of the past, you are now less likely to encounter "boiler plate" conditions.

Eastern skiing is trail skiing except for the "snowfields" at the top of Sugarloaf. Trail selection is excellent, ranging from easy, unintimidating beginners' slopes found virtually everywhere to the icy chutes of Stowe's "Front Four" and the Volkswagen-sized moguls of Killington's Bear Mountain.

Access to all Eastern U.S. resorts is mainly by automobile since there are few resorts of any size near major metropolitan areas. You should keep in mind, however, that some Northern resorts are closer to Montréal than they are to major U.S. cities. Jay Peak and Smuggler's Notch are 2 hours from Montréal; Whiteface, 90 minutes; Stowe and Sugarbush, about 2½ hours.

The size of the ski area becomes more important in the East if you plan on being there for a full week. If you can ski all the trails on your first day, you may get bored by mid-week. But anything with over 2,000 vertical feet is pretty respectable.

THE MIDWEST

This is the training ground for ski vacationers to either the West or East. One might be tempted to neglect these 400–500-ft. vertical mountains, but they play a major role in initiating new skiers. As Bill Hibbard, *Ski Magazine*'s Midwest editor, puts it, "It's not the size that counts, it's the punch." What ski areas here lack in size, they make up in quality: excellent ski schools and lots of lifts like at Boyne, Michigan, which has 11 lifts including three quadruple chairs and snowmaking on 90 percent of its slopes, all on less than 500 ft. vertical. But not all ski chalets in this region are higher than their mountains. Unless you live in the region and have a limited budget, these mountains are not your ultimate ski destination. But as for any of the larger resorts they'll do fine for anyone learning to ski and will cost you less!

THE ROCKIES

This is the region that skiers dream of: Colorado, Utah, Wyoming, New Mexico, and Idaho. Here are the country's oldest destination ski resorts and the ones with reputations as big as their mountains. Skiing here is done mostly between 5,000 ft. and 11,000 ft. with plenty of above-tree-line skiing.

With almost 40 different resorts, Colorado is the most popular destination state. Snow is usually abundant although snowmaking has appeared at several areas since the drought of the early 1980s. But snowmaking is not a staple as it is in the East. It is usually used to start areas up should natural snow not be sufficient by Thanksgiving.

Two of the country's premiere resorts, Vail and Aspen, spearhead Colorado's reputation. But rising stars such as the Winter Park–Mary Jane complex, a favorite of Denverites; the Summit County areas of Keystone, Arapahoe Basin, Breckenridge, and Copper Mountain; and the isolated but high-spirited Steamboat are solid back-ups for the leaders and are quickly developing strong reputations of their own.

Utah, although less heavily frequented, has some of the world's best powder skiing, particularly at Alta and Snowbird and to some extent at Park City and Deer Valley (which is certainly the most luxurious area in the U.S.). And with the developing Utah Interconnect—linking Park City to Snowbird via Brighton and Solitude—the state is tops for skiing. Unusual state liquor and entertainment laws, however, limit the attraction for those looking for more than great skiing.

Difficult to get to but worth every mile is Sun Valley, Idaho, the nation's first world class ski resort, which was opened in 1936 by Averell Harriman. The Sun Valley Lodge has been host to the best, the richest, the most powerful, and the most beautiful. And you can add your name to the list.

For the challenge they don't come much tougher than Jackson Hole, Wyoming, where a 66-passenger aerial tram will take you to some of the country's most devastatingly steep chutes. Skiers entering Corbett's Couloir, for example, must lower themselves from a rope anchored on the cornice or jump it with a Hail Mary!

The Rockies are unquestionably American skiing at its best and your only problem here is choosing among the wide variety of excellent resorts.

THE WEST COAST

This region is fast emerging as a force in the destination area market. It has, in fact, some of the largest ski areas in the country. Mammoth, California, although a solid 6 hours from Los Angeles, is America's busiest resort with somewhere in the vicinity of 1.5 million skier visits annually. Nestled around magnificent Lake Tahoe are half a dozen of the U.S.'s most beautiful areas, led by Squaw Valley, the site of the 1960 Winter Olympics, its neighbor Alpine Meadows, and Heavenly Valley, where a 4,000 ft. vertical makes it the area with the highest vertical drop in the country.

This is skiing in the High Sierra where it's sunny over 80 percent of the time and they measure snowfalls in feet, not inches. If God's a skier, this is where He hangs out! It is one of the few regions in the U.S. where snowmaking firms have not made any major forays. With 400–500 inches of annual snowfall in some areas, the prospects for big sales are dim.

The snow is not, however, the same "champagne powder" as that found in Utah. Because of the milder climate, Sierra snow can often be moist and heavy; some call it "Sierra Cement," but it quickly develops a good, powdery consistency. Snow comes early and leaves late, and ski areas consistently run out of skiers before they run out of snow. If you want to ski late—into June at some areas—you can't go wrong with the West Coast and the Pacific Northwest.

Entertainment around Lake Tahoe is unmatched elsewhere in the skiing world. Nightclubs in nearby Reno and Stateline on the Nevada–California border at Heavenly Valley feature top entertainment and night club acts along with gambling around every corner. All the big Las Vegas clubs are represented here as well: Harrah's, Caesar's Palace, Circus Circus, and the MGM Grand Hotel with its fabulous stage shows.

EASTERN CANADA

Although there is some alpine skiing in Ontario, much of it is "club" skiing and resembles the U.S. Midwest. Eastern Canada destination skiing is basically found in Québec. Skiing and the weather here compare quite well with the American East Coast and New England. But the big difference lies in the culture; this is French Canada, an area unlike anywhere else on this continent. Québecers call it "Skiing *à la Francaise*" and that's 75 percent of the reason skiers are drawn here. The province's highest mountains, Mont Tremblant and Mont Ste Anne, are just slightly over 2,000 vertical ft. and like other eastern centers depend heavily on snowmaking.

Ski season runs from late November to mid-April with Gray Rocks, the dean of Canadian snowmaking, always the last to shut down in mid-May. Best part of the season is mid-February to the end of March.

Here again, a favorable exchange rate for American visitors can weigh heavily in a decision of where to go for a skiing holiday.

WESTERN CANADA

In British Columbia the mountains and climate are similar to the U.S. West Coast with high mountains on the coast and somewhat smaller mountains at higher elevations in the interior. Ninety minutes north of Vancouver is Whistler-Blackcomb, a twin-peak resort that offers the highest vertical drop in North America, 5,280 ft. It is the home of summer racing camps and of Nancy Greene who with Jean Claude Killy in 1966 and '67 won the first two World Cup championships.

In the interior are several smaller but excellent areas where the snow is dry and regular and the crowds nonexistent. Ski areas like Fernie Snow Valley and Kimberley exceed 2,000 ft. vertical while Panorama at Invermere fetches 3,200 ft. These are more or less "local" areas partly because they haven't been discovered yet, partly because their winter tourist industry is not yet sufficiently developed.

On the border between British Columbia and Alberta is every skier's dream—the best helicopter skiing in the world. This is a costly proposition but one every serious skier must at least wish for. Across the Continental Divide lie the Alberta ski centers with the largest, Lake Louise, in a class by itself for all-around fine skiing. Sunshine Village near Banff is the one with the most above-tree-line skiing and the most dependable conditions. It is the last one to close, and only for lack of skiers. Canadian Rockies skiing, while less developed than in the U.S., can certainly match it slope-for-slope. And for Americans coming here the favorable exchange rate makes the trip that much sweeter.

 **ENTERING CANADA.** Customs regulations between the United States and Canada are among the most liberal in the world. Passing from one country to the other is usually a simple matter of presenting some valid and acceptable form of identification and answering a few simple questions about where you were born, where you live, why you are visiting Canada, and how long you will stay.

The identification need not be a passport, although this is certainly acceptable. You can also use a driver's license, birth certificate, draft card, Social Security card, certificate of naturalization, or resident alien ("green") card. Entry procedure for citizens of Great Britain, Australia, and New Zealand is similarly simple.

Canada allows British and American guests to bring their cars (for less than 6 months), boats or canoes, rifles and shotguns (but not handguns or automatic weapons) and 200 rounds of ammunition, cameras, radios, sports equipment, and typewriters into the country without paying any duty. Sometimes they will require a deposit for trailers and household equipment, but these are refundable when you cross back over the border. (This is to guarantee that you do not sell these items in Canada for a profit.) Needless to say, you may bring clothing, personal items, and any professional tools or equipment you need (if you work in Canada) without charge or restriction. It is also a good idea to carry your medical insurance and insurance for boats, vehicles, and personal luggage.

Some items are restricted, however. You need the contract for a rented car. And, if you are going to return home and leave behind a car you rented in the States, you have to fill out an E29B customs form. Tobacco is limited. Dogs, for hunting or pets, are duty-free, but you must bring a certificate from a veterinary inspector to prove that the dog has no communicable diseases. (Cats may enter without restriction.) All plants must be examined at the customs station to preclude the entry of destructive insects. Most important, Canadian officials are diligent in pursuing smugglers of narcotics and other illegal items.

 WHEN TO SKI. All brochures and ski area literature claim ideal skiing and weather conditions extend from November to late April or early May. However, there are definitely periods that are better than others. They wouldn't charge a premium price otherwise, would they?

It is difficult to understand the rush to get out on the boards by mid-November when snow cover is marginal, but in the East enthusiasm brings skiers out early, enticed by the first snowflakes and the cold which makes snowmaking possible. Ski areas searching for added revenues are now into promoting skiing at Thanksgiving, but a ski-week that early, unless it is to learn to ski, will only get you out in the worst part of the season. The snow is thin, machine-made snow only covers a few trails, days are short and often gray, and temperatures are getting colder. Doesn't seem like much fun, does it? On the other hand, in late March and early April when snow depths are at their highest, ski areas are in full operation, and the days longer and the sun warm and inviting, ski areas can't give their ski packages away. But anticipation is half the fun, it is said, and that's why people will pay $25 to ski a few trails at Vail in November but won't take their $5 offer to ski the whole wonderful area in late April.

Short of exceptionally favorable ski weather—meaning lots of early snow— skiing in the East before December 15 is usually dependent on the amount of machine-made snow produced. And while there may have been a good dump or two, the natural snow base is thin and you'll tear the bottom of your skis on all but the easiest runs and those with machine-made snow. By Christmas week ski areas normally have more than 50 percent of their runs open and can be considered to offer good skiing.

In the West early skiing is touch-and-go as well and depends on the timing of the first major storms which can come anytime from October to early December. However, most areas aim to open Thanksgiving on natural snow, or like everyone else, on machine-made.

January is usually a slow month for ski resorts and a good time to catch the best ski areas when they're not too busy. The snow by then is usually quite dry and powdery although temperatures are at their coldest. This is the best time to enjoy the legendary western powder, particularly in the Canadian and American Rockies and more specifically at powder heavens like Alta and Snowbird in Utah and in British Columbia's heli-skiing country.

February to mid-March are the most popular everywhere and for obvious reasons: days are getting longer, the sun's a little higher, and the snow is usually quite dependable almost everywhere. The East gets its largest snowfalls during these months and by then the West has several feet of snow covering the trails. These are the busy times at all resorts and along with Christmas the periods for which you need to make your reservations far in advance.

But from mid-March on, when skiing and weather are often at their best, bookings start dropping off and by early April you can enjoy off-season rates at most resorts. This, in the opinion of many skiers, is the best time of the year unless you're a powderhound. And it will outclass by far any of the early season skiing that is so anticipated.

The Late Season. Finally a word on very late season skiing. While several areas are always trying to push the limits of winter further and further there is a point of diminishing returns for both ski areas and skiers. After April 15 in the East, skiing becomes more of a freak show than real skiing and the areas which remain open do so more for the publicity they generate than for the great skiing they offer. Late season skiing is only good when the nights are cold enough to freeze the snow. When the nights remain well above freezing you ski in heavy corn snow and slush. Turning is difficult and if the same conditions were offered in January they would be called dangerous. So while there is a certain kick out of skiing in May or June, it's far from being good skiing.

The only exceptions to this, of course, are high-altitude areas such as Arapahoe Basin, Colorado, with a summit elevation of 12,450 ft., Snowbird at 11,000 ft., Sunshine Village, Alberta, at 9,000 ft., and Mount Bachelor and Timberline in Oregon with more than 8,500 ft. elevation. At these areas, the snow stays just about all year long.

 **PACKING YOUR BAGS.** Depending on your mode of travel, you'll be more or less restricted as to what you can bring along. But however you travel, there are some essentials you can't do without.

Essential Ski Equipment:
- Skis. Good skis are also available on a rental basis at many resorts and if space is a premium you can opt for this more costly route.
- Boots. Very important. Rental boots are never as comfortable, so don't leave yours behind.

- Poles.
- Ski goggles.

Essential Ski Clothes:
- Long johns.
- Ski socks: (3 pairs).
- Turtlenecks.
- Winter ski suit. If your ski parka is not too wild, wear it on the plane. Ski suits are bulky and not the easiest to pack.
- Lighter jacket or shell which can be worn both on warmer days and after skiing.
- Ski sweater.
- Toque or knitted stocking cap.
- Gloves. Throw in a pair of mittens if you plan to ski during the colder part of the season, light gloves for spring skiing.
- After-ski boots. Nothing is more cumbersome than footwear in your luggage, so bring only a practical type of after-ski wear you can use traveling and going out at night as well.

Now that you've prepared your most important items—the ones that will cost you the most if you have to buy them at the resort—you can start thinking of your leisure wear. Don't get too fancy. Remember that you're on vacation, and your hosts will certainly favor informality. Ski resorts seldom require formal attire. Occasionally, dining rooms in fancier hotels might require a man to wear a jacket (but never a tie) and a woman to be comparably attired, but this is rare. So unless your hotel has warned you about formal attire, or you like the look, don't bring any.

Choose your clothes so you can mix and match with relative ease. Pick your clothes among colors that can all be matched—grays and blues; browns, burgundies, and golds, etc. Avoid bringing clashing colors or a top that can only be matched with one pair of pants or one skirt.

Remember also that all ski resorts have laundry service or at least a laundromat. With two pairs of sports pants and three of everything else you'll have more than you need.

A sweatsuit, a T-shirt, and your bathing suit should also be part of the clothes you bring along on your ski vacation. Many of the resorts have indoor pools and hot tubs are the rage. A sweatsuit's great for wearing around your room, in the morning, after a shower, relaxing . . . anytime actually. And you'll need one pair of sport shoes to wear indoors.

Don't forget your toiletries—and your vitamins.

Putting it all together. A few tips on packing:

Try to pack all your clothes in one bag.

Stuff one of your ski boots with socks and underwear. Goggles go in the other. It's a good idea to keep your boots in a boot bag which can also be stuffed with your gloves, mitts, toque, etc.

Skis and poles go in the ski bag which can also be stuffed with whatever you couldn't get into your one main bag.

Now you're ready to go. Ski bag over your shoulder, boot bag in one hand, main bag in the other. You can carry everything in one load. And that's important at busy airports.

DRESSING FOR WARMTH. It's important to dress efficiently for skiing, and while fashion is of concern to many, function and warmth should not be neglected.

Choose your clothes to fit snugly but not too tight, because tight clothes will restrict movement and make you cold. You'll more often than not find better ski clothes and counseling at specialized ski shops than you would at a larger department store. You'll pay more, however, but you'll get what you need. On the other hand, if you know what you need then shopping around at the department stores will save you money. Once you have the proper outerwear, dressing up for warmth is easy.

Dress in layers. For maximum warmth, do as cross-country skiers do. By layering your clothes you trap warm air between each layer and that helps keep you warm. By dressing in layers, you can also add or remove a layer as the temperature changes.

Upper body. Start with good ski underwear. Avoid cottons which retain little warmth. Ski underwear such as the Lifa brand are a mix of polypropylene and nylon (which keeps you dry) or polypropylene and wool (which keeps you dry and warm). Next, a good turtleneck is essential. Some of the better ones have a zippered neck which allows you to open up a little when it gets warm or if you go inside at lunchtime. Make sure your T-neck is long enough at the waist and the arms. They always shrink up a little in the wash.

Next, a light-to-medium wool sweater or wool flannel shirt, depending on the temperature. In layering there is no need for heavy, bulky sweaters; thin, tightly knit ones are better. In extreme cold you might throw in a breathable shell under your ski jacket. Avoid those rubbery, air-tight shells which will only make you sweaty, clammy, and cold.

Lower body and feet. Your long johns should be of the same material as above. Some come as one-piece units, but two-part jobs are easier to deal with. If you purchase a one-piece unit buy one with a "trap"—a zippered panel at the back.

Your feet will stay warm if you have the right socks and your boots are not too tight. Here again the principle of trapping warm air comes into play. One pair of medium-weight wool socks is all you need. Make sure they are high enough to extend up the calf so they won't bunch up at the top of the boot. Keep them clean, too. This may sound funny to you, but dirt tends to block air circulation and reduce warmth.

Head. Your head is your most efficient heat control valve. Over 50 percent of your body heat escapes through the head. Wearing a toque is therefore extremely important in cold temperatures. Teenagers who ski without head cover in below zero temperatures only look smart to other teenagers who know nothing about staying warm. A good, tightly-knit wool toque ample enough to cover your ears entirely should do the job. Many toques have a polypropylene headband on the inside to prevent itching, but they still itch! A neck gaiter or a scarf are also essential to keeping your neck warm.

Hands. There's a saying, "If you can keep your extremities warm, the rest of you will be warm." Keeping your head, feet, and hands warm **is** very important; cold hands are often a factor in cold skiing. Mitts are the best as they trap the most air. Gore-Tex mitts with a good warm lining are the best. Make sure they are long enough to cover the wrists and have an elastic neck to prevent snow and cold from penetrating. Good ski gloves are also available. Unfortunately, the warmer they are the more expensive they are.

ABOUT SNOWMAKING. Many still refer to it as "artificial snow," as it was called in the early days. This conjures images of pulverized styrofoam, crushed ice, and chemically generated snowflakes engineered in some laboratory. Nothing could be further from reality.

Machine-made snow is the best and most commonly used term nowadays to define "artificial snow." In fact the only thing artificial about it is the way it is made—not by nature but by men and machine. A more apt term would be natural snow made artificially, somewhat like a test-tube baby. It's real in every way.

Machine-made snow is produced simply by blowing water through a gun at a below-freezing temperature. The air pulverizes the water into tiny droplets which freeze on contact with the air when temperatures are below freezing. There are no chemicals added or needed to make snow although areas will sometimes inject a bit of methanol to prevent freeze-up in the the air pipes.

High-tech snowmaking systems make use of computers to keep track of temperature swings, automatically controlling the amount of air needed to produce either the maximum amount of snow or the type of snow wanted.

Machine-made snow has done wonders for ski areas, particularly in the East and Midwest where snow has lately been inadequate. It has created a new standard of quality in terms of coverage. Gone are the rocks, roots, and bare and thin spots that were accepted as part of the game as late as 1980. And while snowmaking does not cover 100 percent of all mountains, the new expectations prevent ski areas from opening trails which are inadequately covered. When one or a few trails are well covered, skiers don't want to ski the rougher, thinly covered natural snow runs.

In the old days (and still today at centers where little or no snowmaking exists) trails were still opened with inadequate cover for lack of anything better. The feeling is "If you're going to open one bad trail you might as well open all of them."

In the East and Midwest, it bears repeating, snowmaking is a must. It is used to guarantee early season skiing usually around mid- to late November, in time for Thanksgiving. Just as importantly it is used extensively through the end of February or early March to build up and maintain a solid base, unaffected by the wild fluctuations of Eastern weather. It is also used to touch up areas that wear down from excess skier traffic and the continued grooming that also affects the snow.

Among the greatest users of machine-made snow in the East are Killington, Vermont, where skiing starts in late October and extends into June, and Gray Rocks, in the Laurentians north of Montréal, certainly the only 600-ft. mountain with a worldwide reputation and skiing every year into May.

Selecting a ski vacation at an Eastern area which has little or no snowmaking is the equivalent of betting on the weather. It's a 50–50 proposition.

Snowmaking, lo and behold, has even made forays into the Rockies where we have always been told that "snow is up to here . . . even up to there!" Well, as competitive and businesslike skiing has become, it only took a couple of lean years in the early 1980s for the tenders to go out for pipes and compressors. But snowmaking here is not used in the same way and is not as critical as it is in the East.

Snowmaking in the Rockies is usually at the lower elevations and is used to start up areas in late November, should there be a shortage from the clouds. It is also used to prevent having to close down and refund deposits mid-winter in the event of a disastrous year as happened in the early 80s. This way, with a few trails covered and open, ski resorts are protected.

The only areas where snowmaking is really not needed is in Utah, where Alta and Snowbird sometimes wish they had a little less snow and a bit more sun, and in the High Sierras, where annual snowfalls of 300–500 inches have proven to be quite satisfactory.

Even European resorts are looking to snowmaking as recent weather patterns in the Alps have played havoc with vacation and World Cup ski race schedules. The dependability of snowmaking has in fact been the saving grace for recent World Cup events which were made up at North American snowmaking resorts after having been canceled for lack of snow in Europe.

One last note about snowmaking: It is more resistant to warm temperatures than natural snow since it has a higher density. Natural snowflakes are star shaped while machine-made snow is more like a solid pellet. It tends to make surfaces a bit harder than natural snow but that's a small price to pay for not damaging your $400 skis.

ABOUT GROOMING. Next to snowmaking, grooming is one of the areas where ski resorts have made their biggest strides. In the 1950s and '60s skiers were still pretty much left to themselves to pack the snow. As pleasant as this may be when the snow is light and powdery, it's no fun having to move "Sierra cement" or trying to catch an edge on boiler plate.

Grooming is one of the most important components of skiing and is something ski publications should do a better job of explaining. Weather being such an important element, saying a slope is "groomed" often projects the wrong idea of what snow conditions are like to the skier unaware of the marvels of modern day technology.

Grooming tractors, "snow-cats" as they are called, cost anywhere from $100,000 to $120,000, and anything costing that much must do everything but climb trees. Attachments such as front end U-blades for pushing the snow and levelling bumps, compacter bars for packing it, powder makers for softening hard surfaces, and hydrostatically-driven snow tillers to break up the hardest surfaces all help make snow surfaces more often than not surprisingly good.

Thanks to this equipment, a mogul-covered run one day can be as flat as a pancake the next. An icy surface in the morning can be turned into a loose granular surface by afternoon.

Grooming and snowmaking is transforming the way people ski. While ungroomed runs in the past caused formidable obstacles to many, they forced skiers to ski more cautiously. You just couldn't go all-out when the moguls were as big as you were. But with today's meticulously manicured slopes skiers have literally grown wings and are negotiating even advanced runs at speeds never possible before grooming.

The nation's top areas often proudly parade in formation their fleet of Piston Bullies, Thiokols, and BR–400 Ski-Dozers, a happy mix of farm machinery and military equipment.

Next time you visit a ski area take a look at its grooming equipment, observe it a work and you'll have an even better grasp of one of the key elements which make skiing a more enjoyable experience.

 **ABOUT SAFE SKIING.** Skiing, like any other sport, has its risks. Yet overall, when ski areas take their responsibilities and skiers respect the Skier's Responsibility Code, the sport of skiing is not a dangerous activity.

The days of broken ankles and legs are far behind us now with important technological advances in skiing equipment and teaching. Sure, people still break a bone from a fall now and then, but these injuries are more and more in the minority. Nowadays injuries and skiing accidents are more often caused by the behavior of skiers.

Grooming removes moguls on on all but the steepest of runs. This reduces the impact and many of the twisting injuries which skiers often experienced when skiing under difficult conditions. But leveling runs has turned them into literal speedways. Inconsiderateness, ignorance of skiing rules, and speed have now become the major culprits in skiing injuries, many of which have become quite serious and sometimes fatal.

In planning your skiing vacation it's important for you to know and apply the rules of safe skiing endorsed by the National Ski Areas Association, Ski Industries America, and the Canadian Ski Council: the Skier's Responsibility Code.

Safety Tips. Here are more common sense suggestions endorsed by the National Ski Areas Association and Ski Industries America.

● If you overtake another skier on the slope call "on your right" or "on your left" so that he will know where to anticipate you.

● Remember that you too were once a beginner. Don't ski too fast or too close to novice skiers.

● If you ski into another skier or cause him to fall, you are legally responsible for stopping and providing assistance.

● Avoid skiing through ski classes. The same goes for race courses unless you are a participant.

● Do not attempt to stop a runaway ski. Instead, shout the warning "Runaway ski" to people below.

● Don't take friends down trails they are not ready for.

● Be especially careful when there are small children on the trail. Even though they may be excellent skiers, they are very light and can be knocked over easily.

● After falling, get up promptly to avoid becoming an obstacle for another skier.

● Ski cautiously through a snowmaking area. Machine snow can be sticky when being made and you can fall if you are not prepared for it.

● Never tamper with ropes, signs, barriers, or markers. They are put up for a good reason.

● Don't cut lift lines, and try to keep off other people's skis while moving through the lift maze.

● Have your lift ticket or season's pass visible for checking so you do not hold up the line.

● Keep out of the way of snow grooming vehicles. Stop and let them pass before proceeding.

● Ski defensively—expect the unexpected. Look ahead. Plan ahead. Be aware of what's around you. Be prepared to stop anytime.

● It is always wise to warm up for any strenuous activity. Skiing is no exception. Do your warm-up exercices at the top of the lift just before your first descent.

● Refrain from littering. Littering on the ski trails not only detracts from the beauty of the mountain but also can cause someone to fall.

● Be careful when carrying equipment in crowded areas. Remember when you turn around, your long skis turn also, sweeping in a wide arc.

● To prevent theft when leaving equipment unattended, lock your skis and poles to one of the ski racks at the area. Use a coin-operated ski lock available at the area or carry a lightweight cable lock with you. If you don't have a lock, separating your skis may help.

SKIER'S RESPONSIBILITY CODE

There are elements of risk in skiing that common sense and personal awareness can help reduce.

1 Ski under control and in such a manner that you can stop or avoid other skiers or objects. Excessive speed is dangerous.

2 When skiing downhill or overtaking another skier, you must avoid the skier below you.

3 You must not stop where you obstruct a trail or are not visible from above.

4 When entering a trail or starting downhill, yield to other skiers.

5 All skiers shall use devices to prevent runaway skis.

6 You shall keep off closed trails and posted areas and observe all posted signs.

THIS IS A PARTIAL LIST. BE SAFETY CONSCIOUS.

Selecting the right trail. Suffice it to say that skiing an "expert" slope doesn't necessarily make **you** an expert! On the contrary, it can make a fool out of you, and, worse, cause injury to yourself and others.

Don't overestimate your capabilities. There's nothing wrong with a bit of extra challenge now and then but skiing over your head is not much fun. You wouldn't have much fun playing tennis against Ivan Lendl; it's no more pleasant to ski down "Suicide Pipeline" when you can barely handle "Easy Street." Particularly at large areas, don't ski without a trail map in your pocket. Know and understand the meaning of trail markings.

TRAIL MARKING SYMBOLS. The symbols shown here comprise the standard international trail marking system.

Remember, these symbols do not tell the whole story. They describe only the relative degree of challenge of a particular trail **compared to all other trails at that area.** Also, gradients and difficulty vary along each trail. Therefore, it is always a good idea to start off on the "easier" trails when visiting a new area.

 **Green Circle.** *Easier* trails and slopes.

 **Black Diamond.** *Most difficult* trails and slopes.

 **Blue Square.** *More difficult* trails and slopes which fall somewhere between easier and most difficult designations.

 **Triangle. Red Border and exclamation point on yellow background.**

This symbol warns of an obstacle ahead. Ski with caution.

Then as you progress towards the area's "more difficult" and "most difficult" terrain you will have a better grasp of the area's level of difficulty. That is why terrain rated "more difficult" at Vail, Snowbird, Squaw Valley, and Jackson Hole may be tougher than the "most difficult" trails at an Eastern area.

Some Colorado areas also have "double black diamond" trails which are either extremely steep or unusually long, mogully, and difficult runs only for very strong or very calm skiers.

If you know and follow the rules and ski with common sense you'll be safe on skis as will everyone else.

NIGHT SKIING. For most nondestination ski areas—day ski areas—the feasibility of maintaining expensive facilities 12 months a year while only operating 4 or 5 months has always been a problem. Nowadays, however, many areas are coming to a fuller realization of their potential by developing summer programs and activities.

They are also trying to maximize their winter utilization by operating longer hours and, simultaneously offering skiers a more flexible skiing schedule. Enter night skiing.

Originally a ski area which opened at night would throw up a few bulbs here and there and charge 50 percent of the day rate to ski "under the stars." In those early days skiers did better skiing under the full moon without lights. Night skiing could rightfully be called an experience, an adventure of sorts.

But nowadays the challenge of night skiing has all but been removed with the installation of high-powered mercury vapor and metalarc 1,000-watt lamps generating in some cases over a million watts of lighting power and rendering the ski slopes bright as day.

As there is no problem playing baseball or football at night, so it is now with night skiing. In fact visibility under modern lighting systems is always constant and often better than by day when "flat light" sometimes enters into the picture. Some areas even counter flat daylight by turning on the lights.

In North America the most sophisticated and extensive night skiing region lies 40 minutes north of Montréal, in the St Sauveur Valley of the Laurentians. Here within a radius of 5 miles there are more than 60 night skiing trails at 7 resorts generating more than 4.5 million watts of brightness for the after-work crowd of skiers. One ski area alone, Mont St Sauveur has 1.1 million watts of power. At night the region radiates as much as a small city and draws a tremendous number of skiers. In fact, Mont St Sauveur night skiers are almost as numerous as its day skiers. This and other areas operate until 10:30 P.M. weekdays and midnight on weekends. Night tickets are sold from 3 P.M.

The only drawback for night skiing is that it tends to be colder at night, so dress warmly and check temperature forecasts. Remember, though, that the overnight low is usually reached in the early hours of the morning just before sunrise. So while temperatures drop steadily during the night they'll normally still be far from the lowest when you finish skiing.

ABOUT SKI LESSONS. Ski lessons are not just for beginning skiers. Most people underestimate the importance of lessons and overestimate their capabilities.

However if you've never skied before, lessons are paramount. Enjoying skiing the first time out can mean a lifetime of fun and enjoyment. Avoid making that first experience a bad one by borrowing a friend's equipment and taking a lesson from yc r neighbor who skis "pretty good." No matter how good a skier your friend might be, if he can't teach your first experience might be disastrous.

By renting equipment the first time out you'll be fitted properly and you'll also avoid purchasing expensive equipment before you know if you'll enjoy the sport.

Instructors are used to beginners; they understand your apprehensions and are trained to analyze your skiing potential. They know which slope is the easiest at their area; which slope teaches best. What may seem like an easy slope to your friend might be too much for your first run.

Learning to ski is no longer the long process it once was. Improvements in teaching progression and the use of shorter skis have made it possible to make parallel turns and ski most intermediate trails within a ski week of lessons. In addition to teaching you to ski, instructors will introduce and familiarize you to your ski equipment, how it works, and how to take care of it for better performance. They'll talk to you about skiing safety, rules of the road and courtesy on the slopes, show you how to ride the lifts, and present the importance of exercising before your first run.

When planning a ski vacation consider booking lessons as well. Resorts offer lessons for all abilities, including racing and touring groups where advanced skiers go with an instructor to explore off-the-track mountain areas you wouldn't normally know about. This is particularly interesting at the larger areas where there is a lot of tree or open skiing such as Alta, Snowbird, Park City, Jackson Hole, Vail, Aspen, Sun Valley, Whistler-Blackcomb, Lake Louise, Mt. Bachelor, and others.

Race training camps are available from the best including World Cup champions Phil and Steve Mahre. Their training sessions run different weeks at Keystone, Colorado, Heavenly Valley, California, and Stowe, Vermont, every winter. Check with the area for schedules and rates.

Refreshers. It's the wise skier who takes a lesson now and again to correct and strengthen technique. Technique evolves and although you might be skiing well, a lesson might help you master those big bumps that give you trouble or help you carve those turns a bit better.

ABOUT SNOW REPORTS. Once you've decided on a skiing vacation, snow reports take on a new meaning and their analysis most often is not that easy. Snow reports come from various sources.

From ski areas or their regional association. Although some can be reliable they are usually given in such a way as to maximize the desirability of skiing at their area. They are usually prepared by the public relations or marketing department instead of the mountain manager or the ski patrol, who are the ones who really know what's happening on the mountain. Most ski areas have recorded snow phones where you can get the latest info. A good snow report will give the date and time of recording. Snowfall in the past 24 hours and up to 7 days can be meaningful, but accumulation "in the last 17 days" doesn't mean much if yesterday there were 2 inches of rain and subfreezing temperatures. Listen for temperatures as well. If it's 40° F and the area claims to be making snow, you can hang up right away.

Snow quality is next. It is either powder, granular, frozen granular, corn, or icy.

Base depths are deceiving unless you know the area and the kind of snow cover it requires to be good. Two feet of base may be nothing in the Sierras while in the East and Midwest it's more than plenty. And with snowmaking in the picture, where are these base depths really taken? We've skied more than our share of ski areas where base depths averaged 20–40 inches and there were still bare patches on many runs. So don't go by who has the biggest base. They may just have the best PR department.

Number of trails open is an important factor to consider. But here again make sure you get complete information. Saying 25 trails open does not indicate the same situation at Killington and Jay Peak—Killington has 100 trails and Jay 32. Thus, there is a better situation at Jay, because Killington would only have

25 percent of its runs open. Ski areas are into little games here, though. Early in the season you'll often discover that the three trails open for skiing are "Upper this," "Lower that," and the "Arrival Plaza." Multiply that by three and you have nine runs open but only three ways down. Other centers will also play the percentage game where one wide trail represents 30 percent of the area's skiing acreage. So as soon as that one run opens up—30 percent of the mountain is open, but it's still only one run.

You can't really knock areas for doing this, though. Giving a snow report for an area is about the same as a parent answering the question, "Do your children look good?" Of course they do!

Some areas do call a spade a spade, however, and you'll need to find out for yourself in the region that interests you. In the East, for example, several state or provincially run areas, such as Whiteface and Gore in upstate New York, Cannon Mt., New Hampshire, and Québec City's Mont Ste Anne, give straight, descriptive reports of conditions. And they usually don't open trails before they're sufficiently covered.

Newspapers should be able to provide some of the best information, but few devote enough space to do the job adequately. There's a lot of tedious repetition in ski reports and newspapers are perfect for the job as readers can select without being subjected to the whole thing. Unfortunately, until they spend some time and allow enough space, newspaper reports will be dated, incomplete, and often edited.

Radio and television are the best sources. They are the most immediate and this is where you'll find more professional reporters. Best reports will be those prepared by a specialist and not read by the staff announcer. In the latter case, you know the report is simply a compilation of what the areas themselves have phoned in. You can trust the guy or gal who calls it bad from time to time, because then you'll know that when it's good, it's truly good. Also follow weather reports. When you hear that the interstate is closed because of a major snowstorm you'll know that the foot and a half of snow reported at the ski area is not wishful thinking by the PR department. Conversely, if television news shows residents of Aspen planting rice, you can bet that skiing will be less than ideal unless it's done from behind a boat.

Here are some definitions to help you better understand snow reports. (See *Glossary* for other ski terms.)

• **Corn snow.** Spring condition. Large ice-like granules sometimes the size of corn kernels caused by the melting of frozen granular.

• **Frozen Granular.** Granular snow which was once wet then frozen together forming a solid mass. This condition can also develop from extreme compacting by skiers. Frozen granular will support a ski pole planted in it while ice will make chips and will not support your pole. **Caution.** Some skiers will call this condition ice and many areas will use the term instead of ice.

• **Granular Snow.** Old snow which is no longer powdery and soft. Cross-country skiers call it hard, grainy snow. It is more abrasive. The snowflake is no longer star-shaped and has become more like a pellet because of aging, wear and tear, or grooming. This condition, contrary to common belief, is not a spring condition. It can happen anytime and it's no deterrent to the quality of skiing.

• **Ice.** Caused by rain followed by a freeze-up, freezing rain, or extreme skier traffic on wet snow.

• **Limited skiing.** Used when skiing at an area or on a certain level of trails is limited to less than 50 percent of the normally available terrain.

• **Packed powder.** Powder snow which has been packed mechanically or by skier traffic.

• **Powder snow.** Snow which is fresh and dry and in its original state. It is not always light but can be as found in the higher elevations. Powder snow can have a variable consistency and will eventually become granular when it becomes more like a pellet than star-shaped. Powder snow, simply said, is dry, soft snow.

• **Sugar snow** is a breakdown of frozen granular snow in cold temperatures.

• **Variable conditions.** Used to describe a wide variety of surface conditions. No one surface type dominates. Often found in springtime, particularly at the bigger mountains where surfaces may be powder at the top and springlike at the bottom or varied from more northerly to more southerly exposed facings.

• **Wet snow.** A deep snowfall of wet snow, while advertised as great by the areas, is often very difficult to handle by skiers and dangerous for beginners or weak skiers. Packed and harder surfaces are often the safest conditions.

● **Windswept or windblown.** Irregular surfaces affected by winds that have formed drifts in some spots and exposed the base in others. Can cause icing.

Beware of adjectives such as **good** to **excellent** which some areas, particularly in the West still use, to describe conditions. They say nothing about skiing and even when there is limited or even bad skiing the minimum rating is often good.

These conditions are, of course, affected and often altered by grooming. You can read about grooming, discussed above.

GETTING IN SHAPE. An important part of getting the most out of your skiing vacation is to be physically prepared for it. Skiing does not require Olympic conditioning, but some preparation will avoid soreness the first few days and prevent injury.

Most recreation and fitness centers as well as your local Y and many ski clubs hold preseason conditioning programs with exercises specifically aimed at preparing your ski muscles. They usually begin in early October and run until the end of November. Taking part in one of these is probably the best; it will put you back in shape for the season together with other keen skiers from whom you can also pick up valuable information on planning your ski vacation.

If joining a fitness group is not convenient for you, remember that fitness can be gained by simply modifying your daily routine a little. Here are some suggestions:

● Going to work or school, park a bit farther and walk the rest of the way. If you use public transit it's even easier. Get off one or two stops before your normal stop and walk. Brisk walking is an excellent exercise. As you feel better, lengthen the walk.

● At work, instead of taking the elevator take the stairs. This will strengthen your leg muscles and will help build-up your cardiovascular capacity.

● Instead of taking the usual coffee break, take an exercise break. Do a few stretching exercises during that time, stretching your back and leg muscles particularly.

● You can strengthen and tone your stomach muscles in your car or sitting at your desk by doing tummy tucks. Breathe out and suck in your stomach, hold for a few seconds, release and repeat. You can also tone and strengthen your buttocks by flexing your buttock muscles right on your chair. Nobody will even notice unless you do it too intensely and start turning pink!

● Remember that alpine skiing is basically an "anaerobic" activity, meaning that it requires more muscle tone, strength, and flexibility than cardiovascular endurance. Plan your exercise accordingly.

● Develop flexibility first. Remember that good, flexible muscles and ligaments will stretch so they won't tear. You can work on flexibility almost anywhere and anytime. Flexibility exercises require no special equipment. Many books are published on the subject. It's good to read a bit since there are good and bad ways of stretching. Stretch gently.

● Develop muscle strength. Walking and climbing stairs are excellent ways of working on a key set of ski muscles. Biking is a fun way to strengthen your legs while having a good time. A bit of supervised weight training is also good if available—but not essential. Sit-ups are great for strengthening stomach muscles. There are a number of ways to do sit-ups; check exercise manuals as well as some good dance exercise publications. Always keep knees slightly bent when doing sit-ups to avoid strain on the lower back, and remember that most of the work in a sit-up is in getting off the ground. After that initial step the load decreases substantially. Thus, many people do the "crunchie," a short sit-up in which the shoulders barely get off the ground. It's a great workout for the stomach.

● Developing quick reflexes is the other important part of getting in shape for skiing. The sport requires that you move quickly and suddenly from time to time and the better your reaction time—your agility—the better and easier you will ski. A lot of jumping exercises will help improve your reaction time, and games such as soccer, basketball, and especially volleyball are excellent for this specific purpose and for all-around skiing preparation.

● Developing balance is another aspect of preparing for the ski season. Most team sports—except maybe baseball—are excellent for this. Simple exercises such as standing on one leg, tieing your shoelaces, and walking on the white line can build agility.

Don't expect skiing to get you in shape. That's the wrong way of going about it. Be prepared and you'll enjoy skiing much more. After your first day skiing you won't be a basket case and will still have enough energy left to enjoy the social side of your vacation.

METRIC CONVERSION

Converting Metric to U.S. Measurements

Multiply:	by:	to find:
Length		
millimeters (mm)	.039	inches (in)
meters (m)	3.28	feet (ft)
meters	1.09	yards (yd)
kilometers (km)	.62	miles (mi)
Area		
hectares (ha)	2.47	acres
Capacity		
liters (L)	1.06	quarts (qt)
liters	.26	gallons (gal)
liters	2.11	pints (pt)
Weight		
grams (g)	.04	ounces (oz)
kilograms (kg)	2.20	pounds (lb)
metric tons (MT)	.98	tons (t)
Power		
kilowatts (kw)	1.34	horsepower (hp)
Temperature		
degrees Celsius	9/5 (then add 32)	degrees Fahrenheit

Multiply:	by:	to find:
Length		
inches (in)	25.40	millimeters (mm)
feet (ft)	.30	meters (m)
yards (yd)	.91	meters
miles (mi)	1.61	kilometers (km)
Area		
acres	.40	hectares (ha)
Capacity		
pints (pt)	.47	liters (L)
quarts (qt)	.95	liters
gallons (gal)	3.79	liters
Weight		
ounces (oz)	28.35	grams (g)
pounds (lb)	.45	kilograms (kg)
tons (t)	1.11	metric tons (MT)
Power		
horsepower (hp)	.75	kilowatts
Temperature		
degrees Fahrenheit	5/9 (after subtracting 32)	degrees Celsius

GLOSSARY OF MAIN SKI TERMS

Aerial tramway. A large lift composed of two cabins holding up to 120 people suspended by a moving cable traveling high above ground. Used mostly where topography requires very long spans.

Après-ski. Social activities at ski resorts after skiing.

Avalanche control. Evaluation of high altitude steep terrain with heavy accumulation of unstable snow and necessary prevention measures such as blasting to release avalanches.

Base. The plastic or polyethylene running surface on the bottom of your skis; also, the amount of packed snow reported by ski areas.

Boiler plate. Solid ice created by rain followed by a freeze-up.

Breakable Crust. A crust which can be broken easily by skiers. Usually caused by freezing rain immediately after a snowfall.

Bunny hill. A gentle slope for beginners.

Carved turn. A long, arc turn made with little or no side-slipping.

Catwalk. A narrow road for vehicular traffic or narrow trail linking two peaks or two trails on a traverse.

Certified. Used by the U.S. and Canadian Ski Instructors' Alliance to indicate a skier has been tested and has passed examinations to become a ski instructor qualified to teach the technique approved by the governing body.

Chairlift. A method of uphill transportation where chairs suspended from a moving cable bring skiers uphill 2, 3, and even 4 at a time.

Chatter. Vibration of skis on hard surfaces that prevents the edges from setting properly.

Christie. Short for Christiania, a turn invented in the latter part of the nineteenth century by the skiers of Christiania, now Oslo. Turn where skis are parallel when the turn is completed.

Chute. A steep, narrow trail.

Corn snow. A type of snow found in the springtime where large ice-like granules, the size of corn kernels, are formed by the melting of frozen granular by the sun.

Cornice. An overhanging ledge of snow or ice.

Crevasse. Deep, dangerous crack found in glaciers.

Crud. Heavy or crusty snow. Occasionally called "death crud" in the Rockies.

CSIA. Canadian Ski Instructor's Alliance. The association of Canadian ski instructors.

CSPS. Canadian Ski Patrol System. The Canadian body of ski safety and first aid volunteers who promote safety on the slopes and administer first aid when needed.

Damping. The quality of a ski to absorb vibration.

Downhill ski. The lower ski, the one normally on the outside of the turn.

Drop-off. An abrupt change from flat to steep.

Edges. Strips of metal on the edge of the ski's running surface to improve grip on the snow.

Edging. A method of controlling side-slippage in a turn. Also used to control speed.

Edgeset. Application of edging just before starting a turn.

Face. The steepest part of a mountain.

Fall line. The line a ball would follow if it rolled freely down the mountain.

Fanny pack. Small pack carried around the waist in which skiers carry their odds and ends.

Flat light. Poor visual condition, usually in haze or cloudy weather, where terrain contours cannot be properly delineated.

Free skiing. Skiing without restrictions. Out of competition.

Frozen granular. A type of snow often mistaken for ice. It is granular snow which became wet then froze together forming a solid mass. It can usually be groomed quite easily.

Giant slalom. A form of alpine ski racing in which a skier must negotiate a series of gates connected by relatively long traverses. It combines elements of both slalom and downhill.

Glade. Ski slope where skiers ski beneath the trees.

GLM. Graduated Length Method of teaching skiing. It is based on the use of shorter skis to make turning easier at first, then progressing to longer ones.

Gondola. A ski lift composed of a series of small enclosed bubbles shaped like eggs carrying anywhere from 3 to 6 passengers. They are loaded from a stationary position and then clamped onto the driving cable.

Grooming. What ski areas do with machinery to improve snow conditions.

Hardpack. Powder snow that has been packed hard by heavy skier traffic.

Herringbone. A method of climbing hills where skis are edged and placed in a reverse-V position in order to prevent backslip. Frequently used by cross-country skiers.

High Season. A time of year when resorts are busiest. In skiing normally the Christmas–New Year weeks, early-February to mid-March, and Easter if it comes early. This is a period of higher rates.

Inside ski. The ski which is on the inside of the turn. The ski which becomes the uphill ski when the turn is terminated.

J-bar. Ski surface lift in the shape of a J carrying one skier at a time.

Lift line. The area where a lift runs, the straight cut through the trees. Also the area where skiers wait to get onto the lift.

Low season. Part of the season which is the least busy. In skiing usually before Christmas, January, and from late March on.

Mashed potatoes. A snow condition encountered in very warm weather when the snow becomes very heavy and difficult to move around.

Meadow. Large, open slope usually with a moderate grade.

Mogul. A bump in the snow formed by the turning action of skiers. Moguls are quite common on steep slopes.

NASTAR. National Standard Race. Giant slalom-type of ski competition offered at many U.S. ski centers and open to anyone. Skiers can compare themselves to a national standard.

NSPS. National Ski Patrol System. The American body of ski safety and first aid volunteers who promote safety on the slopes and administer first aid when needed.

Package tour. A travel arrangement for which a skier pays for a number of services all at once. Package tours can include such things as air fare, transfers, accommodations, meals, and lift tickets. Packages can be more or less comprehensive.

Pomalift. A surface ski lift also known as a "platterpull" consisting of a series of bars at the end of which each has a disk. The skier straddles the bar.

Powder. Fresh, dry snow; snow in its original shape—star-shaped.

Powderhound. Skier who loves powder and will look for it in the most remote parts of a ski area.

Quad. Short for quadruple chair; 4-passenger chairlift.

Rock garden. Expression used to illustrate a condition where many rocks are exposed.

Ruts. Deep tracks in the snow caused by constant turning of skiers in the same area. Most frequently seen on racing courses.

Skating. Skiing on one ski while pushing with the other. A method of traveling on flats or slight grades much like ice-skating. A commonly practiced cross-country skiing technique.

Schussboomer. Skier who skis rapidly and indiscriminantly. Also known as a "bomber."

Snow bunny. A novice or beginning skier. Usually reserved for females.

Step-in binding. Ski binding where the skier need not bend over to connect it with his boot. He merely needs to step into it.

Pre-jump. A method by which a skier jumps before the edge of a bump to avoid being projected too high.

Rope tow. A form of surface lift consisting of a moving rope which skiers grasp to be pulled uphill. It was one of the earliest forms of uphill transport.

Release binding. The piece of equipment that keeps your boots secured to your skis. Usually includes a toe and a heel piece, both of which can release when forces are applied.

Safety binding. A misnomer for release binding.

Schuss. Skiing straight down without controlling speed.

Shovel. The front part of the ski including the upward turning part of the ski near the tip.

Sideslip. A sideways sliding of the skis, releasing the edges.

Sidewall. Side of a ski.

Sitzmark. A hole made when a skier falls in soft snow.

Ski brake. A spring-loaded device included with all modern release bindings to prevent a runaway ski.

Slalom. Old Norwegian word meaning "zigzag" tracks downhill. Also a form of alpine ski racing where a skier must negotiate a number of closely spaced gates in the fastest possible time.

Snowcat. The nickname given to a grooming tractor. It is actually the trade name for Tucker grooming machines.

Snowplow. A basic ski maneuver whereby skis are placed in a V-position much like a snow plow. It is a means of controlling speed and initiating a turn.

Spring condition. A catch-all phrase used to describe the variety of conditions found in the springtime: from frozen granular to mashed potatoes, including the possibility of bare patches.

T-bar. A surface lift in the form of a reversed-T pulled by a moving cable and hauling 2 skiers side-by-side.

Tail. Back end of a ski.

Telemark. A turn originating in the Telemark region of Norway in the late 1800s. It is performed on cross-country or special "telemark" skis by pushing one ski in front and ahead at an angle to the other ski. The leading ski carries much of the weight while the other leg, in kneeling position, helps to maintain balance. It is a turn best performed in deep snow. The technique is quite commonly practiced by skiers in the west and becoming more popular in the east.

Terrain. The skiing surface of a ski area.

Transition. The change in ski terrain going from a flat section to a steeper one or vice-versa.

Traverse. Skiing across a slope at a certain angle with the fall line.

USSA. United States Ski Association. The national federation of American skiers and the sport's governing body.

Wind slab. Snow packed by the wind.

World cup. A series of events run in several skiing disciplines to determine an overall champion every year. The World Cup Circuits regroup the top skiers in alpine, cross-country, freestyle, biathlon, and ski jumping.

Skiing—Where It All Began

A Short History

by
GUY THIBEADEAU

*Guy Thibeadeau has been a ski broadcaster and writer for more than
20 years. He lives in the Laurentians north of Montréal, from where he
operates the MRG Ski Network, broadcasting daily ski and snow reports
to 20 different media. He is a correspondent for several U.S. ski publications.*

Skiing originated in the northern part of Europe and Asia several
thousands of years ago. Skis thought to be more than 5,000 years
old—the oldest known pair in the world—were found in Hoting, Sweden, and are displayed in the Djugarden Museum in Stockholm. The
"Hoting Ski," as it is called, was short and wide, measuring 110 cm by
20 cm (approximately 43 inches by 8 inches). In 1931 a famous rock
carving depicting a ski scene dating back over 4,000 years was found
at Røddøy in Norway; it shows longer skis on two men hunting elk.
Another positive proof of the early beginnings of skiing is a ski tip
found in northern Norway which dates back over 2,500 years. That ski
tip can be viewed today at the Holmenkollen Ski Museum in Oslo.

Skiing that far back, of course, was not a sport; it was merely a more
practical way of getting around in the snow. The evolution of the skis
themselves is quite interesting going, from relatively short skis at first

23

to skis measuring as much as 12 ft., 2½ in. in the seventeenth and eighteenth centuries.

There was also an era when a short and a long ski were used simultaneously—the long one for gliding and the short one, which had elk skin on the bottom for grip, was used for pushing. These were used by the Lapps about 250 years ago.

Skis were used through the ages by northern peoples and their armies to defend their territory. Sixteenth-century records document two major points in Norwegian and Swedish history where skiers played a major role. In 1200 A.D., during the battle of Oslo, King Sverre of Norway equipped his reconnaissance troups with skis to track the Swedish army's position. In 1206, during the Norwegian Civil War, two skiers—called "birch legs" because they wrapped their legs with birch bark for protection—carried two-year-old infant royal Haakon Haakonsson to safety over the snow-covered mountains of Norway in the middle of winter. He was to become Norway's greatest formative leader. A similar story surrounds the founding of Sweden and Gustav Vasa's rescue by skiing woodsmen who took the man who was to become their king from Salen to Mora, a distance of 85 km.

Both events are commemorated yearly by two ski races tracing the historic ski journeys which helped create Norway and Sweden: Norway's Birkebeiner-Rennet, a 55-km race from Lillehammer to Rena and vice versa in alternate years; and Sweden's famed Vasaloppet, where over 12,000 skiers attempt to ski the 85-km distance from Salen to Mora.

But where did skiing as a sport actually begin?

In 1850 Sondre Nordheim, a Norwegian farmhand from Morgedal in the southern Norwegian region of Telemark, found a way of fastening the foot to the ski with a heel binding. Before then skiers wore only toestraps and were unable to turn as their feet would slip out immediately. With the foot properly fastened to the ski, modern skiing could begin—with the slalom.

At about the same period Nordheim had observed that it would be easier to land a jump on the steep part of a slope rather than on the flat. And jumping was on its way to becoming a sport and competitive activity.

In 1870 the same Nordheim developed a ski with sidecut—that is, narrower at the waist than at the tip and tail. This made turning a lot easier, and all ski manufacturers have been making skis with sidecuts ever since.

With his bindings and skis Nordheim developed a way of turning which he called the "Telemark" turn, after the district in which he lived.

As skiing popularity grew in Norway in the 1870s the boys from Telemark were the hottest skiers around with their elegant Telemark turn. Their biggest rivals at ski meets were the fellows from Christiania (the old name for Oslo), who in time developed their own technique, skidding their skis wide apart but more or less parallel. They called it the "Christiania" turn (nowadays still referred to as the Christie).

The first skiing competitions were held in 1843 in northern Norway in the town of Tromsø, north of the Arctic Circle. They were basically straight running events; the first cross-country races. Jumping came next with competitions in Telemark and Christiania in 1866, and then slalom in 1885.

Among the most famous Norwegian Emigrants who spread skiing around the world were John A. "Snowshow" Thompson who in 1856 began carrying the U.S. mail, sometimes 120 pounds of it, across the Sierra Nevada on skis. He did this for 13 years, until 1869, when the first transcontinental railroad was built. And then there is Herman

"Jackrabbit" Johannsen who, in 1986, celebrated his 111th birthday in the Laurentians north of Montréal. From the 1920s through the 1950s Jackrabbit—so named by Canada's Cree Indians for his agility on skis—was instrumental in the development of cross-country and alpine skiing in both the Canadian and American East.

While the sport of skiing originated in Norway, the first signs of an organized technique came out of Austria in 1896 when an army officer, Mathias Zdarsky, set up a military ski school at Lilienfeld and published the first ski instruction manual. He is commonly acknowledged as "the father of alpine skiing." Around 1907, another Austrian, Hannes Schneider, studied and refined Zdarsky's method and developed the Arlberg technique, which made skiing a lot easier, and eclipsed the Telemark method for several decades.

After World War I, Schneider returned home more determined than ever to spread his skiing technique worldwide. Much like St. Peter and the Apostles, Schneider's disciples were sent around the skiing world promoting the philosophy that "skiing is a way of life." Hannes Schneider himself took the Alrberg technique to North Conway, New Hampshire, Herman Gadner to Gray Rocks in the Laurentians, Fritz Loosli to Lac Beauport north of Quebec City, Sepp Ruschp to Stowe, Vermont, Luggi Foeger to Yosemite, Otto Lang to Mt. Rainier, and Friedl Pfeiffer to Sun Valley, Idaho.

From there ski resorts around the world began to develop along the European alpine model through the 1970s when a more modern North American concept began to develop.

The first T-bars were installed in Switzerland in 1935 with the first aerial lift, the Parsenn funicular, erected in Davos in 1932. In the same year Alec Foster built the first rope tow on the "Big Hill" at Shawbridge, north of Montreal. Sun Valley built the first chairlift in North America in 1936 as it became the U.S.'s first world class ski resort. From there ski lifts of all sorts have developed, from T-bars to jet T-bars to platterpulls, J-bars, and double and triple chairs. The first quadruple detachable chair was installed at Breckenridge, Colorado, in 1982, and now the state of the art in uphill transportation is the "Vista Bahn," a detachable quad with a wind-protective bubble installed at Vail, Colorado, for the winter of 1986.

Skiing has now spread around the world wherever there is snow. From Scandinavia, where it was born, to the alpine countries of Europe, where skiing technique evolved, to North and South America, Australia, Asia, Eastern Europe, and such unlikely areas as North Africa, Hawaii, India, Pakistan, and Iran, more than 30 million people throughout the world ski every year.

EASTERN UNITED STATES

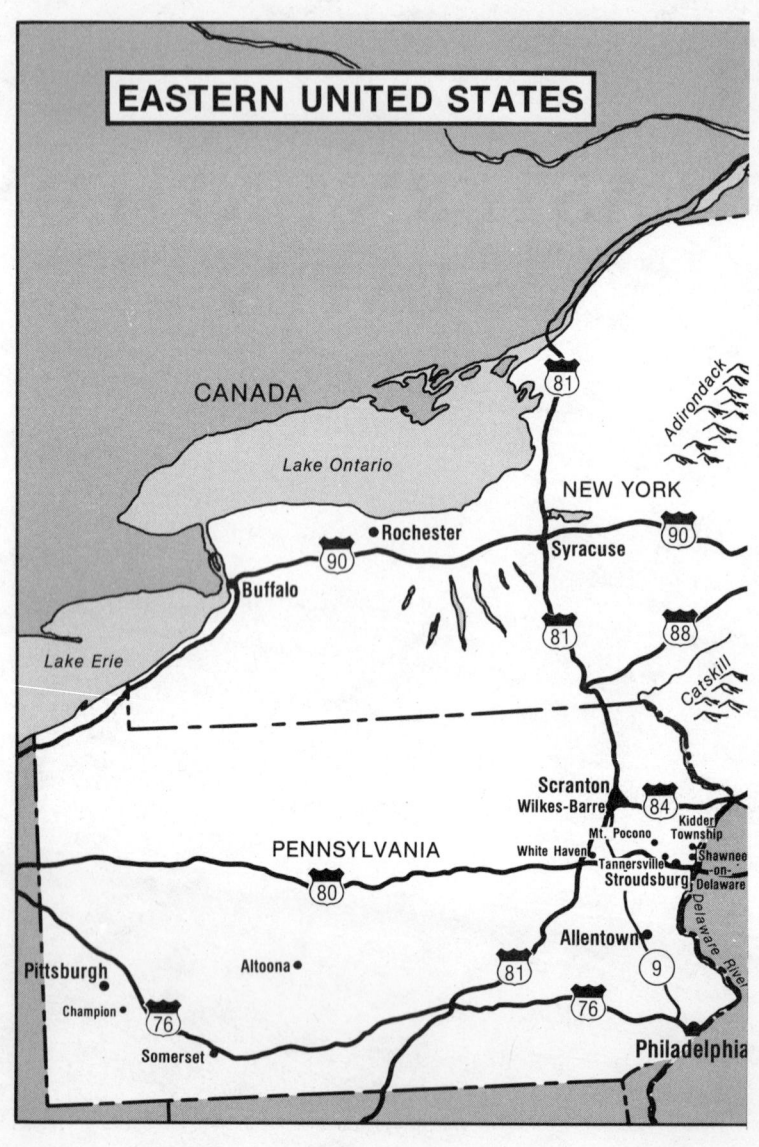

EASTERN UNITED STATES

CANADA

Lake Ontario

NEW YORK

81

Rochester

90

Syracuse

Buffalo

81

88

Lake Erie

Adirondack

Catskill

Scranton

Wilkes-Barre

84

PENNSYLVANIA

Mt. Pocono

Kidder Township

White Haven

Shawnee -on- Delaware

80

Tannersville

Stroudsburg

Allentown

Altoona

81

9

Pittsburgh

Champion

76

76

Delaware River

Somerset

Philadelphia

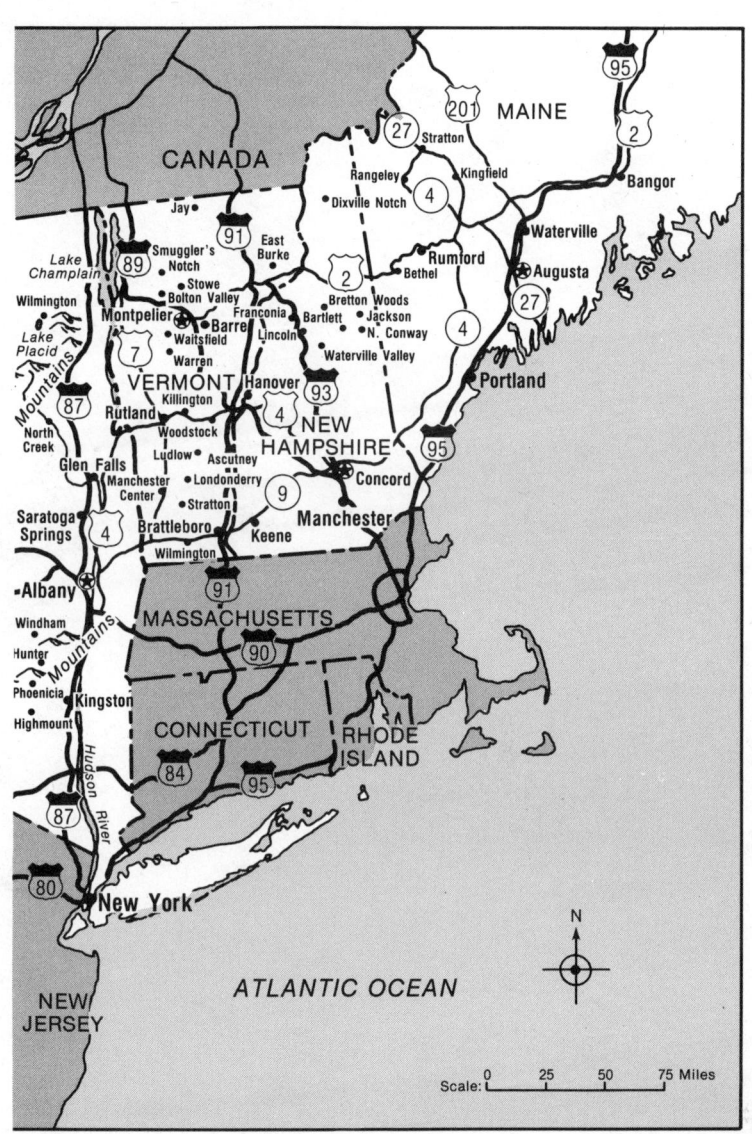

95

MAINE

2

27 Stratton

201

CANADA

Jay

Rangeley   Kingfield

Dixville Notch   4   Bangor

91   East
Burke   Rumford   Waterville

Lake
Champlain 89   Smuggler's
Notch   2   Bethel   Augusta 27

Wilmington   Stowe
Bolton Valley   Bretton Woods
Montpelier   Franconia Jackson
Lake   Bartlett N. Conway
Placid   Waitsfield Lincoln   4
7   Barre   Warren   Waterville Valley   Portland

North   Mountains VERMONT Hanover
Creek   93
87   Rutland Killington   4   NEW
Woodstock   HAMPSHIRE   95
Glen Falls   Ludlow Ascutney
Manchester Londonderry   Concord
Saratoga   Center   Stratton   9
Springs   Brattleboro   Manchester
4   Keene
Albany   Wilmington

Windham   91
Hunter   Mountains MASSACHUSETTS
Phoenicia
Highmount Kingston   90

CONNECTICUT RHODE
87   ISLAND
84   95
Hudson River

80

New York

NEW
JERSEY   ATLANTIC OCEAN   N

Scale: 0   25   50   75 Miles

EASTERN UNITED STATES

by
SARA WIDNESS

Freelance writer and editor as well as publicist for skiing resorts in New England, Sara Widness has been associated for the past decade with the Sunrise Group in Killington, Vermont. She is a former newspaper-woman and was associated with the United Press International in New York City.

A visitor to an Eastern ski slope who had a lot of West Coast skiing under his belt was contemplating his maiden voyage down a Vermont mountain: "I don't know about this," he said. "I'm used to skiing in powder up to my elbows."

His host replied: "Well, you better get used to it, because back here we ski in frozen granular up to our edges."

A skier is a skier is a skier. The experience of exhilarating motion down a mountain trail has much less to do with powder and frozen granular than it does simply with being there in the first place.

And simply by being there, Eastern ski areas provide winter recreation opportunities to literally millions of people who in the last decade have discovered, happily, that the snowmaking technology so adroitly used at the majority of these ski areas today provides, more often than not, a remarkable skiing experience and one that doesn't involve hours and hours of travel and expensive airline tickets.

It's probably impossible to state definitively that snowmaking has created the wonderful ski experiences that exist on the Green Mountains of Vermont, the White Mountains of New Hampshire, or the Longfellow Mountains of Maine. But it is certain that the guarantee

31

of reliable snow cover for a certain number of months every winter has created a sense of confidence in communities surrounding the ski areas, stimulating them to become year-round destination resorts in ways they couldn't be if snow were still an "iffy" commodity.

So the charm of New England, from white steepled churches to Mom and Pop stores, has been packaged as part of the allure, along with Revolutionary War-era country inns and hostelries, to bring people to this region during the long, snowy winters.

The same is true in New York, where ski areas are just starting to stretch and yawn and investigate the year-round opportunities that are knocking there.

In Pennsylvania's Poconos the resort ambience is such that with nary a drop of snow there's still lots of leisure-time activity; the snow just happens to be the frosting on the cake.

Maine

The craggy character of the Maine coastline is reminiscent of the Pacific Northwest. Two of the most exciting cities in the country are called Portland—one in Maine and the other in Oregon. But it may come as a surprise that Maine's mountainous terrain, characterized by the 4,000-foot-high Western Mountains, can evoke memories of the Rockies and the Cascades. There aren't many vistas in the east that span broad valleys and craggy mountains. Such is the drama created in what is known as the Rangeley Lakes Region.

For most skiers and travelers this may be as close as they come to the mystique of Maine's north woods that draws whitewater afficionados, fishermen, and hunters of deer, moose, and elk. But there's plenty of wilderness yet at both Saddleback and Sugarloaf, although Sugarloaf has become a competitive force among Eastern ski areas by virtue of offering the good skiing and sophisticated amenities that today's market demands. Saddleback is just beginning to stretch and yawn and promises to give its neighbor (six miles away as the crow flies) some stiff competition in not too many years.

A third area in Maine, Sunday River, took Maine skiers by surprise a few years back with a "snow is money" corporate approach to running a ski area. Sunday River has always enjoyed proximity to a bit of Maine civilization—Bethel—and is creating its own tour de force, the prerequisite resort village, at the base of its mountain.

Although there are nearly a dozen other smaller ski areas in Maine, these three can be considered destination resorts in the sense that most if not all of the vacation amenities, snowmaking, and efficient lifts are in place and multiplying quickly.

SADDLEBACK SKI AREA

Box 490
Rangeley ME 04970
Tel: 207–864–5921

Snow Report: 207–864–3380
Area Vertical: 1,830 ft.
Number of Trails: 40 on 100
  acres
Lifts: 2 doubles, 3 T-bars
Snowmaking: 90 percent of
  skiable terrain
Season: mid-November–mid-April

Saddleback Ski Area is one of two skiing mountains in Maine to top the 4,000-foot mark. Saddleback is 4,116 feet and Sugarloaf 4,237 feet.

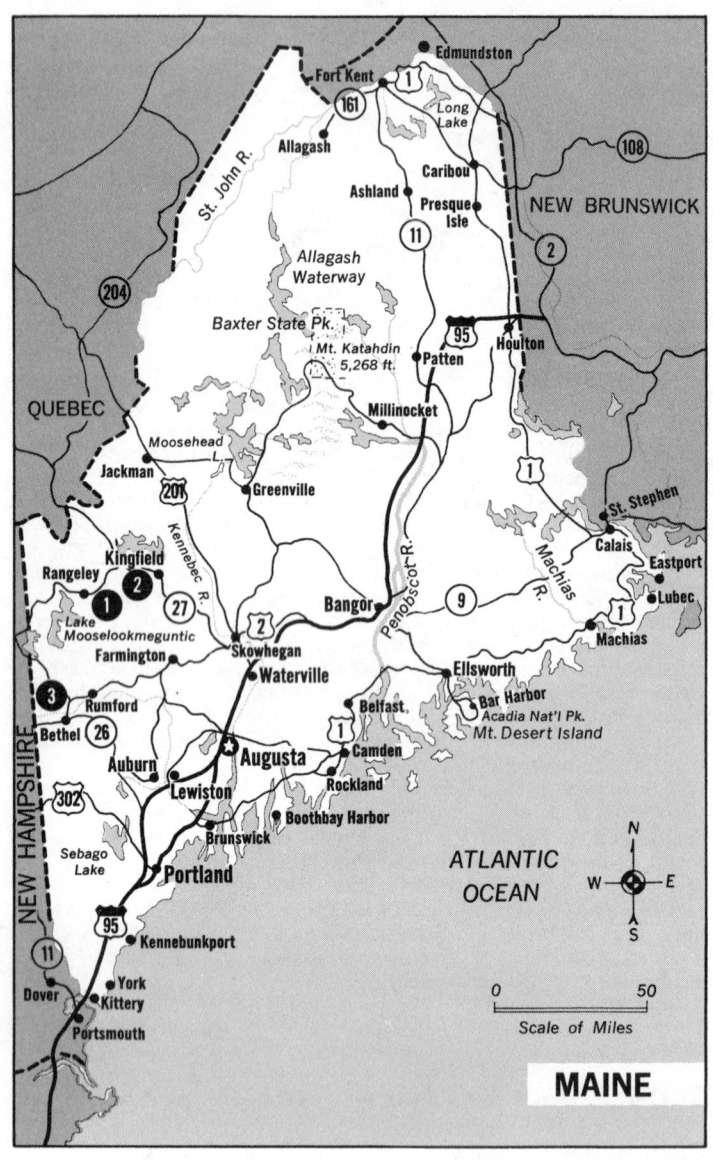

Resorts

1) Saddleback Mountain
2) Sugarloaf/USA
3) Sunday River

Saddleback overlooks much of the Rangeley Lakes Region, and from the summit there are also views of Canada and New Hampshire. This is an area that since the early 1900s has lured visitors with its scenic and wilderness charms.

In the era of the grand hotels, steam locomotives whisked families away from the heat of summer cities to steamships that ferried guests to and fro across the lakes.

In the late 1950s, the recreation focus expanded from just warm weather activities to skiing. Saddleback Ski Area emerged in this decade and by 1968 led the Maine ski industry by being the first major area to install snowmaking equipment. It still leads the Maine snowmaking pack today, with the potential to cover more of its skiable terrain—90 percent—with machine-made snow than any other ski area in the state.

The mood here is laid back and uncrowded. Forty trails are about equally divided among "easiest," "more difficult," and "most difficult" designations. Part of the fun of Saddleback is its fixation on Western lore. These are, remember, the Western Mountains. So it's no surprise that Bronco Buster, a 3,000-foot long black-diamond run from the summit, lures experts to the top. The summit is also accessible to intermediates on Cliffhanger, while the meandering 2.5-mile Lazy River is a favorite with beginners. Youngsters like the snow on White Stallion, while teens prefer Rough Rider and El Hombre, mainly for the moguls.

What could these be—the Buggy, Surrey, Stage Coach, Pony Express, and Wells-Fargo? The lifts, of course. Cars park in the Corral. You buy gas at the Wagon Stop, picnic at the Chuck House and lodge, among others, at the Bunk House (condominiums), and meet your friends at the Trading Post (lodge).

A 1984 acquisition of 12,000 acres of surrounding woodlands will add more names to the cowboy theme, as only 82 acres are now developed. This purchase makes Saddleback one of the largest privately held ski areas in the United States with a skiing potential that lies in a semi-circle of five mountains, only one of which now sports trails.

Practical Information for Saddleback

HOW TO GET THERE. Saddleback is located in the heart of Maine's Western Mountains, 110 miles from Portland and 220 from Boston. It is 7 miles from Rangeley and 12 miles southwest from Sugarloaf/USA.

By air. *Delta, People Express, United,* and *Bar Harbor Airlines* fly to the Portland Jetport. All major and regional airlines serve Boston's Logan Airport. Charter flights on *Mountain Air Services* (864–5307) are available from both Portland and Boston to nearby Rangeley Airport. Call Saddleback's reservation number, 864–5366, to arrange for a shuttle from the Rangeley Airport. Mountain Air Services can make rental cars available.

Ajax (761–5455), *Avis* (800–331–1212), *Budget* (800–527–0700), *Hertz* (800–654–3131), and *National* (800–328–4567) rental car systems are located at the Portland Jetport; all major rental car agencies are available at Logan.

By car. From points south, take the Maine Turnpike north to Exit 12, then Rte. 4 north through Farmington to Rangeley, then drive 7 miles east on the Saddleback Mountain Road to the resort.

TELEPHONES. The area code for all of Maine is 207.

ACCOMMODATIONS. While in the process of becoming a full-fledged, four-season resort whose primary focus is skiing, Saddleback draws on a decades-old collection of inns with a smattering of new inns and lodges primarily in nearby Rangeley. The Rangeley Chamber of Commerce, Box 317 K, Rangeley ME 04970 (207–864–5364) provides information and reservation services for more than 25 establishments including inns, housekeeping cottages, motels, condominiums, and private homes. Trendy pricing hasn't caught on here yet, so expect to find Down East hospitality at bargain prices. Therefore, our selection of accommodations available slopeside and nearby includes only two categories: *Moderate,* $25–$40, with 2-bedroom condos sleeping 4 people, at about $75 per night; and *Inexpensive,* less than $25.

Moderate

Cabin-Condo Care. P.O. Box 155, Rangeley 04970; 864–5241. Fully furnished, trailside condominiums offer ski-trail access. Also available through Cabin-Condo and through Morton & Fubish Rental Agency, Box 160, Rangeley 04920; (864–3340), are a range of privately owned homes, chalets, and cottages on both the mountain and waterfront.

Country Club Inn. P.O. Box 685, Rangeley 04970; 864–3831. A small inn offering fireplaces, dining, and cross-country skiing.

Rangeley Inn & Motor Lodge. Box 398 (Main Street) Rangeley 04970; 864–3341. A restored turn-of-the-century inn with brass beds, oak, and antiques, plus whirlpool baths and dining.

Saddleback Lake Lodge. P.O. Box 610, Rangeley 04970; 864–5501. Multiple bedroom chalets and suites, all with fireplaces and on cross-country trails.

Mountain View Cottages. P.O. Box 284, Rte. 17, Oquossoc 04964; 864–3416. On west shore of Rangeley Lake with views of mountain.

The Swiss Colony. P.O. Box 597, 1½ miles south of Rangeley 04970; 864–3760. On Rangeley Lake, cottages with alpine motif.

Inexpensive

Following is a selection of motels and camps for the budget-minded. *Saddleback Motor Inn,* P.O. Box 468 (off Rte. 4), Rangeley 04970; 864–3434. *Fly Buck Camps,* Box 222 (off Rte. 17), Oquossoc 04964; 864–5575. *Idlewood Lake View Cottages,* P.O. Box 529, Rangeley 04970; 864–5011. *Interlaken Lodge,* Star Rte. 1 (off Rte. 4), Rangeley 04970; 864–3448. *Sequoia,* P.O. Box 208 (off Rte. 17), Oquossoc 04964; 864–3492. *Town & Lake Motel,* Box 47 (off Rte. 4), Rangeley 04970; 864–3755. *True's Cottages,* Box 467 (off Rt. 4), Rangeley 04970; 864–3705.

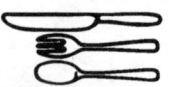

RESTAURANTS. Just as Saddleback accommodations have staved off trendy pricing, so have the region's restaurants. Down East hospitality reigns at the dining places as well as at the lodges and inns. In this selection, the *Expensive* category has been eliminated. Average prices for a meal for one person are as follows: *Moderate,* $10–$18; *Inexpensive,* less than $10. Most restaurants accept MasterCard and Visa, but it's always wise to check before you go.

Moderate

Country Club Inn. Mingo Loop Rd., Rangeley; 864–3831. Enjoy dancing and views over dinner of lobster or other Maine favorites. Reservations suggested.

Oquossoc House. P.O. Box 300, Rtes. 4 and 17; 864–3881. Steaks are a specialty here.

Quimby Pond. Star Rte. 1, Box 109, off Rte. 4, Rangeley; 864–3675. Casual elegance in 14-person dining room. Reservations a must.

Rangeley Inn. Off Main Street, Rangeley; 864–3341. Look for homemade breads and soups.

Saddleback Motor Inn. Off Rte. 4, Rangeley; 864–3434. Family-oriented with salad bar and seafood specialties.

Inexpensive

Doc Grant's. Main St., Rangeley; 864–3449. Family-style dining on home style fare.

The Glass Sneaker. Main St., Rangeley; 864–5616. A cafe with fancy salads.

Mike's Sports Pub & Grub. Main St., Rangeley; 864–5616. A bar and grill with hearty sandwiches and big-screen TV.

The Red Onion. Main St., Rangeley; 864–5022. Pizza and other light fare to eat in or take out.

HOW TO GET AROUND. Access to a **car** is imperative here since there is no public transportation to speak of. Some lodges, however, may supply shuttle service to the slopes; check when making your reservations.

 **SEASONAL EVENTS.** Black-diamond enthusiasts can ski free for 3 days by skiing bronco buster nonstop, top to bottom, during the annual *Bronco Buster Challenge* held in **March.** In 1985 it drew 1,000 skiers! A winter carnival and series of college rodeo weekends offer students discounted skiing. Dog sled racing is big in this neck of the woods, with New England competitions and local Rangeley meets scheduled throughout the winter.

 **OTHER SPORTS AND ACTIVITIES.** The *Ski Nordic Touring Center* (864–5921) at Saddleback offers terrain for all ability levels, with 40 km of groomed trails skirting lakes and mountains on the 12,000-acre preserve. The truly adventurous can trek to the summit and telemark to the base. Guide service for extended tours is available with advance notice.

Other ski touring facilities in the region include the *Winter's Inn* in Kingfield (265–5421) with 35 km of trails; the *Edelweiss* in Rangeley (864–3831) with 30 km; *Akers Ski Center* in Andover (392–4582), with 25 km. In Farmington: *Titcomb* (728–9031), 30 km; *Holley Farm* (778–4869), 10 km (plus an indoor pool and sauna); and *Troll Valley,* (778–2830), 15 km.

Over 100 miles of snowmobile trails are maintained regularly in the Rangeley region. **Ice skating, sledding,** and **tobogganing** are available.

 **NIGHTLIFE.** On weekends and holidays there's mellow folk music in the *Painted Pony Tavern* upstairs in the Saddleback base lodge (864–5921), or wander down to *Mike's Sports Pub & Grub* on Main Street in Rangeley (864–5616) for conversation and big-screen TV. A three-piece combo is often on board at the *Country Club Inn* on Mingo Loop Rd. in Rangeley (864–3831), and weekends at the *Rangeley Inn* on Main St. (864–3341) catch rock 'n' roll and country rock.

SUGARLOAF/USA

Kingfield ME 04947
Tel: 207–237–2000

Snow Report: 207–237–2000 or 1–800–THE LOAF in Maine
Area Vertical: 2,637 ft.
Number of Trails: 58 or 250 acres in four separate areas
Lifts: 1 gondola, 1 triple, 8 doubles, 4 T-bars
Snowmaking: 50 percent of skiable terrain
Season: early November–early May

Down East, surrounded by the lumberjack lore of the deep Maine woods, sits an enigma called Sugarloaf/USA, or "The Loaf" to the locals. How else to describe a ski resort that pays annual tribute to an endangered species by hosting Yellow-Nosed Vole Day, boasts an $8-million hotel/conference center related to Boston's Parker House, has staged the Sugarloaf Schuss annually since 1951, and is surrounded by tongue-twisting geography like Mooselookmeguntic, Azigcohos, and Matawamkeag?

Sugarloaf/USA also has a sizable peak, at 4,237 feet, third among New England ski areas after Whiteface in New York and Killington in Vermont. Look for powder conditions come spring here, especially in a skiable snowfield, unusual to Eastern skiing, above the treeline of this giant in the Longfellow Mountains. In fact, it was discovering this snowfield 35 years ago that warmed the cockles of a few intrepid Maine skiing hearts of money and influence. They formed the Sugarloaf Ski Club in 1950. Donations and volunteer labor by the likes of Robert Bass of Bass Shoe Co. led to the first of what are now 58 trails.

Three decades ago, the nearby hunting lodges and camps, likely as not without electricity and running water, provided overnight accommodations for skiers. A bus parked at the base of Sugarloaf Mountain was equipped with a gas heater, toilets, and six bunk beds—a far cry from the 670 condominiums, some going for as high as $400,000, that add sizzle to Sugarloaf's resort village which, by the way, includes a brand-new, seven-story conference center, laundromat, bank, video rental store, and other shops and restaurants.

Maniacs themselves comprise over 50 percent of the resort's annual visitors who sort themselves out by skiing abilities on 21 expert trails, such as the 9,000-foot Gondola Line, that fan from the summit snowfield, on 15 intermediate trails including the 3.5-mile Tote Road that goes from summit to base, and on 19 novice trails that funnel into the village.

Some of the expert trails are left ungroomed for mogul buffs, and brand-new skiers are encouraged to ski—at no charge—on two easy trails serviced by ski lifts.

On-mountain hosts called Friends of Sugarloaf provide complimentary mountain tours. Seniors over 70 ski free as do youngsters 6 and under, who also get complimentary rental equipment.

Practical Information for Sugarloaf/USA

HOW TO GET THERE. Sugarloaf/USA is located 110 miles from Portland in Maine's Carrabassett Valley. It is just over 200 miles from Boston. **By air.** *Delta, People Express, United,* and *Bar Harbor* airlines fly to the Portland Jetport. All major and regional airlines service Boston's Logan Airport. Service by *Morgan Aviation,* Norridgewock (634–2039) is available between Portland and the Sugarloaf Regional Airport 8 miles away in Carrabassett. Contact Sugarloaf Area Reservations (237–2861) to arrange for pick-up. *Ajax* (761–5955), *Avis* (800–331–1212), *Budget* (800–527–0700), *Hertz* (800–654–3131), and *National* (800–328–4567) rental car systems are located at the Portland Jetport.

By car. Take the Maine Turnpike to Exit 12 to Rte. 4, north through Farmington to Rte. 27, and then north to Sugarloaf/USA.

TELEPHONES. The area code for all of Maine is 207.

ACCOMMODATIONS. The *Sugarloaf Area Chamber of Commerce,* Rte. 27, Valley Crossing, P.O. Box 1980, Carrabassett Valley ME 04947 (207–235–2500), provides information on lodging in nearby towns as well as walk-to-the-slopes accommodations in the resort village that includes nearly 200 studio–5-bedroom condominiums, the 100-room *Sugarloaf Hotel,* and the 26-room *Sugarloaf Inn.* Condominiums range per unit per night from $100 for a 1-bedroom that sleeps four to $250 for 5 bedrooms sleeping 12. Lodging both at the mountain and in nearby towns is generally categorized as *Moderate* ($40–$60) to *Inexpensive* (less than $40) per room per night, double occupancy.

Moderate

Cathy's Place. Rte. 27, Stratton 04982; 246–2922. Motel with restaurant and lounge.

The Chateau. Rte. 27, Carrabassett Valley 04947; 235–2731. A motel with some dorm rooms, restaurant, and sauna.

Hotel Herbert. Rte. 27, Kingfield 04947; 265–2000. A New England country hotel with health club, award-winning chef, and entertainment.

Judson's Sugarloaf Motel. Rte. 27, Carrabassett Valley 04947; 235–2641. A small motel with restaurant, across street from airport.

The Lodge at Sugarloaf/USA. In village 04947; 237–2861. A full-service Dunfey Hotel opening in winter of 1986.

Mountain View Motel. Rte. 27, Stratton 04982; 246–2033. Motel rooms and 2-bedroom apartments.

Sugarloaf Inn Resort. In village 04987; 237–2861. Lodgings include the Sugarloaf Inn and additional 220 condominiums. Amenities include the Sugartree Health Club with indoor pool, saunas, steam room, and Jacuzzis, fitness center, skating pond, restaurant, and lodge. Packages include lift tickets.

Three Stanley Avenue Guest House. 3 Stanley Ave., Kingfield 04947; 265–5541. An old Victorian home with 7 rooms, some shared baths, breakfast served.

The Widow's Walk. Rte. 27, Stratton 04982; 246–6901. Informal 6-room guest house in a Victorian home listed with the National Register of Historic Places. Breakfast served.

Winter's Inn. Winter's Hill, Kingfield 04947; 265–5421. Classic hilltop mansion listed with National Register of Historic Places. MAP available.

Inexpensive

Country Cupboard. Rte. 27, Kingfield 04947; 265–2193. Bed and breakfast inn serves homemade food, shared baths, sitting room with wood stove.

County Seat Inn. Rte. 27, Farmington 04938; 778–3901. Colonial bed and breakfast inn with shared bath; dinner available weekends. Breakfast served.

Lumberjack Lodge. Rte. 27, Carrabassett 04947; 237–2141. Chalet-style apartments at base of mountain sleep up to 8; sauna and game room on premise.

Mountainside Condominium Rentals. In village 04947; 237–2861. Walk to the slopes from mountain homes, most with fireplaces. MAP available.

Stratton Plaza. Rte. 27, Stratton 04982; 246–2000. An old hotel in the process of renovation.

Sugarloafer's Ski Dorm. Tufts Pond Rd., Kingfield 04947; 265–2041. A log fort turned dormitory with optional linen service. MAP available.

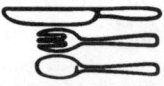 **RESTAURANTS.** Maine lobster isn't the only food served at restaurants in and around Sugarloaf. Continental and ethnic cuisines long ago made inroads to complement Down East specialties. Restaurants listed here are based on price. *Expensive,* $15 and above; *Moderate,* $10–$15; *Inexpensive,* $10 and less. The cost represents the price of a meal for one person, exclusive of drinks, tax, and tip. Unless otherwise noted, restaurants accept major credit cards.

Expensive

The Gladstone. In village; 237–2262. Menus change weekly but might include veal Dijon or chicken Kiev. Also home to Mountain Caterers, which will provide hors d'ouevres and dinners for in-home celebrations.

One Stanley Avenue. 1 Stanley Ave., Kingfield; 265–5541. A lumber baron's mansion that now serves French fare.

The Porter House. Rte. 27, Eustis; 246–7931. A restored 1908 farmhouse offers American menu.

Truffle Hound. In village; 237–2355. Locals enjoy generous discounts from extensive menu that includes rack of lamb.

Tufulio's. Valley Crossing, Rte. 27; Carrabassett Valley; 235–2010. Italian fare.

Winter's Inn. Winter Hill, Kingfield; 265–5421. Priciest restaurant in the area with dessert specialties and monthly concerts served up in a Victorian mansion.

Moderate

Cafe Italiano. Jay; 897–3939. Generous portions, special fast-service menu.

Cathy's Place. Main St., Stratton; 246–2922. A favorite with locals, offering a prime rib special on weekends.

The Chateau/Macho's Hacienda. Rte. 27, Carrabassett Valley; 235–2731. The name says all—French goes south of the border.

Hotel Herbert. Main St., Kingfield; 265–2000. French and Yankee influences both reflected on menu.

Longfellow's. Main St., Kingfield; 265–4394. A big menu includes such diverse types as Yankee, Italian, and Mexican.

The Seasons. In village; 237–2701. A greenhouse environment surrounded by ski slopes.

Other moderately priced restaurants in the region include the *Country Cupboard,* North Main St., Kingfield, 265–2193; *Judson's Sugarloaf Motel,* Rte. 27, Carrabassett Valley, 235–2641; the *Kingfield Woodsman,* Rte. 27, Kingfield, 265–2561; *Stratton Diner,* Rte. 27, Stratton, 246–3111; and *Trail's Inn,* off Rte. 27, Eustis, 246–7511.

Inexpensive

The Bag. In village; 237–2451. Favorite lunch and après-ski eatery offers sandwiches, soups, and entertainment.

Gepetto's. In village; 237–2191. Deli menu includes pizza. No credit cards.

Mountain Deli. In village; 237–2264. Deli lunch and dinner menu, take-out orders. No credit cards.

Porter's Family Restaurant, Rte. 4, Farmington; 778–4352. Serves skiers at breakfast and those en route around lunch and dinner.

Shell Shanty. In village; 273–2403. Wide selection of Maine seafood, other Yankee specialties.

HOW TO GET AROUND. A free **shuttle** makes the rounds of the base village. In fact, the shuttle, in operation since 1972, is a Sugarloaf/USA tradition! The village itself includes a video rental store, bank, laundromat, shops, and restaurants. A **car** is needed to travel beyond the shuttle's route.

SEASONAL EVENTS. *Yellow-Nosed Vole Day* kicks off events in early **December,** with discounts offered on day lift passes to those coming in costume as this endangered species. The *White White World Week Winter Carnival* is a **January** happening that includes the *National Body Sliding Contest* (imagine being wrapped in clear plastic or anything else that makes you slippery!). And the *Maine Lung Association* benefits annually from the World Heavyweight Ski Championships held here—minimum weights, 250 pounds for men, 225 pounds for women.

OTHER SPORTS AND ACTIVITIES. The *Carrabassett Valley Ski Touring Center* (237–2205) is only a mile away from Sugarloaf/USA and offers over 105 km of double-tracked **ski touring** loops. In fact, guests of some of the village condominiums can join this trail system right outside their door. The center also maintains an Olympic-size **ice skating** rink. (See Saddleback Ski Area for additional cross-country facilities nearby.)

The *Sugartree Health Club* at the Sugarloaf Inn Resort (237–2701) offers indoor **swimming,** hot tubs, saunas, steam rooms, **racquetball** courts, and exercise facilities.

Mountain Equestrian Services (237–2400 or 2000) at the base of the lifts gives both **sleigh rides** (a 3-mile loop around the village) and **horseback riding** tours.

Maine's Western Mountains can be explored by **snowmobile** on a series of trails maintained by the Maine Snowmobile Association.

HINTS FOR THE HANDICAPPED. Several nationally ranked handicapped skiers come to Sugarloaf/USA regularly because of the special attention and facilities they receive here, including lift tickets and lessons at half price and the use of outriggers, a special changing room, and the professionalism of six ski school instructors trained to work with amputees, blind and deaf people, and those with cerebral palsy. The ski school donates time to the Maine Special Olympics held annually here. For detailed information, contact the base lodge, 237–2000.

 **DAY-CARE FACILITIES.** The nursery is free midweek (nonholiday) for children ages 2½ years and up. The daily rate is $20 for under 2½ years (by reservation only). Hours are 8:30 A.M.–4:30 P.M. A night nursery, available Monday through Saturday, accepts all ages by reservation only, 6–11 P.M.

The *Little Cub Ski School* for ages 3–6 coordinates learning to ski with nursery play. The Junior Ski School gives 90-minute lessons to ages 7–14; and *SKIwee*, a *Ski Magazine*-endorsed program, involves children ages 4–12 in 6 hours of instruction, lunch, and play. For information on all programs, contact the base lodge, 237–2000.

 **NIGHTLIFE.** You can stay right at Sugarloaf/USA and catch rafter-shakin' music for dancing at *Maxwell*'s (237 –2000) and après-ski and a little night music at *The Bag* (237–2451) and *Gepetto*'s (237–2192). *The Atmosphere* is mellow in the Widowmaker's Lounge (237–2000), also on the mountain, featuring bluegrass and country-rock. And you may be able to carry on a conversation at *The Cirque* at the Sugarloaf Inn Resort (237–2701) where a piano bar sets the pace.

Off the mountain, the *Trail's End,* off Rte. 27 (246–7511) and across the street *Kern's Inn* (246–3333), both in Eustis, offer country-western and rock. The *Herbert* on Rte. 27 in Kingfield (265–2000) can be just about anything when it comes to music, with barber shop, Dixieland, and piano among the possibilities. There's a piano player on board at *Tufulio*'s in Valley Crossing, Carrabassett Valley (235–2010), and you may find soft country and rock at *Longfellow*'s on Rte. 27 in Kingfield (265–4394).

SUNDAY RIVER SKI RESORT

P.O. Box 450
Bethel ME 04217
Tel: 207–824–2187

Snow Report: 800–533–9595
Area Vertical: 1,630 ft.
Number of Trails: 36 or 220
*   acres on two mountains*
Lifts: 2 triples, 3 doubles,
*   1 T-bar*
Snowmaking: 75 percent of
*   acreage*
Season: mid-November–mid-April

A good deal of the charm of Sunday River comes from its proximity —only 6 miles down the road—to the town of Bethel. The name Bethel means "House of God," a label that's stuck since the town was incorporated in 1796, just a few years after it hosted one of the last Indian raids in New England. Originally a Canadian holding, the town was founded in 1774 as Sudbury, Canada.

Perhaps the fact that Bethel is on a major river, the Androscoggin, and an east-west rail line assured that the town would not be just another obscure village in the Maine woods. Situated near the foothills of New Hampshire's White Mountains, Bethel thrived as a summer resort.

In 1959 some folks from Bethel saw the potential of developing skiing in their already popular community. Sunday River was thus created, serving primarily local and Maine clientele until 1972 when an infusion of professional ski area management and new dollars turned what was known as one of Maine's best kept secrets into the fourth largest ski area in Maine and New Hampshire today.

But this growth hasn't touched the character of the surrounding area. There's a notable absence of fast food outlets and a choice of pre-twentieth century inns in and around Bethel that compete with Sunday River's new condominiums.

Barker Mountain and North Peak are the two distinct mountains comprising Sunday River's 36-trail network. The North Peak is just being developed with 3 fall-line trails and a triple chair in place; however, there's potential for a dozen more trails and several additional lifts.

The bulk of the skiing takes place on Barker Mountain where wide-open intermediate terrain makes the average skier smile, especially after enjoying the 2½-mile Lazy River Trail. It's the half-mile Agony Trail, a black-diamond challenge, that attracts the teens, along with the moguls on Cascades and Monday Mourning. Novice skiers can get to the top of Barker Mountain for the views and meander back on the 3-Mile Trail, the longest run on the mountain.

Sunday River claims to be the only place in the country that offers a money-back guarantee if you don't learn to ski in a day. Called the Guaranteed Learn-To-Ski Program, it's open to ages 7–70. If you're not turning, riding the novice ski lift, and having fun, you get your money back!

Practical Information for Sunday River

HOW TO GET THERE. Sunday River is 73 miles northwest of Portland in Maine's White Mountains. **By air.** The Portland Jetport is the nearest gateway, served by *People Express, United, Bar Harbor,* and *Delta* airlines. From the airport, *Oxford Hills Transit* van service is available with advance reservations (824–2187).

Ajax (800–367–2529), *Avis* (800–331–1212), *Budget* (800–527–0700), *Hertz,* (800–654–3131) and *National* (800–327–4567) rental car systems are located at the Portland Jetport. Ajax rental cars (761–5955) may be dropped off at the ski area.

By car. Take the Maine Turnpike to Exit 11, than to Rte. 26 and north through Bethel; follow signs to Sunday River.

TELEPHONES. The area code for all of Maine is 207.

ACCOMMODATIONS. The Sunday River Resort Service, P.O. Box 450, Bethel 04217 (824–2187), or the Bethel Area Chamber of Commerce, P.O. Box 121, Bethel 04217 (824–2282), can provide information on lodging and dining establishments that range from modern on-mountain condominiums to restored country inns and bed and breakfast homes. The on-mountain condominiums offer access to health-spa facilities including indoor swimming, whirlpool, and sauna. Hotel rates are based on double occupancy. Categories determined by price range are: *Expensive,* $75–$110; *Moderate,* $40–$75; *Inexpensive,* under $40. Many include breakfast or MAP plan for two.

Expensive

Bethel Inn & Country Club. Broad St., Bethel; 824–2175. Classic New England inn with swimming and health spa amenities. Rate includes MAP.

Bethel Opera House. The Common, Bethel; 824–2312. An 1884 Victorian theater has been revamped to create 10 contemporary condominiums.

Cascades Condominium Hotel. Trailside; 824–2187. Studio and 1-bedroom units with indoor pool, health spa, and common room with fireplace.

The Madison. Rte. 2, Rumford; 364–7973. A modern motel with health spa facilities. Rate includes MAP.

Merrill Brook Village Condominiums. Trailside; 824–2187. One-bedroom deluxe units with fireplace and hot tub.

South Ridge Townhouse Condominiums. Trailside; 824–2187. One–three-bedroom units with fireplace or woodstove.

Sunrise and Fall Line Condominium Hotels. Trailside; 284–2187. One-bedroom, split-level condominiums housing pool and health-spa facilities. Sunrise has large common room with fireplace. Fall Line has restaurant overlooking pool.

Westways, Rte. 5, Lovell 04051; 928–2663. A New England inn. Rate includes MAP.

Moderate

The Chapman Inn. The Common, Bethel; 824–2657. Historic home on the common has whirlpool, sauna; breakfast included.

Four Seasons Inn. Main St., Bethel; 824–2755. Serves dramatic flaming fruit compotes for breakfast. No children.

Kedarburn Inn. Rte. 35–37, Waterford 04088; 583–6182. Tastefully appointed with game room, lounge with entertainment; breakfast included.

King's Inn. King's Highway, West Bethel; 836–3375. An oasis in the wilderness with the artist's touch much in evidence. A dining table is sized for King Arthur's knights; breakfast included.

L'Auberge. Mill Hill, Bethel; 824–2774. A traditional inn except for the constellation painted on the ceiling. MAP available.

Norseman Inn. Rte. 2, Mayville Rd., Bethel; 824–2002. A country farmhouse with a Scandinavian flair. MAP available.

Old Rowley Inn. Rte. 35–37, North Waterford 04264; 583–4143. An old stage coach stop. Breakfast available.

Philbrook Inn. North West Bethel Rd., Shelburne, NH; 603–466–3831. One of the oldest Colonial inns in the area, in same family for generations. MAP available.

Sudbury Inn. Main St., Bethel; 824–2174. A Victorian dwelling with tin ceilings. Breakfast available.

Sunday River Inn. Bethel; 824–2410. A modern inn with on-premises cross-country center. MAP available.

Inexpensive

The following establishments may be considered for the budget-minded: **Barn Motel,** Rte. 2, Bethel, 824–2898; **Bethel Spa Motel,** Main St., Bethel, 824–2989; **Kimball's Motel,** Rte. 2, Rumford Center, 364–4495; **Lake Christopher Condos,** Rte. 26, Bryant Pond, 665–2500; and **Pleasant River Motel,** Rte. 2, West Bethel, 836–3575.

Inexpensive inns serving breakfast include: **Baker's B & B,** Sunday River Rd., Bethel, 824–2088; **Douglass Place,** Rte. 2, Bethel, 824–2229; **Lake House,** Rte. 35–37, Waterford, 583–4182; **Miller's Inn,** Main St., Bethel, 824–2796; and **Rostay Motor Inn,** Rte. 2, Bethel, 824–3111.

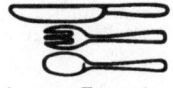 **RESTAURANTS.** As in other parts of Maine, the cost of dining out in the vicinity of the Sunday River Ski Area can be easy on the pocketbook. In this selection, restaurants are listed by category. Categories, determined by price, are: *Expensive,* $15 and above; *Moderate,* $10–$15; *Inexpensive,* less than $10. The price represents the cost of a meal for one person; drinks, tax, and tip extra. Unless specified, restaurants accept most major credit cards.

Expensive

The Lake House. Rt. 35–37, Waterford; 583–4182. Intimate dining in formal atmosphere. Menu includes duck a l'orange.

Moderate

The Bethel Inn. Broad St., Bethel; 824–2175. Classic New England inn with formal dining room overlooking golf course, cross-country skiing. Specialties include chicken pot pie at lunch and lobster at dinner.

The Boiler Room. Rte. 26, Bryant Pond; 665–2500. German food served up in restored clothes-pin mill.

D.W. McKeen's. Access Rd., Sunday River Ski Resort; 824–3232. Seafood, steaks, and veal.

Fall Line Restaurant. Sunday River Ski Resort; 824–2187. Seafood and steak dinners.

The Olde Rowley Inn. Rte. 35–37, North Waterford; 583–4142. Country dining by candlelight, including steak and seafood.

Sudbury Inn. Main St., Bethel; 824–2174. Barbecued ribs are the specialty in this restored nineteenth century inn. Reservations recommended.

Inexpensive

Charlie's Place, Main St., Bethel; 824–2732. A local pizza parlor with take-out service. No credit cards.

Mother's. Main St., Bethel; 824–2589. Old gingerbread house serves a casserole with Maine shrimp, plus tavern sandwiches.

The Only Place. Rte. 2, West Bethel, 836–3663. Claims to have the finest pizza north of Boston. No credit cards.

RFD #1. Main St., Bethel; 824–2810. Look for fish fry, BLTs. Popular with locals. No credit cards.

Saturday Night Out. Sunday River Ski Resort; 824–2187. Pub food and oysters on half shell.

HOW TO GET AROUND. Access to a **car** is imperative here, unless you are staying right at or near the mountain.

 **SEASONAL EVENTS.** On Sundays in **January** and early **February,** the *Equitable Family Ski Challenge* pits family pairs and singles (ages 19–30) on a giant slalom course. And in early February, there's a classic week-long winter carnival in Bethel that offers races, sleigh rides, skating parties, and snow sculpture contests.

 OTHER SPORTS AND ACTIVITIES. Two nearby inns offer **cross-country** ski facilities: the *Sunday River Inn & Ski Touring Center,* Bethel (824–2410), 25 miles of trails; the *Bethel Inn & Country Club,* Bethel (824–2175), 18 miles of trails. The on-mountain condominiums make available to guests, free of charge, indoor **swimming pools,** saunas, and Jacuzzis.

 **HINTS TO THE HANDICAPPED.** A Portland orthopedic surgeon lends his support to Maine Handicapped Skiing that began in 1983 at Sunday River. Modeled after the Handicapped Skiers Program in Winter Park, Colorado, it focuses on skiers affected by various neuromuscular disorders as well as on amputees, the blind, and the deaf. Specialized equipment and a fully trained volunteer staff support the program. For more information write: *Maine Handicapped Skiing,* 400 Range Rd., Cumberland, ME 04110, or call 207–829–3039.

 **DAY-CARE FACILITIES.** At the mountain the *South Ridge Day Care Center* (824–2187) accepts youngsters ages 2–6. Its Sunday Rills Youngster Program for ages 3–6 provides 2 hours of supervised skiing, rental equipment, and lunch, along with day care. The nearby *South Ridge Nursery* accommodates children ages 6 weeks–2 years. Both are open from 9 A.M. to 4 P.M. daily. Children 5 and under ski free.

 **NIGHTLIFE.** There's afternoon entertainment 2–5 P.M. at the *Cascades Lounge* in the Barker Mountain Lodge at Sunday River, 824–2187. After dinner, guests can wander over to *D.W. McKeen*'s (824–3232), on the Access Rd., a local watering hole that offers darts and big-screen TV along with a three-piece band on weekends. In Bethel, there's live bluegrass at the *Sudbury Inn*, Main St. (824–2174) on weekends, and a piano bar at the *Millbrook Tavern*, Broad St., (Bethel Inn, 824–2175).

New Hampshire

The White Mountain National Forest takes up a sizable chunk (730,000 acres) of New Hampshire while encompassing the most dramatic mountains in the eastern United States, the Presidential Range. The granite peaks and outcroppings cut a bold northeast-to-southwest swath through the state, creating imaginary characters such as The Old Man of the Mountain who presides high above the valley near Franconia. This same granite has shaped the character of the people as well, exemplified by miles of stone fences, craggy features, and an accent that stands out between its Vermont and Maine neighbors.

Then there's the formidable presence of Mt. Washington itself, at 6,288 feet the highest mountain in New England and a legend for the highest wind speed ever recorded—231 mph. Some of the most severe weather in the world is found on this mountain.

So it comes as no surprise that skiers must wait until spring to tackle Mt. Washington's snowfields. New England skiers who are in the know flock to Tuckerman's Ravine, a two-mile hike off Rte. 16 in Pinkham Notch, north of Jackson, to soak up the sun and to establish themselves among the raconteurs whose favorite stories are of exploits up the mountain with skis and backpacks, and then the descent down the snowfield, over the lip of the ravine—an incredibly steep way down. Every five years there's a race here, held in April, weather permitting, called the Inferno.

So if Mt. Washington sets the standards for lore and determined hearty adventure (there are no lifts here), what, then, does New Hampshire hospitality offer the rest of us? Plenty!

The foothills on both the eastern and western sides of the Presidential Range are home to seven noteworthy ski areas, with the Balsams also vying for attention near the Canadian border.

Attitash, Mount Cranmore, and Wildcat are all literally within minutes of each other in the Mount Washington Valley on the eastern side of the state. This valley draws its vitality year-round from a healthy tourist town, North Conway, that offers a plethora of factory outlet stores along with a fine collection of lodging and dining establishments.

New Hampshire's I–93 defines the territory on the western side of the Presidential Range, with Bretton Woods, Cannon, Loon, and Waterville Valley ski areas competing for attention with "The Old Man of the Mountain."

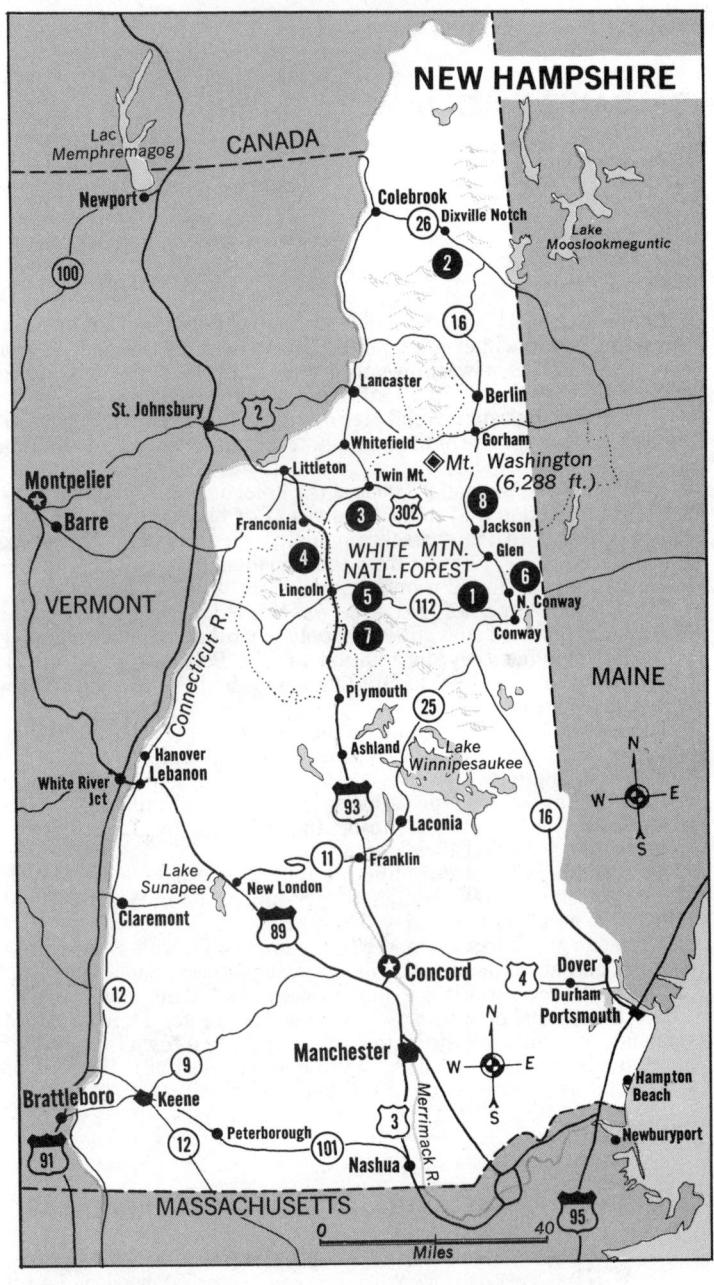

NEW HAMPSHIRE

CANADA

Lac Memphremagog

Newport

Colebrook
Dixville Notch

Lake Mooslookmeguntic

Lancaster
Berlin

St. Johnsbury

Whitefield
Gorham

Littleton
Twin Mt.
◇ Mt. Washington (6,288 ft.)

Montpelier
Barre

Franconia
WHITE MTN. NATL. FOREST
Jackson
Glen

VERMONT

Lincoln
N. Conway
Conway

MAINE

Connecticut R.

Plymouth

Hanover
Lebanon
White River Jct

Ashland
Lake Winnipesaukee

Laconia

Franklin

Lake Sunapee
New London
Claremont

Concord
Dover
Durham
Portsmouth

Manchester

Merrimack R.

Brattleboro
Keene
Peterborough
Nashua

Hampton Beach
Newburyport

MASSACHUSETTS

0   40
Miles

Resorts

1) Attitash
2) Balsams Wilderness
3) Bretton Woods

4) Cannon Mountain
5) Loon Mountain
6) Mt. Cranmore Skimobile
7) Waterville Valley
8) Wildcat Mountain

BALSAM'S WILDERNESS

Dixville Notch, NH 03576
Tel: 603-255-3400

Snow Report: 603-255-3400
Area Vertical: 1,000 ft.
Number of Trails: 12 or 95
*   acres*
Lifts: 1 double, 2 T-bars
Snowmaking: 55 percent of
*   terrain*
Season: mid-November–April

Like many of its New England counterparts, Balsam's Wilderness turned to luring winter guests after having been established for well over a century as a warm-weather mecca. In 1873 the Dix House opened to serve up to 50 guests. This was the precursor to today's 232-room The Balsams Grand Resort Hotel. It was added to over the years, but when the age of the grand hotel began to fade, so too did The Balsams.

In 1954, Neil Tillotson purchased the hotel and surrounding 15,000 acres at an auction and moved a division of his company, Tillotson Manufacturing, to the sparsely populated area (Dixville Notch has about 30 residents), 13 miles from the Canadian border. The Tillotson Rubber Company found a home there.

In 1966 the Wilderness Ski Area was opened, adding a year-round focus to the region. Today, there are only two other grand resort hotels operating, summer only, in addition to The Balsams. They are the Mount Washington Hotel in Bretton Woods and the Mountain View House in Whitefield, NH.

There's not a wealth of alpine skiing here, and it wasn't until Tillotson purchased the estate that winter recreation became part of the four-season offering. However, the 12 trails on 3,482-foot Dixville Peak, including a 2-mile run called the Connecticut Trail, are sufficient when coupled with the lavish resort life style that the 350 employees of the hotel shower on their guests.

As a member of Ski the White Mountains, guests here can also ski at Attitash, Bretton Woods, Cannon, Cranmore, Loon Waterville, and Wildcat at no charge, Monday–Thursday.

If you can pronounce them, the trail names on Dixville Peak are fun, drawing on natural landmarks such as Magalloway, Sanguinary, and Monadnock. Seven trails are marked with black diamonds.

The hotel's Ballot Room is the polling place for Dixville Notch residents, who have the distinction of being the first town in the nation to report the results of their voting in national elections. Hence, Dixville Notch is known as the "First in the Nation."

Practical Information for Balsam's Wilderness

 **HOW TO GET THERE. By car.** Dixville Notch and Balsam's Wilderness can be reached by taking I-91 to St. Johnsbury, VT, to Rte. 2 to Lancaster, NH, and Rte. 3 to Colebrook, NH, then Rte. 26 East to Dixville Notch. Or take I-93 to Lincoln, NH, then Rte. 3 on. **By bus.** *Concord Trailways* (800-258-3722, except New Hampshire) serves the town of Colebrook, 9 miles from Dixville Notch. Call Balsam's Wilderness (255-3400) to arrange for limousine service to the resort.

TELEPHONES. The area code for all of New Hampshire is 603.

 **ACCOMMODATIONS.** There are two sections to **The Balsams Grand Resort Hotel.** Dixville House is the original wooden structure with New England-style rooms, all wallpapered. It encompasses most of the public rooms. Hampshire House, built in 1917, is still known as "the new wing." It was the first steel structure building in New Hampshire and plans for it were exhibited at a long-ago World's Fair.

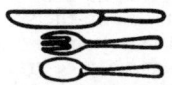 **RESTAURANTS.** Dining out here is actually dining in, with guests in the main dining room required to wear jackets in the evening. The dinners are sumptuous, with table d'hote offerings ranging from appetizers through desserts, fruits, and cheeses. Entrees include prime rib, Maine lobster, Long Island duckling, chicken preparations, veal, fish, and more. At least four vegetables are offered with every meal, and the desserts run the gamut from chocolate fudge cake to strawberry tart and rice pudding. Although all meals are taken in the main dining room, during the day, guests who prefer not to eat at the ski area cafeteria can also stop by the lounge and coffee shop for refreshments. Prices are moderate, $10–$20.

HOW TO GET AROUND. There is a free **shuttle** service that takes guests from the hotel three-fourths of a mile to the ski lifts.

 OTHER SPORTS AND ACTIVITIES. The Balsams/ Wilderness nordic trail system provides nearly 55 km of terrain that meanders in varying degrees of difficulty around Lake Gloirette near the hotel. Days here begin with an aerobics workout. An outdoor rink is lit for after-supper **skating** parties. A pair of draft horses pulls hay wagons for old-fashioned socializing. **Sleds, toboggans,** and **snowshoes** are available. The 15,000-acre Balsams property is laced with state-groomed snowmobile trails, part of a 110-mile trail system.

DAY-CARE FACILITIES. Supervised activities and games are staged in the base lodge daily from 9 A.M. to noon and from 1 to 4 P.M. for children out of diapers and up. The nursery is free to hotel guests and $2.50 an hour otherwise. Babysitting can also be arranged.

NIGHTLIFE. There are three lounges, *La Cave,* the *Wilderness Room Lounge,* and the *Switzerland of America Ballroom* with dancing, nightly music, and entertainment. Full-length feature films are shown regularly in a 265-seat theater.

BRETTON WOODS SKI AREA

Rte. 302, Bretton Woods NH 03580
Tel: 603–278–5000

Snow Reports: 603–278–5051
Area Vertical: 1,500 ft.
Number of Trails: 20 or 180
   acres
Lifts: 1 triple, 2 doubles, 1
   T-bar
Snowmaking: 80 percent
Season: mid-December–mid-April

Bretton Woods Ski Area looks east across the Ammonoosuc Valley straight up to Mt. Washington's 6,288-ft. mass. On late afternoons the vivid pinks and purples of alpenglow off of Mt. Washington are a visual feast. And the area is subject to a local phenomenon known as the Bretton Woods flurries—sunshine predominant not very far away in

North Conway or Twin Mountain, with snow at Bretton Woods. (The 180-in. annual average snowfall is the greatest in New Hampshire.)

Located on a 2,600-acre private preserve in the White Mountain National Forest, Bretton Woods is an anomaly among eastern ski areas. It's one of the newest, having opened for alpine skiing in 1973; and yet it is surrounded by the century-old tradition of a true grande dame among grande dame hotels, the Mt. Washington Hotel, whose massive size puts it in some kind of scale with Mt. Washington.

The setting is dramatic, and the preponderance of easy to intermediate trails, with only a sprinkling of steep and very short black diamond terrain, allows skiers to focus as much on the beauty as on the skis.

Looking back, records show that at one time the region was so popular that 75 passenger trains a day brought guests to three grand summer hotels in the region. The 235-room Mt. Washington Hotel is the only one left, unfortunately, and is off-limits to skiers until it's winterized a few years down the road.

However, in addition to creating one of the most esthetically pleasing base lodges in the country—a spacious, timbered structure—Bretton Woods is also developing a base of slopeside beds and offering a free shuttle service to take people to and fro.

There are only a few ski areas in this neck of the woods that offer night skiing. Bretton Woods is among them, opening two lifts from 6 to 10 P.M. Friday and Saturday nights and Wednesdays during holiday weeks.

This is a popular area with somewhat limited lift capacity, so the mountain has instituted a limited lift ticket policy to help keep waits in lift lines no longer than 10 minutes.

Practical Information for Bretton Woods

HOW TO GET THERE. Bretton Woods is one of four major New Hampshire ski resorts referred to as the Ski 93 Group. The others are Cannon Mountain, Loon Mountain, and Waterville Valley. All are easily accessible **by car** from southern corridors via I–93.

By air. Boston's Logan Airport is the gateway to Bretton Woods and other resorts in the Ski 93 Group. The airport is served by all major and regional carriers. *Bar Harbor* (800–341–1504), *Pilgrim* (800–243–0490), and *Precision* (800–451–4221) airlines fly from La Guardia and Newark airports in the metropolitan New York City area directly to Manchester, NH. Precision also makes daily commuter flights from Boston to Manchester and Laconia, NH.

Car rental agencies available in Manchester are *Avis* (624–4000 or 800–331–1212), *Budget* (668–3166 or 800–527–0700), and *Hertz* (669–6320 or 800–654–3131). Avis also serves the Laconia Airport and *National* (528–1400) will pick up there.

By bus. *Concord Trailways* makes 2 round trips daily from downtown Boston and Logan Airport. For information and schedules, call 800–258–3722. Stops in towns near the Ski 93 Group areas include Campton (Waterville Valley), Lincoln (Loon Mountain), Franconia (Cannon Mountain), and Littleton (Cannon Mountain and Bretton Woods).

TELEPHONES. The area code for all of New Hampshire is 603.

ACCOMMODATIONS. The *Twin Mountain Chamber of Commerce,* P.O. Box 194, Twin Mountain, NH 03595–0194; 846–5407. Lodging information and reservation service for accommodations in and around Bretton Woods. There's really nothing in the expensive range here. **Moderate** is about $30–$50 per night per person, double occupancy; *Inexpensive,* less than $30.

Moderate

Apres Jour Townhouses. Rte. 302, Bretton Woods 03575; 278–1711. Luxury accommodations with fireplaces, in-house cable TV.

Carroll Motel & Cottages. Rte. 3, Twin Mountain, 03575; 846–5553. Motor inn with adjacent cottages, 2 and 3 bedrooms.

The Lodge at Bretton Woods. Rte. 302, Bretton Woods 03574; 278–1000. A contemporary 50-unit inn with indoor pool and sauna, restaurant.

Rosebrook Townhouses. Rte. 302, Bretton Woods 03575; 278–1000. 1 through 4-bedroom fully furnished condominiums with fireplaces, optional maid service. Sleep up to 8.

Thompson's Wallace Hill Inn. P.O. Box 127, Bethlehem 03576; 444–6531. Old house turned country inn, shared bath, lounge, and restaurant.

The Wayside Inn & Motel. Rte. 302, Bethlehem 03574; 869–3364. A 19-room inn with 13 motel units and 180 miles of groomed snowmobile trails adjacent. On-premises dining, lounge, private or connecting baths.

Inexpensive

Boulder Motor Court. Rte. 302 E, Box 2063, Twin Mountain 03525; 10 cottages with mountain views, separate bedrooms, TVs, kitchenettes, some fireplaces.

Carlson's Motor Lodge. Rte. 302, Twin Mountain 03575; 846–5501. 16-unit motor lodge with color TV, breakfast room, recreation room with Ping-Pong and pool table.

Grand View Lodge. Rte. N, Twin Mountain 03575. A New England inn with on-premises dining, lounge.

Northern Zermatt Inn & Motel. Rte. 3, Twin Mountain, 03575; 846–5533. 15 rooms with private baths, color TV, some kitchenettes, public dining.

Lyons Motel. Rte. 3, Twin Mountain 03575; 846–5575. Motel and cottages, some with kitchenettes, on-premises restaurant, salad bar.

The Northlander Motel. Rte. 3, Box 988, Twin Mountain 03575; 10-unit motel with color TV; children under 12 free.

Paquette's Motor Inn. Rte. 3, Twin Mountain 03575; 846–5562. A 29-unit motel with color TV, dining room, fireplace, lounge with large screen TV.

Thimbleberry Bed & Breakfast. Parker Road, Twin Mountain 03575; 846–2211. Antique-decorated rooms, fresh home-baked breads and muffins for breakfast. No smoking.

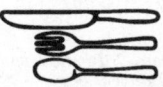 **RESTAURANTS.** The clear mountain air can make a ski traveler hungrier than usual. Luckily, New Hampshire can provide the food to satisfy the inner self. Beef and fowl, seafood and freshwater fish, all are complemented by homemade soups, breads, and pastries. In this region, an *Expensive* meal would cost $15–$20; *Moderate,* $10–$15; *Inexpensive,* less than $10. Most restaurants accept MasterCard and Visa, but it would be wise to check first before going.

Darby's Restaurant and Lounge. *Expensive.* Rte. 302, Bretton Woods 03875; 278–1500. Specialties include prime rib and seafood.

The Grandview Lodge. *Moderate.* Rte. 3, Twin Mountain 03575; 846–5731. The menu ranges from pizza to lobster.

The Shepherd's Inn. *Moderate.* Main St., Bethlehem 03574; 869–5541. Reminiscent of the Great Gatsby era, with Tiffany glass and fancy woodwork. Japanese specialties on Fridays and Saturdays.

Paquette's Motor Inn. *Moderate.* Rte. 3, Twin Mountain 03575; 846–2211. Unique soup bar complements New England fare.

The Wayside Inn & Motel. *Moderate.* Rte. 302, Bethlehem 03574; 869–3364. Continental fare.

Fabyan's Station. *Inexpensive.* Rte. 302, Bretton Woods 03575; 846–2222. Italian specialties served in remodeled turn-of-century railroad station.

Our Place. Rte. 3, Twin Mountain 03578; 846–5578. A truck stop, and you know what they say about truckers.

HOW TO GET AROUND. If you are staying right at the mountain, free **shuttle** service is available. If not, a **car** is a necessity.

 **SEASONAL EVENTS.** Among the area's annual events is the *Presidential Ski Chase*, a 50-km ski marathon and 25-km mini-chase cross-country race, all part of the Great American Ski Chase series. The New Hampshire Special Winter Olympics has also become an anticipated event at the area. And on **New Year's Eve,** there's a celebration that includes a torchlight parade, night skiing, entertainment, dancing, and fireworks. Plus, the full moon beckons at least 2 or 3 times during the season for cross-country enthusiasts to put on their skis for moonlit ski tours.

 **OTHER SPORTS AND ACTIVITIES.** NASTAR races are held here Saturday, Sundays, and daily during holiday periods. The *Bretton Woods Ski Touring Center* (278 –5181), is ranked among the majors in the East with 100 km of groomed and **tracked trails** on 3 major systems. Cross-country headquarters is the riding stable at the Mt. Washington Hotel.

 **DAY-CARE FACILITIES.** Infants from ages 2 months to 3 years are accommodated from 8:30 A.M. to 5 P.M. in a nursery that also provides diaper service. Older children can enroll in the *Hobbit & Pippin Ski School* that specializes in progressive instructional techniques for ages 3–12. This all-day program includes lift tickets, lessons, equipment, lunch, and supervised play/skiing.

 **NIGHTLIFE.** The *Slopeside Lounge* at the Bretton Woods base lodge offers daily après-ski entertainment from 2 to 5:30 P.M. This is also the setting from 8 to 11 P.M. Fridays and Saturdays when a duo or rock 'n' roll group plays music while folks outside enjoy night skiing.

CANNON MOUNTAIN

Franconia NH 03580
Tel: 603-823-5563

Snow Report: 603–823–7771
Area Vertical: 2,146 ft.
Number of Trails: 25 or 107
  acres
Lifts: 2 doubles, 1 triple, 1 80-
  passenger tram, 2 T-bars, 1 poma
Snowmaking: 50 percent of
  terrain
Season: late November–mid-April

Franconia Notch, home to Cannon Mountain, is a windswept, spectacular setting for Franconia Notch State Park, surrounded by vistas of the Lafayette and Franconia ranges.

One of the oldest ski areas in the country, Cannon is geared to skiers looking for challenges, a reputation due in part to its size—4,180 ft.—and a 2,146-ft. vertical. Cannon's biggest draw is the 18–25 crowd out of Boston who delight in the challenges of the mountain's steep terrain.

This is a mountain of American skiing firsts: the first race trail, ski school, aerial tram, World Cup competition, and paid ski patrol. Local artifacts and lore and ski-related miscellany and history from all over the United States are collected at the New England Ski Museum at the base of the mountain.

However, Cannon Mountain, as part of the Franconia Notch State Park, is a state-operated ski area. By definition, this means that private ski area competition over the years pushed Cannon out of its prominent status. A recent $4-million appropriation by the New Hampshire legis-

lature to be shared by Cannon and another state area, Sunapee, will
assist in helping the mountain stay competitive.

Practical Information for Cannon Mountain

 **HOW TO GET THERE. By car.** From Concord NH, which is 75 miles away, take I–93 to Rte. 3 and into Franconia. Cannon is 4 miles south of Franconia. **By bus.** Both Franconia and Littleton (12 miles from Cannon) are served regularly by *Concord Trailways*. Call 823–5661 for information and schedules. (For details on how to get to the region, see Bretton Woods section above.)

TELEPHONES. The area code for all of New Hampshire is 603.

 **ACCOMMODATIONS.** This popular year-round recreation region, offers a variety of lodging accommodations. A selection is presented here. For additional information, contact the *Franconia-Easton-Sugar Hill Chamber of Commerce,* Box D, Rte. 18, Franconia 03580; 823–5661. Rates at these lodgings are per person based on double occupancy for three nights. Categories, determined by price, are: *Expensive,* \$75–\$100 and up, depending on the meal plan offered; *Moderate,* \$50–\$75; *Inexpensive,* under \$50.

Expensive

Franconia Inn. Rte. 116, Franconia 03580; 823–5442. A 29-room traditional New England inn with a ski-touring center, hot tub, sleigh rides, and on-premise dining. MAP available.

Hillwinds Motor Inn. P.O. Box 250, Dow Ave., Franconia 03580; 823–5533. With restaurant, weekend entertainment, this 30-room motel offers a convenient downtown location.

Horse and Hound Inn. Off Rte. 18, Cannon Mountain, Franconia 03580; 823–5501. A traditional 12-room inn at the base of the mountain with cross-country skiing nearby, on-premises pub and dining, fireplaces. Serves breakfast.

Ledgeland. Rte. 117, Sugar Hill 03585; 823–5341. Country inn and housekeeping cottages with fabulous views; completely equipped; open year-round.

Lovett's Inn by Lafayette Brook. Profile Road, Rte. 18, Franconia 03580; 823–5341. A farmhouse built in 1786 that was restored to a 10-room inn boasting stenciled walls and antiques. There are also 6 country cottages. MAP available.

Sunset Hill House. Sunset Rd., Sugar Hill 03585; 823–5522. A 26-room inn with private baths, surrounded by ski-touring terrain.

Moderate

Gale River Motel. Rte. 18, RFD 1, Box 153, Franconia 03580; 823–5655. A 10-room motel with color TV, free in-room coffee, some cottages with multiple bedrooms.

Hill Top Inn. Rte. 117, Sugar Hill 03585; 823–5695. A 5-room bed-and-breakfast Victorian guest house that features hearty farmers' breakfasts.

Raynor's Motor Lodge. Rtes. 18 and 142, Franconia 03580; 823–9586. A 30-room motel with color TV, free coffee, ski racks; massage and MAP available.

Rivagale Inn. 195 Main St., Franconia 03580; 823–9984. A 14-room New England inn with ski lounge. MAP available.

Stonybrook Motor Lodge. Rte. 18, Franconia, 03580; 823–5344. 24 rooms with color TV, lodge with game room, ice skating, cross-country. MAP available.

Inexpensive

Franconia Notch Vacation Rentals. Rte. 18, Mittersill Rd., Franconia 03580; 823–5536. Privately owned vacation homes with 2–4 bedrooms; with fireplace, kitchen, linens, furnishings.

Pinestead Farm Lodge. Easton Rd., Franconia 03580; 823–8121. Simple rooms (6 only) in a New England farmhouse; share kitchen privileges.

Southworth's Bed & Breakfast. Main St., Sugar Hill 03585; 823–5344. Only 3 rooms, but full of character with brass and four-poster beds, shared bath, Continental-style breakfast.

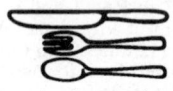 **RESTAURANTS.** One can dine quite inexpensively in the region, meals costing $10–$17 in the *Expensive* category; $7–$10, *Moderate;* and less than $7, *Inexpensive.* We've, therefore, eliminated the lowest category from our selection. Unless otherwise noted, major credit cards are accepted.

Moderate to *Expensive*

Horse and Hound Inn. Cannon Mountain, Franconia; 823–5501. Look for old pine and prints and American food with a Continental accent. There's often live music on weekends.

Indian Head Motel Resort. Rte. 3, Lincoln; 745–8181. Prime steaks and ribs done to your liking.

Lovett's Inn. Profile Rd., Rte. 18, Franconia; 823–7761. One of the few places around where jackets are required for dinner, along with reservations.

Sugar Hill Inn. Rte. 117, Franconia; 823–5621. Country gourmet cooking in a country inn atmosphere.

Moderate

Dutch Treat Restaurant/Lounge. Main St., Franconia; 823–8851. Homemade Italian and American food; children's plates.

Franconia Inn. Rte. 116, Franconia; 823–5542. Describes its fare as classical cuisine prepared in delicate French sauces. Reservations appreciated.

Rivagale Inn. 195 Main St., Box 97, Franconia; 823–9984. New England style home cooking.

Village House Restaurant. Main St., Franconia; 823–5912. Something for everyone here, including children's menu.

HOW TO GET AROUND. Access to a car is imperative here, since public transportation is limited.

SEASONAL EVENTS. Over Washington's Birthday holiday week in **February,** the Franconia community hosts a *Winter Carnival.*

 OTHER SPORTS AND ACTIVITIES. There are 10 miles of **cross-country** terrain right at Cannon and an additional 50 miles in the region. The Ski Hearth Farm in Franconia (823–8047) provides horse-drawn **sleigh** rides, as does the Franconia Inn (823–5442). Also available are **ice fishing, skating, sledding,** and **snowmobiling.** Contact the main lodge, 823–5563.

DAY-CARE FACILITIES. Cannon's Peabody Base Lodge (823–5563) will entertain young ones from age 6 months and up, 9 A.M.–noon and 1–4 P.M. Snacks are provided, but not lunch. The day rate is $15, and reservations are appreciated.

 **NIGHTLIFE.** You can catch live music on the weekends at the *Hillwinds Motor Inn,* Dow Ave., Franconia, 823–5533, and at the *Horse and Hound Inn,* off Rte. 18, Cannon Mountain, in Franconia, 823–5501. The *Baron's Den Lounge* at Mittersill Resort, Rte. 18, Franconia, 823–5511 (a time-share resort) offers entertainment as does the *Village House Restaurant,* Main St., Franconia, 823–5912.

LOON MOUNTAIN

Route 112, Lincoln NH 03251
Tel: 603–745–8111

Snow Report: 603–745–8100
Area Vertical: 2,100 ft.
Number of Trails: 37 or 212
*   acres*
Lifts: 2 triples, 4 doubles, 1
*   tow rope, 1 4-passenger gondola*
Snowmaking: 80 percent of
*   terrain*
Season: mid-November–mid-April

The dying paper mill town of Lincoln, NH got a shot in the arm in 1966 when a former New Hampshire governor, Sherman Adams, began creating Loon Mountain. Ultimately snow farming grew to be a specialty at Loon where a reputation for well-groomed slopes brought sufficient people to mandate a limited lift ticket sale policy on weekends. Today it is the busiest ski area in New Hampshire.

Those who have skied the mountain may be hard-pressed to say just why it's their favorite, except perhaps that it brings out the best in people who seem uncommonly civil and happy even while waiting for lifts. Nearly half of the terrain here is in the intermediate category, but it's always so well groomed that having a good skiing day here is the norm, although the moguls on Angel Street, a black-diamond trail, are purposely left intact.

Recently Loon developed what it calls North Peak, served by its own triple chair and base lodge, and offering spectacular views off the top and challenging terrain.

By virtue of sheer number of trails, Loon today surpasses its next door neighbor, Waterville Valley, some 30 minutes away. Both, incidentally, are ranked among the top 10 ski areas in New England.

A village at the base of the mountain is emerging, bisected by the east branch of the Pemigewasset River. Loon is positioned at the west end of the Kancamagus Highway, an extraordinarily scenic wilderness swath that allows east-to-west movement through the Granite State.

On the mountain, a longtime Loon employee, Bernie Fox, has the distinction of creating what a Boston-based sports magazine, *Sportscape,* calls the best chili in New England. She's the manager of the Octagon Cafeteria, one of six food operations here.

Practical Information for Loon Mountain

 **HOW TO GET THERE.** Loon Mountain is located on Rte. 112, 2 miles from Lincoln and 80 miles from Manchester. **By car.** Take I–93 to Exit 32 onto Rte. 112 East for 4 miles to Loon Mountain. (To get to the region, see Bretton Woods section above.) Shuttle service can be arranged, generally, from various parts of the region by contacting the lodge where reservations are made.

TELEPHONES. The area code for all of New Hampshire is 603.

 **ACCOMMODATIONS.** Lodgings in the communities at and around Loon Mountain range from the simple to the sublime. The sublime can largely be found in the condominiums and townhouses at or near slopeside, where all amenities are available in prices ranging from $135 per room per night

to $380 for two nights in multiple units. Since most of these offer various packages, they are classified here as *Expensive to Deluxe*. The *Loon Mountain Lodging Bureau,* Loon Mountain, Rte. 112, Lincoln NH 03251 (745–8111), provides information and reservation service to a number of area accommodations, including its own on-mountain condos. In the other two categories in this listing, rates are based on per person per night in hotels, motels, and inns. For *Moderate,* expect to pay $20–$30; *Inexpensive,* under $20.

Expensive to Deluxe

Condominiums at Loon Mountain. Lincoln 03251; 745–8111. Fully equipped kitchens, TVs, fireplaces, and woodstoves complement the privacy of these mountain vacation homes.

The Inn at Loon Mountain. Kancamagus Highway, Lincoln 03251; 745–8111. A modern, 45-room inn with windows overlooking Loon's trails or the Pemigawasset River.

Lincoln Station & Riverfront Condominiums. Kancamagus Highway, P.O. Box 477, Lincoln 03251; 745–3441. Free shuttle to Loon from luxury accommodations; 2- 3- and 4-bedroom units; saunas and exercise rooms available.

The Village of Loon Mountain. P.O. Box 508, Kancamagus Highway, Lincoln 03251; 745–3401. 175 luxury townhouses, fully equipped. Free shuttle to Loon, plus indoor pool, sauna, whirlpool, ice skating, and paddle tennis.

Moderate

The Beacon Motel Swim & Tennis Club. Rte. 3, Lincoln 03251; 745–8118. A 100-unit motel with color cable TV, indoor pool, tennis, sauna, Jacuzzi, game room, restaurant, and lounge.

Indian Head Motel Resort. Rte. 3, Lincoln 03251; An 86-unit motel with game and exercise room, indoor pool, sauna, restaurant; live entertainment some evenings.

The Woodstock Inn. Main Street, Box 118, North Woodstock 03283; 745–3951. A 16-room, 100-year-old Victorian inn serves up antiques and meals.

Woodward's Motor Inn. Rte. 3, Lincoln 03251; 745–8141. Restaurant, indoor pool, sauna, racquetball, Jacuzzi, guest laundry in this 58-room motel.

Inexpensive

The Charpentier Bed & Breakfast. Pollard Rd., Box 562, Lincoln 03251; 745–8517. A 6-room country farmhouse with ski loft.

Drummer Boy Motor Inn. Rte. 3, Lincoln 03281; 745–3661. A 57-unit motel, some with kitchenettes, exercise room, Jacuzzi, indoor pool, sauna.

Franconia Notch Motel. Rte. 3, RFD 1, Box 988, Lincoln 03251; 745–2229. A 12-unit motel with color TV (cable), morning coffee,

Kancamagus Motor Lodge. Box 505, Rte. 112, Lincoln 03251; 745–3365. A 34-room motel with cable TV, in-room steambaths, dining room, and lounge.

Red Doors Motel. RFD 1, Box 109A, Rte. 3, Lincoln 03257; 745–2267. 24 rooms with color TV, in-room coffee, game room.

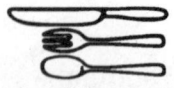 **RESTAURANTS.** At slopeside or in the small communities around Loon Mountain, there is a nice array of dining places serving everything from regional New England dishes to ethnic cuisines. Categories are: *Expensive,* $18 and up; *Moderate,* $10–$18; and *Inexpensive,* less than $10. The costs represent the price for an average meal for one person, excluding drinks, tax, and tip. Unless specified, the restaurants accept most major credit cards, but it is wise to check before you go.

Expensive

D.G. Wagoner's Restaurant and Lounge. At Loon; 745–2278. Salad bar, extensive menu, weekend brunch, entertainment.

Woodstock Inn. Woodstock; 745–3951. A glass-enclosed, year-round porch offers candlelight dining. Breakfasts here are sumptuous and range from red flannel hash to eggs Benedict.

Moderate

The Bear Trap. At Loon; 745–8111. Steaks and chops done to your liking.

The Common Man. Lincoln; 745–3463. Rustic farmhouse serves all-American cuisine.

Half-Baked. North Woodstock; 745–3811. As the name implies, a takeout specialty store with everything from a soup-to-nuts-dinner to Italian fare.

Indian Head Motel Resort. Lincoln; 745–8181. Prime ribs, seafood.

Mt. Adams Inn. North Woodstock; 745–2711. Polish fare, family dining.

Woodstock Station. North Woodstock; 745–3951. Look for a 10-ounce rib eye steak topped with bearnaise sauce.

Woodward's Open Hearth Steak House. Lincoln; 745–8141. Baked stuffed shrimp, among other offerings, besides the steaks.

Inexpensive

The Italian Moose. Lincoln; 745–3339. Casual, family-style dining; Italian specialties.

Truant's Tavern. North Woodstock; 745–2239. A schoolhouse turned fancy with seafood and sandwiches.

HOW TO GET AROUND. It's advisable to have a car here, although some lodging establishments do provide shuttle service to the slopes. Once at Loon, a narrow-gauge 40-passenger steam train provides free shuttle between the two base areas, which are about one-third mile apart.

SEASONAL EVENTS. In early **April** the Governor Adams Cup Race honors Loon's founding father and provides a challenging event for ages 17 and up. And in **March,** the area's handicapped-blind ski program is supported by another fundraising race.

OTHER SPORTS AND ACTIVITIES. *Loon Mt. Ski Touring* (745–2722) offers 20 km of **cross-country** trails that include sights along an old logging road and treks into the Pemigewasset wilderness. Nature and wilderness tours are offered here throughout the winter. NASTAR races are held daily except Tuesdays and Thursdays, and surfboard-like devices called **snowboards,** are championed here (they aren't at most areas). The snowboard is a single ski about 4 feet long and 1 foot wide that is strapped to the feet for descents of the mountain.

Look for **swimming** at Woodward's Motor Inn (745–8141), the Village of Loon Townhouses (745–3401), the Lodge at Lincoln Station (745–3441), Indian Head Resort (745–8181), the Drummer Boy Motor Inn (745–3661), all in Lincoln; and the Alpine Village Townhouses (745–3455) in North Woodstock. Alpine Village and Woodward's Motor Inn (745–8141) also have **racquetball** courts, and there's **tennis** at The Beacon Motel (745–8118) along with swimming in Lincoln. **Ice fishing, skating, sledding,** and **mountaineering** can also be arranged.

HINTS TO THE HANDICAPPED. A young woman named Cindy Buso has spent 10 years developing the Handicapped Skiing Program at Loon Mountain. Various teaching aids are used to compensate for infirmities. This program is combined with the Blind Outdoor Leisure Development (BOLD) Program. In both, the first three lessons are free and include all necessary equipment and lift tickets. In addition, an annual fund-raising race in March helps to support the program. Call the base lodge (745–8100) for details.

DAY-CARE FACILITIES. The *Nursery Ski School* (745–8100) provides ski lessons for ages 3–4 in the Ski Mites Program and accepts infants and up from 8:30 A.M. to 4:30 P.M. The all-day rate is $15 weekdays and $17 weekends.

NIGHTLIFE. Entertainment in this region includes disco at the *Beacon Motel* (745–8118) in Lincoln, a live band or duo on stage nightly (except Mondays) at the *Bear Trap Lounge* at the Inn at Loon Mountain (745–8111), dancing and nightly fun at *Indian Head,* Lincoln (745–8181) and at *King's Court* in Campton (536–3520). *D.G. Wagoner's Restaurant & Lounge* at the Village of Loon (745–2278) also brings in musicians.

MT. WASHINGTON VALLEY SKI AREAS

ATTITASH

Rte. 302, Bartlett NH 03812
Tel: 603–374–2369

Snow Report: 800–258–0316
Area Vertical: 1,550 ft.
Number of trails: 21 or 190
  acres
Lifts: 4 double chairlifts
Snowmaking: 95 percent
Season: late-November–mid-April

Attitash is one of three areas in the Mt. Washington valley which, because of proximity to each other, offer interchangeable lift tickets with the purchase of 3- and 5-day midweek lift ticket packages. The other areas are Wildcat in Pinkham Notch and Black Mountain in Jackson, all of which, in addition to Mt. Cranmore, not only share their skiing but their dining and lodging accommodations as well.

Attitash, located on Rte. 302, 12 miles from North Conway, is an intermediate skier's mountain, with over half of its 21 trails, including the 1¾-mile Northwest Passage, marked for the average recreational skier. However, a 42 percent gradient on Idiot's Option has been known to challenge those with a penchant for black-diamond thrills, and kids and beginners like trails with names like Far-Out. A limited lift ticket sales policy in effect on weekends and holidays helps avoid congestion at the lifts.

The motto of Attitash is "Best skiing in the East, whether it snows or not." And one local fan says, "I really have to say they live up to it—thanks to snowmaking and grooming."

MT. CRANMORE SKIMOBILE

North Conway NH
Tel: 603–356–5544

Snow Report: 603–356–5544
Area Vertical: 1,500 ft.
Number of Trails: 16 or 300
  acres
Lifts: 3 double chairlifts, 1
  poma, 2 trams
Snowmaking: 60 percent
Season: December–April

One of America's oldest ski areas, started in 1938, Mt. Cranmore Skimobile may well be the *raison d'etre* for North Conway. It's here that stories abound of skier-laden snow trains puffing up from the cities in the 1930s. The Mt. Cranmore Skimobile, from whence comes the area's name, was one of the first ski lifts in the United States, and is a series of little cars that run up a track to the top of the mountain. And the Hannes Schneider Ski School, another American skiing first, carries on today with the founder's son, Herbert, as ski meister.

The skiing here is primarily in the intermediate range, but don't be surprised if you see old-fashioned leather ski boots and long skis whipping past on its five black-diamond trails.

The mountain is an east-facing slope that catches the sun on cold days, and it is one of the few ski areas in the country that's really located within walking distance of a real village (as opposed to a village created because of skiing). Skiers can hit the trails in the morning, wander down to North Conway for lunch, and spend the afternoon back on the slopes.

WILDCAT MOUNTAIN

Rte. 16, Pinkham Notch
Jackson NH 03846
Tel: 603–466–3326

Snow Report: 603–466–3326
Area Vertical: 2,100 ft.
Number of Trails: 20
Lifts: 2 doubles, 2 triples, 1 gondola
Snowmaking: 80 percent of terrain
Season: mid-November–late April

With a summit standing at 4,100 ft. and a 2,100-ft. vertical, Wildcat is well named. It's the next best thing to skiing Mt. Washington in this neck of the woods and is the Mt. Washington Valley's biggest ski area. Wildcat is also one of three (including Attitash and Black Mountain) that enjoy interchangeable lift ticket privileges.

Magnificent alpine views are available here even to novice skiers who make descents from the summit. In fact, according to every poll taken, Wildcat always wins the "best scenery in the East" category. From the summit of Wildcat are glimpses of Tuckerman's Ravine across the way. And it was standing on the Mt. Washington side looking over to Wildcat that first inspired some skiers to think of cutting trails on Wildcat.

In 1933 the first race down the Wildcat Trail was held after it was cut by the Civilian Conservation Corps (CCC). Back then, skiers hiked up on fur-lined skis, and if they made three runs a day they were happy. Today, with the gondola, the record is 234 runs down this same trail.

You will find vintage down parkas here and possibly even bear trap bindings sported by loyal long-time followers.

Although the trails are narrow and steep, the preferred style of those who designed the terrain some years back, the narrowness also serves to protect the snow and the skiers from winds that blow over from Mt. Washington.

There's a separate area for beginning skiers—the Snowcat Area—that's served by its own triple chair. Children 13 and under can ride the chair free, if their parents have purchased midweek lift ticket packages.

Practical Information for Mt. Washington
Valley Ski Areas

HOW TO GET THERE. North Conway, is about 130 miles from Boston. **By air.** *Delta, People Express, United,* and *Bar Harbor* airlines fly to the Portland Jetport, 65 miles away. All major and regional carriers serve Boston's Logan Airport. The regional airport in Fryeburg ME, 15 miles from North Conway, accepts private aircraft and charters. *Ajax, Avis, Budget, Hertz,* and *National* rental car systems are located at the Portland Jetport. All major rental car systems are at Logan. National Car Rentals are available through Valley Food and Beverage in North Conway (356–5718).

By bus. *Concord Trailways* (800–852–3317) offers direct bus service daily from Logan and downtown Boston to North Conway. *Vermont Transit/Greyhound* (800–451–3292) offers daily service to the area via Montreal and Portland. For bus information in North Conway, call *The Yankee Clipper Lodge* (356–5736).

By car. Take I–95 North to Spaulding Turnpike in Portsmouth NH, to Route 16 north to North Conway. Routes from North Conway to the individual ski areas will be noted under each area.

TELEPHONES. The area code for all of New Hampshire is 603.

 **ACCOMMODATIONS.** The *Mt. Washington Valley Chamber of Commerce,* North Conway 03860 (356–3171), provides a reservation service for about 100 lodging establishments serving the ski areas. But it should be remembered that the entire valley is a tourist mecca, so you may be staying at a lodging at Attitash, for example, while skiing at Mt. Cranmore. Since most establishments offer packages, lodging rates are based on 3 nights per person, double occupancy. Categories determined by price for the package (unless otherwise stated) are: *Expensive,* $100 and up; *Moderate,* $60–$100; *Inexpensive,* under $60.

Valley Bed & Breakfast (935–3799) is a collection of bed and breakfast establishments serving the Mt. Washington Valley as well as western Maine.

ATTITASH

Moderate

Attitash Mountain Village. Rte. 302, Bartlett 03812; 374–2382. Slopeside 1–4-bedroom condos and motel-style rooms, with mountain views, fireplaces, indoor pool, Jacuzzi, sauna, game room, ice skating, color cable TV. Dining on premises; ski packages available.

The Bernerhof Inn. Rte. 302, Glen 03838; 383–4414. Turn-of-century inn has 10 antique-appointed rooms, a Finnish sauna, some private baths, and serves breakfast in bed. Also look for fine on-premises dining and entertainment. MAP available.

Best Western Storybook Motor Inn. Rtes. 16 and 302, Glen 03838; 383–6800. 53-room colonial inn with dining room, private baths, sauna, laundry, game room. Especially hearty breakfasts served here.

Linderhof Motor Inn. Rte. 16, Box 126, Glen 03838; 383–4334. A Bavarian-style inn offering 33 rooms with 2 double beds, private bath, color TV. Breakfasts available.

The Notchland Inn. Hart's Location, Bartlett 03812; 374–6131. A nineteenth-century inn with 10 antique-filled rooms, private baths, fireplaces, sauna, Jacuzzi, on-premises dining, ice skating. MAP available.

Sky Valley Motel and Chalets. Rte. 302, Bartlett 03812; 374–2322. Great for families. Two- and three-bedroom completely furnished chalets, some with fireplaces.

Inexpensive

Attitash Valley Motor Inn. Rte. 302, Glen 03838; 383–4239. Knotty pine adds warmth to rooms equipped with cable TV, private baths, and in-room coffee. Meals available.

The Country Inn at Bartlett. Rte. 302, Box 327, Bartlett Village 03812; 374–2353. Only 6 rooms in inn, but additional 20 rooms in cottages and one efficiency cottage. Cottages have private baths, cable TV. In the lodge are music room, ski racks, and ski tuning bench.

The Red Apple Inn. Rte. 302, Glen 03838; Motel accommodations with dining and lounge, cross-country out back door, fireplace lounge, country breakfasts.

North Colony Motel. Rte. 302, Bartlett 03812; 374–6679. Modern rooms and cottages just a mile from Attitash.

The Villager Motel. Rte. 302, Bartlett 03812; 374–2742. Motel and housekeeping units, two chalets in quiet valley setting.

MT. CRANMORE SKIMOBILE

Expensive

Cranmore Mt. Lodge. Box 1194, Kearsarge Rd., North Conway 03860; 356–2044. An 11-room inn with shared baths plus 2-room suite with private bath and TV; also 4 rooms in a barn loft, all with private baths and color TV. On-premises ice skating, tobogganing, snowmobiling, and dining. MAP available.

Darby Field Inn. Bald Hill Rd., Conway 03818; 447–2181. 17 rooms (15 with private bath) and what a view of the Mt. Washington Valley! On-premises dining, lounge, cross-country skiing, weekend entertainment. MAP available.

Fox Ridge Resort. Rte. 16, North Conway 03860; 356–3151. A modern resort on a 300-acre hilltop perch. Fine dining, lounge, indoor pool, whirlpool, sauna, color TV. MAP available.

New England Inn. Rte. 16A, Intervale 03845; 356–5541. An 1809 26-room country inn with 14 cottages (9 with fireplaces). Cross-country skiing on premises, sleigh rides, dining. MAP available.

Red Jacket Motor Inn. Rte. 16, North Conway 03860; 356–5411. Modern, if miniature, resort complex set on a hillside. Restaurant, saloon, kitchenettes; indoor pool, whirlpool, sauna, game room, color TV. MAP available.

Snowvillage Inn. Off Rte. 153, Snowville 03877 (near Conway); 447–2818. A pleasant 16-room country inn with cross-country skiing, sauna, library, game room. MAP available.

Moderate

Arends Motel & Inn. Rtes. 16/302, North Conway 03860; 356–2976. A resort motel/inn with 21 motel units, 6 inn rooms, family units. Complimentary Continental breakfast, color cable TV.

The Buttonwood Inn. Box 3297, Mt. Surprise Rd., North Conway 03860; 356–2625. A secluded 8-room bed-and-breakfast inn with private and semi-private baths, TV and game rooms, après-ski room with fireplace, hearty breakfasts. MAP available.

The Center Chimney 1787. River Rd., Box 1220, North Conway 03860; 356–6788. Built as a guest house in 1787 along the Saco River. Offers 4 double rooms; living room with TV, complimentary Continental breakfast.

The Cranmore Inn. Kearsarge St., North Conway 03860; 356–5502. A 25-room inn located near movie theaters, offers 4 suites, 4 private baths, TV room; dining on premises.

Eastern Slope Inn Resort. Rte. 16, North Conway 03860; 356–6321. Downtown location offers 125 rooms, all recently renovated, dining room, pub, sauna, Jacuzzi, year-round pool.

The Hill Cottages. Box 33 MW, Center Conway 03813; 447–5833. Skate and cross-country ski right out the door of 2–4-bedroom completely furnished chalets.

Hitching Post Motel. Box 537. Rte. 16, Conway 03818; 356–2625. 13 motel rooms with or without kitchens; 7 cottages. TV in room, morning coffee.

The Merrill Farm Inn. Rte. 16, Box 2070, Conway 03818 447–3866. 60 rooms with private baths, sauna, Jacuzzi, solar-heated outdoor pool, in-room TV, all in old-fashioned New England setting.

Nereledge Inn & White Horse Pub. River Rd., North Conway 03860; 356–2831. A 1787 inn that serves apple pie for breakfast; 8 guest rooms with shared baths, 2 sitting rooms, dining room and pub.

The 1785 Inn. P.O. Box 9, North Conway 03860; 356–9025. A 14-room inn with shared and private baths, 2 guest living rooms, après-ski lounge, breakfasts.

Vista View Condominiums. Rtes. 16/302, Intervale 03845; 356–2301. Suites sleep up to 4 with single bedroom and queen-size sofabed in living room, color cable TV, stereo, laundry facilities, ski lockers.

Wildflower Guest House. Rte. 16, North Conway 03860; 356–2224. Six rooms in a century-old home with shared parlor with woodstove, and fireplace in dining room. Breakfasts served.

Inexpensive

There's a collection of motels in the area with rates under $45 for three nights per person, double occupancy.

WILDCAT MOUNTAIN

Expensive

Christmas Farm Inn. Rte. 16B, Jackson 03846; 383–4313. A remodeled 18th-century Cape Cod that's full of antiques. Most of the 33 rooms have private baths; cabins and suites also available. On-premises dining, lounge, game room, sauna. MAP available.

The Inn at Thorn Hill. Box SW, Jackson Village 03846; 383–4242. A 22-room inn on a country road, with dining room, game room, and wax room. With MAP.

Nestlenook Inn & Ski Touring Center. Dinsmore Rd., Jackson 03846; 383–9443. A 17-room Colonial farmhouse, 10 bedrooms, most with private baths, 3 cabins. Large screen color TV, sleigh rides, dining. Breakfast and cross-country skiing available.

Wentworth Resort Hotel. Rte. 16A, Jackson Village 03846; 383–9700. A 50-room hotel in the grand style, located on ski touring route. All rooms with private baths, color cable TV. MAP available.

Whitney's Village Inn. Box W, Jackson 03846; 383–6666. An inn and motor lodge with ice skating, tobogganing, and cross-country skiing nearby. 31 of 37 rooms have private baths, 4 with fireplaces. On-premises dining, lounge, pub, game room.

Moderate

Covered Bridge Motel. Jackson Village 03846; 383–6630. 26 rooms with color TV, social room with fireplace, breakfasts served, sauna, Jacuzzi.

The Village House. Box 359, Jackson 03846; 383–6666. A 10-room inn, with private baths, ski waxing room, greenhouse breakfast porch.

Wildcat Inn & Tavern. Rte. 16 A, Jackson Village 03846; 383–6083. A 15-room traditional country inn offering hot tub and sauna, ice skating, sleigh rides, dining and tavern with weekend entertainment.

Inexpensive

Abbott's Ski Lodge. Rte. 16, Jackson 03846; 383–4317. A small inn with 9 rooms, some dorm rooms. Breakfast available.

The Blake House Bed & Breakfast. Box 246 W, Jackson 03846; 383–6983. A guest house offering 5 rooms with shared baths, guest living and dining rooms, breakfast.

Dana Place Inn. Rte. 16, Jackson 03846; 383–6822. A lodge with dining room, pub, hot spa, some condominiums.

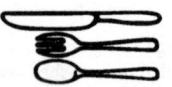 **RESTAURANTS.** Dining out in the Mt. Washington Valley can be a treat to both the palate and the pocketbook. New Hampshire provides tasty food aplenty, not only traditional New England chowders but a wide range of international cuisines as well. Categories based on per person price range used are: *Expensive,* $20 and up; *Moderate,* $10–$20; *Inexpensive,* $10 and under.

Expensive

The Darby Field Inn. Off Rte. 16, North Conway; 447–2181. Sunset views of the valley are served up with gourmet fare. Candlelight dinner and daily specials.

Snow Village Inn. Off Rte. 153, Snowsville; 447–2818. Only one entree is available each day and you place your order before you arrive by making reservations, of course.

Stonehurst Manor. Rte. 16, North Conway; 356–3271. An international elegance is noticed here, with delicacies like veal Oscar and beef Wellington.

Wentworth Resort Hotel. Rte. 16A, Jackson; 383–9700. Waiters are in formal attire here where a specialty is burgundy rack of lamb. Reservations required.

Moderate to Expensive

Dana Place Inn. Rte. 16, North Conway; 383–6822. European-American choices here and a great place for lunch after taking the Ellis River Trail on cross-country skis from the Jackson Ski Touring Foundation.

New England Inn. Off Rte. 16A, Intervale; 356–5541. Authentic New England preparations are featured, including Vermont turkey; children's menu available.

Moderate

Barnaby's. Rte. 16, North Conway; 356–5781. An extensive menu includes roast beef and salad bar.

Bernerhof Inn. Rte. 302, Glen; 383–4414. Austrian cuisine served in turn-of-century inn, includes fondue by the fire.

Daisy's at the Eastern Slope Inn. Main St., North Conway; 356–6321. A choice of elegant or pub dining. As the name says, near the slopes.

The Inn at Thorn Hill. Rte. 112, Jackson; 383–9700. Enjoy American food by candlelight.

Lobster Pot Restaurant at Oxen Yoke. Kearsage St., North Conway; 356–6525. Seafood and prime rib. One of the oldest après-ski places in the area.

Montana's. Seavey St., North Conway; 356–6331. Pastas, veal, and prime rib featured in elegant or pub setting.

Nereledge Inn and White Horse Pub. River Rd., North Conway; 356–2831. English beers and an English pub atmosphere.

The Oxen Yoke. Rte. 16A, North Conway; 356–6525. One of the oldest après-ski places in the area, with substantial hors d'ouevres and seafood.

Snug Harbor. River Rd., North Conway; 356–3000. A colonial home with seafood specialties and a children's menu.

Yankee Smokehouse. Rte. 16/302, North Conway; 356–2687. Eat in or takeout open-pit barbecued chicken and ribs, chili.

Inexpensive

Checkers. Main St., Conway; 447–5524. Pasta specialties and veal dishes.

Poor Dudley's & Dud's Pub. Rte. 16, Conway; 447–4211. Greek salads, stuffed quahogs—clams to landlubbers.

Scarecrow Pub & Grill. Rte. 16, Intervale; 356–2287. Generous portions of such delicacies as cioppino and other Italian fare.

Up Country Saloon. Rte. 16, North Conway; 356–3336. Mexican and American fare.

HOW TO GET AROUND. It's preferable to have a **car** in this region, where public transportation facilities are rare or spasmodic. (See *How to Get There* section above for car rental information.)

SEASONAL EVENTS. The mountain is race oriented, with the Lathrop Ski Camp at Attitash offering race clinics throughout the season. At Mt. Cranmore Skimobile, the *Winterfest Winter Carnival* that rolls by annually in **mid-January** brings racers, snow sculpting, fireworks, and a torchlight parade to all the ski areas in the Mt. Washington Valley.

At Wildcat, recreational skiers can ski like the pros the first weekend of **March** during the annual *Wildcat Challenge* and *Dual Forum Race.* Around **Easter** there's the *Corn Snow Caper,* a rite to spring that includes silly slaloms, a costume contest, snow volleyball, and more. The *New England Handicapped Sportsmen's Association* also benefits from an annual race held here. Just before the ski year ends, an easy giant slalom for skiers 40 years old and up promises a good time during the annual *Old Man of the Mountain race,* named after that formidable craggy face that's a landmark in the White Mountains.

OTHER SPORTS AND ACTIVITIES. Skiing is just one of many attractions in the Mt. Washington Valley. There are community outdoor **skating** rinks in Jackson, North Conway and Conway. **Sleigh rides** are available at New England Inn, Intervale, 356–5541; *Horse Logic Enterprises,* Jackson, 383–4347; and Nestlenook Inn, Jackson, 383–9443. Call the Cranmore Mt. Lodge, North Conway, 356–2044, for information on **snowmobile rides.**

The following establishments have **health/fitness** centers: Mountain Valley Court Club, North Conway (356–5774), racquetball court and fitness center; Mt. Cranmore Racquet Club, North Conway (356–6301) 2 racquetball, 5 indoor tennis, courts, 2 squash courts, 10 Nautilus machines, indoor swimming pool.

Jackson is also home of the *Jackson Ski Touring Foundation* (383–9355), which coordinates trails and activities of 5 major touring areas offering over 200 km of trails. This is the largest ski touring complex in the East, moving ski touring buffs from inn to inn, around villages, or challenging the mountains on backcountry routes.

The five areas comprising the center include the center itself, the *Nestlenook Inn and Ski Touring* (383–9443) and *Linderhof Resort* (383–9443), all in Jackson; the *Intervale Nordic Learning Center* on the grounds of the New England Inn (356–5541), and the *Forest Inn* (356–9772), both in Intervale.

For details on night cross-country skiing, backcountry guided tours and Telemark skiing, contact the *Intervale Nordic Learning Center* (356–3379); *International Mountain Equipment,* North Conway (356–6316); or *Eastern Mountain Sports,* North Conway (356–5433). International Mountain Equipment is also the place to contact for details on **ice climbing expeditions** popular in the area.

Six times a season at Wildcat Mountain there's Super NASTAR, a giant slalom course for NASTAR participants who have won medals. NASTAR is offered Wednesdays, Saturdays, and Sundays all season long.

 **HINTS TO THE HANDICAPPED.** In addition to hosting an annual benefit for the New England Handicapped Sportsmen's Association, handicapped skiers receive complimentary lift tickets. At Mt. Cranmore, special lessons are offered to the handicapped, including hearing impaired, amputees, and highly motivated retarded children. Call 356–5544 for information.

 **CHILDREN'S ACTIVITIES.** In Attitash, the *Attots Clubhouse* accepts children from 1 year old, 9 A.M.–4:30 P.M. daily. Lunch is available as are private ski lessons for the older children. The *Attitash Ski School* involves 6–9-year-olds in an all-day program that involves lunch and two lessons on weekends and during holidays. Young skiers aged 5–14 who want to master the parallel turn can join the *Atticrashers* before moving up to the *Mountain Class* that introduces racing techniques. The weekend-holiday program operates from mid-December to mid-March. For information on any of these programs, call 374–2369.

The Mt. Cranmore Nursery (356–5544) accepts children aged 1–6 from 8:30 A.M. to 4 P.M. daily for $10 a day. The ski school staff will pick up children from the nursery and take them on the slopes for lessons.

At Wildcat Mountain, the *Kitten Club Nursery* (466–3326) accepts children from 3 months to 2 years old by appointment, from 8:30 A.M. to 4:30 P.M. Children 4 years old and under can also take a private ski lesson at $10 through the club's ski school. *SKIwee,* the nationally recognized learn-to-ski program for children, is available for 7–10-year-olds.

 **NIGHTLIFE.** The entire area prides itself on bringing in a variety of live entertainers. Look for rock 'n' roll, lots of loud music, and the under-30 crowd at *Barnaby's* (356–5781), *Bogie's* (356–2472), *Horsefeathers* (356–2687), *Marcello's* (356–2313), and the *Oxen Yoke Inn* (356–6525), all in North Conway; the *Red Parka Pub* (383–4344) in Glen; and *W. W. Doolittle's* (374–6055) in Bartlett, a popular après-ski hangout.

Music on the softer side can be found at *Fox Ridge Resort* (356–3151), the *Darby Field Inn* (447–2181), and *Red Jacket Inn* (356–5411), all in North Conway; and at the *Wildcat Inn and Tavern* (383–4245) and *The Bernerhof* (383–4414) in Glen.

WATERVILLE VALLEY

Waterville Valley NH 03223
Tel: 603-236-8311

Snow Report: 603-236-4144
Area Vertical: 2,020 ft.
Number of Trails: 38 or 196 acres
*   on two mountains*
Lifts: 3 triples, 6 doubles, 1
*   T-bar, 1 poma, 1 J-bar*
Snowmaking: 75 percent of
*   terrain*
Season: mid-November–mid-April

Waterville Valley is a self-contained, privately owned, 500-acre resort favored by Bostonians who travel north 2½ hours into New Hampshire's White Mountain National Forest. In fact, this place is inextricably linked to the Kennedy mystique, as the late Sen. Robert Kennedy lent some financial backing to the area in the mid-1960s and the Kennedy clan subsequently began skiing here.

As with other New England ski areas, it was the summer wilderness ambience that first drew families to the region. These same families then began to see the possibilities of winter recreation and formed ski clubs to cut a few trails on Snow's Mountain in the mid-1930s. Nearby 3,835-ft. Mt. Tecumseh, where the bulk of Waterville Valley's trails are located today, received trail-cutting attention from the Civilian Conservation Corps in the 1930s.

It was the draw of the 1½-mile Mt. Tecumseh Trail that first brought Tom Corcoran, a rising Olympic ski racing hopeful, to the area in 1948. In 1965, after international competition, he returned to create this destination ski resort.

Over half of the area's trails are designed for intermediate-level skiers, with the 3-mile Periphery and nearly mile-long Valley Run two favorites. The steepest trail, with a 38 percent gradient, is Bobby's Run, providing black-diamond challenges along its 3,500-ft. length. The three intermediate trails on Snow's Mountain are accessible only on weekends when the chairlift there is operating.

Given owner Corcoran's own racing background, it comes as no surprise that ski racing is an important element of the ski atmosphere at Waterville. Known as New England's World Cup Resort, it has, in fact, hosted more World Cup events than any other ski area in the country.

The village itself is 1½ miles away from the slopes, but a free shuttle runs back and forth. At the village are inns, condominiums, restaurants, shops, and recreational facilities, all complying with strict zoning codes that call for natural wood exteriors, views from all windows, and nothing higher than 3½ stories. Families with young children are especially welcome here, with free skiing and lodging midweek (nonholidays) to children 12 and under.

Mountain guides are available to orient skiers to the area, and much of the social life revolves around the Waterville Valley Ski Week that couples daily on-slope lessons with a moonlight ski touring party, ski races, and entertainment.

Although Waterville Valley is the most sought-after ski area in New Hampshire, a limited lift ticket sale policy holds lift lines down to about 15 minutes.

Practical Information for Waterville Valley

 **HOW TO GET THERE.** Waterville Valley is located 80 miles from Manchester and 130 miles from Boston. **By bus.** *Concord Trailways* (800–258–3722) provides a daily afternoon trip from downtown Boston and Logan Airport to Campton which is 11 miles from Waterville Valley. Transfers from Campton to the village are available by calling the *Waterville Valley Lodging Bureau* at 800–258–8988. **By car.** From Boston, take I–93 North to Exit 28, then follow Rte. 49 East 22 miles to Waterville Valley. (See Bretton Woods section above for details on getting to the region.)

TELEPHONES. The area code for all of New Hampshire is 603.

 **ACCOMMODATIONS.** The Waterville Valley Lodging Bureau, Waterville Valley NH 03223 (800–258–8988), can make lodging arrangements at three inns and numerous condominiums totaling 3,000 beds within a 5-minute drive of the slopes. All are modern by New England standards, having been built since 1966. Inn rates are per person per night based on double occupancy. Categories determined by price are: *Expensive,* $55; *Moderate,* $30–$55. Condominum rates range upward from $199 for a 1-bedroom unit for 2 nights.

Snowy Owl Inn. *Expensive.* Waterville Valley; 800–258–8988. An 80-room inn with Jacuzzi bathtubs and wet bars in 42 brand-new rooms. Complimentary Continental breakfasts include fresh fruit and homemade breads, plus there's wine and cheese afternoons. Guests have free access to a fully equipped sports center.

Silver Squirrel Inn. *Moderate.* Waterville Valley; 800–258–8988. A 30-room country inn with complimentary Continental breakfasts. Whirlpools and saunas are on premises and guests have free use of Sports Center.

Valley Inn and Tavern. *Moderate.* Waterville Valley; 236–8336. Look for fresh chocolate chip cookies and hot cocoa afternoons and a mint on your pillow at night. Guests have free access to the sports center. Rate includes MAP.

Waterville Valley Condominium Vacations. Waterville Valley; 800–258–8988. Over 150 1–4-bedroom townhouses with well-equipped kitchens, living rooms with fireplaces, and color cable TV. Some have laundry facilities.

Winsor Hill Condominiums. Waterville Valley; 800–343–1286. Eight 1–3-bedroom and 1-bedroom deluxe units.

Village Condominums. Waterville Valley; 236–8301. 25 easy housekeeping units with dishwasher and disposal, laundry, color cable TV, and choice of 1–5 bedrooms. The units flank a central building housing a game room and saunas.

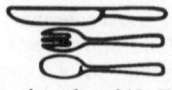 **RESTAURANTS.** Since Waterville Valley is a self-contained resort, skiers dine at on-site restaurants in the village itself. Categories for these eating places are: *Expensive,* $20 and up; *Moderate,* $10–$20; and *Inexpensive,* less than $10. These price classifications are based on the average cost of a meal for one person, excluding drinks, tax, and tip. All accept major credit cards.

O'Keefe's. *Expensive* Waterville Valley; 236–8331. A formal dining room where the specialized fare is seafood and steak. There's a children's menu and choices for dieters. The place turns lively on weekends with live bands.

The Valley Tavern. *Expensive.* Waterville Valley; 236–8336. Candlelight dining in a greenhouse ambience. If you tire of seafood, try their duckling.

Finish Line Restaurant and Lounge. *Moderate.* Waterville Valley; 236–8800. This is informal family dining with a choice of Italian specialties served up with nightly sleigh rides.

Alpine Pine Pizza. *Inexpensive.* Waterville Valley; 236–8338. For afternoon and evening light fare, pizza and submarine sandwiches.

HOW TO GET AROUND. You can leave your car parked for the length of your stay here, for a free **shuttle** makes the rounds continuously between the village dwellings and the mountain.

SEASONAL EVENTS. An outdoor sunrise **Easter** service begins at 5 A.M. every year. Before that, however, in early **February,** WBZ-TV from Boston hosts a *Celebrity Slalom for Wednesday's Child* to raise funds to support adoption programs. World Cup races that attract top international women racers are held usually in **March.**

 OTHER ACTIVITIES. Look for NASTAR recreational **racing** on Wednesdays, Fridays, Saturdays, and Sundays, with a coin-op race course open daily. There's a new **indoor sports** center at the village with an Olympic-size swimming pool, jogging track, tennis, racquetball and squash courts, and exercise and weight rooms. Village guests can **skate** at a covered ice skating rink, take **sleigh rides,** go on moonlight ski tours, and play **platform tennis.** The Snow's Mountain chairlift operates on weekends and holidays to take telemark enthusiasts to a seven-km **cross-country** run. The Waterville Valley Ski Touring Center (236–8311) maintains 60 km of groomed and double-tracked trails that loop from the center through the White Mountain National Forest.

DAY-CARE FACILITIES. The *Waterville Valley Nursery* accepts children from 4 months to 5 years and is open 8:30 A.M.–4 P.M. daily. Older youngsters can enjoy an on-snow play period or learn to ski in two programs, for ages 3–5 and 6–12, through *SKIwee,* a nationally recognized instructional approach to teaching the sport to children.

 **NIGHTLIFE.** *The Sail Loft Lounge* in the Waterville Valley Base Lodge offers après-ski entertainment daily 4–6 P.M. A pianist is on board weeknights at *O'Keefe's* (236–8331), but on weekends live bands invite music for dancing. Boston comedians bring comedy to the *Valley Tavern* (236–8336) where there's also often a trio or piano player.

New York

New York has four principal ski regions. They are the Adirondack North Country Region, dominated by Whiteface and Gore; the Catskills/Hudson Valley Region that includes Hunter, Windham, and Belleayre; the Central Leather Stocking Finger Lakes Region; and the Western Region. In all, New York boasts over 63 places to ski, with over half of these offering night skiing, testimony to the large population centers nearby whose denizens like to breathe the mountain air after work!

Generally, however, New York isn't well known as a destination state when it comes to skiing. What skiers do find, however, are a great number of easy-to-get-to day-trip areas. Many of these are designated as preferred by beginners or by intermediates, so you can mix and match mountains here depending on your skiing ability. Lift tickets are substantially less at the many smaller areas than they are at the destination resorts.

When it comes to destination areas, or major day-trip attractions, attention will focus on only a handful of areas in the Catskills and the Adirondacks. Not included in this roundup, but noteworthy for those seeking a ski vacation experience, are Greek Peak in the Syracuse area and Holiday Valley in southwestern New York.

There's a helpful guide to New York's cold-weather adventures called *I Love New York: Skiing & Winter Sports.* This is available from the *New York State Department of Commerce,* 1 Commerce Plaza, Albany, New York.

BELLEAYRE SKI CENTER

P.O. Box 313, Highmount NY 12441
Tel: 914–254–5600

Snow Report: 800–942–6204
(New York only)
800–431–6012 (outside
New York)
Area Vertical: 1,340 ft.
Number of Trails: 23 or 89
skiable acres
Lifts: 4 double chairs, 2
T-bars, 1 J-bar
Snowmaking: 30 percent
Season: late November–late March

Belleayre Ski Center is owned and operated by the New York State Department of Conservation. The 35-year-old ski area has been pulling skiers up from New York City (3 hours away) for 35 years for enjoyable outdoor recreation and the ambience of the central Catskills.

Skiers who come here are family-oriented and find a friendly atmosphere combined with economical lift tickets. The mountain tends to be less crowded than some of its Catskill neighbors. The skiing encompasses 23 trails that run first off a ridge line, descending straight down to a central plateau and then descending again to a lower base area. The upper half tends to attract intermediate and advanced skiers, while novices prefer the lower mountain and their own learning area. There are base facilities and parking at the top, midsection, and bottom.

Indian lore is strong here, with a favorite novice run called Iroquois and other trails with names like Wanatuska and Utsayantha.

The mountain is a member and founder of "Ski the Catskills," which includes 8 ski areas all within 90 minutes of each other and all accessible from New York State Thruway exits 16–21. These include Bobcat at Andes, Cortina Valley at Haines Falls, Deer Run at Stamford, Holiday Mountain at Monticello, Hunter Mountain at Hunter, Plattekill at Roxbury and Ski Windham at Windham. (Hunter and Windham are covered in this section.)

And for folks who remember childhood tales and American literature, this is the region that Rip Van Winkle made famous! The mountain is surrounded by small but quaint towns. The area tends to be a popular second home haven for people from the New York metropolitan area. However, it hasn't yet been discovered as a winter destination resort area.

Practical Information for Belleayre

HOW TO GET THERE. Belleayre Ski Center is located in the town of Highmount, some 137 miles from New York City. **By car.** Take the New York Thruway to Exit 19 at Kingston, then onto Rte. 28 west for 38 miles to Highmount. Follow signs to the ski area.

TELEPHONES. The area code for the Belleayre area is 914.

ACCOMMODATIONS. For specific information on establishments in the Belleayre area geared to accommodating individuals and groups of 20 or more, contact the Belleayre Lodging Bureau, P.O. Box 313, Highmount, NY 12441; 254–5600; 800–257–7017 in New York; 800–431–4555 out of state. Although most establishments in the area list their rates for a 2-night stay, the following categories are based on a 1-night stay per person, some with MAP: *Expensive,* $40–$60; *Moderate,* $25–$40; *Inexpensive,* less than $25.

Expensive

DeMarfio's Motel & Continental Restaurant. Main St., Fleischmanns 12403; 254–5090. Comfortable motel with fine dining room, cocktail lounge, and game room.

Moderate

The Alpine Inn. Alpine Road, Oliverea 12462; 254–5026. A Swiss-style inn in the Catskills with on-premises nordic skiing, a lighted toboggan run, and snow-tubing. MAP available.

Catskill Mountain Lakehouse. Oliverea Rd., Oliverea 12462; 254–5498. Rooms with private baths, snowmobiles for rent, and fireplace room with pool table. MAP available.

Cold Spring Lodge. Oliverea Road, Big Indian 12410; 254–5711. Cabins with fireplaces, MAP available.

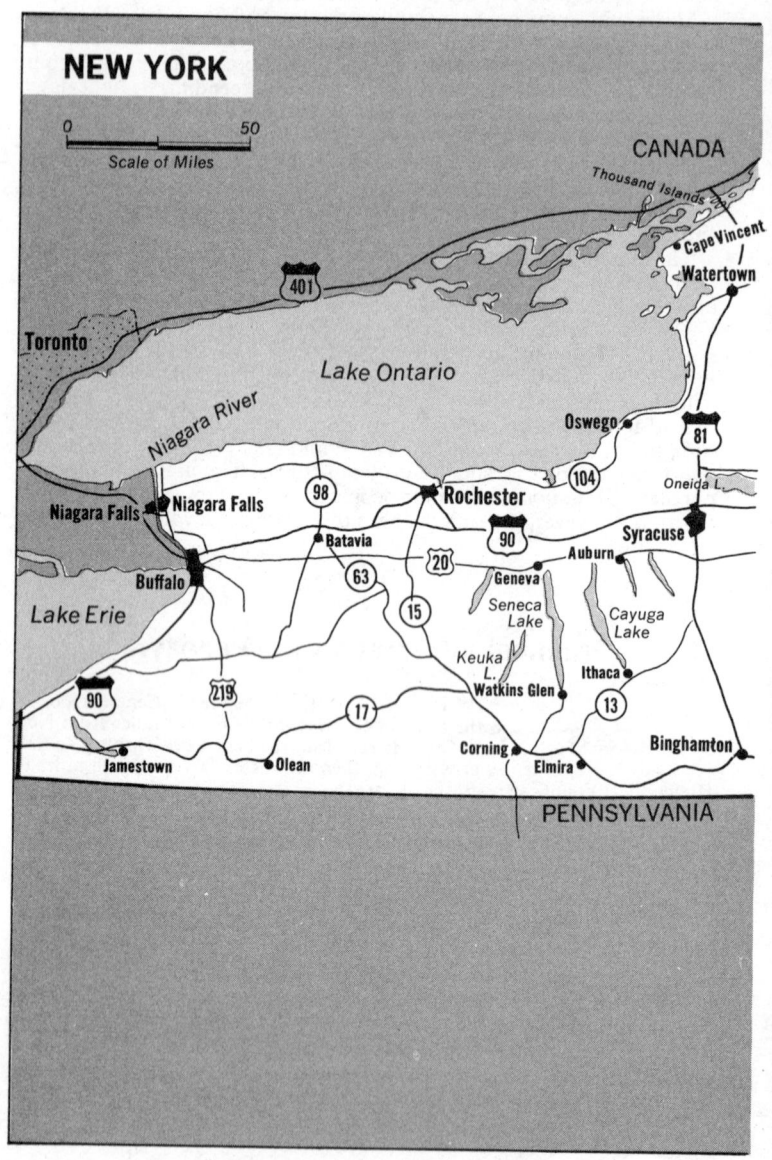

NEW YORK

0   50
Scale of Miles

CANADA

Thousand Islands

Cape Vincent

Watertown

Toronto

Lake Ontario

Niagara River

Oswego

81

104

Oneida L.

98   Rochester

Niagara Falls   Niagara Falls

Batavia

90

Syracuse

Buffalo

20   Auburn

63

Geneva

Lake Erie

15

Seneca
Lake

Cayuga
Lake

Keuka
L.

Ithaca

13

Watkins Glen

219   17

Binghamton

90

Corning   Elmira

Jamestown   Olean

PENNSYLVANIA

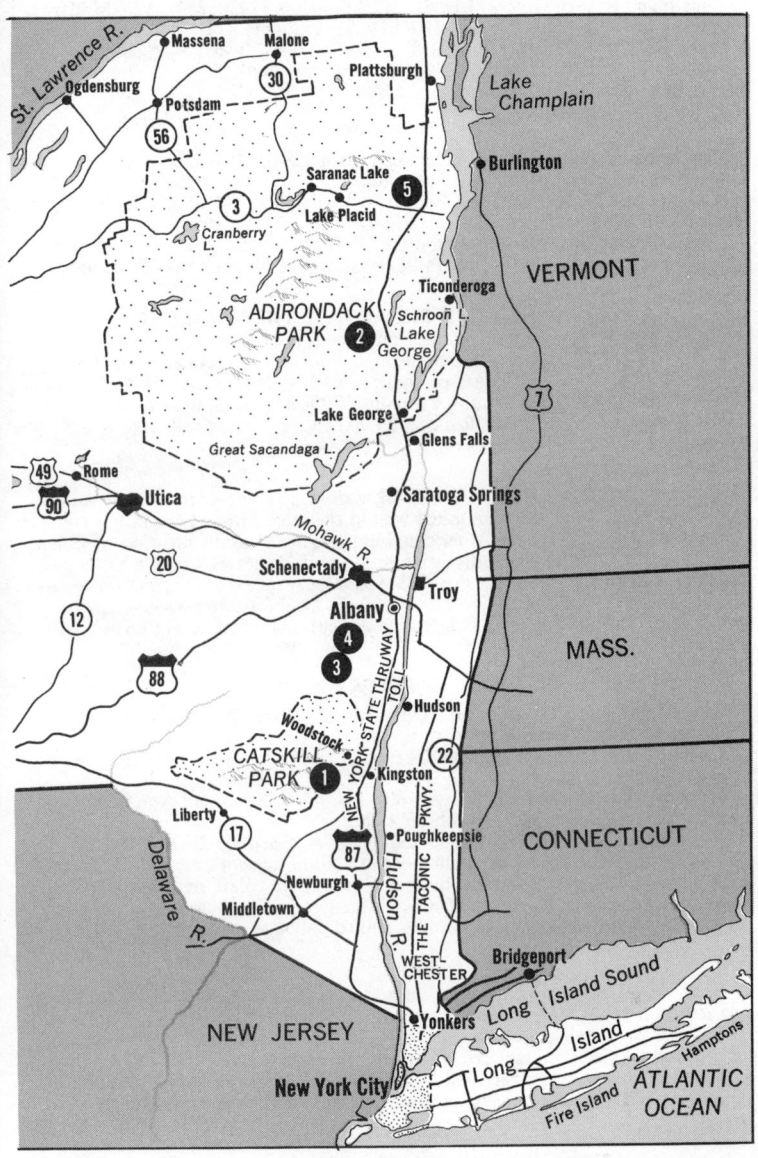

Resorts

1) Belleayre Mountain
2) Gore Mountain
3) Hunter Mountain
4) Ski Windham
5) Whiteface Mountain

Copper Hood Inn. Rte. 28, Shandaken 12480; 688–9962. A resort with indoor pool, sauna, tennis, and ice skating. MAP available.

Northland Resort Motel. Main St., Fleischmanns 12430; 254–5125. Modern motel rooms with color TV and HBO. MAP available.

Pine Hill Arms Hotel. Main St., Pine Hill 12465; 254–5125. 35 rooms with private baths, located at base of Belleayre Mountain, with dining in greenhouse, sauna, hot tub spa, and game room. MAP available.

Inexpensive.

Big Indian Lodge. Oliverea Rd., Big Indian 12410; 254–5266. Cabins with restaurant and game room. MAP available.

Cobblestone Motel. Rte. 214, Phoenicia 12464; 688–7871. Some large efficiencies available in this standard motel.

The Colonial Inn. Main St., Pine Hill 12465; 254–5577. A 27-room inn in the Currier & Ives style that offers horse-drawn sleigh rides. MAP available.

 **BED-AND-BREAKFAST TREASURES.** Two county organizations maintain lists of these economical establishments in the area. Some are in private homes, others in lodges or small inns. For detailed information, contact *Bed-and-Breakfast of Delaware County,* P.O. Box 36, Stamford NY 12167 (676–3104); or *Ulster County Bed-and-Breakfast Association,* SR 108, Rte. 42, Shandaken NY 12480 (688–7101).

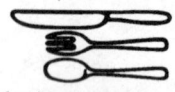 **RESTAURANTS.** Skiers at Belleayre need not spend a fortune to eat well in the area. Most of the fare is standard American, but there are pleasant surprises of Continental cuisine and ethnic dishes as well. In this brief selection categories are: *Expensive,* $15–$20; *Moderate,* $10–$15; and *Inexpensive,* less than $10. Prices reflect the cost for a meal for one person, excluding drinks, tax, and tip. Unless specified, the restaurants listed accept most credit cards.

Expensive

The Alpine Inn. Oliverea Rd., Oliverea; 254–5026. A Swiss inn offering Continental fare. Reservations a must.

Copper Hood Inn. Rte. 28, Shandaken; 688–9962. Rustic fireside dining with home-cooked specialties.

Roxbury Run Restaurant. Denver; 607–326–7577. Swiss and American specialties including duckling and lobster tails.

Val d'Isere. Rte. 28, Big Indian; 254–4646. A charming French provincial restaurant that's pricey for the region but not out of line with New York skiers' expectations. Look for escargot, duck a l'orange, chocolate mousse.

Wild Acres Hotel. Highmount Rd., Highmount; 254–9868. A country club atmosphere with a menu that includes stuffed cabbage.

Moderate

Big Indian Lodge. Oliverea Road, Big Indian; 254–5266. Steaks and seafood are served here, as well as hamburgers.

Catskill Mountain Lake House. Oliverea Rd., Oliverea; 254–5498. Sauerbraten and wiener schnitzel are among the specialties here.

Pine Hill Arms Restaurant and Greenhouse. Main St., Pine Hill; 254–9811. A century-old inn has a greenhouse where Cajun dishes are served.

Inexpensive

DeMarfios Continental Restaurant. Main St., Fleischmanns; 254–9831. Wide-ranging menu, plus soup and salad bar.

HOW TO GET AROUND. A **car** is a must here, although a few lodges will provide transportation to the slopes.

OTHER SPORTS AND ACTIVITIES. There is **ski touring** at the area, and **ice skating, snowmobiling,** and **tobogganning** nearby. The lifts operate 6–10 P.M. Saturdays for night skiing. NASTAR races are held weekends and holidays.

HINTS TO THE HANDICAPPED. There is free skiing for the handicapped through Belleayre's Access Pass.

DAY-CARE FACILITIES. The nursery accepts ages 2–6 for $15 a day, with a *Play and Ski* program for ages 4–6 involving 90-minute lessons to learn how to fall and laugh and how to move with equipment (available weekends and holidays). Children ages 7–8 can join the *Mouse Patrol* for introductory lessons and graduate to the *Kool Kats* (ages 8–12) for more instruction. The *Pied Piper* is an all-day program with lunch, instruction, and on-slope fun.

NIGHTLIFE. Because the ski area isn't yet discovered as a "destination resort," there's nothing nearby resembling a disco or night club. However, there is dancing on Saturdays at *Kass' Inn Resort Hotel*, Rte. 30, Margaretville (586–4861), and at the *Emory Brook* Inn on Main St., Fleischmanns, (254–9831) there's often entertainment.

GORE MOUNTAIN SKI AREA

Peaceful Valley Rd.
North Creek NY 12853
Tel: 518-251-2411

Snow Report: 518–251–2853
Area vertical: 2,100 ft.
Number of Trails: 41 or 170
skiable acres
Lifts: 1 gondola, 1 triple
chair, 4 double chairs, 1 T-bar,
1 J-bar
Snowmaking: 90 percent of terrain
Season: November–April

Gore Mountain Ski Area is located 25 miles from what is known as the Lake George region of the southern Adirondack Mountains. Although not widely recognized, Gore is one of the oldest ski areas in the East. In 1932 the Winter Olympics in Lake Placid gave impetus to the sport of skiing throughout the region. Attention was regained in 1980 with the Winter Games once again in Lake Placid.

The merits of this 3,600-ft. peak, the second highest (after Whiteface at 4,436 ft.) in New York, were duly noted during those first winter games. Uphill transport came by way of cars, trucks, and buses to position skiers for descents down trails that were then gentle but narrow. Open slopes were served by rope tows, thought to be the first lifts in the East. Ski trains used to haul as many as 1,500 skiers from Albany to North Creek where residents opened their homes for accommodations and meals. On one notable day in 1936, the Delaware and Hudson Railroad transported 967 skiers in 14 coaches, and the New York Central carried 850 more in 11 sleepers and four coaches.

World War II put a crimp in the evolution of the ski area, but in 1964 attention was again turned to skiing in the region, and the State of New York began developing Gore. In 1984 it came under the supervision of the Olympic Regional Development Authority.

North Creek itself, two miles away, has a population of 800, and with over 400 beds for tourists is moving, albeit slowly, in the direction of accommodating skiers. However, if après-ski and disco-style nightlife is a must, you won't find it here. The whole region, town and mountain, lends itself to a family experience, a place where you're more than just a number and people get to know you.

North Creek's claim to fame dates back to the turn of the century and a day when Vice President Teddy Roosevelt was hiking in the area. He was contacted by a courier who advised him that President William

McKinley had died. It was from the North Creek train station that Roosevelt was sworn in as President of the United States.

Gore has one of the highest percentages of intermediate terrain—73 percent—of any ski area anywhere, and all of the intermediate trails are over a mile long. The favorite is the Cloud Trail, a full 3½ miles long.

From the top of the mountain there are views of Vermont's Green Mountains and the central and high peaks of the Adirondacks.

Practical Information for Gore Mountain

 **HOW TO GET THERE.** Gore Mountain Ski Area is 30 miles from Glens Falls, 90 miles from Albany, and 30 miles from Fort Edward. It is situated 2 miles from North Creek.

By air. The Albany County Airport is served by *American, Bar Harbor, Brockway, Command, Delta, Eastern, Empire, Mail, People Express, Piedmont, Pilgrim, Ransome, Republic, United,* and *USAir* airlines. All major rental cars are available at the airport.

By bus. *Greyhound* (800–528–0447) and *Adirondack/Pine Hills Trailways* (800–225–6815) lines serve the area.

By car. Take Rte. 87, the Adirondack Northway, to Exit 23; travel north on Rte. 9 to Rte. 28, which leads into North Creek.

By train. There are daily *Amtrak* (800–USA–RAIL) departures from Grand Central Terminal in New York City as well as from the Rensselaer, N.Y., station to the Gore Mountain/Lake George region via Fort Edward. Special ski packages include rail fare, shuttle transportation, lift tickets, and hotel accommodations.

TELEPHONES. The area code for Gore Mountain is 518.

 **ACCOMMODATIONS.** The *Gore Mountain Region Chamber of Commerce*, Box 84, Main St., North Creek 12853 (251–2612) can give information on and make reservations at some area lodges; or contact the individual establishments for information. Because this is a popular tourist region, summer and winter, this list does not attempt to include all of the accommodations around Lake George, about 25 miles away, but focuses on those closer to Gore Mountain. All those listed in this selection, except one, are considered in the *Moderate* category—$40–$70 per person, based on double occupancy. (See *Whiteface* section for listings in Chestertown which might also appeal to Gore Mountain skiers.)

Moderate

Black Mountain Ski Lodge. Star Rte., North Creek, 4 miles west of junction of Rte. 28 12853; 251–2800. 25 rooms, dining room, TV. MAP available.

Garnet Hill Lodge. Off Rte. 28, North River 12853; 251–2821. An old Adirondack lodge in the mountains overlooking Thirteenth Lake. 26 rooms; complete ski touring center; Saturday night smorgasbord. MAP available.

Gore Mountain Lodge. Rte. 28, North Creek 12853; 251–3444; A 14-room motel 4 miles from the mountain. On-premises dining, lounge with fireplace.

Northwind Motel. Peaceful Valley Rd., North Creek 12853; 251–2522. Groups welcome here; dining room. MAP available.

Ridin' Hy Ranch Resort. Sherman Lake, Warrensburg 12885; 494–2742. Lots of activity here with cross-country and horse-drawn sleigh rides. MAP available.

Alpine Motel. Main St., North Creek, 12853; 251–2451. A motel with restaurant. MAP available.

Country Road Lodge. Warrensburg 12885; 623–2207. A bed-and-breakfast establishment, 5 rooms with wood stove in lounge.

Inn on Gore Mountain. Peaceful Valley Rd., North Creek 12853; 251–2111. 16 rooms, closest facility to mountain.

Valhaus Motel. Peaceful Valley Rd., North Creek 12853; 251–2700. 12 rooms, TV, free coffee. Half-mile to mountain access road.

Inexpensive

American Hotel. Main St., North Creek 12853; 251–2500. A small hotel with game room, fireplace in lobby.

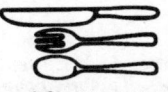 **RESTAURANTS.** As in our listing of accommodations, none of the restaurants in our selection approach being expensive. Most are in the *Moderate* ($10–$15) range; *Inexpensive,* less than $10. The price reflects the cost of a meal for one person; drinks, tax, and tip extra. All but the two inexpensive restaurants listed accept major credit cards. (For a wider selection of restaurants in Chestertown, see the Whiteface Mountain section.)

Northwind Restaurant. *Moderate.* Peaceful Valley Rd., North Creek; 251–2522. A wide-ranging menu of hearty American fare.

Garnet Hill Lodge. *Moderate.* Thirteenth Lake Rd., North River, north of North Creek via. Rte. 28; 251–2821. Mountaintop lodge known for cross-country skiing and fine food, especially Saturday evening buffet.

Inn at Gore Mountain. *Moderate.* Peaceful Valley Rd., North Creek; 251–2111. Look for New Orleans Cajun cooking here, a surprise in the Adirondacks!

Smith's Restaurant. *Moderate.* Main St., North Creek; 251–9965. Steaks, chops, and home-baked goods, with German touch.

Basil & Wicks. *Inexpensive.* Rte. 23, North Creek; 251–2613. A bar serving hamburgers and pizza.

Zio's Pizzeria. *Inexpensive.* Main St., North Creek; 251–2188. The place to go for pizza.

HOW TO GET AROUND. It is practically mandatory to have a car in this region, although some hotels may supply shuttle service. If you do not intend to drive, check when making reservations.

SEASONAL EVENTS. NASTAR races are held weekly here, and recreational and serious amateur racing are important to the winter calendar. The mountain is designated as an alpine training center operated by the New York Ski Education Foundation, New York's major development program for the U.S. Ski Team.

 OTHER SPORTS AND ACTIVITIES. An interesting twist on the winter theme—**horseback riding** through the snow. It's popular in this region, with over half a dozen ranch resorts offering such an experience. These include: *Balsam House,* Friends Lake Rd., Chestertown, 494–2828; *Painted Pony Ranch,* Highway 9N, Lake Luzerne, 696–2421; *Ridin Hy Ranch Resort,* Sherman Lake, Warrensburg, 494–2742; *Sit'n Bull Ranch,* Rte. 418, Warrensburg, 623–3831; and *1000 Acres Ranch,* Rte. 418, Stony Creek, 696–2444. All of the above also offer **sleigh rides.**

Cross-country centers are maintained at *Garnet Hill Lodge,* off Rte. 28 on Thirteenth Lake Rd. in North River, 251–2821, 30 km; *Cunningham Ski Barn,* Rte. 28, North Creek, 251–2466, 50 km; and *Gore Mountain Ski Area,* 251–2466, 10 km.

Warren County, where Gore is located, maintains a total of over 165 miles of groomed and patroled **snowmobile** trails that connect to over 300 miles of state and private trails. To check on conditions, call 793–1300.

And for winter **hikers** and **snowshoe** enthusiasts, the *Department of Environmental Conservation* P.O. Box 220, Hudson St.; Warrensburg 12885 maintains winter trails. Call 623–3671 for details.

The Sagamore Hotel, 110 Sagamore Rd., Bolton Landing 12814, 644–9400, offers 2 indoor **tennis** courts, **racquetball,** indoor **pool,** and complete health **spa** facilities.

HINTS TO THE HANDICAPPED. There is special equipment available at Gore Mountain for handicapped skiers and programs to instruct these skiers in the sport of skiing.

DAY-CARE FACILITIES. The nursery has been supervised by Miss Helen Cornwall since it opened in 1964. It accepts children ages 2–6 from 8 A.M. to 4:15 P.M. daily, at $2 an hour. The Children's Ski School offers instruction for ages 3–12, with 2-hour lessons for ages 6–12 and a Play & Ski Learning Center for ages 3–6 to introduce them to skiing. Both facilities can be reached through the main lodge, 251–2411.

NIGHTLIFE. At the Gore Mountain Lodge, Rte. 28, North Creek (251–3444), there's *Mr. B's Après Lounge,* a place to relax off the trails and listen to music before dinner. You will find folk music, vocal and guitar, at *Basil & Wicks,* Rte. 23, in North Creek (251–2613), and on weekends at the *Balsam House* on Friends Lake Rd., Chestertown (494–2828). Or drive 25 miles to the Lake George region where there are a number of places offering live music and dancing.

HUNTER MT. SKI BOWL

Box 295, Hunter NY 12422
Tel: 518-263-4223

Snow Report: 800–FOR–SNOW
Area Vertical: 1,600 ft.
Number of Trails: 44 or 200
   skiable acres
Lifts: 2 triple chairs, 8
   double chairs, 1 T-bar, 2 pomas,
   1 pony, 2 rope tows
Snowmaking: Nearly 100 percent
Season: early November–late April

Two brothers, Orville and Israel Slutsky, were born and brought up in the Hunter Mountain area. They made their fortunes in the construction trade. While so doing, Hunter, a long-time summer mecca for the New York metropolitan area, fell on hard times as major arteries into the Catskills changed and Hunter was no longer on the beaten path.

The Slutskys, who owned the mountain, offered to give it away for $1 to anyone who would develop it as a ski area. The offer was accepted by Jimmy Hammerstein of the musical family fame. In the fall of 1959, the Hunter Mt. Ski Bowl opened. The Slutskys were brought in to put up the lifts and it was through their insistence from the onset that snowmaking was factored into the mountain's "must have" mix.

The effort of Jimmy Hammerstein and friends to make skiing work here, however, didn't carry over into fiscal acumen, as the major stockholders, like Paul Newman, Kim Novack, and the members of the Modern Jazz Quartet, albeit avid skiers, were, according to a well-placed Hunter source, "terrible businessmen." The effort, in fact, went down the tubes.

The Slutskys rode to the rescue once again and for the past 24 years have owned and operated Hunter, personally making the first runs down the slopes in the morning, day after day, to test the snow conditions. "They love it. They'll be there forever, probably," says the same well-placed source.

Hunter is everyman's mountain in more than one way. Over the years it has tapped into the New Yorkers' penchant for sticking together in groups. Consequently, there are probably more firefighters, police officers, nurses, doctors, and chefs—among other professions and trades—who assemble here to ski together than any other place in the country. Special events and races have grown up around this stick-together-on-skis phenomenon. The result is that everyone feels he or she belongs at Hunter. And the special-interest groups get larger and larger.

Also for everyone is a special place to ski. Hunter One is a learner's area with its own chair and surface lifts and base lodge.

Hunter West is positioned for the advanced skier. And the Hunter Mt. Ski Bowl, the original terrain, is still a free-for-all for everyone, although it tends to attract intermediates.

As ethnic and diverse as the skiers you'll find here is the food service at the Hunter Base Lodge, where staples mean everything, from pizza to sushi.

Hunter is, incidentally, quasi-official headquarters of the ever-growing 70-Plus Ski Club that encourages active participation in alpine skiing by those supposedly "over the hill." An annual race here in honor of these very energetic senior citizens can put younger skiers to shame.

Practical Information for Hunter Mt. Ski Bowl

HOW TO GET THERE. Hunter Mt. Ski Bowl is located right in the town of Hunter in the Catskills, 120 miles from New York City, making it readily accessible by various modes of transportation. **By car.** Take the New York State Thruway to Exit 20 at Saugerties, then follow Rte. 32 north to Rte. 32A and onto Rte. 23A west to the area. **By plane.** The Hunter Mt. Airport (518–0263–4223) nearby has a 2,550-ft. runway that can accommodate single- and twin-engine planes. **By bus.** *Adirondack Trailways* (212–947–5300) buses depart from the Port Authority Bus Terminal in New York City twice daily— 8:30 A.M. and 6 P.M. The bus trip takes three hours.

TELEPHONES. The area code for Hunter Mountain is 518, and for some surrounding towns it is 914.

ACCOMMODATIONS. The Hunter Mountain Reservation Center, Inc., housed in the base lodge (Box 295, Hunter 12442; 518–263–3827) can provide lodging and reservation information as well as suggestions for enter-tainment and services. Since most visitors come to Hunter Mt. Ski Bowl on weekend trips, rates at hotels, motels, and lodges are based on a 2-day weekend per person unless otherwise stated. For those in the *Expensive* category, expect to pay $80–$100; *Moderate,* $60–$80; and *Inexpensive,* less than $60. (For additional lodgings in the area, see *Ski Windham* section. The two ski areas are only 10 miles apart.)

Expensive

Antonio's Motel and Resort. County Rte. 16, Platte Cove, Elka Park 12427; 518–589–5197. A country resort from a restored hotel, offering sauna, indoor pool, Jacuzzi, wide-screen TV. MAP available.

Ramada Inn. Rte. 28. Kingston 12401; 914–339–3900. Offers indoor pool, in-room movie channel and choice of restaurants.

Scribner Hollow. Rte. 23A, Hunter 12442; 518–263–4211. Luxurious suites with double decker living/bedroom combinations, on-premises dining and indoor pool.

Villa Vosilla Resort and Restaurant. Rte. 23 A, Tannersville 12485; 518–589 –5060. An older hotel that has added a new motel section, offering indoor pool, complete gym, Jacuzzi, sauna, and game room. MAP available.

Moderate

Auberge des 4 Saisons Hotel-Motel, Rte. 42, Shandaken 12480; 914–688–2223. 38 rooms (half with private bath), with inn-like accommodations in main house plus a chalet-style motel. Offers French-style cooking. **MAP** available.

Han's County Line Motel & Restaurant. Rte. 32A. Palenville 12463; 518–678–3101. Standard and deluxe motel rooms; some cooking facilities in cabins.

Howard Johnson's Motor Lodge & Restaurant. Exit 20 off I–87, Saugerties 12477; 914–246–9511. Indoor heated pool and sauna, laundry, and game rooms.

The Forester Motor Lodge. Rte. 23A, Hunter 12442; 518–263–4555. A newish motel across the road from Hunter Mountain.

Sun View Motel. Rte. 23A, Tannersville 12485; 518–589–5217. Some apartments with full kitchens, courtesy coffee in country motel.

Eggery Inn. County Rd. 16, Tannersville 12485; 518–589–5363. A 13-room (10 with private baths) bed-and-breakfast that serves dinners on Saturdays.

Washington Irving Lodge. Rte. 23A, Tannersville 12485; 518–589–5560. 28 rooms (five with private baths).

Inexpensive

Greene Mountain View Inn. Church and South Main Sts., Tannersville 12485; 518–589–5511. Essentially a ski lodge with private baths. Breakfast served, along with buffet-style dinners.

The Hunter House. Rt. 23A, Hunter 12442; 518–263–4611. A hotel that has added modern motel units.

Redcoat's Return. Dale Lane, Platte Clove, Elka Park 12427; 518–589–9858. A 14-room inn, 5 rooms with bath; breakfast served.

Sky Top Motel. Rte. 28, Kingston 12401; 914–331–2900. Morning Continental breakfasts and wine and cheese parties in the afternoon.

Sun-Land Farm Motel. Rte. 23A, Hunter 12442; 518–263–4811. A motel with a mainhouse public area; piano and small game room.

Vatra. Rte. 214, Hunter 12442; 518–263–4919. A rustic motel-hotel with home cooking. **MAP.**

Villa Maria. Rte. 23A, Haines Falls 12436; 518–589–6200. An old hotel that has added motel units, indoor pool, sauna and game room. Breakfast available.

Villaggio Resort. Rte. 23A, Haines Falls 12436; 518–589–5000. A motel complex offering indoor/outdoor pool, health club, entertainment, and lounges.

 **BED-AND-BREAKFAST TREASURES.** With an assortment of lodges and country inns situated in the Catskills, visitors are offered a wide choice of bread-and-breakfast establishments. The Hunter Mt. Ski Bowl area is no exception. Some places, like the **Albergo Bed & Breakfast** in Windham (518–734–4499), have combined the European touch with colonial amenities. A few others in the area include **The Eggery Inn,** Tannersville (518–589–5363); **Hunter House,** Hunter (518–263–4611); **The Redcoat's Return,** Elka Park (518–589–6379); **Kaaterskill Lodge,** Haines Falls (518–589–6544); and **Villaggio Resort,** Haines Falls (518–589–5900). Rates at these B&Bs range from $30 to $80 per person. B&Bs are usually not for families and certainly not for all travelers. Be sure to inquire regarding individual credit card policies when making reservations or when checking into the establishment.

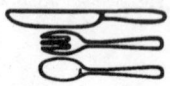 **DINING OUT.** Catskill resorts are well known for their eat-eat-eat type of dining. That's because many of the resorts, particularly those offering package deals, include all-you-can eat provisions with the packages. However, the Hunter area offers visitors the gamut of dining places outside the hotels and resorts. Cuisine ranges from northern Italian to French to American standbys. In this listing, expect to pay $18 to $25 for a dinner for one at a restaurant in the *Expensive* category; *Moderate,* $13–$18; and *Inexpensive,* less than $13. Tips and drinks are extra. Practically all but the inexpensive restaurants accept most major credit cards. However, it is wise to check first.

Expensive

Auberge des 4 Saisons. Rte. 42, Shandaken; 914–688–2223. Obviously French, and one of the better choices in the region, with a 35-year reputation for fine cooking.

Brandywine. Rte. 23. Windham; 518–734–3838. A new restaurant, but with rustic ambience; features northern Italian fare.

Chateau Belleview. Rte. 23A, between Hunter and Tannersville; 518–589–5525. Seafood prepared French style is the specialty, with veal also popular.

Red Coat's Return. Dale La., Elka Park; 518–589–6379. The accent is decidely British, but very homey with an English touch to the menu.

Moderate

Christy's Restaurant. Rte. 23A, Hunter; 518–263–4480. American preparations in family-style environment, great breakfasts.

Fireside Restaurant. Rte. 23A, Hunter; 518–263–4216. Sunday omelets a specialty, plus steaks.

Hans County Line. Rte. 23A, Palenville; 518–678–2264. The range is from waffles to steaks.

Ribcage. Rt. 23A, Haines Falls; 518–589–5502. Chicken and ribs, barbecue style. No credit cards.

Tannersville Yacht Club. Rte. 23A, Tannersville; 518–589–5455. Sandwiches and snacks, plus the singles scene.

Inexpensive

Pete's Place. Rte. 23, Hunter; 518–589–9840. Chili and burgers are served up here. No credit cards.

HOW TO GET AROUND. It is wise to have a **car** at Hunter, particularly if you would like to try the slopes at Windham Ski Area, just 10 miles away. However, as noted in the Accommodations section, some of the lodging places supply **shuttle** service to Hunter Mountain. If you don't plan on driving, check with the hotel or condo when making reservations.

SEASONAL EVENTS. The mountain annually hosts a race event called *The Silver Series,* six contests with prizes of up to $175,000. The winner from Hunter competes in Vail and the winner from Vail comes East to compete at Hunter. Another popular competition is the *Chef's Race* held in mid-**January.** It has become so popular that they've had to be firm about having only chefs enter—no kitchen aides allowed!

What may be the largest amateur race in the world is Hunter's annual *Firefighters Race,* held in early **February.** The event draws up to 225 teams with 5 firefighters on a team going down the course with a 50-foot fire hose.

OTHER SPORTS AND ACTIVITIES. *Villa Vosilla Resort and Restaurant,* Rte. 23A, Tannersville (518–589–5060) makes its indoor **pool,** gym, Jacuzzi, and steam room and sauna available to the public. **Cross-country** skiing is available at *Higher Meadows,* Tannersville (518–589–5361).

CHILDREN'S ACTIVITIES. Hunter offers a child-sitting service at the base lodge, with a specially equipped playroom and a limit of 25 tots. The cost is $18 a day and the service is available from 9 A.M. to 4 P.M. Children aged 3–9 can participate in the *SKIwee/Frosty Ski School* that combines playtime fun and games with on-mountain ski experience. This program is $41 for the all-day (9:30 A.M.–3:30 P.M.) version.

NIGHTLIFE. The "in place" is the *Hunter Village Inn,* Rte. 23A, Hunter (518–263–4788), offering live rock bands that please the young crowd. Look for video replays of skiers on Hunter's slopes during happy hour from 3–6 P.M. at *Aspens,* Rte. 23A, Tannersville (518–589–5052). Evenings and weekends there's dancing to music of the 1950s and '60s.

The Club on Rte. 23 A, Hunter (518–263–4333), offers disco-style music and *Slope's Night Club,* Rte. 23A, Tannersville (518–589–5006), can vary from DJ to live bands.

WHITEFACE MOUNTAIN SKI CENTER

Wilmington NY 12997
Tel: 518–946–2223

Snow Report: 518–946–2223
Area Vertical: 3,216 ft.
Number of Trails: 28 or 142
    skiable acres
Lifts: 8 double chairs
Snowmaking: 93 percent of
    terrain
Season: late November–early April

Whiteface Mountain is a household word among those who can't get enough of the Olympics. Twice this mountain has hosted the winter games, first in 1932 when the town servicing the mountain, Lake Placid, became known as the Winter Sports Capital of the World, and most recently in 1980.

The combination of an exciting mountain (its 3,216-ft. vertical is the greatest in the East) and a town whose *raison d'être* is to woo, wine, and dine tourists makes a ski experience here unforgettable.

The mountain itself is heavy on the "most difficult" side when it comes to trails—44 percent. For intermediates, about 33 percent are marked "more difficult," and beginners can enjoy the rest.

In addition to on-mountain challenges, Lake Placid itself vies for time and attention with its Olympic Center that hosts both sporting events and major entertainers such as Kenny Rogers and Willie Nelson. Mirror Lake, around which the town is clustered, is the setting for ice skating and hockey, and likely as not you'll see horse-drawn sleighs on the ice, too.

There isn't another ski town where thrill seekers can arrange for bobsled and luge runs during a break from skiing. And the shopping, as might be expected, can make rainy day hours pass quickly during a late winter thaw.

Perhaps most noteworthy, however, is the fact that Whiteface Mountain is headquarters for the Olympic Authority and training here goes on year-round. A glass-enclosed elevator to the top of the 90-m ski jump tower is open to visitors who want to sample views of the Adirondack Mountains and perhaps gain a new-found respect for those who pursue this most daring of alpine events.

Practical Information for Whiteface Mountain

HOW TO GET THERE. Whiteface Mountain Ski Center is located in the town of Wilmington, 8 miles from Lake Placid. **By bus.** *Adirondack Trailways* (800–342–4101) and *Greyhound* (563–1480) offer daily bus service to the region. **By train.** Call the *Amtrak Tour Desk* at 800–USA–RAIL for details on ski train packages that include rail fare, hotel accommodations, lift tickets and transfers to and from the Westport station. There are also daily departures from Grand Central (New York City) and Rensselaer stations and other locations on the Amtrak system.

By air. *Brockway Air* (800–338–9100) serves the Adirondack Airport (891–5551) in Saranac Lake, 16 miles from Lake Placid. Airlines serving the Albany County airport include *American, Bar Harbor, Brockway, Command, Delta, Eastern, Empire, Mail, People Express, Piedmont, Pilgrim, Ransome, Republic, United,* and *USAir.* All major rental cars are available at the airport. Fly-drive packages can be arranged through *North Star Tours* (800–338–8898).

By car. Take the New York State Thruway to I–87 to Rte. 73, Exit 30, to Rte. 86. For auto rental information contact *Hertz* at 800–654–3131 or Arnie's Service Station, 523–3158.

TELEPHONES. The area code for the Adirondacks region is 518.

 **ACCOMMODATIONS.** There are over 50 lodging properties in the immediate area. For general information contact the following: *Lake Placid Convention Bureau,* Olympic Center, Lake Placid 12946; 523–2999. *Lake Placid Chamber of Commerce,* Olympic Center, Lake Placid 12946; 523–2445. *Saranac Lake Chamber of Commerce,* 30 Main St., Saranac Lake 12983; 891–1990. *Tupper Lake Chamber of Commerce,* 55 Park St., Tupper Lake 12986–1694; 359–3328. *Whiteface Mt. Chamber of Commerce,* P.O. Box 277, Wilmington 12997; 946–2255.

Hotel rates are based on double occupancy. Categories, determined by price, are: *Expensive,* $50 and up; *Moderate,* $30–$50; and *Inexpensive,* less than $30.

Expensive

Adirondack Inn. 217 Main St., Lake Placid 12946; 253–2424. Beautiful rooms and suites overlooking the lake; free crib or cot for children under 6; restaurant, coffee shop, cocktail lounge; ski plan for individuals or groups.

The Balsam House. Friends Lake Rd., Chestertown 12817 (I–87 exit 23 to Warrensburgh); 494–2828. Beautifully restored inn built in 1865, with 20 uniquely decorated rooms, some with phones. Gourmet restaurant open to the public, offering French cuisine; horse-drawn sleigh rides, snowmobiling available.

Best Western Golden Arrow. 150 Main St., Lake Placid 12946; 523–3353. 74-room resort hotel offering studios, suites; children under 12 free, cribs and cots. Indoor pool, health club, racquetball.

Friends Lake Inn. Friends Lake Rd., Chestertown 12817 (I–87 exit 25); 494–4251. A completely restored 1860s inn with 14 rooms, 7 with private bath. Restaurant open to the public; on-premises cross-country skiing.

Hilton. Mirror Lake Dr., Lake Placid 12946; 523–4411. 178 rooms; children under 18 free, cribs, cots; two indoor pools, restaurant, bar, whirlpool.

Holiday Inn Resort. Olympic Dr., Lake Placid 12946; 523–2556. On hilltop overlooking lake; 182 rooms, children 12 and under free; indoor pool, health spa, and racquetball.

Howard Johnson's. Saranac Ave., Lake Placid 12946; 523–9555. 92 rooms, children 12 and under free; indoor pool, whirlpool.

Mirror Lake Inn. 35 Mirror Lake Dr., Lake Placid 12946; 523–2544. Colonial decor in 72-room inn; penthouse terrace rooms with cathedral ceilings. Under 11 free. Offers health club, gourmet restaurant.

Placid Manor. Whiteface Inn Rd., Lake Placid 12946; 523–2573. Rustic elegance on the lake, view of Whiteface Mountain, with 38 rooms in 10 lodges and cottages. Restaurant and bar on premises.

Ramada Inn. 12 Saranac Ave., Lake Placid 12946; 523–2587. 90 rooms; 18 and under free; indoor pool, whirlpool, restaurant and bar.

Moderate

Alpine Motor Lodge. Wilmington Rd., Lake Placid 12946; 523–2180. Neat, clean rooms in 2-story inn; restaurant with German specialties.

The Bark Eater Inn. Keene 12942; 576–2221. A small country inn offering cross-country skiing, breakfast.

Bonnie View Cottages. Bonnie View Rd., Wilmington 12997; 946–2363. Housekeeping cottages 3 miles from Whiteface.

Grand View Motel. Rte. 86, Wilmington 12997; 946–2209. View of slopes and only 4 minutes from skiing.

The Hotel Saranac of Paul Smith's College. 101 Main St., Saranac Lake 12983; 891–2200. 92 rooms in refurbished hotel first opened in 1927, with original lobby preserved—replica of the foyer in the Danvanzati Palace of Florence, Italy. Restaurant is college-operated training facility.

Hungry Trout. Rte. 86, Wilmington 12997; 946–2217. On Ausable River, only a half mile from Whiteface. A combination motel and restaurant.

The Inn at Whiteface. Rte. 86, Wilmington 12997; 946–2232. Right at the area, views of slopes. Comfortable accommodations.

Interlaken Lodge. 15 Interlaken Ave., Lake Placid 12446; 523–3180. Victorian setting and relaxing atmosphere with 12 guest rooms. MAP available.

Little House Bed & Breakfast. Old Military Rd., Lake Placid 12946; 523–3739. An English-style cottage with view of Whiteface, serving breakfast.

North Country Inn. Rte. 86, Wilmington 12997; 946–2488. Less than 3 miles from Whiteface and offering restaurant with Italian fare.

South Meadow Farm Lodge B & B. Cascade Rd., Lake Placid 12946; 523–9369. A small family lodge located on Olympic cross-country trails, serving breakfast.

Stagecoach Inn. Old Military Rd., Lake Placid 12946; 523–9474. A landmark from the stagecoach days with brass beds, handmade quilts, fireplaces; breakfast served.

Whiteface Mountain Inn. Rte. 86, Wilmington 12997; 946–2155. An old, restored house offering bed & breakfast accommodations, shared baths, excellent breakfasts.

Inexpensive

Ark Lodge. Upper Jay 12987; 946–2276. Only 6 miles from Whiteface with rooms decorated with Olympic memorabilia.

There are a number of inexpensive motel/motor inn establishments in Lake Placid of which the following are just a sampling: *Carriage House Motor Inn,* Cascade Rd., 523–2260; *Edelweiss Motel,* Wilmington Rd., 523–3821; *Hi-Ridge Motel,* Wilmington Rd., 523–3938; *Lake Placid Motor Lodge,* Cascade Rd., 523–2817; *Lakeshore Motel,* Saranac Ave., 523–2261; *Redwood Motel,* Wilmington Rd., 523–2183; and *Village Motel,* Cascade Rd., 523–2150.

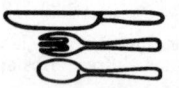 **RESTAURANTS.** There are fine dining spots throughout the Adirondack region, most notably in some of the country inns. Always worth a try for the adventure alone is Hotel Saranac in Saranac Lake, which culinary arts students from Paul Smith's College use as a laboratory-classroom. The emphasis for most restaurants in this region is on straightforward presentation and ample portions. Breakfasts tend to be especially large, perhaps a legacy of the lumbering days when men in the field camps consumed huge breakfasts to start the day. Prices noted are for an average dinner for one person; beverages, tax, and tip extra. *Expensive:* more than $20; *Moderate:* $12–$20; *Inexpensive:* less than $12. Major credit cards are accepted at most places, but it would be wise to check first.

Expensive

The Balsam House. Friends Lake Rd., Chestertown; 494–2828. Elegant dining in a beautifully restored inn built in 1865. Main dining room has candlelight, flowers, and classical music. European chef's specialties include rack of lamb, duckling chambertin, braised sweetbreads, and Adirondack trout.

Friends Lake Inn. Friends Lake Rd., Chestertown; 494–4251. Nicely restored 1860 country inn, reflecting that ambience in the dining room. Daily selections may include snapper en papillote, beef Wellington, or poached salmon with dill hollandaise. Tempting desserts are prepared on the premises.

Rene's. White Schoolhouse Rd., Chestertown; 494–4251. Casual dining in converted 1917 farmhouse. All items are fresh, homemade European fare, including German and Italian dishes and French desserts. Delicious ice cream is also homemade.

Charcoal Pit. Rte. 86 near Cold Brook Plaza, Lake Placid; 523–3050. Fine American fare served in rustic atmosphere with fireplace. Veal Francaise or veal Normandy may be prepared in flambé at tableside. Roast duckling also a favorite. Children's menu available.

Frederick's. Signal Hill, Lake Placid; 523–2310. Gourmet dining overlooking Lake Placid. Tournedos Rossini is a specialty. A seafood platter for two combines lobster, shrimp scampi, scallops, Alaskan crab. Also favored are seafood coquille and veal scallopine; tempting dessert cart.

Interlaken Restaurant. 15 Interlaken Ave., Lake Placid; 523–3180. Dine in a distinctive European atmosphere here, with gourmet menu featuring Swiss and French dishes.

Lake Placid Hilton. Saranac Ave., Lake Placid; 523–4411. Dining room of this hotel offers breathtaking views of the lake and mountains. Menu offers seafood, beef, poultry, and veal dishes.

Steak & Stinger. 15 Cascade Rd., Lake Placid; 523–0027. Despite its name, not only steaks served in this rustic establishment. Continental and American menu also features veal Oscar, shrimp scampi, and chateaubriand.

Moderate

Alpine Cellar. Wilmington Rd., Lake Placid; 523–2180. Excellent German cuisine and atmosphere, including sauerbratern, Alpine schnitzel, and rouladen, plus homemade breads. Children's plate. Dinners only.

Cascade Inn Restaurant. Cascade Rd. and Rte. 73, Lake Placid; 523–2130. Hearty American dishes; nightly specials. Children's portions available.

Hotel Saranac of Paul Smith's College. 101 Main St., Saranac Lake; 891–2200. Fine dining in the hotel's Regis Room; inexpensive buffet Thursday nights; elaborate Sunday brunch. Bake Shoppe features fresh baked goods daily.

Jimmy's. Main St., Lake Placid; 523–2353. Diverse selection of steaks, seafood, chicken, and veal dishes; popular with locals.

Mirror Lake Inn. 35 Mirror Lake Dr., Lake Placid; 523–2544. Home-baked bread and diverse salad bar accompany fresh seafood and veal dishes here. Meal may end with homemade Adirondack maple nut sundae with pure maple syrup, or homemade fudge brownie à la mode. Children's plates available.

Villa Vespa. Saranac Ave., Lake Placid; 523–9959. The town's favorite "nice little Italian restaurant" featuring homemade pastas; fresh seafood daily; unique salad bar. Special pizzas and menu for children.

Inexpensive

Artist's Cafe. Main St., Lake Placid; 523–9493. Overlook Mirror Lake while enjoying a 16-ounce T-bone steak, surf and turf, or steamd shrimp. Children's menu.

Casa del Sol. Rte. 86, east of Saranac Lake; no phone. A Mexican restaurant in the Adirondacks and a favorite with locals. Chili and other traditional Mexican dishes can be tempered to the desired degree of spiciness.

Deer's Head Inn. Rte. 9N, Elizabethtown; 873–9995. The oldest inn in operation in the Adirondacks (since 1818), it reflects German-Swiss influence, with sauerbraten and homemade dumplings a specialty, along with home-baked pies. Children's menu available.

Howard Johnson's. Saranac Ave., Lake Placid; 523–2241. Family-style dining; extensive menu includes inexpensive offerings.

Potluck. Main St., Lake Placid; 523–3106. Specialty foods served in attractive delicatessen setting include hefty sandwiches on hearty breads and pasta salads.

HOW TO GET AROUND. Shuttle service to and from Lake Placid and Whiteface Mountain is available with *Adirondack Express* (523–2335) and *Lake Placid Sightseeing* (523–4430). Or contact the following **taxi** services: *Eddie's Taxi,* 523–2024; *Gene's Taxi,* 523–3161; *Jan's Taxi,* 523–1891; and *M&M Limo and Charter Bus Service,* 523–3611.

OTHER SPORTS AND ACTIVITIES. For information on the over 100 miles of **ski touring** available in the Lake Placid region, contact the *Cascade Ski Touring Center,* Cascade Rd., Lake Placid, 523–9605, or *Mt. Van Hoevenberg,* Cascade Rd., Lake Placid, 523–2811. The latter can also give details on how to arrange for **bobsled** and **luge** rides. The **Sports Office** at Town Hall, Main St., Lake Placid, 523–2591, can give details on **tobogganing** and **snowmobiling.**

NIGHTLIFE. Most of the hotels and dining establishments in the area offer music throughout the evening, in either the lounges or the piano bars. When it comes to places to dance, check out *Mud Puddles* on School St., Lake Placid (523–4446), which attracts a young crowd. So do *Christies* at the Holiday Inn, Olympic Dr., Lake Placid (523–2556), and the *Dancing Bears Lounge* in the Hilton, Mirror Lake Dr., Lake Placid (523–4411). *The Cottage* (523–9845), also on Mirror Lake Dr., draws both locals and visitors, especially in the evening when après-ski hors d'oeuvres are served.

SKI WINDHAM

C.D. Lane Road
Windham NY 12496

Tel: 518–734–4300
Ski Report: 518–734–4300
Area Vertical: 1,550 ft.
Number of Trails: 27 or 180
  skiable acres
Lifts: 3 triple chairs, 2
  double chairs, 1 J-bar, 1 pony
Snowmaking: 95 percent of terrain
Season: mid-November–mid-April

In 1981 Ski Windham made the transition from private club, which it had been since 1965, to a ski resort open to the public. It was purchased by Ski Roundtop, managers of a resort by that name, and Ski Liberty, both in Pennsylvania.

When it was a private club, its clientele tended to be professionals and corporate chiefs, plus a healthy smattering of politicians, all of whom chose Windham to see and be seen.

Today the resort is sought after by people who appreciate the quality represented by the original club environment, plus the quality of grooming of the trails.

The skiing is on 27 primarily fall-line trails. Beginners enjoy a top-of-the-mountain descent on the 2¼-mile Wraparound, the longest trail in the Catskills. Experts prefer the Wheelchair, a steep, moguled run.

The area welcomes skiers of all shapes and sizes, offering free skiing to ages 5 and under and to senior citizens 70 and up. And to make things more comfortable for everyone, a corps of volunteers serves on Ski Windham's Courtesy Patrol Program. Dressed in red and blue parkas, they can give details on just about anything related to skiing and the resort. In turn for their time, they earn extra free skiing!

Practical Information for Ski Windham

HOW TO GET THERE. Ski Windham is located in Windham, about a 2½-hour drive from New York City. **By car.** Take the New York State Thruway (I–87) to Exit 21, then west on Rte. 23 for 25 miles to the resort. **By bus.** There is *Trailways* service twice a day from Manhattan's Port Authority Terminal (212–730–7460). Buses depart daily at 8:30 A.M. and 6 P.M.

TELEPHONES. The area code for this section of the Catskills is 518.

ACCOMMODATIONS. The *Greene County Promotion Department*, Box 467, Catskill 12414 (943–3223), can answer questions about accommodations in the Windham region. Also, the *Ski Windham Lodging Service*, C. D. Lane Rd., Windham 12496 (734–4300), can book reservations at the following establishments that are within a 5-mile drive of Ski Windham. The *Expensive* category here is limited; with a double-occupancy room costing about $75 per night; *Moderate*, $45–$60; *Inexpensive*, less than $45.

Expensive

Albergo Allegria Bed & Breakfast. Rte. 296, Windham; 734–5560. A small country inn that's run European-style, and furnished with antiques.

Moderate

Christman's Windham House. South Road, Windham; 734–4230. A country inn with 4 efficiency apartments.

Hamilton House. Rte. 23, Windham; 734–3190. A motel with some efficiencies available.

Kopper Kettle Motel. Rte. 23, Windham; 734–3575. A 14-unit motel with indoor pool, game room.

Sugar Maples. County Rte. 54, Maple Crest; 734–4000. A resort created from a collection of homes and a motel. A total of 100 rooms with private baths and TV.

Windham Arms. Rte. 23, Windham; 734–3000. A 70-room motel with terraces, color TV, and great views.

Windham Mountain Inn. South Rd., Windham; 734–4270. Some shared baths, pub with fireplace.

Windhaven Motel. Rte. 296, Hensonville; 263–4860. A modern motel with efficiencies.

Inexpensive

Brandow Country Inn. Rte. 23, Windham; 734–3921. Rooms include private baths.

Crest Park Guest Cottages. Rte. 296, Windham; 734–3258. Look for wood stoves and lofts.

Hilltop Acres. Rice Rd., Jewett; 734–4580. A country resort with the European touch; Viennese cooking; MAP available.

Manning's Salisbury Inn. Main St., Maple Crest; 734–9834. A 6-room inn with shared baths.

Parker Inn. Rte. 296, Hensonville; 734–3749. Home-cooked meals, plus on-premises weight and game rooms and ice skating.

Village Inn. Rte. 23, Windham; 734–5308. A country inn atmosphere offering hot tub and TV-game room.

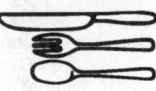 **RESTAURANTS.** Dining in the Ski Windham region is both varied in cuisines and easy on the pocketbook. In this selection, restaurants are listed by price category. Categories are: *Expensive,* $13–$20; *Moderate,* $8–$13; and *Inexpensive,* less than $8. These prices are for a meal for one person, excluding drinks, tax, and tip. Most accept major credit cards. (See *Hunter Mountain Ski Bowl* section for other choices in the area.)

Expensive

Albergo Allegria's La Griglia. Rte. 296, Windham; 734–5560. Northern Italian specialties and fresh game are served here, plus guests get fresh fruit and croissant at breakfast. Rated by some as the best restaurant in the region.

Val d'Isere. Rte. 28, Big Indian, a 20-minute drive from Windham; 914–254–4646. A couple from Brittany and Bordeaux are in charge here, with sirloin steak flambé and fresh fruit tart on the menu. Reservations are suggested.

Moderate

Chalet Fondue. Rte. 296, Windham; 734–4650. Champagne cheese and chocolate are part of the fondue menu, along with goulash and oxtail soups.

Brandywein. Rte. 23, Windham; 734–3838. Look for northern Italian cuisine here.

Point Lookout. Rte. 23, East Windham; 734–3381. An old stagecoach stop serves American and Mexican food.

Thetford's Sir Sirloin Room. Rte. 23, Windham; 734–3322. Prime rib is a specialty here.

Vesuvio's. Rte. 296, Windham; 734–3663. Lobster and Italian specialties are served here.

Inexpensive

The Frog's House. Rte. 296, Hensonville; 734–9817. A pub atmosphere with barbecued ribs and chicken.

Cheers. Rte. 23, Tannersville; 589–5950. A corner-style bar with takeout food including pizza; après-ski fun. No credit cards.

HOW TO GET AROUND. A **car** is mandatory here, although some inns will provide **shuttle** service to the slopes. Once at the resort, there's a bus to transport skiers from the parking lot to the base lodge.

 **SEASONAL EVENTS.** There's a lot of class left over from Windham's private club days, most notably in a torchlight parade that takes place in early **January**. Fifty ski instructors and patrollers descend the Whistler Trail with lit torches. A Viennese dessert buffet follows the dramatic program. And those people who work so hard all year to make the snow to ski on are treated to their own event at Ski Windham. For the past five years the area has hosted the *Northeastern Snowmakers Classic,* a race and party.

OTHER SPORTS AND ACTIVITIES. *Ten Pin Lanes,* South St., Windham (734–3270), offers evening **bowling.** The *White Birches Ski Touring Center,* off Rte. 23 on Navoo Rd., Windham (734–3266), offers 400 acres of private Catskill wilderness for exploration on **cross-country** skis. There are 15 miles of groomed trails at over a 2,000-ft. elevation. (See *Hunter Mt. Ski Bowl* for other activities.)

 **HINTS FOR THE HANDICAPPED.** The *Ski Windham Adaptive Program* encourages people with all kinds of handicaps, including deaf, blind, and orthopedically impaired people, to take part in skiing. Information is available at the Ski School Desk; 734–4300.

DAY-CARE FACILITIES. A nursery is open daily from 9 A.M. to 4 P.M. for children 6 months to 7 years. The day rate is $25. For children 4–7, the *Smokey Bear Ski School* will coordinate a ski lesson through the nursery.

NIGHTLIFE. Ski Windham's *Inside Edge* and *Rathskeller* (734–4300) located in the base lodge are popular après-ski spots. *Jimmy O'Connor's Pub* at the Windham Mountain Inn, South Rd. (734–4270), has live entertainment weekends and has a penchant for Irish music.

And cooking could be evening entertainment. At *Theo's* on Rte. 23 in Windham (734–4455), a popular bar/restaurant, anyone who would like to prepare a specialty is welcome to reserve a "Monday with Theo." The meal is served buffet style. The rest of the week, the international menu comes with a Greek accent.

Tanner's Tool and Die (589–9812), Rte. 23, Tannersville, has for 5 years won the Hunter/Windham award for the best bar. Live bands are featured here.

(See Hunter Mt. Ski Bowl for other choices.)

Pennsylvania

THE POCONOS

The Pocono ski areas of Pennsylvania have an advantage unique in the East. They're within easy striking distance of not only New York City but also of Washington, D.C., and Philadelphia. In the sense that the ski areas near eastern New Hampshire's North Conway region can all be thought of as one ski resort, so can the 17 resorts of assorted sizes and shapes, in the Poconos.

The standards that may apply to "great ski mountains" in other parts of New England don't here, as there's not a vertical over 803 feet. But the four areas that for purposes of this guide are legitimate destination ski areas do share in common 100 percent snowmaking coverage. This translates to highly reliable skiing, with efficient lift systems to get the masses of urban skiers up quickly, and growing resort communities. And it's safe to say from the wealth of condominium development springing up around the mountains that they provide easy-to-get-to weekend alternatives when making the 6- to 12-hour drives into Vermont and New Hampshire may seem a bit much.

The four principal areas are Shawnee Mountain, Camelback, Big Boulder, and Jack Frost Mountain. All are easily accessible from I–80. Two of these, Big Boulder and Jack Frost, are across the road from each other and feature interchangeable lift tickets.

The western Poconos, near Jack Frost and Big Boulder, is a favorite area with cross-country skiers and snowmobilers, with more than 18,000 acres of recreational lands available for exploring. In this Carbon County region there's the annual "Old Time Christmas Celebration" in a town called Jim Thorpe, a nineteenth century community that's sometimes called the "Switzerland of America." This celebration includes townspeople en masse caroling, and a candlelight procession leading to a Christmas tree in the park. Santa is also on board with old-fashioned steam train rides available.

The whole region shares in the fun of the Pocono Winter Carnival that's held in late February. It's a time for ski reps and retailers to show their wares, for arts councils to pull out their finest exhibits and entertainment, for high school ski teams to compete, and for cross country and alpine recreational racers to test their skills against the clock. This effort is coordinated by the Pocono Mountains Vacation Bureau, 1004 Main St., Stroudsburg, PA 18360; 424–6050.

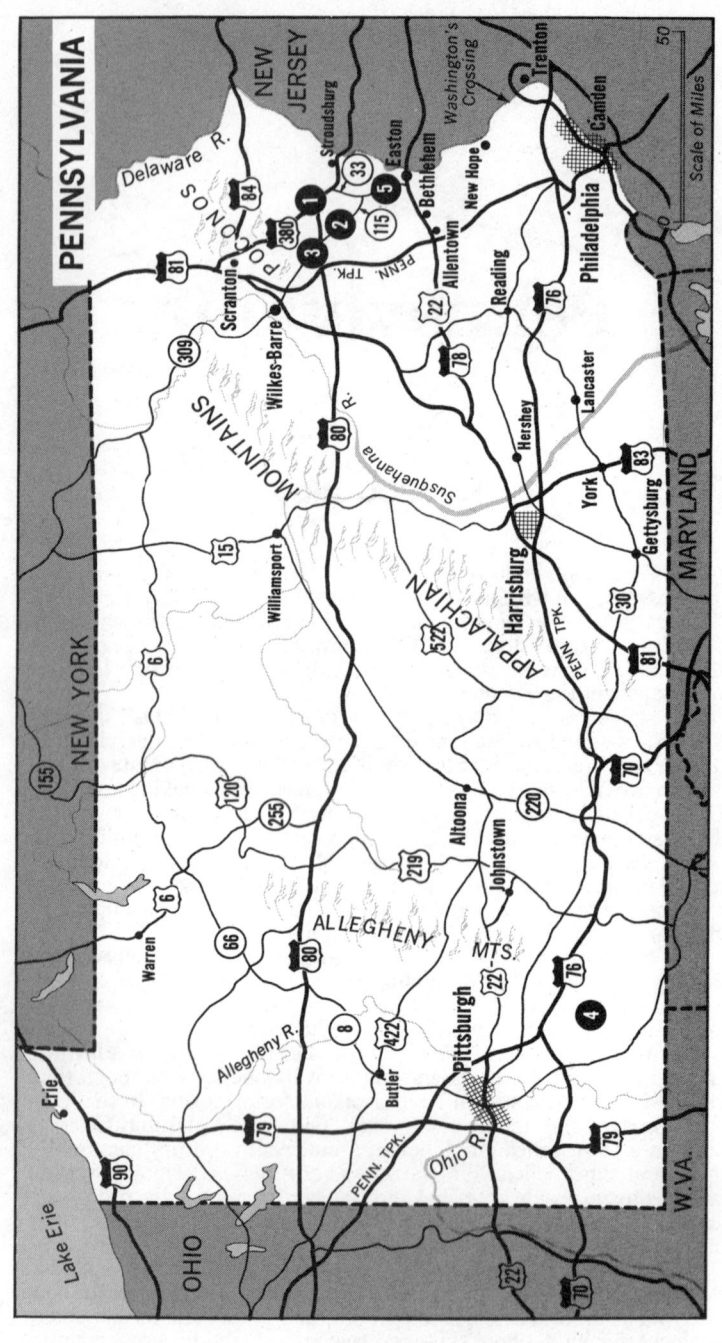

PENNSYLVANIA

Resorts

1) Big Boulder
2) Camelback
3) Jack Frost
4) Seven Springs
5) Shawnee Mountain

A winter wonderland goes undisturbed as this skier maneuvers through snow-covered trees at Quebec's Mt. Sutton.

Photo by Peter Runyon

Alfresco dining is enjoyed by a foursome at the top of the lift at Squaw Valley USA, California. Bearing torches, night skiers create patterns in the snow at Vail, Colorado.

Respites from skiing are offered at many resorts, including sleigh riding in Aspen, Colorado, or ice skating on the outdoor rink at Copper Mountain, Colorado.

Whether schussing down a steep slope at Aspen, Colorado, or gliding through the glades at Mt. Sutton, Quebec, skiers find their own exhilaration in the sport.

Practical Information for the Poconos

HOW TO GET THERE. Getting to the Pocono region is accomplished most easily by following the major auto routes through the region.

By car. From New York City, take the George Washington Bridge to I–80 west to the Delaware Water Gap and into the Poconos. An alternate route is to take the best route to I–78 and follow this and US 22 to Rte. 33 north to the Poconos.

By bus. The area is served by *Pocono Mountain Trails,* Blainstown; 421–1740. *Martz Trailways* has stations in Stroudsburg and Mt. Pocono (421–3040), and *Greyhound* has a station in Stroudsburg (421–4408).

By plane. The Poconos are served by *US Air, Eastern* and *United,* into ABE Pocono Airport (264–2831) in Allentown, and Wilkes-Barre/Scranton Airport (655–3077) in Avoca. There are also smaller commuter airports, including the Pocono Mountain Airport in Mt. Pocono (839–7161); the Stroudsburg Airport (421–8900) and the Birchwood Airpark (629–0222), both in East Stroudsburg; and the Cherry Ridge Airport in Honesdale.

Pocono Limousine Service (839–2111), based in Pocono Summit, services regional and major urban airports (Kennedy, LaGuardia, Philadelphia, Newark, Wilkes-Barre/Scranton, and Allentown/Bethlehem/Easton).

Avis (800–331–1212), *Budget* (800–527–0700), *Dollar* (800–421–6868), *Hertz* (800–654–3131) and *National* (800–328–4567) rental cars are available at Philadelphia, Kennedy, LaGuardia, and Newark airports; all but Dollar are at Allentown/Bethlehem/Easton Airport; and all but Dollar and National are at Wilkes-Barre/Scranton Airport.

TELEPHONES. The area code for the Poconos is 717.

BIG BOULDER SKI AREA

Big Boulder Lake
Kidder Township PA 18624
Tel: 717–722–0101

Snow Report: 717–722–0104
Area Vertical: 475 ft.
Number of Trails: 11 slopes/
*   trails or 65 skiable acres*
Lifts: 5 double chairs, 1
*   triple chair, 1 J-bar*
Snowmaking: 100 percent of
*   terrain*
Season: early December–late March

JACK FROST MOUNTAIN

HCR #1, Box 37-A-1
White Haven PA 18661
Tel: 717–443–8425

Snow Resort: 717–443–8425
Area Vertical: 600 ft.
Number of Trails: 19 trails/
*   slopes or 75 skiable acres*
Lifts: 7 double chairs, 1 T-bar
Snowmaking: 100 percent of
*   terrain*
Season: early December–late March

They're called The Big Two. Together Big Boulder Ski Area in Lake Harmony (Big Boulder Lake) and Jack Frost Mountain in White Haven boast 30 trails serviced by 15 lifts. Both have 100 percent snowmaking coverage and terrain about equally divided among expert, intermediate, and novice skiers.

Their lift tickets are reciprocal, for both daytime hours and for night skiing at Big Boulder from 4 to 10 P.M. 7 nights a week and until midnight Fridays and Saturdays in January and February. And all the slopes are lit! Also unique is a twilight ticket available from noon until 10 P.M. at Jack Frost. Seniors 65 and up ski for only $5.

What the mountains lack in vertical, they make up for in broad slopes and dependable skiing.

Practical Information for Big Boulder/Jack Frost

HOW TO GET THERE. Both are in the western Poconos, Jack Frost 4 miles east of I–80 and the northeast extension of the Pennsylvania Turnpike on Rte. 940; Big Boulder south of the Blakeslee Exit of I–80 on Rte. 903. (See The Poconos section.)

TELEPHONES. The area code for this region of Pennsylvania is 717.

 **ACCOMMODATIONS.** In this two-resort region, the *Expensive* category of accommodations ranges from $50 to $75 per person, based on double occupancy, with some meals included in the higher ranges; *Moderate,* $30–$50; and *Inexpensive,* under $30. Because of their proximity to Camelback Ski Area, Big Boulder/Jack Frost skiers may also choose lodgings from the listings for that resort.

Expensive

The Galleria. Off Rte. 534, Lake Harmony 18626; 722–9111. Offers whirlpool, swimming, and health club in pleasant setting.

Hershey Pocono Resort. Rte. 940, White Haven 18661; 443–8411. Private balconies off rooms, indoor Olympic-size pool, children's activities, and saunas at this noted resort.

Holiday Inn. Rte. 940, Pocono–Lake Harmony, White Haven 18661; 443–8471. Luxurious rooms here in addition to sauna, two restaurants.

Split Rock Resort. Off Rte. 534. Lake Harmony 18624; 722–9111. A lodge and cottages with fireplaces, on-premises indoor swimming, tennis, racquetball, and health club.

Moderate

Blue Heron. Rte. 534, Big Boulder 18624; 443–8428. At entrance to the ski slopes, these 2- and 3-bedroom condominiums feature Japanese soaking tubs.

Greenway Lodge. Rte. 447, Henryville 18332; 629–1991. A top-of-mountain resort offering lounge with fireplace, game room, private baths.

Harmony Lake Shore Inn. Off Rte. 115, Lake Harmony 18624; 722–0522. Right on lake with color TV, refrigerators, and in-room coffee; snowmobile rentals; minutes from ski area.

Naomi Cottages. Rte. 390, Cresco 18326; 595–2432. Fully equipped housekeeping cottages for up to 14, most with log-burning fireplaces.

Snow Ridge Village. Rte. 940, White Haven 18326; 443–8428. Slopeside at Jack Frost, this is condominium living, with cross-country nearby.

Sheraton Pocono Inn. Main St., Stroudsburg 18360; 424–1930. Rooms and suites, recently redecorated, plus indoor pool, dining, and entertainment.

Inexpensive

Antlers Lodge and Cottages. Rte. 611, Swiftwater 18370; 839–7243. A 175-year-old inn also offers cottage living; only minutes from ski areas.

Daniels Top-o-the-Poconos Resort. Rte. 447, Canadensis 18325; 595–7531. A favorite with families, partly because of indoor swimming pool; sauna; dining and cocktail lounge.

Hampton Court Inn. Rte. 940, Mt. Pocono 18344; 839–2119. Lodging is motel-style; on-premises restaurant features charbroiled steaks.

Memorytown USA. Between Rtes. 940 and 611, Mt. Pocono 18344; 839–7176. Cottages and suites, all with fireplaces, some canopy beds; indoor pool.

Richie's Motel. Rte. 940, White Haven 18661; 443–9528. Twin double beds, color TV in rooms; 4 separate dining rooms and 3 bars and lounges on premises.

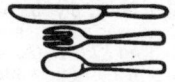 **RESTAURANTS.** As in the case of accommodations, skiers at Big Boulder/Jack Frost may want to check out what the Camelback Ski Area may have to offer in the way of restaurants. In this brief listing, only those dining places nearest to the Big Two are included. Also, many of the area lodging establishments maintain their own dining rooms that are open to the public. Best to call ahead for reservations. Listed here, *Expensive* means $15–$20 for a meal for one person, excluding drinks, tax, and tip; *Moderate,* $10–$15; *Inexpensive,* less than $10. All but the take-out places accept major credit cards.

Iorio's Fireside Inn. *Expensive.* Rte. 115, Blakeslee; 472–9380. If you like lots to choose from, this is it; plus a soup, salad, cheese, and dessert bar to start and top off the meal.

Kelley's Motor Coach Inn. *Moderate.* Rte. 940, Gouldsboro; 842–8417. An authentic English pub and dining room with on-premises bakery, salad bar.

Lake Harmony Lodge. *Moderate.* Lake Dr., Lake Harmony; 722–8368. Overlooking the lake; specialties include Caesar salad and duck a l'orange.

Van Gilder's Jubilee Restaurant. *Moderate.* Rte. 940, Pocono Pines; 646–2377. Everything from steaks to sandwiches here plus a reputation for great breakfasts.

Poco-Mac, Inc. *Inexpensive.* Rte. 115, Lake Harmony; 443–7370. The Poconos version of the American favorite!

HOW TO GET AROUND. A car is a necessity in this area of the Poconos. However, some lodging places may supply **shuttle** service to the mountains. Check when making reservations.

SEASONAL EVENTS. Jack Frost hosts a Special Olympics Qualifier annually in late **January,** and in **March** offers the *52 Association* (for handicapped skiers), a special learn-to-ski program. Everyone in the region enjoys the *Pocono Winter Carnival* held for a week in late **February** and featuring both serious and fun races and good times.

 **Other Sports and Activities.** Look for **tennis, racquetball,** indoor **swimming,** and **health spa** facilities at *Split Rock Resort,* off Rte. 534, Lake Harmony, 722–9111; whirlpool, sauna, exercise equipment, swimming at *The Galleria,* off Rte. 534, Lake Harmony, 722–9111.

The *Hershey Pocono Resort* on Rte. 940, White Haven, 443–8411, features an Olympic-size indoor pool and health spa facilities. And the *Holiday Inn,* Rte. 940, Pocono-Lake Harmony in White Haven, 443–8471, also offers health spa facilities.

Cross-country skiing is popular in the region with a 6-mile trail from Big Boulder to Hickory Run State Park and back. At Jack Frost, 15 km of trails are maintained.

In the nearby town of Jim Thorpe, there's cross-country skiing at Mauch Chunk Lake Park with 20 miles of trails, including the Switchback Railroad bed that traces the route of the first gravity railroad in the U.S. For trail conditions call the park at 325–3669.

 **HINTS TO THE HANDICAPPED.** Handicapped skiers —blind and amputee—can participate not only in beginner instruction at Jack Frost Mountain but also in intermediate and advanced level skiing and introductory racing. The programs are endorsed by the U.S. National Handicap Ski Team, the National Handicap Sports Recreation Association, and the Professional Ski Instructors of America. Jack Frost is the only facility in the area to offer this extended learning progression.

For any handicapped skier, the first day on skis, including lift ticket, rental, and lesson, is free. Ensuing days are available at half price. The beginner instructional program is in conjunction with the 52 Association, a non-profit organization that serves the needs of the severely disabled through its "confidence through sports" concept.

DAY-CARE FACILITIES. There's free babysitting at both areas and free skiing for children under 6 years old (when skiing with an adult). The children's ski school programs at both mountains are dubbed *Kids R Us,* an animated ski school teaching program that involves ages 3–5 in a 3-hour winter experience to familiarize them with the concept of skiing. Games and on-snow fun help get children used to ski equipment. The learn-to-ski terrain earmarked for youngsters at both mountains features colorful animated figures visible from restaurant and lounge areas—so mom and dad can relax. Children under 10 can enroll in a half-day ski and lesson program and those 10 and over can enjoy an all-day, on-slope instructional program.

NIGHTLIFE. The four major resorts in the region all offer music for dancing or entertainment come weekends. These include *The Galleria,* off Rte. 534, Lake Harmony, 722–9111; *Split Rock Resort,* off Rte. 534, Lake Harmony, 722–9111; *Holiday Inn,* Rte. 940, Pocono–Lake Harmony, White Haven, 443–8471; and *Hershey Pocono Resort,* Rte. 940, White Haven, 443–8411. Many smaller places around Lake Harmony offer bands and entertainment on weekends also.

CAMELBACK SKI AREA

Box 168
Tannersville PA 18372
Tel: 717–629–1661

Snow Report: 717–629–1661
Area Vertical: 800 ft.
Number of Trails: 27 or 122
*   acres*
Lifts: 1 quadruple chair, 2
*   triple chairs, 6 double chairs,*
*   1 J-Bar, 1 T-bar*
Snowmaking: 100 percent of
*   terrain*
Season: mid-December–late March

Camelback is a 2,100-foot mountain in the Poconos offering more skiable terrain on its 27 trails than any of its Pocono neighbors.

Popular with New Jersey and New York skiers, the mountain has up to 40 percent of its terrain in the "easiest" category, 20 percent "most difficult," and the rest flagged for the intermediate skier. The upper third of the mountain is quite steep with some challenging expert runs like the Pocket. It also offers gladed skiing at the intermediate level and a wooded terrain called The Meadows for novices.

A virtue of the Poconos ski areas is their commitment to snowmaking, and Camelback is no exception, covering virtually all of its 122 acres with machine-made snow from mid-December to late March. It also runs with the philosophy that skiers can't get too much of skiing, and opens its slopes for skiing from 5 to 10 P.M. nightly.

Practical Information for Camelback

HOW TO GET THERE. Camelback is located 5 minutes from Tannersville via I–80 (exit 45). It is 80 miles from New York City and 90 miles from Philadelphia.

TELEPHONES. The area code for Camelback and the Poconos is 717.

ACCOMMODATIONS. The *Pocono Mountain Vacation Bureau,* 1040 Main St., Stroudsburg (421–5791), can suggest places to stay close to Camelback. There are some 100 rooms right at the slopes and an additional 3,000 in nearby communities. The lodging establishments in this region are very price competitive. Hotel rates are based on double occupancy, per person, mostly MAP. Categories, determined by price, are *Expensive,* $50 and up; *Moderate,* $30–$50; *Inexpensive,* under $30.

For specific mountainside lodging information, call 629–1661, and for condominium lodging, call 629–3661.

Because of the proximity of the three ski areas in this region of the Poconos, Camelback skiers also may opt for lodgings listed for the Big Boulder and Jack Frost ski areas.

Expensive

Caesars Brookdale Resort. Brookdale Rd., Scotrun; 839–8843. A 250-acre estate with cottages and villas besides the main lodge; 55 suites; dining room and bar; indoor pool, whirlpool, and sauna.

The Chateau at Camelback. Camelback Rd., Tannersville; 629–5900. A new resort at the base of Camelback Mountain. Spacious rooms and suites; slopeside rooms with balconies overlooking mountain; restaurant, nightclub, lounge, indoor pool, health club.

Crescent Lodge. Rtes. 191 and 940, Cresco; 595–7486. Lodge, motel rooms, and cottages with color TV and phone; 2 dining rooms; cocktail lounge.

Mount Airy Lodge. At the slopes of Mt. Pocono; 839–8811. Resort estate on 1,500 acres; some suites with sunken Roman baths; dining room and coffee shop; 4 lounges; indoor swimming pool, health club, indoor and outdoor ice skating.

Pocono Gardens Lodge. Paradise Valley, Mt. Pocono; 595–7431. 3-room suites available, with fireplace, Roman bath, heat lamp, stereo, and color TV; also available are chalets with fireplace and terrace; dining room and cocktail lounge; health club, indoor pool, ice skating, snowmobiling, and ice hockey.

Strickland's Mountain Inn Cottages. Rte. 611, Mt. Pocono; 839–7155. Located 1½ miles from ski area; 40 hotel rooms and 71 suites, some with private sauna; 70 cottages and villas; dining room; indoor pool; exercise room.

Moderate

Best Western Pocono Inn. 700 Main St., Stroudsburg; 421–2200. Motor inn in center of town, 10 miles from Stroudsburg Pocono Airport; rooms and suites with color TV; dining room, coffee shop, lounge.

Laurel Grove Inn and Cottages. Rte. 390, Canadensis; 595–7262. Resort motel and cottages on 60 acres; dining room; lounge nearby.

The Overlook Inn. Dutch Hill Rd., Canadensis; 595–7519. A 100-year-old 20-room country inn with crocheted spreads, country furnishings; meals served; no children under 12.

The Pine Knob Inn. Rt. 447, Canadensis; 595–2532. A pre-Civil War country inn decorated with antiques and art, gourmet dining.

Pocono Econo Lodge. Exit 45 off I–80, Tannersville; 629–4100. King-size beds, whirlpool, some deluxe units with fireplaces, color TV (cable).

Towne Motor Court. Rte. 447, Canadensis 18325; 595–2491. A deluxe motel with cabins and housekeeping cottages.

Inexpensive

The following sampling of the many housekeeping cottages and motels are also available for budget-minded skiers.

Alvin's Housekeeping Log Cabins. Rte. 611, Henryville; 629–0667. 4 furnished cabins and 4 efficiency units, all with fireplaces, TVs, kitchens and baths. Just 10 minutes to Camelback.

Elmer's Motel & Cottages. Rte. 611, Tannersville; 629–0330. Family rooms and housekeeping cottages, color TV, just 5 minutes from Camelback.

Fern Rock Cottages. Rte. 611, Scotrun; 839–9311. 1–3-bedroom housekeeping cottages, all with fireplace, TV, baths and kitchens.

Garden Motel. Belmont Ave., Mt. Pocono; 839–9466. A quiet location with modern accommodations; coffee and TV in all units.

Penn's Wood Motel & Cottages. Rte. 611, Tannersville; 629–0131. Only minutes from Camelback, offering winter ski packages, color TV, and pleasant rooms.

Pine Hill Lodge. Rte. 611, Mt. Pocono; 839–9579. A private lodge with 11 bedrooms, fully equipped kitchen, sleeps up to 30. Perfect for a large group.

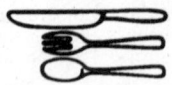 **RESTAURANTS.** Pocono Mountain trout is the specialty of many restaurants in this area. Price categories for the region are *Expensive,* $15 and higher; *Moderate,* $8–$15; *Inexpensive,* under $8. These prices are for one meal, excluding drinks, tip, and tax. Restaurants in the area accept *American Express, MasterCard,* and *Visa* unless otherwise noted.

Expensive

Brass Door Restaurant. Carriage House at Pocono Manor, Rte. 314; 839–7386. A different environment with a paddlewheel, overhead fans, and over-stuffed chairs, reputation for excellent dining. Reservations suggested.

Chateau at Camelback. Rte. 611, Tannersville, 629–5900. A wide-ranging menu in elegant dining room overlooking mountains.

Crescent Lodge Restaurant. Rtes. 940/191, Cresco; 595–7486. An extensive menu with salad bar, lobster included, and prime rib buffet on Fridays. Entertainment weekends.

Fanucci's Restaurant. Rte. 611, Swiftwater; 839–7097. Northern and southern Italian fare served here, including homemade breads, pastas, and desserts.

Homestead Inn. Sandspring Dr., Cresco; 595–3171. A cozy place with homemade soups, breads, and pies, good choice of entrees.

Johnnie's Pocono Summit Inn. Old Rte. 940, Mt. Pocono; 839–7401. For over 50 years a reputation for Italian specialties, especially fresh seafood.

Pump House Inn. Rte. 390, Canadensis; 595–7501. Dine in dining room or wine cellar; enjoy French country cuisine including quiche au fromage and steak au poivre.

Smuggler's Cove Restaurant. Rte. 611, Tannersville; 629–2277. Seafood, steaks, and prime rib are favorites here; separate children's menu; dessert cart and salad bar.

Moderate

Best Western Train Coach Restaurant. Exit 45 off I–80; 629–0113. Authentic railroad dining cars provide the ambience here for steak and seafood specialties.

Cattlemen's Restaurant. Rte. 196, Mt. Pocono; 894–8767. Prime ribs and a stone bar make this country inn a favorite; plus there's piano music Saturday evenings.

Christine's Reeders Inn. Rte. 715, S. Reeders; 629–1210. A Chinese-American restaurant with Cantonese, Mandarin, or Szechuan specialties.

Country Breadboard Family Restaurant and Bakery. Rte. 940, Mt. Pocono; 839–7888. An early American setting with fresh baked goods daily; children's menu.

Hampton Court Inn. Rte. 940, Mt. Pocono; 839–2119. Charbroiled steaks and seafood with claims to meals "fit for a king."

The Inn at Tannersville. Exit 45 off I–80; 629–3131. A rustic environment offering steaks, chops, and seafood by the fireplace.

The Old Heidelberg Restaurant and Lounge. Rte. 611, Swiftwater; 839–9954. Since 1929, offering German, Italian, and American cuisine.

Inexpensive

Antler's Lodge. Off Rte. 611, Swiftwater; 839–7243. A family-run resort that claims excellent food is its priority. Shrimp and veal specialties; children's menu.

Cameltop on Big Pocono Mountain. At Camelback, Tannersville; 629–1661. A great place for lunch with panoramic views of the Poconos.

 **HOW TO GET AROUND.** Driving your own, or a rented, **car** is the best way to get around in the Poconos, particularly if your lodgings are far from the mountain. Some of the nearby accommodations, however, do supply **shuttle bus** service. Check when making reservations.

SEASONAL EVENTS. In late **spring** before the snow melts, crazy hats, games, and prizes compete with the corn snow on the trails during annual *Hi-Jinx Day.* And mid-season there's a 5-day program for recreational skiers designed to hone skiing skills through the *Steve Lathrop Racing Camp.*

 **OTHER SPORTS AND ACTIVITIES.** Complete health and exercise facilities, indoor **pool, sauna,** and **whirlpool,** are available at Caesars Brookdale-on-the-Lake, Scotrun (226–2101), where there's also **ice skating** and **snowmobiling.** Look for hydrospas, indoor roller and ice skating, **racquet-ball, swimming** and whirlpools at *Strickland's Mountain Inn,* Mt. Pocono, 839–7155. *Pocono Gardens* (595–7431) features a health spa and indoor pool, while *The Chateau at Camelback,* Tannersville (629–5900), has a fully equipped health spa and indoor pool and offers a health staff to help with diet planning and exercise programs. *Mount Airy Lodge,* Mt. Pocono (839–8811), features universal and Nautilus equipment, a masseur, whirlpool, indoor pool and saunas, plus exercise classes.

DAY-CARE FACILITIES. The ski area offers child care in a nursery for $2.50 an hour and the Cameland Ski School accepts ages 4–9 for $11 a lesson.

 **NIGHTLIFE.** This is a region where entertainment thrives. For dancing check out *Birchwood Resort,* off Rte. 611, East Stroudsburg, 629–0222; *Caesar's Brookdale on the Lake,* Rte. 611, Scotrun, 226–2101; the *Chateau at Camelback,* off Rte. 611, Tannersville, 629–5900; *Memorytown USA,* off Rte. 611, Mt. Pocono, 839–7176 (country-western bands); *Penn Hills Resort,* Rte. 447, Analomink, 421–6464; *Sheraton Pocono Inn,* Main St., Stroudsburg, 424–1930.

There's also nightly entertainment at *Caesar's Paradise Stream,* Rte. 940, Mt. Pocono, 226–2101; and *Pocono Gardens,* Rte. 940, Mt. Pocono, 595–7431.

SHAWNEE MOUNTAIN

Shawnee-on-Delaware PA 18356
Tel: 717–421–7231

Snow Report: 717–421–7231
Area Vertical: 700 ft.
Number of Trails: 20 or 60
*   skiable acres*
Lifts: 7 double chairs
Snowmaking: 100 percent of
*   terrain*
Season: late November–late March

Trail names here have an Indian ring—Pocahantas, Little Brave, and Chief Thunder Cloud. But the activity might be too much for those long-ago natives, especially on an experimental two nights of the year when the mountain forgets (on purpose) to shut off its night skiing lights (usually it's "lights out" at 10 P.M.) and keeps the lifts operating for skiers 'round the clock.

This area is primarily designed for the beginning–intermediate skier with 7 trails marked "easiest," 10 "more difficult," and 3 "most difficult." A separate beginners' area with its own 2 lifts keeps the just-learning folks out of the mainstream of the action.

Resort activity focuses on the Shawnee Inn at the base of the slopes and at a collection of resort hotels nearby that, like Tamiment, traditionally bring top-flight entertainment to the Poconos for après-ski diversion.

Practical Information for Shawnee Mountain

 **HOW TO GET THERE.** Shawnee Mountain is located in Shawnee-on-Delaware, 4 miles from Stroudsburg which is just about the epicenter of the Poconos. It is 40 miles from Allentown via I–80. Take Exit 52 (the Marshalls Creek Exit) to US 209 north to Shawnee.

HOW TO GET AROUND. If staying right at the mountain, a car isn't necessary. However, it's preferable to have transportation if lodging in a nearby town.

TELEPHONES. The area code for the Poconos is 717.

 **ACCOMMODATIONS.** The *Pocono Mountain Vacation Bureau,* 1004 Main St., Stroudsburg 18360 (421–5791) can suggest places to stay close to Shawnee. For information on condominium and vacation home lodging, contact *Mountain Vacation Properties at Shawnee,* Shawnee on Delaware (421–1500) or *Shawnee Village Vacation Home Rentals,* Shawnee on Delaware (424–1300).

Expensive in this region starts at about $55 (with MAP) per person per night; *Moderate,* $20–$55; *Inexpensive,* $20 and less.

Expensive

Fernwood. Off Rte. 447, Bushkill; 588–6661. This is a year-round resort complete unto itself offering amenities for everybody from families to honeymooners, with indoor tennis and swimming, indoor roller skating, on-premises dining, and nightly entertainment.

Wayne Newton's Tamiment Resort. Off Rte. 209, Bushkill; 588–6652. Another self-contained resort covering 2,200 acres and its own lake. On premises are 4 indoor tennis courts, indoor swimming, snowmobiling, tobogganing, dining, and sometimes big-name entertainment.

Moderate

Glenwood Hotel & Resort Motel. Rte. 611, Delaware Water Gap; 476–0010. A resort offering indoor pool and whirlpool, nightly music for dancing.

Howard Johnson's Motor Lodge. Exit 53 off I–80, Delaware Water Gap; 476–0000. Refurbished rooms, color TV, indoor pool, on-premises dining and lounge; children under 18 free.

The Mountain House. Rte. 611, Delaware Water Gap; 424–2254. A turn-of-the-century inn with country-style meals, private and shared baths.

Pocmont. Off Rte. 209, Bushkill; 588–6671. Suites in main lodge have whirlpool baths; health club offers steam rooms, whirlpool, and exercise equipment; indoor swimming; on-premises dining and entertainment.

Shawnee Inn. Rte. 209, Shawnee-on-Delaware; 421–1500. Lodging right at the mountain with indoor pool and health spa.

Inexpensive

Below is a sampling of motels and housekeeping cottages that offer inexpensive lodging.

Budget Motel. Exit 52 off I–80, Stroudsburg; 424–5451. A new, 110-room, motel with color cable TV and ceramic tile baths and showers. Cribs and rollaways available.

Countryside Cottages. Rte. 611, Stroudsburg; 629–2131. 1- to 4- and even 6-bedroom cottages, some with dorms and two baths; fireplaces, TV; game room.

Shawnee Motor Lodge. Rte. 209, Echo Lake; 223–9247. Rooms with 2 double beds, private bath, color TV, Continental breakfast; restaurant, lounge, and entertainment. Just 2 miles to Shawnee.

Willow Run Cottages. Rte. 209, Stroudsburg; 629–0752. Rustic housekeeping chalets with large decks, completely furnished, fireplace and TV.

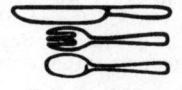 **RESTAURANTS.** A wide variety of dining places to suit every pocketbook is available in the Poconos. Price categories for the region are *Expensive*, \$15 and higher; *Moderate*, \$8–\$15; and *Inexpensive*, less than \$8. American Express, MasterCard, and Visa are accepted at most restaurants.

Expensive

Peppe's Ristorante. Rte. 447, East Stroudsburg; 421–4460. An old-world setting with homemade pastas, other Italian fare. Veal dishes are favorites here.

Top of the World at Saw Creek. Rte. 209, Bushkill; 588–9444. Continental entrees and a seafood menu vie with the views here.

Moderate

Albino's. Washington St., East Stroudsburg; 421–9300. Two dining rooms feature American-Italian offerings plus lots of fresh seafood and veal.

Alternative. Rte. 209, East Stroudsburg; 476–0454. Chinese and Polynesian fare, but a reputation for steaks and seafood.

Bailey's Pub & Steakhouse. Main St., Stroudsburg; 424–9120. Classic English pub with treats like "super nachos" and hickory-smoked baby back ribs.

Live Lobsters at "The Beaver House." Rte. 611, Stroudsburg; 421–1020. Steak and shore here, with whole Maine lobsters featured.

The Country Inn at Stroudsmoor. Off Rte. 191, Stroudsburg; 421–6431. Dinner begins with cocktails by the fire.

Shawnee Inn Dogwood Room. River Rd., Shawnee on Delaware; 421–1500. A beautiful riverside setting with a 100-year-old inn serving American and Continental specialties.

Inexpensive

Casa Mario. Rte. 191, Stroudsburg; 992–3422. Homemade pastas and desserts, with at least 50 entrees to choose from.

Mollie's. Mail St., Stroudsburg; 424–1062. Three meals a day here; basic, hearty food.

HOW TO GET AROUND. As in other parts of the Poconos, a **car** is a necessity in getting about.

SEASONAL EVENTS. As do the other Pocono ski areas, Shawnee participates in the *Pocono Winter Carnival* every year. The specialty here is a costume carnival day with free season passes going to the winners of various costume categories, and free skiing for everyone who uses imagination in their garb!

 **OTHER SPORTS AND ACTIVITIES.** Several establishments in the area offer **health spa** facilities, indoor **tennis**, and **swimming.** These include the Shawnee Inn (421–1500) right at the mountain with indoor swimming, and affiliated with the mountain Shawnee Racquet Club (424–2333) in Eagle Valley Corners. There are 4 indoor tennis and 3 indoor **racquetball** courts, a tanning bed, Nautilus fitness center, whirlpool, and saunas. Fernwood (588–6661) and Tamiment (588–6652) in Bushkill have health club facilities for their guests with gyms, saunas, indoor tennis, whirlpools, and indoor pools. Shawnee Mountain maintains 3 km of **cross-country** terrain right at the area.

 **DAY-CARE FACILITIES.** A service called *Little Wigwam Babysitting*, charges \$2.50 an hour for ages 1 year and up. The *SKIwee* instructional program is available for ages 4–12, and youngsters also enjoy romping in the snow in the *Shawnee Play Park*.

NIGHTLIFE. Right at Shawnee Mountain, the *Easy Bumps Saloon* (421–7231) offers entertainment on Friday and Saturday nights. If dancing is in order, then check out *Caesar's Pocono Palace Resort* on Rte. 209 in Marshalls Creek (226–2101), *Fernwood* on Rte. 209 in Bushkill (588–6661), *Pocmont* off Rte. 209 in Bushkill (588–6671), andTamiment off Rte. 209, Bushkill (588–6652). These establishments also offer nightly entertainment and sometimes, on weekends, big-name entertainment.

SEVEN SPRINGS MOUNTAIN RESORT

R.D. 1, Champion PA 15622
Tel: 814–352–7777

Snow Report: 814–352–7777
Area Vertical: 970 ft.
Number of Trails: 24 or 350
*   skiable acres*
Lifts: 7 triple chairs, 4
*   double chairs, 2 rope tows*
Snowmaking: 100 percent
Season: December 1–April 1

Seven Springs Mountain Resort is more than a ski area, more than a destination resort, more than a major conference center. It's the American family success story, the stuff of legends having to do with entrepreneurship, dedicated families, and hard work.

Of course, its location, 55 miles from Pittsburgh, probably had something to do with it, too.

Seven Springs is Pennsylvania's largest year-round ski resort. Located in Champion, Pa., it is spread over 12,000 acres in Laurel Highlands, a region that includes the most substantial mountains in Pennsylvania, dominated by the 2,900-foot peak that draws Seven Springs' skiers.

There's another ski area nearby, Hidden Valley Resort in Somerset, that shares its 11 slopes and trails with one of the largest ski touring centers in the state, the Hidden Valley Ski Touring Center (30 miles of groomed trails).

Laurel Ridge State Park in Rockwood also has designated a 12-mile cross-country loop. And on state forest and park lands between Rtes. 31 and 30 on Laurel Ridge there are over 50 miles of groomed snowmobile trails.

The beauty of the region and its year-round potential for recreation was first recognized in 1932 by a German immigrant couple who bought 2½ acres of land for $13. They bought here, perhaps not coincidentally in a natural snow bowl, because the terrain reminded them of their native Bavaria. Perhaps it was the influence of the Schwartzwald that led Adolph Dupre to begin creating his dream. One cabin after another was crafted, creating a getaway in the wilderness for people from Pittsburgh.

By 1935 there were automobile engine-powered rope tows helping people up the mountain, and by 1937, the area opened officially for skiing.

Today the resort offers 24 trails—really open slopes—that encompass 350 acres. Eleven trails are designated "more difficult" for intermediates, 4 are earmarked for experts, and 9 for beginners.

An efficient lift system accommodates skiers, as does snowmaking coverage that can blanket 100 percent of the terrain with machine-made snow.

Because it's such a popular place with urban skiers, the resort offers several lift ticket options. For example, after 1 P.M.,lift tickets sold at the day rate include night skiing until 11 P.M. Or, skiers can purchase a less expensive night lift ticket for skiing from 4:30 P.M. on.

Off the mountain, ski guests are welcomed by Somerset County's largest employer at the 385-room main lodge where a winter staff of over 800 people tend to all details of a ski vacation.

Despite its size and success, the Dupre family still maintains hands-on management, and Helen Dupre, widow of the German entrepreneur, is chairlady of the board. This means that the hospitable, club-like environment created over 50 years ago still thrives.

Practical Information for Seven Springs

HOW TO GET THERE. Seven Springs Mountain Resort is 8 miles from Champion and 55 miles from Pittsburgh via the Pennsylvania Turnpike.

By air. The Greater Pittsburgh Airport is served by major airlines. Shuttle service can be arranged from the resort. The Westmoreland County Airport (412–539–8100 in Latrobe, 20 miles away, is served by *Allegheny Commuter Airlines* (412–537–5950). The Seven Springs Airport has a 3,000-ft. paved and lighted runway. Rental car services are available from all major companies at the Pittsburgh Airport. *Budget* (412–539–7100) and *Hertz* (412–539–1512) are available at the Westmoreland facility.

By car. From the east, take Exit 10 (Somerset) off the Pennsylvania Turnpike; at third traffic light off exit ramp, take Rte. 31 west for 7 miles; turn left at Pioneer Park; after 4 miles and at first stop sign, turn right; drive 5 miles to Seven Springs. From the west, take Exit 9 (Donegal) off the Pennsylvania Turnpike to Rtes. 711 and 31; turn right onto Rte. 711 for 2 miles; follow signs in Champion to Seven Springs.

TELEPHONES. The area code for Seven Springs and surrounding communities is 814.

ACCOMMODATIONS. Although there are inns in nearby Somerset that accommodate Seven Springs skiers, most guests who come to the area stay right at the resort, either in the main lodge or in nearby condominiums, townhouses, and cabins that are under resort management. For reservations and information contact the reservation desk at 352–7777.

Accommodations in the **Seven Springs main lodge** are priced from $91 to $99 per room. Most rooms have private balcony or patio and some offer views of skiing activity.

Mountain Villas and Swiss Mountain condominiums and townhouses range from $530 per week for a 1-bedroom unit to $1,210 per week for a 4-bedroom split level home. Condos and townhouses located about ¾ mile from the main lodge range from $330 for a 1-bedroom to $730 for a 4-bedroom home for two nights. All have complete kitchens with dishwasher, and washer and dryer. Most have TV.

Main Lodge suites for up to four people are $275 per day. These include a complete bedroom, sitting room that converts to a sleeping area, refrigerator, color TV, and private balcony or patio.

Cabins with large living rooms, kitchens, bedrooms with bunk beds, and baths can sleep from 14 to 20 people and range from $500 to $700 for two nights.

For off-resort lodgings, there are two inns in Somerset in the *Moderate* price range, where rates, based on double occupancy, range from $50 to $65 per night, EP.

Holiday Inn. Schaffer St., Somerset; 445–9611 or 800–465–4329. Rooms with phone and color TV with HBO; 23 suites; restaurant and lounge.

Ramada Inn. Exit 10, Pennsylvania Turnpike; 443–4646 or 800–2–RAMA-DA. Renovated motor inn with rooms and 4 suites, restaurant, indoor pool, Jacuzzi, and sauna.

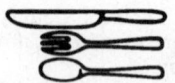

RESTAURANTS. Since Seven Springs is a self-contained ski resort, the dining out here is mostly dining in. Even so, the resort offers a variety of dining accommodations. *Expensive* ranges from $20 to $30; *Moderate,* $8–$20; and *Inexpensive,* less than $8. Two in the *Expensive* category are **La Sorgente,** where reservations are a must for gourmet fare with a French and Italian touch, and the **Oak Room** in the main lodge, which offers an all-you-can-eat seafood buffet on Fridays and a one-price buffet on Saturdays. The **Char 'n Grill Room** *(Moderate)* offers more traditional American food, and **Adolph's Cafe** *(Inexpensive)* in the ski lodge features pastries, international coffees, and Belgian waffles. Guests can also snack at the **Coffee Shop** or at the **Pizza and Pastry Place,** both *Inexpensive* and both in the main lodge.

And something quite new at ski resorts is a light lunch menu at the resort restaurants, designed to offer only 300 calories to weight-conscious skiers. The menu focuses on high-protein foods and low-calorie desserts. There's also a vegetarian salad bar, and a **Mr. Potato Restaurant** in the base lodge encourages healthy eating with a variety of vegetable toppings for baked spuds.

Guests can also dine at the **Pizza & Pastry Place** or at the **Coffee Shop,** both in the main lodge.

OTHER SPORTS AND ACTIVITIES. The resort offers **racing** instruction for NASTAR as well as competitions daily. On premises are an indoor **swimming** pool open weekends until midnight and Mondays–Thursdays until 11 P.M.; **game rooms; bowling** alleys; **minigolf; handball** and **racquetball** courts; **roller skating;** a **health spa** with whirlpool, sauna, and universal gym; **hot tubs** and a **tanning salon.**

If **shopping** is high on the list, the on-premises boutiques' stock ranges from clothing to flowers to leather and gifts.

HINTS TO HANDICAPPED. To accommodate handicapped guests, Seven Springs sponsors Special Olympics and ski races for the blind.

DAY-CARE FACILITIES. Babysitting can be arranged through the main lodge Customer Service Department. There are also complete organized recreational programs for children starting at age 5. The *Tiny Tots Ski School* for ages 3–6 is a combined program of on-slope instruction, indoor play, and lunch. The full-day runs from 9 A.M. to 4 P.M. and is $30.

A *Junior Program* for ages 7–12 involves youngsters in 4 hours of instruction from 10 A.M. to 2 P.M. for $30, including lunch.

NIGHTLIFE. There are five cocktail lounges on premises, with live entertainment in the *Matterhorn Lounge.* Popular here are adult contemporary show bands that provide music for dancing. There's also DJ-style music in three other lounges.

Vermont

New England winters are long, stretching from November until mid-April, challenging Yankee entrepreneurship to turn skis—as well as dollars—on that white stuff that has to be put up with for half a year anyway.

But winters are pretty here, too, nowhere more so than in Vermont, made famous years ago by Margaret Whiting's "Moonlight in Vermont," a melody still faithfully played on the state's easy-listening stations throughout the winter.

So the combination of long winter, snow, and beauty is part of the reason why Vermont leads the pack in the East when it comes to attracting skiers.

But there's something else. The state's Green Mountains, at first glance just rounded hills by western standards, cut a mean and challenging swath from north to south down the state. They're literally the backbone of Vermont, and you can't escape their presence, as anywhere you go you're only a whistle away from skiing.

Vermont ski area operators have been among the most aggressive in the country when it comes to adapting technology that makes the skiing experience more enjoyable for the skier. For example, modern and efficient chairlift systems, well-designed trail networks and snowmaking systems as insurance against lean snowfalls are common parts of the Vermont ski scene, no matter where in the state you go.

The other ingredients that people expect in a vacation today—resort amenities, fine restaurants, and a range of lodging accommodations—have all kept pace with ski area development.

Plus, there's something that doesn't get said very often about the Vermont experience. The state's population is small, only 500,000 people. When guests arrive, anytime of year, they count as one of the Vermont family. And in fact, there are a lot of transplanted New Yorkers and other suburbanites up here because they felt so much at home on their ski vacation.

For seasonal overviews on the Vermont ski experience, contact the Vermont Ski Areas Association, 26 State St., Montpelier, VT 05602, 802–223–2439. They will be happy to send their newest literature.

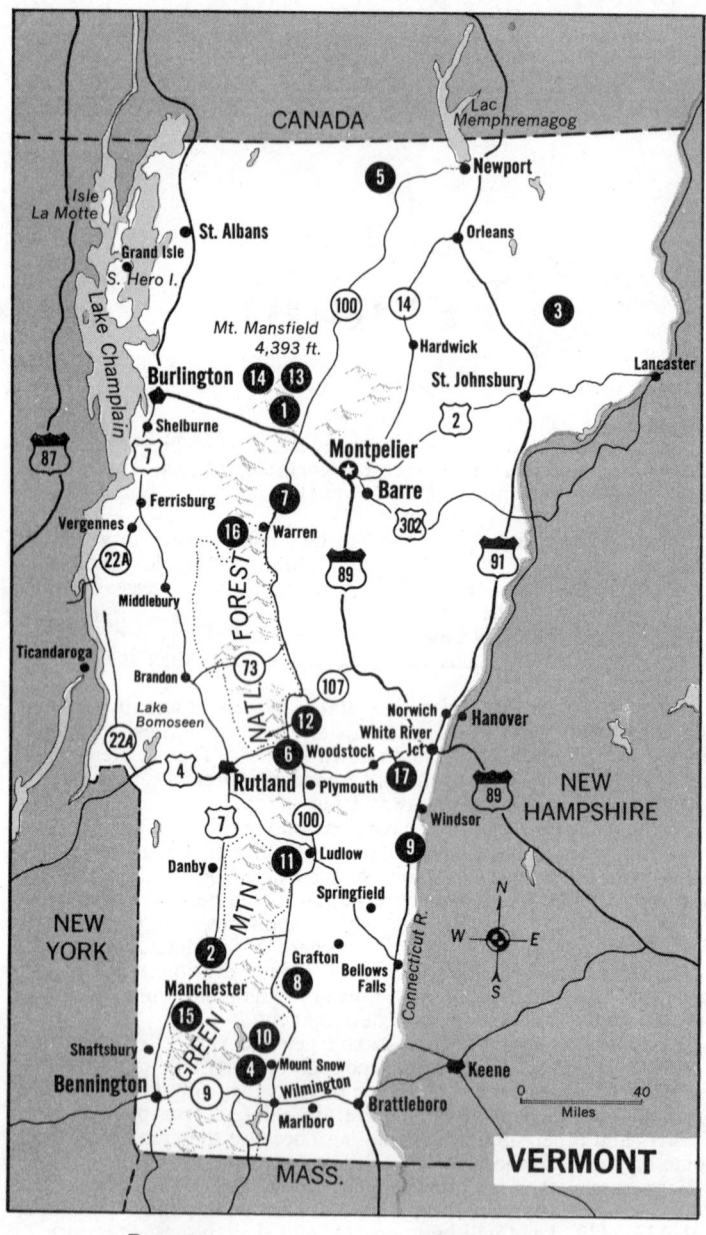

Resorts

1) Bolton Valley
2) Bromley Mountain
3) Burke Mountain
4) Haystack
5) Jay Peak
6) Killington
7) Mad River Glen
8) Magic Mountain
9) Mt. Ascutney
10) Mount Snow
11) Okemo Mountain
12) Pico
13) Smugglers' Notch
14) Stowe
15) Stratton Mountain
16) Sugarbush Valley
17) Suicide Six

SOUTHERN VERMONT

ASCUTNEY MOUNTAIN RESORT

Rte. 44, Brownsville VT 05037
Tel: 802–484–7711

Snow Report: 800–243–0011
Area Vertical: 1,530 ft.
Number of Trails: 31 or 100
* skiable acres*
Lifts: 2 triple chairs, 2
* double chairs*
Snowmaking: 60 percent of
* terrain*
Season: Thanksgiving–April 1

The people behind Mt. Ascutney, Summit Ventures Inc., have as much or more interest in producing a resort, per se, as they do a ski area. This mountain, tucked over on Vermont's Connecticut River side in the small village of Brownsville, has been savored by some devoted skiers for years, although they bemoaned the lack of snowmaking.

Since 1983, however, when Summit took over, that problem has been addressed. Capital construction projects have yielded a first-class condominium hotel, trails have been upgraded, and those who were loyal in the past are Ascutney's cheerleaders today.

The charm of this area is that it's small, very accessible (only 6 miles from I–91), uncrowded, and civilized. There aren't many ski resorts around where guests are greeted at the hotel door and offered assistance with luggage and skis.

Though limited, the black-diamond terrain here on Thunder Road and Sleet Street, among others, can challenge the most expert skier. And for those who like to cruise for awhile, there's a meandering 3-mile run.

Practical Information for Ascutney Mountain

HOW TO GET THERE. Ascutney Mountain is one of six ski resorts detailed in this guide that are located in the southern section of Vermont. The others are Bromley Mountain, Haystack, Magic Mountain, Mount Snow, and Stratton Mountain. Ascutney is located on Rte. 44 in Brownsville. Brattleboro and Manchester are gateways to Ascutney and the other southern Vermont ski resorts.

By air. Direct air service is available on major airlines from Albany NY, which is 78 miles from Brattleboro and 67 miles from Manchester. Connector flights are available from *Precision Airlines* (603–298–5651 or 800–451–4221) and *Command Airway* (603–298–5299), both of which fly into the West Lebanon, NH, airport, 18 miles from the resort. The resort will provide pickup service. Call 484–7711 for details. Precision also flies into the Dillant Hopkins Airport, some 25 miles east of Brattleboro in Keene, NH. Rental car agencies available in Brattleboro are *Hertz* (800–654–3131) and *National* (800–CAR-RENT). In Manchester rental cars are available from *Hand Chevrolet* (362–1754) and *Manchester* Motors (362–1808).

By bus. *Vermont Transit* (295–3011 or 864–6811 in other parts of the state), a division of Greyhound, provides service to Brattleboro (254–6066) and Manchester (864–6811) as well as to White River Junction, which is 16 miles from Ascutney.

By car. Take I–91 north into Vermont to Exit 8 at Ascutney, some 50 miles north of Brattleboro, and onto Rte. 5 north. A few miles later (watch signs) turn onto Black Mountain Rd. and follow it to Rte. 44. Go west 2 miles to the resort.
By train. Amtrak (295–7160) service is available to White River Junction.

TELEPHONES. The area code for all of Vermont is 802.

ACCOMMODATIONS. Ascutney skiers may choose to stay right at the mountain in slopeside condominiums or they may wander as far as the college town of Hanover, NH, home to Dartmouth, about 24 miles away. *Expensive* per weekend (double occupancy) in the region is $80 and up, with *Moderate* from about $40 to $80. *Inexpensive* is less than $40.

Expensive

Ascutney Mountain Resort Hotel. Rte. 44, Brownsville 05037; 484–7711. A full-service resort hotel encompassing 5 colonial-style buildings and offering hotel rooms plus up to 3-bedroom suites that come with fireplace, living room, kitchen, and deck.
Ascutney Mountain Village Condominiums. Rte. 44, Brownsville 05037; 484–7711. Right on the slopes, these condominiums offer 2-room units sleeping up to 6, with full kitchens.
Ascutney Mountainside Condominiums. Rte. 44, Brownsville 05037; 484–7711. Condominium-living offering 2 bedrooms plus sleeping loft, fireplaces or wood stoves, and kitchens with dishwashers and self-cleaning ovens.
The Inn at Weathersfield. Rte. 106, Weathersfield 05151; 263–9217. A 1795 stagecoach stop with private baths, antiques, and working fireplaces; afternoon tea served before 5-course dinner.

Moderate

Holiday Inn. Sykes Ave., White River Junction 05001, 20 miles from the mountain; 295–7537. Après-ski recreation includes indoor swimming, whirlpool, sauna, 2 restaurants and 2 lounges.
Sheraton North Country Inn. Airport Rd., West Lebanon NH 03784, 18 miles from Ascutney; 603–298–5906. Look for indoor pool and Jacuzzi, plus dining and entertainment.

Inexpensive

Cote's Motel. Claremont, NH 03743; 603–542–2231. Just 8 miles from Ascutney, motel offers color cable TV, coffee shop, welcomes groups.
Windsor Motel. Rte. 5, Windsor 05089; 674–9964. Color cable TV and in-room coffee plus hospitality to groups.
Wolpert's Mountain Inn. Windsor 05089; 674–5565. Early American decor view for attention with great views here, just 7 miles from mountain.
Yankee Village Motel. Rte. 5, Ascutney 05030; 674–6010. Large family rooms available, in-room coffee, color cable TV, and coffee shop on premises.

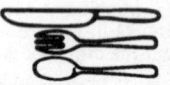

RESTAURANTS. Because Ascutney Mountain is just beginning to flex its muscles as a ski resort, there are limited offerings when it comes to dining out in the area. This situation, however, is expected to change in a few years as more and more skiers are finding this bona-fide skiing destination. In this small selection of restaurants, classifications are as follows: *Expensive,* $12–$18; *Moderate,* $8–$12; and *Inexpensive,* less than $8. American Express, MasterCard, and Visa are generally accepted in the region, but check before going.

Ascutney Harvest Inn. *Expensive.* Ascutney Mountain Resort, Brownsville; 484–7711. A 150-seat dining room offering elegant service in a brand-new restaurant. Fare ranges from international to traditional American, with a gourmet touch. Lobster is on the menu here.
The Ascutney House. *Expensive.* Junction of Rtes. 5 and 131, Ascutney; 674–2664. A restored mansion offering fine American cuisine and billing its ambience as circa 1800.
The Windsor Station Restaurant. *Moderate.* Depot Ave., Windsor; 674–2052. A restored train station now prepares steaks to your specifications, along with veal dishes.

J. P. Mallon's Pub. *Inexpensive.* Rte. 44, Brownsville; 484–7722. A small log cabin specializing in pub food such as sandwiches and stews.

Uptick. *Inexpensive.* Ascutney Mountain Resort, Brownsville; 484–7711. Family-style dining with spaghetti, hot dogs, and top-of-the-list favorite pizza.

 **HOW TO GET AROUND.** It is best to have a **car** at this resort. Some of the mountainside lodging places may have **shuttle** service to the surrounding towns, however. Check when making your reservations.

OTHER SPORTS AND ACTIVITIES. The Sports Center at Ascutney Mountain Resort (484–7711) has a 35 × 70 ft. indoor, heated **swimming pool,** sauna, whirlpool, 2 **racquetball** courts, **weight training** and **aerobics** rooms.

Sleigh rides are offered at the *Kedron Valley Inn Stables* in South Woodstock, 457–1480.

And depending on what's happening on a given weekend, Ascutney skiers often cast an eye toward Hanover NH, where Dartmouth College activities may include college **ice hockey** or **professional entertainers.**

DAY-CARE FACILITIES. The *Nursery* (484–7711) accepts infants through age 6 from 9 A.M. to 4 P.M. daily. Reservations necessary for those under a year old. Lunch can be included. The *Teddy Bear* program takes ages 4–6 on the slopes for introductory lessons, lunch, and combined nursery program. *SkiWee* accepts ages 6–12 for ski instruction made fun.

 **NIGHTLIFE.** *Uptick* at the mountain (484–7711) brings in bands on weekends. The *Winner's Circle Lounge* in the Ascutney Mountain Resort Hotel (484–7711) features jazz musicians on weekends and holidays. Downtown, *J. P. Mallon's Pub* on Rte. 44, Brownsville (484–7722), features a guitarist on weekends.

BROMLEY MOUNTAIN

P.O. Box 1130
Manchester Center VT 05255
Tel: 802–824–5522

Snow Report: 802–824–5522
Area Vertical: 1,334 ft.
Number of Trails: 35 or 157
*   skiable acres*
Lifts: 6 double chairs, one J-bar
Snowmaking: 83 percent of
*   terrain*
Season: November–April

Bromley Mountain has the distinction of being the only south-facing ski area in Vermont. This leads to their claim that they have the earliest and longest-tanned skiers around, and that it's sometimes as much as 10 degrees warmer here than at Stratton or Magic.

Bromley is located right on Route 11, which separates its parking area from the ski lifts. Unlike Stratton and Magic, Bromley makes no pretentions to having a ski village, although there is some slopeside lodging available.

The ski mountain was created in 1937 by Fred Pabst, Jr., of the Milwaukee brewing family. In addition to the mountain itself, Pabst was responsible for some skiing "firsts." He invented the J-bar, pioneered the concept of "snow farming," provided the first base-to-summit snowmaking, and made available the first slopeside nursery facilities.

Bromley is one of those areas that makes all ages feel welcome, with free skiing to ages 6 and younger and by half-price skiing to seniors 65 and older. There's also a Bromley Senior Skiers Club, P.O. Box 1130, Manchester Center VT 05255.

The mountain offers a balanced mix of beginner, intermediate, and expert trails. And everyone ends up at the bottom at the Wild Boar Base Lodge where jockeying for standing-room-only space is as challenging as managing the 3,500-ft. Havoc, a 10-acre, nearly half-mile-long black-diamond trail.

STRATTON MOUNTAIN

Stratton VT 05155
Tel: 802-297-2200

Snow Report: 802-297-2211
Area Vertical: 2,003 ft.
Number of Trails: 60 or 369
skiable acres
Lifts: 1 quadruple chair, 1 triple chair,
8 double chairs
Snowmaking: 62 percent of
terrain
Season: mid-November–early May

It's unclear from the archives how Stratton came to be called Stratton, except that many New England place names trace directly back to King George III of England and his pals. The Indian name for the mountain is Manicknung, or "home of the bear." It was a flourishing New England village of 366 people, according to the 1860 census, but as New Englanders discovered other parts of the country, Stratton's population declined. Even in the early part of this century, people struggled to make a living there, primarily through logging.

In 1959 a visionary named Frank Snyder recognized the possibilities of skiing on this mountain and the advantages of the proximity of a southern-based area to the New York metropolitan market. Three years later, Stratton Mountain opened to skiers.

Fully 57 percent of Stratton's terrain is designated "more difficult" for the intermediate level skier who enjoys the mountain's fall-line skiing. The terrain includes a lower mountain, primarily novice to lower intermediate terrain, and an upper mountain, which is intermediate and advanced terrain. This is one of those areas where there's more than meets the eye, and you have to actually get onto the upper mountain to realize how expansive the terrain is. The Sun Bowl, which benefits from a more southerly exposure, is also popular with intermediate skiers.

Since the early 1980s, Stratton has undergone a renaissance that's included an infusion of more than $70 million for village and mountain modifications. The result is perhaps a contrast to the traditional ski-country image typified by the Stratton Mountain Boys, ski school instructors of an Austrian bent who entertain here in lederhosen. Certainly a 950-car covered parking garage is a first in the East in the ski industry, but the skiers who flock here, primarily from Connecticut's affluent Fairfield County, are accustomed to the kind of sophistication Stratton offers.

A 22-acre village core at the base of the mountain houses 60,000 square ft. of retail space that eventually will have 30 shops and three restaurants in addition to the covered garage. There's a 91-room condo-hotel, a 108-villa complex called Village Watch, and 34 townhouses.

The town of Manchester, 17 miles away, has a collection of outlet designer shops and high-end boutiques. As in other Vermont communities popular with year-round tourists, the area is struggling with its identity—principally, how to retain New England charm while leaping into the twenty-first century. Can hi-tech society coexist with old red barns?

MAGIC MOUNTAIN

Londonderry VT 05148
Tel: 802–824–5566

Snow Report: 802–824–5566
Area Vertical: 1,700 ft.
Number of Trails: 33 or 175
skiable acres
Lifts: 3 double chairs, 1
T-bar, 1 rope tow
Snowmaking: 70 percent of
terrain
Season: late November–April

Magic is the third in the trio of ski areas that make the Manchester/Stratton region of Vermont such a draw for Northeast city skiers.

Because the mountain came under new management in 1985, the area is anticipating many changes in trails, facilities, and programs. The Tower Ski Area Development Corp. won't say exactly what it has up its sleeve except that Magic will move quickly into the mainstream of Vermont ski areas if plans progress on schedule.

In the meantime, locals in this part of Vermont prefer to ski at Magic because of its challenging terrain, offering trails on its west side which are 99 percent black diamond. On its east side are a couple of steep runs and a tree-filled glade. The 2½–mile Magic Carpet is a novice trail, the longest one in this part of the state, and is always well manicured with good snow cover.

One enthusiastic company spokesman describes the mountain as an orange that must be peeled in order to know what's inside; you have to get up on the trails, in other words, and start exploring before you realize the mountain's potential for challenge and excitement.

Practical Information for Stratton, Bromley, and Magic Mountains

 **HOW TO GET THERE.** Stratton Mountain is located 35 miles from Brattleboro and 4 miles from Bondville. (See Ascutney Mountain Resort above.)
By car. Take I-91 north to Vermont Exit 2 to Brattleboro, then Rte. 30 north to Bondville and turn left at the sign. Bromley Mountain is located 6 miles east of Manchester on Rte. 11. Take I-91 to Exit 6 at Rockingham to Rte. 103 west to Chester, then onto Rte. 11 west for 24 miles to Bromley. For Magic Mountain, continue on Rte. 11 through Chester to Londonderry. Look for signs to the mountain.

TELEPHONES. The area code for all of Vermont is 802.

ACCOMMODATIONS. The *Area Lodging Servicer,* Metcalf Building, Peru, VT 05151 (824–6915) handles reservation requests for lodging in all the mountain towns adjacent to and including Stratton, Bromley, and Magic resorts. In addition, there are slopeside condominiums at Bromley ranging from $310 per unit for 2 nights for 2 people. Contact Bromley Mountain, P.O. Box 1130, Manchester Center VT 05255; 824–5522.

Categories for hotel and motel accommodations in the area are: *Expensive,* $65 and up; *Moderate,* $25–$65; *Inexpensive,* $25 and under.

Expensive

Barrows House. Rte. 30, Dorset 05251; 867–4455. A country inn in a charming town. Rambling, 200-year-old house with 27 rooms; on-premises cross-country ski center with rentals and instruction. MAP available.

Bromley Village. Rte. 11, Peru 05152; 824–5522. On-mountain 1–4-bedroom condos provide convenient, forget-your-car accommodations.

Dorset Inn. Rte. 30, Dorset 05251; 867–5500. This country inn goes back to 1796, making it the oldest continuously operated establishment of its kind in the state. Located in picturesque village. MAP available.

The Equinox. Manchester Village 05254; 362–4700. A newly restored resort hotel in the grand style where the Green Mountain Boys met to plan their siege against the British and where Mrs. Abraham Lincoln once summered. This is a re-emerging grande dame with several restaurants and MAP available.

Liftline Lodge. Stratton Mountain, just off Rte. 30, 05155; 297–2600. Walk to the ski lifts; some apartment units. Hot tub, sauna, spa, gym, lounge, and entertainment on premises, plus a restaurant specializing in wild game. MAP available.

Stratton Mountain Inn. Stratton Mountain 05155; 297–2200. A full-service resort hotel right at the mountain; walk to lifts, other village facilities. Color TV, lounge, dining, entertainment. MAP available.

Stratton Village Lodge. Stratton Mountain 05155; 297–2200. A luxury, 91-room hotel with kitchenettes and walk-to-lifts convenience; also near Stratton recreation and village facilities. MAP available.

Moderate

Alpenrose Inn. Off Rte. 30, Bondville, 05340; 297–2750. A quiet country inn offers seven rooms, all with private baths. Guests enjoy homemade breakfasts and dinners. MAP.

The Barn Lodge. Bondville 05340; 297–1877. A ski lodge offering cross-country ski facilities; special rates to children and groups. MAP.

Birkenhaus. Stratton Mountain 05155; 297–2000. An Austrian lodge with 20 double rooms or bunk rooms, all equipped with refrigerators and coffee makers.

Blue Gentian Lodge. Rte. 11, Londonderry 05148; 824–5908. All rooms with private baths, fireplace in lounge, playroom, 2 miles cross-country terrain, color TV. MAP available.

Bromley Sun Lodge. Bromley Mountain, Peru 05152; 824–6941. A modern, 51-room resort hotel on the slopes of Bromley; rooms with 2 double beds; pool, sauna, game room, lounge; ski out your door to slopes.

Bromley View Inn. Rte. 30, Bondville 05340; 297–1459. A 12-room, homey inn near cross-country trails; hot tubs, exercise equipment; hearty breakfasts; MAP available.

Dostal's Resort Lodge. Magic Mountain, Londonderry 05148; 824–6700. Walk to Magic Mountain ski slopes from 50-room Austrian hotel/lodge only 9 miles from Bromley and 14 miles from Stratton; heated indoor pool, two whirlpool spas.

Johnny Seesaw's. Rte. 11, Peru 05152; 362–2637. Rustic, casual log ski lodge near Bromley Mountain with accommodations from bunk rooms to cottages with fireplaces; it's a converted roadhouse and speakeasy; game room, lounge with entertainment; favorite with families.

Marble West Inn. Box 22, Dorset 05251; 867–4155. In Vermont's marble country, an elegant, 6-guest-room home in the National Register of Historic Places. Near cross-country trails of lovely Merck Forest. MAP available.

Nordic Inn. Rte. 11, Landgrove 05251; 824–6444. Intimate, five-room inn with licensed pub, 12 miles of cross-country nearby. MAP available.

Red Fox Inn. Bondville 05340; 297–2488. A converted barn serves as dining room for 10-guest-room Vermont home.

Kandahar Resort Lodge. Jct. Rtes. 11 and 30, Manchester Center 05255; 824–5531. A full service, 1841 inn. Offers two double beds, TV, and private baths; lounge, sauna, on-premises dining.

Haig's. Rte. 30, Bondville 05340; 297–1300. A lodge at the foot of Stratton Mountain with private baths, ski lockers, fireplaces in rooms; music video, game room, dancing, and on-premises dining.

Wiley Inn. Rte. 11, Peru 05152; 824–6600. A meandering, 200-year-old inn 1 mile from Bromley; family suites, fireplaces, and homemade raisin bread.

Inns in the moderate range offering breakfast include:

Bear Creek Resort. Rawsonville 05155; (at base of Stratton Mountain); 297–1700. Look for Jacuzzi, sauna, on-premises dining; free shuttle to the slopes and access to cross-country trails.

Dovetail Inn. Box 976, Dorset 05251; 867–5747. A home on the village green turned to bed-and-breakfast, with private baths. Ask for a breakfast basket to be delivered to your room. Near cross-country skiing.

Inn at Sunderland. Box 2440, Arlington 05250; 362–4213. A Victorian era farm house with old-fashioned high ceilings, ornate woodwork. Breakfast served by fireplace. 20 minutes to Stratton.

Inn on Magic Mountain. Magic Mountain, Londonderry 05148; 824–6100. Popular with families, suites (four with fireplaces) include adjoining bunk rooms; whirlpool, sauna, game rooms; ski to Magic lifts; 9 miles to Bromley, 14 miles to Stratton.

Inexpensive

Brook-n-Hearth. Box 508, Manchester 05256; 362–3604. A home with individual suites and rooms, private baths, lounge, game room, breakfast available.

Inn at Manchester. Box 345, Manchester 05254; 362–1793. A Victorian mansion that offers game room and lounge, fireplaces, breakfasts, and MAP weekends/holidays.

Sunny Brook Lodge. State Park Rd., Jamaica 05343; 874–4891. Rooms with double and twin beds, lounge with TV, breakfasts.

White Pine Lodge. Rte. 11, Londonderry 05148; 824–3909. Completely furnished 2- and 3-bedroom apartments with kitchens, some fireplaces; sleep up to 9; cross-country just out the door.

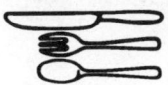 **RESTAURANTS.** These three ski areas share lodging, dining, and après-ski facilities. *Expensive* restaurants will cost $15–$20 for a meal; *Moderate,* $10–$15; and *Inexpensive,* under $10. Most accept major credit cards, but it would be wise to check before you go.

Expensive

Barrows House. Rte. 30, Dorset; 867–4455. Country inn dining, extensive wine list. Specialties include native pheasant, Vermont lamb. Reservations recommended.

Birkenhaus. Stratton Mountain, Stratton (off Rte. 30); 297–2000. Wiener schnitzel and other Continental preparations in Austrian ambience.

Equinox Hotel. Main St., Manchester Center; 362–4700. A grand hotel dining room in newly refurbished establishment once popular with many presidents.

Feathers at Bear Creek. Rawsonville; 297–1700. Such items as sweetbreads and pork tenderloin are staples. Reservations suggested.

Four Columns Inn. Rte. 30, Newfane. A country inn offering award-winning dining. Menu includes bouillabaisse and a saute of rabbit. Reservations recommended.

Reluctant Panther Inn. Manchester Village; 362–2568. A select menu includes brace of quail and five-course, prix fixe dinners. Reservations suggested.

Sage Hill Restaurant. Stratton Mountain Inn, Stratton (just off Rte. 30); 297–2500. Prime rib prepared with Yorkshire pudding is a specialty.

Three Mountain Inn. Rtes. 30/100, Jamaica; 874–4140. A small New England inn with a French twist to the menu.

Toll Gate Lodge. Rte. 11, near Manchester Center; 362–1779. Jackets required here. Award-winning kitchen includes a chateaubriand bouquetiere for two and sweetbreads.

Moderate

Angelo's Ristorante Italiano. Main St., Manchester Center; 362–2408. Homemade sausage, Italian chicken and veal preparations.

Chantecleer Restaurant and Lounge. Rte. 7, Manchester Center, 362–1616. A varied menu with fondue and frogs legs Provencale.

Dorset Inn. Village Green, Rte. 30, Dorset; 867–5500. New England fare served three times daily. Specialties include roast Cornish hen, sauteed fresh calves liver.

Jade Garden. Rtes. 11/30, Manchester Center; 362–4006. Oriental preparations include Peking duck.

Jamaica House. Rte. 30, Jamaica, 874–4400. Boasts area's largest menu including fresh seafood and Italian specialties.

Johnny Seesaw's. Peru; 824–5533. Something for everyone with home-baked bread served, with all entrees tending toward Yankee.

The Londonderry Inn. Rte. 100, South Londonderry, 824–5226. Dinner menu changes daily with unusual preparations of old favorites such as curried lamb.

Popover's Restaurant & Lounge. Rtes. 30/100, Rawsonville, 297–1146. A limited menu includes frog legs with pine nuts and chicken flambéed in Scotch.

Tenderloins Bar & Grill. Stratton Mountain (just off Rte. 30); 297–2200. Located at the Stratton cross-country touring center. Limited menu ranges from beef tenderloin to grilled swordfish.

Inexpensive

Garlic John's. Rtes. 11/30, Manchester; 362–9843. A long list of Italian specialties with discounts for children's dinners.

Gurry's. Rtes. 11/30, Manchester Depot, 362–9878. Mostly pizza, burgers, Italian specialties, but steak and seafood also available.

Friendly's. Manchester Center; 362–3056. Family dining with good service.

Taco House. Manchester Center; 362–9894. Spicy Mexican specialties.

HOW TO GET AROUND. A **shuttle** bus makes a continuous loop around Stratton, covering the village lodging, sports center, and base lodge. As yet there is no service between the two other mountain resorts. It would be best to have a car in these parts, particularly if you want to ski at each of the three mountains or enjoy the New England countryside.

HINTS TO THE HANDICAPPED. Through the ski school at Stratton, there's a handicapped skiers program with one-to-one instruction by a specially trained staff. Bromley can also provide instruction as well as some special equipment for handicapped, blind, and hearing impaired skiers.

CHILDREN'S ACTIVITIES. Stratton accommodates skiing families through a variety of child-oriented programs. The *Baby Cub Nursery,* a certified day-care center, provides indoor activities and supervision for ages 6 weeks–3 years at $22 a day. Lunch is included and the program is open 8:30 A.M.–3:45 P.M. Ages 3–6 can join the *Little Cub* program that includes indoor supervision and ski lessons. The *Big Cub* program enrolls youngsters 6–12 in a Junior Ski School for structured lessons, supervised skiing, and lunch.

At Bromley, the state-accredited nursery has been in operation for 41 years—16 years under the directorship of Lorraine Harrington, who minds children aged 1 month–6 years with tender loving care. The nursery is open 9 A.M.–4 P.M.; full-day fee: $20–$22. Bromley's *Junior Ski School* has several programs, including the *Snoopy Ski School* for ages 6–14, *Ski & Play Hour* for ages 3–5, and an all-day supervised skiing program from 10 A.M. to 3 P.M. (weekends and holidays only) for those old enough. Fee: $25.

NIGHTLIFE. The Stratton Mountain Boys perform for après-ski relaxation at the Stratton Mountain Lodge (297–2211) right at the mountain. These are ski instructors who are skilled at yodeling and the wearing of lederhosen.

Come evening, *Haig's* in Bondville (297–1300), provides a hi-tech environment with video and simultaneous disco.

Alfie's Dancing, Rtes. 11/30, Manchester (362–2637), offers 4 dance floors with music ranging from top-40 to oldies; live bands weekends, and a DJ on board the rest of the week.

Tenderloins Bar & Grill, Stratton Mountain (297–2200) is a night club with music for dancing. And a bar called *The Wentworth* at the Stratton Mountain

Inn (297–2200) has nightly musical entertainment for dancing, ranging from bluegrass to contemporary and jazz.

MT. SNOW SKI RESORT

Mt. Snow VT 05356
Tel: 802–464-3333

Snow Report: 802–464–2151
Area Vertical: 1,700 ft.
Number of Trails: 57 or 305
*   acres*
Lifts: 1 gondola, 5 triple chairs,
*   6 double chairs, 1 rope tow*
Snowmaking: 80 percent of
*   terrain*
Season: early November–early May

If you're a New Yorker and a skier, chances are you know Mt. Snow, a 1,000-acre resort in the Green Mountain National Forest only 213 miles from Manhattan and within striking distance of millions as an easy-to-reach weekend destination.

It didn't take long after it was created in 1954 for Mt. Snow to become one of the best-known and best loved of ski areas, unique for its architecture, Oriental gardens and pools, and Fountain Mountain, a 150-foot geyser that would shoot up from Snow Lake and freeze, creating a unique ski hill.

These amenities, curiously out of touch with their time, might have been more at home now except that they were done away with when the new management, Ski Ltd., that runs Killington, emphasized the best possible skiing experience for customers and decided these amenities were frills.

With the help of computerized snowmaking operations, the best possible skiing is being accomplished. And as this sunny mountain (it claims the sun shines here 50 percent of the time) grows and thrives, so too do the nearby towns of Wilmington and West Dover which, as in many other rural New England communities, have been revitalized by winter tourism.

The result today is the ability to move what might seem to be a metropolis of skiers into Vermont, wine and dine them admirably, offer a variety of terrain, including the North Face's expert trails, and keep them hurrying back for more.

The trail mix is light on the advanced and beginner ends (15 percent each) with 70 percent in the intermediate range. Most of these trails are on Main Mountain, some as long as 2.5 miles and 100 yards wide. The North Face focuses on upper-level skiing and its Ripcord is one of the steepest trails in New England. The result of the heavy focus on the average recreational skier is that management calculates that 90 percent of Mt. Snow's skiers can fully enjoy 90 percent of the terrain.

HAYSTACK

P.O. Box 425
Wilmington VT 05363
Tel: 802–464-7272

Snow Report: 802–464–7272
Area Vertical: 1,400 ft.
Number of Trails: 30 or 135
*   skiable acres*
Lifts: 2 triple chairs, 2
*   double chairs, 3 T-bars*

*Snowmaking: 65 percent of
terrain
Season: Weekends Thanksgiving–
mid-December, then daily
to April.*

Haystack Ski Area is located only 4 miles from Mt. Snow. In fact, a 5-mile nordic-alpine experience is a run along the ridge line that connects the two areas.

As such, it's not a destination resort, as it hasn't yet developed its base facilities to the extent that much of the nearby competition has.

But it's an absence of development, management claims, that brings a loyal breed of skiers back year after year, with some parents who learned to ski here now introducing their own youngsters to the sport at Haystack.

The base lodge is situated between the upper mountain, composed primarily of intermediate terrain, and the lower mountain, which is reserved for novice skiers. Forty percent of the terrain is "more difficult," 33 percent "easiest," and 27 percent "most difficult."

Trail names here have a farming theme, such as Hay Fever, Hay Seed, Pitchfork, and Last Straw. And because of the mellow atmosphere, skiers don't feel obliged to dress to the hilt to tackle the slopes. Blue jeans (with long johns underneath) are quite appropriate here.

The mountain was begun in 1964, receiving national attention early in its history as a center for handicapped skiing programs. At the time it was built, the base lodge was one of the largest in the country. There have been several management changes over the years, with the present owners anticipating a year-round resort in the region.

Practical Information for Mt. Snow and Haystack

HOW TO GET THERE. Mt. Snow and Haystack are 30–35 miles west of Burlington, and 5–9 miles north of Wilmington. (See Ascutney Mountain Resort above.)
By car. Take I–95 north to I–91 to Burlington Exit 2 onto Rte. 9. Drive west to Wilmington, where you take Rte. 100 north. At Coldbrook Road, turn left and drive 3 miles to Haystack. For Mt. Snow, stay on Rte. 100 for a few more miles into the ski resort.

New England Shuttle Service (464–8660) serves gateway airports, bus terminals, and railroad stations. *Buzzy's Taxi Service* (464–5431) provides 24-hour **taxi** service in the area. Rental cars are available through Mt. Snow Vermont Tours Inc. (464–2076).

TELEPHONES. The area code for all of Vermont is 802.

ACCOMMODATIONS. The *Mt. Snow Vacation Service,* Mt. Snow VT 05356 (464–3333) can give specifics on and make reservations for more than 50 inns, lodges, and condominium complexes in the region. There are three separate condominium complexes located at the base of Mt. Snow, offering slopeside, walk-to-lift, and mountain view units. Amenities include indoor pool, whirlpool, Jacuzzis, saunas, and exercise-game rooms. A 2-day weekend here starts at $420. In our selection of other possibilities, rates are per person for a 2-day stay, with meals included. Categories are: *Expensive,* $60–$80; *Moderate,* $40–$60; and *Inexpensive,* less than $40.

Expensive

Deerhill Inn. Valley View Rd., West Dover; 464–3100. Views of Deerfield Valley from 17 guest rooms, some with canopy beds. Afternoon tea is served here. MAP available.

Hermitage Inn. Coldbrook Rd., Wilmington; 464–3511. A 29–room inn that reaches toward the deluxe category, with a dining room that often serves fresh game from its own game farm. There are over 55 miles of cross-country terrain just outside the door. MAP available.

Inn at Sawmill Farm. Rte. 100, West Dover, 464–8131. Lots of elegance; superb meals, wide selection of wines and tasteful furnishings in the luxurious rooms. Restored group of farm buildings.

North Branch Club. Handle Rd. Ext., West Dover; 464–3319. Ski to the lifts and back to the lodge; 18 rooms, some with fireplaces, heated pool, saunas. MAP available.

Snow Lake Lodge. Mountain Rd., Mt. Snow; 464–3333. The hub of Mt. Snow off-slope activities; a full-service resort lodge offering easy access to the slopes. MAP available.

White House of Wilmington. Rte. 9, Wilmington; 464–2135. Turn-of-the-century mansion boasts 8 fireplaces, ski touring center, indoor pool, sauna, steam room; knolltop site with great views.

Moderate

Andirons Motor Lodge. Rte. 100, West Dover; 464–2114. Dining room, 2 lounges, 3 fireplaces, indoor pool, sauna, whirlpool; game room, in-room movies, cable TV. MAP available.

Encore at the Slopes. Handle Rd., at base of Mt. Snow, West Dover; 464–5112. 48 rooms, indoor pool, exercise equipment, Roman whirlpool, large-screen TV. MAP available.

Four Seasons Inn. Rte. 100, West Dover; 464–8303. 24 rooms, sauna, game room with fireplace, color TV.

The Inn at Mt. Snow. Rte. 100, West Dover; 464–5550. 22 rooms just 300 yards from lifts, with California hot tub and sauna, video movies. MAP available.

Kitzhof. Rte. 100, West Dover; 464–8310. 23 rooms, family-style meals and sleigh rides, whirlpool, and sauna.

Nutmeg Inn. Rte. 9, Wilmington; 464–3351. A 1787 country inn by Deerfield River converted to 9-room inn; bar, fireplace, library, delicious home cooking.

Red Cricket Inn. Rte. 100, West Dover; 464–8817. Only thing warmer than the homecooking are the 2 fieldstone fireplaces; sauna, cable TV; moonlight horse-drawn sleigh rides and fondue parties. MAP available.

Tamarack at Mt. Snow. Upper Handle Rd. (Rte. 100), Mt. Snow; 464–8850. Attractive, well-appointed rooms, restaurant, close to base area, cable TV.

Inexpensive

Whippletree. 1 Tannery Rd., West Dover; 464–5485. 7 rooms; breakfast included in rates.

Snow Vista. Mt. Snow Village Loop, West Dover; 464–5575. 5 rooms with guest refrigerator; use of kitchen to prepare lunches.

Old Red Mill. Rte. 100, Wilmington; 464–3700. 24 rooms, private baths. MAP available.

Misty Mountain Lodge. Stowe Hill Rd., Wilmington; 464–3961. 10 rooms in a farmhouse offering old-fashioned home cooking.

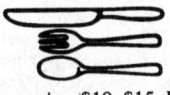 **RESTAURANTS.** There are some 35 restaurants in the region, offering everything from wild game to pizza. In this region a meal for one person costing $15 and more, excluding tips, drinks, and tax, would be categorized as *Expensive;* $10–$15, *Moderate;* and less than $10, *Inexpensive.* In our sampling, major credit cards are accepted unless otherwise noted.

Expensive

Deerhill Inn. Off Rte. 100, West Dover; 464–3100. A small, intimate dining room offering American and European preparations in gourmet fashion.

The Hermitage. Coldbrook Rd., Wilmington; 464–9350. Specials include pheasant, quail, goose, and duckling from on-premises game farm.

Inn at Sawmill Farm. Rte. 100, West Dover; 464–8131. A quiet and formal Vermont country inn with what is generally considered the most prestigious gourmet dining in the valley.

Le Petit Chef. Rte. 100, Wilmington; 464–8437. Country dining with French touch in renovated farmhouse.

Two Tannery Road. Tannery Rd., West Dover; 464–2707. Look for duckling, veal, seafood, and tasty desserts.

The White House. Rte. 9, Wilmington; 464–2135. An old mansion with four-season patio lounge offers Continental fare.

Moderate

Andirons/Dover Forge. Rte. 100, West Dover; 464–2114. Three separate dining rooms offering American fare.

Fennessey's Parlor. Rte. 100, West Dover; 464–9361. Steaks, prime rib, and seafood offered here.

Matterhorn of Dover. Rte. 100, West Dover; 464–8011. Prime rib is a specialty, followed by after-dinner sleigh ride.

Poncho's Wreck. South Main St., Wilmington; 464–9320. Mexican food, steaks, fresh fish served in casually rustic environment.

The Roadhouse. Rte. 100, Wilmington; 464–5017. A rustic setting with garden-fresh veggies, homemade bread, and wood stove.

Inexpensive

Deacon's Den Tavern. Rte. 100, West Dover; 464–9361. Super sandwiches, free soup after skiing; live bands weekends.

TC's Tavern. Rte. 100, West Dover; 464–9316. Italian specialties and takeout service. No credit cards.

Elsa's. Rte. 100, West Dover; 464–8425. Deli and restaurant with takeout service. No credit cards.

 **HOW TO GET AROUND.** The *Mt. Snow Valley Shuttle Service* (464–8660) offers daily service from mid-December to mid-March between Mt. Snow and the lodges and businesses along Vermont Rte. 100. There is **bus** service between the ski area, Snow Lake Lodge, and base-of-mountain condominiums, although all are within walking distance of the lifts and trails.

 **SEASONAL EVENTS.** Mount Snow hosts the *Equitable Family Ski Challenge* races from **January** to **March.** The first weekend of March begins special *Festival of Spring* weekends that take place around St. Patrick's Day and on Easter, the latter with a sunrise service and egg hunt. Early **April** is *Sugar on Snow Weekend* with a maple sugaring demonstration. Throughout the winter, there are races of all kinds for the recreational skier, including NASTAR Wednesdays and Saturdays and coin-op racing Wednesdays–Sundays.

Haystack participates in *National Learn To Ski Week* in late **January**, a program that offers special rates on equipment, lessons, and lift tickets for first-time skiers. It hosts a *Carnival Week* in mid-January with races, barbecues, entertainment, and assorted events, and it offers complimentary skiing on the first day of skiing in early winter.

 **OTHER SPORTS AND ACTIVITIES. Cross-country** skiing is available in Wilmington at the *Hermitage Inn,* Coldbrook Rd. (464–3511), *White House,* Rte. 9 (464–2135), *Sitzmark Lodge,* East Dover Rd. (464–3384), and in West Dover at *Timber Creek Condominiums,* Rte. 100 (464–2323). Haystack's 50 km of trails interconnect with Mt. Snow's at Hermitage Inn.

Horseback riding and **sleigh rides** are found at the *Matterhorn* on Rte. 100, West Dover (464–8011), in a dinner/sleigh package. *Adams Farm* at the junction of Rte. 100 and Higley Hill Rd. in Wilmington (464–3762), also offers hot chocolate and a trip to a log cabin en route. *Flame's Stables,* Rte. 100, Wilmington (464–8329), and the *Red Cricket Inn,* Rte. 100, West Dover (464–8817), both offer sleigh rides to guests.

Snow Lake Lodge (464–3333), right at Mt. Snow, has a **fitness center** open to the public. The *Andirons Motor Lodge* on Rte. 100, West Dover (464–2114), offers indoor **swimming,** sauna, and whirlpool.

Other accommodations with **pools** for guests are the *North Branch Club,* Handle Rd. Ext., West Dover (464–3319), *Encore at the Slopes,* Handle Rd., West Dover (464–3391), *White House of Wilmington,* Rte. 9, Wilmington (464–2135), *Mt. Snow Resort Center Condominiums* at the mountain, (464–3333), and *McNamara Real Estate,* Rte. 100, Wilmington (464–2172).

There's a **bowling** alley at *North Star Bowl,* Rte. 100, Wilmington (464–5148); and look for guided **snowmobile** tours at *Wheeler Farm,* Rte. 100, Wilmington (464–5225). *Lake Whitingham* near Mt. Snow fills the bill when it comes to **ice fishing** —a do-your-own-thing place.

HINTS TO THE HANDICAPPED. Both resorts are equipped with special programs for handicapped skiers including the blind, deaf, amputees, single-limb handicapped, and slightly mentally retarded.

 **CHILDREN'S ACTIVITIES.** Mt. Snow takes good care of families and recently instituted what it calls a *Teddy Bear Ski Week.* Children 12 years old and under bring a teddy bear or other stuffed friend to obtain a free 5-day ticket. They use a special children's lift, join races, and stage a teddy bear parade. The *Children's Learning Center* is a complete learning facility with a rope tow and terrain garden. *For Parents Who Ski* involves children ages 3–12 in instruction, supervised skiing, and lunch. The *Pumpkin Patch Nursery* provides child care services for infants to age 8. For reservations call 464–8501. *SKIwee,* the nationally recognized children's learn-to-ski program, is also available here.

At Haystack, the *Little Stack Nursery* accepts children ages 2–6 (toilet-trained only) from 9 A.M. to 4 P.M. There's optional lunch and lessons, and on Tuesdays (Men's Day) and Thursdays (Ladies' Day) nursery rates are half price. For information and reservations, contact the base lodge, 464–7272.

 **NIGHTLIFE.** They don't call Mt. Snow the Mountain of Pleasure and the Valley of Fun for nothing. Right on the mountain, *Snow Barn* (464–3333), a night club with cover charge, features live band or DJ entertainment nightly on an oak dance floor. The *Snow Lake Spiral Lounge* in the Snow Lake Lodge, also on the mountain (464–3333), has nightly entertainment and a piano bar. The *Deacon's Den,* Rte. 100, West Dover (464–9361), features bands every weekend with a cover charge. The nearby *Silo,* Rte. 100, West Dover (464–5820), also has bands on weekends (no cover charge).

Weekend entertainment comes to *Poncho's Wreck,* South Main St., Wilmington (464–9320), and to the *Andirons,* Rte. 100, West Dover (464–2114).

On Saturday afternoons the place to be is in Wilmington at *North Country Fair* on Rte. 100 (464–5697).

At Haystack slopeside, on Saturdays and holidays there's low-key, top-40 music, live, in the *Hayloft Lounge.*

CENTRAL VERMONT

KILLINGTON SKI AREA

Killington VT 05751
Tel: 802–422–3333

Snow Reports: 802–422–3261
Area Vertical: 3,160 ft.
Number of Trails: 100 or 637
  skiable acres
Lifts: 3 quadruple chairs, 4
  triple chairs, 7 double chairs,
  3.5-mile gondola, 2 surface lifts
Snowmaking: 60 percent of
  terrain
Season: mid-October–mid-June

Killington Ski Area encompasses more mountains than you have fingers on one hand. They're up to six now and there are always plans afoot to add more. More trails (100), more lifts (17), and more skiable acres (637) await skiers here than at any other ski area in the East. In fact, this is the place where skiing superlatives have come to roost: more snowmaking, longest season, steepest trail (on Bear Mountain with pitches of up to 62 degrees), longest run (the Juggernaut, 10 miles) and the longest alpine ski trail in the United States) . . . the list goes on and on.

And it goes without saying that this area packs the skiers in—but with the finesse that goes along with high-speed lifts, interconnected mountains, and great variety of terrain so that except for acres of automobiles you'd never know you were among the madding crowds. For example, you begin your skiing day where you choose—purchasing your ticket at one of a half-dozen ticket outlets spread out over the six-mountain complex.

A long time ago, early in Vermont's history, a Rev. Samuel Peters stood at the top of Killington Peak, 4,241 ft. high, and christened what he saw below *Verd Mont,* meaning "green mountains." Today there's a nifty restaurant at the peak, accessed by the 3.5-mile gondola, the longest aerial tram in North America, and the Killington chairlift. From the summit (accessible when snows melt), there are 360-degree views of five states and Canada. But even in winter the vistas are spectacular and can be enjoyed by novice skiers who can get down from the top of any of the six mountains on trails marked "easiest."

Over the years Killington management has gone for what the avid alpine enthusiast most desires—dependable snow conditions on diverse skiing terrain. The result is today's 38 miles of snowmaking and enough skiing to keep even the hardest skier challenged by variety for days.

In addition to providing the best possible skiing experience, the ski area has also paid attention to booking ski vacation packages. They offer one-stop shopping through a lodging bureau and a streamlined system for obtaining lift tickets, ski school vouchers, and rental equipment.

There's an emerging village at the base of Snowshed, a teaching-learning hill, where high-rise condominiums, hotels and restaurants, shops, and health spa facilities are mushrooming. But the area for years has depended on the entrepreneurial spirit of innkeepers for miles around to provide the bed base for the ever-growing body of Killington skiers.

There's no ski town, per se, in the sense of a Stowe or North Conway. Skiers gravitate to Rutland or Woodstock for movies and other activities. But they don't have to leave the mountain to find a wealth of excellent lodging and dining establishments that line the Killington Rd. from Rte. 4 to the mountain.

PICO SKI RESORT

Sherburne Pass
Rutland VT 05701
Tel: 802–775–4345

Snow Report: 802–775–4345
Area Vertical: 1,967 ft.
Number of Trails: 30 or 130
  skiable acres
Lifts: 2 triple chairs, 5
  double chairs, 1 poma, 1 T-bar
Snowmaking: 45 percent of
  terrain
Season: Thanksgiving–early May

Pico Ski Resort sits right on Rte. 4, a big, bold mountain with long, winding trails spanning its nearly 2,000-ft. vertical drop and snatches of glade skiing among the trees. This is primarily an intermediate's choice, with 60 percent of the trails marked "more difficult," 20 percent "most difficult," and 20 percent "easiest."

Although a mountain that over the years has been run by families and for families, it attracts skiers seeking something a little lower-key in terms of resort ambience than its neighbor Killington.

The mountain was first opened for skiing in 1937 by owners Brad and Janet Mead. Brad Mead brought two novelties to American skiing: the first T-bar to be installed in the United States, and the first Swiss ski instructor, Mr. Karl Acker. Acker coached the Mead's daughter, Andrea, who some years later was to purchase the first-ever U.S. medal in Olympic ski events, in 1948, and Andrea went on to capture a 1952 gold medal. Acker later bought the resort from the Meads.

The present owner, Bruce Beldon, has created today's 30-trail network and is beginning base-of-mountain expansion with a condominium-sports center complex now under construction.

Practical Information for Killington and Pico

 **HOW TO GET THERE.** Killington and Pico are 2 of the 4 ski resorts located in central Vermont that are detailed in this guide. The other two are Okemo Mountain Resort and Suicide Six Ski Area. Rutland is the gateway to these areas. Killington and Pico can be considered a single destination, for they are practically next-door neighbors. Although they don't offer reciprocal ski lift tickets, they do share the bounty of lodging and dining in the area.

Pico Ski Area is on US 4, 9 miles east of Rutland, while Killington is at the junction of US 4 and Rte. 100 in Sherburne, 16 miles east of Rutland.

By air. The Rutland Airport is served by *Precision Airlines* (773–2735) from New York and Boston. The airport also has facilities for private aircraft. *Mountain Aviation* (776–5591) offers aircraft tie-downs, refueling, mechanics, and pilot and passenger lounge. *Budget* (422–9713) or 800–527–0700) rental cars are available here. The Lebanon NH airport, 39 miles from Killington, is served by both *Command Airways* and *Precision,* from Boston and New York. *Hertz* (800–654–3131) rental cars are available here.

By bus. *Vermont Transit Lines* (773–2774) offers direct daily service through Rutland and to Killington from major eastern cities.

By car. Via Connecticut Turnpike: Take I–95, then I–91 to Bellows Falls VT. Take Exit 6 to Rte. 103 and follow it to Rte. 100, then north to US 4, and on to Pico, then Killington. Via the New York Thruway: Exit 24 at Albany and take Northway (I–87) to the Fort Ann/Rutland exit. Pick up Rte. 149 and drive east to US 4, which leads to both ski areas.

TELEPHONES. The area code for all of Vermont is 802.

 **ACCOMMODATIONS.** Lodges, inns, and hotels in this area serve both Killington and Pico skiers. The *Killington Lodging Bureau,* Killington Ski Area, Killington 05751 (422–3333), can make reservations for lodging and meal packages and can also reserve ski lift and lesson packages for skiing at Killington. *Pico Rentals,* Pico Ski Area, Sherburne Pass, Rutland 05701 (775–1927), can also book reservations.

Condominium lodging is popular in this region, with walk-to-the slopes accommodations at both Killington and Pico. Based on 2 people for a 3-night stay, the condominiums start at $105 and range up to $270. A new alpine village, *Sunrise Mountain Village,* off Bear Mountain Rd., Killington 05751 (422–9292), offers a self-contained resort at its 550-unit condominium community near Bear Mountain. In addition to luxury 1–4-bedroom condos, the resort offers complete health spa facilities and on-premises dining at the Bistro Restaurant. Guests here enjoy ski-on/ski-off access to Bear Mountain, one of Killington's 6 peaks.

Mountain Green Condominiums on Killington Rd. (422–3101) provides walk-to-the-slopes convenience with a health spa, pool, and dining for guests staying in suites of 1–4 bedrooms.

There are also many chalets and vacation homes, including the *Hawk Mountain Corporation's* extensive listings of luxury dwellings. Their address is Rte. 100 North, Pittsfield 05762; 746–8911.

Since most lodgings in the area operate on package deals, the rates of establishments listed below are based on 3-night stays per person. Categories are *Expensive,* $120–$200; *Moderate,* $80–$120; and *Inexpensive,* less than $80. All those in the expensive range, as well as many others, include the Modified American Plan, with 1 or 2 meals provided.

Expensive

Cascades Lodge. Killington Rd., Killington 05751; 422–3731. One of the newest properties, right near the base area. Candlelight dining, lounge with fireplace, and king size TV. Indoor pool, sauna, whirlpool, exercise and game rooms.

Cortina Inn. Rte. 4, Mendon 05751; 773–3331. Vest pocket resort, a little of everything. Superb dining; fireplaces in some rooms; indoor pool, sauna, whirlpool, exercise and game rooms. Shuttle to ski area, cross-country skiing.

Little Buckhorn Lodge. Killington Rd., Killington 05751; 422–3314. Family-style meals, home cooking, fireside lounge; 22 rooms, fireplace, lounge, sauna.

The Inn at Long Trail. Rte. 4, Mendon 05751; 775–7181. Historic country inn with large hot tub, some fireplace suites, Irish pub.

Grey Bonnet Inn. Rte. 100, Killington 05751; 775–2537. Antiques combine with indoor pool, whirlpools, sauna, tanning room, exercise and game rooms; color TV.

Killington Village Inn. Killington Rd., Killington 05751; 422–3301. With fireplaces, close to slopes, courtesy shuttle; on-premises lounge and dining.

Mountain Top Inn. Chittenden 05737; 483–2311. A 1,000-acre resort with spectacular views, 50 guest rooms, and 15 cottages; horse-drawn sleigh rides, ice skating, sauna, whirlpool spa, exercise/game rooms, cross-country.

Pico Bavarian House. Rte. 4, Mendon 05751; 773–6331. Bavarian charm includes game room, skating pond, easy access to Pico's slopes.

Red Clover Inn. Off Rte. 4, Mendon 05701; 775–2290. Takes up to 38 guests who enjoy French country cuisine, a favorite dining spot with locals; TV/billiard room.

Red Rob Inn. Killington Rd., Killington 05751; 422–3303. Free shuttle to slopes, outdoor whirlpool, library, game room, sociable lounge with great hors d'ouevres.

Summit Lodge. Killington Rd., Killington 05751; 422–3535. An antique-decorated inn with racquetball, whirlpool, saunas, massage and game rooms, ice skating; 5 fireplaces, on-premises dining.

Tulip Tree Inn. Off Rte. 4, Chittenden 05737; 483–6213. 24-person capacity in charming country inn.

The Mountain Inn. Killington Rd., Killington 05751; 422–3595. A luxury hotel with whirlpool, steambaths, saunas, game room; on-premises dining, lounge.

Moderate

Alpenhof. Killington Rd., Killington 05751; 422–9787. Near slopes, rooms with private baths, dorms and chalets with fireplaces; sauna, whirlpool, game room, video movies; 7-item breakfast buffet and homemade soup in front of fire.

Brandon Inn. Rtes. 7 and 73, Brandon 05733; 247–5766. A 1786 inn that offers horse-drawn sleigh rides and ice skating; on-premises dining.

Chalet Killington. Killington Rd., Killington 05751; 422–3451. Children under 6 free (except holidays) here; sauna, whirlpool, exercise and game room; Continental breakfasts served.

Greenbriar Inn. Rte. 4, Killington 05751; 775–8799. Mountain views, Jacuzzi, sauna, fireplace lounge; each room has private bath, color TV, refrigerator, phone; Continental breakfasts served.

Holiday Inn of Rutland. S. Main St., Rutland 05701; 775–1911. Kids under 20 free in parents room; indoor pool, health complex; free in-room coffee; on-premises dining.

Mountain Meadows Lodge. Rte. 4 East, Killington 05751; 775–1010. Large comfortable rooms (for up to 6) with private baths; BYOB lounge, game room, sitting room with color TV; complete ski touring center.

Rutland TraveLodge. S. Main St., Rutland 05701; 773–3361. 75 rooms with luxury apartments and executive suites. Indoor pool, saunas, complimentary coffee in rooms, color TV (cable); on-premises dining.

Inexpensive

Comfort Inn at Trolley Square. 19 Allen St., Rutland 05701; 775–2200. 114 deluxe rooms; indoor pool, sauna, Jacuzzi.

Edelweiss Motel and Chalets. Rte. 4 West, Killington 05751; 775–5577. Spacious rooms with color TV, coffee in room, game rooms, exercise area, fireplace lounge, hot tub, sauna; some kitchenettes and some chalets with fireplaces.

Grande Finale. Rte. 4 West, Mendon 05751; 773–2155. An 1853 farmhouse welcomes children under 12 free; rooms with private bath, color TV.

Swiss Farm Lodge. Rte. 100, Pittsfield 05762; 746–8341. A dairy farm that opens its doors to guests, uses own maple syrup and honey.

Turn of River Lodge. Rte. 4 East, Killington 05751; 422–3766. A rustic lodge with hug stone fireplace in lounge, set-up bar; rooms with private and shared baths; some dorms; family-style Continental breakfast.

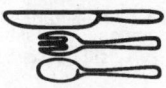 **DINING OUT.** Visitors to this region don't *have* to take all their meals at their lodging places—although most inns and lodges offer fine and substantial fare. If you choose to dine out, there is a wide selection of restaurants, serving not only New England dishes but Continental and ethnic specialties as well. Furthermore, you'll find that the price is right throughout the region. Listings here are based on the following price ranges, excluding tips and drinks: *Expensive,* $15–$20; *Moderate,* $8–$15; *Inexpensive,* under $8. Major credit cards are accepted, unless otherwise noted.

Expensive

The Alpine Inn. Killington Rd., Killington; 422–3485. An intimate restaurant, lacking in ambience, but made up for by excellent, award-winning cuisine. A treatment of salmon is particularly noteworthy. Reservations suggested.

Annabelles' Restaurant. Jct. Rte. 100 and Rte. 107, Stockbridge; 746–8552. A converted farmhouse offers a la carte and fixed price menu in greenhouse or just-like-home setting. Reservations suggested.

Cortina Inn. Rte. 4, Mendon; 773–3331. The breakfast buffets here are not to be missed and dinners range from Continental to New England treatments. Reservations appreciated.

Hemingway's Restaurant. Rte. 4, Killington; 422–2886. A country home turned very elegant in a most rural setting. Service with flair; excellent wine selection and creative menu. Reservations suggested.

The Mountain Inn. Killington Rd., Killington; 311–3595. A casual atmosphere with varied menu focusing on Continental treatments.

Moderate

Back Behind Saloon Restaurant. Rte. 4, West Bridgewater; 422–9907. A converted railroad car provides setting for casual dining; home-made cole slaw part of experience; varied menu.

Casa Bianca Restaurant. Grove St., Rutland; 773–7401. Italian specialties include home-made pastas, veal parmigiana. This is the in place for locals seeking Italian fare.

The Bistro. Sunrise Mountain Village, off Bear Mountain Rd., Killington; 422–3822. A 50-seat dining room overlooking Northeast Passage chairlift offering ski-in-for-lunch convenience from Sun Dog Ski Trail; candlelight dinners.

Countryman's Pleasure Restaurant. Townline Rd., Mendon; 773–7141. It's a country farmhouse offering Austrian specialties such as raspberry-Black Forest tortes and glazed wiener apple strudel. Children's menu.

Ernie's Grill. 37 N. Main St., Rutland; 775–0856. One of Vermont's best-known restauranteurs, Ernie Royal, presides over the kitchen here, with prime rib and superb service among the specialties.

Hawks River Tavern. Rte. 100, Plymouth; 672–5300. A tiny restaurant offering creative cuisine.

Red Clover Inn. Off Rte. 4, Mendon; 775–2290. A country inn that's becoming a favorite with the locals. Look for homemade breads, soups, and desserts; veal and seafood specialties.

Sirloin Saloon. Main St., Rutland; 773–7900. Extensive salad bars, children's menu, oyster bar, and seafood/steak specialties.

Inexpensive

Casey's Caboose. Killington Rd., Killington; 422–3795. A large menu served up in turn-of-century railroad cars. There's literally something for everyone here.

Charity's 1887 Saloon Restaurant. Killington Rd., Killington; 422–3800. Practically everyone turns up here sometime for French onion soup, steaks, seafood, quiche, sandwiches.

Pasta Pot. Rte. 4, Killington; 422–3004. Northern and southern-style pasta dishes, plus vegetarian treatments.

Zorba's Tavern. Killington Rd., Killington; 422–3600. Homemade pizza, pasta, subs, spaghetti, and salads; plus pool table, TV, arcade, and jukebox.

 **HOW TO GET AROUND.** Some area lodges provide a **free shuttle** service to and from the slopes. The *Mountain Bus* (422–9713) provides daily (8:30–10:30 A.M. and 3–5 P.M.) service on the mountain road, picking up skiers from lodges and shops and taking them to and from the mountain. This same service operates evenings from 4:30 P.M. to 2:30 A.M. A one-way ride costs $1.

 **SEASONAL EVENTS. Killington:** The *Bear Mountain Mogul Challenge* attracts upwards of 200 thrill-seekers in **mid-March,** as they set their target on the 62-degree pitches that characterize the steepest terrain in New England. Two other events, a **May Day** Fun Slalom and a **June 1** Fun Slalom are annual happenings that go a long way to publicize the resort's long-lived ski season!

Pico: The *Harry Chapin Memorial Slalom,* held the last week in **December,** remembers the contribution to Rutland and the Pico Ski Club that the singer made prior to his untimely death. This is an amateur race for young skiers. *Club Weekend* is a traditional competition among ski clubs to determine the best club racers and is held the third weekend in **March.**

OTHER SPORTS AND ACTIVITIES. The following establishments have **health club facilities** open to the public:

Brookside Tennis & Racquetball, 40 Curtis Ave., Rutland; 775–1971. Tennis, **racquetball,** nautilus and Jacuzzi, saunas, health bar.

Cortina Health Club, Rte. 4, Mendon; 773–3331. Indoor **pool,** saunas, game room, masseur, exercise room.

Killington Health Club, Killington Rd., Killington; 422–9370. Lap pool, whirlpools, sauna, steambath, tanning rooms, racquetball, exercise rooms.

The Spa, 132 Granger St., Rutland; 775–6565. Nautilus, and free weight equipment; sauna, jacuzzi, and tanning beds.

Summit Lodge, Killington Rd., Killington; 422–3535. 16-person Jacuzzi, whirlpool, 2 saunas, racquetball.

There's **ice skating** at the Summit Lodge and at Hawk Center, Jct. Rtes. 100 and 107; 746–8911.

Ski touring is popular in the region, with the *Killington Gondola* providing access to the 10-mile long Juggernaut Trail. There's also ski touring at *Mountain Meadows Ski Touring Center,* Rte. 4, Killington, 775–7077; *Mountain Top Ski Touring Center,* Mountain Top Rd., Chittenden, 483–2311 (110 km of trails); *Trail Head Ski Touring Center,* Rte. 100, Stockbridge, 746–8038; and *Woodstock Ski Touring Center,* Rte. 106, Woodstock, 457–2114.

Sleigh rides are offered at the Mountain Top Inn and at *Hawk Resort's Salt Ash Colony* on Rte. 100, Plymouth; 672–3811.

 **HINTS TO THE HANDICAPPED.** Both ski resorts offer specialty programs to organizations for the handicapped and can accommodate the handicapped individually through their ski schools. Contact the respective ski resort for detailed information on programs available.

 **DAY-CARE FACILITIES. Killington.** *The Children's Center* (422–3333) provides day-long child and infant care for ages infant–8 years. The charge is $21 for ages 2–8 and $30 for infants. Lunch is included.

Through the center ages 4–8 can enjoy an *Introduction to Skiing* program that involves a 1-hour lesson, rental equipment, use of beginners' tow, and games. Ages 6–12 are eligible for regular lift and lesson programs that involve a 2-hour class, or they can join the *Superstars All-Day Skiing Program* that includes lessons, lunch, and videotaping, all for $45.

Pico. The *Pico Nursery* accepts toddlers (post diaper) to age 6 from 9 A.M. to 4 P.M. daily. There's optional ski school instruction. For ages 6–12 a mountaineering program offers 4 hours of instruction, lift ticket, and lunch for $34. As participants in Pico's *Mt. Explorer's Club,* they receive special badges.

 **NIGHTLIFE.** Three **on-mountain** (Killington Rd.) hot spots, the *Pickle Barrel,* (442–3035), the *Wobbly Barn Steakhouse* (422–3392), and *The Nightspot* (422–9885), offer nightly live band entertainment and dancing all with cover charges.

In Rutland, *The Ritz* at 21 Center St. (775–3365) is the area's first video dance club; cover charge here, too.

Many establishments offer vocal and instrumental soloists as part of the après-ski and dinner ambience. And the *Mountain Inn* on Killington Rd. (422–3595) features honky-tonk piano entertainment. It's probably safe to say that the entertainment overall matches the diversity of ski terrain in the central Vermont region.

OKEMO MOUNTAIN RESORT

RFD #1
Ludlow VT 05149
Tel: 802–228–4041

Snow Report: 802–228–5222
Area Vertical: 2,150 ft.
Number of Trails: 58 or 200
skiable acres
Lifts: quadruple chair 2
triple chairs, 3 double chairs,
2 pomas
Snowmaking: 60 percent of
terrain
Season: mid-November–mid-April

For years Okemo has tantalized the nearby town of Ludlow, at the bottom of its access road, by the possibility that it, too, might someday become the kind of sought-after resort that puts smiles on merchants' faces as it fills their coffers.

And for years Okemo tried to live up to expectations but never quite made it. Then along came Tim and Diane Mueller, a young couple experienced in developing and managing warm-weather resorts in the Caribbean. An infusion of capital, engineering, and good taste has brought Okemo to life in just a couple of years, allowing Ludlow and surrounding Black River Valley to serve winter tourists and to weather its transition from a once-thriving textile mill town to tourist center.

The spiffiest new lifts in the state (perhaps in New England) are now here. A road from the summit turns ski trail come winter, offering beginners 4½ miles of gentle terrain. There are two steep gladed areas for more advanced skiers, and some hair-raising terrain such as Double Diamond and Outrage.

Quality is being stressed here, from Diane Mueller's personal interest in creating attractive signage to the Okemo Ski Patrol that in 1983–84 received the National Ski Patrol of the Year Award.

A 50-ft. clock tower and white stucco archway mark the entrance to the base lodge facilities, around which are clustered a 76-room hotel. A bellman will help with luggage and ski equipment, escort guests to their condominiums, and light the fire in the fireplace.

For busy executives who can't leave their offices behind, there's an executive suite with phones and a secretary.

In 1985 Okemo celebrated its thirtieth birthday. This is one resort that wears its years well and, in fact, looks younger than it ever has!

Practical Information for Okemo Mountain

HOW TO GET THERE. Okemo is located in Ludlow. (See Killington and Pico section for regional details.) **By car.** Take I-91 to Vermont Exit 6 onto Rte. 103 to Ludlow, and follow signs for Okemo Mountain Resort. **By bus.** *Vermont Transit* (228–5274) provides regular daily bus service to Ludlow.

TELEPHONES. The area code for all of Vermont is 802.

ACCOMMODATIONS. *Okemo's Lodging Service,* RFD 1, Ludlow 505169 (228–5571) can arrange accommodations at the 76-room Okemo Mountain Lodge in the base area, or at the slopeside Kettlebrook Condominiums, or at any of the more than 30 establishments offering over 2,300 beds within a 10-mile radius of the mountain. Rates are based on double occupancy per person. Categories, determined by price, are *Expensive,* $70 for rooms up to $135 for condo efficiency units; *Moderate,* $50–$70; *Inexpensive,* under $50.

Expensive

Castle Inn. Box 157, Proctorsville 05153; 226–7222. Quarrystone construction marks this turn-of-the-century inn complete with oak paneling, hand—carved plaster ceilings, and old-time elegance. MAP available.
Echo Lake Inn. Box 154, Ludlow 05149; 228–8602. A rambling turn-of-the-century structure offers country elegance. MAP available.
The Governor's Inn. 86 Main St., Ludlow 05149; 228–8830. This 100-year-old-house was once home to a former Vermont governor. Today it offers creative gourmet fare. With MAP.

Kettle Brook Condominiums. R.F.D. 1, Ludlow 05149 (on Okemo Mountain); 228–5571. 66 slopeside homes in New England contemporary design, 1–3 bedrooms, with fireplaces; convenient to skiing.

The Mill Hotel. 145 N. Main St., Ludlow 05149; 228–5566. A restored nineteenth century mill now houses 1–3-bedroom hotel units with kitchens and fireplaces.

Okemo Inn. R.F.D. 1, Box 133, Ludlow, 05149; 228–8834. An 1810 structure at the base of the mountain, filled with American antiques.

Okemo Lantern Lodge. Box 247, Proctorsville 05153; 226–7770. Victorian gingerbread is still alive and well in this antique-filled dwelling. Breakfast available.

Okemo Mountain Lodge Condominiums. R.F.D. 1, Ludlow 05149 (Okemo Mountain); 228–5571. 76 one-bedroom efficiency units clustered courtyard style around main ski lodge. No charge for children 12 and under. Walk to lifts.

Moderate

Black River Inn. 100 Main St., Ludlow 05149; 228–5585. A stately brick home that's enjoying the new life generated in town by the ski resort.

Combes Family Inn. R.F.D. 1, Ludlow 05149; 228–8799. 10 rooms in total, divided between motel units (with 2 double beds, no phones or TVs), and rooms in inn with hall baths.

Country Peasant Inn. Rte. 100 South, Ludlow 05149; 228–8926. A 6-room inn near pond, shared bath. Breakfast served.

Golden Stage Inn. Box 218, Proctorsville 05143; 226–7744. Built in 1795. Country quilts and plants decorate this 10-room inn (6 with private baths). MAP available.

Mount Holly Lodge. Rte. 155, East Wallingford 05742; 259–2351. A fieldstone fireplace in the living room and player piano in the lounge add sparkle to this establishment that also serves breakfast.

Old Town Farm Inn. R.F.D. 4, Chester 05143; 875–2346. Breakfast served in a colonial farmhouse offering 10 guest rooms (3 with private baths).

The Timber Inn Motel. Rte. 103 South, Ludlow 05149; 228–8666. You'll find sauna, Jacuzzi, color TV, and a restaurant.

The Winchester Inn. 53 Main St., Ludlow 05149; 228–3241. An 1813 Colonial inn with dining room and lounge.

Inexpensive

There's a host of motels in the inexpensive range. These are the *Abby-Lyn Motel,* Junction Rtes. 106/10, North Springfield 05150, 886–2223; *Inn Towne Motel,* 112 Main St., Ludlow 05149, 228–8884; *Pa-Lo-Mar Motel,* 2 Linhale Dr., Springfield 05156, 885–4142; and *Rockingham Motor Inn,* Box 30, Bellows Falls 05101, 463–4636.

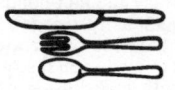 **RESTAURANTS.** Dining out in the Okemo Mountain area presents the visitor with choices similar to other ski areas in central Vermont. Restaurants nearest the resort may be a bit pricier, but all in all the average remains about the same. So does the fare. Categories, determined by price, are *Expensive,* $15 and up; *Moderate,* $9–$15; *Inexpensive,* less than $9. Most places accept MasterCard and Visa unless otherwise noted.

Expensive

The Governor's Inn. 86 Main St., Ludlow; 228–8830. Chef Deedy Marble was named one of four "outstanding innovative chefs in Vermont." Dinners begin at 6 with hors d'oeuvres in the parlor, followed by a single 7 P.M. seating in a Victorian dining room with waitresses in period dress. Braiséd quail and sherried apricot soup may be on the menu. Reservations are requested.

The Castle Inn. Rte. 103, Proctorsville; 226–7222. The mahogany Oval Dining Room is the setting for such entrees as roast duckling grand marnier in this architectural landmark.

Moderate

Black River Inn. 100 Main St., Ludlow; 228–5585. A 5-course menu-du-jour begins at 7 P.M. in this 1835 country inn. Seating by reservation only.

The Clock Works. Okemo Mountain Resort (on the mountain); 228–2800. Italian preparations are the specialty here, along with seafood and steaks.

Echo Lake Inn. Box 154, Ludlow; 228–8602. Fresh herbs and spices from a summer garden garnish home-cooked winter meals.

Michael's Seafood and Steak Restaurant. Rte. 103, Ludlow; 228–5622. Beef and seafood preparations are served here along with a well-stocked salad bar.

Nikki's Restaurant. Foot of Okemo Mountain access road, Ludlow; 228–7797. Offers regional fare ranging from New England pork filet to grilled Atlantic swordfish; eclectic interior.

Okemo Lantern Lodge. Box 247, Proctorsville; 226–7770. Call by 4 P.M. for a reservation and look forward to New England and Continental cuisine.

Winchester Inn. 53 Main St., Ludlow; 228–3241. A 14-item menu includes seafood, steaks, lamb, and veal.

Backside Restaurant. Rte. 103, Mt. Holly; 259–2826. Look for clambakes on Wednesdays, with stir fry and Mexican fare also on menu.

Chuckles. Rte. 103, Ludlow (near Okemo access road); 228–5530. Lobsters and prime rib served in relaxed setting.

Mount Holly Lodge. Rte. 155, East Wallingford; 259–2351. Home-cooked meals served with soup, salad and biscuits.

Okemo Inn. R.F.D. 1, Box 133, Ludlow; 228–8834. Family-style meals with traditional baked breads and home-made soups. Make reservations a day in advance.

HOW TO GET AROUND. A car to the resort is mandatory; however, once at Okemo, everything is within walking distance of the slopes and trails. The resort provides **shuttle** service from the lower parking lots to the base lodge.

 **SEASONAL EVENTS.** In **February,** a cherry-pie-eating contest on George Washington's birthday is an emerging tradition, and the West Indies comes to Okemo once a year when guests are encouraged to don festive cottons for an evening of authentic West Indies food and calypso music. The resort hosts the *Equitable Family Ski Challenge* throughout the winter and a number of serious racing events.

OTHER SPORTS AND ACTIVITIES. There's **ice fishing** on nearby Echo Lake. The Plymouth Village Ski Touring Center in Plymouth and Fox Run Ski Touring Center in Ludlow both offer **cross-country** terrain.

 **CHILDREN'S ACTIVITIES.** Okemo's state-approved *Day-Care Center* (228–4041) is open for ages 18 months –8 years. Ages 3 and 4 can *"Get Acquainted with Your Ski Equipment"* through a special program. The center is open from 8:30 A.M. to 4:30 P.M., free Monday through Friday and non-holiday periods, and $12 weekends and holidays. *SKIwee,* the nationally recognized program to help children learn to ski, is offered here. And Okemo has created a children's race course called Hot Dog Hill that involves following an instructor over moguls, around turns, and through tunnels, with colorful cartoon characters greeting young skiers along the way.

 **NIGHTLIFE.** Through the influence of the ski resort, the town of Ludlow is just beginning to come alive at night, with at least three establishments offering entertainment, usually live bands, on weekends. These are *Chuckles,* Rte. 103, Ludlow, 228–5530; *Michael's Seafood and Steak Restaurant,* Rte. 103, Ludlow, 228–5622; and the *Pot Belly Pub,* Main St., Ludlow, 228–9813.

SUICIDE SIX SKI AREA

Woodstock VT 05091   *Snow Report: 802–457–1622*
Tel: 802–457–1666   *Area Vertical: 650 ft.*

Number of Trails: 18 or 100
skiable acres
Lifts: 2 double chairs, 1 J-bar
Snowmaking: 50 percent of
terrain
Season: mid-December–March

A jump away from the Village of Woodstock, with its Paul Revere church bells and covered-bridge New England atmosphere, is Suicide Six, known in an earlier day (and on current topographical maps) simply as "Hill 6." It was here in 1937 that Bunny Bertram opened what is America's oldest continually operating ski tow. The area, which was then little more than a heart-stopping, steep, open slope, was sold in 1961 to Rockresorts. Today it provides family-oriented skiing on 18 trails.

Trails range from the scenic beginners' run, "Easy Mile," to the sheer drop of The Face, training ground for generations of Olympic and national trainees from nearby Dartmouth College.

Perhaps the main reason to come to this area, however, is that it's a wonderful excuse to spend time in Woodstock, either at the elegant Woodstock Inn, enjoying tea, perhaps, or wandering down the colonial-home-lined streets. For connoisseurs of pretty towns, this one rates high on most lists. It's charming without being quaint, sophisticated (and pricey) without being trendy.

Practical Information for Suicide Six

HOW TO GET THERE. Suicide Six Ski Area is 3 miles north of Woodstock. (See Killington and Pico section for regional details.) **By car.** Take I–95 into Vermont to Exit 9, then US 5 north to Rte. 12, which leads into Woodstock. **By bus.** Woodstock is served daily by *Vermont Transit,* 457–1325.

TELEPHONES. The area code for all of Vermont is 802.

ACCOMMODATIONS. The region offers a wide assortment of lodging establishments, ranging from motels to guest houses and charming colonial inns furnished with antiques. There are also a number of bed and breakfast treasures scattered throughout the region. Reservation services for these places are handled through *Vermont Bed and Breakfasts,* Box 139, Browns Trace, Jericho VT 05465 (899–2354), or *Christian Hospitality,* P.O. Drawer D, Middleboro MA 02346 (617–947–2356), which handles reservations for bed and breakfast establishments throughout New England.

Rates for hotels and inns listed here are based on double occupancy, with many places including breakfast and some having MAP. Categories determined by price are *Expensive,* $50 and up; *Moderate,* $35–$50; and *Inexpensive,* less than $35.

Expensive

The Jackson House. Rte. 4, Woodstock 05091; 457–2065. An 1890 Victorian landmark with 11 antique-furnished rooms, 9 private baths; fireside parlor, library. Breakfasts served.

Juniper Hill Inn. Juniper Hill Rd., Windsor 05089; 674–5273. A stately Vermont mansion with 14 guest rooms and oak paneled great room. Antiques, of course, and breakfasts served.

Kedron Valley Inn. Rte. 106, South Woodstock 05071; 457–1473. Rooms dispersed among 1828 inn, 1824 tavern, or log cabin motel annex. Skating on pond; on-premises dining that has good reputation with locals.

Lincoln Covered Bridge Inn. Rte. 4, West Woodstock 05091; 457–3312. A country inn with 6 guest rooms, private baths, choice of queen, king or twin beds; lounge; breakfasts served.

The Quechee Inn at Marshland Farm. Club House Rd., Quechee 05059; 295–3133. A 1793 Vermont farmstead with 22 guest rooms, private baths; breakfasts served, dinners by reservation.

Woodstock Inn and Resort. US 4, on the Green, Woodstock 05091; 457–1100. Luxurious colonial-style inn, handsome quilts on beds. Fine dining by candlelight; night-time sleigh rides; coffee shop and lounge.

Moderate

The Corners Inn. Rte. 4, Bridgewater Corners 05035; 672–9968. Early American decor in this 6–room inn.

Echo Lake Inn. Rte. 100, Tyson 05149; 228–8602. An authentic colonial inn has welcomed travelers for 175 years; 25 modern rooms.

The Inn at Weathersfield. Rte. 106S, Weathersfield 05151; 263–9217. A 1795 stagecoach stop with 10 rooms; serves afternoon tea.

October Country Inn. 8 miles west of Woodstock, Bridgewater Corners 05035; 672–3412. A 10-room rambling farmhouse with home cooking.

The Village Inn at Woodstock. US 4, Woodstock; 457–1255. A Victorian mansion with 9 guest rooms, oak wainscoting, tin ceilings; dining room.

Inexpensive

Liberty Hill Farm. Rte. 100, Rochester 05767; 767–3926. A working dairy farm with cross-country trails at door, 5 guest rooms, shared bath; farmstyle breakfasts and dinners.

 **BED-AND-BREAKFAST TREASURES.** These are scattered throughout the region. Some are located in charming and lovingly restored old houses. Generally private baths are less common than they are in hotels, but the guest gets to stay in a family setting at inexpensive rates. Contact the *Woodstock Chamber of Commerce,* 18 Central St., Woodstock 05091 (457–2389) for a brochure that lists these establishments in the region.

 **RESTAURANTS.** Since the region is hardly a self-contained resort, visitors here have a choice of places to dine out, either in country elegance, family-style, or old world settings. Offerings are just as varied—Vermont turkey and other regional fare to Continental cuisine and ethnic specialties. The price classifications of the following restaurants are based on the cost of an average three-course dinner for one person for food alone; beverages, tax, and tip would be extra. *Expensive:* $15 and up; *Moderate:* $9–$15. Most places accept major credit cards, but it would be wise to call ahead first.

Expensive

Barnard Inn. Rte. 12, Barnard; 234–9961. An inn offering Continental cuisine under the direction of Swiss chef; jackets required for men.

Lincoln Covered Bridge Inn. Rte. 4, Woodstock; 457–3312. Northern Italian specialties are favored here, and after-dinner coffees are a must. Reservations requested.

The Prince & the Pauper. Woodstock Village; 457–1818. The evening starts in the lounge and moves to a candlelight dinner that will have a Continental touch. Reservations essential.

The Quechee Inn at Marshland Farm. Club House Rd., Quechee; 295–3133. Country elegance overlooking Ottauquechee River; entrees varied but always come with freshly baked rolls and desserts. Jackets and reservations requested.

Moderate

Bentley's Restaurant. Elm St., Woodstock; 457–3232. Plants, antique wood, and interesting menu mark this establishment.

Enes' Table at Valley View Motel. Rte. 12, Woodstock; 457–2512. Family restaurant specializing in Italian food; reservations appreciated.

Juniper Hill Inn. Juniper Hill Rd., Windsor; 674–5273. Four-course, single-entree dinners with all fresh ingredients; single seating at 7 P.M. after cocktails and complimentary hors d'oeuvres by the fire.

Rumble Seat Rathskeller. Woodstock East; 457–3609. Located in the cellar of the 1834 Stone House; offers European-style dining.

The Village Inn of Woodstock. 41 Pleasant St., Woodstock; 457–1255. Roast fresh Vermont turkey and homemade desserts are only the beginning here; also enjoy natural oak woodwork, tin ceilings, and stained glass windows. Reservations requested.

HOW TO GET AROUND. Because Suicide Six is not a self-contained ski resort, it is best to have a **car** — particularly if you would like to explore some of the Vermont countryside. Some accommodations, however, have **shuttle** service to the ski area. Check when making reservations, for driving mountain roads during ski season can be hazardous.

SEASONAL EVENTS. The *Woodstock Inn & Resort* offers a wassail celebration in early **December** that includes a lavish medieval feast, King Arthur style, and a torchlight parade plus lighting of a yule log and Christmas tree. Come spring, there's *Spring Fling* in **March** where you can ski all day for $1. *Seniors on Snow* is a winter activity for people born before 1935 and helps older people enjoy the pleasures of cross-country skiing by guiding them gently into the sport.

OTHER SPORTS AND ACTIVITIES. The *Woodstock Ski Touring Center,* Rte. 106, Woodstock (457–2114), is headquartered at the Woodstock Country Club and its **cross-country** trails cover 75 km of terrain in the Green Mountains. **Sleigh rides** and day/night outdoor platform **tennis** are available through the *Woodstock Inn and Resort,* on the Green, Woodstock, 457–1100. Sleigh rides are also at *White Birch Farm,* off Stage Rd., Barnard, 457–2768; *Quechee Inn,* Club House Rd., Quechee, 295–3133; *Kedron Valley Stables,* Rte. 106, South Woodstock, 457–1480; and *Salt Ash Stables,* Rte. 100, Plymouth, 672–3811.

HINTS TO THE HANDICAPPED. At the *Woodstock Ski Touring Center* (457–2114) there's been a focus on cross-country lessons for the visually handicapped, including *Ski for Light* sponsored by the Sons of Norway. Suicide Six Ski Area can also accommodate handicapped skiers on a request basis.

DAY-CARE FACILITIES. There are no facilities for child care at the area. For information on babysitters in the region, call the *Woodstock Sunshine Nursery,* Linden Hill, Woodstock, 457–1201; or the *Unitarian-Universalist Church* Nursery School, Rte. 4, Woodstock, 457–2557.

NIGHTLIFE. About four times a year there's dancing at the Woodstock Inn on the Green in Woodstock, but the rest of the time look for disco action at *Bentley's Restaurant,* Elm St., Woodstock, 457–3232; and bluegrass and a dance floor at *Spooner's Restaurant,* east end of Woodstock, 457–4022.

NORTHERN VERMONT

BOLTON VALLEY RESORT

Bolton Valley VT 05477
Tel: 802–434–2131

Snow Report: 802–434–2131
Area Vertical: 1,100 ft.
Number of Trails: 30 or 100
  skiable acres
Lifts: 4 doubles, 1 pony
Snowmaking: 40 percent of
  terrain
Season: November–mid-April

The newest of Vermont's major ski resorts may also be the state's oldest ski area. A world traveler and colorful character named Edward Bryant came through Vermont after World War I. He began carving ski trails 2,600 ft. up on Bolton Mountain. Strapped into 7-foot skis with a Sou'western on his head, he christened his work the Heavenly Highway and Bolton Mountain trails and invited his friends to come skiing. He also built a rustic cabin called Bryant Lodge. This was in the late 1920s.

Along came the Depression and then World War II. He tried but failed to get financial backing to put in a rope tow and base lodge, and he died in 1951.

For years after, the only activity on Bolton Mountain was lumbering. In 1964 a University of Vermont graduate, Ralph Des Lauriers, started re-creating Bryant's dream.

Today 30 trails are concentrated on Ricker Mountain, adjacent to Bolton, and the trails that Bryant cut are part of the resort's extensive cross-country network.

Bryant would be amazed to see the self-contained resort village that has developed in 20 years, only minutes from downtown Burlington, the largest city in Vermont.

The resort takes its name from the nearby town of Bolton, chartered by King George III in 1763. Settlers then paid an annual tax of one ear of Indian corn and looked after the towering white and other pine trees suited to mast making. A century later, in 1847, Irish immigrants by the hundreds staged a demonstration called the Bolton Revolt. They wanted their pay for work they had done on the Central Vermont Railroad, called the Iron Ligament, that snaked through the nearby Winooski Valley.

The first hostelry in town was the James Moore Tavern, an establishment commemorated by one of the same name at the resort. And local lore has been kept alive by the likes of the Bolton Outlaw, a trail named in honor of early poachers in the area, and the Beech Seal Trail, derived from punishment inflicted on trespassers by a beechwood wand wielded by Vermont's early lawmakers, the Green Mountain Boys. Another trail, Peggy Dow's Hymn Book, has a long story all of its own, and Bear Run recalls Bolton's first inhabitants.

If you've guessed the mood is folksy here, you're right. Likely as not Des Lauriers is found mingling in the dining room with guests, dressed in ski warm-ups from an early day tour of the mountain and topped with a tweed sports coat.

The trails are primarily in the beginner-intermediate range. The resort village, nestled at the base, provides restaurants, a grocery store, sports center, hotel, and range of condominiums.

Practical Information for Bolton Valley

 **HOW TO GET THERE.** Bolton Valley is one of 7 ski resorts located in northern Vermont that are detailed in this guide. The others are Burke Mountain, Jay Peak, Mad River Valley, Stowe, Sugarbush, and the Village at Smugglers' Notch. Burlington is the gateway to these resorts.

By air. The Burlington International Airport (863–2874) is served by *Delta* (658–2515), *Eastern Express* (800–327–8376), *People Express* (863–2509 or 864–1594), *Piedmont Airlines* (800–448–4104), *Piedmont Commuter–Brockway Air* (800–438–7833), *Pilgrim* (800–243–0490), *United* (800–241–6522), and *USAir* (862–9611). The airport's Ground Transportation desk (863–1889) can give details on shuttle service to the various ski areas. Car rental agencies located at the airport are *Avis* (864–0411 or 800–331–1213), *Budget* (658–1211 or 800–527–0700), *Hertz* (864–7409 or 800–654–3131), and *National* (864–7441 or 800–328–4567).

By bus. *Vermont Transit,* a division of *Greyhound Lines* (800–642–3133) serves Burlington and most adjacent towns.

By car. From Albany NY, take I–87 north to Exit 19 onto Rte. 109; travel east to Fort Anne NY, onto Rte. 4 to Whitehall; then take Rte. 22 north to Vergennes and onto Rte. 7 into Burlington. To drive to Bolton from the north, take Exit 11 off I–89. From the south, take Exit 10 off I–89; follow Rte. 2 to the Bolton Valley access road, then drive 4 miles to the resort.

By train. *Amtrak* serves Waterbury and Essex Junction in Vermont.

TELEPHONES. The area code for all of Vermont is 802.

 **ACCOMMODATIONS.** There are more than 1,150 beds in 2 lodges, an inn, and condominiums within walking distance of the lifts and trails. Rates at these establishments are based on double occupancy. Categories, determined by price, are: *Expensive,* $100–$150, depending on size of suites or units; *Moderate,* $75–$100.

Trailside Condominiums. *Expensive.* Bolton Valley Resort; 802–434–2769. Over 100 completely furnished 1–4-bedroom units with fireplaces (wood is free), private decks, and color TV. Cribs are provided at no charge and daily maid service is available for a small fee.

The Chateau at the Lodge. *Expensive.* Bolton Valley Resort; 802–434–2131. Luxuriously appointed suites with kitchenettes and fireplaces.

Black Bear Inn. *Moderate.* Bolton Valley; 802–434–2126. A 20-room country inn appointed with handmade quilts and wall hangings. Children under 6, free.

The Lodge at Bolton Valley. *Moderate.* Bolton Valley; 802–434–2131. A newly decorated 85-room lodge with private balconies and fireplaces. Children under 6, free.

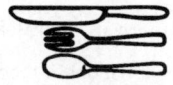 **DINING OUT.** There's a tendency for guests to stay put at this resort, because there is little besides the resorts attractions nearby. Although there are numerous restaurants in both Burlington and Montpelier, most guests consider the 20-mile drive to either city too much to take after a hard day's skiing. Besides, the lodge dining rooms offer a wide selection from light meals to full-course dinners. Expect to pay $15 and up at an *Expensive* place; $10–$15 at a *Moderate;* and less than $10, *Inexpensive.*

The Fireside Restaurant. *Expensive.* Bolton Valley Lodge; 434–2131. Candle-light dining and menu offering nouvelle cuisine. Hearty country breakfasts are a specialty. Reservations preferred for dinner.

The Black Bear Lodge. *Moderate.* Bolton Valley; 434–2161. Country-inn style dining features regional cooking. Dinner by reservations only.

Last Run Cafe. *Inexpensive.* Bolton Valley Lodge; 434–2131. Light meals include soups, sandwiches, and quiche.

Sports Club Lounge. *Inexpensive.* Bolton Valley Sports Center; 434–2131. Light meals and gourmet munchies.

James Moore Tavern. *Inexpensive.* Bolton Valley Lodge; 434–2131. Hearty hot sandwiches and full-course lunches overlooking slopes.

Also available are light meals at the cafeteria and, weather permitting, at the **Barbecue**—al fresco dining on ribs and chicken.

HOW TO GET AROUND. Since this is a legitimate, self-contained destination resort with the slopes within walking distance, having a car here is unnecessary.

 **SEASONAL EVENTS.** Bolton Valley hosts the *National Equitable Family Ski Challenge* race series from **December to February** and every Saturday hosts a NA-STAR race for amateur ski racers. *Spring Thing Weekend* in late **March** brings a carnival atmosphere to the slopes with costumes, confections, and zany fun. And if you happen to celebrate a birthday while here, you can ski free for the day through the *Bolton On Your Birthday* program.

 OTHER SPORTS AND ACTIVITIES. Partly because of its base elevation, at 2,150 ft. the highest in the state, the resort's 6,000 private acres are blessed with early and late season snows. This means that its 100-km **cross-country** center gets snows earlier and later than other ski touring centers in Vermont and, increasingly, people come here because of the combination of extensive alpine and cross-country terrain. A wilderness trail is open at times connecting to Stowe Valley and the Trapp Lodge complex there. Those interested in Norpine and telemarking can purchase a one-ride lift ticket that brings skiers to a 3,400-ft. elevation for a 5-mile descent. Guided backcountry tours can be arranged by calling 802–434–2131.

The Sports Center that's within walking distance of restaurants and lodging houses two **tennis** courts, an indoor pool, tanning room, and lounge.

 HINTS TO THE HANDICAPPED. The *Sports Center* and activities at the Bolton Valley Lodge are accessible to the handicapped, and the lodge is one of the few at a ski area that is serviced by an elevator. The *Bolton Valley Ski School* also directs some programs for handicapped skiers. Both the sports center and the ski school can be contacted at the main lodge, 434–2131.

 **CHILDREN'S ACTIVITIES.** Because the resort lends itself so well to the family ski experience, Bolton Valley emphasizes programs for children. The *Honey Bear Nursery,* open from 8:45 A.M. until 4:30 P.M., accepts infants up to age 6. Advance reservations are urged (802–434–2131). Children from 3 to 5 in the program enjoy outside pre-ski play. The cost is $22 per child. *Bolton Bears & Cubs,* for ages 6–12, takes youngsters on the mountain from 9:30 A.M. until 2 P.M. with supervised instruction and skiing, lunch, and camaraderie. The program is $34 a day.

The *Pied Piper of Bolton* offers evening respite to parents who may yearn for quiet getaway time. Children meet in the Honey Bear Nursery at 5:30 P.M. for optional dinner and quiet games until 9 P.M.

And if parents are feeling a wee bit guilty for taking children out of school for a ski vacation, the *Bolton Mountain School* offers a certified Vermont teacher four days a week (Monday–Thursday) who will supervise homework assignments for grades 1–8. The cost is $25 per child ($12 for each additional child in a family).

 **NIGHTLIFE.** The *James Moore Tavern* in the Bolton Valley Lodge is different from night to night. One evening may be subdued folk music; the next the rafters will be ringing to rock 'n' roll. This is the resort's social center, with video games downstairs for youngsters and the slopes lit for night skiing from 7 to 10 P.M. nightly (except Sunday). The *Sports Center* also hosts

social activities with bridge and backgammon tournaments and volleyball matches vying for attention with Trivial Pursuit wars.

BURKE MOUNTAIN

Box 77, East Burke VT 05832
Tel: 802–626–3305

Snow Report: 802–626–3305
Area Vertical: 2,000 ft.
Number of Trails: 30 or 130
  skiable acres
Lifts: 2 double chairs, 3 pomas
Snowmaking: 25 percent of
  terrain
Season: December–April

Burke Mountain, with a 2,000-ft. vertical, is a monadnock. This means that it's a free-standing mountain unrelated to nearby mountains. From the peak there are views of Mt. Mansfield (Stowe), Jay Peak, and even Mt. Washington over in New Hampshire, plus vistas of surrounding farmlands in valleys formed by glaciers millennia ago.

The mountain first attracted attention as a recreation area back in the 1930s, when the Civilian Conservation Corps (CCC) built a fire lookout tower at the top and an access road that subsequently became the key to a few ski trails that were developed. After this quiet start, a group of local people bought the mountain and put in a lift in an effort to create activity for the community. Eventually it was sold to the present owner, Doug Kitchel, who comes from the family that created the Crayola Coloring Company. Under his management, the mountain has evolved to today's 30 trails, primarily in the upper intermediate range and with a popular hill for novice skiers.

The area attracts primarily family skiers who drive up from Massachusetts and Connecticut. There's a loyal following of people who favor the low-key, uncrowded ambience that this undiscovered resort still offers.

Practical Information for

Burke Mountain

HOW TO GET THERE. Burke Mountain is located 1 mile east of the town of East Burke. (For regional details, see Bolton Valley above.) **By car.** Take I–91 to Exit 23 to Rte. 114 north to East Burke. **By bus.** *Vermont Transit* (226–9316) serves Lyndonville, 5 miles away. **By air.** Caledonia State Airport (626–3353) in Lyndonville offers a 3,300-ft. runway for private aircraft.

TELEPHONES. The area code for all of Vermont is 802.

ACCOMMODATIONS. Part of Burke's charm is that it is still relatively undeveloped and undiscovered, with some condominiums at the mountain and a sprinkling of small motels and inns in nearby East Burke and Lyndonville. *Expensive* here is $50 and up per room per night, double occupancy; *Moderate,* $35–$50; and *Inexpensive,* less than $35.

Expensive

Burke Mountain. Slopeside condominiums; 626–3305. Choice ranges from private room with bath to studios, efficiencies, and 1–4-bedroom units, some with lofts. Units available for 2–night stays for 4–11 people.

Moderate

Changing Seasons Motel. Rte. 5, Lyndonville; 626–5832. A motel offering Jacuzzi and sauna plus cable TV.
Colonnade Motor Inn. Rte. 5, Lyndonville; 626–9316. 40 new rooms with phones, cable TV; only 6 miles from the mountain.
Darion Inn. Off Rte. 114, East Burke; 626–5914. A Vermont country inn with private baths, cross-country skiing, and good meals.
North Star Farm. Off Rte. 114, East Burke; 734–9645. A farmhouse that can hold groups of up to 12; sauna on premises.
The Old Cutter Inn. On Burke Mountain, East Burke; 626–5152. A small country inn with fireplace in après-ski lounge; 9 rooms, one apartment; MAP available.

Inexpensive

Burke Green Guest House. RR 1, East Burke; 467–3472. An 1840 farmhouse with a bed/sitting room that holds up to 6. Bed and breakfast hospitality.
The Garrison Inn. Burke Hollow Road, East Burke; 626–8329. Just 5 minutes from mountain, inn with private baths, living room with fireplace, and hearty breakfasts.
House in the Wood. One mile from ski area, East Burke; 626–9243. On-premises rec room with fireplace and shuffleboard; children welcome and meals available.

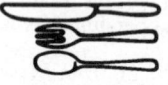 **RESTAURANTS.** Continental and ethnic cuisines complement Vermont staples such as roast turkey, griddlecakes with pure maple syrup, and country-style sausage. Price ranges in this listing are based on a meal for one person, excluding drinks, tax, and tip. *Expensive:* $12–$15; *Moderate,* $9–$12; *Inexpensive,* less than $9. Unless specified, MasterCard and Visa are accepted.

The Old Cutter Inn. *Expensive.* On Burke Mountain, East Burke; 626–5152. A Continental touch to the menu; dinners only.
Ashley's Restaurant. *Moderate.* At Colonnade Motor Inn, Rte. 5, Lyndonville; 626–9316. Regional American menu, with salad bar.
Willy's Restaurant. *Moderate.* East Burke Village; 626–8475. Bavarian cuisine is favored here, along with fresh seafood, steaks, and chops; there's also a bar menu offering lighter fare.
Trinket's Restaurant. *Inexpensive.* At Changing Seasons Motor Lodge, Rte. 5, Lyndonville; 626–5832. An all-American menu with hamburgers a staple. Credit cards for motel guests.

HOW TO GET AROUND. Public transportation is scarce in the region, so it's best to have a car. If you don't bring your own, a *Budget* rental office (800–527–0700) is located in Lyndonville.

 **SEASONAL EVENTS.** In late **spring** the mountain hosts its annual *Burke Mountain Stampede,* which is a first-one-down-wins after a mass start on a downhill course. Burke is home to the Burke Mountain Academy, which accepts 60 students in grades 9–12 who are interested in developing ski racing skills while pursuing their studies. Because of the intensive race-training that goes on here season-long, skiers can often view these students whizzing by or involved in any number of a series of amateur racing events.

OTHER SPORTS AND ACTIVITIES. *Total Fitness Inc.,* 58 Broad St., Lyndonville, 626–5430, offers an indoor **pool, sauna, spas,** tanning booth, isokinetic machines, Olympic weights, treadmills, **bicycles,** and a trek machine.

The *Burke Mountain Ski Touring Center* at the mountain maintains 60 km of **cross-country** trails. Cross-country skiing is a specialty of the Darion Inn off Rte. 114 in East Burke (626–5914), with about 25 km of trails.

There's a **skating rink** at the Burke base lodge facility.

DAY-CARE FACILITIES. The *Burke Mountain Nursery* (626–3305) accepts children ages 4 months–7 years for $2 an hour or $10 all day.

NIGHTLIFE. Other than après-ski activities at various lodgings, about the only offering in the area is the *Packing House Lounge* on Hill St. (Rte. 5) in Lyndonville (626–8777), which is open daily with live entertainment on Wednesdays, Fridays, and Saturdays.

JAY PEAK SKI RESORT

Jay VT 05859
Tel: 802–988–2611

Snow Report: 514–866–1284, from Montréal 802–988–2611
Area Vertical: 2,153 ft.
Number of Trails: 32 trails or 200 skiable acres
Lifts: 1 triple chair, 2 T-bars, 1 60-passenger aerial tram
Snowmaking: 50 percent of terrain
Season: mid-November–early May

Skiers looking for an international flavor at an American ski resort might well head to northern Vermont's Jay Peak, only a few miles from the Canadian border. They speak French as well as English up here, and in fact a sister ski resort, Mont St Sauveur, northwest of Montreal, is under the same management. The Canadian owners have brought a European flair in the past few years to what's called Vermont's Northeast Kingdom, a region distinguished by its wild beauty that's occasionally interrupted by pockets of civilization. Jay itself is a four corners town with a country store and an inn, and the nearest town of any size is Newport, 20 miles away.

In this most rural, farm-oriented country, 30–year–old Jay Peak Ski Resort is carving out a name for itself, offering a large mountain experience without the resort rush experience that sometimes comes at more populated areas. The Canadian Maritime winds do their share to make sure there's lots of snow at Jay. The two distinct mountains that form the ski resort also help as moist air tends to move over the mostly flat terrain before it bumps into the mountains and drops its load of water and, in winter, snow. It can be raining just about everywhere else in the region and Jay will be getting snow.

The resort itself is service-oriented; for example, the Hotel Jay offers valet unloading, a courtesy patrol, and attentive guest services. There's a high repeat business here, good marks for an area that takes a little longer to get to.

Pratical Information for Jay Peak

 **HOW TO GET THERE.** Jay Peak Ski Resort is located 4 miles from Jay, 45 miles from St. Albans, and 75 miles from Burlington. (For northern Vermont regional details, see Bolton Valley above.)

By train. *Amtrak* (527–7706) serves St. Albans from most eastern cities in the U.S. **By bus.** *Vermont Transit,* a division of Greyhound, stops at the Troy General Store (744–2200), 8 miles from Jay. If staying at the Hotel Jay, call 800–451–4449 to arrange for shuttle service to the hotel.

By car. From eastern New England, take I–93 north to I–91; get off at Exit 26 and follow signs to Jay. From New York take I–87 to Rouses Point and follow Rte. 105 east from St. Albans.

TELEPHONES. The area code for all of Vermont is 802.

 **ACCOMMODATIONS.** Perhaps because of its far north location, Jay has not yet experienced the emergence of condominiums and resort village ambience that have become staples of other New England ski areas. In fact, it claims to offer a ski vacation experience the way it was 20 years ago. But it has collected as many types of lodging as are available in the area into a central lodging guide, and a call to the *Jay Peak Lodging Association,* Jay, VT 05859 (988–4363), can book accommodations at slopeside or in nearby towns.

There are some lodging bargains to be found here. Following are examples. *Expensive* lodgings are limited, with the Hotel Jay offering a slopeside room at $70 per person per night, double occupancy, with MAP. *Moderate* is from $40 to $60; *Inexpensive,* less than $40.

Expensive

Hotel Jay. Jay Peak; 988–2880. Located at the base of Jay Peak, with 48 rooms, all with private baths, color TV, and balconies. Lounge, dining room, living room with fireplace, game room, sauna/Jacuzzi. A definite Continental touch in evidence here.

Moderate

Alpine Haven. Rte. 242, Montgomery Center; 326–4567. 2–6-bedroom chalets, located 6 miles from Jay.

Black Lantern Inn. Rte. 118, Montgomery; 326–4507. Built as a stagecoach stop in 1803. Soups to desserts are all homemade; taproom, TV room, fireplace room available for relaxation.

Cedarwood. Rte. 242, Jay; 988–4459. A full-service, 26-room (all private baths) lodge with cross-country skiing on premises, dining available.

Inglenook Lodge. Rte. 242, Jay; 988–2880. Large rooms with private baths, dining on premises, just 1 mile from skiing; sunken fireplace lounge, indoor pool, sauna, and racquetball courts.

Inn at Trout River. Rte. 118, Montgomery Center; 326–4391. An 11-room country inn, with private baths; on premise dining, pub.

Jay Village Inn. Rte. 242, Jay; 988–2643. A country inn near the mountain, combination rooms with suites offering private baths. On-premises dining and player piano in Barney's Pub & Fireplace Lounge.

Inexpensive

Eagle Lodge. Rte. 242, Montgomery Center; 326–4518. A Vermont-style lodge run by Vermonters with home-cooked meals served buffet style.

Gramp Grunts Motel. Rte. 118, Montgomery Center; 326–4572. Look for heated waterbeds with down comforters, color TV, queen size beds, modern baths, and large towels.

Granny Grunts Dorm. Rte. 118, Montgomery Center; 326–4572. Reputation as the top ski dorm in the East; maintains two vans for shuttle from Amtrak and Burlington airport. 18 rooms with fireplace, pool table, sauna.

In addition to a sprinkling of motels, there are also guest houses (including chalets and apartments) with costs ranging per unit or room from $13 to $100. Among these are the *Gingerbread Chalet,* off Rte. 242, Jay (988–4363), and *Bernal Lodge,* Rte. 243, North Troy (988–2527).

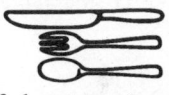 **RESTAURANTS.** Meals may, on occasion, push over $20 (*Expensive*) in this region, with *Moderate* in the $10–$15 range, and *Inexpensive* less than $10. Following is a selection of what the area has to offer. Unless specified, restaurants accept MasterCard and Visa.

Expensive

On the Rocks. Rte. 58, Hazen's Notch, Montgomery Center; 326–4500. One of Vermont's most talked-about places with fine food and ambience. Reservations for dinner a must.

Moderate

The Belfry. Rte. 242, Montgomery Center; 326–4400. Formerly an old schoolhouse, now a combination pub/restaurant offering casual fare such as steaks, potato skins, fresh fish.

Black Lantern Inn. Rte. 118, Montgomery; 326–4507. Candlelight dining here with varied menu. Reservations requested.

Brandys at Cedarwood. Rte. 242, Jay; 988–4459. Located in Jay Village, this establishment offers a combination of French and American cuisine. Also on premises the Woodworks Pub.

Heermansmith Farm Inn. Coventry Village, Coventry; 754–8866. A country setting for fine dining enhanced by slate stone fireplace. Reservations suggested.

Hotel Jay. Jay Peak; 988–2611. Right at the mountain is one of the finest restaurants in the area offering a complete menu including seafood, beef, and veal; excellent wine selection.

Inglenook. Rte. 242 (Upper Mountain Rd.), Jay; 988–2880. An American setting with unusual appetizers, good wine selection.

Jay Village Inn. Rte. 242, Jay; 988–2643. A country inn with candlelight ambience. Menu offers rack of lamb rosemary and steak au poivre; reservations suggested.

Inexpensive

The Border Dining Room & Lounge. N. Main St., Derby; 766–2213. Menu in both French and English with choices of seafood, steaks, and New England dinners; entertainment Friday and Saturday nights; fresh seafood and roastbeef buffet Fridays.

Mill Hollow Pub. Rte. 100, Westfield; 744–6512. Fare ranges from steak to pizza. No credit cards.

Starr's Village Motel. Railroad St., North Troy; 988–4763. Home cooking three meals a day; dining room and coffee shop.

HOW TO GET AROUND. It is best to have a **car** in this region. However, some accommodations may have **shuttle** service to the ski area. If you don't plan to drive your car (or a rented one), check with the hotel when making reservations.

SEASONAL EVENTS. As far as the mountain management knows, Jay has the only downhill event for amateur racers event in the East—the *George Syrovatka International Downhill,* held in mid-**March.** It attracts speedy skiers in numbers of up to 150 and ages ranging from 9 to 62.

OTHER SPORTS AND ACTIVITIES. The *Jay Swim and Racquetball Club* at Inglenook, Rte. 242, Jay (988–2880), offers an indoor **pool** and **racquetball** courts to skiers on a day-membership basis. There are numerous opportunities for **cross-country** skiing, at the *Jay Peak Ski Touring Center* at the mountain (988–2611), with over 20 km of trails; *Hazens Notch Ski Touring,* Rte. 58, Montgomery Center (326–4708), with 30 km of groomed trails and 12 km of maintained trails. *Heermansmith Farm Ski Touring Center,* Coventry Village, Coventry (754–8866), a 14-km trail system; and *Cross Country* at Cedarwood, Rte. 242, Jay, 15 km of trails. **Snowmobiling, sledding, ice fishing,** and **skating** are also available in the region.

HINTS TO THE HANDICAPPED. The aerial tram is accessible to the handicapped by an elevator. The Jay Peak Ski School (988–2611) will also give instruction and assistance to handicapped skiers upon request.

CHILDREN'S ACTIVITIES. The *Child Care Center* (988–2611) at Jay Peak accommodates children ages 2–7 providing indoor fun and games. It's open from 9 A.M. to 4 P.M. daily. Rates are $18 a day per child. Add $14 for two 45-minute lessons in conjunction with Learn to Ski programs through *Kinderschool* and *SKIwee.*

NIGHTLIFE. Saturday nights there's action right at Jay Peak with live bands playing music for dancing at the inn. In nearby Montgomery a place called the *Thirsty Boot,* at end of Rte. 242 (326–4572), has disco entertainment with an occasional sprinkling of live bands. And *Cedarwood,* Rte. 242, Jay (988–4459), has occasional live band music. At *On the Rocks,* Rte. 58 in Hazen's Notch, Montgomery Center (326–4500), there's piano music on Saturdays.

STOWE

Stowe VT 05672
Tel: 802–253–7311

Snow Report: 802–253–8521
Area Vertical: 2,350 ft.
Number of Trails: 44 or 370
  acres
Lifts: 1 triple chair, 8
  double chairs, 4-passenger
  gondola
Snowmaking: 60 percent of
  terrain
Season: mid-November–late April

A few years back Stowe had an identity crisis. It changed its name to Mt. Mansfield, after the 4,393-ft. mountain that's the highest in Vermont and where the skiing here is concentrated. (Stowe Village, 6 miles from the mountain, is the name of the town.) But people were confused, so today Stowe is back to being Stowe, for decades a household word among eastern skiers until Killington started coming on strong in the 1970s. Stowe's title as Ski Capital of the East may have slipped somewhat, but there's probably not another town in the state that throws its support behind a mountain as wholeheartedly as this one. Makes for sophisticated but nice mix of mountain, lodging, dining, and après-ski.

Stowe, perhaps more than any other eastern ski resort, has put eastern skiing on the map. Since the early 1930s it has competed with the likes of Sun Valley, out in Idaho. In 1985, a survey of 1,000 ski industry executives and professional ski instructors ranked the resort as one of the top 10 ski resorts in the country. And Abby Rand, a noted ski and travel writer, has named Stowe as one of the world's top 10 resorts.

A variety of exciting terrain has a lot to do with its ranking. The 4.5-mile Toll Road to the Mt. Mansfield summit is a meandering scenic trail for novices. Expert slopes known as the "Front Four" are the stuff of legends: The Goat, Starr, Liftline, and National. And a second mountain, Spruce Peak, offers terrain for beginners and intermediates. Not to be overlooked is that 32 of the 44 trails are over a mile long.

Either Phil or Steve Mahre, celebrity Olympic racers, is on hand during Mahre Training Center weeks in January, February, and March. The week-long program helps skiers of all ability levels to improve by emphasizing natural abilities. The Mahre brothers are passing on the techniques that have made them the skiing greats of the decade. The program is also available in Heavenly Valley, California and Keystone Resort, Colorado.

Perhaps because Stowe itself itself is such a mature resort with a loyal following of old-time skiers, the area welcomes seniors 70 years old and over with free lift tickets and complimentary ski lessons.

Practical Information for Stowe

HOW TO GET THERE. Stowe is in north-central Vermont, 40 miles from Burlington and 10 miles from Waterbury. (For northern Vermont regional details, see Bolton Valley above.) **By car.** Take I–89 to Exit 10, then follow Rte. 100 north to Stowe.

TELEPHONES. The area code throughout Vermont is 802.

ACCOMMODATIONS. The *Stowe Area Association Lodging Bureau,* P.O. Box 1230, Stowe VT 05672 (253–7321) can make arrangements for lodging at some 60 accommodations ranging from bunk rooms to luxurious inns. For some reason known only, perhaps, to real estate sales people, condominium development hasn't quite caught on in this area yet. The few there range up to $70 a night.

There are two ski dorms: the *Round Hearth,* R.R. 1, Box 2240, Stowe (253–7223), and *Winterhaus,* R.D. 1, Stowe (253–7731), that offer lodging, breakfast, and dinner for only $23 per person per night.

Country inns, hotels, and a sprinkling of resorts take up the lion's share of visitors' attention. In the selection below, *Expensive* includes those with rates from $60 upward per person, based on double occupancy (with MAP); *Moderate,* $30–$60; and *Inexpensive,* less than $30.

Expensive

The Inn at the Mountain. Rte. 108; 253–7316. A slopeside inn plus condominium complex with chairlift to Mt. Mansfield. Rooms (all spacious, some 2-room suites) include steam bath and refrigerator. MAP available.

Ten Acres Lodge. Luce Hill Rd., Stowe; 253–7638. Individually decorated rooms and dining by candlelight; comfortable, elegant decor; spacious rooms, 2 queen-size beds, some 2-room suites. MAP available.

Topnotch at Stowe. Rte. 108, Stowe; 253–8585. They don't make many places nicer than Topnotch, first because of its dramatically high perch, second because of the generous size of both room and bath, with guest rooms resembling mini-suites, equipped with a library and sitting area. Afternoon tea is served here, with four-indoor tennis courts and a health spa. MAP available.

Trapp Family Lodge. Luce Hill Rd., Stowe; 253–8522. Home of the *Sound of Music* Von Trapp family. An elegant brand-new lodge replaces one destroyed by fire a few years ago, with on-premises dining, and only a short walk from the Austrian tearoom and spectacular alpine views. MAP available. Cross-country skiing is the favorite activity here.

Moderate

Anderson Lodge. Rte. 168, Stowe; 253–7336. A small, Tyrolean-style inn with an Austrian chef. MAP available.

Butternut Inn. Rte. 108, Stowe; 253–2477. Antiques, afternoon tea and quail for dinner come with cozy rooms and pine-paneled ambience. Some chalets available. MAP available.

Edson Hill Manor. Off Rte. 108, Stowe; 253–7371. There are 40 km of ski touring trails here; rooms with fireplaces, on-premises dining. Parts of Alan Alda's movie *Four Seasons* were shot here. MAP available.

Green Mountain Inn. Main St., Stowe; 253–7301. An authentic country inn, some rooms with canopy beds, offering game room, sauna, Jacuzzi, and formal and casual dining. MAP available.

Golden Eagle Resort Motor Inn. Rte. 108, Stowe; 253–4811. Oversized beds and fireplaces, balconies, some kitchenettes; sauna, whirlpool and exercise room. MAP available.

Mountaineer. Rte. 108, Stowe; 253–7525. Enjoy a heated indoor pool and candlelight dinners, plus a fireside lounge and game room. MAP available.

The Salzburg Motor Inn. Rte. 108, Stowe; 253–8542. Comfortable accommodations near cross-country and indoor tennis and pool, with a game room, lounge, and on-premises dining. MAP available.

Scandinavia Inn & Chalets. Rte. 108, Stowe; 253–8555. Kids love the video games, on-premises dining with family-style meals, sauna and Jacuzzi. MAP available.

Town & Country Motor Lodge. Rte. 108, Stowe; 253–7595. In town near the shops and movies, offering an indoor pool, game room, sauna, and Jacuzzi.

Inexpensive

Fiddler's Green Inn. Rte. 108, Stowe; 253–8124. Private or connecting baths in old-fashioned inn, complimentary hors d'ouevres.

The Gables Inn. Rte. 108, Stowe; 253–7730. Antiques, country bedrooms, wide plank floors, hot tub, and game room.

Grey Fox Inn. Rte. 108, Stowe; 253–8921. Casual and comfortable 18-room inn with game room and sauna, serving homebaked bread and desserts.

Logwood Inn. Off Rte. 108, Stowe; 253–7354. Lodge—genuine log construction–and chalet with library.

Quality Inn. Rte. 100, Stowe; 253–7355. A 48-room resort hotel with exercise room, lighted skating pond, sauna, Jacuzzi, and free shuttle to slopes.

Siebeness Lodge. Rte. 108, Stowe; 253–8942. A hot tub, fireplace lounge, and cross-country skiing right out your door are specialties here.

Ski Inn. Rte. 108, Stowe; 253–4050. A country inn offering good food.

Spruce Pond Inn. Rte. 100, Stowe; 253–7087. A country inn where reservations are requested for dinner; offers cross-country skiing.

Stowe Bound. Rte. 100, Stowe; 253–4515. Colonial guest house and sheep farm offers German cooking with natural foods.

Stoweflake Resort. Rte. 100, Stowe; 253–7305. A 75-room resort hotel with some condominiums; indoor pool, Jacuzzi, health spa.

The Yodler Motor Inn. Rte. 108, Stowe; 253–4836. Some kitchenettes available in motel accommodations offering home cooking.

BED-AND-BREAKFAST TREASURES. The Stowe area hosts several of these accommodations for the budget-minded. They do not all have rooms with baths; most lack TV's and telephones. But all offer warm hospitality. A selection of them, all in Stowe, is listed here.

In the *Moderate* range (about $25 a night) are: *Charda Inn,* Rte. 100, 253–4598; the *1860 House,* Stowe Village, 253–7352; *Guest House Christel,* Rte. 108, 253–4846; and *Stowe-Away,* Rte. 108, 253–7574.

In the *Inexpensive* range (under $20) are: *Golden Kitz Lodge and Hotel,* Rte. 108, 253–4217; *Lower Village Inn,* Rte. 100, 253–7787; *Nichols Lodge,* Rte. 100, 253–7683; the *Pub at Stowe,* Rte. 108, 253–8669; and *Timberholm Inn,* off Rte. 108, 253–7603.

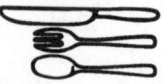

RESTAURANTS. In addition to restaurants referred to briefly in the Accommodations listings above, the community offers some 35 eateries with French, Italian, German, Greek, Hungarian, English, and New England fare. *Expensive* for a meal for one would be $20 and up; *Moderate* is from $10 to $20; and *Inexpensive,* less than $10.

Expensive

The Inn at the Mountain Restaurant and Tavern. Rte. 108, Stowe; 253–7311. A slopeside location with a tradition of excellence focusing on European dishes with an Austrian flair. Smorgasbord lunches and candlelight dining are featured.

Stowehof Inn. Edson Hill Rd.; 253–8500. The Alpine architecture is complimented by European cuisine in this secluded mountain inn, although the dining room is in Early American motif with large stone fireplace and high beamed ceilings.

Ten Acres. Luce Hill, Stowe; 253–7638. An old New England inn that delivers Continental preparations with local ingredients such as Vermont-grown lamb.

Topnotch at Stowe. Rte. 108, Stowe; 253–8585. A dramatic setting with award-winning fare, extensive wine selection, formal and informal dining.

The Trapp Family Lodge. Luce Hill, Stowe; 253–8511. The famous singing Trapp Family presence is alive here, with a main dining room in the handsome rebuilt main lodge and the nearby Austrian tea room where the pastries rival their Alps counterparts.

Moderate

Alpine Lodge. Rte. 108, Stowe; 253–7700. German and other international dishes receive the gourmet touch here.

Cafe Mozart. Pond Rd., Stowe; 253–9900. European pastries and freshly ground coffee follow American and Continental meals.

Charda Inn. Rte. 100 N. Stowe; 253–4598. This is a late-eighteenth century brick dwelling turned restaurant with gracious hospitality.

Foxfire Inn. R.D. 2, Stowe; 253–8459. A long, long menu featuring southern Italian cooking with a lecture, if you wish, on what constitutes each dish!

Hob Knob. Rte. 108, Stowe; 253–8549. Fresh salmon and roast duckling prepared to order.

The Partridge Inn. Rte. 108, Stowe; 253–8000. Look for Cape Cod seafood specialties.

Restaurant Swisspot. Main St., Stowe; 253–4622. Authentic beef and cheese, plus chocolate, fondues—all served in Swiss ambience.

Scandinavia Inn & Chalets. Rte. 108, Stowe; 253–8555. Smorgasbord on Sundays, Swedish pancakes with lingonberries on breakfast menu.

The Shed. Rte. 108, Stowe; 253–4364. An extensive menu in a casual greenhouse environment; wonderful waffle and omelet bar during Sunday brunch.

Stoweflake Inn. Rte. 108, Stowe; 253–7355. Prime rib, fresh fish, and Yankee cooking in main dining room; light menu in lounge.

Town & Country Lodge. Rte. 108, Stowe; 253–7595. New England, family-style, casual dining; salad bar.

Whiskers. Rte. 108; 253–8996. A Victorian mansion that's kept the old-fashioned touches of Tiffany-style lamps and antiques, with menu ranging from prime rib to seafood (including lobster), plus salad bar.

The Yodler. Rte. 108, Stowe; 253–4836. New England hot buffet dinner is featured on Saturdays.

Inexpensive

The Bistro at Topnotch. Rte. 108, Stowe; 253–8585. Still the same great views, but this time with more casual dining offering fondues and salad bar.

Estia Pizza Restaurant. Rte. 108, Stowe; 253–7880. There's Greek food here in addition to pizzas, with emphasis on fresh ingredients.

Stowe Away. Rte. 108, Stowe; 253–7574. Vegetarian, seafood, and Mexican dishes on the menu here, served fireside.

 **HOW TO GET AROUND.** Stowe provides free **shuttle bus** transportation between the ski area and Stowe Village every half hour and continuously between the Mansfield and Spruce base lodges. In addition, many of the hotels in the area provide free shuttles to the ski area. Check when making reservations.

Clark Taxi (253–4250) and *Russell Taxi* (253–7224) are on call in the area.

SEASONAL EVENTS. *Stowe Winter Carnival Week,* usually held in mid-**January,** has been popular since 1921. Known as "king of the winter carnivals," the events range from black tie affairs to dog sled races, church suppers, and snow sculpting. The Wintermeister is part of the fun. This is a winter triathlon involving a cross-country giant slalom and speed skating. Serious ski racers of all ages flock here for various events throughout the season, and **Easter Sunday** sees a gondola ride to the top of the mountain for a service and an optional ski down, with costume parade.

OTHER SPORTS AND ACTIVITIES. The *Mt. Mansfield Touring Center* (253–7311), along with the *Trapp Family Ski Touring Center* on Luce Hill (253–8511), *Edson Hill Manor,* off Rte. 108 (253–7371), and *Topnotch at Stowe,* Rte. 108 (253–8585) offer 100 miles of interconnecting **cross-country** trails. A 4-mile recreation path in and around Stowe Village, popular in snow-less weather for **jogging** and **cycling** also attracts cross-country enthusiasts.

Sleigh rides are available from *Stowehof* on Edson Hill (253–9722) and the Trapp Family Lodge (253–8511). There's **skating** in town at the *Jackson Arena,* and public indoor **swimming pools** at the *Town & Country Motor Lodge,* Rte. 108 (253–7595), the *Salzburg Inn,* Rte. 108 (253–8541), the *Peacock Motel,* Rte. 100 (253–7244) and *Stoweflake,* Rte. 100 (253–7355). Other accommodations offering swimming, to guests only, are *Notchbrook Resorts,* Rte. 108 (253–4882), *Mountainside Resort,* Rte. 108 (253–8610), and *Sullivan Real Estate,* Rte. 108 (253–8132).

The Topnotch (253–8585) has four **indoor tennis** courts open to the public; the *Green Mountain Inn Health Club,* Main St. (253–7301), offers **racquetball,** Jacuzzi, whirlpool, steam and dry sauna, Nautilus and exercise equipment; the *Golden Eagle,* Rte. 100 (253–4811), has the same facilities as the Green Mountain Inn except for racquetball.

HINTS TO HANDICAPPED. The Stowe Ski School will teach handicapped people in private lessons. Call 253-7311 for information and reservations.

DAY-CARE FACILITIES. A day-care center called *Pooh's Corner* is located at Spruce Peak and operates in conjunction with the *Winnie the Pooh Ski School* to involve children ages 3–4 in ski lessons. The rate is $3 an hour or $18 a day, without lessons. *Kanga's Pocket,* a nursery, accepts children ages 2 months–3 years at a daily rate of $28. The center is open from 8:30 A.M. to 4:15 P.M. The *Stowe Ski School* hosts a Mountain Adventure Program for ages 7–12 that includes instruction, supervised skiing, and lunch, from 9:30 A.M. to 3 P.M.

NIGHTLIFE There's an endless list of restaurants and inns that offer piano bars, duos, and folk guitar-style entertainment nightly. *Stowehof* on Edson Hill Rd. (253 –9722) and the *Trapp Family Lodge* on Luce Hill (253– 8511) both offer romantic evening sleigh rides. Live band music of all varieties is available in town at *B. K. Clarks,* Rte. 108 (253–9300), jazz, rhythm and blues; *Ladies Invited,* Rte. 108 (253–9077), offers a changing menu; the *Matterhorn Night Club,* Rte. 108 (253–8198), has music from the '40s and '50s; and the *Rusty Nail Saloon,* Rte. 108 (253–9444), offers top-40 and hard rock.

SUGARBUSH SKI RESORT

Warren VT 05674-9993
Tel: 802–583–2381

Snow Report: 802–583–SNOW
Area Vertical: 2,600 ft. (Mt.
Ellen), 2,400 ft. (Lincoln Peak)
Number of Trails: 81 or 330
acres
Snowmaking: 45 percent of area

Lifts: 3 triple chairs, 9
double chairs, 1 T-bar, 2 pomas
Season: late October–mid-May

In Vermont's Mad River Valley, or "The Valley" as it's known locally, three distinct mountains compete for attention with fine restaurants and shops, all comfortably at home in a bucolic working farm community.

The mountains are Sugarbush North and Sugarbush, comprising Sugarbush Ski Resort in Warren, and Mad River Glen in Waitsfield. The valley itself is narrow, marked by a river of the same name, white-steepled churches, country schoolhouses turned boutiques and carefully preserved covered bridges.

Sugarbush emerged in 1957–58, quickly becoming the "in" place among the East's sophisticated skiers, and was dubbed at one time "mascara mountain" for its collection of chic.

With this sophistication came folks like Armando Orsini, the New York restaurateur who converted a haybarn with crystal chandeliers and strains of Vivaldi into today's Common Man Restaurant, a very uncommon place, and Henri Borel, proprietor of Chez Henri, one of the most elegant French restaurants in Vermont.

Twenty years later Solon Automated Services purchased Sugarbush and its neighbor (then Glen Ellen, now Sugarbush North) and began scheming trails and lifts that would connect the two mountains. This is still a few seasons away, but a courtesy shuttle scoots skiers back and forth.

When the resort first opened, there were perhaps 50 beds nearby for skiers; today the collection of condominiums alone at the base of Sugarbush total over 4,000 beds. And as with other healthy resort communities, country inns and lodges in the locale are thriving.

Management claims that Sugarbush/Sugarbush North is a ski area built for skiers and by skiers. All of the trails on Sugarbush, itself a giant bowl, come to a central hub at the base. Experts stick to the upper levels, intermediates to the middle, and novices enjoy lower terrain.

An advantage to upper-level skiers offered by both mountains is upper-elevation lift service that allows them to stay put near the top, avoiding long runs back to the base in order to get back to the exciting terrain.

At Sugarbush North, novice skiers can ride to the summit to enjoy spectacular 360-degree views. Here the Rim Run, a 2½-mile trail down the spine of the Green Mountains, exposes Camel's Hump and Mt. Mansfield (Stowe) on the right, and the Adirondacks of New York and Lake Champlain on the left. On a clear day, New Hampshire's White Mountains are also visible. Overall, nearly a quarter of the trails are in the "easiest" category, nearly 50 percent "more difficult," and 30 percent are "expert."

Skiers of all ages are very much at home here with free ski programs for youngsters 6 and under and senior citizens 70 and older.

Like previous owners, the newest proprietors of Sugarbush, are attentive to many of the smallest details that can make the difference between a nice and an excellent ski vacation experience. For example, there's the convenience of a cable TV system that provides 24-hour information on ski conditions, nightlife, and events in the area. This is available in many of the nearby accommodations.

MAD RIVER GLEN

Waitsfield VT 05673   *Snow Report: 802–496–3551*

Tel: 802–496–3551

Area Vertical: 2,000 ft.
Number of Trails: 30 or 85
*   skiable acres*
Snowmaking: 10 percent of
*   terrain*
Lifts: 3 double chairs, 1
*   single chair*
Season: mid-December–late April

Mad River Glen is one of the three ski areas (Sugarbush and Sugarbush North) that make the Mad River Valley one of Vermont's most popular winter destinations. Mad River doesn't have the glitter and glamor of its next-door neighbors, but its low-key, just-give-'em-good-skiing approach to running a mountain produces loyal fans who come back generation after generation.

One of the reasons it exacts great loyalty from its skiers, perhaps, is due to bumper stickers that say: "Mad River Glen—Ski It If You Can." Management, however, says not to be intimidated: "You can!"

The mountain was developed—about as much as it still is today—back in 1949. Its specialty is steep, twisting, fall-line trails, a favorite of New York investment banker Roland Palmedo who first saw potential in this Vermont mountain.

Today's owner, Betsy Pratt, says she doesn't see much need to change what people keep coming back for—the challenging terrain as well as a dedicated crew of chairlift operators and cafeteria staff who have been serving Mad River skiers for years. JoAnn Eurich, for example, is celebrating her 30th year as a Mad River staff member, beginning as a dishwasher and now helping manage the base lodge restaurant.

Although there is some lodging at the base of the mountain, Mad River is happy to share the largesse of the valley with its skiers.

The terrain includes 40 percent "most difficult" trails, 40 percent "more difficult," and 20 percent "easiest." The trails are named after animals, with birds and periwinkles going to the beginning skiers, and Panther, Lynx, and Catamount the purview of the experts.

Practical Information for Sugarbush
and Mad River Glen

HOW TO GET THERE. Sugarbush is located in the town of Warren, 55 miles from Burlington and 20 miles from Waterbury. Mad River Glen is located 5 miles from Waitsfield, on Rte. 17. (For northern Vermont regional details, see Bolton Valley above.) **By car.** To get to both resorts, take I–89 north to Exit 91 at Middlesex, then onto Rte. 100B south, which merges into Rte. 100. At Rte. 17 follow the signs to each resort.

By limousine. *Mad River Transit* (486–4278) makes 4 trips daily between the Burlington Airport and the Mad River Valley. They also have a rental car service.

TELEPHONES. The area code for all of Vermont is 802.

ACCOMMODATIONS. Sugarbush Village is a mature resort village at the base of Sugarbush that's characterized by a greater variety of condominium architecture than you'll find at any other resort in the state. Although most of the 4,000 condo beds are in the village, condominium complexes also dot surrounding hills and sprout along the Sugarbush Access Rd. to the mountain. In addition, there are numerous country inns and lodges in the three valley towns of Warren, Waitsfield, and Fayston.

Sugarbush Reservations, Sugarbush Ski Resort, Warren VT 05674–9993 (800 –451–5020) can assist in providing information and making reservations at both resorts. In the region, a per person per night rate, double occupancy, in the *Expensive* range is $45–$60; *Moderate* is between $30 and $45.

Expensive

The Hotel Sugarbush. Village Gate, Mountainside, and Castlerock condominiums, Box 234, Sugarbush Village, Warren 05674; 583–2381. Accommodations for 2 people for 2 nights, include 1–3-bedroom dwellings. All have private baths, including hotel suites, and walk-to-slope and activities convenience.

The Bridges Resort & Racquet Club. Sugarbush Valley 05674; 583–2922. Accommodates up to 600 guests in 1–3-bedroom condominiums with fireplaces, fully appointed kitchens, access to pool, saunas, game room, indoor tennis and squash courts, party lounge. Free shuttle to slopes.

Sugarbush Inn. Sugarbush Access Rd. Warren 05674; 583–2301. Elegant country inn with beautifully decorated private and public rooms serves afternoon tea to guests. Offers pool, sauna, Jacuzzi, ice skating, and free shuttle to slopes, plus cross-country skiing nearby. MAP available.

South Village. Warren 05674; 583–2381. Condominiums include *Snow Creek,* walk-to-lift convenience in 2-bedroom/2-bath luxury units; and *South Village Villas,* most modern dwellings with solar spaces and skylights. Both offer complimentary coffee.

Tucker Hill Lodge. R.F.D. 1, Box 147, Waitsfield 05673; 496–4580. Country sophistication, excellent dining, extensive cross-country center, and changing rooms. Accommodates 68. MAP available.

Moderate

Madbush Resort. Rte. 100, Waitsfield 05673; 496–3966. A traditional inn with the modern touches of a hot tub, sauna, cable TV, refrigerator in room. Some 4-person lofts; cross-country nearby and shuttle to slopes. MAP available.

Golden Horse Lodge. Sugarbush Valley, Warren 05674; 583–3200. A 12-room Bavarian-style lodge with private baths. On-premises dining.

Beaver Pond Farm. Box 306, Golf Course Rd., Warren 05674; 583–2861. Serves country breakfast and après-ski complimentary hot cider and munchies. A restored farmhouse for 10.

Lareau Farm Country Inn. Rte. 100, Waitsfield 05673; 496–4949. A 150-year-old farmhouse with antiques, country breakfasts.

Mad River Barn. Rte. 17, Waitsfield 05673; 496–3310. Offers cross-country skiing and sauna. Spacious guest rooms, children under 10 sleep free in same room with parents. MAP available.

Millbrook Lodge. Rte. 17, Waitsfield 05673; 496–2405. An 1865 farmhouse turned country inn with antiques, hand stenciling, and quilts. MAP available.

Mountainview Inn. Rte. 17, Waitsfield 05673; Seven rooms decorated with antiques and quilts. MAP served family style at harvest table.

Valley Inn. Rte. 100, Waitsfield 05673; 496–3450. More quilts and tastefully decorated rooms, sauna, ski tuning and game rooms, bar, on-premises dining.

Powderhound Resort. Rte. 100, Warren 05674; 496–5100. A combination of condominium convenience with country inn ambience; 2-room suites with kitchenettes, color TV; dining, lounge game room, hot tub, and shuttle.

The Battleground. Rte. 17, Waitsfield 05673; 496–2288. A resort offering 2, 3, and 4-bedroom, 2-bath townhouses with fieldstone fireplaces, fully equipped. kitchens, lighted paddle tennis court, and cross-country trails.

Snow Goose Inn and Restaurant. Rte. 100B, Moretown 05660; 496–3532. A contemporary inn offering waterbeds, private baths, candlelight dining, and desserts before bed.

White Horse Inn. German Flats Rd., Waitsfield 05673; 496–3260. Inn with private baths, lounge with pool table.

Inexpensive

Carpenter Farm. Box 2710, Meadow Rd., Moretown 05660; 496–3433. Private and shared baths, sauna, and cross-country trails at this small country inn.

Christmas Tree Inn. Sugarbush Access Rd., Warren 05674; 583–2211. No phones, but handmade quilts and the Vermont country ambience, plus hearty breakfasts.

Golden Lion Inn. Rte. 100, Warren 05674; 496–3084. Private baths, queen and double beds in spacious rooms.

Mad Ellen. Carroll Road, Waitsfield 05673; 496–3401. A lodge easy on family budgets with semi-private baths. MAP available.

Mooselips Motel. Rtes. 17/100, Waitsfield 05673; 496–3937. Two-room suites sleep up to 6, with cable TV and phones in room. On-premises dining, large-screen TV, video jukebox, pool table in lounge.

Pitcher Inn. Box 408, Warren 05674; 496–3831. A 26-bed inn downtown in village, great breakfasts.

Schultze's Ski Lodge. Rte. 100, Moretown 05660; 496–2366. A lodge with semi-private baths, breakfast that includes homemade breads. Kitchen privileges at dinner time.

Snuggery Inn. 2 miles from Sugarbush North, Waitsfield 05673; 496–2322. One of the original valley lodges offering hot tub and ice skating. MAP available.

South Hollow Farm. R.R. 1, Box 287, Warren 05674; 496–5627. Restored farmhouse; sledding and cross-country. Breakfasts served.

Wait Farm Motor Inn. Rte. 100, Waitsfield 05673; 496–2033. Ten motel rooms with cable TV and private baths; village location.

Weathertop Lodge. R.D. 1, Box 151, Waitsfield 05673; 496–4909. Family-run lodge with sauna; serves breakfast.

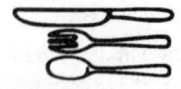 **RESTAURANTS.** The Mad River Valley is establishing a reputation for not only outstanding skiing but also exemplary dining experiences. *Expensive* here means meals costing $15–$20; *Moderate,* $9–$15; *Inexpensive,* less than $9. An unusual twist in a ski resort community is the *Green Mountain Coffee Roasters Cafe and Espresso Bar,* in the Mad River Green Shopping Center on Rte. 100 in Waitsfield (496–5470), where you can enjoy fine coffees along with croissants, pastries, and chocolate truffles. Major credit cards are accepted, unless otherwise noted.

Expensive

Chez Henri. Sugarbush Village, Warren; 583–2600. An authentic French bistro offers veal sweetbreads in a rich wine sauce and a noontime French onion soup that's as close to the real thing as you'll find in New England.

The Common Man. German Flats Rd., Warren; 583–2800. A barn turned posh serves European fare to strains of Vivaldi under crystal chandeliers.

Millbrook Inn. Rte. 17, Waitsfield; 496–2405. Eclectic menu includes authentic Indian cuisine and gourmet vegetarian dishes.

The Phoenix. Sugarbush Village, Warren; 583–2777. Stained glass and wonderful, myth-making desserts. Reservations requested.

Sam Rupert's Restaurant. Sugarbush Access Rd., Warren; 583–2421. A greenhouse atmosphere with interesting menu.

The Sugarbush Inn. Sugarbush Access Rd., Warren; 583–2301. Two restaurants here. The Terrace Room is a greenhouse setting; the Onion Patch serves steaks and seafood.

Tucker Hill Lodge. Rte. 17, Waitsfield; 496–3983. Fresh seafood is a specialty, as are interesting and unusual preparations of old New England favorites.

Waitsfield Inn. Rte. 100, Waitsfield; 496–3979. Classic and American culinary traditions here.

Moderate

Beggar's Banquet. Rte. 100, Fiddlers Green, Waitsfield; 496–4485. Noted for hearty soups, salads, entrees, plus Mexican night on Sundays.

The Den. Rte. 100, Waitsfield; 496–8880. Look for house steaks and seafood.

D. W. Pearl's. Rte. 100, Waitsfield; 496–8858. Soup and salad bar, great breakfasts.

Huckleberry's. Rte. 100, Warren; 496–5100. A family restaurant with an Italian and northern European flair. Reservations requested.

Mad River Barn. Rte. 17, Waitsfield; 496–3310. Informal dining with homemade breads and desserts.

Mother Machree's at Gallagher's. Jct. Rtes. 17/100, Waitsfield; 496–8800. Dine here and skip the cover charge at Gallagher's bar later on.

Old Tymes. Sugarbush Village, Warren; 583–2001. Green Mountain memorabilia transform a long-time farmhouse and classic menu.

Inexpensive

The Odyssey. Sugarbush Village, Warren; 583–2001. Pizza and homemade Italian specialties.

Bridge Street Cafe. Bridge Street, Waitsfield; 496–3474. Mom's kitchen with homemade muffins, soups.

HOW TO GET AROUND. There is a **shuttle** between Sugarbush and Sugarbush North that runs every 15 minutes. Many area lodges also provide free shuttle service to the slopes.

**SEASONAL EVENTS.** At Mad River Glen, a prespring ritual is the *Mogul Contest and Groundhog Watch* on **February** 2, Groundhog Day. Family races are popular throughout the season, and in mid-**March** there's an annual *Telemark Festival.* At Sugarbush, *March Madness* begins on the first of **March** and continues to **April** 1, offering mogul contests, ski club races, snow golf, tug-of-wars, and something special every day. Toward the end of the season, the annual *Tucker Hill Triathlon* (496–3203) combines canoeing, cycling, and cross-country skiing. On **Easter,** there's a costume parade and candy hunt.

OTHER SPORTS AND ACTIVITIES. Ski **touring** is popular in the Mad River Valley at *Tucker Hill Lodge,* Waitsfield, 496–3203; the *Rossignol/Sugarbush Inn Ski Touring Center,* Warren, 253–2301; *Blueberry Lake Cross Country Center,* Warren, 496–6687; *Mad River Barn,* Warren, 496–6550; and *Ole's Cross Country Center,* Warren, 496–6687. In all there are nearly 150 km of marked and groomed trails.

The *Sugarbush Sports Center,* one of the finest facilities of its kind at a ski resort in New England, offers 3 **tennis,** 2 **squash,** and 2 **racquetball** courts; an indoor **pool,** exercise room with universal gym; hairstyling salon, saunas, steam room, Jacuzzi, and whirlpool.

The *Bridge's Resort and Racquet Club* in Warren (583–2922), provides a heated pool, saunas, two squash and two tennis courts to the public.

Competitive amateur skiers can pit themselves daily against the clock on a Dual Automatic (coin-op) Race Course that is a modified giant slalom challenge. This program is available on both mountains.

**HINTS TO THE HANDICAPPED.** Although neither Sugarbush nor Mad River Glen has any formal handicapped programs, the ski school at each resort can accommodate skiers with disabilities or impairments on a one-to-one basis. Contact the main lodge at each resort for specific information and reservations. Sugarbush, 853–2381; Mad River Glen, 496–3551.

**DAY-CARE FACILITIES.** At Sugarbush, the *Valley Day School Nursery* (853–2381) accepts infants on up from 8:30 A.M. to 4:15 P.M. daily at $3.75 per child per hour, with reduced rates for additional children from the same family. State-certified facilities at the resort include a special crib room for infants. For older children, there's a ski playground dubbed the *Land of the Mogul Mice,* where youngsters under 6 can ski free. The *Sugar Bear* is a program for children up to 10 years old that includes supervised skiing and lunch.

At Mad River Glen, a nursery called the *Cricket Club* (496–3551) offers an all-day—8 A.M.–4 P.M.—child care program with ski instruction available.

**NIGHTLIFE.** Find lively après-ski entertainment nightly at *Gallaghers,* Jct. Rte. 17/100 in Waitsfield (496–8800), part of a complex that includes dining at Mother Machree's. The *BassTavern* (583–3100) on the Sugarbush Access Rd. in Warren houses a disco, and the elegant *Chez Henri Restaurant* in Sugarbush Village (583–2600) also provides disco entertainment.

One of the most popular night spots in the valley is *The Blue Tooth* on the Sugarbush Access Rd. in Warren (583–9912), billing itself as a cozy mountain saloon. *Edison's Studio* on Rte. 100 in Waitsfield (496–2336) shows movies nightly with deli food and cocktails available.

The *Wunderbar* in the Valley House at Sugarbush Ski Resort (583–2381) is home to a folk singer, and a number of inns feature nightly entertainment, usually of the mellow folk rock or piano bar style. On the right night you can dance at the *Sugarbush Sports Center* at Sugarbush Village (583–2391) when there's live entertainment at its Gallery Restaurant overlooking the tennis courts.

THE VILLAGE AT SMUGGLERS' NOTCH

Smugglers' Notch VT 05464
Tel: 802–644–8851

Snow Report: 802–644–8851
Area Vertical: 2,610 ft.
Number of Trails: 41 or 246
    skiable acres
Lifts: 4 double chairs, 1 handle tow
Snowmaking: 17 percent of
    terrain
Season: late November–late April

According to the folks at Smugglers, the name refers to a colorful character who enjoys a rich lifestyle but who does so without paying the duty customarily charged. Actually, "the Notch" is the closest thing to a hairpin curve in Vermont and is, except in winter, the route linking Stowe to Smugglers'.

Three interconnected mountains, Madonna (2,100-ft. vertical), Sterling, (1,500-ft. vertical), and Morse (1,150-ft. vertical), are the skiing peaks here. The concentration of expert-level skiing is on Madonna, with a 54 percent pitch on a black-diamond stretch called Freefall. Nearly half of the overall terrain is rated for intermediates, and the easiest trails for novice-beginners are concentrated on Morse Mountain. Sterling offers both open and gladed trails with the 2.5-mile Rum Runner a favorite of novice skiers.

Because all of the vacation activity is focused on a self-sufficient condominium village at the base of the mountains, Smugglers has recognized its value to families as an easy-to-get-around resort. Cars can be parked and forgotten as everything is within walking distance of the condominiums.

Village amenities include, in addition to sports facilities, a grocery store, post office, and a variety of restaurants. Like its counterpart Bolton Valley Resort, Smugglers is designed to keep people in the village and there's little tourist activity nearby.

To keep guests abreast of what's happening at the resort, the Smugglers' Ski School staff takes an active part in daily activities, serving as on-mountain hosts, joining Friday and Sunday night prime rib dinners with guests, and staging a 3 P.M. daily bonfire where parents pick up children from ski lessons, chat over the day, and enjoy hot chocolate and cider. At the bonfire the ski school instructors/snow hosts outline the coming evening's activities. There's also a daily newspaper published by the resort called *The Smuggler Says* that chats about activities, weather, and ski tips.

The pièce de resistance of the 5-day ski week is a Thursday evening torchlight parade of ski school instructors.

Practical Information for the Village at Smugglers' Notch

HOW TO GET THERE. The Village at Smugglers' Notch is 28 miles northeast of the Burlington International Airport and 5 miles southwest of Jeffersonville on Rte. 108. (See Bolton Valley above for northern Vermont regional details.) Call the resort at 644–8851 to arrange for limo service at the airport. **By car.** From Burlington take Rte. 15 east to Essex Junction and Jeffersonville and Rte. 108 south to Smugglers.

TELEPHONES. The area code for all of Vermont is 802.

ACCOMMODATIONS. Lodging choices are made simple at this self-contained village. You either want a private motel-type room with bath, a 5-bedroom condominium, or something in between. Some condominiums are efficiencies with a kitchenette, and there are deluxe studios. Daily maid service is optional. Two-night per person weekend rates, including lift tickets for two days of skiing and lessons range from $115 to $170, depending on size and luxury of the unit.

RESTAURANTS. Guests take their meals at on-premises restaurants. Given the limited number of restaurants, there are really only two price ranges: *Moderate,* $10–$15 per person, and *Inexpensive,* less than $10.

The Barn Restaurant. *Moderate;* 644–8851. There's a nightly theme for the popular international buffets.

Chez Moustache. *Moderate;* 644–5567. Dine on appetizers or enjoy full-course dinners.

The Crown & Anchor Pub Restaurant. *Moderate;* 644–2900. An English pub ambience features a la carte dining.

The Tack Room at the Salty Dog. *Moderate;* 644–2734. There's a European flair to preparations here.

Base Lodge Cafeteria. *Inexpensive;* 644–8851. The place for everybody's favorite hamburgs and hotdogs.

McPherson's Pub. *Inexpensive;* 644–8851. Hot sandwiches and cheese plates are specialties.

HOW TO GET AROUND. A free shuttle bus positions itself in center village evenings to take guests to and from the variety of entertainment. On busy days, a shuttle will also take guest skiers from the lower mountain to upper-mountain lifts.

OTHER SPORTS AND ACTIVITIES. There are two indoor **tennis** courts, a heated indoor **pool, sleigh rides,** and outdoor games such as broomball and snow soccer to complement the skiing. The resort also maintains over 23 miles of **cross-country** trails. *Norland Villa,* one of the condominium clusters, also has a Scandinavian spa or public sauna that includes a hot whirlpool, steam room, and cold shower massage. Complimentary juice is served; bathing suits are mandatory.

HINTS TO THE HANDICAPPED. The ski school staff here is equipped to work with blind skiers through the BOLD program. Call the resort for information: 644–8851.

 **CHILDREN'S ACTIVITIES.** The *Woodshed Nursery* is open to ages 6 months–6 years from 8:30 A.M. to 4 P.M. The *Little Smugglers' Ski School and Camp* provides ski lessons for ages 3–6. The school is a 1¾-hour session with hot chocolate; the camp is a 5½-hour program that includes two ski lessons and lunch. Ages 7–12 can participate in the school and camp with specialized ski lessons, and ages 13 and older can join the *Young Adults Ski School,* which is heavy on skiing and can include introduction to racing.

Part of the fun of the Smugglers' children's programs is a *Cookie Monster Race* held Thursdays and Sundays. Wee racers run an obstacle course, and at check points they have to eat chocolate chip cookies! Everyone's a winner with buttons and prizes.

A special note: Two mothers experienced in rearing children in Vermont's snowy mountains have written a book called *The Book on Family Ski Vacations* that tells you how to read between the lines of ski area literature, how to equip and dress a child for snow country, things to remember to bring in the car, and even games to play along the way. For a free copy of this Smugglers' sponsored project, contact the resort's public relations office (802–644–8851).

NIGHTLIFE. Because this is a self-contained village, guests tend to stay put day and night, and after-dinner action takes place throughout the village. Nightly entertainment at the *Smugglers' Lounge* can be a piano player or a duo; there's relaxed piano-bar music from 4 to 6 P.M. at the *Club Lounge,* followed by nightly live entertainment from 9 P.M. to 1 A.M.; a DJ is on board with music for dancing at *The Snow Snake;* and there's live rock during the week at the *Salty Dog.* On weekends and some other occasions a live rock band appears at *The Meeting House.*

MIDWESTERN
UNITED STATES

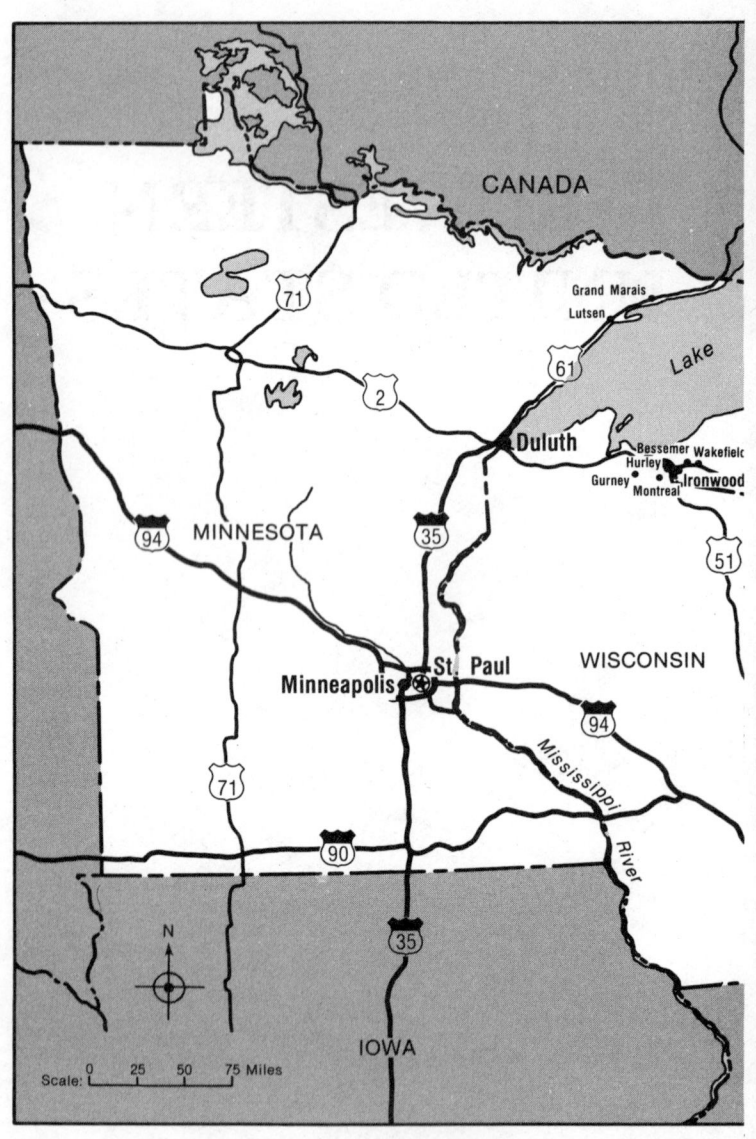

CANADA

71

Grand Marais
Lutsen

61

Lake

2

Duluth

Bessemer Wakefield
Hurley
Gurney   Ironwood
Montreal

MINNESOTA

35

51

Minneapolis ☒ St. Paul

WISCONSIN

94

Mississippi

94

71

90

River

N

35

IOWA

Scale: 0   25   50   75 Miles

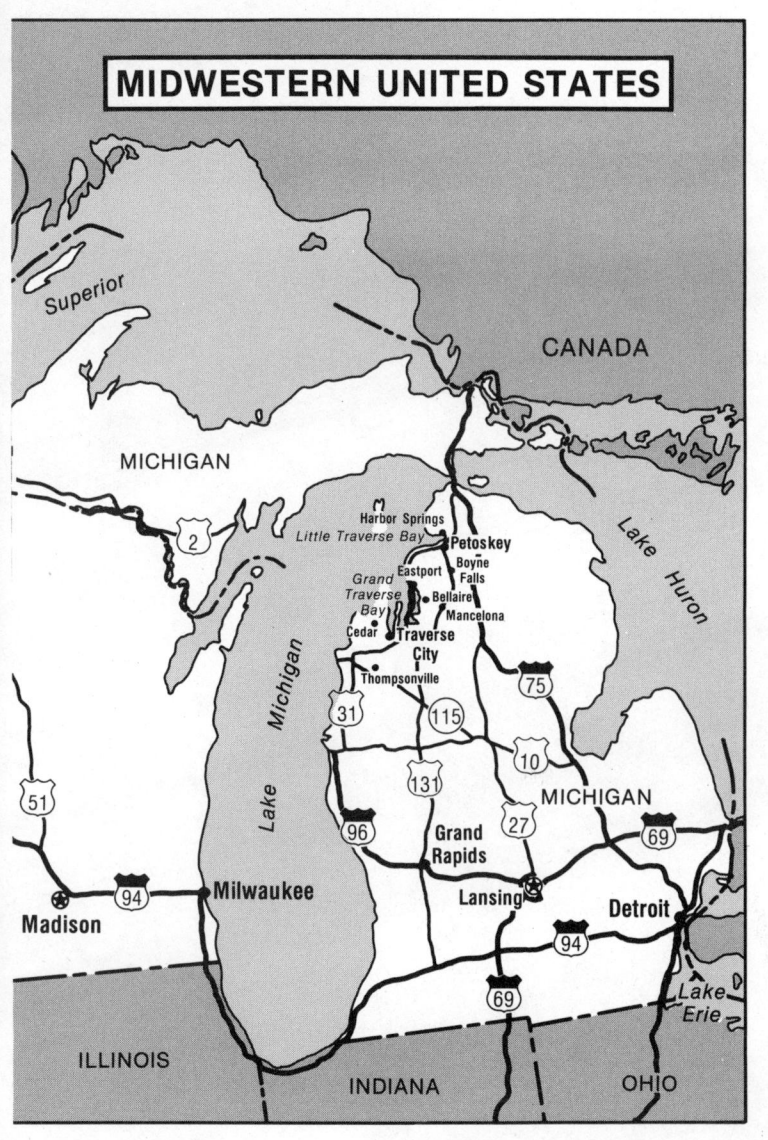

MIDWESTERN UNITED STATES

Superior

CANADA

MICHIGAN

Lake Huron

Harbor Springs
Little Traverse Bay
Petoskey
Eastport
Boyne
Falls
Grand
Traverse
Bay
Bellaire
Mancelona
Cedar
Traverse
City
Thompsonville

Lake Michigan

75

31

115

10

131

MICHIGAN

96

Grand
Rapids

27

69

51

94

Milwaukee

Lansing

Detroit

Madison

94

69

Lake Erie

ILLINOIS

INDIANA

OHIO

MIDWESTERN UNITED STATES

by
SARA WIDNESS

As in the Eastern United States, modern snowmaking technology at most Midwest ski areas provides winter recreational fun for millions. The long-established Midwest summer resort communities that combine the beauty of lakes and mountains are rapidly becoming sensitive to the advantages of selling snow.

There is absolutely no rule of thumb to go by in choosing what will be the "right" resort for your ski vacation. Families will lean toward the availability of children's programs and amenities; young people will especially want a choice of après-ski activity; ski fanatics will look for a variety of challenging terrain; new-to-the-slopes skiers will look for sound ski instructional programs.

And there are, of course, many other variables to consider.

The right mind set, however, is perhaps the most important variable.

Just like theater, not every ski area is a heart-of-Broadway experience. But you can enjoy some fine performances in the few Midwest ski resort areas. And it's putting forth their best that motivates the folks behind the skiing you're bound to enjoy.

With most Midwest ski destinations located in Michigan, we've divided that state into Lower and Upper Peninsula, with the latter spilling over to a select area in Wisconsin.

Michigan

LOWER PENINSULA

In the northwestern corner of Michigan's Lower Peninsula are four major ski resorts all using Traverse City as their hub. They are Hilton Shanty Creek and Schuss Mountain Resort, 45 and 42 miles northeast of the city, respectively; Crystal Mountain Resort, 28 miles southwest; and Sugar Loaf Resort, 18 miles northwest.

Traverse City itself is the tourist center of this part of Michigan, with a cosmopolitan environment and lots of professionals enjoying the recreation the region offers.

Primarily, the tourist facilities, both lodging and dining, are geared to warm-weather water pursuits; however, an increasing number recognize the popular winter tourist attraction called snow that falls in great abundance in the region, and many offer "off season" rates during the winter months for cross-country and alpine skiers and snowmobile enthusiasts.

Traverse City also enjoys the title of Cherry Capital of the World. A one-time lumbering center, it also made history when wood from this region rebuilt Chicago after the famous Chicago fire.

Guests come here year-round to enjoy the accomplishments of students at the Interlochen Arts Academy, and a winter event, the North American VASA Race, attracts the top U.S. cross-country skiers and those from 11 foreign countries.

CRYSTAL MOUNTAIN

Thompsonville MI 49683
Tel: 616-378-2911

Snow Report: 616-378-2911
Area Vertical: 757 ft.
Number of Trails: 20 or 78
*   skiable acres*
Lifts: 1 quadruple chair, 3
*   double chairs, 1 rope tow*
Snowmaking: 95 percent of
*   terrain*
Season: late November–early April

Crystal Mountain is a self-contained resort on Michigan's Lower Peninsula that combines its 20 alpine trails with a 22-km cross-country facility that also provides access to an additional 15 km of state-maintained trails. There's not only night skiing on 12 mountain trails, but

Resorts

1) Big Powderhorn
2) Blackjack
3) Boyne Highlands
4) Boyne Mountain
5) Crystal Mountain
6) Hilton Shanty Creek
7) Indianhead Mountain
8) Nubs Nob
9) Schuss Mountain
10) Sugar Loaf
11) Whitecap Mountain

some of the cross-country terrain also benefits from electricity and there are guided moonlight ski tours.

The area vertical is big by Midwest standards, with trails primarily in the intermediate category (45 percent) 25 percent marked for novices, and 30 percent for advanced skiers.

There's an innovative way to sell lift tickets here, with tickets sold in 4-hour time increments to attract day skiers who can't or don't want to ski the full day.

Crystal Mountain has been in the business of attracting skiers for 25 years, but skiing in the area actually came about in the early 1950s when a local high school principal rigged up a rope tow in his own backyard, then caught "ski fever" and went looking for bigger mountains.

Beginning skiers are still catered to here, with a free rope tow and beginner's area open any time.

SCHUSS MOUNTAIN RESORT

Schuss Mountain Rd.
Mancelona MI 49659
Tel: 616–587–9162

Snow Report: 616–587–9162
Area Vertical: 400 ft.
Number of Trails: 17 slopes or 50
*   skiable acres*
Lifts: 1 triple chair, 2
*   double chairs, 2 rope tows*
Snowmaking: 100 percent of
*   terrain*
Season: December–March

HILTON SHANTY CREEK

Bellaire MI 49615
Tel: 616–533–8621

Snow Report: 616–533–8621
Area Vertical: 325 ft.
Number of Trails: 17 or 50
*   skiable acres*
Lifts: 3 double chairs, 1 rope tow
Snowmaking: 95 percent of
*   terrain*
Season: December–March

A very recent acquisition has joined Schuss Mountain and Hilton Shanty Creek under the same management—makes sense as the two are only 2½ miles down the road from each other. Both, therefore, are fortunate to be positioned in the snowbelt that graces this part of the northern Lower Peninsula of Michigan, but both still rely heavily on snowmaking to augment Mother Nature's largesse.

Schuss has been around since 1967 when it got a lot of publicity for marketing itself as the Kingdom of Schuss, complete with a village square entered over a moat and through a covered gatehouse. Vestiges of this romance still remain, but over the years the resort has become a full-service, year-round facility.

The architecture at Shanty Creek is newer but on winter weekends the rates stay the same for reciprocal lift and lodging packages.

The terrain at Shanty Creek is geared to the beginner–intermediate skier, while that at Schuss Mountain is for the intermediate–advanced skier.

Between the two resorts the region offers 700 accommodations, including on-mountain hotels, condominiums, and chalets/private homes.

SUGAR LOAF MOUNTAIN RESORT

Cedar MI 49621
Tel: 616–228–5461

Snow Report: 616–228–5461
Area Vertical: 440 ft.
Number of Trails: 24
Lifts: 5 double chairs, 1 J-Bar
Snowmaking: 80 percent of
*   terrain*
Season: early December–April

Sugar Loaf celebrated its twenty-first birthday in 1986. It seems to offer two mountains in one, a unique situation where you can ski virtually all around the peak. The front face is primarily clear cut with trails defined for all level skiers, including the black-diamond Awful Awful Trail that's touted as the steepest terrain in the Midwest.

The mountain's back face offers a series of gladed runs, primarily for intermediate-level skiers. In all, the mountain offers 20 percent "easiest" terrain, 40 percent "more difficult" and 40 percent "most difficult." Its vertical, at 440 ft., is hefty for the Midwest.

Thirteen kilometers of cross-country terrain weave through the mountain's base area, offering skiers a choice of either alpine or cross-country skiing.

Practical Information for Lower Peninsula

Ski Resorts

HOW TO GET THERE. By air. Cherry Capital Airport, 3 miles southeast of Traverse City, is served by three commuter lines: *Republic Express* (800–441–1414) from Detroit; and *American Eagle* (800–433–7300) and *Midstate* (800–654–3131) both from Chicago. Car rentals at the airport are available from *Avis* (800–331–1212), *Hertz* (800–654–3131), and *National* (800–328–4567). *Champagne Flight* (947–4646) in Traverse City provides a **shuttle** limousine service. The Antrim County Airport in Bellaire can service a variety of planes, including a DC–9, for skiers going to Hilton Shanty Creek or Schuss Mountain. At the base of Sugar Loaf there is also a 4,300-ft. all-weather airstrip.

By car. From Detroit, follow I–75 north to Grayling; then Rte. 72 west to Kalkaska, and north on US 131. Two of the ski areas—Hilton Shanty Creek and Schuss Mountain Resort—are within a few miles of each other off US 131. To get to Crystal Mountain, stay on Rte. 72 to Traverse City, then take Rtes. 31 and 115 to the ski area. For Sugar Loaf, follow Rtes. 72 and 22 out of Traverse City.

TELEPHONES. The area code for this region of the Lower Peninsula is 616.

ACCOMMODATIONS. An organization has been established to give information and book reservations at many establishments in the region. It's called *Michigan RSVP* (Reservation Service & Vacation Planning) and it can be contacted at P.O. Box 512, Traverse City 49685; 947–1166.

At Sugar Loaf **mountainside,** there are 150 rooms in the base lodge and another 150 rooms in townhouse accommodations. Rates, including lift tickets, start at $45 per person per night, double occupancy. Contact *Central Reservations,* Sugar Loaf Mountain Resort, Cedar 49621; 228–5461. Mountainside lodging at Shanty Creek and Schuss Mountain is coordinated through *Schuss Mountain Resort,* Schuss Mountain Rd., Mancelona 49659; 587–9162. Condominium prices range from $110 to $180 per night, depending on size of unit, and private homes from $165 to $220.

In this selection of accommodations, those listed under Traverse City Area could serve skiers at all four areas. However, Crystal Mountain, located 28 miles away from Traverse City, has a cluster of accommodations near the mountain. They are listed separately.

Hotel rates are based on double occupancy. Categories, determined by price, are *Expensive,* $70 and up; *Moderate,* $40–$70; and *Inexpensive,* less than $40.

TRAVERSE CITY AREA

Expensive

Grand Traverse Resort Village. US 31, Acme 48610; 938–2100. Geared for holidays with indoor pool, sauna, Jacuzzi, exercise equipment, whirlpool, indoor racquetball and tennis courts; ice-skating and cross-country skiing; condominium and motel accommodations.
Waterfront Inn/Best Western. 2061 US 31, Traverse City 49684; 938–1100. A modern motel facility with an indoor pool, prides itself in offering fine dining.

Moderate

Chateau Reef. P.O. Box 295, Suttons Bay 49682; 271–3634. Near a quaint, artsy village, 14 units on the beach, some housekeeping units.
Colonial Inn. 460 Munson Ave., Traverse City 49685; 947–5436. A 44-unit motel with in-room heart-shaped whirlpools, on-premises sauna, Jacuzzi and exercise room.
Crystal Mountain. Rte. 115, Thompsonville 49683; 378–2911. 85 lodge rooms, 20 chalets, some luxury accommodations in resort setting.
Driftwood Motel. 1861 US 31, Traverse City 49685; 938–1600. A 39-unit motel on the beach with indoor pool, Jacuzzi, some housekeeping units.
Fox Haus Motor Lodge. 704 Munson Ave., Traverse City 49685; 947–4450. An 80-unit motel with some housekeeping units, sauna, game and exercise rooms.
Hilton Shanty Creek. Bellaire 49615; 533–8621. 410 units include lodge and chalet accommodations, indoor pool, full-service health club.
Munson Motor Inn. 417 Munson Ave., Traverse City 49685; 947–9520. A 21-unit motel offers special senior rates and is known for friendly hospitality, free coffee.
Pine Crest Motel. 360 Munson Ave., Traverse City 49685; 947–8900. A 32-unit motel located near Northwestern Michigan College.
Red Lion Motor Lodge. Suttons Bay 49682; 271–6694. A friendly staff with location on the West Grand Traverse Bay; some housekeeping units.
Schuss Mountain Resort. Mancelona 49659; 587–9162. 215 units divided among hotel, condo, and chalet accommodations; indoor pool, sauna, Jacuzzi.
Shoreside Inn. 5841 US 31, Acme 49610; 938–1888. A 16-unit motel on the water on East Bay Beach; near marina.
Sugar Loaf Resort. Cedar 49621; 228–5461. 250 units in lodge and townhouse accommodations, some with fireplaces; sauna, Jacuzzi.

Inexpensive

The following establishments fall into the inexpensive category during the winter months, which is considered "off season" in the Traverse City region. In Traverse City (49685): *Bayshore Motel,* 833 E. Front St., 946–4798; *Best Value Motel,* 828 East Front St., 947–4330; *Cedar Lake Motel,* 11998 West Bayshore Dr., 946–7442; *Days Inn,* 429 Munson Ave., 941–0208; *D'Orr Haus Motor Lodge,* 894 Munson Ave., 947–9330; *Parkview Motel,* 825 E. Front St., 947–8218; *Ranch Rudolf,* 6841 Brownbridge Rd., 947–9529; *Sleepy Hollow Motel,* 939 S. Memorial, 943–4740.

Outside of town are *Knollwood,* 5777 US 31, Acme 49610; 938–2040; *Granada Inn,* 720 N. Cedar, Kalkaska 49646; 258–9131; *Leelanau Country Inn,* 149 E. Harbor Hwy., Leland 49654; 228–5060; *Maple Lane Resort,* 8720 Dorsey Rd., Empire 49630; 334–3413; *Wayside Motel,* Rte. 2, Box 472, Suttons Bay 49682; 271–3636.

BED-AND-BREAKFAST TREASURES. In Traverse City, these establishments include *The Broadbrick Inn,* 6369 Secor, 946–0650; *The Cider Mill,* 5515 Barney Rd., 947–2833; *Flower House Inn,* 3975 E. Longlake Dr., 946–4895; *Javor Homotel,* 922 W. Front St., 941–1233; *Painted Pony Inn,* 8392 West M–72, 947–9117; *Vintage House,* P.O. Box 424, Northport 49670, 386–7228; *Warwickshire Inn,* 5037 Barney Rd., 946–7176; *Wood How Lodge,* 611 W. 8th St. (near Northport) 49670, 946–3941.

CRYSTAL MOUNTAIN AREA

The Brookside Inn. *Expensive.* US 31, Beulah 49617; 882–7271. Look for canopy-covered waterbeds, a Polynesian spa, and rooms with log stoves, some with saunas and steam baths.

Hotel Frankfort. *Expensive.* Main St., Frankfort 49635; 882–7271. Under same management as Brookside Inn, with similar amenities.

The Beach House. *Moderate.* Beulah 49617; 882–5075. A one-time boarding house with antiques and rooms overlooking Crystal Lake.

Sunny Woods Resort Motel. *Moderate.* US 31, Honor 49640; 325–3952. Offers motel accommodations.

Hammer's Riverside Resort. *Inexpensive.* US 31, Benzonia 49616; 882–7783. Individual housekeeping cabins.

Mountain Valley Motel. *Inexpensive.* Cadillac Hwy., Thompsonville 49683; 378–2990. A 20-unit motel with indoor swimming pool.

Pine Knot. *Inexpensive.* US 31, Beulah 49619; 882–7751. A motel with some kitchenette units.

The Plaza Motel. *Inexpensive.* US 31, Benzonia 49616; 882–4314. Housekeeping units.

Rosier's Motel. *Inexpensive.* US 31, Benzonia 49616; 882–4891. A modern, 13-unit motel.

RESTAURANTS. Throughout this region of the Lower Peninsula, the visitor will find many places to dine out. What he or she won't find, however, are high prices. In this selection, restaurants are listed by price category: *Expensive,* $12 and up; *Moderate,* $7–$12; *Inexpensive,* less than $7. Unless specified, those listed in the moderate and expensive ranges accept American Express, MasterCard, and Visa.

Expensive

The Jordan Inn. 228 Main St., East Jordan; 536–2631. European country cuisine.

Hannah Lay Room. Grand Traverse Resort Village, US 31, Acme; 938–2100. Rack of lamb, roast duckling and chateaubriand for two, and souffles are specialties.

Hilton Shanty Creek. Bellaire; 533–8621. American and European cuisine with breathtaking hilltop view.

Reflections Restaurant & Lounge. 2061 US 31, Traverse City; 938–2321. Waterfront views and fresh seafood specialties.

The Rowe Inn. On East Jordan Road, Ellsworth; 588–7351. One of the area's best, offering European-flair dining.

Tapawingo. Lake St., Ellsworth; 588–7971. Michigan-grown foods of the season are specialties.

Moderate

Bowers Harbor Inn. 13512 Peninsula Dr., Traverse City; 223–4222. Elegant dining in century-old mansion, extensive wine list. Reservations suggested.

Campbell's of Torch. East Torch Lake at Clam River, Torch River; 377–4171. Family dining with emphasis on Italian foods, chicken, and seafood.

Crystal Mountain. Rte. 115, Thompsonville; 378–2911. Look for 20 percent discount for seniors and children between 5 and 6 P.M.

Dills Olde Towne Saloon. 4235 Union, Traverse City; 947–7534. A century-old lumbering saloon offers seafood and fresh meats.

Embers on the Bay. 5555 US 31, Acme; 938–1300. Famous for one-pound pork chops.

Giovanni's. 9205 US 31, Interlochen; 276–6244. Italian specialties.

Hearthstone Restaurant. M–88, 2 miles south of Bellaire; 533–6531. Steaks and chops.

La Senorita. 1245 S. Garfield Ave., Traverse City; 947–8820. Mexican foods to warm the inner skier.

Mr. Steak & the Traverse Bay Tavern. 2030 S. Airport Rd. and 714 Munson, Traverse City; 946–0981. Steaks and seafood.

Park Place Hotel. 300 East State, Traverse City; 946–5000. Choice of old-fashioned dining or an 1890's pub menu.

The Pinestead Reef. 1265 US 31, Traverse City; 947–5493. Views of East Bay over dinner.

Ricciardi's. Downtown Charlevoix; 599–9492. Italian-American dining.

The Sawmill. 236 E. Front St., Traverse City; 946–9160. A rustic sawmill ambience.

Sugar Loaf Resort. Cedar; 228–5461. Choice of Tonelli's Pizzeria & Finer Delicatessen or the Four Seasons Dining Room with extensive menu.

Sydney's. 128 East Front St., Traverse City; 947–6770. Freshly made pastas, deli-sandwiches, and old-fashioned soda fountain.

West Wharf. 13641 West Bayshore, Traverse City; 947–7079. Seafood, beef, and chicken treats.

Inexpensive

Bonanaza Family Restaurant. 1112 S. Garfield Ave., Traverse City; 941–7472. Salad bar and family-style dining.

China Fair. 1357 S. Airport, Traverse City; 941–5844. Cantonese, Mandarin, and Szechuan choices.

Conley's Irish Pub. 221 E. State, Traverse City; 947–3400. Sandwiches plus boiled dinners.

Cheepeng. 3650 US 31 South, Traverse City; 947–2703. Cantonese and Mandarin choices.

Sleders Family Tavern & Victorian Porch. 717 Randolph, Traverse City; 947–9213. Open since 1882, so they must be doing something right.

Union Street Station. 117 S. Union, Traverse City; 941–1930. Vegetarian, some ethnic specialties.

U & I Lounge. 214 E. Front St., Traverse City; 946–8932. The place for Greek food.

CRYSTAL MOUNTAIN AREA

Moderate

The Brookside Inn. US 31, Beulah; 882–7271. Look for country-cured ham and antique-filled walls.

The Cabbage Shed. Alberta; 352–9843. Homemade soups are specialties in this rustic, homey setting.

The Frontenac. Frankfort; 352–7111. Steaks and a special salad served in a taco are favorites here.

Hotel Frankfort. Main St., Frankfort; 882–7271. Steaks are specialties here.

The Sail Inn. US 31, Benzonia; 882–4971. Seafood specialties and a salad bar displayed in a sailboat lure patrons here.

INFORMATION SERVICES. For information on the region, contact the *Traverse City Ski Council,* 2616 McClintock, Bloomfield Hills, MI 48013; 313–332–5050; and the *Traverse City Chamber of Commerce,* 202 E. Granview Parkway, Traverse City, MI 49684; 947–5075. For details on facilities near Crystal Mountain, contact the *Benzie County Chamber of Commerce,* 826 Michigan Ave., Benzonia, MI 49616; 882–5802.

HOW TO GET AROUND. A **car** would be extremely helpful, especially if you intend to ski all four areas. However, there is some **shuttle** service available. A free shuttle, for instance, makes regular runs between Schuss Mountain and Hilton Sandy Creek, a 2½-mile trip. Some lodging establishments in the region may also supply shuttle service. If you do not intend to drive, be sure to check when making reservations.

SEASONAL EVENTS. Sugar Loaf in early **December** hosts a pre-season race camp for young racing hopefuls. Shanty Creek hosts a *Bavarian Weekend* in **January** and also gets into the craziness of an *Irish Weekend.* In mid-**February,** around a Valentine's Day theme, Sugar Loaf hosts an annual *Sweetheart Cup,* a race that pits couples against couples. The *Schuss Cup Weekend* is held in **March** at Schuss Mountain; it involves an obstacle race plus a slalom over a pond of ice cold water. Something called a *Tutti-Frutti Contest* goes on at about the same time, involving stuffing fruit into snowsuits.

OTHER SPORTS AND ACTIVITIES. At *Crystal Mountain,* there's a **bonfire** right at the mountain which serves as a welcoming party just for kids. On Tuesdays, **tubing** is popular—using old-fashioned inner tubes on the slopes. And Wednesdays, there's a romantic **hayride** for guests.

At *Schuss,* there is **cross-country** skiing available with 19 km of trails connecting to Shanty Creek's ski-touring network, for a total of 28 km of terrain. Schuss also has horse-drawn **sleigh rides** during the week as well as **saunas** and indoor **pools.**

At *Shanty Creek* there are 2 **racquetball** courts, indoor pools, and a fully equipped **health spa** with aerobics classes, sauna, steam room, and Nautilus. Skiers at Shanty Creek who purchase a day lift ticket can also ski free until 10 P.M.

Sugar Loaf boasts an outdoor heated pool, open year-round, that lures skiers off the slopes, as well as 4 indoor **tennis** courts and a game room.

NASTAR races are a staple at all four resorts.

HINTS TO THE HANDICAPPED. All of the "Big Four" ski resorts participate in programs for the handicapped. At Crystal Mountain, for instance, racing events are conducted for the *Blind Outdoor Leisure Development* (BOLD) program. Special attention is also given at the resorts for people with other physical disabilities or impairments. Contact the base lodge at each ski area for details.

CHILDREN'S ACTIVITIES. Crystal Mountain claims its day-care programs aren't just depositories for kids. It recently introduced a *Mountain Midgets* program for ages 3–4 that combines nursery care, lunch, snacks, and equipment with supervised skiing activities in a special terrain garden. Gentle inclines and walk-up mats facilitate learning and development of coordination. Children, ages 5 and up, can enroll in a 10 A.M.–4 P.M. program that includes instruction, lots of skiing fun, lunch, and hot chocolate. There's also an *Elf Club* program for ages 5–8. *Pooh's Corner* offers day-care for tiny ones 10 A.M.–4 P.M. daily and 8 A.M.–5 P.M. weekends. At *Schuss Mountain Inn,* day-care is available at no charge for guests 2–6 years old, and for $10 a day for non-guests. The *Royal Elf Club* takes children ages 5–9 and involves them in half-day and full-day instructional fun on snow.

At *Shanty Creek,* kids ages 5–10 can join the *Kids' Academy* for a lesson/ski experience from 10:30 A.M. to 4 P.M. The nursery accepts infants to age 10 from 9:30 A.M. to 12:30 P.M. and from 1:30 to 6:30 P.M.

At *Sugar Loaf,* the *Kids Club* offers all-day supervision on skis for ages 5–12. A nursery accepts non-skiing youngsters from 10 A.M. to 5 P.M.

For detailed information and reservations, contact the base lodge at each ski resort.

NIGHTLIFE. Bands light up the Traverse City night at the *Holiday Inn,* 615 East Front St., (947–3700), and the *Pinestead Reef,* 1265 US 31 (947–5493), both offering top-40 and easy listening entertainment. Look for jazz at the *Union Street Station,* 117 S. Union St. (941–1930).

There's entertainment also at *JRR's Warehouse Saloon,* 205 Lake, Traverse City (941–4422).

Nightlife is focused right at the mountains, too, with entertainment Tuesday–Saturday nights at Hilton Shanty Creek and Schuss. Trios are the standard fare at Shanty Creek, and live contemporary music at Schuss. You will also find après-ski activities at Sugar Loaf Resort and Grand Traverse Resort Village.

For skiers at Crystal Mountain, the *Frontenac* in Frankfort (352–7111) offers a dinner theater. Folk singers appear at the *Cabbage Shed* in Alberta (352–9843), and a pianist is on board at the *Hotel Frankfort* in Frankfort (882–7271). Saturday nights there's live entertainment on the third floor of the base lodge.

The lodge at Sugar Loaf features entertainment six nights a week with rock bands on weekends and a piano player weeknights.

LITTLE TRAVERSE BAY REGION

Three ski resorts in northwestern Michigan share the attractions of the Little Traverse Bay Region, whose claim to fame is year-round recreation. These are Boyne Highlands and Nub's Nob, both in Harbor Springs, and Boyne Mountain, about 35 miles away across the bay in Boyne Falls.

Like most of their midwestern counterparts, these ski areas augment Mother Nature's natural bounty with snowmaking systems that cover 90 percent of the skiable terrain, assuring seasons that last from late November to mid-April.

Since the 1800s this region of Michigan has been primarily in the summer resort business, thanks to the beauty of Lake Michigan. However, in the past 25 years, it has also grown to be the winter capital of the Midwest.

BOYNE HIGHLANDS

Harbor Springs MI 49740
Tel: 616–526–2171

Snow Report: 616–526–2171
Area Vertical: 520 ft.
Number of Trails: 17 or 225
*   skiable acres*
Lifts: 3 quadruple chairs, 4
*   triple chairs, 1 rope tow, 1 T-bar*
Snowmaking: 90 percent of
*   terrain*
Season: late November–mid-April

BOYNE MOUNTAIN

Boyne Falls MI 49713
Tel: 616–549–2441

Snow Report: 616–549–2441
Area Vertical: 460 ft.
Number of Trails: 17 or 325
*   skiable acres*
Lifts: 4 quadruple chairs, 6
*   double chairs, 1 rope tow*
Snowmaking: 95 percent of
*   terrain*
Season: late November–mid April

These two resorts are under the same management, although about 25 miles apart, and offer interchangeable lift tickets and similar programs and amenities.

Boyne Mountain, home of the first chairlift in northern Michigan, was founded in 1960 by Everett Kircher, and 4 years later he purchased Boyne Highlands. Together they comprise 10,000 acres in Charlevoix and Emmet counties.

Much of the skiing at Boyne Mountain is geared to the advanced skier, with 55 percent "most difficult," 25 percent "more difficult," and 20 percent "easiest." At Boyne Highlands the split among all three skiing levels is about equal.

There's night skiing on Saturdays at Boyne Mountain, and at both areas, first-time-ever skiers are eligible for free ski lessons.

At Boyne Highland's there's access to two cross-country trails via a ride on a chairlift with a total of 26 km of ski touring terrain overall. And at the Boyne Mountain Nordic Cross Country Complex, look for 42 km of ski touring terrain.

NUB'S NOB

Harbor Springs MI 49740
Tel: 616–526–2131

Snow Report: 616–526–2131
Area Vertical: 427 ft.
Number of Trails: 19 or 110
  skiable acres
Lifts: 3 double chairs, 1
  triple chair, 1 quadruple chair,
  1 rope tow, 1 poma lift
Snowmaking: 90 percent of
  terrain
Season: late November–early April

If there was ever any question about where good snow's to be found, the answer lies at Nub's Nob, where the mountain's official snowmaker, Jim Dilworth, made skiing history by taking his snowmaking expertise to the winter Olympic games in Sarajevo in 1984. When not traveling to the Olympics, he sticks close to home protecting the 110 skiable acres at Nub's Nob.

The mountain has been serving skiers for over 25 years, offering 30 percent "easiest" terrain, 40 percent "more difficult," and 30 percent "most difficult." The mountain claims to have more sunshine than its neighbors and says its open slopes are protected from the wind.

The resort offers night skiing from 6 to 10 P.M. Mondays–Wednesdays (after the holidays) and NASTAR is popular here.

In addition to turning out great snow, Nub's Nob pays attention to the details like offering palatable cafeteria food. Specialties include a chicken sandwich (without the skin) and others geared to low cholesterol diets.

Practical Information for Little Traverse

Bay Resorts

HOW TO GET THERE. Boyne Highlands and Nub's Nob are both located approximately 5 miles from Harbor Springs, 10 miles from Petoskey, and 275 miles from Detroit. **By car.** From Detroit, take I–75, Michigan's principal north-south highway, and follow it most of the way northward. At Indian River, go east on Rte. 68, which leads into Rte. 31. Follow signs to the two resorts. For Boyne Mountain, leave I–75 at Gaylord, then go west on Rte. 32 and a short distance north on Rte. 131 to the ski resort.

By air. The Emmet County Airport (539–8441) serves commuter lines from both Detroit and Chicago. From Detroit, *Republic Express* (800–441–1414) flies in daily, as does *American Eagle* (800–433–7300) from Chicago. At the airport, car rentals are available from *Hertz* (800–654–3131); at press time, the airport was in the process of instituting limousine service. Call 539–8635 for information. Also, within walking distance of the Boyne Mountain ski area is a paved and lighted 4,200-ft. airstrip for private aircraft.

TELEPHONES. The area code for the Little Traverse Bay region of Michigan is 616.

ACCOMMODATIONS. Lodging at **mountainside** has all sorts of possibilities in condominium and hotel settings. Each of the main lodges at the three ski resorts can serve as central reservations for mountainside and other lodgings. At Boyne Highlands, *Bartley House* on Hedrick Rd. (526–2183) offers 65 rooms in a hotel setting with all the amenities of a resort. The *Boyne Highlands Inn* (526–2171) at that mountain has 165 rooms in a Swiss alpine motif.

At Boyne Mountain, there's a choice of the 110-room *Boyne Mountain Lodge* or 1–3-bedroom *Mountain Villa Condominiums,* all offering walk-to-the-slopes convenience. Although a lodge, there are also some mini-suites available. Contact the lod : for details, 549–2441.

The *Petoskey Regional Chamber of Commerce,* P.O. Box 306, Petoskey MI 49770 (347–4150), also provides information on lodgings most accessible to the three ski areas.

There are a number of condominium/private home complexes open to skiers. In this region, categories by price are *Expensive,* $60–$100, which is the category of mountainside accommodations listed above; *Moderate,* $40–$60; *Inexpensive,* less than $40. The rates are per person per night, based on double occupancy.

Expensive

Birchwood Farm Estate. Box 497, Harbor Springs 49740; 526–2156. 3–5 bedroom homes.

Graham Real Estate. Main St., Harbor Springs 49740; 526–6251. 2–3 bedroom homes, most with fireplaces.

The Harborage. 500 Front St., Boyne City 49712; 582–9622. A condominium marina on Lake Charlevoix with 2–4 bedroom homes.

Harborside Inn. Main St., Harbor Springs 49740; 526–6238. 24 luxury suites with fireplaces, whirlpool baths, kitchens, color TV.

Wildwood on Walloon. 2775 Wildwood Harbor Rd., Boyne City 49712; 582–9616. Fireplaces and 3–6-bedroom suites on Walloon Lake.

Moderate

Alpine Resort. 1116 W. Gruler, Petoskey 49770; 347–8501. Condominiums that sleep up to 12 in well-appointed units with fireplaces.

Best Western Inn. US 131, Petoskey 49770; 347–3925. A 63-unit motel with cable TV, indoor pool, game room, restaurant, and lounge.

Birchwood Inn. M–119, Lake Shore Dr., Harbor Springs 49740; 526–2151. 44 rooms overlooking Little Traverse Bay; cable TV; Continental breakfasts served.

Foster Boat Works Inn. 111 Pine River La., Charlevoix 49720; 547–9955. 1-bedroom condo units, some with lofts, fireplaces, whirlpools.

Hamlet Village Resort Homes and Condos. Pleasantview Rd., Harbor Springs 49740; 526–2641. Featured are fireplaces, whirlpool spa, and access to Nub's Nob chairlifts.

Harbor Cove. Box 544, Harbor Springs 49740; 526–2159. Cross-country ski out the door of these 2–4-bedroom townhouses.

Hayner's Motel. Rtes. 31/131, Petoskey 49770; 347–8717. Enjoy indoor pool, Jacuzzi, and TV with HBO at this 92-unit motor lodge.

Hideaway Valley Condominiums. Box 544, Harbor Springs 49740; 526–2159. A secluded wooded setting for these 3–4-bedroom townhouses; cross-country skiing and snow-mobiling on premises.

Holiday Inn Lodge. US 131, Petoskey 49770; 347–6041. A 144-room inn with swimming, sauna, whirlpool, and color TV.

Inn on the Hill. US 131, Petoskey 49770; 347–4193. A new, 30-room chalet with charming decor on a quiet hill.

Lakeside Condominiums. 453 E. Lake St., Petoskey 49770; 347–3572. Located between Petoskey and Harbor Springs, condo units come with indoor pool/spa, cross-country skiing; studios–4 bedrooms available.

Land Masters. Rte. 2, Pleasantville Rd., Harbor Springs 49740; 526–2641. Both resort homes and condos here; accessible to chairlifts; cross-country skiing at doorstep.

North Arm Resort. Jones Landing, Petoskey 49770; 347–8432. Fully furnished chalets sleep up to 8; lodge with fireplace.

Stafford's Bay View Inn. US 31, Petoskey 49770; 347–2771. A Victorian era country inn with private baths, on-premises dining.

Trout Creek Condominiums. Pleasantview Rd., Harbor Springs 49740; 526–7722. Fine views of Boyne Highlands from these 1–3 bedroom condo units.

Weathervane Terrace Hotel. 111 Pine River La., Charlevoix 49720; 547–9955. A 68-room hotel with Jacuzzi, wet bars, kitchenettes, hot tub, and some water beds; views of Lake Michigan.

Inexpensive

Bartley House. Hedrick Rd., Harbor Springs 49740; 526–2183. Right at the foot of a Boyne Highlands chairlift, offering heated pool, saunas, game room, on-premises dining.

Cliff Dweller Lodge. 2724 Boyne Mountain Rd., Boyne Falls 49713; 549–2231. A 52-room lodge with heated outdoor pool, saunas, game room, and on-premises dining.

Best Western of Mackinaw City. 112 Old US 31, Mackinaw City 49701; 436–5544. Offers 60 soundproof rooms sleeping up to 8, with TV, refrigerators.

Golf View Motel. US 31, Petoskey 49770; 347–8281. A 20-room motel only 6 miles from Nub's Nob.

Ramada Inn of Mackinaw. 450 South Nicolet, Mackinaw City 49701; 436–5535. There's an indoor rec center here with pool, sauna, and game room; 164 rooms, plus on-premises dining.

Sundown Motel. 525 W. Mitchell St., US 31, Petoskey 49770; 347–2561. Soundproof rooms, near restaurants and lounges, holds groups of up to 100.

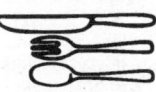 **RESTAURANTS.** Because this is a four-season resort area, there's a collection of fine restaurants, with *Expensive* meals costing $12 and up; *Moderate,* $8–$12; *Inexpensive,* less than $8. Again and again you will find white fish on the menu in both fancy and plain eateries. This is a regional favorite. Try it—you'll like it. American Express, MasterCard, and Visa are widely accepted, but check first, particularly at the inexpensive places.

Expensive

Arboretum. M–119, Lake Shore, Harbor Springs; 526–6291. As the name suggests, a tropical environment with varied menu ranging from fish to lamb.

Boyne Highlands. Hedrick Rd., Harbor Springs; 526–2171. The main dining room offers lobster, when available, and candlelight dinners; overlooking the slopes.

Duffy's of Harbor Springs. Rte. 2, Pleasantview Rd.; 526–2189. Steak and seafood hit the spot here, along with great bread and salad bar; live entertainment in the pub.

The New York. 101 State, Harbor Springs; 526–5901. Since 1904, a Victorian setting with hardwood floors and Tiffany-style lamps. Varied menu.

Stafford's Pier Restaurant. 102 Bay, Harbor Springs; 526–6201. Meals come with soup, salad, and bread, with specialties being steak, seafood, and prime rib.

Walloon Lake Inn. 4178 West St., Walloon Lake; 535–2999. A country inn overlooking the lake, offering gourmet dining with emphasis on fresh local fish.

Moderate

Bootlegger's Cafe. US 131 S, Petoskey; 347–1651. Not one but four dining rooms with the Prohibition-era theme, featuring prime rib and salad bar.

Crow's Nest Restaurant. 4601 N. State Rd., Cross Village; 526–6011. A house-turned-restaurant that still keeps on with home cooking, specializing in seafood and steaks.

Duffy's of Charlevoix. US 31 N, Charlevoix; 547–4021. Kansas beef, frogs legs, and fettuccini Alfredo are among favorites, with an Irish folk singer on call in the pub.

Grey Gables Inn. 308 Belvedere, Charlevoix; 547–9261. Look for elegance in this century-old inn with extensive menu and entertainment nightly (except Mondays).

Holiday Inn, US 131, Petoskey; 347–6041. Seafood buffets Fridays, steak buffets Saturdays, with great views and entertainment nightly.

Inland House. US 31, Conway; 347–8127. Crooked Lake is the vista here, with menu including shrimp, beef, and sandwich specials.

Juilleret's of Petoskey. Jct. US 31/131, Petoskey; 347–7300. Look for whitefish and prime rib here, with nightly specials.

Northwood Restaurant. US 31, Oden; 347–3894. This is the place to come for fish 'n' chips.

Park Garden Cafe. 432 East Lake St., Petoskey; 347–8251. This is the oldest saloon/eatery in town, with tin ceiling and carved walnut bar. Favored by locals and visitors for good food.

Inexpensive

Bar Harbor. 100 State, Harbor Springs; 526–2671. A bar that serves up hamburgers to its hungry customers.

Legs Inn. Lake Shore Dr., Cross Village; 526–5087. A rustic setting where ethnic fare is favored.

Petoskey has a **McDonald's** on US 31 North, and Charlevoix has one on US 31 South. The Petoskey **Big Boy** (347–2931) is located at the corner of US 31 and US 131, and offers takeout service, too.

HOW TO GET AROUND. If you book at one of the mountainside accommodations, a vehicle is hardly necessary. Some of the hotels and other lodgings in the surrounding area may supply **shuttle** service to the slopes. Check when making your reservations. However, it is advised to have access to a **car** in this region for the freedom it offers in dining out or trying your skiing skills at any of the three slopes.

SEASONAL EVENTS. At Nub's Nob a torchlight parade on **New Years Eve** adds a thrilling and romantic glow to the slopes. Boyne Highlands hosts the *National Pro Ski Racing Team* in **January.** Also at that ski area, mid-**March** brings on *Crazy Spring Day Celebration.* At Boyne Mountain there's a *Spring Carnival* right after **St. Patrick's Day** with live entertainment in the afternoons, special bands in the evenings, a costume party, and on-slope events. Similarly, Nub's Nob is festive in March with a *Mardi Gras* that brings out the costumes, contests, and goofy fun.

OTHER SPORTS AND ACTIVITIES. There are outside heated **pools,** 2 outdoor Jacuzzis, and **ice skating** available at Boyne Highlands. Also **sleigh rides** can be arranged through *Sogonosh Stables* in Harbor Springs, 526–5766. The *Little Traverse Racquet Club,* 611 Woodview Dr., Petoskey (347–5450), offers indoor **tennis, racquetball,** and a health spa.

At Boyne Mountain look for an outdoor heated pool, outdoor Jacuzzi, ice skating, and a sauna. Call 549–2441.

At Nub's Nob, there are 9 km of cross-country terrain, with an additional 26 km at Boyne Highlands; 526–2171.

CHILDREN'S ACTIVITIES. Youngsters aged 8 and under can use the rope tow at Boyne Highlands without a lift ticket. Both this resort and Boyne Mountain also take pride in their *Austrian Children's Program* that involves children in lessons, lunch, dinner, and evening activities. The full-day program begins after breakfast and continues until 9 P.M. For ages 3–6 there's a nursery at each resort that operates 9 A.M. to noon, and 1–5 P.M. Babysitters for toddlers can also be arranged.

At Nub's Nob, children 12 years old and under ski free—except holidays, evenings, and weekends. There's no nursery on-premises, but the *Holy Childhood Nursery* on Main St. in Harbor Springs (526–2815) will assist skiers with non-skiing tots.

For any of the on-premises programs, contact the base lodge at each of the three resorts.

 **NIGHTLIFE.** There are live bands weekends at Boyne Mountain's *Day Bar* and nightly in its *Snowflake Lounge.* At Boyne Highlands look for a trio performing six nights a week in the *Slopeside Lounge,* and Warren Miller ski movies two nights a week. Also at Boyne Highlands, from 4–7 P.M. Saturdays the troops are called out to rock 'n' roll.

At the *Holiday Inn,* US 131, Petoskey (347–6041), there's disco entertainment, and the piano reigns supreme at *Grey Gables Inn,* 308 Belvedere, Charlevoix (547–9261), and at the *Perry Davis Hotel* in downtown Petoskey (347–2516).

Sean Ryan, an Irish folk singer, performs regularly at *Duffy's of Charlevoix* on US 31 North (547–4021), while at *Duffy's of Harbor Springs,* Pleasantview Rd. (526–2189), the mood switches to instrumental with a group called the Keel Haulers (four talented musicians) on board.

UPPER PENINSULA

BIG POWDERHORN MOUNTAIN

Bessemer MI 49911
Tel: 906–932–4838

Snow Report: 906–932–4838
Area Vertical: 600 ft.
Number of Trails: 23 or 180
*   skiable acres*
Lifts: 7 double chairs
Snowmaking: 85 percent of
*   terrain*
Season: late November–early April

BLACKJACK

Bessemer MI 49911
Tel: 906–229–5115

Snow Report: 906–229–5115
Area Vertical: 465 ft.
Number of Trails: 16 or 380
*   skiable acres*
Lifts: 4 double chairs, 2 rope tows
Snowmaking: 20 percent of
*   terrain*
Season: late November–March

INDIANHEAD MOUNTAIN

Wakefield MI 49968
Tel: 906–229–5181

Snow Report: 906–229–5181
Area Vertical: 638 ft.
Number of Trails: 15 runs or 130
*   acres*
Lifts: 1 triple chair, 1 quadruple
*   chair, 2 double chairs, 3 T-bars*
Snowmaking: 90 percent of
*   terrain*
Season: late November–early April

WHITECAP MOUNTAIN

Box D, Montreal WI 54550
Tel: 715–561–2227

Snow report: 715–561–2227
Area Vertical: 400 ft.
Number of Trails: 32 or 450
*   skiable acres*
Lifts: 1 quadruple chair, 4
*   double chairs, 2 rope tows*
Snowmaking: 50 percent of
*   terrain*
Season: Thanksgiving–early April

Blackjack is a mile as the crow flies from Indianhead, and Big Powderhorn is only 5 miles away. These three ski areas and a fourth, Whitecap in nearby Montreal, Wisconsin, comprise a group called Ski the Summit located on the western tip of the Upper Peninsula of Michigan. The region is characterized by rugged hills with wilderness forest near Lake Superior's south shore.

Because of its northern location, the area's residents resemble their Canadian neighbors in speech characteristics, although the region is strongly ethnic with a blend of Finns, Italians, and Slavs who came decades earlier to work the iron and copper mines.

The romance of the territory was captured in Edna Thurber's novel about the lumber industry, *Come and Get It,* and some old-timers still recall the roaring '20s when Al Capone and his brother ran a hotel in the area and there were almost as many bars as residents on Silver Street in Hurley, still the place for après-ski action with 28 bars for the population of 2,200.

The region's ski areas attract Chicago, Milwaukee, and Minneapolis-St. Paul skiers. "Thank God Wisconsin is flat," says an Indianhead spokesman who cherishes the Milwaukee market.

Because of the snowbelt that hugs the lake's south shore, the region gets reliably heavy snowfalls averaging 211 inches a year. However, snowmaking is also used at all the areas. Once on the mountains, skiers discover they're actually on a ridgeline facing west and looking out toward Lake Superior beyond the Ottawa National Forest.

The four resorts offer interchangeable lift tickets and naturally share their lodging and dining facilities with each other.

For more information on any of the areas, contact the *Upper Peninsula Travel and Recreation Association,* P.O. Box 400, Iron Mountain, MI 49801; 906–774–5480. Also of assistance to skiers is the *Ironwood Chamber of Commerce,* 100 East Aurora St., Ironwood, MI 49938; 906–932–1122.

Practical Information for
the Upper Peninsula Areas

HOW TO GET THERE. By car. These resorts are all reachable via US 2, an east-west highway in Michigan's Upper Peninsula which leads off I–75, the major north-south highway, just north of the Mackinaw Bridge. From Wisconsin, US 2, is reached via US 141, leading north from Green Bay. Big Powderhorn Mountain is located off US 4, 3 miles from Bessemer; Indianhead is 1½ miles from Wakefield; Blackjack is 6 miles east of Ironwood; and Whitecap is 18 miles west of Ironwood. Look for signs for each turn-off.

By air. There is regularly scheduled service via *Simmons Airlines* (932–5808) and *Midstate Aviation* (800–825–0522) into the Ironwood Airport from St. Paul and Chicago airports. Each ski area provides **shuttle** service for its guests.

By bus. *Greyhound* provides service to the Ironwood bus depot (932–4221) from Wisconsin and Illinois; *Four Star Bus Lines,* from Minneapolis-St. Paul; and *Wisconsin-Michigan Trailways,* from Wisconsin, Michigan, and Minnesota.

TELEPHONES. The area code for the three Michigan mountains is 906, and for the Whitecap Mountain area it is 715.

ACCOMMODATIONS. There are lodging operations connected with all 4 mountains. They are *Big Powderhorn Lodging Association,* Powderhorn Rd., Bessemer, MI 49911 (906–932–3100), servicing 3,000 beds within 1½ miles of the mountain, mainly in chalets and condominiums; *Blackjack Lodging Reservation Inc.,* Blackjack Rd., Bessemer 49911 (906–229–5157), servicing 290 beds, mostly condominiums; *Whitecap Mountain Management Co.,* Box E, Montreal, WI 54550 (715–561–2776), servicing an estimated 500 slopeside beds, mostly condominiums with some motel units; and *Indianhead Reservations,* Indianhead Mountain, Wakefield, MI 49968 (906–229–5181), servicing a combination of chalets and lodge rooms.

Because of the mix of lodging available, mountainside accommodation can be considered inexpensive to upper moderate, predicated mostly on number of people per unit.

Expensive in this region is $70 and up per room per night, with *Moderate* $40–$70, and *Inexpensive,* less than $40.

Expensive

Powdermill Inn. Off US 2, Bessemer 49911; 906–932–0880. This is an A-frame, chalet-type building built of logs and glass, and rooms offering access to indoor swimming, whirlpool, sauna, restaurant and game room.

Moderate

Circle Hills Resort. Rte. 513, Ironwood 49938; 906–932–3857. Luxury condominium living includes access to indoor pool, restaurant, and lounge.

Hiawatha Lodging. US 2, Ironwood 49938; 906–932–5416. This is a lodging referral service offering a variety of establishments with some including health spa and swimming amenities.

Haven North Condos. Off Hwy. 51, Hurley, WI 54534; 715–561–5626. Completely furnished 1–3-bedroom condos with fully equipped kitchens, cable TV, maid service, fireplaces; access to indoor swimming and saunas at Holiday Inn across the street.

Holiday Inn. Off Hwy. 51, Hurley, WI 54534; 715–561–3030. Offers indoor recreation center with pool, whirlpool, saunas, exercise equipment, restaurant, and lounge; snowmobile trails out front door.

Rainbow Motel & Chalets. Rtes. 64 and 107, Silver City 49953; 906–885–5329. Housekeeping units include color TV, with access to sauna, spa, exercise room, and Jacuzzi.

Towne House Motor Inn. Half-block off business Rte. 2, Ironwood 49938; 906–667–0243. A downtown location with weekend entertainment, restaurant, lounge; some king size beds; newest facility in town.

Inexpensive

Armata Motel. US 2, Ironwood 49938; 906–932–4421; 12 ground floor units with color TV, tubs and showers; car plug-ins.

Best Western Cloverland. US 2, Ironwood 49938; 906–932–1260. A popular place but doesn't take any ski reservations until after Nov. 1.

Crestview Motel. US 2, Ironwood 49938; 906–932–4845. In-room coffee, cable TV, and free use of sauna come with rooms.

Davey's Motel. US 2, Ironwood 49938; 906–932–2020. 24 motel and housekeeping units, color TV, daily family rates, and special welcome to snowmobilers.

Hedgerow Lodging. US 2, Bessemer 49911; 906–663–6950. Individual A-frame chalets with kitchens.

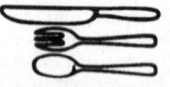 **RESTAURANTS.** Whether you dine in Michigan or in Wisconsin, you can expect fine German and Scandinavian dining rooms serving fresh fish from the abundance of waterways in this region. Restaurant price categories are: *Expensive,* $12 and up; *Moderate,* $8–$12; and *Inexpensive,* under $8. The price is an average cost for one meal for one person, excluding drinks, tax, and tip.

Expensive

Carlin Club. Presque Isle, WI; 715–686–2255. People come here for the German motif, carried out in both the menu and the decor.

Powdermill Inn. Powderhorn Road, Bessemer; 906–932–0800. A copper-and-stone fireplace, cathedral ceilings, and lots of glass add character to the inn that offers a full menu specializing in steaks.

Moderate

Alpen Inn. Big Powderhorn Mountain; 906–667–0211. A country setting on the side of a ski trail; diners can choose from a full menu and watch the night skiers schussing down the trails under the lights.

Blackjack Inn. Blackjack Mountain; 906–229–5115. Warm paneling adds coziness to this inn that faces the slopes; family fare is the menu's theme.

Branding Iron. Silver St., Hurley, WI; 715–932–3425. Grill your own steaks here, or they'll do it for you.

Caribou Lodge. Big Powderhorn Mountain; 906–932–4838. A salad bar and buffet are the draw here, in addition to action on the slopes.

China Sea Palace. US 2, Superior House; 906–932–5744. This is a hexagon-shaped log building that serves up Chinese specialties.

Circle Hills Resort. Rte. 513, Ironwood; 906–932–3857. This is a small restaurant, with lounge, that offers a full menu.

Connie's Supper Club. Silver St., Hurley, WI; 715–561–9807. Italian specialties are the draw here, as well as steaks.

Liberty Bell Chalet. Half-block off Main St., Hurley, WI; 715–561–3753. Caesar salad, Italian offerings, and the ubiquitous pizza are musts here.

The Lodge Restaurant. Off US 2, Indianhead; 906–229–5181. There are great buffets, fish fries, and ethnic fare here.

Snowflake. Big Powderhorn Mountain; 906–932–4838. The Wednesday smorgasbord is popular; a full menu offered other nights.

Towne House Motor Inn. Suffolk St., Ironwood; 906–932–2101. Red and black is the motif here, with a lounge, salad bar, and special nights focusing on Mexican cuisine and surf and turf.

Inexpensive

Angelo's Pizza. Rte. 2, Ironwood; 906–932–2424. Deep-pan pizza give this place a name.

Don & GG's. US 2, Ironwood; 906–932–2312. A lounge that serves pub fare, including hearty sandwiches.

Grampa Tony's. US 2, Ironwood; 906–932–0596. Lots of food is the order of the day; great for families who love Italian spices.

Windjammer. Silver St., Hurley, WI; 715–561–9800. The lounge here is shaped like a ship; the food is American and Italian.

HOW TO GET AROUND. A **car** is a necessity in the region. However, some lodging establishments, particularly those at the mountains, may furnish **shuttle** service. Check when making your reservations.

SEASONAL EVENTS. A regional calendar features *New Years torchlight parades* on **December 31** at Big Powderhorn, Blackjack and Whitecap, *winter carnivals* in mid-**January** at Blackjack and Whitecap, followed by *spring carnivals* in early **March** at these two areas. **St. Patrick's Day** is big at both as well.

OTHER SPORTS AND ACTIVITIES. The *Indianhead Health & Racquet Club* (906–229–5151) offers an indoor **pool, racquetball,** Nautilus, aerobics, tanning bed, and sauna. **Sleigh rides** are also available at the Indianhead lodge.

At Big Powderhorn Mountain look for an indoor pool and saunas, an **ice skating** rink, and **sleigh ride.** Whitecap has a heated and lighted indoor **tennis** court.

Cross-country skiing abounds in this region, with 30 km of groomed trails at Big Powderhorn, accessed by a free shuttle from the mountain. Whitecap has 20 km of trails, and Blackjack has 32 km. For additional information on cross-country skiing, call *Michigan Tourist Information,* 906–932–3330. NASTAR is offered at all four ski areas.

Snowmobiling is also popular in the region, and Michigan Tourist Information can provide specifics on where trails are maintained and marked.

Ice skating is also offered at Indianhead and at the community college in Ironwood, 906–932–0602.

HINTS TO THE HANDICAPPED. Free use of equipment, lessons, and lift tickets are available at Indianhead (906–229–5181) to amputees and the blind. In fact, there's an amputee on the resort's ski patrol who works with the handicapped in between patrol duties. Big Powderhorn (906–932–4838) also offers free skiing to the handicapped, and Blackjack (906–229–5115) has an instructional program for the visually impaired.

DAY-CARE FACILITIES. At Indianhead there's *Kinderschule,* which includes all-day babysitting and lunch for ages 2½ and up, with ski lessons available for ages 4–7. The hours are 9 A.M. to 4 P.M. Two nights a week, there's also a special evening children's program.

They call it *Kinderschool Program* at Big Powderhorn Mountain, with babysitting for ages 2 and up and lessons for ages 4 and up.

At Blackjack, a *Kinderkamp Nursery* offers free child care to ages 2 and up when parents purchase lift tickets. Evening babysitting is also available to Blackjack lodging guests. A *Kinderschool Program* is also available at Whitecap.

Contact the base lodge at each of the ski areas for information and reservations.

NIGHTLIFE. There's plenty of après-ski activity in the region, with a number of establishments offering dancing and entertainment. These include: *Alpen Inn* at Big Powderhorn Mountain, 906–667–0211; *Booby Hatch,* 2 blocks off US 2, Bessemer, 906–663–4694; *Branding Iron,* Silver St., Hurley, WI, 906–932–3425; *Caribou Lodge,* Big Powderhorn Mountain, 906–932–4714; *China Sea Palace,* US 2, Superior House, 906–932–9839.

A favorite place of the young crowd is *Horse's Corral,* Silver St., Hurley, WI; 715–561–9945. Live bands play at *Towne House* on Suffolk St., Ironwood; 906–932–2101.

There's also music aplenty at *Dudley's Saloon* at Indianhead Mountain, 906–229–5181; *Logger's Lounge* at Blackjack Mountain, 906–229–5115; *Powdermill Inn,* Bessemer, 906–932–0800; *Ski High* at Indianhead Mountain, 906–229–5181; *Snowflake* at Big Powderhorn Mountain, 906–932–4838; and *The Vertical Drop,* Indianhead Mountain, 906–229–5181.

Minnesota

LUTSEN MOUNTAIN

Box 128
Lutsen MN 55612
Tel: 218–663–7281

Snow Report: 218–663–7281
Area Vertical: 1,008 ft.
Number of Trails: 27 or 200
*   skiable acres*
Lifts: 3 double chairs, 1 poma
*   lift, 1 T-bar*
Snowmaking: 70 percent of skiable
*   terrain*
Season: Thanksgiving–April

Lutsen, located on the north shore of Lake Superior, is the largest ski area in mid-America, spread over 1,500 acres and incorporating four large mountains.

These are Ullr, with runs for beginning and intermediate skiers; Eagle Mountain, with extra-long runs and spectacular views of Lake Superior and the surrounding wilderness; Mystery Mountain, with a summit chalet and mile-plus runs; and Moose Mountain, offering the most challenging terrain and the area's greatest vertical drop.

The mountains themselves rise 1,000 and more vertical feet above the shore of the world's largest fresh-water body, Lake Superior. The views from the summit span hundreds of miles of blue water contrasting with the rocky coast of Minnesota's North Shore. The Superior National Forest, a wilderness area with moose, bear, and timber wolves, borders the ski area.

The base-of-mountain village includes a total of 88 condominiums and a recreation area; and all along the Lake Superior shore are a variety of lodges and condominiums offering accommodations, food, and entertainment.

Because of proximity to Lake Superior and its peculiar climatic conditions, the area receives twice the natural snowfall of inland areas of northeastern Minnesota, and by early December most of the mountain's trails are also assisted by an efficient snowmaking system drawing water from the scenic Poplar River that roars by through gorges and over falls and rapids.

Practical Information for Lutsen Mountain

 **HOW TO GET THERE.** Lutsen Mountain is located 1 mile from the town of Lutsen on Minnesota's North Shore of Lake Superior. It is 90 miles northeast of Duluth and about 75 miles south of the Canadian border. It is some 240 miles north of Minneapolis–St. Paul.

By car. From Minneapolis–St. Paul, take I–35 north to Duluth; follow Superior St. through Duluth to 10th Ave. E.; turn right 1 block to London Rd. which becomes US 61; follow 61 to Lutsen, then take County Rd. 36, left, to Lutsen Mountain.

TELEPHONES. The area code for northern Minnesota is 218.

 **ACCOMMODATIONS.** Both on-mountain and all along Hwy. 61 bordering Lake Superior's North Shore, there is a variety of accommodations in this region. Condominiums can be a bit pricey, but the cost can be kept down if shared by more than two people. Categories in this selection, determined by price, are *Expensive*, $70–$225 per night, depending on the size of the unit; *Moderate*, $30–$70; *Inexpensive*, less than $30.

Expensive

Blue Fin Bay on Lake Superior. US 61, Tofte 55615; 663–7227. Located on a point jutting out into Lake Superior, offering lakeside motel units and townhouses; restaurant and lounge.

Chateau LeVeaux Condominium Resort & Motor Inn. US 61, Tofte 55615; 663–7223. Motel units and housekeeping condos with fireplaces; pool, whirlpool, sauna, game room.

Sea Villas. US 61, Lutsen 55612; 663–7212. Luxury condominiums right on Lake Superior and part of Lutsen Resort. Private lakeside decks offer spectacular views of lake.

The Village at Lutsen Mountains. County Rd. 36, Lutsen 55612; 663–7241. Nestled in the valley of Lutsen Mountains ski area, efficiency–3-bedroom housekeeping condominiums offer ski in, ski out convenience to both cross-country and alpine facilities; pool, whirlpool, fireplaces.

Gull Harbor Condominiums. US 61, Tofte 55615; 663–7205. Luxury condominiums on a cliff overlooking Lake Superior; sauna and whirlpool.

Moderate

Aspenwood Resort-Motel. US 61, Tofte 55615; 663–7978. European and housekeeping plans available in complex that includes whirlpool, sauna, game room, homemade pizza shop, and lounge.

Cascade Lodge. US 61, Grand Marais 55604; 387–1112. Main lodge and log cabins with fireplaces overlooking Lake Superior and surrounded by Cascade River State Park; cross-country trails nearby; housekeeping and MAP available.

Hungry Jack Lodge. Gunflint Trail, Grand Marais 55604; 388–9979. A log lodge with game room and lounge, offering lakefront rustic but fully modern cabins; housekeeping and MAP plans available, with family style meals served in the fireside dining room; sauna, cross-country skiing, and snowmobile routes.

Lutsen Resort. US 61, Lutsen 55612; 663–7212. A rustic, old-lodge atmosphere right on Lake Superior, with pool, whirlpool, saunas, recreation room, dining room, lounge, cross-country trails; housekeeping and MAP plans available.

Nor'wester Lodge. Gunflint Trail, Grand Marais 55604; 388–2252. Housekeeping cabins near snowmobile and cross-country trails; dining room on premises, and housekeeping and MAP and American meal plans available.

Solbakken Resort. US 61, Lutsen 55612; 663–7566. Secluded housekeeping cabins nestled on Lake Superior's shore offering spacious lake homes with fireplace, and economical kitchenette motel units; access to cross-country trails.

Thomsonite Beach. US 61, Lutsen 55612; 387–1532. Small and large luxury housekeeping apartments and guest house with fireplaces, decks, and kitchens; plus motel units, all nestled on shore of Lake Superior with access to cross-country trails.

Inexpensive

Bear Track's Bally Creek Camp. US 61, Grand Marais 55604; 387–1162. Bunk-style cabins styled after old logging camps, but rustic and tastefully nestled in woods, offering lodge-to-lodge skiing with 125 miles of groomed cross-country trails out the door; saunas.

Bearskin Lodge. Gunflint Trail, Grand Marais 55604; 388–2292. Secluded lakefront cabins and 3-bedroom housekeeping lodges with fireplaces; main lodge offers family-style meals and sauna; access to cross-country skiing.

Best Western Superior Inn. US 61, Grand Marais 55604; 387–2240. Modern units located right on the harbor, in town.

Best Western Cliff Dweller. US 61, Lutsen 55612; 663–7273. One-bedroom units overlooking Lake Superior, with restaurant.

Fenstad's Resort. US 61, Little Marais 55604; 226–4724. Housekeeping lakeshore cabins on the beach and rocky shoreline; fireplaces and kitchens; groomed cross-country trails outside door.

Golden Eagle Lodge. Gunflint Trail, Grand Marais 55604; 388–2203. A family resort offering modern but secluded lakeshore housekeeping cabins with fireplace stoves, on groomed and tracked cross-country trails; sauna, food shop. Two cabins are handicap accessible and barrier-free.

Gunflint Lodge. Gunflint Trail, Grand Marais 55604; 388–2294. Family-oriented northwoods resort near cross-country skiing.

East Bay Hotel. US 61, Grand Marais 55604; 387–2800. Located right on the bay in downtown Grand Marais; on-premises restaurant and bar.

Sandgren Motel. US 61 Grand Marais 55604; 387–2975. Motel units right in town.

Shoreline Motel. Broadway, Grand Marais 55604; 387–2633. A multi-story motel located on the bay downtown; great views.

Sugar Beach Resort. US 61 Tofte 55615; 663–7595. Housekeeping cabins, some with fireplaces; near Lake Superior.

Turner's Skyport Lodge. Devil's Track Lake, Grand Marais 55604; 387–1411. A family resort with combination modern motel units and housekeeping cabins; full-menu restaurant; on-premises cross-country skiing, snowmobiling, ice fishing, and skating.

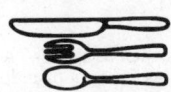 **RESTAURANTS.** Dining out in this region is still reasonably easy on the pocketbook. Most restaurants offer American fare, with a regional favorite being fresh fish hauled in from Lake Superior. Restaurants are listed here by price category. *Expensive:* $10–$16; *Moderate:* $5–$10; *Inexpensive:* less than $5. MasterCard and Visa are accepted at those in the expensive and moderate categories.

Expensive

Blue Fin Bay Restaurant. US 61 Tofte; 663–7227. Fine dining on a point jutting out into Lake Superior; varied menu with sandwiches available in the Bridge Bar.

Lutsen Resort Dining Room. US 61, Lutsen; 663–7212. Right on Lake Superior; fine dining in a beautiful lodge atmosphere, varied menu.

Moderate

Cascade Lodge Restaurant. US 61, Grand Marais; 387–1112. A superb view of Lake Superior from the popular, full-service dining establishment offering extensive American menu.

Grand Marais Common Ground. US 61, Grand Marais; 387–2193. Fine dining in a rustic atmosphere, offering Lake Superior fish, ribs, steaks, and bakery; cocktails and lake-view dancing with live entertainment.

Harbor Light Supper Club. US 61, Grand Marais; 387–1142. A full service supper club offering dancing with live music on weekends, imported wines and liquor, varied menu.

Upper Deck Restaurant. US 61, Grand Marais; 387–1597. A full-service restaurant offering American menu; located on the harbor with great view of Lake Superior.

Inexpensive

Best Western Cliff Dweller Restaurant. US 61, Lutsen; 663–7848. Good food in a warm but casual atmosphere, family dining overlooking Lake Superior.

Lutsen Mountains Chalet Cafeteria. County Rd. 36, Lutsen; 663–7281. Breakfast and lunch for skiers, including sandwiches, chili, soups, hamburgers, and beverages.

Sven & Ole's Pizza. 9 W. Wisconsin, Grand Marais; 387–1713. Pizza in a Norwegian atmosphere, also sandwiches, salads and soups, available for both sit-down or takeout.

HOW TO GET AROUND. Access to a **car** is a necessity in this region. Some of the lodging establishments, however, may supply **shuttle** service to the mountain. Check when making reservations.

 **SEASONAL EVENTS.** The annual *Cindy Nelson Cup* downhill ski race is held in early **January.** This event has been hosted by the George Nelson family since 1977 in honor of their daughter, the area's most renowned international ski racer and an Olympics bronze medal winner.

In the annual *Koo Koo Can-Am Speed Skiing Race,* held in mid-**winter,** downhill skiing speeds of more than 70 mph are reached as competitors ski in an all-out tuck from top to bottom of Koo Koo run on Eagle Mountain.

The *Moose Mountain Downhill,* held in early **March,** is the only professional downhill race in the Midwest.

 OTHER SPORTS AND ACTIVITIES. The 35-km Lutsen Mountains Trail System (**cross-country**) connects with the 200-km North Shore Trail System. With a Norpine ticket, cross-country skiers can ride the chairlifts to the summits and ski down for miles. The *Grand Marais Municipal Pool,* Tourist Park (US 61), is an Olympic-size indoor **pool.**

HINTS TO THE HANDICAPPED. The Moose Mountain Downhill Race, an annual event, accommodates handicapped skiers with a special division for them. For information, contact the main lodge, 663–7281.

DAY-CARE FACILITIES. *Kinder School* (663–7281) is open to ages 3–7 and is offered on weekends and holidays. The program includes 5 hours of indoor and outdoor play, with a minimum of 2 hours instruction by a ski school instructor specially trained to teach children.

 **NIGHTLIFE.** US 61 reverberates on weekends when the musicians come to town, although they hang around nightly at the *Grand Marais Common Ground* (387–2193), with everything from jazz to country and rock 'n' roll.

The *Harbor Light Supper Club* in Grand Marais (387–1142), offers music for dancing that includes country rock and swing. The *Dockside* at Lutsen Resort in Lutsen (663–7212), plays a variety of recorded music to woo guests to a lighted dance floor. Lutsen Mountain's *Chalet Bar* (663–7281) brings in variety entertainment and specializes in rock 'n' roll.

For those seeking a quiet background-music atmosphere, the *Bridge Bar* at the Blue Fin Bay Restaurant in Tofte (663–7227), features duos and soloists and lots of folk music.

WESTERN UNITED STATES

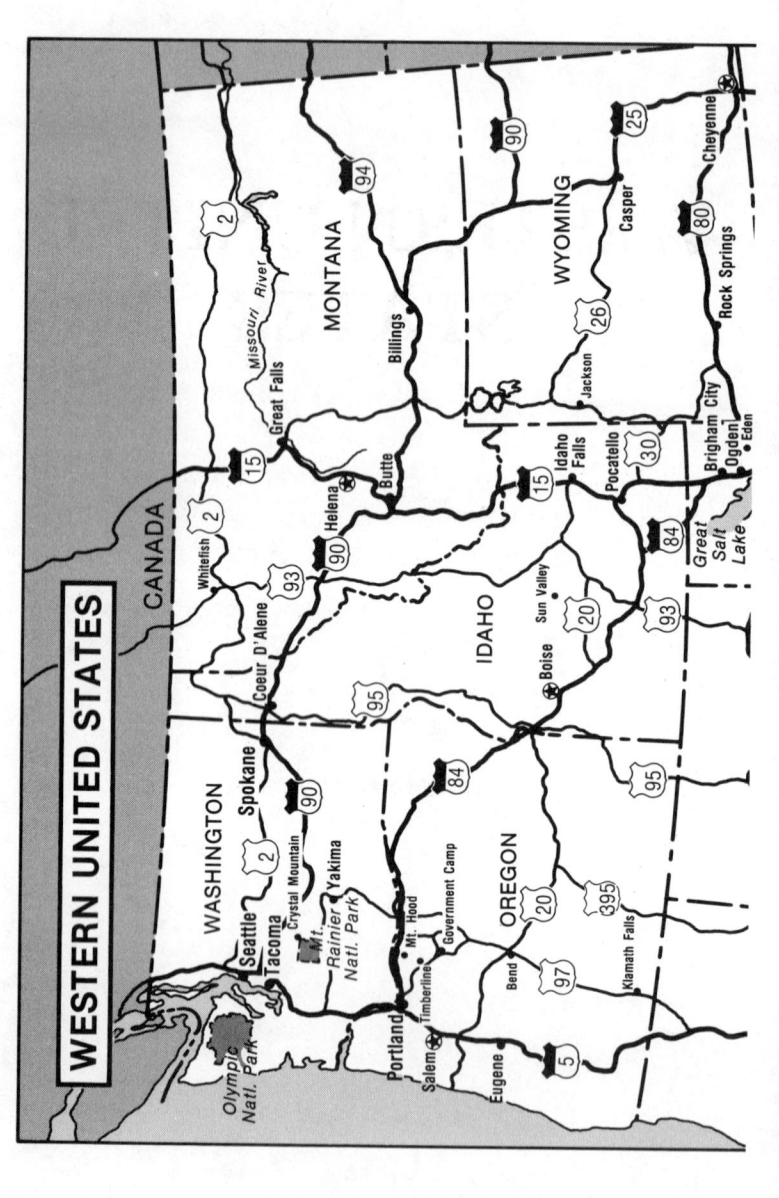

WESTERN UNITED STATES

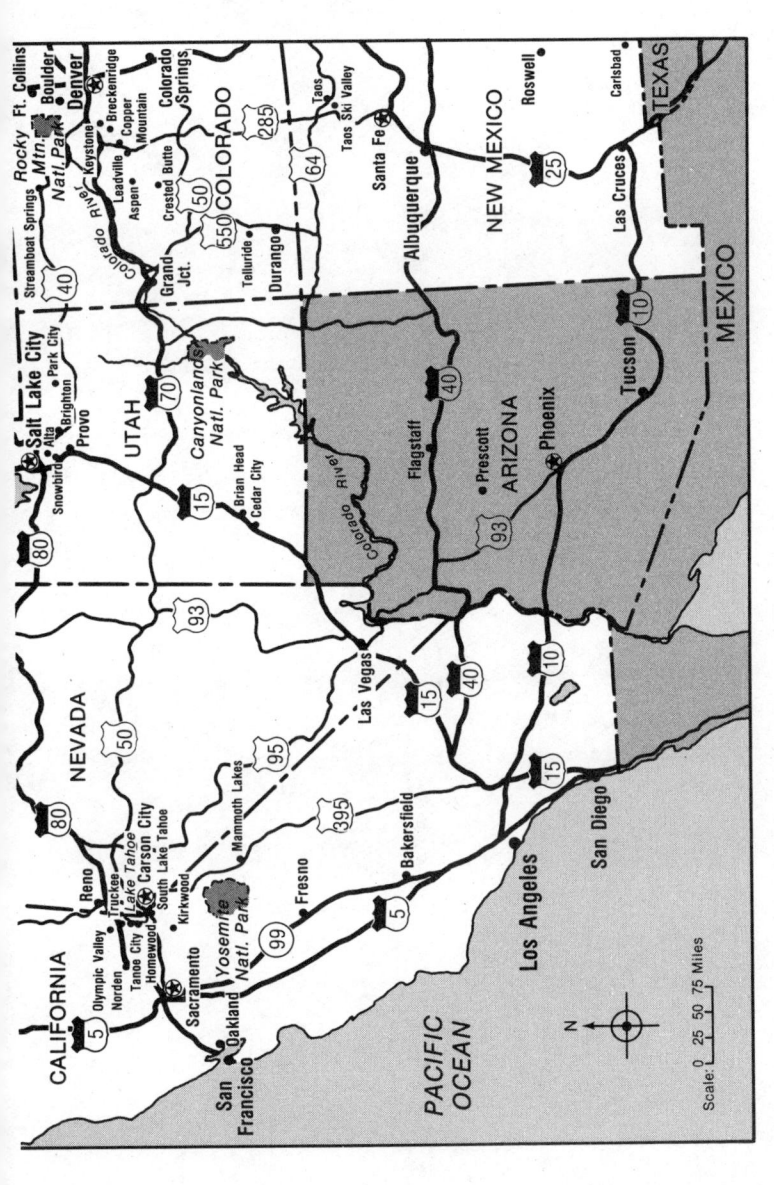

WESTERN UNITED STATES

by
DIANA HUNT

Diana Hunt writes for national and Rocky Mountain publications and is a member of the U.S. Ski Writers Association, Aviation/Space Writers Association, and Colorado Press Women. She has been editor for Pam Am's in-flight Clipper *magazine.*

The Rocky Mountain West offers the best skiing in the world. That is a grandiose claim to live up to, but difficult to dispute.

Certainly Europe has the ambience, the excitement of something different, the possibility of skiing from town to town and even country to country via enormous ski "circuses." Eastern Canada has a French flavor; South America, New Zealand, and Australia the lure of summer skiing. But only the Rockies (and this includes the Canadian Rockies) have consistent snow conditions. When you plan a ski vacation, you know you will have something to ski on. Snow depths here are measured in feet rather than inches. Yes, snow depths vary, but even in years with "low" snowfall, the Rocky Mountains are superior to just about any place in the world.

The snow is also the driest you'll find anywhere. Because the storms travel from the Pacific, over the Sierra Mountain Range and across deserts before hitting the barrier of the Rocky Mountains, much of the moisture has already been taken out. The resulting snowfall creates the famed "champagne powder" the Rocky Mountain resorts love to talk about—fluffy, light stuff that floats away from your skis.

Guest facilities are among the best in the world, particularly in world-class resorts such as Sun Valley, Aspen, Vail, Deer Valley, and

Beaver Creek. Mountain chic is the in look, featuring massive stone fireplaces, cedar wood walls, decor in forest green, mountain sky blue, leaded crystal. Swimming pools and hot tubs are de rigueur. Unlike the fine hostelries of Europe, however, guests can feel comfortable coming to dinner dressed as casually or as elegantly as they wish. Of all the ski resorts in the United States, only The Lodge in Sun Valley requires a tie and jacket for weekend dining.

Activities other than skiing are plentiful and becoming more so. Vacationers will find everything from dog sledding to hot air ballooning to roller skating, tennis, or ice skating.

The resorts vary so widely in style that there is at least one ski area to appeal to everyone. Colorado and Utah boast the most sophisticated resorts in terms of guest and mountain facilities.

If it's glamor you're looking for, put on your Bogner outfit and trip the light fantastic in Deer Valley, Aspen, Vail, or Beaver Creek. The patriarch of them all in the glamor category, however, is Sun Valley, Idaho. If it is old-fashioned hard skiing with a European touch of atmosphere, go to Taos or Alta. If it's just plain hard skiing, stay in Jackson Hole. You want diversity? Go to Lake Tahoe in California, offering 22 ski areas, countless gambling tables, and big name entertainment. Here you can ski both California and Nevada in the same day, this country's closest version to the Swiss-Italian ski crossing.

You like the vast ski circuses of Europe? Try Utah's Interconnect. Do you want to stay in a city and have a choice of ski areas or other activities? Make reservations in Salt Lake City, Utah, or Reno. A huge mountain? Go to Mammoth Mountain in California or Vail, Colorado. Sun and ski? Colorado, Utah, New Mexico, or California record the greatest percentage of sunshine during the winter months.

A quiet retreat with quality service? Stay at Beaver Creek, Colorado, Sun Valley, Idaho, or Deer Valley, Utah. A quiet retreat for a low-key and low-budget vacations? Then head for Grand Targhee, Wyoming, or Winter Park or Telluride, Colorado. If a lively singles scene is on your agenda, go to Aspen or the Lake Tahoe area. A family vacation where the kids and parents can each ski at their own ability level or ski together? Snowmass and Breckenridge in Colorado or Park City in Utah. Steep and Deep? Snowbird and Alta in Utah, Jackson Hole, Wyoming, Taos, New Mexico, or Squaw Valley, California. Perfect grooming conditions without the surprises of moguls or catwalks? Then it is Deer Valley, Keystone, or parts of Copper Mountain for you. To soak up that Western flavor, head for Steamboat Springs or Purgatory in Colorado or Jackson Hole, Wyoming.

Lodging prices in this section are quoted for a regular winter season. Add about 15 percent for Christmas holidays and deduct 15 percent for the low season prior to Christmas and after March.

California

HEAVENLY VALLEY

P.O. Box AT
South Lake Tahoe CA 95705
Tel: 916–541–1330

Snow Report: 916–541–SKII
Area Vertical: California—3,600 ft.
Nevada—2,900 ft.
Number of Trails: over 20 square
  miles
Lifts: 1 aerial tramway, 6
  triple chairs, 10 double
  chairs, 9 surface lifts
Snowmaking: 30 percent of
  area
Season: mid-November to mid-May

Unique among ski areas, Heavenly lies in two states—California and Nevada. In terms of skiable acreage, it is the largest ski area in North America with 9 peaks, multi-mile runs, and an amazing 3,600-foot vertical drop. It is a balanced mix of half intermediate, one-quarter beginner, and one-quarter expert terrain. It is often called the "upside-down" mountain because most of the beginner and intermediate terrain is located at upper elevations—a treat for those who don't usually get a chance to ski or see the view from the summit. There are well-groomed runs, wide-open bowls, and timbered glades. Mott Canyon, on the Nevada side, is an ungroomed run with lots of trees and cliffs to test out the experts' abilities. The ski area stretches along the south shore of what has been called the most beautiful alpine lake in the world.

If all this beauty is too much and you feel the need of concrete beneath your boots, Reno, South Lake Tahoe, and Lake Tahoe are not far away for 24-hour après-ski diversion. On top of that, summer is high season in the gaming casinos. Wintertime prices to lure skiers to the tables and entertainment are ridiculously low by Colorado or Utah standards. You can get a dinner special for the price of one drink in the glitzy spas of Vail, Aspen, and Deer Valley.

However, even paradise has its flaws—San Franciscans relentlessly pursuing their pleasures blanket the entire area on weekends. The base lodges on the California side are usually crowded, but the Nevada day lodges are rarely so jammed. It is worth the steep road to the Nevada side for shorter lines and more ski runs.

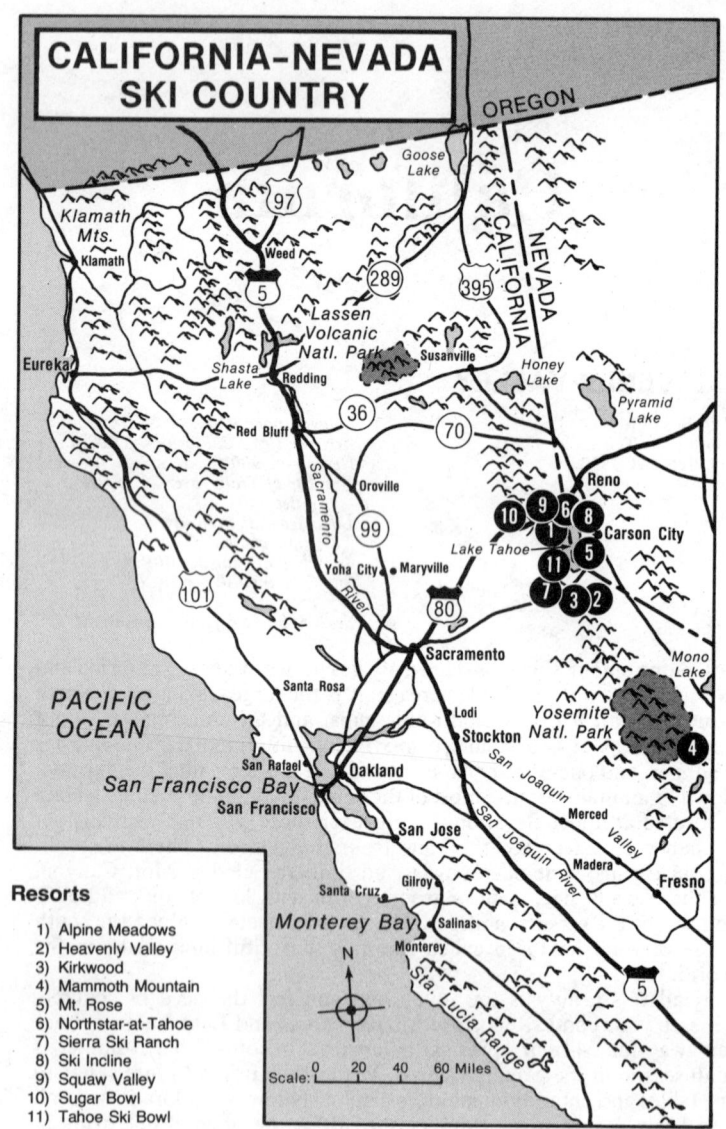

CALIFORNIA–NEVADA SKI COUNTRY

Resorts

1) Alpine Meadows
2) Heavenly Valley
3) Kirkwood
4) Mammoth Mountain
5) Mt. Rose
6) Northstar-at-Tahoe
7) Sierra Ski Ranch
8) Ski Incline
9) Squaw Valley
10) Sugar Bowl
11) Tahoe Ski Bowl

Practical Information for Heavenly Valley

HOW TO GET THERE. By air. *Air Cal,* 702–323–6060, serves South Lake Tahoe airport from major California cities. It is a short drive to the ski area via taxi, rental car, or bus. Reno's Cannon International Airport is 55 miles from Heavenly, and is served by major national and international airlines. *LTR Stagelines* has daily scheduled **bus** service between the Reno airport and South Lake Tahoe hotels, motels, and casinos. Call 702–588–6633 for schedules and fare information. Rental cars are also available.

By bus. *Greyhound Bus Lines* has 12 daily buses between South Lake Tahoe and San Francisco; 14 daily buses between Reno and San Francisco. The Lake Tahoe terminal can be reached at 916–544–2241.

By car. Heavenly is 180 miles east of San Francisco via I–80 to Sacramento, then US 50 to South Lake Tahoe. Reno is approximately 75 minutes away via US 395 and 50.

Skiers can rely on the *Skier's Shuttle* bus which operates from most South Lake Tahoe locations to Heavenly's California and Nevada base facilities. One way fare is $1. For more information call *City Bus Information,* 916–544–2266. Some casino hotels have complimentary 24-hour shuttles to the ski areas.

TELEPHONES. The area code for the Heavenly Valley area is 916; for all of Nevada it is 702.

ACCOMMODATIONS. Heavenly Central Reservations can book lodging in many of the major hotels with casinos, lodges, and condos; call 702–588–4584. Buses pick up skiers from Heavenly, Kirkwood, and Sierra Ski Ranch. For motel or hotel reservations for any of the 10,000 rooms in the South Lake Tahoe area, call the Visitors Bureau, 800–822–5922 in California and 800–824–5150 outside California. For a free travel planner, write South Lake Tahoe Visitors Bureau, P.O. Box 17727, South Lake Tahoe CA 95706.

Hotel rates are based on double occupancy. Categories, determined by price, are: *Expensive:* $50 and up (includes all casino hotels, with some starting at $90); *Moderate:* $40–$50 weekends and $30–$40 midweek; *Inexpensive:* $30–$40 weekends and $25–$30 midweek. For accommodations on the north shore of Lake Tahoe, see sections on Tahoe and Reno.

Caesars Tahoe. *Expensive.* P.O. Box 5800, Stateline NV 89449; 702–588–3515 or 800–648–3353. The most recent addition to the gaming scene. Opulent facilities, lavish rooms, top-name entertainment, decadent appointments. For show information, call 800–648–7469.

Harrah's Tahoe. *Expensive.* P.O. Box 8, Stateline NV 89449; 702–588–6611 or 800–648–3773. Has a worldwide reputation for quality and service; the sound-proofed accommodations are elegant; there's even a choice of pillows.

Harvey's Resort. *Expensive.* P.O. Box 128, Stateline NV 89449; 702–588–2411 or 800–648–3361. The first gaming property at Lake Tahoe and now the largest.

Matterhorn Motel. *Moderate.* P.O. Box 7277, South Lake Tahoe CA 95731; 916–541–0367. European charm, quiet, suites available, central location.

Tahoe Beach and Ski Club. *Moderate.* P.O. Box 1267, South Lake Tahoe CA 95705; 800–822–5962. Remodeled in oak and tile; condos have hot tubs, kitchens, heated pool.

Walley's Hot Springs. *Moderate.* P.O. Box 26, Genoa NV 89411; 702–782–8155 or 702–833–6556. Bed and breakfast cottages; use of mineral springs, swimming pool; good restaurant; 20 minutes from Heavenly Valley.

Lazy S Lodge. *Inexpensive.* P.O. Box 7676, South Lake Tahoe CA 95731; 916–541–0230. Quiet cottages, studios, spa, central to ski areas.

7–11 Motel. *Inexpensive.* P.O. Box 153, South Lake Tahoe CA 95705; 916–544–3640. At the foot of Heavenly Valley, a block from the lake; free casino bus.

South Lake Tahoe American Youth Hostel. *Inexpensive.* 1043 Martin St.; 916–544–3834. Family units with kitchens and fireplaces; free shuttle bus to casinos.

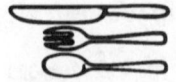 **RESTAURANTS.** Heavenly Valley has plenty of places to eat in between skiing. On the California side, the base lodge, Top of the Tram (2,000 ft. above Lake Tahoe) and Sky Meadows (at the base of Sky Chair) both have cafeterias, barbecues, and dining rooms and cocktail service. On the Nevada side, Boulder Base Lodge, Stagecoach Lodge (at the base of Stagecoach Lift), and East Peak Mid-mountain Lodge (the base of East Peak and Dipper chairs) have eats and drinks and outdoor sundecks.

Restaurants are listed in order of price category. *Expensive:* $18 and up; *Moderate:* $10–$18; *Inexpensive:* less than $10. These prices are for a meal for one person, excluding drinks and tip. The above listed on-mountain cafeterias are inexpensive and generally do not take credit cards. Other sit-down restaurants honor most major credit cards. The buffets at the casinos in South Lake Tahoe are considered great bargains; check them out, but don't bet your skis. For other restaurants in the South Lake Tahoe area, see section on Kirkwood Ski Area.

Christiania Inn. *Expensive.* Across the road from the Tram at Heavenly Valley at 3819 Saddle Road; 916–544–7337. A country-style inn serving gourmet meals by fireside; popularized by *Bon Appétit* and *Cosmopolitan* magazines; major credit cards; reservations.

Stetson's. *Expensive.* In Del Webb's High Sierra Hotel/Casino; 702–588–6211. Decorated with Stetsons, of course; excellent presentation of mesquitebroiled specialties; reservations.

Eagle's Nest. *Moderate.* At the Nevada base area, 472 Needle Peak Rd.; 702–588–6492 or 702–883–6478. Features American and Italian dishes amidst Victorian ambience.

Edelweiss. *Moderate.* Tahoe Season Resort on Keller and Saddle Roads; 916–541–6700. Informal dining with a view of the ski area; Tyrolian/German cuisine; major credit cards.

Oglebee's. *Inexpensive.* Ski Run and US 50; 916–544–2429. Open for 3 meals a day, beer/wine only in the wood and plank building, popular with Tahoe locals.

HOW TO GET AROUND. A complimentary **shuttle bus** runs between the California base lodge and accommodations in the area and from the casinos to the Boulder base lodge in Nevada, 7 A.M. to 5:15 P.M. For schedule information, call the ski area, 541–1330.

 **SEASONAL EVENTS.** The major event in **January** is *South Lake Tahoe's Winter Carnival* with barrel races, snow sculptures and costume competitions. *John Denver's Celebrity Classic* is the biggest thing to hit Heavenly each **February.** A bit less glamorous is the *Truckee Dog Sled Races* each **February.** In **March** the *FIS World Cup Men's Slalom* lights up the slopes. The USSA Cross Country Championships are scheduled here mid-**March** through 1988. The annual *Silver Dollar Downhill* race is open to USSA-licensed racers in **April.**

 OTHER ACTIVITIES. In addition to skiing North America's biggest mountain complex, there is **helicopter skiing** through the Ski School; 541–1330, ext. 255. Instruction in Spanish and Japanese is available; also private lessons. **Cross-country** skiers are welcome as long as they wear safety straps. Nearby Royal Gorge Cross Country Ski Resort is a must for any XC fan. There are 255 km of machine groomed track—56 trails for beginners, intermediates, and experts.

For an unusual, close-up look at Lake Tahoe, book onto the rather grand old sternwheelers, the *Tahoe Queen* or the *M.S. Dixie* (leaving from Zephyr Cove). Cruises offer a bit of adventure, dining, drinking, and live music. Call for reservations aboard the *Dixie* at 588–3508 or 882–0786. The *Tahoe Queen* cruise heads across the lake to the north shore ski resorts, even in winter; call 541–3364.

DAY-CARE FACILITIES. Call the South Lake Tahoe visitors center, 541–5255, or the ski area, 541–1330, and ask for child care recommendations.

 **NIGHTLIFE.** The California base lodge has live music and dancing. In town, *Hodge's* and *Rojo's* have live entertainment and dancing. The casinos all feature lounge acts and revues for various tastes. *Crystal Cabaret* at Caesars is all glitter; *Harrah's* revue is a sizzler. The mainstay of nightlife in town, of course, is the gambling, from the luxurious Harrah's to the more homey *Barney's Club.* Big-name entertainment usually is headlined at *Caesars* and *Harrah's.*

MAMMOTH MOUNTAIN

P.O. Box 24
Mammoth Lakes CA 93546
Tel: 619–934–2571

Snow Report: 619–934–6166 (local)
213–935–8866 (Southern
California)
Area Vertical: 3,100 ft.
Number of Trails: 150, the
longest run 2.5 miles
Lifts: 2 gondolas, 3 quad
chairs, 6 triple chairs, 16
double chairs, 2 T-bars, 2
pomas, 1 Mighty Mite
Snowmaking: none
Season: November–June

Mammoth Mountain is well named—32 lifts, 42,000 skiers per hour transported uphill, 51 restaurants in the area, plenty of California sunshine, and people, lots of people. Los Angelenos crowd here by the thousands on weekends, but weekdays can be comparatively empty.

The reputation for "Sierra Cement" aside, this is one big and diverse mountain. Best time to check out those California tans is May and June—skiing sometimes goes until July 4th. There seems to be more sunning than skiing during the "summer" ski season.

Situated south of the Lake Tahoe ski areas, down the spine of the Sierras, Mammoth draws primarily from the southern California crowd. In addition to the 150 trails, there are open bowls and wide open slopes. There are so many lifts and runs that it's a good idea to stay with your skiing mates rather than trying to meet them somewhere on the mountain later in the day. Parking near the lifts is a problem; best thing to do is leave the car at a lodge and take one of the shuttle buses to the lifts.

Mammoth is an expired volcano, the hills above 9,700 ft. covered with what is called asbestos soil, and nothing grows. The view of the Sierras from the summit at 11,053 ft. looks down onto the desert and the Inyo National Forest, and gives you a feeling of being on top of the world.

Practical Information for Mammoth Mountain

HOW TO GET THERE. By air. *Mammoth Air Shuttle* has scheduled service on Thursdays, Fridays, Sundays, and Mondays from Orange County and Burbank to Mammoth; call 619–935–4737 or 800–446–4500 *Alpha Air* offers daily service between Mammoth and Los Angeles and Oakland; call 800–824–2610 or, in California, 800–421–9353. Rental cars are available from the Mammoth Lakes airport to the Mammoth Mountain Ski Area.

By car. From Los Angeles it is a 300-mile, 6-hour drive via US 395 to Rte. 203 to Minaret Rd. From the San Francisco area take Hwy. 80 to US 395, or Hwy. 50 to South Lake Tahoe, then Hwy. 19 or Hwy. 89 to US 395. In the spring when Tioga Pass is open, the drive goes through Yosemite.

By bus. *Greyhound Bus* serves the town of Mammoth Lakes twice daily from the north and south. *Skier's Express* runs on Fridays and Sundays between Mammoth and southern California; call 213–321–1221. *Hot Dogger Tours* has scheduled service between Mammoth and Los Angeles, Orange County, and Mojave; call 714–523–5982 or 213–698–6211.

TELEPHONES: The area code for the Mammoth Lakes area is 619.

ACCOMMODATIONS. Within walking distance of the lifts are condos and lodges owned by the ski area. (These are the first two listed below.) Mammoth Mountain, P.O. Box 24, Mammoth Lakes, CA 93546; 934–2571. There are also condominium complexes within walking distance of Warming Hut II, at the edge of town, and there are 30,000 rooms in the town of Mammoth Lakes, 4 miles away. Categories, based on price, are: *Expensive:* up to $290 per night for a one-bedroom condo; *Moderate:* $55–$180; and *Inexpensive:* $20–$70 for hotel and motel rooms.

Mammoth Mountain Inn. *Expensive.* Motel, hotel, and condo units at the slopes totaling 200 rooms. A 5-day package, double occupancy, in a hotel or motel room is available.

Alpha Air. *Expensive.* At the slopes; 934–2581. Special rate includes the flight with a 3-, 4-, or 5-day midweek package.

Arrowhead Condos, Chateau Blanc, Heritage Condos, Val D'Isere Condos, Woodlands Condos. *Expensive.* All these condos are reached at Box 8527, Mammoth Lakes CA 93546; 800–MAMMOTH. Also in the *Expensive* category is **1849 Condos,** Box 835, 800–421–1849; and **Snowbird Condos,** Box 7013, 934–8270.

In the *moderate* category are: **Discovery 4,** Box 789, 800–538–4751; **Mammoth Estates Condos,** Box 1117, 800–228–2884; **Mammoth Points Condos,** Box 1595, 934–4100; **St. Moritz Villas,** Box 7833, 800–858–7900; **La Vista Blanc, Tyrolean Village,** and **Sierra Manors,** Box 8527, 800–MAMMOTH.

Inexpensive places, mostly motels in town, include **Innsbruck Lodge,** Box 758, 934–3035; **Lapplander Lodge,** Box 931, 934–2873; **Laurel Lodge,** Box 122, 800–257–3781; **Ponderosa Lodge,** Box 380, 934–2468; **ULLR Lodge,** Box 53, 934–2454.

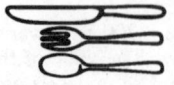

RESTAURANTS. On the mountain itself, there are 6 self-serve restaurants and 2 with table service. Mammoth Mountain Inn serves all meals. Mammoth Lakes boasts 45 restaurants. Most take major credit cards. Price categories are based on an average dinner for one. *Expensive:* $15–18; *Moderate:* $10–15; *Inexpensive:* less than $10.

Altitude 9000. *Expensive.* In the Mammoth Mountain Inn across the parking lot from the ski area's main lodge; 934–2581. The dining room has an open feel, with exposed beams; American and Continental dishes (pepper steak is good), an extensive wine list; reservations suggested.

Roget's. *Expensive.* Hwy. 203 and Minaret Rd.; 934–4466. Considered the finest restaurant in the area; Continental cuisine with unusual dishes; dinners only; Sunday brunch; reservations.

The Mogul. *Moderate.* Old Mammoth Rd. across from the Mammoth Mall; 934–3093. Homemade soups, salad bar, steaks, seafood, poultry; dinners only.

Rafter's. *Moderate.* Old Mammoth Rd. south of Hwy. 201; 934–2536; Mountain rustic, American menu (the petite top sirloin is particularly popular); dinner only and live entertainment.

Whiskey Creek. *Moderate.* Main St. and Minaret Rd., 934–2555. Terribly trendy; beef, seafood.

Bergers. *Inexpensive.* Minaret Rd.; 934–6622; supposedly has the best burgers in town; lunch and dinner.

Las Montanas. *Inexpensive.* Main St.; 934–9014. Mexican food and good margaritas; generous portions, dinner only.

Swiss Cafe. *Inexpensive.* Old Mammoth Rd.; 934–6196 Good for an early breakfast before hitting the slopes; fresh croissants, muffins, the usual eggs and pancakes; also lunch and dinner.

 **HOW TO GET AROUND.** Unless staying at the slopeside Mammoth Mountain Inn, a car is convenient. The ski area runs a **shuttle bus** service throughout the lodge parking lot. The *Warming Hut II,* at the edge of Mammoth Lakes, has a service which makes a loop through the condo area. It is suggested you park close to Chairs 2, 4, 10, and 15 and ski directly to your car. The town of Mammoth Lakes and the ski area run a 50-cent shuttle service with five routes looping between town and various drop-off points at the mountain. Call 934–2571 for information and schedules. *Quicksilver Bus Service,* 934–3838, has daily scheduled runs from the village to the airport and to the ski area lodges; the company also offers charter and taxi service in the village of Mammoth Lakes.

 **SEASONAL EVENTS.** The latest Warren Miller ski movie usually opens the ski season in **mid-November** at Warming Hut II. Various ski clubs and other interest groups hold their races throughout the season. The Village Championships, which began in **January,** culminate in team events in early **April,** spiced with local rivalries. A summer race camp follows in early **June.**

 OTHER SPORTS AND ACTIVITIES. If you have the energy or inclination for something else besides downhilling, you're in luck. There are many miles of cross-country trails, and rentals are available (at the slope and in town). For **helicopter skiing** in the Sierra Madres, try *Mammoth Heli-ski,* 934–4494; P.O. Box 600, Mammoth Lakes CA 93546.

There is **ice skating** at Convict Lake, with skate rentals at the *Ski Surgeon,* 934–6376. **Sleds** are available at *Kittredge Sports,* 934–7566, or *Filson's,* 934–2290; **sleigh rides** from *Sierra Meadows,* 934–6161. There are 200 miles of **snowmobile** trails; for information call *DJ's Snowmobile Rentals,* 935–4880. **Tobogganing** and **tubing** are also available.

Racing is a big deal here. There are mid-week race camps and 3- and 5-day camps. The *Alpine Athletic Club* is a racing program for adults. Each Wednesday sees an FIS-style World Cup amateur slalom and giant slalom.

 **DAY-CARE FACILITIES.** The Mammoth Mountain Inn operates the *Small World Day Center;* daily and weekly programs include ski lessons for toddlers (18–30 months) and pre-school or school age children (30 months–12 years), night babysitting, and infant care (newborn–18 months). Call 934–2581 and ask for the day-care center.

The Mammoth Mountain *Ski School* has special instructors who teach children ages 6–12 ski techniques; lessons are in the mornings and afternoons. Pre-school, ages 4–6, have half-day sessions. Call the ski school at 934–2571, ext. 3285 or 3287.

NIGHTLIFE. Mammoth Inn has a bar and lounge, as does *Yodler.* Fifteen more lounges, plus a movie theater and swimming pools are in town. The *Creekside,* Main St. and Minaret Rd., 934–2555, often has a live band and *Rafters,* Old Mammoth Rd., 934–2536, has live entertainment. Check the local papers for what is hot in town.

SQUAW VALLEY USA

P.O. Box 2007
Olympic Valley CA 95730
Tel. 916–583–6985

Snow Reports: 916–583–6955
Area Vertical: 2,700 ft.
Number of Trails: all open bowls
  encompassing 8,000 acres
Lifts: 16 double and 5 triple
  chairlifts, 2 gondolas, 1 tram
  and 2 poma lifts.
Snowmaking: none
Season: mid-November–early May

Squaw Valley is immense. Nestled among six Sierra mountain peaks overlooking Lake Tahoe, Squaw has thousands of acres of open skiing on an average annual snowpack of 400 inches. Squaw is best known as the home of the 1960 Winter Olympics, but you don't have to be an Olympic-caliber skier to love it. Seventy percent of the terrain is for beginner and intermediate skiers, while there are plenty of ungroomed peaks and steep verticals for the experts. Even on the super-crowded weekends, experts can find solitude on hair-raising pitches. Most runs are above timberline, are broad, and have plenty of room for turns. As one local described it, Squaw Valley is the Porsche of ski areas. Most of those Porsches come from San Francisco.

With the Siberia Express, the world's fastest chairlift, a 125-passenger gondola, a cable car, and chairlifts dotted around the snowscape, over 33,000 skiers an hour can be transported uphill.

Practical Information for Squaw Valley

HOW TO GET THERE. The closest gateway by **air** is Reno's Cannon International Airport, served by 12 carriers. Ground transfer is 45 minutes via *See Tahoe Tours;* call 702–832–0713 for details on frequent departures; also *Sierra Nevada Stage Lines,* 702–359–1750; and *Silver State Stage Lines,* 702–348–7121. Taxi service is available through Carson City White Cab, 883–4447; Reno-Sparks Cab Co., 331–4141; Whittlesea Checker Taxi, 323–3111 or 322–9191; or Yellow Deluxe Cab Co., 331–7171.

Four-wheel drive and skierized cars are available for rental in Reno. Companies include (all area code 702): *Alamo,* 327–0400; *American International,* 329–2050 or 800–527–0202; *Avis* 785–2727 or 800–331–1212; *Budget,* 800–527–0700 or 785–2545; *Dollar,* 800–421–6868 or 348–7770; *Hertz,* 785–2511 or 800–654–3131; *National,* 800–CAR–RENT or 785–2756; *Rent a Dent,* 322–3529; *Thrifty,* 329–0096 or 800–367–2277; and *Ugly Duckling,* 800–THE-DUCK.

By automobile, Squaw lies 200 miles east of San Francisco via I–80 and Highway 89, 5 miles north of Tahoe City. US 395/580 runs from Oregon to Southern California. The phone number for Reno AAA is 702–826–5322; for Incline Village AAA, it is 916–546–7083.

Amtrak's *California Zephyr,* called the most scenic train ride in America, stops daily in Reno: mornings westbound, evenings eastbound. Call 800–USA–RAIL for reservations and information. For Reno ticket office, call 702–329–8638.

TELEPHONES. The area code for Squaw Valley is 916; for Reno, it is 702.

ACCOMMODATIONS. For information on lodgings, contact Squaw Valley Central Reservations, Squaw Valley USA, Box 2007, Olympic Valley CA 95730; 800–824 –7954; in California, call 800–545–4350; locally, 916– 583–5585. Shuttle to the ski area is available from all lodge locations except the Super 8 Motel. Squaw Valley itself is a residential area with no hotels and just a few shops in the village core. However, that may change in a few years. Rate categories are based on 7-night, 6-day packages per person, double occupancy. *Expensive:* $500–$750; *Moderate:* $400–$500; *Inexpensive,* $300–$400. Daily rates and condos, where available, are slightly higher.

Olympic Village Inn. *Expensive.* Box 2648, Olympic Valley; 916–583–1501 or 800–VILLAGE. Outdoor heated swimming pool and 5 outdoor spas, restaurant, and bar. Nightly rates also available.

Squaw Village Lodge. *Expensive.* This new development, at the base of Super Spruce lift has a full-facility health club. Six-day lift tickets available.

The Tavern Inn. *Expensive.* P.O. Box 2741; 916–583–1504. Two miles from the area, condos are complete with fireplace, washer/dryer, spa.

River Ranch Lodge. *Moderate to Expensive.* Box 197, Tahoe City CA 95730; 916–583–4264. On the river, 4 miles from the area, near Truckee. Rustic lodge atmosphere.

Christy Hill Inn. *Moderate.* 1 Christy Hill Place; 916–583–RENT. European style bed and breakfast, located ½ mile from the slopes; restaurant on premise.

Granlibakken Resort. *Moderate.* Box 6329, Tahoe City CA 95730; 916–583– 4242. 8 miles from the area; saunas, hot tubs, full breakfast daily. One-bedroom condos and bedrooms available.

Mayfield House. *Moderate.* An old Tahoe residence, beautifully restored and refurbished in Tahoe City, 8 miles from Squaw; 916–583–1001.

Pepper Tree Inn. *Inexpensive.* 1877 N. Lake Blvd., Tahoe City CA 95730; 916–583–3711. Has a 7-night package.

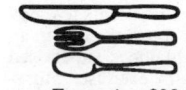

RESTAURANTS. Variety is the spice of food fare at Squaw Valley, where cuisine ranges from Continental to ethnic to basic American. Restaurant categories listed here are based on a meal for one, with beverages and tips extra. *Expensive:* $20 and up; *Moderate,* $10–$20; *Inexpensive,* less than $10. All restaurants listed take major credit cards unless otherwise noted.

Christy Hill. *Expensive.* In the Christy Hill Inn; 583–8551. Has both a fixed-price menu (for $35) and an a la carte choice. Imaginative cuisine. Reservations necessary.

La Petite Pier. *Expensive.* 7250 N. Lake Blvd., Tahoe Vista, a 20-minute drive from Squaw; 546–4464. Fine French cuisine. Reservations suggested. Fixed-price and a la carte menu.

Wolfdales. *Expensive.* On the west shore of Lake Tahoe, near Homewood, a 20-minute drive from Squaw; 525–7833. One of the best, if not the best, in the area. Their specialty is fish dishes with Japanese touches. Reservations suggested. Open Fridays, Saturdays, and Sundays only.

Fabio's. *Moderate.* In the parking lot of Squaw Valley; 581–0329. Features northern Italian dishes. Owner Fabio is a flamboyant character who likes to keep his customers amused.

Jake's on the Lake. *Moderate.* 788 N. Lake Blvd.; Tahoe City; 583–0188. Serves Continental dishes and daily specials.

O B's. *Moderate.* Commercial Row, Old Truckee, 8 miles north of Squaw; 587–4164. California cuisine. It's worth a trip to Truckee to see this old railroad and lumbering town, then have a delightful dinner here. The town's Main St. is the real thing, not refurbished but very "in" right now.

Bacchi's Inn. *Inexpensive.* Lake Forest Rd., 1 mile north of Tahoe City; 583–3324. Italian food, all you can eat—minestrone soup, bread, and antipasto, all for the low price of $3.95. No credit cards.

La Chamois. *Inexpensive.* In Tahoe City; 583–5404. Not French, as you may assume, but a pizza, soup, and sandwich shop. No credit cards.

Hasta de Lago. *Inexpensive.* 760 N. Lake Blvd., Tahoe City; 583–0385. Tasty Mexican fare, done to your favorite degree of "hotness."

HOW TO GET AROUND. The village core of Squaw is all ski, so everything is within walking distance. **Shuttle buses** provide transportation among the hotels and into Tahoe City as well.

OTHER SPORTS AND ACTIVITIES. Every ski area has its **amateur races.** But at Squaw, there is a different flavor—you can race at night. If you still have the energy by the end of the afternoon, recreational skiers can enter a series of eight races starting in **January.** For further information, call Squaw Valley Competition Services, 583–7664. For plain old **night skiing,** the illuminated slopes of Searchlight are lit during the Christmas and New Year's holidays. The lift runs 4–9 P.M. and lift tickets cost (during the 85/86 season) an extra $6 for adults. Snowboards are allowed.

Snowfest is the annual winter carnival which takes place throughout the North Lake Tahoe area at the end of **February**–beginning of **March.** Activities include ski races, dances, wine tastings, tournaments, and parades. For details of which activities are scheduled at various resorts, contact Snowfest, P.O. Box 7590, Tahoe City CA 95730; 916–583–7625.

Cross-country skiing is available at the *Squaw Valley Nordic Center.* Their moonlight skis with fondue are wonderful; call 583–8951 for information. *Royal Gorge Cross Country Resort,* with 47 groomed trails, is on old Hwy. 40, off I–80 in Soda Springs; 916–426–3871.

Snowmobile rentals are available at the *Tahoe City Recreational Area* (the golf course); call 583–1516. The *Snowmobile Connection* is in North Lake Tahoe at Hwy. 267 and 28; 546–9909. Also in North Lake Tahoe is *Snowmobiling Unlimited* on N. Lake Blvd.; 583–5858.

Sledding can be enjoyed on the golf course, at the town park in Tahoe City, and at Granlibakken Resort. In fact, the resort has special saucers to sled on; no charge for guests, a rental fee for others. Call 583–4242 for prices and hours.

Sightseeing and **gambling** in nearby Reno is a big draw for the ski resorts in the area. (See Reno).

CHILDREN'S ACTIVITIES. Squaw's philosophy is that skiing is a family affair. To that end, *Ten Little Indians Snow School* provides a way for parents to enjoy skiing while children aged 3–5 years spend the day in an entertaining and educational environment. The schedule includes supervised activities that introduce children to skiing; also arts and crafts, exercises, storytelling, and rest periods. Skiing takes place in a specially designated area. Children must be toilet trained.

The *Snow School* is near the bottom of Cornice I Lift. Sessions begin at 8:30 A.M. or 1 P.M. Call the school's office at 583–4743 for information.

For children too young to ski, parents may enroll them in *Wee Care.* It is $3.50 per child from 8 A.M. to 6 P.M.; after 6 it is $4 for the first child and $2 for each additional child. Check with the ski area, 583–6985, for details.

NIGHTLIFE. Life after skiing at Squaw Valley centers around going to dinner and then getting a good night's rest for the next day of skiing. However, *Bar One,* at the base of Squaw Valley, 583–6985, is considered by aficionados as the best après-ski place in the country. It features live music. Also, *Jake's* and *O B's* restaurants are known to swing into the night.

California/Nevada State Line

There is nothing quite like the Tahoe Basin, cut by the imaginary California/Nevada boundary. Twenty-one ski resorts cluster around the pristine lake—this country's largest concentration of ski facilities and one of the world's most beautiful destinations.

On the Nevada side of the border, gambling is a year-round, 24-hour activity, punctuated by skiing in winter. Of all the gambling resorts in North America, Harrah's Tahoe Hotel is the only one to have been awarded the Mobil 5-Star and AAA's 5-Diamond awards. A stay in the Tahoe area is a trip to two worlds: the glitz and glitter of nonstop nightlife and the beauty and serenity of the Sierra Nevada Mountains and the high desert country. There is even a cultural side–Reno has both chamber and philharmonic orchestras.

Staying at an expensive place is easy. Look for *Harrah's,* 219 N. Center St., Reno, 329–0411 or 800–648–3773. Rates $63–$75; 5 restaurants. *Caesars Tahoe, Flamingo Hilton, Caesars Palace, MGM Grand* in Tahoe, and in Reno the *MGM Grand Hotel,* 2500 E. 2nd St., 789–2000 or 800–648–5080, 800–851–8817 from Canada; rates $49–$73. *Eldorado,* 4th & Virginia Sts., Reno, 786–5700 or 800–648–5966. Rates $30–60, 5 restaurants. *John Ascuaga's Nugget,* 1100 Nugget Ave., Sparks; 356–3300 or 800–648–1177; rates $49–$60 with 9 restaurants. *The Wingfield House,* 219 Court St., Reno, is a historic mansion overlooking the Truckee River. Three guest rooms with semi-private bath and breakfast, $90–$125 a night; 800–FOR–RENO.

There are plenty of inexpensive motels and rustic cabins. For example, the *Center Lodge,* 200 S. Center St., Reno, is $25; 329–9000. *Long Horn Motel,* 844 S. Virginia St., Reno, has rates from $20–$24; 322–2633. The *Zephyr Motel,* 4401 W. 4th St., Reno, has a room rate of $18.50 with weekly rates of $90 for kitchenettes. *Reindeer Lodge,* 9000 Mt. Rose Hwy., Reno, is a rustic lodge with four guest rooms at $14.50 per person double occupancy, $25 single occupancy, including breakfast; 849–9902. Call the *Reno/Sparks Convention and Visitors Authority's Information/Reservation Referral Service* at 800–FOR–RENO; write the *Tourism Department,* P.O. Box 11430, Reno NV 89510, and ask for their invaluable *Travel Planner.* The major hotels all have ski packages, which generally include room, lift tickets, two drinks, buffet breakfasts, discount coupons and the like.

Ski Tahoe North offers special ski packages in the north shore lodges with interchangeable lift tickets. The ticket is valid at 9 areas: *Alpine Meadows, Homewood, Mt. Rose, Northstar-at-Tahoe, Ski Incline, Slide Mountain, Squaw Valley USA* (see *California* section above), *Sugar Bowl,* and *Tahoe Ski Bowl.* Write *Tahoe North Visitors and Convention*

Bureau, P.O. Box 5578, Tahoe City CA 95730; call 800–822–5959 in California or 800–824–8557 outside California.

There's plenty of sightseeing, too, including Harrah's automobile collection and gun collection, the *Wilbur D. May Museum and Arboretum, Liberty Belle Saloon's* slot machine collection, and the new 5-acre *Great Basin Adventure. Tahoe Tours,* 702–832–0713, *Silver State Stage Lines,* 702–348–7121, and *Sierra Nevada Stage Lines,* 702–359–1750, have group tours; call for rates. The tourist literature also includes addresses of courthouses where couples can be married and a lawyer referral service for those who want to get a quick (6-week residency) divorce.

There are over 100 restaurants on the North Shore alone. In addition to the ever-present gambling, there are countless lounges, saloons with any type of music you want to hear or dance to. For information on North Lake Tahoe activities and ski facilities, call *Ski Tahoe North,* 800–822–5959 in California or 800–824–8557 outside California; write *Tahoe North Visitors and Convention Bureau,* P.O. Box 5578, Tahoe City CA 95730. Major destination resorts along the north shore are *Alpine Meadows, Northstar-at-Tahoe, Squaw Valley USA,* and a dozen more.

Nearby *Incline Village,* nestled on the north shore of the lake, is the place to be for those who are looking for luxury. There, homes nestled in remote alpine settings are available for rent by the weekend or month. There are also condominiums, intimate hotels like the *Lakeside Tennis and Ski Resort,* and big-time places like the *Hyatt Lake Tahoe Resort Hotel & Casino,* Lakeshore and Country Club Dr., 831–1111 or 800–228–9000. Rates range from $70–$78 for rooms, $148–275 for suites.

At the opposite end of the spectrum is *Haus Bavaria,* 593 N. Dyer Circle, 831–6122. As the name suggests, it is an Austrian-style chalet, with 5 guest rooms and a minimum stay of two nights; $50 for one person, $60 for two, with full breakfast. Head off to Ski Incline, Squaw, or Alpine Meadows for skiing.

South Lake Tahoe also has its share of superb skiing, nightlife, and fine dining. Near the town are the country's largest resort, *Heavenly Valley* (see *California* section), *Kirkwood,* and several smaller areas and cross-country centers. For information write *South Lake Tahoe Visitors Bureau,* P.O. Box 17727, South Lake Tahoe CA 95706; 800–822–5922.

Twelve air carriers serve Reno, with 61 daily scheduled departures. Charter service and air taxis are also available.

All major and many minor rental car agencies are represented at the airport, from *AA Auto Rentals,* 323–3514, to *Wild West Auto Rentals,* 329–2050 or 800–824–0698.

Amtrak stops in the heart of Reno on E. Commercial Row at Lake St. The *California Zephyr* is the most scenic train ride in America, crossing three mountain ranges on its 2,427-mile transcontinental journey. Call 800–USA–RAIL or the Reno Ticket Office, 329–8638, for reservations and information. Amtrak also stops in nearby Truckee.

ALPINE MEADOWS SKI AREA

P.O. Box AM
Tahoe City CA 95730
Tel: 916–583–4232

Snow Report: 916–583–6914
Area Vertical: 1,797 ft.
Number of Trails: 100 trails
*   over 2,000 acres on two*
*   mountains; longest trail is*
*   2.5 miles*
Lifts: 11 double chairs, 2
*   T-bars.*

*Snowmaking: On 100 percent of
beginner trails, 10 percent of
intermediate trails
Season: mid-November–Memorial Day*

Alpine Meadows is a ski cruiser's paradise. Most of the intermediate runs are on the front side with varying degrees of pitch and slant, and are groomed to perfection every night. There are powder areas and steep challenges for experts, particularly Wolverine Bowl. Experts should also look for Art's Knob, Our Father, and nearby Hail Mary.

Skiers can follow the sun around the mountain for the best exposure; good spring corn snow is found on Ward and Scott Peaks. Check the information desk in the base lodge for free guided tours. The quickest way onto the slopes is to buy lift tickets at the base of Subway Chair. The base lodge includes a cafeteria, full-service restaurant, bar, repair and ski shop, and a large sundeck. Alpine Meadows has the longest spring skiing season in the Tahoe area and sunshine an average of 80 percent of the entire ski season.

Practical Information for Alpine Meadows

HOW TO GET THERE. By car. Tahoe City is 6 miles and Reno is 58 miles from the ski area via I–80. San Francisco is 200 miles west; Sacramento is 120 miles. Take I–80 east to Lake Tahoe turn-off, Hwy. 89 to Alpine Meadows Rd.; it is 3 miles to the ski area. For more details and maps, contact the *California State Automobile Association,* 942 Hwy. 89, South Lake Tahoe CA 95706; 541–4434.

By air. The closest airports are Reno (see *Reno* section for airline listings), Sacramento, and the Lake Tahoe Airport on Hwy. 50, served by *AirCal,* 800–4–AIRCAL, and *Pacific Coast Airlines,* 800–322–8881 in California, 800–235–6967 in Nevada. Small planes can land at the Truckee-Tahoe Airport, 2 miles east of Truckee, 10 miles north of Lake Tahoe; aircraft tie-down area, 24-hour flight operations.

Dollar and *National* rental cars are available in Reno by booking through the Tahoe North Visitors and Convention Bureau, 800–824–8557, or in California only, 800–822–5959); also—and in Reno *Budget,* 702–785–2541 or 800–527–0700. For limousine service, call *Alpine Limousine,* 577–2727, or *Bell Luxury Limousine,* 800–BEL–LIMO. *Tahoe Transportation, Inc.,* 583–1422, serves North Tahoe, Truckee, and Alpine Meadows from Reno's Cannon International Airport.

In Lake Tahoe, rental companies are *Dollar* and *National* through the *Tahoe North Visitors and Convention Bureau; Thrifty,* 587–2588; and *Budget,* 583–8941.

By train. *Amtrak* stops in Truckee; for schedule call 800–USA–RAIL, or in California only, 800–872–7245.

By bus. *Trailways,* 323–4511, and *Greyhound,* 323–4511, provide eastbound and westbound service to the Truckee depot on Commercial Row.

TELEPHONES. The area code for this region of California is 916, and for all of Nevada it is 702.

ACCOMMODATIONS. Call the *Tahoe North Visitors and Convention Bureau,* 800–822–5959 (California only), or 800–824–8557 (outside California), or write to them for information and reservations at P.O. Box 5578, Tahoe City CA 95730. They handle 115 properties along the North Shore from Truckee to Incline, including facilities at Alpine Meadows. Those skiing at Alpine Meadows prefer to stay at or near the ski area.

Condo and room rate categories are based on per person, double occupancy rates. *Expensive:* $80–$120; *Moderate:* $50–$80; *Inexpensive:* $40–$50.

Alpine Place One and Two. *Expensive.* Within walking distance of the slopes; 583–8213. Condos of 2, 3, and 4 bedrooms, with fireplaces, TV, kitchens, babysitting, and day-care; 2-bedroom goes for $100–$115 a night with a two-night minimum and a $200 deposit. Shuttle bus available to the slopes, a quarter of a mile away.

River Run. *Expensive.* On the access road to Alpine Meadows, along the Truckee River; 583–0137. Condominiums of 1 bedroom to a 3-bedroom with loft.

River Ranch. *Moderate.* Overlooking the Truckee River at the entrance to Alpine Meadows; 583–4264. Rooms with antique furnishings and views, restaurant and lounge, complimentary breakfast in your room; two-night minimum. "The coziest hotel in the Sierras."

Pepper Tree Inn. *Moderate.* P.O. Box 29, in downtown Tahoe City; 583–3711. Comfy lodgings with hot tub and pool; pets permitted.

Alpine Motor Inn. *Inexpensive.* At the base of Alpine Meadows Road along the Truckee River; 583–4266. Continental breakfast, hot tub, racquetball courts at an additional charge; two-night minimum.

For lodgings other than along the North Shore, see sections on *Reno* or *South Lake Tahoe.*

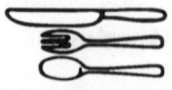 **RESTAURANTS.** In the ski area itself, *Kealy's Pub* (583–4232) in the base lodge serves hearty fare and the mid-mountain lodge has an *Alpine Deli.* Listed here is a small selection of restaurants nearest the ski area. For a wider selection of dining places closer to Tahoe City, see sections on *Heavenly Valley* and *Northstar* ski areas. For an *Expensive* meal here for one person, expect to pay $20 and more; *Moderate:* $10–$20; *Inexpensive:* less than $10. All accept most major credit cards.

River Ranch. *Expensive.* At the entrance to Alpine Meadows, overlooking the Truckee River; 583–4264. Features intimate fireside dining on Continental cuisine.

Steven at Incline Village. *Expensive.* 341 Ski Way, in the bullwheel building of the lift, Nevada side; 832–0222. Sophisticated dining with a great view. Open for lunch and dinner only.

Swiss Lakewood. *Expensive.* Hwy. 89, 6 miles south of Tahoe City; 525–5211. European food, featuring quail and fondue bourguignonne. Dinner only.

Cantina Tres Hombres. *Moderate.* 8791 N. Lake Blvd., Kings Beach; 546–4052. Mexican food with a western flair.

Donner's Ski Ranch. *Moderate.* Old Hwy. 40, Norden; 426–3635. Basic American foods with western accent; a favorite of locals.

Pfeiffer House. *Moderate.* One-half mile south of Tahoe City, along I–80; 587–1377. An oldtime favorite of frequent Tahoe skiers; menu features schnitzel and sauerbraten; dinner only.

Donner Lake Kitchen. *Inexpensive.* 13440 Donner Pass Rd.; 587–3119. Hearty skiers' breakfast and lunch. Open 7 A.M.–2 P.M. daily.

 **HOW TO GET AROUND.** Most accommodations have **shuttle** service to the ski area. The ski area operates a free daily shuttle pickup service at several places along the north and south shores of Lake Tahoe, 583–2371; *Tahoe Area Regional Transit* (TART) operates a public **bus** on a daily schedule in the North Lake Tahoe area, 583–2371.

 **SEASONAL EVENTS.** Snowfest is the big **winter** celebration all along the North Shore, with hundreds of events taking place in late **February** and early **March.** The Great Ski Race is held the first Sunday in **March** and follows a scenic and historic ski route from Lake Tahoe to Truckee, 30 km away. It is the largest cross-country ski event in California, with nearly 1,000 entrants. For information, write Tahoe Cross-Country Ski Center, P.O. Box 1632, Tahoe City CA 95730; 583–0484.

OTHER SPORTS AND ACTIVITIES. The *Tahoe Nordic Ski Resort,* 2 miles northwest of Tahoe City, has 50 km of cross-country terrain with lake views. **Sledding** and **snowmobiling** are available in Tahoe City. Take a ride to Incline Village to see the unusual *Doll and Toy Museum.* They have a wonderful collection of china dolls made in 19th-century Germany, replicas of English royalty, popular storybook dolls from the early 20th century; Country Club Mall, Incline Village, 831–7680. Free admission, but donations are accepted. The *Cobblestone Cinema* in Tahoe City features current movies. Also in Tahoe City are numerous art galleries, and the *North Tahoe Fine Arts Council* puts on productions throughout the year; call 546–5562 or 583–9048.

DAY-CARE FACILITIES. *Alpine Place One and Two* provides babysitting. The *Children's Snow School* takes youngsters aged 3–6; full-day lessons are $36.

NIGHTLIFE. *River Ranch* has a cozy lounge. There is no dearth of night spots around Lake Tahoe, Tahoe City, Truckee, Tahoe Vista, South Lake Tahoe, Incline Village, Sparks, or Reno; it's a matter of how much a person can take. Pick up the local newspapers or a copy of *Key* magazine for the latest happenings.

KIRKWOOD

P.O. Box 1
Kirkwood CA 95646
Tel: 209–258–6000

Snow Report: 209–258–3000
Area Vertical: 2,000 ft.
Number of Trails: 50 trails,
*   2,000 acres; the longest run is*
*   2.5 miles*
Lifts: 2 triple chairs, 7 double
*   chairs, 1 surface lift*
Snowmaking: none
Season: Mid-November to May

Kirkwood is south of Heavenly Valley (see *California* section) by a mountain peak or two and only 30 minutes from the town of South Lake Tahoe. The Sierra Crest rises 2,000 ft. above Kirkwood's mountain meadow, providing some of the most diverse skiing terrain in the country. There is everything—chutes, good steep pitches, tree skiing, open bowls, and gentle novice terrain on the Hay Flats. The panoramic view from the top of Wagon Wheel chairlift, at 9,500 ft., is from the High Sierras to the central valley of California. The resort is still in the "undiscovered" phase.

The little village of Kirkwood includes six condominium complexes, all within a few minutes of the lifts. The two base lodges both have rental and ski shops, cafeterias, and sit-down restaurants.

Practical Information for Kirkwood

HOW TO GET THERE. For transportation to South Lake Tahoe and Reno, see *Heavenly Valley* section. Kirkwood is 30 miles southwest of South Lake Tahoe on Hwy. 88 at Carson Pass. **By car.** From Reno, take US 395 south to Minden, then Hwy. 88 west to Kirkwood. It is about 1½ hours from Reno's Cannon International Airport. The skier's **shuttle** provides scheduled service from South Lake Tahoe locations to Kirkwood Ski Resort; call 258–6000 for schedules. **Taxis, rental cars,** and complimentary casino/hotel **vans** are also available.

TELEPHONES. The area code for the Kirkwood area is 209.

ACCOMMODATIONS. Kirkwood Central reservations system, P.O. Box 1, Kirkwood, CA 95646, 258–7247, can arrange moderately priced lodging at one of the five local complexes—a total of 84 condominiums—owned and operated by Kirkwood. For accommodations in nearby South Lake Tahoe, see *Heavenly Valley.* For lodging information and rates for the South Lake Tahoe area, call 800–822–5922.

Ski packages are available for downhill skiers as well as cross-country skiers, from $65 a night per person, double occupancy. Lodging ranges from double rooms to 3-bedroom condos with kitchens, fireplaces, and the usual resort amenities.

Base Camp, across the street from Solitude and Cornice Lifts in the main base area, has 1- and 2-bedroom condos.

Edelweiss, at Kirkwood's Timber Creek base area, offers access to Hole in Wall and Bunny Chair lifts; 1-, 2-, and 3-bedroom condos, some with lofts.

Sun Meadows, across from Solitude and Cornice lifts, is the newest complex; health club, conference facilities, restaurant, double rooms, 1-, 2-, and 3-bedroom condos with views of Thimble Peak and Kirkwood Meadow.

Thimblewood, close to the Timber Creek base area, features 1-bedroom, 1-bath condos; views of Kirkwood Meadow.

Whiskey Run, adjacent to Red Cliffs day lodge at the base area, has 2-bedroom, 3-bath condos with ski-in/ski-out accessibility.

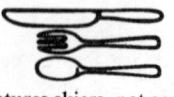

RESTAURANTS. There are many fine places to dine at Kirkwood, with many more to offer if the skier decides to cross the Nevada border where casinos lure gamblers by serving up great buffets at little cost. But this guide features skiers, not gamblers, and restaurants listed here are on the safe-bet side of the border.

Price categories are based on a meal for one, excluding beverages and tip. Restaurants are listed in order of price category. *Expensive:* $15–$25; *Moderate:* $10–$15; *Inexpensive:* less than $10. All restaurants listed accept major credit cards unless otherwise noted. Abbreviations for credit cards are: A, American Express; MC, MasterCard; and V, Visa.

Expensive

Chez Villart. 584 Emerald Bay Rd.; 916–541–7868. French cuisine, intimate atmosphere, beer or wine; closed Mondays; reservations suggested.

Fresh Ketch. 2435 Venice Dr.; 541–5683. Open 7 days a week, featuring seafood, poultry, steaks; dockside dining and boat parking; weekend brunch. Won local chamber "best interior design" award.

Le Cordon Bleu. US 50 at Logan Shoals; 588–5762. Features lakeside dining on rack of lamb, chateaubriand; Sunday brunch; closed Mondays and Tuesdays; reservations suggested for dinner.

Ristorante Tre Fontaine. 3140 US 50 in South Lake Tahoe; 577–2016. Serves French and Italian dishes, beer and wine; free limousine service to and from the main strip of town. MC, V only.

Moderate

The Chart House. Kingsbury Grade; 702–588–6276. Serves up the usual fare of steaks, prime rib, and salad bar; great view of Lake Tahoe.

Nephele's. 1169 Ski Run Blvd; 541–8130. Serves steaks, seafood, chicken teriyaki; extensive California wine list.

Zachary's. Round Hill Mall in Zephyr Cove; 588–2108. Features Continental cuisine, scampi, duck; closed Sundays. MC, V only.

Inexpensive

Bandana's. 3737 US 50; 541–8646. Pizza, other Italian dishes, salad bar, beer/wine, food to go. MC, V only.

Cantina Los Tres Hombres. 765 Emerald Bay Rd.; 544–1233. Mexican specialties; no reservations.

Donner House. 2600 Lake Tahoe Blvd.; 541–9610. A casual spot for family dining, sandwiches to steaks.

HOW TO GET AROUND. If you stay in the village of Kirkwood, no transportation is needed. Everything is within walking distance, including the grocery store and restaurants. The town of South Lake Tahoe operates a 24-hour free transportation system on the US 50 corridor and in the area's residential neighborhoods; call 916–544–2266 for fares and schedules.

SEASONAL EVENTS. Early **December** features the *Telextreme Telemark Race Series;* the *New Year's Eve Torchlight* parade is an annual event; mid-**January** is the *Kirkwood Classic Cross Country 15K* race; a snow sculpture contest takes place mid-**February.**

Check the *South Lake Tahoe Chamber of Commerce,* 3066 US 50 (541–5225) for up-to-date information; closed Sundays. The *Visitors Coupon Information Center,* 4093 US 50 (544–0374; 800–237–3536) hands out complimentary packages with discounts for dining and entertainment.

OTHER SPORTS AND ACTIVITIES. Kirkwood has one of the largest **cross-country** centers in the country. Seventy-five km of groomed track cover some 4,000 acres. The interconnecting trail system provides a challenge for all ability levels and includes pine forests, open meadows, and ridges with spectacular views of the Sierra Nevada crest. Lessons, clinics, guided tours, and video reviews are available.

DAY-CARE FACILITIES. For children aged 3–8 years, there is child care available at *Red Cliffs* lodge; 9 A.M.–4:30 P.M. with lunch, $25; half days with no lunch, $10. The *Mogul Mountain* takes children, 4–12, who are ready to ski out to the slopes from Red Cliffs lodge; all day (10:30 A.M.–4 P.M.) with lunch is $25. Mogul Mountain has its own grooming and its own platter lift. For reservations and information, contact the ski school at 258–6000.

NIGHTLIFE. There's the usual après-ski activities in the lodges and restaurants. But for those who prefer après-ski, there are the headline entertainers in the casinos at Lake Tahoe, Nevada. Also the all-night gambling, from baccarat (James Bond's favorite) to blackjack, craps, roulette, and slot machines. Favorites among those who can bear to face the blinding snows the day after are the Cascade Room in *Caesars Tahoe Resort,* 702–588–3515, and *Harrah's Lake Tahoe,* 702–588–6611. Fair warning: Take with you only what you can afford to lose.

NORTHSTAR-AT-TAHOE

P.O. Box 129
Truckee CA 95734
Tel: 916–562–1010

Snow Report: 916–562–1330
Area Vertical: 2,200 ft.
Number of Trails: 46, longest is
*   2.9 miles*
Lifts: 1 six-passenger gondola,
*   3 triple chairs, 5 double*
*   chairs, 2 surface lifts*
Snowmaking: First 1,000 ft.
*   of vertical*
Season: Thanksgiving–April

Northstar is called the Sierra's most complete resort. They gear themselves for the family vacation with a classic distribution of ski terrain—25 percent beginner, 25 percent expert, and 50 percent intermediate. The north-facing, wind-protected bowls offer some of the best powder skiing around. Steep chutes, long, lazy meandering runs, and fantastic scenery keeps everyone happy. Lift ticket sales are limited so that on sell-out days, lift line waits should be no more than 20 minutes.

There are plenty of amenities off the slopes as well. The village mall houses shops, meeting facilities, sundeck with barbeque pit, and restaurants. The Recreation Center is great for après-ski relaxation with spas, saunas, and game rooms.

Lake Tahoe's north shore is 6 miles by road and the naughty California/Nevada border only 15 minutes away.

Practical Information for Northstar-at-Tahoe

HOW TO GET THERE. The Truckee/Tahoe Airport is only 3 miles from Northstar and the *Amtrak* stop in Truckee is about 6 miles away on California Hwy. 267. *Sierra Tahoe Aviation,* 587–4433, comes into Truckee. Reno is 40 miles southeast and San Francisco is 196 miles west. Major national airlines serve Reno's Cannon International Airport, 785–2575.

TELEPHONES. The area code for Northstar-at-Tahoe is 916; for all of Nevada it is 702.

ACCOMMODATIONS. Lodging on the North Shore stretches from Incline Village to Tahoe City. Many of the establishments include interchangeable lift tickets valid at 9 areas. For specific information on the 80 or so lodges in the region, contact the *Tahoe North Visitors and Convention Bureau,* P.O. Box 5578, Tahoe City CA 95730; 583–3494, or 800–822–5959 in California and 800–824–8557 outside California.

For reservations at the base village, call 562–1113, or 800–811–5987 in California and 800–824–8516 outside California. Lodging categories are based on rates per person, double occupancy. *Expensive:* $80 and up; *Moderate:* $50–$80; *Inexpensive:* under $50. Packages of 3–6 nights are available and include lift tickets. Studio to 4-bedroom condos with full kitchens, fireplaces, hot tubs, saunas, and shuttle service throughout the complex range from $93 a night for a studio to $200 for a 4-bedroom; 3- and 4-bedroom houses range from $170 to $225 per night.

River Run Condominiums. *Expensive.* On the access road to Alpine Meadows overlooking the Truckee River; 583–3494. Nightly rates for accommodations ranging from 1-bedroom to 3-bedrooms with loft.

Pepper Tree Inn. *Moderate.* P.O. Box 29, downtown Tahoe City; 583–3711. Has hot tub, pool; pets permitted.

River Ranch. *Moderate.* P.O. Box 197, Tahoe City; 583–4264. Set on the Truckee River and all rooms have a view; antique furnishings; complimentary breakfast.

Tahoe City Travelodge. *Moderate.* P.O. Box 84, Tahoe City; 583–3766. Motel overlooks lake; phones, color TV, complimentary coffee; heated pool and hot tub; restaurant and lounge.

Seven Pines Motel. *Inexpensive.* P.O. Box 232, Kings Beach; 546–9886. Standard motel facilities.

Tamarack Lodge. *Inexpensive.* P.O. Box 69, Mammoth Lakes; 934–2442. Features rustic-style rooms and housekeeping cabins. Restaurant; cross-country ski school.

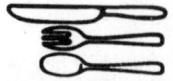

RESTAURANTS. All along the north and west shores of Lake Tahoe, the visitor may take his pick of places offering a wide variety of cuisines. On the mountain, *Big Springs* day lodge has a cafeteria, snack bar, and hot dog bar. Nearby is a wine and cheese house, and in the mall at the base area is a deli. For more substantial meals, one would have to visit towns in the area. Following is a selection, listed in order of price category. *Expensive:* $20–$30; *Moderate:* $10–$20; *Inexpensive:* less than $10.

Le Petit Pier. *Expensive.* 7250 N. Lake Blvd., Tahoe Vista; 546–4464. A classic French restaurant with set menus, attentive service, set details.

Jakes-on-the-Lake. *Moderate.* Boatworks Marina at 780 N. Lake Blvd., Tahoe City; 583–0188. It is "in" and reservations are necessary; diners can watch the colors over the lake change with the sunset; mostly seafood, dinners only.

Schaffer's Mill Restaurant and Lounge. *Moderate.* At the base mall of Northstar, serves 3 meals a day, popular with skiers staying in the base complex.

Swiss Lakewood. *Moderate.* Hwy. 89, 6 miles south of Tahoe City; 525–5211. Tahoe's oldest eatery, it serves European cuisine, mostly veal, fondue, Bourguignonne, quail, chateaubriand; reservations required; dinners only.

Donner Lake Kitchen. *Inexpensive.* 13440 Donner Pass Rd.; 587–3119. Open 7 days a week till 2 A.M., with skiers mostly ordering from the lengthy breakfast menu.

Squeeze Inn. *Inexpensive.* Main St., Truckee; 587–4814. Serves a great variety of omelets for breakfast and lunch.

HOW TO GET AROUND. A free skiers' **shuttle** is available between Tahoe Vista/Kings Beach and Northstar; call 562–1010.

SEASONAL EVENTS. Santa plays a big part in Northstar's 4-day **Christmas** celebration, especially when he passes out candy to the children in ski school, child-care centers, and any and all skiers on the slopes. The *Truckee Dog Sled Races* are held each **February** at the airport. The races feature over 70 teams from the western U.S. with the huskies covering distances of 3–14 miles. Weight pulling is exciting, too; the record for one dog is 1,600 pounds. Snowfest lasts for 10 days in late February and early **March,** with more than 100 events taking place at various north shore locations. The *Restaurant Relay* is at Northstar, where teams of waiters must perform specified culinary tasks while racing on cross-country skis.

OTHER SPORTS AND ACTIVITIES. The *Northstar Nordic Center* maintains 40 km of double-track **cross-country** trails. Guided tours, gourmet ski tours, off-track tours, telemark lessons, races, and clinics are scheduled throughout the season. The tracks wind through forests overlooking the Martis Valley and the Sierra Nevada. Skiers will see *Schaffer's Camp,* once the hub of frenzied activity during the west's logging era. Northstar Nordic Center, P.O. Box 129, Truckee CA 95734; 562–1010.

Other cross-country ski centers are *Big Chief Guides Nordic Center* on Hwy. 89 between Truckee and Squaw Valley, P.O. Box 5669, Tahoe City CA 95730, 587–4723, with groomed trails providing access to over 4,000 acres of wilderness; and *Tahoe Cross-Country Ski Center,* 2½ miles east of Tahoe City, P.O. Box 1632, Tahoe City CA 95730; 583–9858 or 583–0484; over 60 km of trails providing spectacular views of the lake.

Snowmobiles can be rented from *Snowmobile Rentals,* Tahoe City, 583–3595; *Snowmobiling Unlimited,* Carnelian Bay CA, 583–5858; *Renegade Snowmobile Tours,* Incline Village NV, 832–0482. In Incline Village the *Outdoorsman,* 832–0482, rents **sleds.**

CHILDREN'S ACTIVITIES. The SKIWEE program offers all day lessons for children 5–12. The price of $40 includes 5 hours of lessons and lunch. Call *Ski School* at 562–1330. For younger kids who are toilet trained, a child-care center at the base mall has all-day activities.

NIGHTLIFE. *Rendezvous Bar,* 562–1010, in the base mall has live entertainment and is popular on weekends. There is the usual gambling, big name entertainers, and hot spots in Tahoe City, Incline Village, and Reno. There are also bars overlooking the lake for quiet drinks. Pick up the visitors guides and the weekly entertainment guide, *Key,* or the local newspaper for the latest happenings.

OTHER LAKE TAHOE SKI AREAS

The major California/Nevada ski areas that a visitor would ski have been detailed. There are, however, numerous smaller areas in the Lake Tahoe area, both in California and Nevada. These include:

Boreal Ridge
Truckee CA
Vertical drop 600 ft.
Night skiing

Donner Ski Ranch
Norden CA
Vertical drop 800 ft.

Echo Summit
South Lake Tahoe CA
Vertical drop 550 ft.

Granlibakken
Tahoe City CA
Vertical drop 280 ft.
Oldest ski resort in Tahoe and
   least expensive lift ticket

Homewood
Homewood CA
Vertical drop 1,650 ft.
Most protected from winds

Mt. Rose
Reno NV
Vertical drop 1,400 ft.
Has highest base elevation
   in the area

Sierra Ski Ranch
Twin Bridges CA
Vertical drop 2,210 ft.

Ski Incline
Incline Village NV
Vertical drop 900 ft.
Charming ski area with top-of-the-line
   accommodations

Slide Mountain
Reno NV
Vertical drop 1,450 ft.
Locals call it "steep and cheap"; shares
   the mountain with Mt. Rose; look for
   interchangeable lift ticket in future

Soda Springs
Soda Springs CA
Vertical drop 700 ft.
Open weekends and holidays

Sugar Bowl
Norden CA
Vertical drop 1,500 ft.
Access gondola brings overnight guests
   across railroad tracks to the base area

Tahoe Donner
Truckee Ca
Vertical drop 600 ft.
What they call a "confidence builder"

Tahoe Ski Bowl
Homewood Ca
Vertical drop 600 ft.

Colorado

ASPEN

P.O. Box 1248
Aspen CO 81612
Tel: 303–925–1220

Area Vertical: 3,370 ft.
Number of Trails: 620 acres of
   groomed trails at Aspen Mountain,
   longest run 3.0 miles 402 acres
   of groomed trails at
   nearby Buttermilk/Tiehack,
   part of the Aspen complex
Lifts: On Aspen Mountain, 8
   chairlifts. On Buttermilk/
   Tiehack, 6 chairlifts
Snowmaking: 35 percent of
   terrain
Season: Mid- to late-November–
   mid-April.

Mention Aspen to skiers and they're bound to get a faraway look in their eyes and a faint smile on their lips. Mention Aspen to Hollywood types and they're likely to produce an all-knowing grin with a few dollar signs in their eyes.

Aspen is a mecca to skiers and to the glamour crowd. It has long been a haven for film stars. Jimmy Buffet, John Denver, Jill St. John, Leon and Jill Uris, and Goldie Hawn call Aspen home at least part of the year.

The first silver prospectors staked their claims in 1879. By the 1880s, Aspen had become one of the biggest silver towns in the west. In 1892, it was served by two railroads, had a fancy hospital, a courthouse, opera house, a first-class hotel, six newspapers, and nearly 12,000 people. Repeal of the Sherman Silver Act in 1893, however, dropped the price of silver and made Aspen destitute; by the 1930s, only 600 people lived in the town. At that time, the ski industry began to stir, and it blossomed after World War II to what it is today.

The turn-of-the-century Victorian mining town atmosphere has been preserved and updated. The modern mansions on the hills surrounding the colorful town just add to the "upscale" feeling. Aspen Mountain, called "Ajax" by the longtime skiers, juts up from downtown and the area couldn't be more perfect if it were a movie set.

Planned for the 1986–87 season is a gondola lift, touted as being the nation's longest and as having the world's greatest vertical rise.

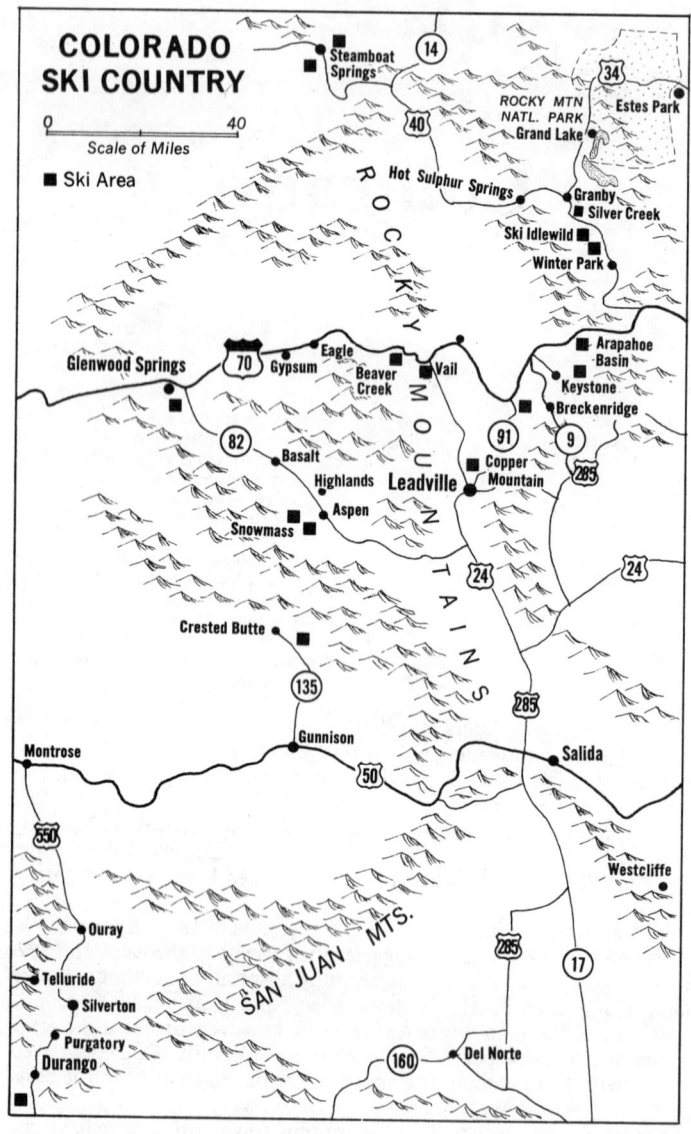

COLORADO
SKI COUNTRY

0   40

Scale of Miles

■ Ski Area

Practical Information for Aspen

HOW TO GET THERE. Aspen is in the White River National Forest, 205 miles from Denver. **By air.** *Rocky Mountain Airways* and *Aspen Airways* fly from Denver to the Aspen/Snowmass Airport four miles from town. Taxis are available between the airport and town lodging. Taxis and limos are also available for the ride from Denver's Stapleton Airport to Aspen.

By bus. *Trailways* runs between Denver and Aspen and Grand Junction and Aspen. *Aspen Limousine and Bus Service* provides the same service; 925–2400. Reservations are suggested.

By train. Daily transcontinental service on *Amtrak* stops at Glenwood Springs. Without prior arrangements, the taxi to Aspen is $55; however, divide that among five people and it's $11 per person. Eastbound trains arrive at 3 P.M. and westbound trains at 1 P.M. Make advance reservations through Amtrak or your travel agent to book a *Mellow Yellow Taxi* at a special rate between Glenwood Springs and the Aspen area; 925–2282. *High Mountain Taxi* also serves this route; 925–8294.

By car. It is 145 miles from Denver via I–70 to Glenwood Springs, then Hwy. 82 into Aspen. From Colorado Springs, take Hwy. 24 to Hwy. 82, 160 miles (See *Practical Information* for Southern Colorado). From Grand Junction take I–70 east to Glenwood and Hwy. 82 to Aspen, 140 miles.

TELEPHONES. The area code for all of Colorado is 303.

ACCOMMODATIONS. Contact the *Aspen Resort Association,* 700 S. Aspen St., Aspen CO 81611; 925–9000, or in Colorado, 800–421–7145, for lodging reservations. There's a lodge for every taste and nearly every pocketbook.

Lodging in town is within a maximum of an eight-block walk to the base of Aspen Mountain; also the free shuttle runs regularly through town to the mountain and to Buttermilk, Snowmass, and Aspen Highlands. Many hotels have shuttle service to and from ski areas and the airport. The listings here will give an idea of the range of lodgings available. Price categories are based on rates per person, double occupancy. *Expensive:* $75–$120; *Moderate:* $50–$75; *Inexpensive:* under $50.

Expensive

Aspen Club. 1450 Crystal Lake Rd.; 925–8900. A condominium complex specializing in physical fitness, a half-mile from town, with 2-bedroom units with fireplaces. Restaurant, cocktail lounge, fitness center, pool, sauna, hot tubs, steam rooms, running track, and indoor tennis.

Aspen Ski Lodge. 101 W. Main St.; 925–3434. One- and 2-bedroom units with outdoor decks. Some have kitchenettes, fireplaces, Jacuzzis. Heated outdoor pool and hot tubs, gourmet breakfast and health club privileges.

Aspen Square. 617 E. Cooper Ave.; 925–1000. Condominium with studios, 1- and 2-bedroom units. Fireplaces, private balconies, heated swimming pool, Jacuzzi, saunas, daily maid service.

The Gant. 610 West End Ave.; 925–5000. One- to 4-bedroom units in this condominium resort. Two heated pools, whirlpools, saunas, and 5 all-weather tennis courts.

Lift One. 131 E. Durant Ave.; 925–1670. Full-service condominiums at the base of Aspen Mountain; 1- to 3-bedroom units. Pool, sauna, Jacuzzi. Convenient to restaurants and nightspots.

ULLR Lodge. 520 W. Main St.; 925–7696. Family-style establishment with whirlpools, heated pool, game rooms, European ambience.

Moderate

The Brass Bed. 926 E. Durant Ave.; 925–3622. Small, old-world-style facility with brass beds in the rooms. Full breakfast buffet.

Limelight Lodge. 228 E. Cooper Ave.; 925–3025. Lounge, heated pool, sauna, complimentary breakfast, refrigerators.

St. Moritz Lodge. 334 West Hyman Ave.; 925–3220. 1930s lodge with European flavor. Apartments, rooms with private baths, inexpensive dorm rooms with shared baths. Fireplace in lobby, TV lounge, library, and game rooms; après-ski refreshments, but no restaurant. Heated pool, sauna, Jacuzzi. Condos are also available.

Inexpensive

Little Red Ski Haus. 118 E. Cooper Ave.; 925–3333. Friendly Victorian house, recently renovated; complimentary breakfast; three lounges, quad and single rooms.

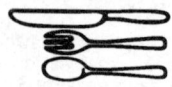 **RESTAURANTS.** On Aspen Mountain, the mountaintop *Sundeck* offers the usual ski fare with indoor and outdoor seating. *Bonnie's Restaurant* is mid-mountain in Tourtelotte Park serving good ol' American food and delicious European specialties. The outdoor deck is *the* place to meet and to be seen. *Ruthie's* is near Ruthie's Run with cafeteria-style service plus gourmet dining in the *Polo Lounge,* 925–2244.

On Buttermilk, *Cafe Suzanne,* located at the bottom of lift 3, features French country food, outdoor tables, wine, and beer. *The Cliff House,* at the top of lifts 5 and 2, offers cafeteria-style dining and a sundeck with a spectacular view. *Little Switzerland* at the bottom of lift 1, features cafeteria-style dining and a sundeck. *Romeo's,* located at the bottom of lift 4 at Tiehack, has cafeteria-style dining, a sundeck, wine, and beer.

In town, there are over 80 restaurants, most of them excellent and most with prices comparable to New York or San Francisco. *Expensive* restaurants run around $18–$30 for entrees; *Moderate,* $12–$18; *Inexpensive,* under $12. All restaurants listed take MasterCard and Visa unless otherwise noted.

Expensive

Abetone Restaurant. 620 E. Hyman Ave.; 925–9022. Northern Italian dinners, seafood, and vegetarian dishes. Reservations encouraged.

Charlemagne. 400 W. Main St.; 925–5200. Fine French food.

Maurice's. 700 Ute Ave.; 925–7822. Continental and French cuisine.

Parlour Car. 615 W. Hopkins Ave.; 925–3810. French cuisine in a restored railroad car.

Ute City Banque. 501 E. Hyman Ave.; 925–4373. An eclectic variety of dishes for lunch and dinner. Reservations encouraged.

Moderate

Chart House. 219 E. Durant Ave.; 925–3525. For steaks and salad bar.

Copper Kettle. 535 E. Dean Ave.; 925–3151. A different country's cuisine is featured each night. The restaurant is decorated with paintings and the wine cellar is extensive. Advance reservations necessary.

Crystal Palace. 300 E. Hyman Ave.; 925–1455. Victorian style with dinner; shows twice a night. Do make advance reservations.

Poppie's Bistro Cafe. 834 W. Hallam Ave.; 925–2333. For quail, fish, beef dishes.

Inexpensive

Eastern Winds. 520 E. Cooper Ave.; 925–5160. Polynesian and American dishes.

Home Plate. 333 E. Durant Ave.; 925–1986. For meals in a home-cooked style.

Mother Lode. 314 E. Hyman Ave.; 925–7700. Italian food in surroundings of brick walls with music.

The Shaft. 534 E. Cooper Ave.; 925–1483. For great ribs, chicken, steak—good value.

Skier's Chalet Steak House. 710 S. Aspen St.; 925–3381. Prime ribs and steaks.

Takah Sushi. 420 E. Hyman Ave.; 925–8588. For Japanese food.

 **HOW TO GET AROUND.** There is free **bus** service around town and to the ski areas of Aspen Mountain (in town), Buttermilk, Aspen Highlands, and Snowmass. **Taxi** (Mellow Yellow, 303–925–2282, or High Mountain, 303–925–5245) and horse-drawn sleighs from the mall are other means. Aspen is compact enough to **walk** nearly everywhere and the center of town is a mall with no vehicular traffic permitted. Unless you're staying at a remote lodge or friend's house, you won't need a car.

SEASONAL EVENTS. *Subaru Aspen Winternational* is the **January** carnival; it features the top amateur racers in world competitions on Aspen Mountain. *Banana Days* are held each **March** with parties, contests, special events, and discounted lodging.

 OTHER SPORTS AND ACTIVITIES. There are guided **cross-country** tours on the *Tenth Mountain Trail,* a hut-to-hut European-type experience. Moonlight dinner tours, cookhouse lunches, and cross-country lessons are available at Ashcroft, a ghost town 12 miles up Castle Creek Rd. There are 30 km of cross-country trails. Check *Aspen Touring Center,* Box 2432, Aspen CO 81612, 925–7185, or the Tenth Mountain Trail Hut System, 925–7625. A system of well-equipped shelters in the *Alfred A. Braun Hut System* connects Aspen with Crested Butte. Cost is $15 per person per night; call 925–7162. Ski rentals are available from *Ute Mountaineer,* 925–2849.

Snowshoe rentals are available from *Ute Mountaineer;* in fact, all kinds of touring equipment can be rented there.

Helicopter skiing is available through *Colorado First Tracks* during February and March; 925–7735.

In season, there are deep-powder **snowcat tours** (call Aspen Club, 925–8900) as well as guided out-of-bounds skiing for powder freaks.

 **DAY-CARE FACILITIES.** Aspen Mountain has no child-care or children's ski school facilities, but several in-town nursery services are available; 925–1940 for information. *Aspen Sprouts* day care takes 1–5-year-olds, and is located at the Aspen Airport Business Center; 920–1055. Buttermilk Mountain operates the *Powder Pandas Ski School* for ages 3–5. Beginner to advanced instruction, rental equipment, private ski hill, lunch and snacks. Write Box 223, Woody Creek CO 81656, or call 925–6336. Also, see *Snowmass* section for children's programs there.

Preschool story hour is Wednesday mornings at the *Pitkin County Library,* 120 E. Main St.; school-age children have story hour Wednesday afternoons. A children's film program is held here Friday afternoons from the end of December to early March; call 925–7124. Teens will enjoy hockey or figure skating at the *Aspen Ice Garden,* open 7 days a week; 925–7485.

The *Aspen Center for Environmental Studies* at the Hallam Lake Wildlife Sanctuary (925–5756) offers guided walks and snowshoe hikes Monday–Friday and an open house on Sunday afternoons; animals and educational displays.

NIGHTLIFE. An amazing choice of activities is offered. If you can both ski and party, there are rewards. Among the best known is *Andre's,* 312 S. Galena Ave., a disco where glimpses of movie moguls are possible. The *Tippler Oyster Bar,* 535 E. Dean Ave., is a must after skiing and later at night. *Little Nells,* 611 E. Durant Ave., at the bottom of Aspen Mountain, is lively. *The Paragon,* 419 E. Hyman Ave., blares disco music 'til the wee hours; *Little Annie's,* 517 E. Hyman Ave., and *O'Leary's Pub,* 521 E. Hyman, are favored gathering and meal spots for locals.

For those of a more cultural bent, an old favorite for dinner theater is the *Crystal Palace,* 300 E. Hyman Ave., 925–1455, an elegant red velvet Victorian restaurant where waiters present zany revues; reservations needed for dinner and show. Next door is *Grand Finale* with a delightful show of Broadway and Hollywood tunes; reservations for dinner and show at 925–1488. There are also four movie theaters in town.

BEAVER CREEK

P.O. Box 915
Avon CO 81620
Tel: 800–525–2257;
   from Denver, 949–5750

Snow Report: 303–476–4888 or
*   303–534–1245*
Area Vertical: 3,340 feet
Number of Trails: 42 named
*   runs on 689 acres, longest*
*   run 4 2/3 miles*
Lifts: 5 triple chairs, 3
*   double chairs*
Snowmaking: on 165 acres
Season: Late November–mid-April

Beaver Creek is the home of multimillionaires and families alike. With second homes costing $600,000 for starters, these people have some cash to spend. The masses can enjoy the resort both winter and summer, but it's not the cheapest vacation. The 1986–87 winter will be its seventh season and the lift lines are still short. There is an unhurried, European, up-scale atmosphere to the narrow valley.

Beaver Creek had been selected as the site of the 1976 Winter Olympics, but the Colorado voters vetoed any such antics in their backyard. As a result, Vail Associates (developers of the new ski area) took time to plan and develop a balance between the pristine environment, lodging and recreation needs, and private homes to create what they considered the perfect resort experience to complement their own sprawling Vail Valley. Since its opening in 1980, every house, condominium complex, hotel, and support building has been carefully blended into the pine and aspen trees. Cars are directed immediately to underground parking garages and that's the last people see of a car until they leave. If you must ride, a horse-drawn sleigh will pick you up.

The resort is due for completion in the mid-1990s at a price tag of more than $1 billion. Among those who were the first to build at Beaver Creek are former President Gerald Ford, his Secret Service bodyguards, and former ambassador to Belgium, Leonard Firestone.

Practical Information for Beaver Creek

HOW TO GET THERE. By air. *Rocky Mountain Airways* flies 2 to 9 flights daily from Denver into its private airport at Avon Stolport, just 3 miles from the Village of Beaver Creek. Some lodge shuttles meet flights at no charge; make advance arrangements when booking accommodations; for schedules, call 534–2291. Taxi service provided by *Louie's Casual Cabs*, 476–TAXI, and *Going Places*, 476–6816 or 321–5246. *Carey American Limousine* provides service to Avon; charters available, 393–0653; *Colorado Mountain Express*, 949–4227, limousine service which drops you off at the door, makes 7 daily trips from Stapleton Airport in Denver.

By bus. *Trailways* provides frequent service from Denver and Grand Junction to Vail, where you can take a shuttle bus to Beaver Creek during the winter season for $1.

By car. Beaver Creek is 10 miles west of Vail, just off I–70 in the White River National Forest. By car, it is 100 miles, or a little over a 2-hour drive, west from Denver on I–70. From Grand Junction it is 100 miles east on I–70. Rental cars are available from agencies at Denver's airport. In nearby Avon there is *Avis*, 800–332–0169; *Budget*, 800–527–0700; *Hertz*, 800–654–3131; and *National*, 800–328–4567.

TELEPHONES. The area code for all of Colorado is 303.

ACCOMMODATIONS. Currently, Beaver Creek has accommodations for 1,600 guests (with projected room for 10,500 at completion) in condos, hotels, and private houses. There are 8 condominiums or hotels plus luxury private houses with 5 to 7 bedrooms for large groups. Reservations can be made by contacting *Central Reservations,* Box 7, Vail CO 81658; 800–525–2257 in or out of Colorado.

All rooms are pricey. One-bedroom condos range from $120 to 265 a night; a hotel or lodge room is $80–$180 a night, double occupancy. Super deluxe 5-bedroom homes rent for $425 a night; 6-bedrooms for $550 a night; 7-bedrooms for $650 a night. The Hyatt Corporation expects to open a 350–450 room luxury hotel this year, and the Plaza Lodge is expected to open next year. The following list will give you an idea of what's available. All have whirlpools and saunas; none accept pets.

The Centennial. 180 Offerson Rd., Avon; 845–7600. Condos and lodge rooms; swimming pool.

The Charter at Beaver Creek. At base of Beaver Creek Mountain, 120 Offerson Rd., Box 5310, Avon; 949–6660. The first to open, with 1- and 2-bedroom condos and lodge rooms, indoor and outdoor swimming pools, golf course, and 2 restaurants.

Creekside at Beaver Creek. P.O. Box 2017, Avon; 949–7071. Two-bedroom condos, indoor and outdoor pools.

Kiva. 135 Offerson Rd., Avon; 949–5474. Condos and large rooms; restaurant, tennis courts.

Park Plaza. P.O. Box 36, Avon; 845–7700. Newest lodging, has 36 2- and 3-bedroom luxury condos, pool, and restaurant.

Post Montane. 76 Avondale Lane, Avon; 845–7500. Hotel and suites; restaurant.

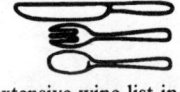

RESTAURANTS. Continental breakfast and lunch are served at the midmountain *Spruce Saddle* with a cafeteria and outdoor barbecues for warm spring-ski days. *The Rafters* has sit-down dining, Continental menu, and an extensive wine list in Spruce Saddle; reservations suggested, 949–6050. At the base area, *McCoy's Bar and Restaurant* serves breakfast and lunch, cafeteria-style, and après-ski cocktails, hors d'oeuvres, and entertainment; outdoor barbecues in good weather.

At *Expensive* restaurants listed below, entrees cost $18–$22; *Moderate,* $12–$18; *Inexpensive,* under $12. All restaurants listed take Visa and MasterCard unless otherwise noted.

There are a number of less-distinguished and less-expensive restaurants in nearby Avon. See also the *Vail* section.

Mirabelle. *Expensive.* At the entrance to Beaver Creek, 55 Village Rd., Avon; 949–7728. By far the most outstanding restaurant at the resort. French cuisine served in a restored wooden Victorian farmhouse, once the largest residence in the town of Avon and a place of some social importance at the turn of the century. Some claim it is the finest restaurant in the mountains—no small compliment. Cash only.

First Season. *Moderate.* In the Charter House at the base of Beaver Creek Mountain; 949–6660. Continental cuisine 7 nights a week, reservations required.

Kiva Club. *Moderate.* In the Kiva, 38340 US 6 and Hwy. 24, Avon; 845–7793. Lunch and dinner southwestern style. Reservations.

Legends Restaurant. *Moderate.* In the Poste Montane, 76 Avondale Lane, Avon; 949–5540. Three meals, plus weekend brunch.

Drinkwater Park. *Inexpensive.* In the Village Hall at base of the mountain. A favorite of locals, offering Mexican food 7 days a week. No reservations.

Zambini's. *Inexpensive.* Downstairs in the Village Hall. Serves pizza, salads, quiche.

HOW TO GET AROUND. Shuttle buses run from the base area, where day skiers park their cars, to the mountain, stopping along the way to pick up skiers in front of their condominiums.

SEASONAL EVENTS. The *Silver Series* races begin in **January,** along with the *City Challenge* races. In **February,** the *Mountain Man Winter Triathlon* is held in conjunction with *Avon Winterfest.* In **March,** it's the *Legends of Skiing* and the *Jerry Ford Celebrity Cup,* and in **April** the *Cindy Nelson Invitational.*

DAY-CARE FACILITIES. A toddler's program, called *Small World Play School,* is for nonskiing infants and toddlers. The play school is located at the Golf Course Clubhouse and parents can register infants from 2 months of age; advance registration is recommended. Infants and toddlers cost $28 per day, $76 for 3 days, $115 for 5 days; includes lunch and snacks. Parents should supply any special food and diapers. Contact Small World Play School at 949–5750.

For toilet-trained children, the *Children's Skiing Center* meets at the Village Hall; lunch and ski lessons provided, ages 3–12; call 949–5750. Prices are $28 for one day, $76 for 3 days, and $115 for 5 days.

NIGHTLIFE. Evenings in Beaver Creek tend to be on the quiet side, with people lounging in front of a fire or broiling in hot tubs. *Drinkwater Park* in the Village Hall has live entertainment, mostly folk, some rock, during the busiest months of the ski season. To find the action, head to Vail where you can dance the night away.

BRECKENRIDGE

P.O. Box 1058
Breckenridge CO 80424
Tel: 303–453–2368

*Snow Report: 303–453–6118,
    900–410–SNOW
Area Vertical: 2,583 ft.
Number of Trails: 1,441 acres,
    100 runs, longest run 3 miles
Lifts: 2 quad chairs, 1
    triple chair, 10 double
    chairs, 1 T-bar, 1 platter-pull
Snowmaking: on 300 acres.
Season: mid-November–mid-April*

Breckenridge was the center of a thriving group of villages and mining camps that sprang up during the gold fever of the 1860s. The largest single gold nugget ever found in the United States, weighing 13 pounds, 7 ounces, was unearthed here in 1887.

After World War II, the mining stopped and the town was almost forgotten. As late as the mid-1950s, Breckenridge was included in listings of Colorado ghost towns. In fact, through a surveyor's oversight, Breckenridge was not even part of the nation until 1936. Special ceremonies brought what was called the "Kingdom of Breckenridge" into the United States.

Early visitors were charmed by the Victorian buildings and miners' cabins (some date back to the 1840s), and in 1961, the Breckenridge Ski Area opened.

Over the years, Breckenridge has gained in popularity, and today it is a lively vacation spot, both summer and winter. Century-old businesses line the main street, and there are hundreds of shops and restaurants of all descriptions and price ranges. The ski mountain is just a few miles outside the town limits.

Practical Information for Breckenridge

 **HOW TO GET THERE.** The resort is located in the Arapaho National Forest, 85 miles west of Denver.

By air. Stapleton Airport in Denver is the gateway. Limousines, taxis, and charter coaches are available from Stapleton upon request. For buses to Breckenridge, see below.

By bus. *Trailways* operates daily service to Frisco and Breckenridge from Denver's Stapleton Airport and Denver downtown; about $11 one way. **Chauffered vans:** *Resort Express,* 800–334–7433; *Summit Taxi,* 800–321–5246; cost approximately $25 one way.

By car. A two-hour drive west via I–70 from Denver, through the Eisenhower Tunnel, which cuts through the Continental Divide, to exit 201, Colorado Rte. 9, about 9 miles from Frisco. From Colorado Springs, it is 150 miles via I–25, I–70, and Rte. 9. Three rental car agencies have drop-off services in Breckenridge: *Enterprise,* 800–525–3897; *Ajax,* 800–525–3852; and *Hertz,* 800–645–3131.

TELEPHONES. The area code for all of Colorado is 303.

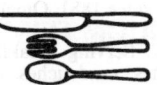 **ACCOMMODATIONS.** The *Breckenridge Resort Chamber* represents 95 percent of the available lodging and is the central reservations facility. Call 800–221–1091; in Colorado, 453–2918; from Denver, 623–5381. Write Box 1909, Breckenridge CO 80424. There are more than 100 condominium complexes, motels, and family-style lodges in the town and base area of Breckenridge, and 21,000 people can be housed. The following list should give you some idea of what's available.

Expensive: ranging from $90 to $350 per night, depending on the size of the unit; *Moderate:* $75–$115; *Inexpensive:* $50–$75.

Expensive

Beaver Run. Box B, Breckenridge; 453–6000. Top-of-the-line ski-in, ski-out property at the base of Peak Nine. It includes a complete commercial center, pool, hot tubs, saunas, steam and exercise rooms, day care.

Hilton Hotel. 800–321–8444. Top of the line ski-in, ski-out property. 6,000 square ft. of meeting space, indoor pool, Jacuzzi, health club, and restaurant.

Park Place. 325 Four o'Clock Rd.; 453–9344. Spacious 2-bedroom units, hot tubs. Easy access to shuttle, town, and slopes; access to pool, whirlpool, hot tub, sauna.

Village at Breckenridge. Main St. and South Park Rd.; 453–2000. Condominium resort complex between the banks of the Blue River and the base of the ski lifts, cross-country, ice skating.

Moderate

Four O'Clock Lodge. 550 Four O'Clock Rd. in Upper Four Seasons Village; 453–6228. Within walking distance of the slopes and town, studios to 3-bedroom lofts. Access to an amenities area with pool, whirlpool, sauna, hot tub.

Wedgewood Lodge. 535 Four O'Clock Rd.; 800–521–2458. Victorian townhomes located as a ski-home property, features fireplaces, hot tubs, sauna.

Inexpensive to Moderate

Brass Bed Inn. 229 S. Main St.; 453–0843. Bed and breakfast inn in a restored, late-1800s Victorian home. Swedish breakfast included.

Fireside Inn. 114 French St.; 453–6456. Restored Victorian home in town with dorms, private rooms, and family-style group dining.

O'Brien's Lodge. 212 N. Ridge St.; 453–0588. Has everything from dormitory to 1–3-bedroom accommodations.

Copper is considered to be at the high end of affordable resorts, popular with families and groups. Because it's visible from I–70, it gets a lot of drop-ins for day-skiing.

Practical Information for Copper Mountain

HOW TO GET THERE. Copper Mountain is in the Arapaho National Forest, 75 miles west of Denver.

By air. Denver's Stapleton Airport is the gateway with connections by bus (see below) or rental car. All major car agencies are represented at the airport. *Summit Taxi* has a Denver Special, $15 per person from Stapleton to Copper Mountain.

By bus. *Trailways, American Limousine,* and *Resort Express* all shuttle between Stapleton Airport and the ski area. Call Apex Travel at 968–2310.

By car. Take I–70 west from Denver 75 miles through Eisenhower Tunnel to exit 195. The resort claims that there are no mountain passes to cross from Denver, but this is misleading; Eisenhower Tunnel cuts through the Continental Divide at 11,600 ft. and climbing from 5,280 ft. at Denver is no small task. Alternatively, you can go via Loveland Pass. From Colorado Springs, it is 90 miles via US 24 and Colorado Rte. 9; from Grand Junction, 180 miles east on I–70 to Exit 195.

TELEPHONES. The area code for all of Colorado is 303.

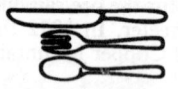

ACCOMMODATIONS. There are approximately 2,800 pillows in 22 hotel and condominium units plus a 225-room Club Mediterranee in the village. Reservations are made through *Copper Mountain Lodging Services,* Box 3001, Copper Mountain CO 80443; 800–525–3878 outside Colorado, 800–332–3828 inside Colorado. If they're booked, additional lodging is available at the mountain and in the surrounding Summit County area through the *Copper Mountain Resort Association,* 800–525–3891 outside Colorado, or 968–6477.

Nearly all the lodges have a choice of *expensive* to *moderate* hotel rooms and condos. The average price runs $43 per person, maximum occupancy. For example, **Mountain Plaza** and **Village Square** are both at the base of the mountain, and have saunas, shops, and Jacuzzi. A one-bedroom apartment at either is $150 per night; a studio with kitchen, fireplace, and pull-out sofa, or a hotel room, is $100 a night.

Inexpensive motels can be booked in nearby Frisco at **A & B Court Apartments,** 310 Main St., (668–3587), or **Sky Vue Motel,** 305 S. Second Ave., (668–3311). In Dillon, the **Tenderfoot Motor Lodge** (22784 U.S. Highway 6, 468–2254), is moderately inexpensive.

Club Med runs from mid-December to mid-April. The nightly per person rate, including lift ticket, Club Med ski school, and three meals is $119 double occupancy; a 7-night package is $830. Contact Club Mediterranee, 50 Beeler Place, Copper Mountain CO 80443; 800–528–3100 outside Colorado, 968–2161 in state.

RESTAURANTS. *Solitude Station* at mid-mountain offers the skier hearty cafeteria-style fare, as does the *Center Cafeteria* at the base area; upstairs from the latter is *Jacques' Loft,* a full-service restaurant and après-ski lounge. *B-Lift Pub* is open for three meals a day, mostly burgers. *Union Creek* also has a cafeteria for skiers.

Ten other restaurants in town offer a variety of cuisines at reasonable prices. Entrees at *Expensive* establishments are $9–$17; *Moderate,* $6–10; *Inexpensive,* under $5. All restaurants listed take Visa and MasterCard unless otherwise noted.

Expensive

Barkleys. 620 Main St., Frisco; 668–3694. Good steaks, prime rib, chicken, fish. Reservations recommended.

Blue Spruce. 120 W. Main St., Frisco; 668–5243. A fine Continental restaurant; no reservations.

Farley's. 104 Wheeler Pl., Copper Mountain; 968–2577. Specializes in prime rib, steaks, nightly specials. Reservations recommended.

The Plaza. Mountain Plaza, at center of base area; 968–2882, ext. 6505. An elegant restaurant featuring Continental cuisine, classical guitar music during dinner. Reservations needed.

Moderate.

The Clubhouse. At B-Lift. Mexican food is served American-style at this skier's hangout. Breakfast, lunch, and dinner served in winter. No reservations.

Columbine Cafe. Village Square; 968–2882. Après-ski entertainment, pasta, steak, chicken, salads. No reservations.

Racquets. In the Copper Mountain Racquet and Athletic Club; 968–2882. Features prime rib and Polynesian dishes. Reservations recommended.

Tuso's. 104 Wheeler Pl.; 968–6090. A wide menu, including Mexican and Italian food.

Inexpensive.

The Copper Still. Snowbridge Square; 968–2020. Deli foods, snacks, and soups. No reservations.

The Scoop. Mountain Plaza Building; 968–6168. Croissant sandwiches, ice cream, chocolates. Lunch only. Call for credit card information.

Soupy Sales. Village Square; 968–2629. Known for the stuffed potatos, chili, and soups. Breakfast and lunch only.

Vlasta's Pizza. Snowbridge Square; 968–2323. Deli foods, breakfast, lunch, and dinner.

 **HOW TO GET AROUND.** The *Summit Taxi Service,* 668–3565, and the free *Summit Stage* operate throughout the county. Within Copper Mountain Resort, there is a **free shuttle** service. Much is within walking distance from the base of the mountain, but if you care to venture afield, a **car** is needed.

 **SEASONAL EVENTS.** Early season ski clinics for recreational skiers in **December** have become a standard. Women's cross-country ski series are in early **February,** followed by the Subaru U.S. Alpine Championships. Resort seminars offer programs on a variety of professional and personal subjects, **December** to mid-**April.**

 OTHER SPORTS AND ACTIVITIES. Cross-country skiing is available on 25 km of maintained double tracks at Union Creek. Track fees are $4 for adults; a ticket for K-lift and the tracks is $7. Lessons, clinics, and a women's cross-country series are part of the nordic program. Rentals are available. Call 968–2882, ext. 6342.

Ice skating on West Lake is held noon to 9 P.M., no charge; skate rentals at *Turning Point Sports/Gorsuch Ltd.* in Village Square, 968–2048. **Sleigh rides** follow the base of the mountain daily except Sunday; call 968–2232 for reservations.

The Racquet and Athletic Club offers **racquetball, Nautilus equipment, weight room, aerobics,** and **pool** with four 25-yard lap lanes, **saunas, hot tubs,** a **massage therapist,** two **indoor tennis courts,** nursery, restaurant and bar. Daily fees for resort guests; call 968–2882.

 **CHILDREN'S ACTIVITIES.** Call for day-care information, 968–2882, ext. 6345. *Belly Button Babies* is for tots 2 months to 2 years. Rates for 1986 were $27 a day, $18 for a half-day. *Belly Button Bakery* operates daily for kids 2 years and up, teaching them cooking, baking, arts and crafts, and outdoor snow play. Costs in 1986 were $27 a day, $18 for a half-day.

Junior Ranch is a learn-to-ski program for 4-, 5-, and 6-year-olds. A full day of supervised indoor and outdoor activity, $24; a half-day (12:45–3:30 P.M.) was $18 during 1986. Ski equipment and lunch money are needed; reservations recommended (968–2882). *Senior Ranch* is a ski-school program for 7–12-year-olds, beginners to hot-shots. All-day instruction; lunch money needed; 1986 costs were $24 a day and $18 a half-day (12:45–3:30 P.M.). *Newcomer* packages for children are for those who have never skied. They include lift tickets, lessons, and ski rentals; one day, $30; two days, $60; three days, $90. For children who have skied before, the lift/lesson/rental package prices are: one day, $39; two days, $74; three days, $108.

 **NIGHTLIFE.** The nightlife won't overwhelm you at Copper Mountain, but some good sounds come from the background guitar music at *Plaza Restaurant. Clubhouse*, at B-Lift, features live entertainment Tuesdays–Sundays, 3:30–7:30 P.M. *Rock and Top 40* is featured at *Columbine* in Village Square, Tuesdays–Saturdays, 9 P.M.–1 A.M. *O'Shea's*, in the Copper Junction Building at the base area, has live country-western music during the winter only. Movies are put on twice-weekly by the Resort Association; call for schedules and location, 968–6477. The Center features après-ski entertainment six nights a week. VCR rentals and two game rooms (Snowbridge Building and Copper Junction) round out après-ski life.

CRESTED BUTTE MOUNTAIN RESORT

P.O. Box A
Mt. Crested Butte CO 81225
Tel: 303–349–2333; 349–2211

Snow Report: 303–349–2323
Area Vertical: 2,150 ft.
Number of Trails: 51 on 420
　　acres, longest run 1.9 miles
Lifts: 3 triple chairs, 1
　　enclosed double cabin, 5
　　double chairs, 1 T-bar
Snowmaking: 40 percent
　　(160 acres)
Season: November–April

Unlike the other Colorado mining towns, Crested Butte never became a ghost town. Amax Mining Company still takes a good deal of molybdenum from the area, sparking classic confrontations between miners and environmentalists. This rather remote town, in the Gunnison Valley, is listed as a National Historic District.

Crested Butte's weatherbeaten Victorian buildings reflect the price of survival in the harsh high-country winters. But behind the sometimes scruffy 1880s facades are gourmet restaurants, boutiques, and art galleries. The ambience is Victorian without the self-conscious cuteness of Aspen and Breckenridge.

The ski area, Mt. Crested Butte, is three miles up the road from the town. Here the condos are modern, with views of the Elk Mountain Range and Ragged Wilderness Areas that will take your breath away. The ski area is actually the other side of Aspen Mountain and hardy cross-country skiers make their way across the summit in winter; hikers do it in summer. A dirt road between Aspen and Crested Butte is open only in summer and is an arduous drive.

The area's self-proclaimed fame stems from its 405 acres of expert, out-of-bounds skiing and its being the center of the rebirth of the telemark turn in cross-country touring. Strong skiers hire a guide to take them to the "Outer Limits" for endless powder, both downhill and for those on skinny skis. Groomed trail skiing is for strong intermediates.

Crested Butte is very affordable. The area attracts college students from nearby Western State College in Gunnison, and singles and families from the Southeast and Texas. It is strictly a destination area, too remote from any population center to attract day-skiers. Bargain hunters can do well here.

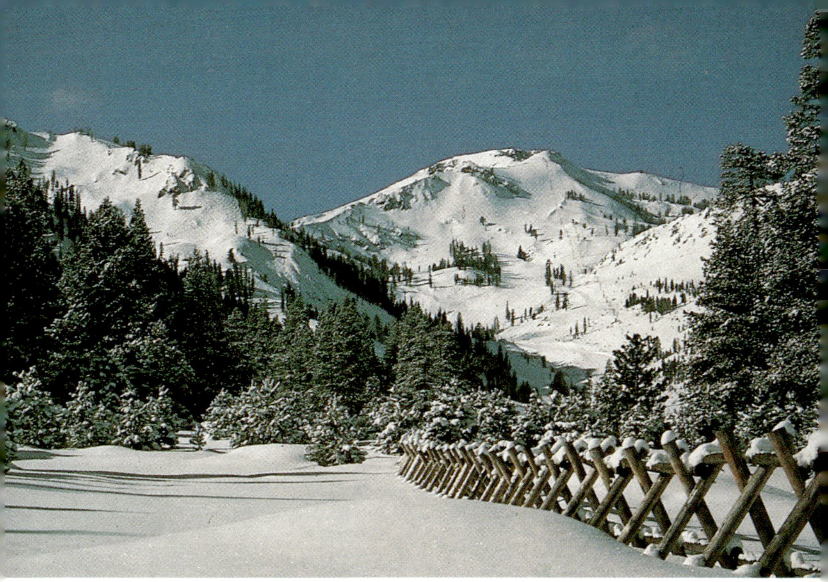

At an elevation of 8,900 feet, Squaw Peak looms above this peaceful setting in Squaw Valley USA, California. Up, up, and away go the gondolas at Killington, Vermont, to lift skiers high above the snow-topped trees on the slopes.

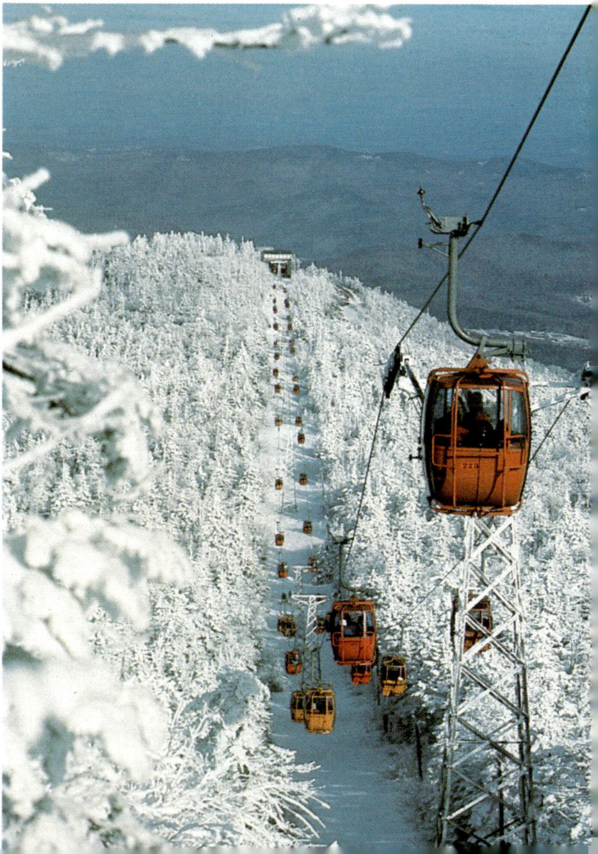

Photo by Bob Perry

Photo by Bob Perry

A sextet of expert skiers at Aspen, Colorado, enjoy a fine day for the sport, while at Killington, Vermont, youngsters get their ''ski legs'' under trained supervision.

Fireworks light up the sky as a climax to night skiing at Vail, Colorado.

Photo by Don Weil

Skiing knows no season. At Aspen, Colorado, a
family of four makes its way to the slopes through
gently falling snowflakes. At Silver Mountain,
British Columbia, a brave soul doesn't need a beach
to get her suntan.

Practical Information for Crested Butte

 **HOW TO GET THERE.** Crested Butte is in the Gunnison National Forest, 230 miles southwest of Denver. **By air.** Gunnison is the closest gateway, 30 miles downvalley in west central Colorado. *Air Atlanta* operates charters from Dallas, Atlanta, and Houston. *Trans Colorado* serves Gunnison daily from Denver, Colorado Springs, and Albuquerque. *American Airlines* operates from Chicago, Dallas, Houston, and Los Angeles. *Crested Butte* Aviation flies between Crested Butte and Aspen. Call 349–7334 for information.

From Gunnison Airport, taxis, 349–5749, and limousines, 349–5874, operate daily schedules to Crested Butte. Rental cars are available at the airport from *Coopers,* 349–5749.

By car. It is a 5-hour drive over Monarch Pass from Denver via US 285, US 50, and Rte. 135.

By bus. *Trailways* runs from Denver, Colorado Springs, and Grand Junction to Gunnison.

 **ACCOMMODATIONS.** There are 5,000 pillows in 34 condominium complexes and 9 lodges in the town of Crested Butte and the new Mt. Crested Butte. Contact *Central Reservations,* 349–2222 or 800–525–4220 to arrange lodging, lift tickets, ski rental, and lessons. Accommodations categories are determined by price. *Expensive:* $150 for a 1-bedroom condo, up to $320 for a 3-bedroom condo; *Moderate:* $130–$145 for a 2-bedroom condo; and *Inexpensive,* about $30 per person per night in a lodge room.

Crested Mountain. *Expensive.* 21 Emmons Rd.; 349–7555. Located on Warming House hill, each unit has a whirlpool, fireplace, and use of heated pool and health spa.

Mt. Crested Butte Hotel and Resort. *Expensive.* P.O. Box 5033; 349–2060. New in 1986, this 263-room hotel managed by AirCoa is ski-in/ski-out at the base of Keystone and Silver Queen lifts; 2 restaurants, lounge, 2 bars, pool, spa, indoor tennis, sun deck.

Penthouse. *Expensive.* 21 Emmons Rd., atop the Conference Center; 349–7555. Primarily 1-bedroom units, slanted, wood ceilings, pool, hot tubs. Tops at this resort is the 3-bedroom, 3-bath condo with a 2-½-story living room with rock wall fireplace, private hot tub, private deck, and sauna.

Irwin Lodge. *Expensive.* P.O. Box 457; 349–5140. Located in the wilderness, accessible only by snowcat or snowmobile, guests stay a minimum of 3 days in this rustic but luxurious lodge. Guided cross-country skiing or downhill with snowcats; meals included.

Mountain Sunrise Condominiums. *Moderate.* 15 Marcellina La.; 349–2828. Attractive townhouses located several blocks from the slopes. Skiers can take the shuttle bus, walk, or drive to the main lot; Jacuzzi and sauna.

Plaza Condos at Wood Creek. *Moderate.* 11 Snowmass Rd.; 349–2130. Spacious complex has sauna, outdoor hot tubs, restaurant; a 4-minute walk to the lifts.

Elk Mountain Lodge. *Inexpensive.* 129 Gothic Ave.; 349–5114. In the town of Crested Butte; rooms do not have private baths.

Four Seasons Lodge. *Inexpensive.* 416 First St.; 349–5336. Also in town; basic accommodations.

 **RESTAURANTS.** Most of the good restaurants are in town, but several lively après-ski spots are at the mountain. Restaurants are listed in order of price category. *Expensive:* $13–$20; *Moderate:* $8–$12; *Inexpensive:* less than $8. MasterCard and Visa accepted unless otherwise noted.

Penelopes. *Expensive.* 120 Elk Ave; 349–5178. A long-time favorite of locals and visitors in the know, it is a cheery, sunny place with lots of ferns and antiques; Sunday brunch is especially good.

Skyland Resort and Country Club. *Expensive.* 385 Country Club; 349–6129. Good basic American food.

Slogar's. *Expensive.* 517 Second Ave.; 349–5765. Dining in dark Victorian atmosphere.

Soupcon. *Expensive.* 127 Elk Ave.; 349–5448. Small, elegant log cabin in an alley behind the Forest Queen; basically a very French menu; try the roast duck.

Artichoke. *Moderate.* 433 Emmons Rd.; 349–5400. Specializing in steaks, chops, and artichokes; also huge burgers for lunch.

Bacchanale. *Moderate.* 208 Elk Ave.; 349–5257. Delightful Italian dishes.

Forest Queen. *Moderate.* 129 Elk Ave.; 349–5336. Located in the oldest building in Crested Butte; American fare.

Jeremiah's. *Moderate.* 129 Elk Ave.; 349–5336. American menu.

Angelo's. *Inexpensive.* 501 Elk Ave.; 349–5708. Pizza; no credit cards.

Donita's Cantina. *Inexpensive.* 332 Elk Ave.; 349–6674. Good Mexican food.

Tincup. *Inexpensive.* Mt. Crested Butte; 349–2055. Chicken, chopped steaks.

Wooden Nickel. *Inexpensive.* 222 Elk Ave.; 349–6350. A must—serves hearty portions of steak, ribs, lobster; a local favorite with a noisy, rah-rah atmosphere.

HOW TO GET AROUND. The *Mountain Express* resort **shuttle** operates free of charge from 7 A.M. to midnight between town and the mountain. Call 349–5616 or 6298 for schedule. Having a car gives visitors more flexibility.

SEASONAL EVENTS. *Western State College winter weekend* is always in early **December.** The infamous *Al Johnson Memorial Uphill-Downhill* race is held the end of **March,** while winter is "flushed out" by celebrating *Flauschink* in early **April.**

 OTHER SPORTS AND ACTIVITIES. The **cross-country's** Telemark turn is said to have been rediscovered and perfected here. Certainly, cross-country skiing is important at this resort, with guided tours into the awesome wilderness areas as well as 13 km of groomed tracks as part of the nordic program. Contact Rick Borkovec, director, at 349–2333 or the *Ski Touring Center* at 349–2250.

For Outer Limits skiing, call the ski school at 349–2252. **Ice skating** is available at the mountain, 349–2292; **sleigh rides,** 349–2211. **Snowshoe** rentals are available through *Alpineer,* 349–5582. Skyland Resort has **racquetball** courts, 349–6131.

 **DAY-CARE FACILITIES.** Children 6 months to 3 years are taken at *Buttetopia Ski and Day Care Center* in the Whetsone Building, 349–2209. Another section takes care of 3–7-year-olds. The older kids get ski instruction, indoor supervision, lunch; $30 for a full day, $15 for a half day without lunch.

Buttetopia also has a special class for parents and their children together to teach the parents how to ski safely with their kids and how to continue their learning mode after the formal instruction is over. Cost is $10 an hour.

ABC-on-Skis is a beginner skiing program for 3–8-year-olds who are toilet trained; full day, 9 A.M.–4:30 P.M., is $35, with lunch, nursery care, ski equipment, and lessons; no lifts are used.

NIGHTLIFE. *Black Bear Bar,* 11 Snowmass Rd., and *Kochevar's Saloon,* 127 Elk Ave., have live music or disco dancing. *Rafter's Nightclub* in the Gothic Building at the base area has live bands except Monday nights; good for après-ski. Check out *Donita's Cantina* on Thursday nights for $4 liters of margaritas. *Eldorado Cafe,* upstairs next to the post office, serves burgers and has pool tables and live entertainment.

The *Crested Butte Mountain Theatre,* 132 Elk Ave., 349–5685, has performances year round. The *Crested Butte Society,* 349–6355, sponsors activities for artists, dancers, and musicians.

KEYSTONE

P.O. Box 38
Keystone CO 80435
Tel: 303-468-2316

*Snow Report: 572–SNOW (Denver
   direct); 303–468–4111
   (outside Denver)
Area Vertical: 2,360 ft.
Number of Trails: 680 skiable
   acres, 40 miles of trails;
   open bowl, glade, and trail
   skiing, 49 trails
Lifts: Keystone Mountain: 1 six-passenger gondola, 3 triple chairs, 8
   double chairs 2 poma lifts.
   Arapahoe Basin: 1 triple
   chair, 4 double chairs
Snowmaking: 75 percent of area
   (484 acres)
Season: Keystone: late
   October–early May
    Arapahoe Basin: late
   November–mid-June*

Keystone is the ultimate planned village. This "full-service" four-season resort consists of the Keystone Lodge and 900 condominium units mostly clustered around a central lake and immaculate village. Every building has been built with materials and colors that blend with the environment, maintaining a feeling of the natural landscape. It is almost too perfect—and those coming from high-stress situations could decompress too quickly.

Like most mountain communities, Keystone first saw the light of day with the quest for gold. The settlement was established by 1880 in a wide valley bisected by the Snake River, the craggy Continental Divide towering above. With the wane of the gold and silver booms, Keystone had little more than a few weathered boards to show for its former life. In the 1950s, a strange breed started coming to Arapahoe Basin a few miles from Keystone to slip and slide down the snow—skiers. It wasn't until the late 60s, though, that skiers started having an impact on the economy. Even then, Summit County was just the high area to drive through on the way to Aspen.

The Keystone Mountain resort was created in 1970; the mountain itself is perhaps a mile from the planned village, while Arapahoe Basin is several miles away at the base of Loveland Pass. The entire operation is under the management of Ralston Purina Company, and the corporate hand can be felt, particularly in the efficient, formal service and employee attitudes. Today, the Summit County ski areas, marketed as "Ski the Summit" form the biggest resort cluster in the country and host more skiers than the Aspen complex.

Keystone is considered to be at the upper end of affordability, with enough elegant dining and shopping for those who want to spend a few more dollars. The resort attracts well-to-do and upper -middle-income families, mostly from the Midwest, Southeast, Texas, and Oklahoma.

Practical Information for Keystone

HOW TO GET THERE. Keystone is in the Arapaho National Forest, 75 miles west of Denver.

By air. Denver's Stapleton Airport is the closest gateway, with scores of airlines from all major American cities, and rental cars available. Scheduled chauffered van service via *Resort Express* is available from the Airport for $22.50 per person one way; 800–334–7433.

By car. Drive 75 miles west from Denver via I–70, through Eisenhower Tunnel, to Exit 205, then 6 miles east on US 6. In good weather, go through the spectacularly scenic Loveland Pass by exiting I–70 just before the tunnel, and taking US 6, past Loveland and Arapahoe ski areas to Keystone. From Colorado Springs, it is 145 miles via I–25 and I–70; from Grand Junction it is 180 miles east on I–70 over Vail Pass to Exit 205, then 6 miles east on US 6.

By bus. Trailways has daily bus service from Denver's airport to Frisco, with some schedules direct to Keystone. It's a short taxi ride from Frisco to Keystone.

TELEPHONES. The area code for all of Colorado is 303.

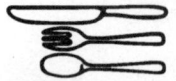

ACCOMMODATIONS. For reservations, call 468–4242 or write *Keystone Central Reservations,* Box 38, Keystone CO 80435. In Denver, call direct: 534–7712. Information for all accommodations: 468–2316.

Categories are determined by price. *Expensive:* $107–$132 per night for hotel rooms; $132–$375 a night for studio units to 4-bedroom condos. *Moderate:* $121–$300 per night for studios to 4-bedroom condos. *Inexpensive:* $110–$243 for studios to 4-bedroom condos. Ask for "Premium" when making reservations at an expensive establishment, "Deluxe" at moderate establishments.

Expensive

Keystone Lodge. Box 38; 468–2316. Keystone's full-service hotel, the lodge holds awards for the superiority of its guest facilities. Each of the 152 rooms has a mountain view; the heated indoor–outdoor pool has complete cocktail service. There is a sauna and hot therapy baths. No pets.

Most of the following accommodations range from studio units to 4-bedroom condos. Private homes are also for rent. **Argentine, Plaza Mall, Edgewater,** and **Lakeside** are all on Keystone Lake at the center of the village; 2-minute shuttle ride to the mountain.

Willows, Decatur, Montezuma, and **Lenawee** are on the east side of Keystone Lake; 2-minute walk to village center, 2-minute shuttle ride to mountain.

Chateaux d'Mont and **Lancaster Lodge** are at the base of Keystone Mountain.

Moderate

Pines, Soda Spring, Homestead/Lodgepole, Quicksilver, Tennis Townhouses, St. John; 5-minute walk from village center; no pets.

Inexpensive

Flying Dutchman, Wild Irishman, Key Condo, Keystone Gulch. These are standard accommodations, but hardly cheap. Farther from the Village, they don't have the wonderful views.

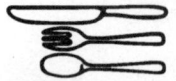

RESTAURANTS. There are 10 restaurants in the village, including the *Keystone Lodge,* Keystone Ranch, a few miles from the village at the golf course, and historic *Ski Tip Lodge,* a restored stagecoach stop from the 1860s, now an unusual dining and lodging experience.

At the base of the mountain is *Gassy's,* open for lunch and dinner. Good crepes can be had from the *Greatest Crepe Wagon,* parked at the base area. *Last*

Lift Bar is good for snacks and drinks. The *Summit House* at the top of Keystone Mountain is a multileveled cafeteria and soup bar, with outdoor barbecues in good weather. *Mountain House* and *River Run Plaza* offer cafeteria food.

Entrees in *Expensive* restaurants will run $17–$20; $10–$15 in *Moderate;* under $10 in *Inexpensive.* All restaurants listed take Visa and MasterCard unless otherwise noted.

Garden Room. *Expensive.* In the Keystone Lodge; 468–2316. For Continental meals prepared tableside. Reservations recommended.

Bentley's. *Moderate.* Overlooking Keystone Lake; 468–6610. Burgers as well as Italian-American dishes. Reservations accepted.

Bighorn Steakhouse. *Moderate.* In the Keystone Lodge; 468–2316. Serves steaks and offers a 28-item salad bar.

The Navigator. *Moderate.* At Keystone Lake; 468–5600. For seafood; reserve in advance.

Edgewater Cafe. *Inexpensive.* In Keystone Lodge; 468–4127. Open in winter for three meals. Reservations accepted.

Last Chance Pizza. *Inexpensive.* Argentine Plaza, Keystone Village; 468–4186. Good pizzas and a young crowd.

OUTSIDE KEYSTONE RESORT

Blue Spruce Inn. *Expensive.* 12 West Main, Frisco; 668–5243. Known for its Continental menu; steaks and ribs.

La France. *Expensive.* 25 Chief Colorow, Dillon; 468–6111. Elegantly French. No credit cards.

Keystone Ranch. *Expensive.* At the Keystone Ranch golf course in the resort, a few miles from Keystone Village; 468–4161. Outstanding six-course dinners, fixed price of $30, all in an elegant ranch setting. Reservations recommended.

Ski Tip Ranch. *Expensive.* On Montezuma Rd., 2 miles east of Keystone Village; 468–9928. For dining in a cozy guest ranch—the oldest in Colorado. Call for prices and credit card information.

Old Dillon Inn. *Moderate.* 305 Dillon La., Silverthorn; 468–2791. Mexican food, loud music, and weekend entertainment make this the most popular hangout for locals.

Claim Jumper. *Inexpensive.* 805 North Summit Rd., Frisco; 668–3617. For pizza and chicken.

Whiskey Creek. *Inexpensive.* 912 North Summit Rd., Frisco; 668–5595. For Mexican food and fine margaritas.

 **HOW TO GET AROUND.** A free **shuttle** operates continually from the Keystone Lodge and all condos to the Village, Mountain House, River Run Plaza, Arapahoe Basin, and Keystone Ranch for dinner. For information, call the *Transportation Center,* 468–4200. Within Summit County the free **bus** service, *The Summit County Stage,* runs from Keystone to the neighboring "Ski the Summit" areas of Breckenridge and Copper Mountain from mid-November until late April.

 **SEASONAL EVENTS.** *Grand Marnier National Ski Club Championships* race off in **March.** *Colorado Special Olympics* for mentally handicapped athletes also holds regional championships in March. *World Professional Skiing Championships* ushers in **April,** as does spring skiing with a week-long *Hawaiian Beach Party* at the top of Keystone Mountain.

Special at **Christmas** is an Elizabethan-style dinner with madrigal entertainment, reminiscent of Tudor England. Presented in the Conference Center of the Keystone Lodge, this is an unusual and memorable way to spend Christmas—$37 per person; call 468–2316.

 OTHER SPORTS AND ACTIVITIES. Cross-country skiing is on 26 miles of prepared trails. Lessons and tours by day or evening offered; Telemark lessons with lunch and lift ticket are $35 per day. Contact Jana Hlavaty, Keystone Resort, Box 38, Keystone CO 80435; 468–2316.

Helicopter skiing is available through *Rocky Mountain Heliski* out of Dillon; call 468–8253.

Ice skating is popular on Keystone Lake; the *Keystone Center* is the largest maintained outdoor facility in the country. Rink admission is $2.50; skate rental $2.50; 468–2316, ext. 3980.

DAY-CARE FACILITIES. They're free—if kids are 18 months and under and stay in the same lodge room or condo unit with their parents. The *Children's Center* in the Mountain House at the base of Keystone Mountain will take care of children from 2 months. It is open 8 A.M.–5 P.M. daily; advance reservations required, 468–4182. Care for infants 2–11 months is $35 a day or $5 an hour; you supply the baby food. All-day child care—12 months and up—is $30, lunch included, or $4.50 an hour. Evening babysitting may be reserved through the Children's Center.

At Arapahoe Basin, the center accepts children 18 months and older from 8:30 A.M.–4:30 P.M. daily; call 468–2316; ext. 62–210 for reservations. Prices are the same as Keystone Center.

Snow Play Program, 468–4182, is for children 3 years and older. It offers sledding and skating. Children should be toilet-trained and dressed for outdoors. Keystone Mountain only; $32 a day including lunch; half-day for $25 (8 A.M.–1 P.M. or noon–5 P.M.).

Junior Ski School is for ages 3–12; $40 a day includes lift ticket, rental equipment, lunch, and 4 hours of lessons; reservations required at the ski school, 468–2316.

NIGHTLIFE. You won't disco the night away in Keystone, but there are several lounges for après-ski and après-dinner drinks. The *Tenderfoot Lounge,* in the Lodge, is elegant with a spectacular view of the Gore Range. *Bentley's* occasionally has live entertainment and *Last Chance Saloon* usually has nightly entertainment. See *Restaurants* section for addresses.

PURGATORY

P.O. Box 666
Durango CO 81302
Tel. 303-247-9000

Snow Report: 303–247–9000
Area Vertical: 2,022 ft.
Number of Trails: 600 skiable
　　acres, longest run 2 miles
Lifts: 4 triple chairs, 5
　　double chairs
Snowmaking: 100 acres served
　　by 3 lifts
Season: late November
　　(Thanksgiving)–early April

Durango, in southwest Colorado, has long been a summer tourist destination. Purgatory Ski Resort came to life in 1965 and the winter season has increased in importance since then. This area will come of age in the mid-1990s with the completion of a master development plan.

Durango was named after Durango, Mexico; its past is rich with Spanish history. Spanish prospectors came through in 1765 and 1776; at that time the river upon which Durango is located was named Rio de las Animas (River of Lost Souls). Durango was located by fiat of the Denver and Rio Grande Railroad in 1880, when the company decided to locate the railroad depot a few miles below the existing Animas City. By the end of that year, the town had 500 buildings and a population of about 3,000.

Today, Durango still remembers Spanish and Native American heritage. It is surrounded by wilderness areas, close to the New Mexico border, yet it is a substantial town of over 16,000 population, many of them ranchers, college faculty, artists, and small business owners. It is a Registered National Historical Landmark—not cutesy like Aspen or Breckenridge, not weatherbeaten like Crested Butte, but, with its southwestern charm, enjoyable and affordable as ski vacations go.

Practical Information for Purgatory

 **HOW TO GET THERE.** Purgatory is located in the San Juan National Forest, 340 miles southwest of Denver, 25 miles north of Durango.

By air. La Plata Airport, 20 miles south of Durango and 45 miles south of Purgatory, is the gateway to Purgatory. Direct flights are scheduled from Denver, Dallas/Ft. Worth, Houston, Albuquerque, Phoenix, and Tucson on *America West, Trans-Colorado, Mesa Airlines,* and *Aspen Airways.* Common fare rates are available from Denver to Durango in conjunction with package tours; charter flights also go into La Plata. The *Air Shuttle* operates between the airport, Durango, and the ski area; $5 to Durango, $10 to Purgatory. Call 259–LIFT for schedules; prices subject to change without notice. Rental cars are available.

By bus. *Trailways* has regular service to Durango; 247–1581. The *Lift* regularly runs between Durango and Purgatory, $5 round-trip. Call 259–LIFT. Charters are available by contacting *Purgatory/Durango Central Reservations,* 800–525–0892 out of state, 800–358–3400 in Colorado.

By car. From Denver to Purgatory is a 340-mile drive via US 285, US 150, and US 550 in the southwest corner of the state. From Grand Junction it is 150 miles south on US 50 and US 550. Flagstaff, Arizona, is 319 miles to the south, Albuquerque is 212 miles via Hwy. 44 to US 550; Phoenix, 456 miles. Durango is 25 miles south on US 550. Rental cars available at La Plata Airport are *Avis,* 800–331–1212, and *National,* 800–328–4567.

TELEPHONES. The area code for all of Colorado is 303.

ACCOMMODATIONS. At Purgatory, there are accommodations for 700 people with up to 2,500 planned for 1993. In Durango, there are over 10,000 pillows with prices for all pocketbooks. Midway between the ski area and town is another fine resort, **Tamarron** (Box 3131, Durango CO 81301). Accommodations are deluxe, there are 13,000 sq. ft. of conference facilities, a separate small ski area, and two gourmet restaurants. Call 800–525–5420; in Colorado, 247–8801. Tamarron offers a free shuttle to Purgatory and into Durango.

Durango Reservations, Box 3418, Durango CO 81301 (800–525–9090 or 259–4142 in Colorado) represents Best Western and condominium properties in town and at the ski area. *Purgatory/Durango Central Reservations,* 534 Main Ave., Durango CO 81301 (800–358–3400 in Colorado and 800–525–0892 out of state), represents a majority of lodging both in town and at Purgatory. Following is a sample of what's available. *Expensive:* $165–$220 a night (depending on size of unit); *Moderate:* $45–$165; *Inexpensive:* $25–$45.

Expensive

Cascade Village. 50827 Hwy. 50 North; 259–3500. A mile north of Purgatory; two-bedroom units available.

Eolus Condominiums. Box 666, Durango; 247–9000. Slopeside lodging.

Village Center. Box 666, Durango; 247–9000. Slopeside 2-bedroom units.

Moderate

Angel Haus. Box 666, Durango, at base of Purgatory Mountain; 247–8090. Reasonably priced one- and two-bedroom condominiums.

Best Western General Palmer House. 567 Main Ave., Durango; 247–4747. Historic, 19th-century house with Victorian decor; restaurant, and bar.

Best Western Lodge at Purgatory. 49617 US 550, Durango; 247–9669. Western-style lodge; restaurant and lounge.

Strater Hotel. 699 Main Ave.; 247–4431. Built in 1882 and authentically restored, this is an outstanding facility.

Inexpensive

Alpine North Motel, 3515 Main Ave.; 303–247–4042. Basic motel facility.
Durango Hotel. 543 E. Second Ave.; 247–9905. One block from the train depot, with 40 dorm rooms and cooking facilities.
Pino Nuche Pu Ra Sa. Box 347, Ignacio; 563–4531. 25 minutes south of Durango on Hwy. 172. This is a motel and visitor center with restaurant, pool, and meeting rooms run by the Southern Ute Tribe. The name means "gathering place of the Pine River Indians."

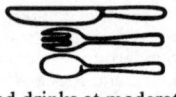 **RESTAURANTS.** With over 30 restaurants in Durango and a half-dozen at the mountain plus the restaurants at Tamarron, one need not go hungry. **At the mountain,** *Farquhart's North* in the village serves lunch, dinner, and drinks at moderate prices. *Powderhouse* is mid-mountain next to Pitchfork, with outdoor barbecues and home-style favorites; *Dante's* is mid-mountain by Chair 5, with cafeteria, sit-down dining, a greenhouse, and *Dante's Den and Lounge. Sterling's* is in the Village Center, and is a cafeteria, with outdoor sundeck and lounge. *Doe's Deli* and the *New York Bakery* are also in the center.
Expensive restaurants have entrees running $15–$25; *Moderate,* $9–$15; *Inexpensive,* below $9. All restaurants listed take Visa and MasterCard unless otherwise noted.

Expensive

The Ore House. 147 Sixth; 247–5707. One of the oldest restaurants in town, rustic and casual with extensive wine selection.
The Palace. 1 Depot Pl.; 247–2018. Victorian decor with a wide variety of entrees.
Sweeney's Grubstake. 1644 County Rd. 203; 247–5236. At the north end of town, serves steaks, seafood, and huge salads.

Moderate

The Atrium. 21382 Highway 160; 385–4834. Basic American fare.
Francisco's. 619 Main Ave.; 247–4098. For Mexican food, steaks and seafood. Children's menu available.
Katie O'Brien's. 152 E. Sixth; 247–9083. Steak and seafood in a Victorian atmosphere.
Lost Pelican. 658 Main Ave.; 247–8502. Good seafood, salads, and soups, with happy hour in The Nest.
New York Bakery. 327 W. Needles; 259–6477. Although known for their scrumptious desserts, they have a full menu as well.

Inexpensive

Father Murphy's. 636 Main Ave.; 259–0334. Pub atmosphere, serving pasta, burgers, and soups. No credit cards.
Griego's Taco House. 1400 E. Second Ave.; 247–3127. The name says it. No credit cards.
Hoop's Hickory House. 3690 Main Ave.; 259–5666. Pit-smoked barbecue and burgers.
Mr. Rosewater's Delicatessen. 552 Main Ave.; 247–8788.
Olde Tymer's, 1000 Main Ave.; 259–2990. Casual surroundings, with menu of burgers, soups, pasta.
Pronto's. 160 E. Sixth; 247–1510. For Italian food.

 **HOW TO GET AROUND.** Major **car** rental agencies are at the Durango airport (see *How to Get There*) and many visitors opt for the convenience of their own vehicle. A **shuttle** service operates regularly to and from Purgatory and within Durango on all major arteries. Tamarron runs a regular free shuttle between the resort, Purgatory, and town.

SEASONAL EVENTS. *Snowdown Winter Carnival* is celebrated late **January** through early **February;** mid-**March** sees *Wolverton Days* cross-country championships, and *The Sunburst Festival* welcomes spring skiing.

OTHER SPORTS AND ACTIVITIES. *Purgatory Ski Touring Center* maintains 15 km of **trails** across US 550 from the entrance to Purgatory Village. Lessons, rentals, Telemark clinics are available; a trail ticket is $3. Contact directors Tony Forrest and Ken Emrick, 247–9000.

For real excitement, book a day with *Telluride Helitrax* and head for 500 square miles of untracked powder in the San Juans; intermediate to expert skiing. Day **heli-skiing** begins at $60 for one run or $210 for all day (4 runs). Group rates available, prices subject to change. Gourmet lunches and beverages included in the full day. Extended heli-ski packages are available, and there are scenic flights for non-skiers. Contact Purgatory Ski Resort at 247–9000, ext. 140. *Rent-a-Snowmobile* does just that in winter, 3600 Main Ave., Durango; 259–1252. *Black Thunder* also rents **snowmobiles;** contact Purgatory or Cascade Village for reservations. **Sno-Cat tours,** nearby **ice fishing, ice skating, tennis, tubing,** and **sleigh rides** can be arranged. Call the Chamber of Commerce, 247–8900.

DAY-CARE FACILITIES. Call 247–9000 at Purgatory Ski Resort for information and reservations. The *Teddy Bear Camp* operates during ski season for children 2 months–6 years of age. Day care is $23 a day, $13 a half-day, lunch included. The ski school is $33 a day, $16 a half-day with lunch and ski lessons; skis and boots are available with the program. Children should be provided with adequate warm clothes, goggles, and sunscreen.

Older children can go into ski school, $27 a day with lunch and lift ticket; lift tickets (12 and under) are $8 a day, and a season's pass for children 12 and under is only $25.

NIGHTLIFE. Yes, there is life after skiing, at least if you go into Durango. *The Sundowner,* 3777 Main Ave., features country-western music both après-ski and after dining; popular with the older crowd. The *Diamond Belle Saloon,* 699 Main Ave., a historic Durango landmark, is right out of the Old West—those swinging doors have been swinging for over a century; elegant Victorian atmosphere, ragtime piano. The *Old Muldoon,* 561 Main Ave., is for popcorn and for meeting singles. *Sundance,* 602 Second Ave., features country-western dancing, live music, and a Western flavor—you'll feel comfortable in your cowboy hat and boots. *Sixth Street Parlour,* 110 W. Sixth, has contemporary live sounds. Another gathering spot with no planned entertainment is the *Ore House,* 147 Sixth.

There are even night-time activities that do not have to do with drinking. Bowl at *Durango Bowl,* 760 Camino del Rio; 259–1012. See a movie, or attend the live theater—*Abbey,* year-round (128 E. Sixth; 247–2626).

SNOWMASS

P.O. Box 5566
Snowmass Village CO 81615
Tel: 303-923-2010

Snow Report: 303–925–1221
Area Vertical: 3,596 ft.
Number of Trails: 1,500 acres
of tree-lined trails; longest
run 3.7 miles
Lifts: 11 double chairs, 2
triple chairs, 1 platter pull
Snowmaking: 55 most heavily
trafficked areas
Season: late November–mid-April

The wide open valley that is Snowmass is no longer Aspen's stepsister, "Snowmass-at-Aspen," but has its own distinctive personality. Snowmass is a premier year-round resort.

This rich valley was a haven for cattle ranches in the 1880s. The railroad at Woody Creek was nearby for transport to Denver's slaughterhouses and mining activity down the road at Aspen drew families to homestead the pristine valley. Living there was not without hardships, though: the Ute Indians made a last-ditch stand against the whites by burning the forest land. Today the Snowmass skier knows that area as the "Big Burn."

Ranching continued, even as mining gave out. There are still descendants of those original ranching families in the Snowmass area—the Anderson Ranch houses an arts center and the Hoaglund Barn is quarters for the Alpine Bank.

Bill Janss of Sun Valley fame saw the Snowmass valley and realized its potential for skiing. He bought up over 3,400 acres and made an agreement with the Aspen Skiing Company to take control and create the ultimate in ski areas. In December 1967, Snowmass-at-Aspen was born. Originally, the plans called for 26,000 guests and residents in 7,480 units, but public concern over growth caused the master plan to be revised.

Today, 7,500 people can be accommodated in 7 lodges and 22 condominium complexes, 95 percent of which are adjacent to the slopes for ski-in, ski-out convenience. Aspen Skiing Company still owns and operates the Snowmass Ski Area, and the Snowmass Company Ltd. is the main landowner and developer. Snowmass is modern, well planned, and efficient.

You'd better have deep pockets, though, if you plan to vacation here—Snowmass is a class act and charges class-act prices, though you can save up to 40 percent on lodging during early December, most of January, and April.

Practical Information for Snowmass

 **HOW TO GET THERE.** Snowmass is in the White River National Forest, 200 miles southwest of Denver. **By air.** All major airlines fly into Denver's Stapleton Airport; connect via *Aspen Airways* (398–3744 or 800–332–1332) or *Rocky Mountain Airways* (398–3896) to the Snowmass/Aspen Airport. In winter, there are flights into Grand Junction and connecting ground transportation to the airport. Courtesy cars, taxis, and limousines are available at the airport; so are rental cars: *Avis,* 800–331–1212; *Budget,* 800–0900; and *Hertz,* 800–654–3131.

By bus. *Trailways* has daily schedules to the Snowmass/Aspen Airport and into Aspen from Denver and from Grand Junction; call 292–2291.

By train. *Amtrak's* California Zephyr stops eastbound at 3:15 P.M. and westbound at 1:30 P.M. in an extravagantly scenic route from Denver across the Rockies. Advance arrangements should be made for connecting ground transportation from Glenwood Springs to Snowmass through Amtrak or your travel agent; *Mellow Yellow* **taxi** service has the route; 925–2282. Call Amtrak at 800–421–8320 or in Denver at 893–3911.

By car. Go west on I–70 from Denver to Glenwood Springs, then Hwy. 82 to Snowmass, 200 miles. From Grand Junction it is 128 miles east on I–70 to Glenwood, Hwy. 82; 10 miles west of Aspen on Hwy. 82, 6 miles west of the Snowmass/Aspen Airport.

TELEPHONES. The area code for all of Colorado is 303.

ACCOMMODATIONS. Contact *Central Reservations* at Box 5566, Snowmass Village CO 81615, 923–2010, for accommodations in the Village. In addition, there are nearly 8,000 pillows in Aspen, 12 miles down-valley (see section on *Aspen*).

A sampling of what's available follows. All properties are ski-in, ski-out with the exception of the Snowmass Club, which is three miles away on the golf course; a free shuttle service runs between the mountains and the club. Rates are based on double occupancy for a one-bedroom condo. *Expensive:* $175–$225; *Moderate:* $110–$175; *Inexpensive:* less than $100.

Expensive

Crestwood. Box 5460, Snowmass Village; 923–2450. Attractive condominium complex with 1–3-bedroom units featuring fireplaces and private balconies with barbecues; some with saunas. Heated pool.

Snowmass Club. P.O. Drawer G-2, 0239 Snowmass Circle, Snowmass Village; 923–5600. Ski lodge and villas at base of Snowmass Mountain ski area. Spacious rooms and condominium units with private balconies. Restaurant, bar, lounge. Indoor and outdoor tennis courts; squash and racketball courts; indoor and outdoor pools; health club; dog sledding.

Woodrun Place. 0425 Wood Rd., Snowmass Village; 923–5392. Luxurious condominium accommodations, with all the amenities.

Moderate

Stonebridge Inn. Box 5008; Snowmass Village; 923–2420. Rooms with restaurant and lounge.

Timberline. Box I–2, Snowmass Village; 923–4000. Condominium units with rustic Western atmosphere.

Inexpensive

Pokolodi Lodge. Box B–2, Snowmass Village; 923–4310. Family-oriented lodge on hillside, 50 yards from ski lift. Pool and Jacuzzi. Restaurants nearby.

Snowmass Inn; 923–4202. Comfortable accommodations.

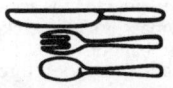

RESTAURANTS. Six restaurants are **on the mountain.** *Sam's Knob* is a typical cafeteria; upstairs is a fairly good sit-down restaurant, *Top of the Knob.* The expanded *Ullrhof,* at the base of the Big Burn, serves usual ski fare, as does *Elk Camp* cafeteria. *High Alpine* also offers a buffet line, and an elegant restaurant, *Gwyn's,* gives reasonable value for high-quality food, large portions, and a fine wine list.

Expensive restaurants have entrees for $15–$25; *Moderate,* around $10; *Inexpensive,* $5–9. Nearly all accept credit cards, but call to be sure.

Expensive

Chez Grandmere. 0016 Kearns Rd.; 923–2570. Exclusive establishment that has room for only 34 at its once-nightly seating. Price-fixed, 5-course meal.

Four Corners. In the Snowmass Club; 923–5600. Known for game specialties. Members and club guests only.

Krabloonik. At the dog kennels (see "Other Sports and Activities" below); 923–3953. In spectacular setting and with homespun atmosphere, serving gourmet game cuisine. Ski in for lunch; dinner reservations required.

Moderate

Cafe Rendez-vous. In Village Mall; 923–4989. Country fresh cooking for breakfast and dinner. Reservations suggested.

La Pinata. 65 Daly La.; 923–2153. Good Mexican food and margaritas.

Pippin's. In the Hotel Wildwood, 40 Elbert La.; 923–3550. Steak and lobster. Elegant dining with wonderful views and a harpist.

Shavanos. 20 Village Sq.; 923–4292. New American and Continental food; overlooks Snowmass Mall.

Tiffany Green. In the Stonebridge Inn; 923–2420. Hearty breakfasts and a skier's dinner featuring the finest in Colorado beef.

Timberline Restaurant. Snowmass Village; 923–4004. Affordable family dining with a cozy atmosphere. European and American cuisine.

The Tower Restaurant. On the Mall; 923–4650. Serves pasta, seafood, steaks —a lot of food for the money.

Inexpensive

Cheese Shop Cafe. 45 Village Mall; 923–2597. Features cheese omelets, soups, salads, quiches, and sandwiches.

Mountain Dragon. On the Mall above Sports Kaelin; 923–3576. Specializing in Mandarin and Szechuan cuisines.

Mountain Charley's. On the Mall; 923–4996. For breakfast and sandwiches at lunch.

Mama Maria's Pizza & Subs. Snowmass Center; 923–5250. Specializing in pizza, subs, and antipasto salads.

Pour La France. 0016 Kearns Rd. 923–5990. For soups, salads, pastries, specialty coffee drinks. Take-out service available.

Stew Pot. 15 Village Mall; 923–2263. Featuring homemade soups, stews, homemade bread, and sandwiches.

The Timber Mill. 105 Village Sq. 923–4774. Cafeteria-style breakfasts and lunches.

 **HOW TO GET AROUND.** Intravillage bus service is available at no charge between the day-skier lot and Lift One; check the *Transportation Department* at 923–3777 for specific times. The *Roaring Fork Transit Agency* offers daily bus service between Snowmass and Aspen, with many stops in between. It costs $1.50 and runs from early morning to late at night. *Aspen Skiing Company* runs free shuttle buses between Snowmass, Buttermilk, and Aspen from 8 A.M. to 4:45 P.M. for skiers; schedules are posted at the Snowmass Bus Stop and the Information Booth, or call 925–8484, 923–2085, or 923–2000, ext. 240.

Aspen Limousine (925–2400), *High Mountain Taxi* (925–TAXI), and *Mellow Yellow Taxi* (925–2282) offer services.

 **SEASONAL EVENTS. January** is time for the winter celebrations—in Aspen and Snowmass it's Winterskol, featuring a chili shootout, hot-air balloon race, Telemark cross-country, uphill/downhill race series, torchlight parade, and the Mad Hatter's Ball. The Snowmass/Ute Series 30K Touring Race is mid-**March** and Banana Season coincides with Spring Carnival in early **April,** when everyone goes bananas in the warm sunshine.

 OTHER SPORTS AND ACTIVITIES. Learn more about plant and animal adaptations to winter by joining a *Snowshoe Tour*. Four days a week at 10 A.M., the group treks through the snow to see the winter outdoors in a way few ever experience it. Skiers or non-skiers and children over 8 welcome; wear warm clothing and flat-heeled boots. Reserve at least a day in advance through the *Snowmass Resort Association,* 923–2000, or 892–7100 from Denver. The cost of $12 per person includes guide, equipment, and instruction for 3-hour hike; lunch is on your own.

Over 50 km of maintained **cross-country** trails linking the Snowmass Club Touring Center and Owl Creek Trail to Aspen's Buttermilk Mountain are free. The *Aspen/Snowmass Nordic Council* grooms the trails; for more information call 925–4790. Rentals, tours, and lessons at the Snowmass Club Touring Center, 925–3148.

The largest full-time **dog sled** kennel in the world is in Snowmass. Visitors can take a half-day dog sled ride pulled by 13 huskies from *Krabloonik Kennels* and then top it off with a gourmet game meal in Krabloonik Restaurant's hand-hewn log cabin. Advance reservations required, 923–4342.

Snowmobiles are available to rent in the Maroon Creek Valley at *T–Lazy–7 Ranch,* 925–4614. **Horse-drawn sleighs** whisk guests to a secluded mountain cabin for a barbecue and western entertainment; departures 5:30 and 8 P.M. Reserve in advance at the Information Booth in the Mall, or call 923–2000, ext. 249.

If you want to get above it all, take a **hot-air balloon ride** in the morning; it includes complimentary champagne upon landing. Call *Unicorn Balloon Company,* 925–5752, for information and reservations.

For other activities, there's **swimming** in one of 47 heated outdoor pools and Jacuzzis for guest use in the village. Those staying in the Snowmass Club have use of the full-service athletic club and indoor tennis courts, and they can have a Personal Fitness Profile done to improve their athletic performance and eating habits.

 **CHILDREN'S ACTIVITIES.** Snowmass is geared toward families, and there are excellent facilities for kids. Winter programs include *Snowmass Snowbunnies* for 1 ½–3-year-olds, and, with a **ski** program, for 3–6-year-olds. The program includes snow games, ski films, and arts and crafts. Daily, 9 A.M.–3:30 P.M.; weekly rates and evening baby sitters also available; call 923–4620. In the recreation building, one level below the Mall.

Ski classes for children from post-kindergarten age through pre-teens meet at the Ski School Youth Center at 9:30 A.M. for lessons, special races, and picnic; call 923–4873. *Kinderheim Ski School and Nursery,* for 1½–6-year-olds features an indoor program plus skiing and sledding; 8:30 A.M.–4 P.M.; 923–2692.

A teen program for 13–19-year-olds is exclusive at the Ski School. Grouped by ability, students are led by an instructor through lessons, videotaping, racing, picnics, and after-ski activities, including sleigh ride barbecues; call 923–4873.

 **NIGHTLIFE.** Snowmass is more sedate than its neighbor Aspen; so for heavy nightlife and the singles scene, head for Aspen. But "downtown" Snowmass Village isn't entirely quiet. The après-ski crowd heads for *Timber Mill,* 105 Village Sq., for live music until 5:30 P.M. or so. The *Tower Magic Bar* puts on a spontaneous magic show 7 nights a week. For late night disco, go to the *Stonebridge Inn,* 300 Carriage Way, 10 P.M.–2 A.M. The *Piano Bar* in the *Snowmass Club,* 0239 Snowmass Club Circle, is quietly elegant, but for members only.

The *Repertory Theater* performs for 6 weeks in winter; for tickets contact the Snowmass Resort Association or the ticket hotline, 923–2618. Then there's always the movies.

STEAMBOAT SPRINGS

2305 Mt. Werner Circle
Steamboat Springs CO 80487
Tel: 303–879–6111

Snow Report: 303–879–7300
Area Vertical: 3,600 ft.
Number of Trails: 91 trails on
*   1,450 acres, longest run 3 miles*
Lifts: 1 six passenger gondola,
*   7 triple chairs, 9 double*
*   chairs, 1 ski school chair,*
*   1 mighty mite*
Snowmaking: 170 acres served by
*   10 lifts*
Season: late November (Thanks
*   -giving weekend)–mid-April*

The Ute Indians considered the Yampa Valley, with its numerous hot mineral springs and abundant hunting and fishing, to be their summer playground. Trappers came upon the area in the mid-1800s and gave present-day Steamboat Springs its name because of the chugging sound made by the bubbling mineral springs.

Mining had its turn in the valley, but farming and ranching have been the mainstay of the economy. Even today, the alfalfa hay is widely known for its high quality. Steamboat Springs is a thriving town of over 6,000 inhabitants. There happens to be a big mountain nearby, and through the years the town has produced more than its share of Olympic and national champions. The area is wide open and sunny, the mood is friendly, the dress casual; if you don't own a cowboy hat when you arrive, you probably will before you leave.

Steamboat Springs is geared to families, as are its prices—at the low end of affordable.

A new $8–million, 8–passenger gondola will be in operation during the 1986–87 skiing season. Known as the "Silver Bullet," it will run the same route as the old gondola, from the base to Thunderhead. The speedier "Silver Bullet" will operate closer to the ground, thereby allowing it to operate in windy weather when the old gondola often had to be shut down.

Practical Information for Steamboat Springs

 **HOW TO GET THERE.** Steamboat Springs is in the Routt National Forest, 157 miles northwest of Denver. **By air.** All the major airlines serve Denver's Stapleton Airport. *Rocky Mountain Airways* makes connections to the Bob Adams Field/Routt County Stolport, 2 miles west of town and 5 miles from the ski area. Taxis from the airport to the lodges cost between $5 and $10, depending on the lodge location. There are also rental cars at the airport: *Budget,* 800–527–0700; and *National,* 800–328–4567.

In late December 1986, *American Airlines* was scheduled to fly directly to Steamboat Spring's Yampa Valley Regional Airport, near Hayden, from Chicago and Dallas-Fort Worth. One nonstop roundtrip daily was scheduled, while two roundtrips were slated for weekends. Flights are to continue through early April to accommodate the skiing season.

By bus. *Trailways* runs an express bus between Denver's Stapleton Airport and Steamboat Springs from mid-December to early April; one-way fare is $24. Advance reservations during February and March recommended; call 879–0740 locally or, in other parts of Colorado, 800–332–3204; write Box 774408, Steamboat Springs CO 80477. Regularly scheduled buses run from Denver and from Salt Lake City (340 miles west).

By car. From Denver, Steamboat Springs is 157 miles via I–70 through the Eisenhower Tunnel to Exit 205; follow Hwy. 9 to US 40, over Rabbit Ears Pass and into the Yampa Valley. From Grand Junction, drive east on I–70 to Hwy. 131 at Wolcott, then onto US 40 in the valley, a total of 200 miles. From Laramie, Wyoming, it is 122 miles via Hwy. 230, Hwy. 127, Rte. 14, and US 40.

TELEPHONES. The area code for all of Colorado is 303.

 **ACCOMMODATIONS.** The *Resort Association* serves as the central reservations office for lodging; call 879–0740, or write Box 774408, Steamboat Springs CO 80477. Twenty lodges are within walking distance of the slopes and another 55 hotels, condominiums, and townhouses make up a total of 14,000 pillows in town and at the base area. Below is a sampling of what's available.

Hotel rates are based on double occupancy. *Expensive:* $100–$300; *Moderate:* $70–$100; *Inexpensive:* $60–$70.

Expensive

Bear Claw Condominiums. 2420 Ski Trail La.; 879–6100. Top-of-the-line accommodations, right against the lifts and partway up the mountain.

La Casa. 2700 Village Dr.; 879–6006. One-bedroom condos available.

Dulaney Condos. 2700 Village Drive; 879–6006. Same complex as La Casa; also one-bedroom suites.

Sheraton at Steamboat. Box 773419; 879–2220. A luxury hotel at the base area, good après-ski activities and close to restaurants and shopping.

Moderate

Best Western Ptarmigan Inn. 2304 Après-Ski Way; 879–1730. Adjacent to gondola station at base of Mount Werner. Family-style restaurant and lounge; heated pool and sauna; games room and ski shop.

Glen Eden Ranch. 54737 Routt County Rd. 129, Clark; 879–3906. 18 miles north of town; rustic cabins with kitchens and fireplaces; free shuttle to ski area.

Harbor Hotel. 703 Lincoln; 879–1522. Renovated Victorian-style rooms; comfortable place.

Holiday Inn. 3190 S. Lincoln; 879–2250. A mile from the base area gondola; free shuttle service, outdoor pool, restaurant, and cocktail lounge.

Overlook Hotel. Box 770388; 879–2900. One mile south of town; shuttle service. Most units with mountain views. Dining room and lounge with entertainment. Indoor pool, whirlpool with sauna.

Thunderhead Lodge. 35215 Mt. Werner Way; 879–2220. At the ski area, with heated pool. A Sheraton property.

Moderate to Inexpensive

Scandinavian Lodge. Box 5040; 879–0517. Above the ski area, ski to the lifts and ski tour out the back door. Prices include three outstanding meals.

Inexpensive

Rabbit Ears Motel. 201 Lincoln Ave.; 879–1150. Close to downtown restaurants and shopping; take shuttle to ski hill.

Whistler Mountain Townhomes. 2304 Après-Ski Way; 879–1730. Less than a mile from the ski hill on bus route.

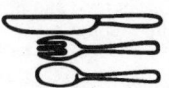 **RESTAURANTS.** There are two restaurants on the ski mountain. At the top of the gondola is the mid-mountain *Thunderhead* with the usual ski-time cafeteria food. The best deal is to hop the gondola early, have the special skier's breakfast at Thunderhead, and be skiing while the crowd is still riding the lifts. Also a pleasant lunch spot is the casual, sit-down *Stoker Bar* on the first level.

Rendezvous Saddle Restaurant in the Priest Creek area has seating for 600 inside and outdoors; included inside is the dining room *Ragnar's,* noted for its fine food and Norwegian specialties; make reservations during February and March; 879–6111.

At or near the base area are 14 restaurants.

Entrees at *expensive* restaurants are $13–$16; *Moderate,* $9–$12; *Inexpensive,* under $9. All restaurants listed take MasterCard and Visa unless otherwise noted.

AT OR NEAR THE SLOPES

Cipriani's. *Expensive.* In the Thunderhead Lodge, 35215 Mt. Werner Way; 879–2220. Features northern Italian cuisine, good wine list. Reservations recommended,

Mattie Silk's. *Expensive.* In Ski Times Sq., 1890 Mount Werner Rd.; 879–2441. A delightful, split-level restaurant featuring veal, pork, duck, and lamb in a candle-lit atmosphere. Fifty imported beers. Children's menu. Reservations suggested.

Remington's. *Expensive.* In the Sheraton, 2200 Village Inn Ct.; 879–2220. Overlooking the Headwall of the ski area. Children's menu available. Open winters only, reservations recommended.

Don Amigos. *Moderate.* 1910 Mount Werner Rd.; 879–4270. An old-time hangout in Steamboat. Good Mexican food and lots of activity. Dinner only. Children's menu.

Soda Creek Cafe. *Moderate.* In Thunderbird Lodge, 35215 Mt. Werner Way; 879–2220. Specializes in German food; also burgers and sandwiches. Cheerful atmosphere and German beers and wines. Children's menu.

The Tugboat. *Inexpensive.* 1860 Mount Werner Rd.; 879–9990. Another local favorate. Noisy, western atmosphere serving burgers and beer. Open for three meals.

IN AND AROUND TOWN

L'Apogee. *Expensive.* 810 Lincoln St.; 879–1919. Probably the most expensive place in town, it is classic French. Blackboard menu, fresh vegetables, extensive wine list. Reservations recommended.

Brandywine. *Expensive.* 57 ½ Eighth St.; 879–9939. Beef, seafood, and good after-dinner drinks are served in a Victorian setting. Children's menu. Reservations needed during February and March.

The Coral Grill. *Expensive.* In Sundance Plaza on Angler Dr., off Hwy. 40; 879–6858. The specialty is Maine lobster, swordfish, salmon—in fact, all the seafood. Oyster bar and good sushi.

CJ's Cafe. *Moderate.* 903 Lincoln Ave.; 879–9754. Seafood, vegetarian meals, steaks, fresh fruit drinks in tropical surroundings. Lunch and dinner. Children's menu.

The Cove. *Moderate.* 709 Lincoln Ave.; 879–7720. Cantonese food and exotic drinks.

Mazzola's. *Moderate.* 440 S. Lincoln Ave.; 879–2405. Italian dishes, pizza, salad bar. Lunch weekdays, dinner daily, children's menu.

Pine Grove. *Moderate.* 1465 Pine Grove Rd.; 879–1190. Contemporary western atmosphere in a converted barn. American menu and children's menu. Award winner. Dinner only in winter.

The River Bend. *Moderate.* Five miles west of town, across from the golf course, 26795 Routt County Rd. 40; 879–1615. American menu featuring barbecued ribs. Free transportation for four or more. Children's menu. Lunch and dinner.

Soupçon. 912 Lincoln St.; 879–5016. Homemade breads and quiches in a quaint atmosphere, with fresh flowers, small tables.

Cantina. *Inexpensive.* 818 Lincoln Ave.; 879–0826. Mexican food and pizza. Crowded with locals for breakfast; good margaritas in the evening.

Double-R Bar-B-Q. *Inexpensive.* 1124 Yampa; 879–7427. Great for barbecues, sandwiches, chicken, hoagies. No credit cards.

The Shack. *Inexpensive.* 740 Lincoln Ave.; 879–9975. Good for a quick breakfast or lunch. Call for credit card information.

Sidestep. *Inexpensive.* 738 Lincoln Ave.; 879–9933. Burgers and Mexican food. Breakfast, lunch, and dinner. No credit cards.

 **HOW TO GET AROUND.** *Steamboat Springs Transit* (SST) connects points west of the city limits to town and to the ski area; check schedules at lodge, but extra **buses** are put on during ski season; 50¢ a ride, but for savings buy tokens in quantity at any lodge or store. For schedule information, call 879–3717. For **taxis,** call *Steamboat Taxi Service,* 879–3111.

 **SEASONAL EVENTS.** There is almost always something special going on in cowboy country. Three- and six-day *Billy Kidd Race Camps* are scheduled throughout the winter. In mid-**January,** the most unusual ski area event happens—the *Cowboy Downhill;* top rodeo riders from the Pro Rodeo Tour come up from Denver's annual National Western Stock Show and try their skill. The oldest continuous *Winter Carnival* in the West takes place for a week in early **February** with a fun mixture of cowboys, skiers, and hot-air balloons. The *Junior National Championships* are the end of February, the *National Masters Championships* in **March;** spring officially arrives in early **April** with the *Steamboat Springs Stampede.*

 OTHER SPORTS AND ACTIVITIES. Cross-country is avidly pursued in Steamboat. Besides ski touring from the Scandinavian Lodge, the *Ski Touring Center* maintains 12 miles of trails; guided tours on Rabbit Ears Pass, moonlight tours by appointment; lessons, call 879–8180. Other lodges that offer cross-country skiing are *Bear Pole Ranch, Dutch Creek Guest Ranch, Elk River Guest Ranch, Glen Eden, Home Ranch, Post Ranch, Red Barn Ranch,* and *Vista Verde Guest Ranch.* Anyone can ski here—it's open forest land.

Ski powder by **snow cat;** contact the *Steamboat Powder Cats,* 879–5188.

Dog sledding is nearby at *Dog Sled Adventures,* 879–5280. **Ice fishing** is at Steamboat and Dumont Lakes; license required, call 879–1870 for information. **Ice skating** is at Howelson Hill in town, open to the public at no charge. Rent skates at *Ski Haus,* 1450 Lincoln; 879–0385. **Sledding** is also popular at Howelson Hill for young children; call 879–4300.

Sleigh rides go from *All Seasons Ranch,* 879–2606; *Double Runner Ranch,* 879–6459; *El Rancho,* 879–9988; *Red Barn Ranch,* 879–4580; *Vista Verde Guest Ranch,* 879–3858. **Snowshoeing** expeditions head out from Elk River, Red Barn, Vista Verde, and Post ranches. **Snowmobiles** can be rented at Dutch Creek, Elk River, Post, and Red Barn ranches.

Enjoy **hot mineral pools** any time of year in town at the public pool and at the *Steamboat Springs Health & Recreation Association,* 879–1828. Year-round early morning **balloon rides** are available through four hot-air balloon companies—*Balloon Colorado,* 879–4932; *Balloons Over Steamboat,* 879–3298; *Balloon the Rockies,* 879–7313; and *Pegasus Balloon Tours,* 879–7529.

HINTS TO THE HANDICAPPED. For ski instruction by appointment for the visually impaired and some physically disabled, contact the *Steamboat Ski School,* 2305 Mount Werner Circle, Steamboat Springs CO 80487; 879–6111.

CHILDREN'S ACTIVITIES. "Kids ski free" was started at the Steamboat Ski Area and they have made a high art of it. The Ski Corporation even publishes a newsletter for children called *Skids,* which lists all the special activities and rates for kids of all ages. The *Kids Ski Free Program* stipulates that children 12 and under can ski free with parents who purchase 5 or more day lift tickets and who are staying a minimum of 5 nights at a participating Steamboat Chamber/Resort Association lodging property. Children also stay free in the same room with their parents and will have free ski rentals when their parents rent skis for the same period of time. The offer is not valid during the Christmas/New Year's holiday. Call Steamboat Ski Corporation for more details, 879–6111.

In addition, the *Kiddie Corral Child Care* accommodates children 6 months to 6 years of age; day supervision with games, crafts, movies $20 a day, second child $14 a day, plus $4 for lunch for kids over 2; $16 a half day, $12 for second child. The Kiddie Corral Ski School is for young skiers 3–5 years of age who are toilet trained. Lunch, lift privileges, and lessons, $27 a day; $20 a half day; $70 for three days; $100 for 5 days. Ground floor, Gondola Building; 879–6111, ext. 216.

The ski school has lessons for kids 6–15. Group lessons are $16 for two hours, $29 for all day; for details, call 879–6111, ext. 222.

Kids seem to be the only ones who have energy for night skiing; take them to Howelsen Hill in town; Tuesdays–Fridays, 6–9 P.M.

Off the slopes, children will enjoy the Hydro Tube and swimming at the *Steamboat Springs Health & Recreation Association,* Lincoln St., in town; 879–1828.

If you want to leave junior at home while you party, many lodges provide a list of qualified baby sitters; inquire at the front desk or call the Chamber/Resort Association for a list; 879–0880.

NIGHTLIFE. Join the *Steamboat Stompers* for square dancing the first and third Friday of the month, 8 P.M., at the Community Center, Lincoln Ave.; 879–5837 for details. Once a week, *Vista Verde Ranch,* 31100 Routt County Rd. 64, Clark, hosts square dancing; 879–3858.

Much of the late-night action is at the ski area. The *Tugboat,* 1860 Mount Werner Rd., is lively into the wee hours, often with live entertainment. *Hershey's Bar* in the Clock Tower has a deejay spinning disco tunes; mostly a young crowd. The *Inferno* in Gondola Square has live bands after skiing and late night. A little more conservative is the *Conservatory* in Thunderhead Lodge; comfortable lounge, entertainment. The *Hatch* in the newly renovated Harbor Hotel has good country-western bands. *Glen Eden Ranch* has a pleasant lounge with western music. (See *Accommodations* above for addresses.) For the 18–21 set, *Steamboat Suds* is a 3.2 percent beer pub one mile west of town.

Bowlers can head to *Sno Bowl II* just west of town; call 879–9840 for a lane. Three movie theaters have first-run films. The *Steamboat Arts Council* holds dance concerts and melodramas, and there are other local talent displays throughout the year; call 879–4434.

TELLURIDE

P.O. Box 307
Telluride CO 81435
Tel: 303–728–3856 and 800–525–3455

Snow Report: 303–728–3856
Area Vertical: 3,155 ft.
Number of Trails: 38 on 470
acres, longest run 2.85 miles
Lifts: 9 double chairs
Snowmaking: 120 acres served
by 4 lifts
Season: late-November (Thanks-
giving)–mid-April

This tiny Victorian gem lies at the end of a box canyon in a remote southwestern Colorado valley in the spectacular San Juan Mountains. Typically, Telluride sprang to life as a bustling mining camp: gold and silver miners thronged the streets and the exuberant red-light district was famous for miles around. The name Telluride comes from the rare, lustrous crystalline element tellurium, found in compound with gold or silver.

Following the gold rush, Telluride slumbered for over half a century. Young people seeking an alternative life style migrated to this remote town in the 1960s and saw the charm of the elegant Victorian buildings; they stayed, renovated the houses, and carefully preserved the amalgam of gothic and Victorian styles. Today, Telluride is registered as a National Historic District; it is a self-contained, dramatic mountain hideaway with one main street, a two-block walk from the backcountry.

Probably because it's not very easy to get to, the area offers the best value of all Colorado resorts, with good services and accommodations. Telluride attracts vacationers from the West and Southwest.

Practical Information for Telluride

HOW TO GET THERE. Telluride is located in the Uncompahgre National Forest, 325 miles southwest of Denver.

By air. Telluride's new airport, located 5 miles from town, has daily round-trip flights from Denver, Albuquerque, and Phoenix on *Mesa Airlines.* Montrose, Durango, and Grand Junction airports are gateways to Telluride also. *America West* flies to Phoenix and Austin/Durango daily; there are connections on America West to San Diego, Ontario, Los Angeles, San Jose, and San Francisco. America West or *Trans-Colorado* flies from Albuquerque to Durango daily. There is service from Los Angeles, San Diego, Dallas, and Houston into Grand Junction on *Frontier Airlines.* Trans-Colorado and *Aspen Air* connect with major airlines at Denver's Stapleton Airport for Montrose. Aspen Air also serves Montrose from Aspen and Denver. *Telluride Transit* meets all flights with 24-hour advance reservations in Montrose, Grand Junction, and Durango. For information on schedules, contact the Telluride Ski Resort, Box 307, Telluride, CO 81435; 728–3856.

By bus. *Trailways* serves Montrose. *Telluride Transit* provides ground transportation to Telluride with 24-hour advance reservations, 738–4105, or Telluride Central Reservations Transportation Desk, 800–525–3455. The Montrose/Telluride trip is $15 per person one-way; Durango/Telluride, $35 per person one-way; Grand Junction/Telluride, $30 per person one way.

By car. Denver is a long drive on US 285, US 50, US 550, and Rtes. 62 and 145. Durango is 125 miles south via Rte. 145, Rte. 62, and US 550; Montrose is 67 miles north via US 550, Rte. 62, and Rte. 145. Grand Junction is 125 miles north via US 789, US 550, Rte. 62, and Rte. 145. Car rentals from Montrose include *Budget,* 800–527–0700; and *Hertz,* 800–654–3131; in Grand Junction, *Avis,* 800–331–1212, Budget, Hertz, and *National,* 800–328–4567; in Durango, Budget, Avis, and Hertz.

TELEPHONES. The area code for all of Colorado is 303.

 **ACCOMMODATIONS.** *Telluride Central Reservations* handles lodging, information, and reservations for all properties in town. Box 1009, Telluride CO 81435; 800–525–3455; 728–4431 in Colorado. With only 10 lodges totaling 3,500 pillows, the area fills quickly during holiday periods. The base of the ski area is 4 blocks from town, 6 blocks from Main Street condos.

Expensive: $105–$180 a night, depending on the size of the facility; *Moderate:* $80–$105; *Inexpensive:* $30–$50.

Bachman Village. *Expensive.* 105 S. Davis, near entrance to town; 728–4226. The new, deluxe, Victorian-style homes here are ideal for 6 to 8 people.

Graysill Condos. *Expensive.* Liftside; 728–4431. Fine accommodations with Jacuzzis, washers/dryers; 2-bedroom units available.

LuLu City Condos. 728–4387. Most condos are liftside. All units have phones, TV, hot tubs, steam showers, and saunas.

Beaver Pond Condos. *Moderate.* 105 S. Davis, in town; 728–3970. One- to three-bedroom condos, some with steam and Jacuzzis.

Ore Station Lodge. *Moderate.* 260 S. Aspen; 728–4311. Studio to 3-bedroom condos, furnished in antiques and oak furniture.

Telluride Lodge. *Moderate.* 666 W. Colorado Ave., at the base of the area; 728–4446. Oldest ski lodge in Telluride Valley, 4 blocks from historic downtown; common hot tub.

Johnstone Inn. *Inexpensive.* 403 W. Colorado Ave.; 728–3316. Three blocks from Coonskin Lift. A Victorian-style bed-and-breakfast establishment.

New Sheridan Hotel. *Inexpensive.* Box 980, 231 W. Colorado Ave.; 728–4351. Smack in the middle of town, this is a Victorian beauty built in 1895 and renovated in 1977. Free ski shuttle to mountain, 6 blocks away.

Oak Street Inn and Youth Hostel. *Inexpensive.* 134 N. Oak; 728–3383. Two shared saunas, TV in lounge.

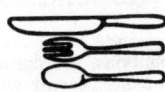 **RESTAURANTS.** At the mountain, cafeteria food is available at the base of the second lift and at midmountain. Brunch at *Gorrono Ranch Restaurant,* after catching the first tracks in the morning, is popular. For groups, box lunches are prepared by *Monika's,* 219 E. Colorado Ave., 728–3305; *Baked-in-Telluride,* 127 S. Fir, 728–9902; and the *Deli-Downstairs,* 217 W. Colorado Ave., 728–4617,

For a small town, Telluride has a relatively large number of restaurants and bars—at last count, 20 in town plus 3 at the base or middle of the mountain.

Expensive restaurants have entrees ranging from $13 to $20; *Moderate,* $8–$12; *Inexpensive,* under $7. Call restaurants for credit card information.

Expensive

Cimarron Restaurant. 150 W. San Juan Ave.; 728–3377. Features hand-cut steaks, seafood, and a salad buffet.

Julian's. In the New Sheridan Hotel, 231 W. Colorado Ave.; 728–3839. Features northern Italian cuisine. Breakfast, lunch, and dinner, Wednesday–Monday (closed Tuesdays).

The Senate. 123 S. Spruce; 728–3201. A historic bar with intimate dining from a Continental menu. Scrumptious desserts, live entertainment.

Silverglade. 115 W. Colorado Ave.; 728–4943. The specialty is California style mesquite-broiled fresh fish.

Moderate

Excelsior Cafe. 200 W. Colorado Ave.; 728–4250. Marvelous Continental breakfasts; soups, fondues, espresso, pastries until 10:30 P.M.

Floradora Saloon. 103 W. Colorado Ave.; 728–9937. Extensive lunch and dinner menus. Char-broiled burgers, salad bar. Open late.

Monika's Gourmet Carry-out. 219 E. Colorado Ave.; 728–3305. Exceptional carry-out food; full dinner not available. Closed Sundays.

O'Willy's. 114 E. Colorado Ave.; 728–4969. Serves Buffalo burgers, prime rib. Happy hour and live entertainment.

Sofio's. 110 E. Colorado Ave.; 728–4882. Telluride's Mexican restaurant.

Inexpensive

Baked-in Telluride. 127 S. Fire; 728–9902. Light fare.

Deli Downstairs. 217 W. Colorado Ave.; 728–4617. Sandwiches, salads, pastries.

The Underground. 121 W. Colorado Ave.; 728–4790. Ice cream parlor, hamburger grill, and video-game center. Open until 11 P.M.

HOW TO GET AROUND. A free **shuttle bus** makes the loop from town to the mountain—Coonskin and Meadow lifts—every 40 minutes in ski season; a free bus circulates in town every 10 minutes during ski season and summer festivals. **Taxis** are available by calling 728–4384. Nearly everything is within walking distance, and the base area is only 4 blocks from most lodges.

SEASONAL EVENTS. The *Mayor's Cup,* followed by the *Invitational Governor's Cup* are in mid-**January**— fun if you follow politicos. *Coonskin Carnival* is Telluride's answer to the winter blahs in early **February;** *Spring Fling* heralds spring's arrival at the end of **March.**

OTHER SPORTS AND ACTIVITIES. *The Nordic Center Guides,* 728–3404, introduces **cross-country** skiers to the backcountry with picnics and lessons; 10-km and 17-km ski tracks. Trail fee is $4, equipment rental available, $9 a day. Telemark lessons are available on the mountain for $18. Inquire about guided tours through *Central Reservations,* 728–3455, or 800–525–3455 outside Colorado. For those who like to ski tour the backcountry on their own, call 728–3856 for information on trails from the town park to Lizard Head Pass and Sunshine and Wilson mesas.

Heli-skiing is available, even for the not-so-fantastic skier; contact *Heli-Trax,* 728–4909, and find the hidden basins in the San Juan Mountains. **Ice skating** is available on the town pond; skating parties every Wednesday evening with a bonfire and music; rentals from Olympic Sports at $1.50/pair, 226 W. Colorado Ave.; 728–3501. **Roller skating** all year at the *Quonset Hut,* Columbia and Townsend, 728–3851, rentals $2.50 a pair.

HINTS TO THE HANDICAPPED. Skiing is free for those with sight or hearing impairment or with a variety of other physical handicaps. For details and reservations, contact the Ski School, 728–3856.

DAY-CARE FACILITIES. Children 1½–7 years old are cared for at the *Meadows Child-care Center* during ski season. The program includes organized play, story reading, learning concepts; $25 a day with lunch; $4 an hour; call 728–3856. For 4–12 year-olds ready to ski, the rates are $35 a day, $25 a half day. Lift tickets for children 4 and under are free with the purchase of an adult ticket; tickets for kids 5–12 are $11.

Underground for Kids, 121 W. Colorado Ave., is an ice cream parlor with video games and other kid entertainment. *The Teen Center,* at Columbia and

Townsend, has special programs once a week throughout the year and is open to visitors.

NIGHTLIFE. While visitors may not be overwhelmed by the choice, there are enough evening activities to keep most busy during their stay. *Fly Me to the Moon Saloon,* 132 E. Colorado Ave., features live music, a dance floor, pool, and pizzas from 3 P.M. to 3 A.M. The historic *Sheridan Bar,* 225 W. Colorado Ave., has scheduled live entertainment until 2 A.M. *Trinity Tavern,* 200 W. Colorado Ave., has disco, pizza, entertainment; all saloons close by midnight on Sundays.

VAIL

P.O. Box 7
Vail CO 81658
Tel: 303–476–5601, 800–525–3875
   outside Colorado

*Snow Report: 303–476–4888, or
   303–534–1245
Area Vertical: 3,150 ft.
Number of Trails: 89 trails on
   10 square miles (largest single
   mountain complex in U.S.),
   longest run 4 miles
Lifts: 1 gondola, 9 double
   chairs, 3 triple chairs, 4 quad
   chairs, 1 T-bar
Snowmaking: on 279 acres
Season: late November–late April*

What is now known as Gore Creek Valley was once a high mountain pasture cradled by the Gore and Sawatch mountain ranges that provided a rich summer hunting ground for the Ute Indians. Sir St. George Gore, a baronet from Ireland known as Lord Gore, spent the summers of 1854–56 with famous mountain man Jim Bridger on the east side of the Gore Range. Gore killed every animal he could raise his rifle at before he was "requested" to return home (see Winter Park section). Five years later, when Bridger returned, he named the mountain range and valley after Lord Gore though Gore never set foot that far west.

The intrusion of the white man searching for gold and silver in the 1870s and 1880s was the last straw for the Utes. Leaving the mountains, they set "spite fires" that burned thousands of acres of timber (see Snowmass section). Years later, the wide-open terrain so devoid of trees became Vail's famous "back bowls." Like the "Big Burn" at Snowmass, Vail's back bowls are a magnet drawing skiers of advanced ability.

With the exception of a few sheep ranchers, the Gore Creek Valley slept until 1940, when U.S. Highway 6 followed the passes from Denver and wound through the valley. Charlie Vail was in charge of construction for the Colorado Department of Highways, hence the name Vail Pass. The Tenth Mountain Division trained 20 miles away near Leadville during World War II, and many of the men came back to these mountain valleys after the war. It was one of those veterans who saw the possibilities of the incredible ski terrain in the Vail Pass area.

Land was bought up and Vail rose from the ground in one summer, opening in December 1962. Today, the simulated Swiss village is the largest single mountain skiing complex in Colorado. Vail became the Western White House during President Ford's term of office, and the Fords continue to vacation in Vail and maintain a second home in Vail Associates' Beaver Creek, 10 miles west. Vail Village has 5,000 permanent residents. It is second only to Aspen in glitter and glamour, with a bit of suburban quality. The cost may not be in the stratosphere, but it's still for the more affluent.

Practical Information for Vail

 **HOW TO GET THERE.** Vail is in the White River National Forest, 100 miles west of Denver.

By air. All major airlines serve Denver's Stapleton Airport. *Vail Guides* (949–1000) has taxi service and *Trailways* and *Carey American Limo* (393–0653) have bus service; *Colorado Ground Transportation* (288–5669) and *Colorado Mountain Express* (949–4227) limo service, drop people off at the door, and also have bus transportation from Denver's airport. *Summit Taxi* serves Vail ($17.50 one way) as well as Summit County (476–6816 or 800–321–5246). *Rocky Mountain Airways* makes connections to the Avon Stolport, 10 miles west of Vail at Beaver Creek. There is a general aviation airport at Eagle, 30 miles west of Vail, but there is no connecting ground transportation except taxi or rental car.

By bus. *Trailways* serves the Vail Transportation Center from downtown Denver and Stapleton Airport (along with *Carey American Limo*—see "By air" above) and from Grand Junction.

By car. From Denver, Vail lies 100 miles west on I–70. From Grand Junction, it is 150 miles east on I–70; Colorado Springs is 145 miles away via I–25 and I–70. *Budget,* 800–527–0700, *Hertz,* 800–654–3131, and National, 800–328 –4567, rental car companies are in Vail; all the major rental car companies are at the Denver airport.

ACCOMMODATIONS. Twenty thousand guests can be accommodated within a 5-mile radius of Vail Village. Contace *Vail Resort Association,* 241 E. Meadow Dr., Vail CO 81657; outside Colorado, call 800–525–3875; in state call 476–5677 or Denver direct 628–6624.

All establishments are in the village within walking distance of slopes, shopping, and dining.

In this listing, price categories are determined by the size of the unit as well as the amenities offered. *Expensive:* $140–$675 per night; *Moderate:* $100–$400 per night for double rooms and 1–3-bedroom condos; *Inexpensive,* $90–$175 per night, depending on the size of the unit.

Expensive

Antlers Lodge at Vail. 680 West Lionshead Pl.; 476–2471. Spacious lodge with studios to 3-bedroom units equipped with fireplaces and balconies. Saunas, heated outdoor pool, and Jacuzzi overlooking Gore Creek.

Landmark Condominiums. 610 W. Lionshead Circle; 479–1350. One- to 3-bedroom units.

The Lodge at Vail. 174 East Gore Creek Dr.; 476–5011. European-Alpine design houses hotel and 1–3-bedroom units. Restaurant and lounge, swimming pool, saunas.

Vail Athletic Club. 352 East Meadow Dr.; 476–0700. Rooms and suites with balconies; many with kitchens, fireplaces. Swimming pool, sauna, massage, steam rooms, exercise rooms; racquetball, handball, and squash courts.

Moderate

Christiana. 356 E. Hanson Ranch Rd.; 476–5641. Located at foot of mountain within walking distance of shops, restaurants and lifts. Rooms and apartment units. Heated pool, sauna.

Enzian Lodge. 705 Lionshead Circle W.; Box 1776; 476–2050. Two blocks from gondola ski lift. Heated pool, Jacuzzi, bar, and lounge. Some rooms with fireplaces.

The Lodge at Lionshead. P.O. Drawer 1868, 380 E. Lionshead Circle; 476–2700. Studios and apartments facing Gore Creek. Most units with fireplaces and balconies. Two heated pools, saunas, laundry facilities.

Marriott's Mark Resort. 715 W. Lionshead Circle; 476–4444. Rooms and condominium units 200 yards from Lionshead gondola. Restaurants, lounges, athletic club, racquetball courts, and swimming pool.

Vail Racquet Club Condominiums. 4690 Racquet Club Dr.; 476–4840. At base of Vail pass in East Vail. Units with fireplaces and balconies with barbecues. Restaurant, 3 indoor tennis courts, squash and racquetball courts, health spa, exercise room.

The Westin Hotel. 1300 Westhaven Dr.; 476–7111. In Cascade Village, to west of Vail Mountain. Rooms and suites with balconies; some with fireplaces. Formal restaurant for northern Italian and Continental cuisine; The cafe is for light meals; lounge and bar. Two outdoor heated pools, indoor tennis courts, racquetball, handball, and squash courts. Limo service to lifts; ski trail to return to hotel.

The Willows. 74 East Willow Rd.; 476–2231. 300 yards from chairlift. Units with fireplaces, balconies, sauna, and whirlpool.

Inexpensive

Best Western Inn at West Vail. 2211 N. Frontage Rd.; 476–3890. Two miles west of Lionshead ski area. Health club with pool and sauna. Free shuttle service.

Roost Lodge. 1783 N. Frontage Rd.; 476–5451. A long-time favorite of those on a budget. Bus or drive to village.

Sitzmark Lodge. 183 Gore Creek Dr.; 476–5001. Comfortable rooms with balconies. Restaurant and lounge, outdoor pool, whirlpool, and sauna.

Vail Village Inn. 100 East Meadow Dr.; 476–5622. At entrance to village. A variety of rooms and condo units. Cocktail lounge and large heated pool.

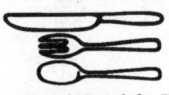 **RESTAURANTS.** Dining in Vail presents another array of choices—72 to be exact. On-mountain food service includes cafeterias at *Mid-Vail* (outdoor barbecues in good weather), *Eagle's Nest, Golden Peak,* and *Lionshead Gondola Building.* Snack facilities are at *Far East Shelter* at Lift 14 (also outdoor barbecues) and *Wildwood Shelter* at Lift 3. Full-service, sit-down restaurants are *The Cook Shack* at Mid-Vail (nouvelle cuisine), *The Wine Stube* at Eagle's Nest (international dishes), and *Frasier's* at Lionshead (homemade soups, breakfasts, sandwiches).

The *Expensive* restaurants listed here have entrees ranging from $17.50 to $45; *Moderate,* $12–$18; *Inexpensive,* under $12. All restaurants listed take Visa and MasterCard unless otherwise noted.

Expensive

Alfredo's. In the Westin Hotel, 1300 Westhaven Dr.; 476–7111. Northern Italian cuisine in an elegant setting. Serving dinner and Sunday brunch. Reservations suggested.

Ambrosia. 17 E. Meadow Dr.; 476–1964. Extensive Continental menu and good dessert selection served in a French provincial setting. Dinner only. Reservations recommended;

Cyrano's. 298 Hanson Ranch Rd.; 476–5551. Full Continental menu and good California wine list. Serves breakfast, lunch, dinner, and brunch. No reservations.

The Left Bank. 183 Gore Creek Dr.; 476–3696. Très French and très expensive, with only two seatings each night. Reservations needed several weeks in advance; dinner only in winter.

Maison Creole. In the Vail Athletic Club, 352 East Meadow Dr.; 476–0700. New Orleans-style cooking served in mountain art deco surroundings. Open for three meals, plus Sunday brunch. Reservations recommended.

Tea Room Alpenrose. 100 E. Meadow Dr.; 476–3194. German specialties and mouth-watering pastries. Lunch and dinner.

The Wildflower. In the newly renovated Lodge at Vail, 174 E. Gore Creek Dr.; 476–5011. Sunny spot with silk flowers all around, serving nouvelle cuisine. Price-fixed dinner for $45. Reservations recommended.

Windows at the Top of the Mark. 715 W. Lionshead Circle; 476–5011. Gourmet dining in a refined and formal atmosphere. Dress for dinner here. Reservations suggested.

Moderate

The Chart House. 610 W. Lionshead Circle; 476–1525. Known for its steaks and salad bar, this is one of the largest restaurants in Vail. No reservations.

Sweet Basil. 193 E. Gore Creek Dr.; 476–0125. A local favorite. Sunny restaurant with local art on display, homemade desserts.

Tyrolean Restaurant and Lounge. 400 E. Meadow Dr.; 476–2204. Specializes in game dishes served in rustic Austrian elegance. Reservations recommended.

Inexpensive

Los Amigos. 318 E. Hanson Ranch Rd.; 476–5847. Vail's oldest Mexican restaurant serves huge portions and good margaritas. No reservations.

Blu's Beanery. 193 E. Gore Creek Dr.; 476–3113. Offers a choice of omelets, pasta, salads, steaks for brunch and dinner. No reservations.

Bully III Chop House. 20 Vail Rd.; 476–4152. A breakfast buffet and a prime rib dinner buffet; also nightly specials. Make reservations.

Szechwan Lion. 304 Bridge St.; 476–4303. Extensive Chinese menu for lunch and dinner. Reservations accepted.

Torino's. 2111 N. Frontage Road W.; 476–0122. Features Italian dishes, pizza, sandwiches. Takeout for lunch or dinner, too.

 **HOW TO GET AROUND.** Within Vail Village is a free **shuttle bus** service, the third-largest municipal bus system in the state. Between Vail and Beaver Creek, the shuttle costs $1. For information, call 476–7000. The village is planned as a pedestrian mall, and shops, dining, lodging, and the base area are all within walking distance; however, if you're carrying skis and boots, it can sometimes be a long walk.

 **SEASONAL EVENTS.** *WinterFaire* is the annual winter carnival in mid-**January;** at the end of January is the *Professional Mogul Classic.* At the end of **February**–beginning of **March** is the *American Ski Classic* with *World Cup* races, the *Gerald Ford Celebrity Cup,* and *Legends of Skiing. Mountain Madness* celebrates the zaniness of spring skiing a few weeks before **April** closing.

 OTHER SPORTS AND ACTIVITIES. The **cross-country** skiing center, 476–5601, teaches basic-to-advanced track skiing and use of touring skis; Telemark clinics are held; full or half-day tours are available. Gourmet lunches (Thursdays only) and a Vail-to-Red Cliff tour for 6 or more people can be planned by advance registration; call 476–3239, ext. 4380. *Eagle River Mountain Guides* offers half and full-day and supper tours; call *Western Sports* at 476–3296 for reservations. Experienced cross-country skiers can head out from the top of China Bowl or from the top of Vail Pass for backcountry skiing.

If you can ski Vail's back bowls with confidence, then **helicopter skiing** might be for you. *Vail Heli-ski* takes skiers to out-of-bounds areas in Vail Valley, Resolution Peak, and other spots for $250 a day. Write Box 54, Vail CO 81658 or call 949–5113 for information.

Piney River Ranch, 8 miles from Vail, offers **snowmobile** excursions, **snowcat** tours, and backcountry ski tours: 884 Spruce Ct., Vail CO 81658; 476–3941. **Sleigh rides** start from the golf course every night; 476–1154. **Snowshoe** walks and backcountry **hikes** are offered through *Vail Nature Center,* 476–7000, ext. 227; *Vail Mountaineering,* 476–1414; and *Eagle River Mountain Guides,* 476–3296. **Ice skating** is available at *Dobson Ice Arena,* 321 E. Lionshead Circle, 476–1560; $2.50 admission, $1 skate rental.

For a nice diversion, visit the *Colorado Ski Museum,* located between Vail Village and Lionshead; exhibits portray the history of Colorado skiing and the individuals who made it happen. Call 476–1876 for hours.

HINTS FOR THE HANDICAPPED. For ski instruction by appointment for people who are blind or have other physical disabilities, contact *Vail Ski School,* Box 7, Vail CO 81658; 476–5601, ext. 4324.

DAY-CARE FACILITIES. There are a number of baby-sitting services; lodges maintain lists of qualified sitters, and the *Vail Youth Center* in Lionshead Parking Structure Building provides sitters; call Robin Olsen at 476–1365. Or try *Lois Brenden Day Care,* 476–0640; *Ingrid Turnbull,* 476–3136; *Pinwheel Professional Babysitting Service,* 949–4997; *Vail Babysitting, Inc.* 827–5279. *Rumpelstiltskin School* is for ages 1–5, weekdays only; 949–4590. *Children's Skiing Center* is day-care for ages 3–6, toilet trained, 476–2626; *ABC Children's Acres* for ages 2–5, 476–1420.

Vail Children's Skiing Center has ski programs for toilet-trained kids aged 3–6 and youngsters 6–13 at Golden Peak and Lionshead; $28 a day for lessons with supervision, without lunch; $78 for 3 days; $115 for 5 days.

NIGHTLIFE. *Sheikas Night Club,* 220 E. Gore Creek Pl., is a wild and glitzy disco. It has live entertainment, and caters to folks in their forties. The *Clock Tower Cafe,* 232 Bridge St., has a romantic piano bar, Tuesday–Saturday evenings. *Cyrano's,* 298 Hanson Ranch Rd., and the *Red Lion Lounge,* 304 E. Bridge St., are considered the "hot spots." *Mickey's* at the Lodge at Vail, 174 E. Gore Creek, has entertainment; the *Shadows at the Mark,* 715 W. Lionshead Circle, is a disco.

Call *Vail Institute for the Performing Arts* for information on local theatrical and musical productions; 476–1000.

WINTER PARK

P.O. Box 36
Winter Park CO 80482
Tel: 303–726–5514, 800–453–2525
   for reservations outside Colorado

Snow Report: 303–892–0961
Area Vertical: 2,200 ft.
Number of Trails: 60 trails on
   826 acres, longest run 2 miles
Lifts: 2 quad chairs, 3 triple
   chairs, 12 double chairs
Snowmaking: 11 trails (220
   acres), serviced by 6 lifts
Season: mid-November–late April

Middle Park and the Fraser Valley were lush summer hunting grounds for the Ute Indians. Irish baronet Lord Gore heard of the paradise for hunters in this part of the American West and headed for what was probably the most bizarre hunting party ever to hit these shores. For two summers, 1854–56, Lord Gore, accompanied by the famous scout Jim Bridger, devastated the local wildlife while living like a king in a striped silk tent with a brass bed and down-filled mattress, linen coverings, trunks of clothes, barrels of delicacies, leather-bound books, wines and liqueurs, pewter mugs, a bathtub, hand-carved and inlaid rifles, packs of hounds, a collapsible raft, and a fur-covered potty. The baronet's personal possessions alone filled 28 vehicles. The mountain range and valley named for Lord Gore were never visited by him; instead he spent his time east of the pass in Middle Park and its environs.

It wasn't the miners who overran the Indian's territory here; it was the railroaders and ranchers. A railroad route linking the Plains states to the west coast via Denver was built over the Continental Divide and through Middle Park. Later, the Moffatt Tunnel was built under the Divide, bypassing the tortuous 11,600-foot Rollins Pass. It was the opening of this tunnel in 1928 that brought the first skiers to the area. (Robert Black's book, *Island in the Rockies,* gives a complete account of the fascinating railroad history of this remote country.)

Enthusiastic Denverites rode the train as far as west Portal Station (so named because it was the entrance on the west side of the Continental Divide). They would hike up the mountain and ski down, making perhaps two runs a day and staying overnight in the railroad construction shacks. Winter Park ski area was born. It became part of the Denver Mountain Parks system in 1940, making it the second-oldest ski area in the state. (The oldest area is Berthoud, a small area a few miles away on top of the Divide.) Today, Winter Park is still owned by the City of Denver, administered by a management company and run as a not-for-profit entity—unique in resort operations in this country. The little mountain town of Winter Park, two miles north of the ski area, grew after the ski area was in existence.

Winter Park prides itself on being a "people's resort": rates are consistently less than those at other Colorado resorts.

Practical Information for Winter Park

HOW TO GET THERE. Winter Park is 67 miles northwest of Denver in the Arapaho National Forest.

By air. Denver's Stapleton Airport is the closest gateway for all major airlines. From the airport, *Trailways,* the *Express (Gray Line),* and *Frontier Airlines Ski Shuttle* serve Winter Park; call *Winter Park Central Reservations* for schedules, 726–5587 or 726–8015. *Home James* taxi service, 726–5060, and *Grand Connection,* 726–5252, provide on-call and scheduled service.

By bus. *Trailways* serves Winter Park and nearby Fraser from downtown Denver and the airport; 980–0730 or 292–2291. (See "By air" for more buses from the airport.)

By train. *Amtrak's* transcontinental California Zephyr serves Winter Park daily; train depot is Fraser, 2 miles from the town of Winter Park, 4 miles from the ski slopes. Most lodges provide free shuttle service. The area shuttle bus, *The Lift,* meets all trains, no charge; *Home James* taxi service is also available, 726–5060. On weekends, the *Denver and Rio Grande Railway* runs a ski train between Denver's Union Station and the Winter Park base area. Arrival is 10 A.M.; the train waits on a siding for the return trip at 4 P.M. Since the early 1950s, the ski train has climbed 4,000 feet in altitude, gone through 29 tunnels and carried hundreds of young skiers each weekend in the 1915 vintage passenger cars; $13 round trip. Call 800–USA–RAIL or 778–6158 in Denver for reservations.

By car. Winter Park is 67 miles northwest of Denver via I–70 to Exit 232, then onto US 40 over Berthoud Pass to the ski areas; the town is 2 miles farther. All major rental car agencies are represented at the Denver airport. In Winter Park there is *National,* 800–328–4567, and *Hertz,* 726–8993 or 800–654–3131.

TELEPHONES. The area code for all of Colorado is 303.

ACCOMMODATIONS. *Winter Park Central Reservations* handles the majority of lodging in the Fraser Valley; write Box 36, Winter Park CO 80482; call 726–5587 or 800–453–2525 outside Colorado. Categories, determined by price, are: *Expensive,* $90–$140 a night, for studios to 2-bedrooms; *Moderate,* $80–$100 for 1-bedroom condos, double occupancy to $37 per person for a 2-bedroom, 4-person occupancy; *Inexpensive,* $10–$30 per room, double occupancy.

Expensive

Creekside Condominiums. 145 Arapahoe Rd.; 726–9461. One-bedroom units, double occupancy are available.

Iron Horse Resort Retreat. 257 Grand County Rd. 70; 726–8851. Winter Park's only ski-in, ski-out property offers full hotel service, a health club, restaurant, and lounge. Studios, to 2-bedrooms.

Moderate

Meadow Ridge Resort. Box 203, Winter Park Ranch; 726–9411. Condominium resort community, 4½ miles west of ski area. One- to 3-bedroom units, each with fireplace and sun deck. Restaurant, bar, pool, sauna, and whirlpool, tennis and racquetball courts, ice rink.

Winter Park Tennis Club. Next to Meadow Ridge complex, Box 377, 628 Cranmer, Fraser; 726–9703. Huge condominiums with wonderful views.

Hi Country Haus Condominiums. Box 3095, 78727 US 40; 726–9421. Located 2 miles from ski hill. All units with fireplaces. Games room, indoor pool, sauna, Jacuzzi.

Snowblaze Athletic Club. Box 404, 79104 US 40; 726–8501. Full athletic club facilities, sauna in every condo. Two-bedroom, four-person units available.

Timber Run Condominiums. Box 1356, Forest Trail; 726–8085. Two-bedroom, four-person units.

A number of mountain inns serve breakfast and dinner family-style; most cost in the range of $33–$60 a night per person with two meals. Contact: *Arapahoe Lodge,* 78594 US 40, 726–8222; *Beaver Village,* 79303 US 40, 726–5741; *Brenner's Lodge,* Box 15, 219 Vasquez Rd., 726–5313; *Timber House,* 196 Grand County Rd. 716, 726–5477.

Inexpensive

Alpenglo Motor Lodge. 78641 US 40; 726–5294. Basic accommodations, on a per person basis.

Morning Star Ranch. 933 Grand County Rd. 8; 726–8118. In the woods, only 10 minutes from the ski area. Small, country-style facility; double occupancy.

Olympia Motor Lodge. 78572 US 40; 726–8843.

Sundowner Motel. 78869 US 40; 726–5452.

Viking Lodge. 78966 US 40; 726–8885.

YMCA of the Rockies (Snow Mountain Ranch). Box 558, 1344 Grand City Rd., Granby; 887–2152. A real bargain, 20 minutes from Winter Park with miles of cross-country trails and Olympic-size pool. Rustic cabins are $10 a night per person.

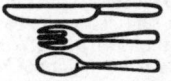 **RESTAURANTS.** There is a broad selection of eateries for a small town. **At the ski area,** the *Mary Jane Center* has a cafeteria and a sit-down restaurant, the *Club Car.* In the lower level of Mary Jane Center is the *Bratskeller* for quick snacks and barbecues, open weekends and holidays only. On the Winter Park side, the midmountain *Snoasis* is a cafeteria, and downstairs is *Mama Mia's* pizzeria; at the base, *West Portal Station* is a cafeteria and has an après-ski lounge, the *Derailer Bar. Stoney Lonesome Coffee & Tea Market* serves croissant sandwiches, homemade soups, salads, divine pastries for sit-down or take-out; a small bar carries the beverage of your choice.

Entrees at the Expensive restaurants listed below run $17–$30; *Moderate,* $7–$17; *Inexpensive,* under $6. All restaurants listed take Visa and MasterCard unless otherwise noted.

Expensive

Expectations at the Slope. 1161 Winter Park Dr., Old Winter Park; 726–5727. Fine Continental food served in a small dining area. Dinner only. Reservations suggested.

The Hideaway. 78260 US 40; 726–9921. Darkly dramatic with madrigal music in the background. Excellent service. Entrees include Tasmanian lobster, Alaskan king crab, Nova Scotia scallops, veal, lamb, shrimp, prime rib (with advance notice). Dinner only; reservations needed.

The Peck House. Empire; 569–9870. Thirty miles south of the ski area on US 40 (but worth the trip), this original stagecoach house established in 1862 is the oldest hotel still operating in Colorado. Fine dinners served in the Victorian dining room. Reservations recommended. Rooms are available—some are said to be haunted.

Moderate

Deno's Coachman Tavern and Restaurant. 78911 US 40; 726–5332. A favorite local hangout featuring American dishes, late-night snacks, burgers.

Gasthaus Eichler. Park Place. 726–5133. Classic German food in a European atmosphere. Good fattening desserts. Breakfast and dinner.

Doc Susie's. 78336 US 40; 726–8104. A bit of New England in the Wild West. Breakfast is a specialty here—the owners claim to have originated eggs Benedict. Lunch and dinner menus.

Lani's Place. Cooper Creek Square; 726–9674. Light, cheery oaken surroundings. Mexican specialties, also takeouts. Lunch and dinner.

Restaurant on the Ridge. At Meadow Ridge Resort; 726–9411. Continental menu for dinner, including oysters, other seafood, and chicken Wellington. An elegant place. For breakfast and lunch, the menu is Mexican (with other specialties). Sunday brunch, children's menu. Reservations recommended for dinner.

The Shed. 78672 US 40; 726–9912. Good steaks; also chicken and burgers. Dinner and breakfast. No reservations.

Inexpensive

Carver Brothers Bakery. 93 Grand County Rd.; 726–8202. Egg breakfasts, fresh pastries; lunch and dinner selections include soups, stews, sandwiches. No credit cards.

Fred & Sophie's. 78884 US 40; 726–5331. Soups, sandwiches, barbecued ribs, lunch and dinner.

Hernando's Pizza Pub. 78260 US 40; 726–5409. Features pizza and other Italian dishes served in a casual atmosphere around a huge fireplace. Carryouts available. Lunch and dinner.

The Kitchen. 78542 US 40; 726–9940. Hearty breakfasts, some Mexican specialties served at this local favorite. Casual spot for breakfasts only. No credit cards.

HOW TO GET AROUND. During ski season *The Lift* connects all the lodges to the town and to the ski areas of Winter Park and Mary Jane; runs every 20 minutes, free; 726–5514 or 8253.

 **SEASONAL EVENTS.** There always seems to be something happening at Winter Park. Because of its nonprofit status, the area hosts more than its share of civic and amateur, as well as pro, events. In **December,** Christmas festivities include a visit by Santa, Christmas Eve church services at the base area, and a torchlight parade. *Winter Wild West Week* is the town's Old West version of winter carnival at the end of **January.** The *First Interstate Bank Cup* is the pro race held in early **February,** while a variety of pro and amateur qualifier races are held throughout February. *The Golden Bunny Race* for kids highlights **Easter,** the *Mascot Race* is in early **April,** with *Spring Splash* (skiing into a pond of water) closing the season in mid-April.

 OTHER SPORTS AND ACTIVITIES. Available is **Snow-Cat skiing** (conditions permitting) in Parsenne Bowl above the Mary Jane area. Racing clinics, mountain guides, freestyle, and jumping programs are available; for some seldom-skied, hard-to-find challenging terrain, sign up with the "Jane Gang," the ski instructors on the Mary Jane Mountain. Never-Ever ski packages, STAR test, NASTAR, and the Ski Blast Weekend workshops are offered through the ski school.

Cross-country enthusiasts can head for nearby Idlewild, 756–5564, with a nordic center in the town; *Snow Mountain Ranch/YMCA of the Rockies* with 26 miles of groomed trails, 887–2152; *C Lazy U Ranch* near Granby for outstanding trail systems, 807–3344; or *Soda Springs Ranch* near Grand Lake, about 30 miles from Winter Park, 627–3486.

Snow tubing at *Fraser Valley Sports Center,* 726–5954, is uncontrolled fun; $5 an hour for an inner tube and rope tow. **Snowmobiling** is available from *Beaver Village,* 726–9247; $20 for an hour's guided trip up to the summit of the Continental Divide; also available from Snow Mountain Ranch/YMCA. **Ice skating** is available at Beaver Village (skate rental for a small fee), and Meadow Ridge, 726–9401—$3–$4 per hour skate rental. **Sleigh rides** are scheduled from Meadow Ridge, Beaver Village, Idlewild, and from McLean Real Estate Office by *Winter Park Sleighrides,* 726–5557 or 8605. **Racquetball, swimming,** and **weightlifting** can be enjoyed by guests of Snowblaze, Meadow Ridge, and Iron

Horse. **Roller skating** and **basketball** are available year-round at Snow Mountain Ranch, along with indoor miniature golf.

DAY-CARE FACILITIES. For reservations for programs listed below, call 726–5514. An infant nursery for children 6 weeks–18 months is available at the ski area on a limited, space-available basis; parents must provide lunch. The nursery for children 18 months–8 years includes all-day supervision and lunch for $25 a day.

Some lodges can arrange for qualified baby sitters. *Mountain View Day Care* provides child care for infants to 4 year olds; $20 a day includes indoor and outdoor activities, lunch, and a snack; call 726–8951 for reservations.

CHILDREN'S ACTIVITIES. Children 3–4 years old, mature enough to ski, and toilet trained can be part of *Penguin Peak;* $35 a day includes all-day supervision, games, ski lessons, play, and lunch. *SKIwee* is for kids 5–7; 3 hours of instruction, lunch, lift ticket, progress pin and card; $35 a day, $90 for 3 days, $135 for 5 days. *The Rangers* are 8–13-year-olds; lessons, lift tickets, lunch, special stickers and pins for $35 a day ($20 for beginners), $90 for 3 days, $135 for 5 days. Lift tickets for children 13 and under are $9 a day.

NIGHTLIFE. Nighttime activities are as casual as the life style in Winter Park. After skiing, late evening usually finds music and dancing at *The Slope,* 1161 Winter Park Dr., in Old Town Winter Park. The *Stampede,* 145 Forest Trail Rd., has recorded disco music, dancing, and an oyster bar, and is a good meeting place. If you want to run into your ski instructor or other locals, head for *Deno's* on US 40, no entertainment but lots of lively conversation. *Gasthaus Eichler,* Park Pl., celebrates "Stammtisch Hour" from 5 to 6 P.M. by the fireplace with special German après-ski treats.

Idaho

SUN VALLEY

Sun Valley Company
Sun Valley ID 83353
Tel: 208–622–4111

Snow Report: 800–635–4150
Area Vertical: 3,400 ft.
Number of Trails: 66 on 1,275
  acres
Lifts: 8 double and 8 triple
  chairlifts
Snowmaking: 20 percent of
  terrain
Season: late November–early May

Sun Valley celebrated its golden anniversary in 1986. For 50 years, Sun Valley has been synonomous with style and glamour.

Before 1936 there was no destination ski resort in the United States. Averell Harriman, chairman of the board of the Union Pacific Railroad, set out to find a place to build a self-sustaining resort in the European tradition served by his railroad. In a rather remote Idaho valley of sheep ranches he found his ideal combination of mountain terrain and valley floor near the ramshackle mining town of Ketchum. He wanted people to ride his train beyond the Mississippi River, and this resort idea might even get the more adventurous off the train and onto the slopes.

The Sun Valley Lodge opened for business a few days before Christmas 1936. The original concept was to offer exquisite food, impeccable service, and nightly entertainment in a mountain region that was neither too high, too windy, too remote, or too near a town. The elegance established at the beginning has always attracted celebrities, from East Coast notables to Hollywood stars. Hemingway, Cooper, Gable, Colbert, Crosby, Garland, Monroe, Eastwood, and Duchin have all added glitter to this already glamorous resort.

All this and skiing, too. Baldy and Dollar mountains are groomed to perfection. There is a wonderful 3-mile run, 5 on-mountain restaurants (complete with etched glass and brass, even in the cafeterias). Skiers can follow the sun through a day of skiing on the different faces of the mountains. The world's first chairlift went into service in Sun Valley, with a design based on a device used to load bananas onto fruit boats.

In the 1940s, the Union Pacific sold some of the 4,300 acres around Sun Valley for development. In 1964 the railroad sold the resort. This was the start of major changes and Sun Valley has since been developed as a vacation village for families while still attracting the rich and famous. Condos, lodges, and hotels are in several locations—around the original Sun Valley Lodge, near Mt. Baldy, and in the town of

Ketchum. With a year-round population of 3,000, Ketchum is unpretentious but exhibits quaint restaurants, western bars, and art galleries. Because the local population is so small, there are no weekend lift lines. Nearly all the skiers are destination visitors.

Sun Valley today is established as a cultural center as well as a summer and winter destination. One thing which won't change—the omnipresence of Mt. Baldy. It can be said that Sun Valley is the *grande dame* of skiing resorts.

Practical Information for Sun Valley

HOW TO GET THERE. By air. Gateways to Sun Valley are Salt Lake City, Boise, Idaho Falls, and Twin Falls. *Horizon Airlines* flies to Hailey (12 miles from Sun Valley) from Salt Lake and Boise. Call 800–453–2737. Charter carriers from Salt Lake to Hailey are *Barken International,* 801–322–0655; *Mercury Aircourier,* 801–531–6149; *Interwest Aviation,* 801–359–2085; *Key Airlines,* 801–539–2805; *Salt Lake Beechcraft,* 801–364–6438; *Trans West Air Charter,* 801–566–1675; and *Sky Hawk,* 801–539–2550.

From Boise, air charters are *Executive Charter* (Lear jet) 208–384–7580; and *Sun Valley Airways,* 208–788–3225. Twin Falls charters are *Reeder Flying Service,* 208–733–5920; and *Sun Valley Airways,* 208–788–3225. Sun Valley Airways also flies from Idaho Falls.

Bus service is available to Sun Valley from Salt Lake City, 5 hours via *Lewis Bros. Stages,* 801–359–8677; and *Trailways,* 801–328–8121. From Twin Falls, a 2-hour ride, call *D Bus Company,* 208–733–8003, or *Sun Valley Stages,* 208–733–3921. Boise, 3 hours away, has bus service on *Apollo Transit,* 208–336–7240; *Trailways,* 208–343–7531; and *Sun Valley Stages,* 208–733–3921. Idaho Falls, 3 hours drive, serves Sun Valley via *Greyhound,* 800–528–0447; *Sun Valley Stages,* 208–733–3921; and *Teton Stage Lines,* 208–529–8036.

Car rental agencies which have drop-off service in Sun Valley are Avis, Hertz, and National. Others are round trips only. In Salt Lake, the following agencies rent cars—(all 800 numbers): *American International,* 527–0202; *Avis,* 331–1212; *Budget,* 527–0700; *Dollar,* 421–6868; *Hertz,* 654–3131; *Holiday,* 237–2804; *National,* 328–4567; and *Payless,* 541–1566.

In Twin Falls, call (all 208 area code): Avis, 733–5527; Budget, 734–4067; Hertz, 733–2668; National, 733–3646. In Boise, call American, 343–8100; Avis, 383–3350; Budget, 383–3090; Hertz, 383–3100; National, 383–3210; and Payless 342–7780. Idaho Falls has Avis, 522–4225; Budget, 522–8800; Econo, 524–6140; Hertz, 529–3101; National, 522–5276; and Payless, 529–1529.

For additional assistance, call the Sun Valley reservations office, 800–635–8261, or in Idaho, 800–632–4104.

TELEPHONES. The area code for Sun Valley and most of Idaho is 208; for Salt Lake City and all of Utah it is 801.

ACCOMMODATIONS. Lodging is grouped into four areas around the mountain complex. For reservations and information on all accommodations, write the Sun Valley Company, Sun Valley ID 83353; 208–622–4111.

The most *expensive* and luxurious accommodations are in the tiny village of Sun Valley. Each lodge in the core village is adjacent to the shopping and restaurant mall. Hotel room rates range from $85 to 195 per night; 1-bedroom condos start at $180; 3-bedroom condos start at $315 per night.

Sun Valley Lodge and Inn received the AAA Four-Diamond Award for 1985. The **Lodge** is a full-service hotel with glass-enclosed, heated swimming pool, massage, sauna, newly appointed interior, and the Duchin Dining Room and Lounge. It is considered the hub of activity in the village. Seven nights ranges from $434 for a standard room to $819 for a parlor suite, per person, double occupancy. Includes 6-day lift ticket.

The **Inn** is a Tyrolean-like hotel with family-style cafeteria, 2 restaurants, meeting room, bell service, telephones, and glass-enclosed heated pool. Same rates as the Lodge.

The luxury **Lodge Apartments** are adjacent to the Lodge, available in 1, 2, and 3-bedroom units. Cozy living rooms, fireplaces, kitchens, telephone, daily maid service. Rates from $434 (studio) to $934 (2-bedroom) double occupancy for a 7-night package with a 6-day lift ticket.

Wildflower Condominiums are similar in appearance and have the same rate structure. The shuttle bus takes approximately 15 minutes to Mt. Baldy, 5 minutes to Dollar Mountain—an ideal beginner's hill.

Within walking distance of the village are clusters of condominiums in Elkhorn Village at the base of Dollar Mountain. Rates are *moderate* with hotel rooms averaging $45–$60 a night. **Village I** and **II, Atelier, Snowcreek, Dollar Meadows,** and **Cottonwood** all have studio to 4-bedroom units with rates at $479 per person for a 7-night package, double occupancy, to $342 per person for 8 people in a 4-bedroom unit, 7 nights with 6-day lift tickets. In all units, children under 11 stay free when in the same room with parents. Special packages are available during Singles Week, Snowball Week and Winter Carnival in January and Ski Club Week in March. Skiers who are better than beginners will want to take the 10-minute shuttle ride to Mt. Baldy, Warm Springs stop. Contact the *Elkhorn Resort at Sun Valley,* Elkhorn Rd., P.O. Box 1067, Sun Valley ID 83353; 622–4511 or 800–635–9356 out of state, or 800–632–4101 in Idaho.

Moderate to *expensive* lodging is found in Warm Springs at the base of Mt. Baldy—it's a short walk to the lifts. Prices range from $63 for a studio up to $315 for a 4-bedroom suite. Contact *Warm Springs Resort,* Box 228, Sun Valley ID 83353; 726–8274 or 800–635–4404.

The fourth area is the town of Ketchum itself. Contact *Sun Valley Ketchum Central Reservations,* P.O. Box 979, Sun Valley ID 83353; 726–0147 or 800–635 –4156. Lodging is moderately priced. The **Tamarack Lodge** (Box 2000, Sun Valley ID; 726–3344) is just a few blocks from the center of town, and has a small indoor pool.

Christiana Lodge (Best Western), 209 Walnut, Ketchum ID 83353; 800–534 –3241. A few minutes walk from a variety of shops and restaurants. About a 7-minute shuttle ride to Mt. Baldy.

Most of the hotels and lodges in each area have some *inexpensive* rooms for under $40 a night. Group rates often bring prices down to the inexpensive level.

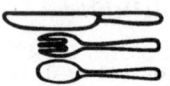 **RESTAURANTS.** For information and reservations for all Sun Valley restaurants, stop by the Restaurant Reservations Booth in the Lodge lobby between noon and 8 P.M. daily, or call 622–4111, ext. 2435. Restaurants are listed in order of price category. *Expensive:* $15–$25; *Moderate:* $8–$15; Inexpensive: less than $8. These prices are for a meal for one person, exclusive of drinks and tip. All but the inexpensive restaurants, snack bars, and cafeterias accept major credit cards.

Expensive

Lodge Dining Room presents elegant dining in a grand manner. White-glove service, French cuisine, extensive wine list. *Do* dress for the part. Live entertainment nightly. For reservations call 622–4111, ext. 2150. Sunday brunch—a must—is served from 8:30 A.M. until 2 P.M.; no reservations for brunch.

Christiana Lodge. 209 Walnut St., Ketchum; 726–3388. Huge upholstered couches against a two-story rock wall. Expect a leisurely dinner, Continental menu; reservations recommended.

Moderate

Duchin Dining Room. In the Lodge; 622–4111, ext. 2144. Open for lunch and dinner, Saturdays until midnight. A family place, American menu, no reservations required.

El Torito. Sun Valley Village Mall; 622–4111, ext. 2260. Serves Mexican specialties, full bar service, takeout orders.

Ram Dining Room. Sun Valley Mall; 622–4111, ext. 2225. A steak and seafood house; most entrees cooked on an open grill. Good cheese and chocolate fondues. Reservations not required.

The Ore House. Sun Valley Mall; 622–4111, ext. 2471. Features steak, seafood, salad bar, happy hour-and-a-half.

River Street Retreat. 12 River St., Ketchum; 726–9502.

 **HOW TO GET AROUND.** The village itself is quite compact and an automobile is unnecessary. Condos are within easy walking distance of Sun Valley Village, but the lodges do provide complimentary **bus** service. Continuous round trips by bus go from the village and the lodges to Dollar and Baldy mountains. The Sun Valley-Ketchum area provides public buses within the Sun Valley, Elkhorn, Ketchum, and Warm Springs areas. Taxis are also available. The two ski mountains are several miles from the Sun Valley area. Warm Springs is near Mt. Baldy.

 **SEASONAL EVENTS.** There is a New Year's Eve celebration with a big band sound, *Singles Week* is in mid-**January**, Winter Carnival at the end of January, *Sun Valley Celebrity Ski Invitational* the last weekend of January, and *North American Airlines Ski Federation* visits in mid-**March.**

 OTHER SPORTS AND ACTIVITIES. For those who want to improve or just brush up, the ski school will accommodate. Classes with private or group instruction are available. NASTAR races run every Tuesday through Friday. If skiers can pry themselves off Baldy, they will find some of the finest **cross-country** skiing in the country. There are groomed trails as well as guided backcountry **tours** and **helicopter skiing** to find your own wilderness. Beginning cross-country skiers can stay at the *Nordic Center* (25 miles of groomed trails) and *Wood River Nordic*—both offer track and Telemark lessons within the village. If it's forests you want, head for Wood River Valley, Galena, and Busterback Ranch tour centers. If you are a strong nordic skier, go with the *Sun Valley Trekking* Company, which offers hut-to-hut skiing in the Sawtooth Wilderness area. Actually, accommodations are in domed tents called yurts and the dinners are scrumptious. For information on any of the above, call *Sun Valley Nordic Ski Touring Center* at 622–4111, ext. 2250 or 2251, or write Box 272, Sun Valley ID 83353. The *Sun Valley Cross-Country Ski Association* publishes a free map and guide to the entire backcountry area. Write the association at Box 3636, Sun Valley ID 83353, for a copy.

Close behind skiing comes **ice skating.** Sonja Henie starred here in the movie *Sun Valley Serenade* in 1941, and skating has been alive and well ever since. The huge rink behind the lodge rents skates. Skating goes on year-round with an indoor rink; competition hockey on weekends. Information at The Lodge.

The town of Ketchum has become a thriving **arts** community with a ballet foundation, two theater groups, and first class preparatory schools. It is the kind of unpretentious resort town where Mariel Hemingway can walk down the sidewalk without a second glance from anyone.

Speaking of Hemingway, nightly horse-drawn **sleigh rides** glide under the moon and across the golf course to Papa Hemingway's hunting cabin for a fine family-style dinner. For reservations, call ext. 2435, with 48 hours advance request.

There's **bowling** in the lodge basement, first run **movies,** and special **theater** and **dance** performances at the Opera House and, of course, the perfect après-ski relaxation in the glass-enclosed heated pools at the inn and lodge; cocktail service at the lodge pool.

 **DAY-CARE FACILITIES.** *Playschool* is a program of planned activities for children, including swimming, ice skating, and 2 hours of ski school. Call 622–4111 for details or go to the blue building north of the Sun Valley Mall. Children 5 years old and older are enrolled in the *Sun Valley Ski School.* Ski/play activities are designed to teach sound skiing fundamentals while having fun.

NIGHTLIFE. The *Ram Bar* features après-ski Mondays through Fridays with Mike Murphy. There is entertainment nightly at the lodge dining room. Check out some of the western bars in Ketchum. For the most up-to-date information. call ext. 2435.

Montana

THE BIG MOUNTAIN

P.O. Box 1215
Whitefish MT 59937
Tel: 406–862–3511

*Snow Report: 406–862–3511,
    800–548–3390*
Area Vertical: 2,170 ft.
*Number of Trails: 43 runs on
    33 miles of terrain;
    longest run is 2.5 miles*
*Lifts: 4 triple chairs, 2
    double chairs, 1 T-bar,
    1 platter lift*
Snowmaking: none
Season: late November–April

In glacier country of northern Montana, Big Mountain is just that. Although only 6,770 ft. at the summit (lower than the base elevations of the Colorado ski areas), Big Mountain is the predominant geographical feature hereabouts. From the nearest town of Whitefish, 8 miles away, the ski trails on the mountain are clearly visible. Families from the northern Rockies and Canada are attracted to the area because of the reasonable costs, and the area promotes that image.

On weekends, Calgarians, (the city is only 320 miles away) descend by the busload on Big Mountain. But weekdays are not crowded. Kids with parents on 5- and 6-night packages stay and ski free during low season. At certain lodges, kids stay free during the entire season.

The back side of the mountain has just been opened up with 8 new trails, primarily intermediate, and a new Summit House with snackbar. Most of the mountain is rated intermediate, with 20 percent each for beginner and expert terrain. There is night skiing Tuesday–Saturday nights. The base area has a lodge, cafeteria, stores, restaurants, and a ski shop.

Practical Information for Big Mountain

 **HOW TO GET THERE. By air.** Glacier Park International Airport in Kalispell is 19 miles from Big Mountain, and is served by *Western Airlines, Frontier,* and *Cascade.* Rental cars are available at the airport. **By car.** Big Mountain is 8 miles north of Whitefish, off US 93. Kalispell, at US 93 and US 2, is 23 miles; Glacier National Park is 28 miles; Missoula is 137 miles via Hwy. 93N; Great Falls, 230 miles; Spokane, WA, 270 miles; and Calgary 320 miles.

By bus. Charter buses ply between Calgary and Big Mountain for weekend and week-long trips. A daily bus runs from Whitefish to the area; call 862–3511 for schedules.

By train. *Amtrak's* Empire Builder stops daily both eastbound and westbound in Whitefish, just 8 miles from the slopes.

TELEPHONES. The area code for all of Montana is 406.

 **ACCOMMODATIONS.** Fifteen hundred guests can stay within walking distance of the slopes. Skiers should pick up major provisions for their condos in Whitefish, as the small convenience store at the slopes has a limited food supply. Call central reservations, 862–3511, for all base lodging; they will also assist on lodging in Whitefish. Hotel rates are per person, based on double occupancy. Categories, determined by price, are *Expensive,* \$75 and up; *Moderate,* \$45–\$75; and *Inexpensive,* less than \$45.

Anapurna Alpine Homes. *Expensive.* P.O. Box 55; call central reservations, 862–3511. These are a variety of units at the base of the area, all within walking distance of the lifts. Some are ski-in, ski-out. All units are rented on a nightly basis, with a discount for 5 nights or more.

Edelweiss. *Expensive.* At slopeside; contact central reservations, 862–3511. This is the newest, poshest accommodations at the area.

Grouse Mountain Lodge. *Expensive.* 1205 Hwy. 93W, Whitefish 59937; 862–3000; or in Montana, 800–621–1802; outside Montana, 800–321–8822. Highly recommended by AAA, this resort overlooks golf course; large rooms, bar, and grill.

Kandahar Lodge. *Expensive.* P.O. Box 1659; phone central reservations, 862–3511. Amenities include sauna, Jacuzzi, cedar-wood decor, single hotel rooms or 3-bedroom condos; located above the ski area road near the entrance to the parking lot, a short walk to the base area and can be skied to from Triple Three Chairlift; also served by a shuttle bus.

Alpinglow Inn. *Moderate.* Base area overlooking Flathead Valley; 862–6966 or central reservations. Amenities include saunas, heated pool, whirlpools; nightly and package rates with meals available.

Chalet Motel. *Moderate.* 6430 Hwy. 93S, Whitefish; 862–5581. In town; has pool.

Allen's Motel. *Inexpensive.* 6540 Hwy. 93S, Whitefish; 862–3995.

Cadillac Hotel. *Inexpensive.* 10 Central Ave., Whitefish; 862–3015. Has a restaurant and lounge; private baths.

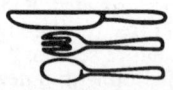 **RESTAURANTS.** There are a cafeteria and four restaurants at the base with a good selection in the town of Whitefish. Since dining at the base is rather limited, we list only two categories here: *Moderate,* \$10–\$18; and *Inexpensive,* less than \$10. Those prices are based on the cost of an average dinner for one person for food alone; beverages, tax, and tip extra. Major credit cards accepted.

Alpinglow Inn. *Moderate.* At the base area; 862–6966. Overlooks the picturesque Flathead Valley through high glass windows; open to the public for breakfast.

4Bs Restaurant. *Moderate.* At the base area; 862–3511, ext. 244. Serves three meals a day, either in the cafeteria or in the dining room; the atrium offers a great mountain view.

Bierstube. *Inexpensive.* At the base area; 862–3028. A bit rowdy, but serves the best burgers in these parts; open daily until 5 P.M.

Moose's. *Inexpensive.* On the mountain; 862–7771. Serves soup, pizza, and sandwiches 10 A.M. –10 P.M. daily.

 **HOW TO GET AROUND.** Everything is accessible from the small base village **by foot.** A **bus** makes the regular run between Whitefish and Big Mountain for a minimal fare; call 862–3511 for details. Check with central reservations as to which lodges on the mountain road have free shuttle service. Otherwise, a **car** is convenient.

 **SEASONAL EVENTS.** In December, local media personalities battle it out on Big Mountain's race course. Each *Glacier Sprints and Glides* highlight Whitefish. Whitefish *Winter Carnival* takes place in early **February** each year, with parades, street games, contests, races, and dogsled and balloon rides. In **March** the *Doug Betters Winter Classic* features pro football players and the media racing each other for charity. *Spring Rendezvous* is at the end of **March.**

 OTHER SPORTS AND ACTIVITIES. A mapped, 3-mile **cross-country** trail starts from the top of Tenderfoot Chairlift. Additional **ski touring** is in nearby Flathead National Forest and Glacier National Park. Ski rentals are available at *The Big Mountain Ski Shop;* call 862–3511. **Sleigh rides** are available during the week; call 862–2538 for information. Nearby is **snowmobiling, ice skating, snowcat rides;** check the ski area at 862–3511 for details.

 **DAY-CARE FACILITIES.** *Alpinsnack Day Skier Center* has child-care facilities at the ski area. They take kids of all ages, even in diapers, for $2.50 an hour, $2 out of diapers, second child $1.50 an hour; call 862–3511 for further information. Advance notice is required for children under 1 year of age.

 **NIGHTLIFE.** At the base village, there is music various nights of the week at *4Bs, Moose's, Hellroaring Saloon and Eatery,* and the *Bierstube.* Whitefish has a number of lively night spots.

BIG SKY RESORT

P.O. Box 1
Big Sky MT 59716
Tel: 406–995–4211, 800–548–4486

Snow Report: 406–995–4211,
    800–548–3390
Area Vertical: 2,800 ft.
Number of Trails: 55 miles of
    groomed trails,
    longest run 3 miles
Lifts: 2 four-passenger
    gondolas; 1 triple
    chair, 3 double
    chairs, 1 rope tow
Snowmaking: 17 percent of
    terrain
Season: mid-November–end of
    April

Montana is not big-time, party-scene skiing. The ski areas are modest in comparison to their brethren throughout the Rockies and California, but that same, light Rocky Mountain powder falls on the slopes. The resorts can be considered regional destination areas, drawing mainly families and students in the northern (and Canadian) Rockies.

Big Sky (just look up to see where it got its name) was a dream of Chet Huntley—half of the Huntley-Brinkley news team. When he retired from television, Huntley moved to this pristine mountain land and forged his ski area. He *is* the history of the ski business in this part of the world.

Basically, Big Sky is a good intermediate mountain and people move around well so that crowds are rarely in evidence. There are open bowls and tree-lined and meadow runs. There are steep, expert faces and mogul runs and smooth, wide beginner slopes.

Skiers can follow the sun by starting at Mad Wolf chair, heading to the bowl or gondola 2; and toward afternoon skiing the front side and Ram's Head chair. Experts like to climb from Lone Peak chair to the

Little Rock Tongue for open bowl skiing or tight tree turns. Check with the ski patrol for areas that are open. Summer skiing is available in June, depending on conditions; call the resort for information.

Practical Information for Big Sky

GETTING THERE. By air. The closest commercial airport is Bozeman. Scheduled flights are via *Northwest Orient, Western, Frontier, United,* and *Big Sky Airlines.* Rental cars are available from *Avis, Hertz, Budget, National,* and *American International.* Head south 45 miles on Hwy. 191 to the resort.

By car. Big Sky is 45 miles south of Bozeman, 18 miles north of Yellowstone National Park. From Bozeman, drive west on Rte. 307 about 10 miles, then south on Hwy. 191. Highways are kept in good driving condition in winter; motorists can get weather information and road reports on all radio stations or call in-state 800–332–6171 or out of state 444–6339. Within a 100-mile radius of Bozeman call 586–1313.

TELEPHONES. The area code for all of Montana is 406.

ACCOMMODATIONS. There is slopeside lodging at Huntley Lodge and condos with many more beds a short distance away in Meadows Village. Call or contact *Big Sky Lodging,* P.O. Box 1, Big Sky, MT 59716; 800–548–4486 or 995–4211. Hotel rates are per person, based on double occupancy. Categories determined by price are *Expensive,* $65–$150; *Moderate,* $40–$65; and *Inexpensive,* less than $40.

Huntley Lodge (see above). *Expensive.* A resort hotel at the base of the lifts with a spectacular view of the Spanish Peaks and Lone Mountain. Heated outdoor pool, ice skating rink, some private Jacuzzis, convention facilities; units range from studios to 3 bedrooms.

Lone Mountain Ranch. *Expensive.* Box 145, Big Sky 59716; 995–4644. A few minutes down the road from the ski area, this rustic but deluxe property consists of log-and-stone cabins with all conveniences, meals in the ranch dining room. It draws primarily cross-country skiers, but downhillers are permitted as well; weekly rates with meals only.

Buck's T-4 Lodge. *Moderate.* Box 895, Big Sky 59716; 995–4111 or 800–528–1234. Best Western establishment; has lounge, restaurant, Jacuzzi, free shuttle service to the ski area.

Coral Motel. *Inexpensive.* Box 204, Canyon Route, Gallatin Gateway 59730. Rustic setting with lots of cowboy charm, there are 7 units and mom's family-style home cooking. Five miles from Big Sky.

Mountain Lodge. *Inexpensive.* Box 46, Big Sky 59716; 800–831–3509 or 995–4560. Rooms have 4 beds; price includes lift tickets; basic and clean. A short walk to the slopes.

In Bozeman there is a choice of moderate and inexpensive motels, including a **Holiday Inn, Super 8,** and **Best Western.**

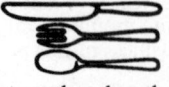

RESTAURANTS. Six restaurants are found at the base area and about the same number within a short driving distance. Prices are moderate in comparison to other ski resorts. The price classifications of the following restaurants are based on the cost of an average three-course dinner for one person for food alone; beverages, tax, and tip extra. *Expensive:* $18–$28; *Moderate:* $12–$18; *Inexpensive:* less than $12. Major credit cards are accepted.

Furst Place. *Expensive.* Meadow Village Center; 995–4794. Considered the best spot by locals; fireside dinners only of Continental dishes, including seafood, veal, game, steaks; reservations requested.

Lone Mountain Ranch. *Expensive.* Rte. 64 near the ski area; 995–4644. Has the best sleigh ride dinners ever; gourmet meals prepared on a wood-burning stove, light by kerosene lantern; fixed price. Guests at ranch get first chance, but it is possible to make a reservation.

Fondue Stube. *Moderate.* In the Huntley Lodge; 995–4221. Serves chicken, beef, and seafood fondue; two nightly seatings; call for reservations.

Huntley Lodge dining room. *Moderate.* 995–4211. Serves buffet breakfast and Continental dinners. Reservations suggested, especially for the Austrian folklore dinners when Austrian ski-school instructors entertain.

Corral. *Inexpensive.* US 191; 995–4795. Features family-style dining, open 7 A.M. to 9 P.M. with breakfast all day; children's menu.

M.R. Hummers. *Inexpensive.* Mountain Mall at the base of the slopes; 995–4543. Popular, packed with skiers; good sandwiches, snacks, steaks, ribs, lunch and dinner.

Mountain Lodge. *Inexpensive.* Base area; 995–4560. Famous for its pizza; also good hamburgers and sandwiches. Open for breakfast, lunch, and dinner.

Snoshoe Inn. *Inexpensive.* 3 miles from entrance on US 191; 995–4565. Open for 3 meals a day; hearty breakfasts, sandwiches, and steaks.

 **HOW TO GET AROUND.** Shuttle busses run between the base area, the condominium complexes, and Meadow Village. Huntley Lodge and some condos are at the base area within walking distance. However, if skiers want to do any exploring outside the area, it is necessary to have a car.

 **SEASONAL EVENTS.** Mid-December features the *National Team Biathlon Race* at Lone Mountain Guest Ranch, followed by *St. Nick's Nordic Festival.* In **January,** *Western Winter Carnival* is a rip-roarin' weekend of craziness and it's the *Vikings Rivalry* at Lone Mountain, while **March** brings the *Mad Wolf Classic,* a three-pin race from Big Sky Ski area to Lone Mountain Guest Ranch. *Old Days Spring Carnival* brings out all the crazies during **mid-April,** featuring the "2-jump inner-tube" competition.

 OTHER SPORTS AND ACTIVITIES. Sleigh rides available from Lone Mountain Guest Ranch (995–4644) and *Buffalo Horn Outfitters* (check for details at Huntley Lodge activities desk, 995–4211). **Cross-country skiing** at the area offers 13 nordic trails with 45 miles of terrain; also from Lone Mountain Ranch and into Yellowstone National Park; **snowcat tours** and **snowmobiling** into Yellowstone as well—contact Huntley Lodge). Bring your own skates to enjoy the **skating rink** behind Huntley Lodge.

 **DAY-CARE FACILITIES.** Children 1 year old and older can go to the *First Run Child Care Center* on the lower level of the Mountain Village Mall for programmed activities and lunches. Children 3–5 years can join the *Ski Club,* which offers a full day of skiing and other recreational activities. Call Big Sky Resort at 995–4211.

 **NIGHTLIFE.** In Mountain Village Mall, check into *Whiskey Jack* for loud music and a young crowd; *Caboose* for a bit on the more mellow side. *Chet's Bar* in Huntley Lodge usually has live entertainment. *Buck's T-4* also offers music on some evenings.

New Mexico

TAOS SKI VALLEY

P.O. Box 90
Taos Ski Valley NM 87571
Tel: 505–776–2291

Snow Report: 505–758–0088
KKIT radio weatherline:
505–758–4267
Area Vertical: 2,612 ft.
Number of Trails: 73
Lifts: 6 double chairlifts, 1
triple chairlift, 1
poma, 1 pony
Snowmaking: 15 percent of
acreage
Season: Thanksgiving–mid-April

Taos skiing owes its existence to one person—Ernie Blake. In the early '50s, Ernie Blake commuted from his work at one ski area in New Mexico to another in Colorado in his Cessna 170. He was always looking for the perfect ski location as he flew over the Sangre de Cristo mountain range of the southern Rockies. He spotted the old mining town of Twining, New Mexico, that showed promise. In 1954 he and a friend climbed the mountains in over 3 feet of powder and found the skiing challenging and the location remote enough to build a destination resort. As a bonus, it was close to the famous artists' colony and ancient Indian pueblo of Taos. In 1955 the resort opened, and today Ernie Blake still runs his "perfect" ski location.

The tree line in the southern Rockies is at 12,000 ft. (twice that of the Alps). Part of the magic of Taos is the variety of hidden powder bowls, glades, and chutes beginning at 11,819 ft. and plunging to the village at 9,207 ft. All this snow under the blue New Mexico skies and warm sun! If you check a world atlas, you'll see Taos is the same latitude as the southernmost tip of the Greek islands.

Taos is home to the famed "Al's Run," a gravity-defying vertical plummet. Since this is the first run any skier sees in Taos, Blake put up a sign that says, "Don't panic—we have easy runs, too." And its true. There are meandering trails with wide, lazy turns, well-groomed trails cut through the forest, and those wide-open bowls. But make no mistake; by and large, this is a difficult ski area.

Blake puts his personal touch on nearly everything at Taos. He created the "Martini Trees." At the base of certain spruce trees, skiers can find ice-cold martinis buried in glass *porrons* (wine bottles)—said to help one's self-confidence. His ski school is based on the European tradition that *everyone* takes lessons. Highlight of ski school could be Ernie's history of ski talk. In fact, the entire ski village has a European ambience, with French and German spoken as much as English. The

Swiss, French, and German chefs vie with one another for fine aprés-ski feasts at the village lodges. All the bistros, shops, and lodges are within walking distance, making the atmosphere intimate, *gemmutlich, sympathetique.*

Practical Information for Taos

HOW TO GET THERE. Albuquerque is the closest commercial airport, served by most major airlines. *Jetaire Airlines* has daily flights between Albuquerque and Taos; call 800–538–2473. From Albuquerque, Taos is a 3-hour drive, (143 miles). Denver's Stapleton Airport is 281 miles away, or nearly a 6-hour drive; Colorado Springs airport is a 5-hour drive.

Faust's Transportation runs a **shuttle** service between the airport and the ski area twice a day. For reservations and information, call 758–3410. Skierized **rental cars** are available from *Avis* at Taos Ski Valley or at the Albuquerque airport; call 800–331–1212 or, in Taos, 776–2670. Also check *Taos Rent A Car* at 758–8911, 758–9301, or 758–4053.

TELEPHONES. The area code for all of New Mexico is 505.

ACCOMMODATIONS. Packages are offered for 3–7 days. Most popular in this rather remote resort is the 7-day Learn-to-Ski-Better package, which includes lodging, three meals a day, 6-day lift ticket, and 6 days of lessons. You can stay in the old Indian town of Taos and visit the pueblo which has been continuously inhabited since 1200. For reservations contact the *Taos Valley Resort Association,* P.O. Box 85, Taos Ski Valley NM 87571; 800–992–SNOW (7669) or 776–2233 within New Mexico; or *Taos Central Reservations,* P.O. Box 1713, Taos NM 87571, 800–821–2437, or 758–8522 within New Mexico. Categories, based on price range for the package, are: *Expensive,* $750–$900; *Moderate,* $400–750; *Inexpensive,* less than $400.

Hotel Edelweiss. *Expensive.* On the slopes; 776–2301. Features a 7-day ski package with breakfast and dinner, 6 days of lifts, and lessons; double occupancy.

St. Bernard condos, 776–8506, or **Hotel,** 776–2251. *Expensive.* Both on the slopes; 7-day ski package with three meals a day, 6 days of lifts and lessons, double occupancy.

Thunderbird Lodge and Chalets. *Expensive.* On the slopes; 776–2280. The full 7-day ski package ranges from $760 to $825.

Villacito Condos. *Expensive.* Box 49, Arroyo Seco NM 87514; 776–8778. Located 13 miles from the slopes; large units with hot tubs, washer/dryer, and phones. Offers 7-day package with 6 days of lift tickets and lessons; double occupancy.

Austing Haus. *Moderate.* Box 8, Taos Ski Valley NM 87571; 776–2649. Two miles from the slopes; 7-day packages with lifts and lessons; double occupancy; hot tub, restaurant, and game room.

Quail Ridge Inn. *Moderate.* Box 707, Taos, NM 87571; 800–624–4448 or 776–2211. A family resort and conference center, 14 miles from Ski Valley in Taos; has a lounge and restaurant, racquetball, tennis, phones, pool, hot tub, sauna, fireplaces. Offers a 4-day package with lift tickets for a 1-bedroom.

Abominable SnowMansion. *Inexpensive.* Box 3271, Taos NM 87571; 776–8298. A dormitory facility 10 miles from the slopes. Rate includes 7 nights lodging, 6 days of lift tickets, and lessons. There are hearty home-cooked meals; bed and breakfast packages also available.

Kachina Lodge Best Western. *Inexpensive.* Box NN, Taos NM 87571; 758–2275. Eighteen miles from the ski slopes. Lounge and nightclub, hot tub, laundry. A 4-night stay is offered with lift tickets, double occupancy.

RESTAURANTS. Since many ski packages include meals, most visitors opt to stay at Ski Valley. But there are many good restaurants in Taos—reached via the daily shuttle service—to lure skiers from the mountain. In this selection, restaurants are listed by price category. *Expensive:* $15–$25; *Moderate:* $8–$15; *Inexpensive:* less than $8. These prices are for an average meal for one, excluding beverages, tax, and tip. All restaurants in the moderate and expensive categories accept major credit cards.

Expensive

Doc Martin's. Taos Inn, N. Pueblo Rd.; 758–2233. The Spanish influence is felt here like nowhere else; the historic inn oozes with authenticity. The menu offers superb northern New Mexican dishes and seafood, extensive wine list; reservations are recommended.

Hotel St. Bernard. At the slopes, Taos Ski Valley; 776–2251; full service bar, nightly entertainment, extensive menu, big-screen video. Reservations suggested.

Sagebrush Inn. S. Santa Fe Rd., Taos; 758–2254. Award-winning menu includes steaks, prime rib, seafood, vegetarian dinners, salad bar, Chinese dishes. Live entertainment nightly; reservations a must.

Whitey's. In the historic Dorothy Brett house, Ski Valley Rd. at the blinking light in Taos; 776–8545. International dishes of seafood, lamb, steak, beef Wellington, chef's choices; intimate atmosphere. Reservations required.

Moderate

Apple Tree Restaurant. 26 Bent St., Taos; 758–1900. Intimate and charming with four dining rooms; the best *chile rellenos* in Taos, Hunan-style shrimp, good seafood, steaks, desserts, wine list; serves Sunday brunch 10 A.M.–3 P.M.; reservations recommended.

Carl's Gourmet Deli & Cajun Cookin'. In Pueblo Alegre Mall, Taos; 758–1637. Serves spicy hot Cajun specialties for lunch and dinner; overstuffed New York deli items and gourmet lunches to go for the slopes; beer and wine; open daily 11:30 A.M.–9:30 P.M.

The Garden Restaurant. On the Plaza in Taos; 758–9483. Extensive selection of Mexican, Italian, and vegetarian items; beer and wine.

Phoenix Restaurant. Taos Ski Valley at the base of Kachina Lift; 776–2291; Serves hamburgers, chili, soups, sandwiches, beer and wine. View of the highest peaks in New Mexico.

St. Bernard Rathskeller. At the ski area; no phone. Serves sandwiches, homemade soups, stews; eat inside or on the sundeck.

Inexpensive

Comidas del Mante. S. Santa Fe Rd. between Randall Lumber and Ranchero Boots in Taos; 758–9317. Mexican cooking.

Floyd's Restaurant and Lounge. S. Santa Fe Rd., Taos; no phone. American and Mexican food.

Mainstreet Bakery. Guadalupe Plaza, Taos; 758–9610. Delicious "health food."

Rucksack. On the lower level, west end on Hondo Lodge, sells snack items.

Snack Bar. On the main floor of the Ski Center, serves light lunches and snacks.

HOW TO GET AROUND. *Faust's Transportation* has local *bus, taxi,* and *charter* service. A daily skiers' **shuttle** serves the Taos motels, the Town Ticket Office, and the ski slopes (reservations required). Thursday mini-tour and shopping shuttle from the Ski Valley to town. Call 758–3410.

E.S. Lawrence Gallery, Kit Carson Rd. in Taos, sponsors a **shuttle** service to accommodate skiers staying in Taos Ski Valley. Starting mid-December, the bus departs the ski area at 5:30 P.M. Tuesdays–Fridays, dropping passengers at the Gallery; it returns about 9 P.M. Many of the local merchants stay open on ski shuttle nights.

SEASONAL EVENTS. The *Summit Series Telemark Race* is in mid-**January** and the *Michelob Light Pro-Race* is at the end of **February** each year. The *Marlboro Coin-op Race Course* operates daily throughout the season. NASTAR is available for recreational racers to compete against each other; races on Sundays, Wednesdays, and Fridays.

OTHER SPORTS AND ACTIVITIES. The big thing at Taos Ski Valley is the ski school. Owner Ernie Blake's philosophy is that skiers must learn more here than they could anywhere else. So whether you are a beginner or an expert, to be part of the scene you take part in the ski school program. For those who have never skied, there is the Yellow Bird Program.

In Taos, the many **art galleries** are worth visiting. The *Millicent Rogers Museum,* 4 miles north of Taos off Rte. 3, 758–2462, displays Hispanic and native American arts and gifts. First run **movies** are featured at the Plaza Theatre and High Society Cinema; 758–9715. Guided **snowmobile** tours are conducted at *Moreno Valley Recreation* in Angel Fire; 758–3088 or 377–2321. An hour from Taos via US 64 and US 285 south treat yourself to the *Ojo Caliente Mineral Springs* and therapeutic **massage.** Open Mondays–Thursdays, 1–7 P.M., Fridays–Sundays, 8 A.M.–noon and 1–8 P.M.; call 583–2233 for an appointment.

DAY-CARE FACILITIES. Baby-sitting arrangements can be made for infants younger than 3 years old. *Kinderkafig* is for children 3–6. The 3- and 4-year-olds are in a program which includes an hour of skiing in the morning and in the afternoon plus various outdoor and indoor activities and lunch rest time; 5- and 6-year-olds meet for 2 hours of ski lessons in the morning and afternoon plus lunch.

The *Junior Elite Program* is for 7–12-year-olds with 2 hours of ski instruction in the morning and afternoon plus a weekly ski school race and videotape critique. The *Elite* is for 13–18-year-olds with 2 hours of morning instruction. All lift tickets and ski school classes can be purchased at the ski school office or next door at the ticket office. Call Taos Ski Valley, 776–2291 for free information and schedules.

NIGHTLIFE. Most of the nightlife centers around the ski lodge activities. Many have nightly entertainment, everything from country-western to jazz. After a hard day of keeping up with instructors, most skiers call it an early night.

The *Thunderbird Lodge,* Taos Ski Valley (776–2291), holds a jazz festival each January with the country's top performers, something jazz buffs should keep on their calendar. It equals any gig seen in New York.

For those who do drive or take the shuttle into Taos, there are several places with lively activity. Kachina Lodge, 758–2275, features music from punk to country during the week.

Ogelvie's Bar and Grille, on the Plaza, 758–8866, is a good gathering spot, especially on weekends when live entertainment is featured; unusual drinks.

Adobe Bar, in Taos Inn, 758–2233, features live entertainment, Happy hour from 5 to 6 P.M., with oysters, shrimp, and the best margaritas in the West; definitely a spot not to be missed. Good for artist watching—R.C. Gorman spends a lot of drinking time here.

Oregon

MT. BACHELOR

P.O. Box 1031
Bend OR 97709
Tel: 503-382-2442, 800-547-6858

Snow Report: 503-382-7888
Area Vertical: 3,100 ft.
Number of Trails: 40 on 6,000
acres
Lifts: 5 triple chairs, 5
double chairlifts
Snowmaking: none
Season: mid-November–July

Like the entire Pacific Northwest, the weather and snow conditions at Mt. Bachelor can be changeable: rain slickers sold in many sport shops are an indication of its fickleness. But spring and summer skiing is among the best anywhere.

The Northwest destination resorts aren't anything like the slick resorts of California and Colorado. These areas draw mainly families from Canada and northwestern United States, with fewer choices of lodges and restaurants in the immediate vicinity of the ski areas. Yet they are not without their charm. The views from these ancient volcanoes are totally different from the Rockies or the Alps in that each mountain stands alone, with the other volcanic cones off in the distance. The summit of Mt. Bachelor provides a 360-degree panoramic view, with the Three Sisters, Hood, St. Helens, and Rainier standing like faraway sentinels.

The skiing at Bachelor's summit is 360 degrees, too. If one side isn't good, just traverse to another. So skiers won't get lost in a sudden whiteout, a cat track—Catchline—will bring skiers to the front side of the mountain.

Closer to the base of Bachelor, there are fine tree skiing, glades, powder runs in Outback, and groomed trails. Four-day lodges surround the base of the hill, each with its own restaurant, parking lot, ticket office, rental shop, and set of lifts. Access to the summit is via the Sunrise Lift, so start from Sunrise Lodge. Below the summit are beginning and intermediate runs; day-care facilities are in Sunrise Lodge. Blue Lodge also has good beginning and intermediate trails starting from it.

The main lodge accesses more expert runs; then there's Cinder Cone and the Outback for powder freaks.

The summit chair opens the area to summer skiing and to passengers with nothing more than shoes on their feet. The lift actually operates through Labor Day, shutting down for just a few months until the beginning of the season in November. This is high desert country, and the "in" thing during spring and summer is to ski the summit in the

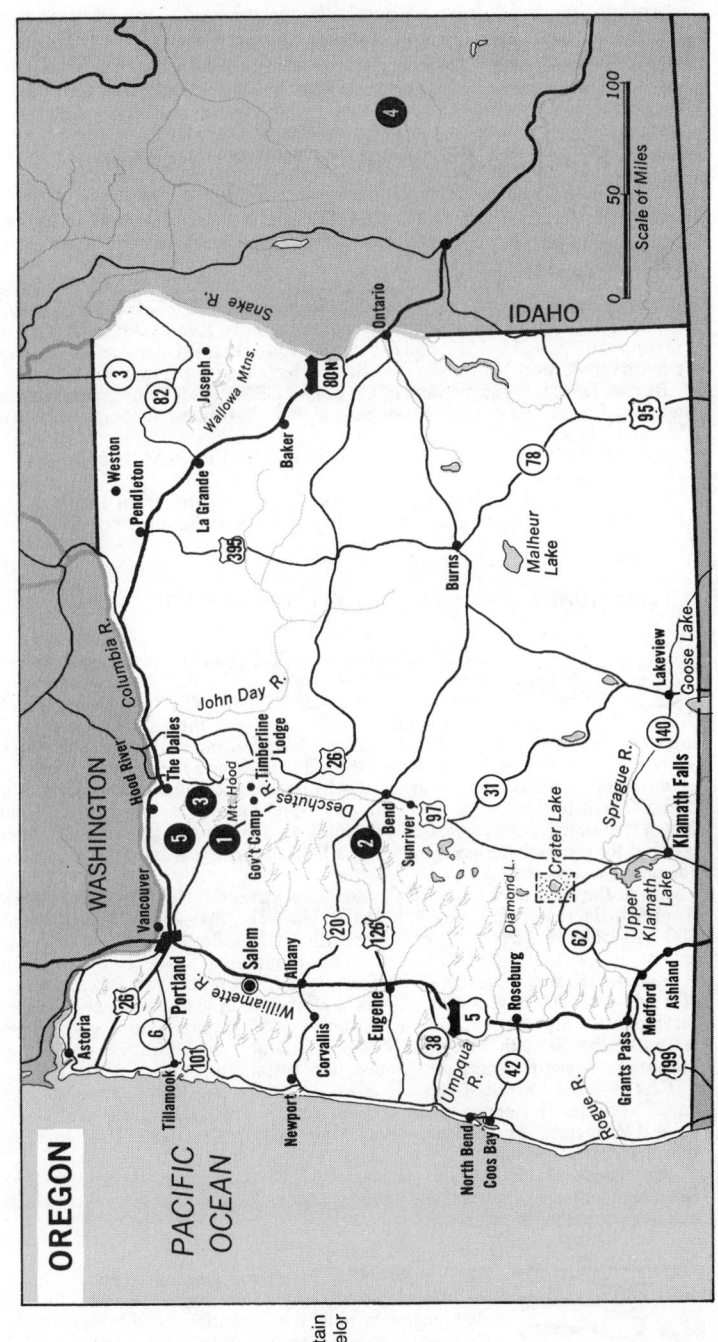

Resorts

1) Mirror Mountain
2) Mount Bachelor
3) Mount Hood Meadows
4) Sun Valley
5) Timberline

morning, then head down to Bend, 40 minutes and many thousands of feet in elevation away to golf, tennis, raft, or hike.

Practical Information for Mt. Bachelor

HOW TO GET THERE. Mt. Bachelor is 22 miles west of Bend, on scenic Century Drive. Bend is in the center of Oregon.

By air. *Horizon Air* serves the Redmond/Bend Airport from San Francisco, Portland, and Seattle; call 382–2124. Airport limousine service goes into Bend, 15 miles from the airport. Rental cars at the airport are *National,* 800–328–4517, and *Hertz,* 800–654–3131. Private aircraft can land at Sunriver Airport; 17 miles from Bend. Hertz cars are available.

By car. Bend is at the junction of US 97 and US 20. It's 3 hours from Portland away via US 26 and US 97. From Seattle, it is 334 miles, 7 hours, via I–5 to Portland, then US 26 to US 97.

By bus. *Pacific Trailways* operates from Portland to Bend daily; also daily between Bend and Mt. Bachelor.

By train. *Amtrak's* Coast Starlite serves West Coast cities from Seattle to San Diego. The train stops in Chemult, south of Bend, with limousine or rental cars from there.

TELEPHONES. The area code for all of Oregon is 503.

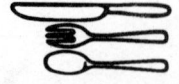

ACCOMMODATIONS. For all lodgings near the ski area, contact *Mt. Bachelor Central Reservations,* P.O. Box 1031, Bend OR 97709; 382–8334. There are no accommodations at the base of the mountain, but there are some lodges and motels along Century Drive leading to the base and a wide variety of lodgings in the town of Bend, 22 miles away. Sunriver, a smaller community 18 miles away, also has a selection of accommodations for a total of 3,500 beds in the general area. All offer 7-night packages, which include one day of free skiing. Rates are based on double occupancy. Categories, determined by price for the package, are: *Expensive,* $300 and up; *Moderate,* $200–$300; and *Inexpensive,* less than $200.

Inn of the Seventh Mountain Condos. *Expensive.* On Century Dr., 14 miles from Mt. Bachelor; P.O. Box 975, Bend; 382–8711, 800–452–6810 in Oregon, 800–547–5668 in western states. suites with kitchen, fireplace, TV; whirlpools, saunas, ice skating rink; bus service to the mountain.

Sunriver Resort. *Expensive.* On Century Dr., 18 miles from Mt. Bachelor; 800–547–3922 in Oregon, 800–452–6874 elsewhere in U.S. Resort also has bus service to the area, heated indoor swimming pool, Jacuzzis, store, golf course.

Inn of the Seventh Mountain Lodge. *Moderate.* Same address and phone number as Seventh Mountain Condos. TV; restaurant, lounge, snack bar.

Best Western Entrada Lodge. *Moderate.* Century Dr., Bend; 382–4080. Borders Deschutes National Forest, 2 miles west of Bend. Charming rooms with color TV; Jacuzzi, sauna, heated pool. Full breakfast available. Free après-ski refreshments in season.

Riverhouse Motor Inn. *Inexpensive.* On US 97, north of Bend; 389–3111. Seventeen suites; restaurant and lounge, sauna, Jacuzzi. Cross-country skiing and snowmobiling available.

RESTAURANTS. Five on-mountain restaurants are in the four-day lodges and the Nordic Lodge. Sunday champagne brunch is a tradition at the main lodge. However, après-ski activities take place in the individual lodges as well as in Bend and in Sunriver. Restaurants are listed here in order of price category. *Expensive:* $15–$25; *Moderate:* $7–$15; *Inexpensive:* less than $7. All sit-down restaurants accept major credit cards.

Expensive

Cyrano's Restaurant. 828 N.W. Wall St., Bend; 389–6276. Holds less than 30 diners, so reservations are required. The 6-course meal changes monthly.

Le Bistro. 1203 N.E. Third St., Bend; 388–7274. In a redecorated church; gourmet menu features saddle of lamb and scampi; closed Sundays and Mondays.

The Meadows Dining Room. In Sunriver Lodge; 593–1221. Fancy service with a fancy menu, including duck and fresh fish.

Moderate

The Brass Wok. At the Riverhouse; 389–7579. Serves Szechuan and Mandarin style Chinese dishes; food to go.

The Ore House. 1033 N.W. Bond St., Bend; 388–3891. Features that plush San Francisco style of all restaurants in the Ore House Chain; good steaks, salad bar; open daily.

Pine Tavern. 967 N.W. Brooks, on Mirror Pond, Bend; 382–5581. The town's oldest tavern, serving American menu, Sunday brunch; reservations required.

The Riverhouse. 3075 N. US 97, Bend; 389–8810. French and Continental cuisine; open 7 days a week, 3 meals a day.

Inexpensive

Bentley's American Grill. 119 N.W. Minnesota, Bend; 389–9878. Serves brunch and lunch; hamburgers, soups, salads.

Bonanza. 1245 S. US 97, Bend; 389–2852. Features the largest salad bar in central Oregon, all-you-can-eat soup and salad; children's menu.

Mexicali Rose. 301 N.E. Franklin, Bend; 389–0149. As the name implies, south of the border dishes, as hot as you want 'em.

Poppy Seed Cafe. At the Inn of the Seventh Mountain; 387–8711. Good for fish and chips, sandwiches, family-style dinners; airy atmosphere, with plenty of greenery.

 **HOW TO GET AROUND.** A **shuttle bus** operates daily from Bend and several lodging properties to Mt. Bachelor; call 593–2255 for the schedule. The more expensive lodges have complimentary bus service; otherwise a car is necessary. TLC, or the **Limousine** company, has a chauffered presidential limousine for hire; 389–5202. Call-A-Cab **taxi** service is 382–1687.

 **SEASONAL EVENTS.** A Thanksgiving cross-country ski clinic is an annual **November** activity. In **January** the *Sun Cup Downhill and Super "G"* is held; **February** it's the *Police/Fireman Winter Olympics* and the *Northwest Cup Giant Slalom.* In **March** or **April,** Easter brings the *Gourmet Picnic Tour Easter Egg Hunt* and *Family Relay;* **May** starts the "Summit Season" (usually the best skiing at the summit) with reduced ticket prices; the *Pole Pedal Paddle Cross Country Race* is mid-May. *Cross-Country US Ski Team* spring training camp is in late May–early June; junior cross-country camps during the month of **June;** *Bob Beattie Summer Camps* for adults and juniors are May–July in the summit's permanent snow fields. For details on any event, call the ski area at 382–2442 or 382–2607.

 OTHER SPORTS AND ACTIVITIES. Besides skiing for 10 months of the year, there is an extensive **nordic trail system.** Fifty km of machine-groomed, marked, and patrolled trails begin near the main parking lot at Bachelor and lead into the Deschutes National Forest. The Nordic Lodge at the base, adjacent to the main lodge, has snacks, ski school, rentals, and repairs. Daily trail pass is $6 for adults, $3.50 for children 12 years old and under, $3 for seniors. Lessons in telemarking and racing are available.

Snowmobile trails are marked to Elk Lake and Cascade Lakes. Also, tours are available through Sunriver Resort; call 382–2124, ext. 418. **Sleigh rides** are from the Inn of the Seventh Mountain, 382–8711; also *Wildcat Packers and Outfitters* run sleigh and dinner rides, 389–9458. Pick up a copy of *Our Town*

guide to Bend and vicinity for the latest in activities and events as well as maps of the area.

DAY-CARE FACILITIES. There are two day-care centers at Mt. Bachelor, at the main and Sunrise lodges. Rates are $15/per day or $3 an hour for ages 6 weeks–6 years; reservations recommended; 382–2442. Planned activities; lunch must be provided by parents. For advance booking, write Mt. Bachelor Day-Care Center, P.O. Box 1031, Bend OR 97709. Children's ski school is for youngsters 7–12; *Tiny Tracks* is a ski school for 4–6-year-olds; full day lesson, $18. Contact the ski school at 382–2442.

NIGHTLIFE. The town of Bend is usually hopping, and depending on the crowd at the Inn of the Seventh Mountain and Sunriver Resort, those places can be lively as well. *Brandy's,* 197 N.E. Third in Bend has nightly entertainment; 382–2687. *El Crab Catcher* at the Seventh Mountain has après-ski hour with ski movies, entertainment, and dancing; 389–2722. *The Riverhouse* features bands from the Northwest, happy hour; 389–3111. The *Pine Tavern,* 382–5581, and *DeJola's,* 338–1288, are often packed with après-skiers.

OTHER OREGON SKI AREAS

Mt. Hood is another of those extinct volcanos that dominate the Oregon landscape. The 11,245-foot mountain has three day-ski areas on its slopes—Mt. Hood Meadows, Timberline, and Mirror Mountain. Mt. Hood is about 70 miles east of Portland via Hwy. 84N and Hwy. 26. Mirror is the smallest and closest to Portland; Timberline has nice beginner and intermediate terrain for both summer and winter skiing, while Mt. Hood Meadows is the most diverse, with runs for all ability levels.

MT. HOOD MEADOWS

P.O. Box 47
Mt. Hood OR 97041
Tel.: 503–337–2222

Snow Report: 503–337–2222, 503–227–SNOW
Area Vertical: 2,777 ft.
Number of Trails: 40 on 2,000 acres, longest run 3 miles
Lifts: 1 triple chair, 7 double chairs, 1 rope tow
Snowmaking: none
Season: mid-November–mid-May

There are some 2,000 skiable acres on the eastern flank of Mt. Hood. Included is a good mix of groomed slopes, gentle beginners, fun intermediate cruisers, and short—but—steep advanced terrain. Most of the skiing is in the trees, protected from the wind. The Texas Chair serves areas above timberline, but runs only when weather conditions permit. The most famous run is Heather's Canyon, a 3-mile long outback trail for experts reached only from Texas Chair. There is night skiing from five of the lifts on the front of the mountain.

The main base lodge and a smaller lodge below the Meadows Chair include bars, a deli, snack bar, and bakery; there is usually live entertainment during the late afternoon hours. Rental skis are available.

TIMBERLINE SKI AREA

Timberline OR 97028
Tel: 503–226–7979, in
   Oregon 800–452–1335

Snow Report: 503–222–2211
Area Vertical: 2,000 ft. winter, 2,500 ft. summer
Number of Trails: 28 on 1,000 acres
Lifts: 5 double chairs, 2 rope tows
Snowmaking: none
Season: mid-November–mid-April, mid-May–Labor Day

Obviously, what separates Timberline from other ski areas is the full summer ski season. Skiing in summer starts 1,000 feet higher than in winter, from 6,000 to 8,500 feet on the treeless section of Mt. Hood for glacier skiing. Temperatures can range from blizzards to swimsuit sun. Lifts open early in the morning and close early in the afternoon to avoid the mushy midday conditions. More than a dozen race camps hold clinics here each summer, and Olympic team members and hopefuls attend.

Winter skiing is in the protected wooded area with lots of good beginner and intermediate runs. Some runs are lit for night skiing.

The Wy'East day lodge sells tickets, food, 3 meals a day, drinks, and rental equipment.

MIRROR MOUNTAIN

P.O. Box 400
Government Camp OR 97028
Tel: 503–272–3522

Snow Report: 503–224–9221
Area Vertical: 1,400 ft.
Number of Trails: 31 on 400
　　　skiable acres
Lifts: 4 double chairs, 7 tow
　　　ropes
Snowmaking: none
Season: late November–mid-April

The terrain consists of mostly open slopes, north facing. This is the oldest ski area on Mt. Hood. Two day lodges have cafeterias, and the West Lodge has a bierstube.

Practical Information for Other Oregon Ski Areas

HOW TO GET THERE. Portland is reached by major **air** carriers and **Amtrak.** Mirror Mountain is 53 miles east on US 26, next to the village of Government Camp. Timberline is 60 miles from Portland via US 26 to Government Camp/Timberline. Trailways serves Timberline from Portland; 297–8801.

Mt. Hood Meadows is 67 miles from Portland via I-84 and Rte. 35, and is 10 miles from Government Camp. For **bus** service to Mt. Hood Meadows, call 297–8801.

TELEPHONES. The area code for all of Oregon is 503.

ACCOMMODATIONS. Most skiers drive to one of the areas for the day, but some do stay at one of the most unique lodges in the country—Timberline Lodge, Timberline OR 97028. This is a huge stone castle built during the WPA era. It is a National Historic Landmark, with hand-crafted details such as decorative animals atop posts, wrought iron hinges, and door ornaments. Each of the 57 rooms is different. Rates range from $36 to $100 per person, double occupancy for the night. For reservations, call 800–452–1335 in Oregon; 800–547–1406 in Washington, Idaho, Utah, Nevada, and northern California; 503–231–5400 from other locales.

There is also lodging in Government Camp and the Town of Welches, with an average room cost of $40 a day.

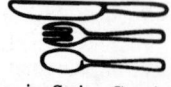

RESTAURANTS. The day lodges all have cafeterias. Grill your own steak at *Charlie's Mountain View Restaurant* in Government Camp; *moderate.Chalet Swiss,* US 26 at Welches Rd. near Rippling River Resort, specializes in Swiss Continental food, with veal, cheese fondue, and raclette; open Wednesday to Sunday; 622–3600. The *Cascade Dining Room* in Timberline Lodge serves American and Continental dishes; an elegant atmosphere, with meals costing $15–$25.

HOW TO GET AROUND. A **car** is a necessity, since there is no public transportation available to these ski areas.

SEASONAL EVENTS. Timberline has 24-hour skiing on **New Year's Eve;** the Golden Rose Celebrity Ski Classic takes place the end of **May. Summer** and night skiing are popular.

 OTHER SPORTS AND ACTIVITIES. The *Nordic Center* is located at Hood River Meadows at Mt. Hood Meadows ski area, by the lower parking lot. There is a fee for **track skiing** on the 26–km trail system. Telemarking lessons are available. At Timberline, class and private lessons are offered at the *White River Nordic Center;* there are day and night tours with a wilderness gourmet meal. Call the ski areas for details.

 **CHILDREN'S ACTIVITIES.** Timberline offers a *SKIWEE* program for kids 3–12. Rates are $40 per child per day, including full-day lesson, lift ticket, rental, and lunch. Register at the ski school desk in the Wy'East Day Lodge; 503–231–5402. Mt. Hood Meadows has children's classes at the ski school.

 **NIGHTLIFE.** With everyone rushing back to Portland, there is not a lot of it. What there is will be found at Timberline Lodge, in the *Rams Head Bar* overlooking the lobby or in the *Blue Ox Bar.*

Utah

Seven Wasatch Front ski areas are within an hour of the international airport of Salt Lake City. The canyons stretch like fingers from the Great Salt Basin, each catching the Pacific storms, which have been dried and salted from moving across the Salt Lake. Little Cottonwood Canyon, home of Alta and Snowbird, catches the majority of the storms, and snowfall is measured in feet, not inches. Four ski resorts are described in detail here, followed by a listing of seven other ski areas as well as the Ski Utah Interconnect.

ALTA

Alta UT 84092
Tel: 801–742–3333

Snow Report: none
Area Vertical: 2,000 ft.
Number of Trails: open and bowl
skiing on 1,700 acres;
longest run 3 miles
Lifts: 8 double chairs, 3 rope
tows
Snowmaking: none
Season: mid-November–May

Alta is the oldest ski area in Utah. In 1938, the Collins single chair was installed at Alta—the third in North America. It was made from used mining equipment, and a lift ticket was 15¢ a ride. But skiing in Utah remained for those living in the Wasatch Front communities, a select group of powder aficionados, and to some World War II snow troops training at Alta until the advent of Alta's upstart neighbor, Snowbird.

Alta is and will remain a holdout of another era. It offers stupendous skiing, period. No fancy amenities, no high tech, high speed, detachable lifts, no glamor, no high prices. It is no-frills skiing. But then, after days of attacking the slopes, not many people have the will or energy to do much more than eat a hearty meal and collapse into bed.

Skiing in Alta is reminiscent of Europe in that there are no formally marked, highly groomed trails—just pistes that leave the skiers to use their imagination to negotiating the trees and canyons they encounter on the downhill trip. Some beginner and intermediate terrain is groomed, but most of the skiing is in powder or as it falls. The philosophy of skiing in Alta is dramatically opposed to Stein Eriksen's philosophy over in the next canyon at Deer Valley, where not a snowflake is

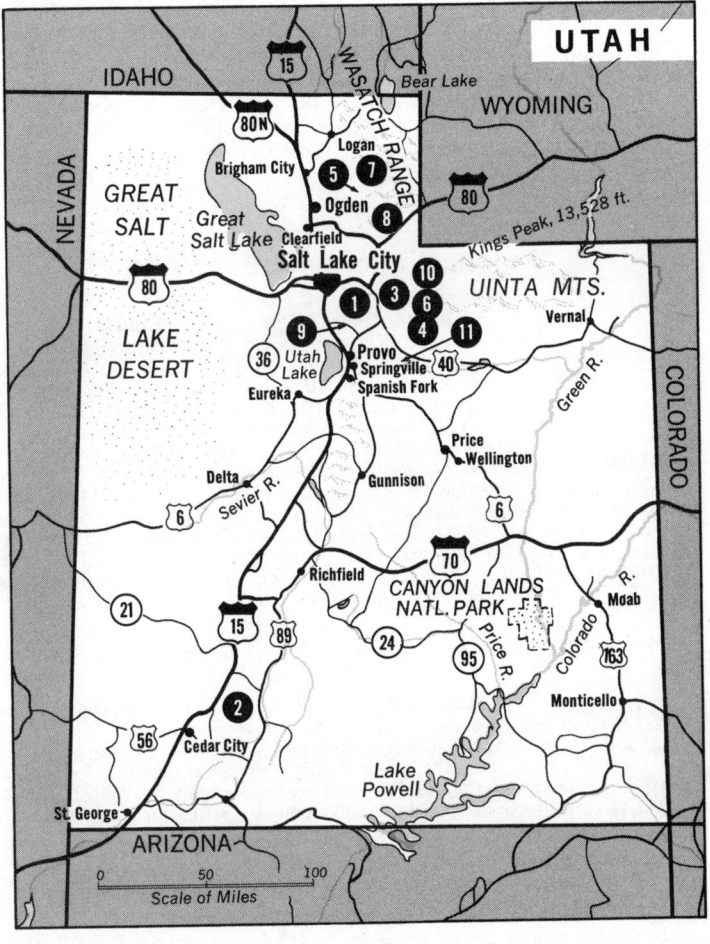

Resorts

1) Alta
2) Brian Head
3) Brighton
4) Deer Valley
5) Nordic Valley
6) Park City
7) Powder Mountain
8) Snowbasin
9) Snowbird
10) Solitude
11) Sundance

out of place. Terrain is rated 25 percent beginner, 35 percent intermediate, and 40 percent advanced—far more advanced terrain than any other destination area except perhaps Taos in New Mexico (the two are soulmates). The front part of the mountain is primarily advanced, and can be scary to those not up to its demands. However, the intermediate runs are accessed by lifts not visible from the base. There is plenty of expert-only, out-of-bounds terrain, but check with the ski patrol to see if the routes are safe. The Utah Interconnect is caught here, as well as a ski route to Snowbird, a mile and a half west.

There isn't a formal base lodge and the guest lodges are as old-fashioned as the facilities. Lodges offer modified American and full American plans, so guests often ski back for lunch.

Practical Information for Alta

HOW TO GET THERE. Alta is 26 miles southeast of Salt Lake City, just past Snowbird, at the end of Little Cottonwood Canyon. Take I-80 to Wasatch Blvd. and then onto Rte. 210. It can be a quick 45-minute drive from the airport, but if it's snowing and there is avalanche danger, it could take days. The narrow mountain road is frequently closed during storms.

By air. Major airlines serve Salt Lake's International Airport (for a list of the airlines and rental car companies, see Practical Information for Park City). *Hosking Helicopter* lifts skiers to Alta in just 15 minutes for approximately $300.

By bus. *Utah Transit Authority* provides scheduled bus service for $7 per person, one way; call 263–3737 for times. *Lewis Brothers* (359–8677) and *Carey-Bonneville* (364–6520) have **limousine** service; *City Cab* (363–5014), *Ute Cab* (359–7788), and Yellow Cab (521–2100) will take skiers for their usual mileage fee.

TELEPHONES. The area code for all of Utah is 801.

ACCOMMODATIONS. All lodges (excluding condominiums)—a total of seven properties—operate on modified American and full American plans, with packages of 3, 5, or 7 nights. Meals add about $25–$35 a day per person. Contact *Alta Travel & Reservation Service,* Alta, UT 84092; 801–742 –2040. All lodges can be contacted individually by writing to them at Alta UT 84092, or calling their numbers in this listing.

A popular alternative is to stay in Salt Lake City and drive up each day to ski. There are 10,000 beds in Salt Lake, everything from deluxe to motel-cheap. Contact the *Utah Travel Council,* Council Hall/Capitol Hill, Salt Lake City UT 84114 (801–533–5681), for a list of accommodations.

In this list of lodgings at the resort, we consider *Expensive,* $100–$140 per night for two in a studio condo or $500–$675 for a 7-day package, double occupancy in a 1-bedroom; *Moderate,* daily rates of $65–$100 per person or a 7-day package at $300–$500; *Inexpensive,* less than $65 per day or a 7-day package at less than $300.

Blackjack Condominium Lodge. *Expensive.* Situated between Alta and Snowbird; 742–3200. Free shuttle to both ski areas, fireplaces, game room; accommodations range from studios to 3-bedroom units.

Hellgate Condominiums. *Expensive.* Halfway between Alta and Snowbird; 742–2020. Free shuttle to slopes, firewood; 1- and 2-bedroom condos.

Alta Lodge. *Moderate.* 742–3500. Ski-in, ski-out accommodations from dorm rooms to deluxe rooms with fireplaces and balconies, saunas, whirlpools, bar; often called the classic ski lodge; MAP plan only, with lift passes included in price.

Alta Peruvian Lodge. *Moderate.* 742–3000. With outdoor Jacuzzi, pool, sauna; rooms range from dormitory style to 2-bedroom suites; full American plan only and lift passes included.

Goldminer's Daughter Lodge. *Inexpensive.* At the base of the lifts, next to the parking lot; 742–2300 or 800–453–4573. Has ski and repair shop, hot tubs, sauna, game room, mini-gym; MAP and lift tickets.

Rustler Lodge. *Inexpensive.* 742–2200. With heated pool, hot tubs, sauna; another classic lodge with dorm rooms to large suites; MAP plan and lift tickets included in rates.

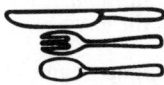

RESTAURANTS. Since the lodges all serve breakfast and dinner (some include lunch), meals are usually taken where you stay. If you are staying elsewhere and want to eat at one of the lodges, you can make reservations, providing the lodges are not booked with their own customers. Popular among these are *Goldminer's Daughter* and *Rustler.* All places are considered *moderate,* in the $8–$15 price range. The two on-mountain cafeterias are at Alpenglow and Watson Shelter, and are open for lunch.

HOW TO GET AROUND. Once at the ski area, one can walk or take the free **shuttle bus** to lifts, lodges, and restaurants. Those staying in condos would want a **car** if they intend to eat out.

SEASONAL EVENTS. Spring skiing in "sugar snow" is heavily promoted, since the snow outlasts the visitors.

OTHER SPORTS AND ACTIVITIES. There is unlimited terrain for **cross-country** skiers; instruction is available through the *Alf Engen Ski School;* 742–2600. For the Interconnect, see the section on Ski Utah Interconnect.

CHILDREN'S ACTIVITIES. The *Children's Ski School* meets at the Albion Ticket Office at 10 A.M. and 2 P.M. daily; call ski school, 742–2500. The *Children's Center,* located upstairs in the Albion ticket and ski school building and operated by *Vesla Barne Day Care Inc.,* is for youngsters 2–12 years. Open from 9:30 A.M. to 4:30 P.M.; lessons, lunch, and day-care are available; call 742–3042.

NIGHTLIFE. Contrary to popular opinion, one can drink alcoholic beverages in Utah—you just have to know how. State liquor stores sell packaged liquors, beer, and wines; locations can be found in the local telephone directory under "Utah State Government." The stores accept cash only and are closed Sundays and holidays.

In designated restaurants, mini bottles of liquor and tenths and fifths of wine are sold to patrons; customers may also bring their own "brown bag bottles" into the restaurants, but there is a hefty charge for corkage and set-ups.

Private clubs are establishments which sell drinks over the bar to members and guests; consider the membership fee a cover charge. The Chamber of Commerce has a list of private clubs.

Beer bars sell beer only, but "brown bagging" is permitted; fees for corkage and set-ups. Grocery stores sell 3.2 beer.

Evening hours at Alta, however, revolve around lodge life. There may be movies planned, folk dancing, special talks, costume parties, bridge or chess games, or just conversation and marshmallow-toasting by the fire.

DEER VALLEY RESORT

P.O. Box 1525
Park City UT 84060
Tel: 801–649–1000

*Snow Report: 801–649–1000 or
   649–2000
Area Vertical: 2,200 ft.
Number of Trails: 42 trails on
   280 acres
Lifts: 7 triple chairs, 1 double
   chair*

*Snowmaking: on 24 percent of
skiable terrain
Season: Thanksgiving weekend
through Easter weekend
(snow permitting)*

One thing you should know about Deer Valley: It is **expensive**. But what the heck, if you can afford to ski Deer Valley in the first place, you won't care how much everything else costs. It is the Riviera of ski areas.

The creators of Deer Valley are hotel and mountain engineering experts. The folks who brought you the luxurious Stanford Court Hotel in San Francisco bring you the elegent Deer Valley. Every creature comfort is looked after. Certainly, no one should have to stand in line, so the number of lift tickets sold is limited to an uncrowded capacity. Attendants are on hand to unload and watch skis while you park, stow your gear, assist you in getting into bindings, and load you up again at the end of a ski vacation. If you rent equipment at the area, they promise to have your equipment waiting for you at the Snow Park Lodge shop—designed for the conditions that day, with your boots warm and your skis waxed. Overnight storage is complimentary, and next day lift tickets may be purchased from 3:30 to 5 P.M. daily.

Deer Valley is actually two mountains, Bald Mountain and Bald Eagle Mountain, with 15 percent of the area designated as beginner terrain, 50 percent intermediate, and 35 percent advanced. That plentiful Utah powder is groomed to perfection, with no catwalks, no moguls, no surprises, just great cruising. Flagstaff Mountain is targeted for future development. At build-out, Deer Valley will have 80 ski runs and 15 lifts on 660 acres of terrain with a capacity of 8,000 skiers on all three mountains. Olympic gold medal winner Stein Eriksen holds forth as the director of skiing. His input is seen in all aspects of what is as close to ski perfection as possible. Two day lodges, Snow Park at the base and Silver Lake at mid-mountain, have all the amenities, including elaborate buffets, dining, rentals, ticket office, child care, a photo shop, and ski school, all set in brass and wood and etched glass. Information desks are located in Snow Park and Silver Lake day lodges. Marquees at the top of Bald Mountain and outside the two day lodges give current information on trail conditions and restaurant usage.

Deer Valley is adjacent to the old mining town and current ski town of Park City. Many of the original Victorian era buildings have been renovated, giving the town a charming frontier ambience. There is a wide choice of shops, restaurants, lodging, and nightlife.

Practical Information for Deer Valley

HOW TO GET THERE. The nearest airport is Salt Lake City International, served by major national carriers. *Hosking Helicopter* will transfer passengers to Park City; service and rates are determined by individual requests; P.O. Box 160, Bountiful UT 84010; call 801–295–3402.

By car. Located in Park City, Deer Valley is a 45-minute drive via I–80 from Salt Lake City International Airport. Rental cars from the airport include *Alamo,* 539–8780 or 800–327–9633; *American International,* 322–2488 or 800–527–0202; *Hertz,* 539–2683 or 800–654–3131; *National* 539–0200 or 800–CAR–RENT.

By bus. From the airport, *Lewis Brothers Stage* serves Park City with buses, vans, limos; call 359–8677 for schedules. *Red Horse Express* has scheduled service hourly to Park City.

TELEPHONES. The area code for all of Utah is 801.

ACCOMMODATIONS. Rentals at Deer Valley are available by the day or week. For accommodations, contact *Deer Valley Lodging,* P.O. Box 3000, Park City UT 84060; 649–4040 or 800–453–3833. Condominiums form clusters at the base area of Snow Park Village and at mid-mountain at Silver Lake Village. Concierge, valet, and daily maid service are available at all lodgings. *Expensive* is the word for this resort, with some accommodations reaching to the posh or *Deluxe* category, Expect to pay $100–$300 for 1-room lodgings and $400–$840 a night for 2-bedroom suites.

Listed below are the accommodations available at the resort. For less expensive lodgings, one can mingle with the masses in the town of Park City. Contact the *Park City Chamber of Commerce,* P.O. Box 1630, Park City UT 84060; 649–6100. (See Practical Information for Park City.)

Stein Eriksen Lodge (Silver Lake Village). P.O. Box 3177, Park City; 649–3700 or 800–453–1302. Top of the line in this top-of-the-line resort. It could be considered downright ostentatious with so much custom work and spaciousness. It's a ski-in, ski-out lodge at mid-mountain Silver Lake Village. Old world elegance, massive beams, huge fireplaces, health club, pool, afternoon tea. Booked direct only.

Cache. P.O. Box 3000, Park City; 649–4040. In the Silver Lake area, condos with glassed-in Jacuzzis; walking distance to lifts.

The Cottages. P.O. Box 3000, Park City; 649–4040. Individual 4-bedroom cottages with Jacuzzi and sauna; ski-out access only.

La Maconnerie. P.O. Box 3000, Park City; 649–4040. Has 3- and 4-bedroom suites, swimming pool, Jacuzzis; ski-in, ski-out.

Pinnacle. P.O. Box 3000, Park City; 649–4040. 4- and 5-level apartments with saunas, pool tables, outdoor Jacuzzis.

Scheduled to open for the 1986–87 season is **Aspen Hollow,** private wooded residences of 3 and 4 bedrooms, Jacuzzis. Contact Deer Valley Lodging.

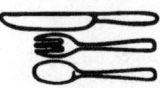

RESTAURANTS. Dining seems to be as important as skiing at Deer Valley. In fact, it is definitely the highlight of a skiing vacation here, with fine Continental or American cuisine offered at the posh lodges. But if you prefer cocktails with your meals, check when making reservations how the Utah liquor laws dictate the serving of alcoholic beverages. Price categories, based on an average three-course dinner for one, excluding tip or drinks, are: *Expensive,* $18–$28; *Moderate,* $10–$18; *Inexpensive,* less than $10. All restaurants accept major credit cards.

Expensive

Cafe Mariposa. In Silver Lake Lodge; 649–1005. Must be experienced. It is the ultimate in skier dining, to say nothing of dining anywhere. Lunch and dinner with full table service feature innovative dishes, elegantly served, with the fireplace crackling for atmosphere. Look around—there will probably be familiar faces, from Justice Sandra Day O'Connor to Charlton Heston. Reservations required.

Glitertind Gourmet Room. In the Stein Eriksen Lodge; 649–3700. Oozes with Norwegian atmosphere. Old World specialties and smorgasbord; dinners only; reservations suggested.

Philippes. In Stag Lodge, Royal St., Deer Valley; 649–2421. French Provençal restaurant, open for 3 meals a day; creative dishes change weekly; winner of the Silver Spoon Award from Gourmet Diners Club of America; reservations required for dinner.

Moderate

Birkebeiner Deli. In the Stein Eriksen Lodge; 649–1005. A New York-style delicatessen, open from 9 A.M. to 11 P.M. Deer Valley's version of a family restaurant.

The Huggery. In Snow Park Lodge; 649–1007. Serves breakfast, lunch, and dinner in self-service buffet, closed Sundays and Mondays.

Inexpensive

The Snuggery. In Silver Lake Lodge; 649–1000. Has a self-service buffet for Continental breakfast and lunch.
The Stew Pot. In Deer Valley Plaza; 645–STEW. Features stews, soups, sandwiches, salads for lunch and dinner; open until 9 P.M.

 **HOW TO GET AROUND.** If skiers want to visit Park City in the evenings, a **car** is necessary. The *Park City Transit* **shuttle bus** operates between the ski lodges and condos and into Park City during the day. In Deer Valley itself, everything is within walking distance or a lift ride.

SEASONAL EVENTS. The *Steve Garvey Celebrity Classic* and the *Coca Cola Cup Race* are the two annual events.

OTHER SPORTS AND ACTIVITIES. Guests at Stein Eriksen Lodge can use the health club and tackle an exercise program under an instructor's direction. Most of the lodges have **swimming pools. Ski racing** is set up on Little Reb run at the base of Bald Mountain; practice on the self-timed course, then race in the *Medalist Challenge;* race clinics available. Race tickets purchased at the course. (For additional activities, see Practical Information for *Park City.)*

 **CHILDREN'S ACTIVITIES.** Snow Park Lodge at the base area has a child care center with separate areas for different age groups. For children 3–12, there is a daily schedule of indoor and outdoor activities; half- and full-day programs, with or without lunch. The nursery accepts infants 6–35 months; call for reservations at 649–1000; ext. 1622.
The ski school accepts children for group lessons, half or full day; for youngsters under 4, private lessons only. Contact the *Ski School* at 649–1000; ext. 1638.

 **NIGHTLIFE.** There are several lounges for quiet, elegant evenings with friends. The *Après-Ski Lounge* in Snow Park Lodge is open until 6 P.M.; serves beer, set-ups. *Troll Hallen Lounge* in Stein Eriksen Lodge features hors d'oeuvres until midnight. Other choices are one's own bar in a condo or to head for Park City.

PARK CITY SKI AREA

P.O. Box 39
Park City UT 84060
Tel: 801–649–8111, 800–222–PARK

Snow Report: 801–649–9571
Area Vertical: 3,100 ft.
Number of Trails: 82 on 2,200 acres
Lifts: 1 gondola, 5 triple chairs, 8 double chairs
Snowmaking: on 350 acres
Season: mid-November through end of April

Park City is an old mining town that went broke, then was revitalized by the creation of a ski area. Silver was discovered in 1868 and miners flocked to the mountain town from around the world. They hauled away more than $400 million in silver. The crash of 1929 sealed the fate of the silver mining town, but about then the townfolk began sliding downhill on long boards. The first lift to take these fanatics up the mountain was installed in 1945 and the ski era had begun.
Many of the original Victorian buildings are intact and delightfully restored, giving the place a definite Western frontier ambience. There

is a multitude of lodgings, restaurants, and night spots, 50 shops, and 15 art galleries. Both families and singles will be comfortable here. Park City is also home of the United States Ski Team.

Park City is Utah's largest ski area with 2,200 acres of skiing, including 650 acres in 5 open bowls, groomed trails, long mogul runs, and specially cut tree runs. Old weathered mining buildings are on the mountain, one serving as a restaurant and inexpensive overnight lodging. Night skiing is on the 1¼-mile Payday intermediate run, the longest lighted run in the Rockies, and on the novice First Time. You can pick up the Interconnect here (see Ski Utah Interconnect). Truly, skiers from beginners to experts will have fun at Park City because the terrain is so diverse. To ski and sun all day, start at the Pioneer Lift and the Prospector Lift in the morning and early afternoon, and spend the rest of the day near the Motherload and King Consolidated chairs.

The Town Lift opened in 1986. This triple chair takes skiers from the old Coalition Mine Building (Park City's logo, the building burned to the ground in 1981), near the bottom of historic Main Street, to mid-mountain. The lift parallels the tramway towers that carried silver, lead, and zinc from the Silver King mine to the Coalition Building. Tickets can be purchased at the lift; skiers may ride the Town Chair down at the end of the day.

Practical Information for Park City

HOW TO GET THERE. Park City is 27 miles east of Salt Lake City. **By air.** *Western Airlines* has its hub in Salt Lake; in addition, the airport is served by *American, America West, Continental, Delta, Eastern, Frontier, Republic, Trans World,* and *United.*

Hosking Helicopter leaves Skypark Airport in Salt Lake for the base of the mountain at Park City Ski Area; ski area employees meet flights with lift passes; baggage is delivered to lodges. For service and rates, call 295–3402.

By car. Take I–80 from Salt Lake to Rte. 224, a 40-minute drive on good highways. Major rental car firms are located at the airport: *Rent A Car,* 800–527 –0202 or 322–2488; *Ajax,* 800–421–0896 or 521–2649; *Avis,* 800–331–1212 or 539–2683; *Budget,* 800–527–0700 or 801–363–1500; *Dollar,* 800–421–6868 or 521–2590; *Hertz,* 800–654–3131 or 539–2683; *Holiday,* 800–327–3631 or 539–0200; *National,* 800–328–4567 or 539–0200; *Ute,* 800–328–4567 or 539–0200; *A–1 Compact Auto Rental,* 532–2001; *Alamo,* 800–327–9633; *Auto Rent,* 800–453–4495 or 322–2529; *Thrifty,* 800–367–2277 or 328–2545; and *Agency,* 800–321–1972 or 534–1622.

Park City isn't out of range of a **cab.** Call *City Cab* (363–5014), *Ute Cab* (359–7788), or *Yellow Cab* (521–2100).

By bus. *Trailways* and *Greyhound,* both 800–872–7245, serve Salt Lake City from all over the U.S. The area is well served by scheduled bus from the airport and some downtown pickups. *Lewis Brothers* (359–8677) serves the area from both locales; their "Red Horse" departs from the airport every hour on the half-hour and departs from Park City on the hour; $10 round trip. There is also *Park City Transportation* limousine service (800–637–3803), $44 for 1–4 passengers; and *Carey-Bonneville Limousine Service* (364–6520). Bus service leaves for Alta and Snowbird weekends on demand at 8 A.M., returns 5 P.M.; $14 round trip.

By train. *Amtrak's* "California Zephyr" pulls into downtown Salt Lake City from the West Coast and from Denver; 800–872–7245.

TELEPHONES. The area code for all of Utah is 801.

ACCOMMODATIONS. Resort Center at the base of the mountain is expanding, with nearly 90 new condominiums ranging from studios to 4 bedrooms. Included is a fitness center, a dining club, and meeting space. There is a total of 12,000 pillows in a 5-mile radius of Park City. *Park City Ski Holidays,* P.O. Box 4409, Park City UT 84060 (649–0493 or 800–222–PARK), is an affiliate of the ski area and represents 2,500 lodging units. *Advance Reservations, Inc.,* P.O. Box 1179, Park City UT 84060 (649–7700 or 800–453–4565), represents most of the other properties, including bed and breakfast establishments and deluxe homes.

In our list, *Expensive* ranges from $90 to $250 for 1-bedroom suites, double occupancy; *Moderate,* $50–$90; and *Inexpensive,* less than $50.

Expensive

Blue Church Lodge & Townhouses. In "uptown" Park City historic district, one block from Main Street's activities. Listed on the National Register of Historic Sites, this recently remodeled lodge features elegant condos from 1 to 4 bedrooms; fireplaces, lounge, indoor and outdoor spas, game room.

Park Station Condominium Hotel. 950 Park Ave., next to the Town Lift and walking distance from historic Old Town. Full hotel service in hotel rooms to 3-bedroom condos, 24-hour front desk, Jacuzzi, ice skating rink.

Silver King Hotel. 1485 Empire Ave., 150 yards to lifts. Features studios to penthouse suites; 24-hour front desk, concierge, swimming pool, sauna, whirlpool, Continental breakfast, gift shop, underground parking.

Moderate

Four Seasons. 2000 Prospector Ave., ¾ mile from lifts. Underground parking, fireplaces, pool, hot tub.

Old Miners' Lodge Bed & Breakfast. 615 Woodside Ave. 3/5 mile to lifts. This 1893 building is in the historic district, restored to the original trappings; includes full breakfast, wine or cider after skiing, use of community living room and library, outside hot tub; each room is named after a historic Park City person.

Prospector Square Hotel. Conference Center and Athletic Club. This is a complete facility just a few minutes by bus from downtown Park City and the lifts, includes 100 hotel rooms, 180 studio units, seven 3-bedroom condos and 5 private homes. Guessts have use of the athletic club with pool, Jacuzzi, masseuse, steam room, gym, racquetball courts, sauna, weight training room, and lounge.

The Yarrow Hotel and Conference Center. 1800 Park Ave., a short bus ride to town and the lifts. A full service hotel with swimming pool, sauna, Jacuzzi, ski rental and repair and National Car Rental office.

Inexpensive

Alpine Prospector's Lodge. 151 Main St., close to restaurants and shops; 16 rooms, 4 baths, sauna, lounge.

Chateau Après Lodge. 1299 Norfolk Ave., 150 yards to lifts. Dormitories and rooms; 132-guest capacity.

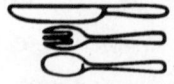

RESTAURANTS. Park City gives the impression of being a steak and prime ribs town, but 10 mountain restaurants and a variety of others in town should satisfy anyone's appetite. *Expensive* restaurants have entrees in the $15–$25 price range; *Moderate,* $8 – $15; and *Inexpensive,* less than $8. The town restaurants take major credit cards. (See Practical Information for Deer Valley for additional listings.)

The **on-mountain** eateries, all in the inexpensive–moderate range, include *Summit House,* at the top of the gondola and the Prospector, Pioneer, Motherlode, and Thaynes chair lifts; *Snow Hut,* at the bottom of Prospector; *Midmountain Restaurant,* next to the Angle Station of the gondola; and *Base Cafeteria,* in the gondola building.

Adolph's. *Expensive.* 1541 Thaynes Canyon Rd.; 649–7177. Serves Swiss specialties in a Tyrolean decor overlooking the golf course; closed Mondays; reservations suggested.

Claimjumper. *Moderate.* 536 Main St.; 649–8051. Features buffalo steak, prime rib, and other hearty entrees; Western decor, open 6–10 P.M.

Grub Steak. *Moderate.* Prospector Square; 649–8060. Casually Western; American dishes of chicken, steak, ribs; serves 3 meals daily and Sunday brunch.

Cicero's. 306 Main St.; 649–6800. A turn-of-the-century parlor room, complete with trophies from the hunt; entrees include duck, chicken cordon bleu, prime rib; lunch and dinner.

Baja Cantina. *Inexpensive.* Park City Resort Center; 649–BAJA. Park City's answer to the ubiquitous Mexican fare; lunch and dinner; no reservations.

Eating House. *Inexpensive.* 317 Main St.; 649–8284. Basic restaurant serving breakfast all day; evening entrees include seafood, soup, salad bar, and sandwiches.

 **HOW TO GET AROUND.** A car is neither necessary nor desirable. A free **shuttle bus** serves the lodges, historic Main Street, and the base area between 7:45 A.M. and 12:30 A.M. Call *Park City Transit* (649–6660) for details. *Park City Taxi* (649–8567) is available from 7 A.M. to midnight; call for service.

 **SEASONAL EVENTS.** The **Christmas Eve** torchlight parade is the highlight of the holiday festivities. Each **February** is the local winter carnival. World Cup races are held in **March** and in **November.** There is usually a *U.S. Ski Team Celebrity Classic* in February or **April.** Easter egg hunt and sunrise service round out the year.

 OTHER SPORTS AND ACTIVITIES. Recreational **racing** is usually big at most areas—the *Marlboro Ski Challenge* is the deal here. Run daily on an electronically timed race course, the dual slalom enables friends and families to race against each other. Group races and obstacle races can be arranged by prior notice; contact the ski area marketing department, 649–8111. The ski areas of Deer Valley and Park West are a snowball's throw away, and worth a day or two away from Park City's slopes.

To get a bird's eye view of the area in a **hot air balloon,** contact *Balloon the Rockies,* P.O. Box 399, Park City UT 84060 (645–8188), for morning rides. The same company puts together **snowmobile** tours for a rabbit's eye view of the surroundings.

Cross-country ski with the *Norwegian School of Nature Life,* P.O. Box 4036 (in Main Street Memorial Building, New Park Cyclery, Emporium Plaza and Rte. 248 at Kearns Blvd.); 649–2320 or 649–9461. Ski lessons, long and short day tours, cabin treks into the Uinta Mountains, and overnights are all available.

Piute Creek Cross Country, Rte. 1A, Kamas UT 84036, at the Upper Loop Rd., offers tranquil and secluded guided day **tours,** overnight bunk and breakfast tours, and rentals from a rustic base camp.

White Pine Ski Touring Center, P.O. Box 680393, at the Park City Golf Course (645–7555), has complete services, 9 km of prepared **track,** group and private **instruction,** overnight **excursions,** and a rental and repair shop.

Sleigh rides in the evening and dinner at the edge of the golf course are offered by *Park City Sleigh Company,* P.O. Box 680096 (in Park Meadows Racquet Club); 649–3359.

Ice skaters can enjoy *The Skaters Center* at Park City Resort Center, an outdoor rink at the base of the mountain; open 7 days a week, rental, lessons, broomball; 645–7555.

 **CHILDREN'S ACTIVITIES.** *Kinder-Ski-Kare* at the ski area, for children enrolled in ski school lessons, provides supervised play for ages 3–6; call 649–8111, ext. 314. *Merry Pop-ins* offers babysitting service in hotels and condos for infants and children at any time of day or night; contact them at P.O. Box 39, Park Meadows Plaza D-100; 649–5900. *Miss Billie's Kids Campus,* Star Route, across from Park West Ski Resort, takes care of children up to age 9; licensed by the state; 649–9502.

NIGHTLIFE. Park City visitors not only ski here, they party. Prowl Main St. or the Base Plaza—Most expensive and moderate lodges have lounges. Favorites are the *Cowboy Bar,* Main St.; the *Club* on Main St.; *Rusty Nail* at the Plaza. *Sneakers* (Park Meadows Racquet Club) is a bit ritzier.

For live entertainment, plays and musicals, head for the Egyptian Theater, 328 Main St. Movie buffs can see the latest films at *Holiday Village Cinemas III,* 1776 Park Ave.

SNOWBIRD SKI AND SUMMER RESORT

Snowbird UT 84092
Tel: 801–741–2222, 801–521–6040
    Salt Lake City

Snow Report: 801–742–2222,
    801–521–6040
Area Vertical: 3,100 ft.
Number of Trails: 38 designated
    trails, longest run 2.5 miles
Lifts: One 125-passenger tram,
    7 double chairs
Snowmaking: none
Season: end of November–mid-June

Snowbird popularized skiing in Utah. Starting in the 1970s, the cognoscenti of the skiing world descended on the newly opened planned resort. Snowbird, the giant killer, catered to the upscale crowd, a group far different from that at neighboring Alta. Today, the skiing crowd is more a mix of in-fashion types and utilitarian-clad midwesterners.

From narrow Little Cottonwood Canyon, four stark concrete buildings dominate the base area while the huge tram makes a dramatic climb to the top of Hidden Peak. The terrain is vast, consisting of two north-facing bowls with 1,900 acres. With 50 percent advanced or expert runs, it is as challenging as Alta. But there are delightful civilized intermediate and beginner runs through stands of spruce and pine and one can buy a less-expensive lift ticket valid for chairlifts only. The tram serves the mostly strong intermediate-to-expert terrain of Peruvian Gulch and Gad Valley. Beginner skiers cluster around Chickadee chair. Ask the tram operator or locals about out-of-bounds skiing and the chute to Alta.

Because the area can be intimidating, the establishment has provided free guided tours to acquaint newcomers to the area and find the runs best suited to their ability. Tours depart at 10 A.M. and 1 P.M. daily from the Plaza Deck. The extended spring and summer skiing is usually off the Gad I chairlifts or alternatively, from the aerial tram.

Practical Information for Snowbird

HOW TO GET THERE. Snowbird is 45 minutes from the airport and 35 minutes from downtown Salt Lake City, via I–15 South to Wasatch Blvd. then east on Rte. 210 into Little Cottonwood Canyon. You can literally leave home on an early morning flight and be on skis that afternoon. (See *Practical Information* for Park City for list of airlines and rental car companies.) *Hosking Exploration Helicopters,* 295–3402, takes four people to Snowbird for a total of $330–$350 one way.

By bus. *UTA* (Utah Transit Authority) runs scheduled service from the end of November through Easter weekend from the airport and downtown to Snowbird, starting at 7 A.M. Rates are $6 one way from the airport. Call 263–3737 for information. *Lewis Brothers Stages,* 359–8677, has charter buses and minivans; *Trailways,* 328–8121, has charter buses; *Mountain Transfer,* 800–453–

4522, and *Carey-Bonneville,* 364–6520, have charter vans. **Taxi** service is about $35 one way; see *Practical Information for Alta* for numbers.

TELEPHONES. The area code for all of Utah is 801.

ACCOMMODATIONS. The village consists of four lodges, the tram building, and shops, boutiques, and groceries in Snowbird Center. Reservations for any of Snowbird's lodges is made through *Snowbird Corporation,* Little Cottonwood Canyon, Snowbird UT 84092; 800–453–3000 or 801–532–1700; 800–742–2222.outside continental U.S. Snowbird lift vouchers with packages are exchangeable at Alta, Park City, and Deer Valley (the last two have an additional charge). Nightly rates and packages of 3, 4, 5, and 7 nights are available.

Salt Lake City has 10,000 beds plus restaurants and culture. The 35-minute drive from downtown is not difficult except when it's snowing; there is extreme avalanche danger in the narrow canyon, and Rte. 210 is often closed or clogged with cars. The *Utah Travel Council,* Council Hall/Capitol Hill, Salt Lake City UT 84114, 801–533–5681, has information on a stay in Salt Lake.

Expensive: nightly per room rates of $256–$359 for a suite; per person costs of $987 to $1,383 for a 7-night package. *Moderate:* nightly per room rates of $103–$112 for a 1-bedroom or studio; per person rates of $861–$1,000 for a 7-night package. *Inexpensive:* nightly rate of $32 for a dorm; a 7-night dorm package for $385.

The Cliff Lodge is a full-service hotel with health and beauty spa, meeting and convention space; 24-hour front desk, covered parking, steam room, herbal wraps, exercise studio, juice bar; total of 532 rooms from 2-bedroom to a corner deluxe suite.

Iron Blosam Lodge has time-shares, with limited rental rooms; two pools, steam room, Jacuzzi, weight room, saunas, physical therapist, game room, valet parking. Each room has its own balcony, from studio units with 1 bed to a 2-story loft suite.

The Lodge at Snowbird has a pool, saunas, valet parking; 160 condos with a choice of dormitories, bedrooms, and loft suites.

Turramurra Lodge has the usual heated swimming pool, saunas, valet parking, within easy walking distance of the center. Each of the 73 units, ranging from standard bedroom units to 2-level loft suites, has a private balcony.

RESTAURANTS. There are only 10 restaurants at the base and one on-mountain, but there is a good variety. Unless otherwise noted, the phone number for all restaurants is 742–2222. A state liquor store is in Snowbird Center and bottles may be taken into any of the restaurants. *Expensive* is in the $15–$20 range; *Moderate,* $10–$15; and *Inexpensive,* less than $10. Major credit cards accepted.

Golden Cliff Dining Room. *Expensive.* In the Cliff Lodge. Airy, open to the second story, dinner music, warm ambience; menu features Continental dishes of veal Oscar, salmon; also Italian and barbecue nights; huge breakfast buffets.

Forklift. *Moderate.* Level 3 of the Snowbird Center. Open for 3 meals a day; beef, fish, pasta entrees for dinner; burgers, soups, and salads for lunch.

Lodge Club. *Moderate.* Level 1 of the Lodge at Snowbird. An intimate club serving veal, chicken, beef, good appetizers.

The Steak Pit. *Moderate.* Level 1 of the Snowbird Center. Specializes in great steaks; also seafood and unlimited salad fixings. Often crowded, so dinner reservations are necessary (521–6040).

Wildflower Restaurant. *Moderate.* Level C of Iron Blosam Lodge. The newest restaurant at the resort; family-oriented with entrees from sandwiches to fish; breakfast and dinner only.

Birdfeeder. *Inexpensive.* A quick snack bar on the outdoor plaza, Level 3 of the Snowbird Center.

Mid-Gad. *Inexpensive.* Located at the top of the Mid-Gad chair. Good for lunch without having to come down the mountain.

Mexican Keyhole. *Inexpensive.* In the Cliff Lodge. Features superb Mexican dishes; cozy decor.

HOW TO GET AROUND. Everything is within easy walking distance. *BART* (Bird Area Rapid Transit) provides free **shuttle service** to and from the main and Gad Valley parking areas and the Snowbird Center for day skiers and lodge guests. A shuttle operates to Alta every 30 minutes for $1 one way. Transportation to Park City may be arranged through the lodge front desk.

SEASONAL EVENTS. Festivities always take place during **Christmas;** *Winterfest* is celebrated from mid- to end of **January;** *USSA Masters Series Race* is in early **February,** and the *Telemark Series* is in mid-**April.** *NA-STAR* races are every Tuesday, Thursday, and Friday.

Spring skiing season is the first two weeks in **May,** with terrain open in the Gad Valley. **Summer skiing** goes to **mid-June,** with Little Cloud Chairlift and the aerial tram open from 7:30 A.M. to 1 P.M. daily. Summer race camps are open to intermediate and advanced skiers of any age from the end of May to mid-June; the fee is approximately $550 and includes instruction, ski conditioning such as hiking, swimming, tennis, ski films, and lectures, meals, and lodging; contact *Snowbird Ski School Office,* 742–2222 or 521–6040, ext. 4170.

OTHER SPORTS AND ACTIVITIES. Nordic and alpine **touring** is available along the ridges on the upper half of Little Cottonwood Canyon. Most of the **cross-country** skiing leaves from Alta and White Pine.

Helicopter skiing into virgin powder snow is available through *Wasatch Powder Guides* (742–2800).

CHILDREN'S ACTIVITIES. Complimentary child care is available for guests of the Cliff Lodge. Children enrolled in the Children's Ski School are also cared for when not in lessons; they must be 3 years old and toilet trained. *Kinderbirds* takes 4–5-year-olds for ski lessons and supervised activities. There is a Cookie Dual Race for all kids in ski school every Thursday afternoon on Chickadee, followed by an ice-cream party.

In-room babysitting services for infants to 3 years of age are available with 2 weeks prior notice to the individual lodge or by calling 801–742–2222.

NIGHTLIFE. Evening entertainment centers around the lodge lounges. Particularly popular are *Eagle's Nest Lounge,* with a great raw seafood bar and live entertainment; on Level C of the Cliff Lodge. The *Lodge Club,* Level 1 of the Lodge at Snowbird, is lively after skiing. The *Tram Room Bar,* Level 1 of the Snowbird Center, has live entertainment, pool tables, large screen TV; the loudest place in the village, good for burning up any extra energy.

OTHER UTAH AREAS

Brian Head Ski and Summer Resort
P.O. Box 8
Brian Head UT 84719
In the south of the state, this area is only 150 miles north of Las Vegas and an easy trip for Californians; low-key family resort.

Brighton Ski Bowl
Brighton UT 84121
25 miles up Big Cottonwood Canyon from Salt Lake City

Nordic Valley
P.O. Box 178
Eden UT 84310
The third area near Ogden

Powder Mountain
P.O. Box 68
Eden UT 84310
Near SnowBasin, in the Golden Spike Empire

SnowBasin
P.O. Box 200, Dept. UP
Huntsville UT 84317
In the "Golden Spike" area near Ogden.

Solitude Ski Resort Company
P.O. Box 17557
Salt Lake City UT 84117
23 miles up Big Cottonwood Canyon from Salt Lake City

Sundance
RR #3, Box A–1
Sundance UT 84604
South of Salt Lake, near Provo, is Robert Redford's ski area. Always active in the performing arts, the area is a family oriented resort. It's been a sleeper, but is on the verge of expansion and promotion.

SKI UTAH INTERCONNECT

The Interconnect could well be North America's largest skiable area. Actually, locals have skied this route for years, but few tourists dared into the backcountry.

Because the resorts of the Wasatch Front—those closest to Salt Lake City—are only a few miles apart as the crow flies but miles away via circuitous canyon roads, the idea of tying the areas together by a network of trails is an exciting one. The Interconnect currently combines five resorts, all of which can be visited in one day with a guide, 40 lifts and over 250 runs. The five-area tour covers more than 20 miles of backcountry terrain and groomed trails.

You should be at least a strong intermediate skier to attempt the tour, just because you are likely to encounter a variety of conditions during the trip. Start at Park City's Jupiter Peak, ski down the back side to Brighton and over to Solitude, do some hiking to Alta, then cross over Sugarloaf and Mt. Baldy to Snowbird. A van takes you back to Park City. Or reverse the procedure and start at Snowbird.

The Interconnect is becoming a reality, with new lifts being put in to eliminate some of the more difficult touring sections. It is certainly North America's answer to the European ski circuits—of skiing from town to town. This is not so much a novelty, as it is in Europe, but a backcountry experience for which one should be prepared. It is a great way to see a number of resorts you are not likely to visit by staying in one area—but you must always ski with a guide. For additional information on the Interconnect Adventure, contact *Ski Utah, Inc.*, 307 W. 200 South, Salt Lake City UT 84101; 801–534–1779. Day trips and extended trips are available.

Washington

CRYSTAL MOUNTAIN RESORT

P.O. Box 1
Crystal Mountain WA 98022
Tel: 206–663–2265 or 2264

Snow Report: 206–634–0200;
  634–3771; 967–SNOW
Area Vertical: 3,100 ft.
Number of Trails: 31 on 1,681
  acres
Lifts: 3 triple chairs, 6
  double chairs
Snowmaking: none
Season: end of November–April

Ski conditions in Washington State are like that in Oregon—unpredictable. One statistic sets the percentage of sunshine during the ski season at 2 percent, versus 70 percent in most California and Colorado areas. Certainly bare bones amenities if compared to major resorts, at least the lodges and restaurants are clustered around the base of Crystal Mountain, the only such area in the Pacific Northwest. But if you ski hard enough, a hot Jacuzzi and clean sheets are all that is important.

And you can ski hard at Crystal. There is a lot of expert terrain, ungroomed outback, and mostly unmarked areas. There is only 10 percent beginner terrain, while advanced and expert terrain make up 70 percent. Much of the steep and deep resembles more famous areas such as Snowbird or Jackson—but the snow is laden with that Northwest wetness. There are extensive open areas as well as glade skiing.

A day lodge has a cafeteria and a bar and a restaurant at the summit house. This essentially is a day area for Seattle residents or a low-key destination area.

Practical Information for Crystal Mountain

HOW TO GET THERE. Crystal Mountain is in the Mt. Baker-Snoqualmie National Forest, on the northeast boundary of Mt. Rainier National Park. It is 76 miles from Seattle, 64 miles from Tacoma, and 67 miles from Sea-Tac International Airport. Sea-Tac is served by major national and international air carriers.

By car. Take I–5 from Seattle to Exit 142A to Auburn, follow Rte. 164 to Rte. 410, east for 33 miles to the Crystal Mountain turnoff; go 6 miles up the road to the resort. Rte. 410 is closed to the east during winter months.

Buses run twice daily from Enumclaw on Rte. 164; call 663–2265 for schedules and rates.

TELEPHONES. The area code for Crystal Mountain is 206.

ACCOMMODATIONS. Lodging at Crystal Mountain is moderate by ski area standards. Prices range from $50 per night for a room to $88 for a family unit. There are also rates for packages up to 5 nights. Reservations for most lodges can be arranged by calling 663–2558, or writing to the lodge of your choice c/o Crystal Mountain WA 98022. All are quite near the ski area, and all guests register at the Silver Skis Chalet office (listed below).

Alpine Inn Hotel; 663–2262. Basic accommodations with private bath.

Crystal Chalets; 663–2558. Comfortable chalets nestled in the trees, with fireplace; sleep 1–4 people; some meal packages available.

Crystal House Hotel; 663–2558. Comfortable chalets nestled in the trees, with fireplace; sleep 1–4 people; some meal packages available.

Crystal House Hotel; 663–2558. In the heart of the valley, with standard rooms by the night and 5-night packages; breakfast and dinner included in the packages.

Silver Skis Chalet; 663–2558. Modest lodge geared for families or groups. A standard unit contains kitchen-living area and fireplace and sleeps 2–6 people; heated outdoor pool.

Village Inn; 663–2558. Next door to Crystal House, features country-style compact rooms; some meal packages.

RESTAURANTS. Since Crystal Mountain is a self-contained ski resort, visitors generally take their meals at the resort restaurants, where dining costs are *moderate* by ski resort standards, ranging from $7 to $15 for a dinner for one person, excluding tip, beverages, and tax. All restaurants can be reached through the resort's main telephone number, 663–2265.

Alpine Inn Restaurant has a varied menu and a fine wine selection; open 7 days a week serving 3 meals a day until 9 P.M.

Crystal Inn Restaurant also features fine dining; open until 9 P.M. weekdays and 10 P.M. weekends.

Rafters is a full-service restaurant in the new lodge serving breakfast, lunch, and après-ski hors d'oeuvres.

Sporting Elk Cellar in the Alpine Inn serves snacks in the European rathskeller tradition.

The Summit House, perched at the top of Crystal Mountain at 6,872 ft., is the highest restaurant in Washington State. Who cares if you ski or not? Just relax and enjoy the spectacular view of 14,410-ft. Mt. Rainier in the distance. Fast foods during ski season; full-service "sunset dinners" during the summer.

HOW TO GET AROUND. Everything at the ski area itself is within walking distance, so no transportation is needed.

SEASONAL EVENTS. The **New Year's Eve** Torchlight Parade is an annual party. The *City League Team Race Series* program pits business rivals against each other on Wednesday and Sunday races during **January** and **February,** with finals held in early **March.**

OTHER SPORTS AND ACTIVITIES. The *Crystal Mountain Athletic Club* provides instruction for serious racers for national and international competition. Contact the club at 11425 136th Ave. East, Puyallup WA 98373; 848–6389. **Cross-country** lessons are available at the ski school, as are downhill lessons.

DAY-CARE FACILITIES. *Crystal Mountain Childcare Center* (663–2300) is open from 8 A.M. to 4:30 P.M. for ages 2 and older. Rates are $12.50 a day or $1.75 an hour; reservations recommended. It is located in the Poolside Building next to the Crystal Inn Restaurant; supervised play. They serve a choice of grilled cheese, hamburgers, or sandwiches with fries for modest prices.

NIGHTLIFE. Besides the restaurants, there is *Rafters Lounge* with entertainment Saturdays and Sundays. The *Pub* serves beer and wine on the D level of the new lodge. Other than that, take a hot tub and get a good night's sleep to attack the mountain the next day.

Wyoming

GRAND TARGHEE SKI RESORT

Alta WY via Driggs ID 83422
Tel: 307–353–2304

Snow Report: 800–443–8164;
*   800–443–0637 in Wyoming*
Area Vertical: 2,200 ft.
Number of Trails: 20 groomed
*   trails, 1,500 skiable acres*
Lifts: 3 double chairlifts,
*   1 rope tow*
Snowmaking: none
Season: mid-November–mid-April

Grand Targhee is on the "sunny side of the Tetons." Situated on the Idaho–Wyoming state line, Grand Targhee nestles up to the Teton Peaks, which soar high as a dramatic backdrop. The Teton Valley once was a battleground for Indians, fur trappers, and mountain men. Today, the valley is a thriving tourist and farming community.

The west slope doesn't have the reputation for being as cold as Jackson Hole, yet an average of 500 inches of snow falls there each winter. The powder skiing is about the best you can find, and the slopes are not as steep as in many resorts, taking away the sometimes terrifying pitch proclaimed in larger, better-known ski areas. Intermediate terrain makes up 70 percent of the mountain, 10 percent is beginner, and 20 percent is advanced. Besides the groomed trails, there are glades, bowls, and acres and acres of open skiing, which is especially delightful after a fresh snowfall.

The base area is smaller than at many other areas, with all base facilities within 50 yards of the lifts. While locals who know their powder flock to Targhee, the slopes stay uncrowded, the ambience is uncommercial, and the prices are relatively inexpensive. It is not easy to get to, but the trip is worth it. The view from the summit includes three states, two national parks, the Jedediah Smith Wilderness, and the three Tetons as they were first seen by the French fur trappers in the 1820s.

Practical Information for Grand Targhee

HOW TO GET THERE. By air. Fly into Idaho Falls, ID, 87 miles to the west, on *Western* or *Cascade Airlines.* Or fly into Jackson, 42 miles to the east, via *Western* or *Frontier* (see Practical Information for *Jackson Hole*). With 48 hours notice, the resort shuttle will meet incoming and outgoing flights at the Avis counter; $20 one-way, minimum of two people; children 12 and under are free with parents. For large groups, *TWA Services,* 307–344–7311, runs charter buses as does *Teton Stage Line,* 208–529–8036. Traveling time is about an hour and a half from Jackson and two hours from Idaho Falls. Rental car listings are at the airports. General aviation (including private and charter flights) can use Driggs Airport, 13 miles from Grand Targhee. The runway is asphalt, 5,200 ft. long, and at 6,200 ft. elevation. Call *Red Baron Flight Services,* 208–354–8131. With 48 hours notice, a resort van will meet incoming flights; $20 one way. In Driggs, rental cars are available from *Grand Teton Motors,* 208–354–2320.

By car. From Idaho Falls it is 87 miles via Rtes. 26, 31, and 33 to Driggs, then up the narrow, twisty road to Grand Targhee. From Jackson Hole it is 42 miles over Teton Pass and up the one and only road to the base area. From Salt Lake City it is a 5-hour drive.

The *Targhee Express* **bus** goes between Targhee and Jackson every Tuesday and Friday, departing Jackson Hole at 8 A.M., and departing Targhee at 4:30 P.M.; call 353–2304 for information.

TELEPHONES. The area code for all of Wyoming is 307; for this section of Idaho it is 208.

ACCOMMODATIONS. The base area is compact, with three lodges, the restaurant, bar, cafeteria, nursery, ski shop, gift shop, outdoor pool, and hot tubs. Kids 12 years and under are free at Targhee. On 2-day packages, one child per paid adult will lodge and ski free when staying in the same unit; on 3-day or longer packages, one child per paid adult will lodge and ski free and get a free shuttle pass and small-fry lesson. Seniors 65 and over deduct $8 per day from regular season ski packages.

Rates at Grand Targhee are in the *moderate* category when compared to other resorts. On a 5-night, 4-day package with a half-day group ski lesson, for example, the **Targhee Lodge** is $192 per person, double occupancy. The **Teewinot Lodge** is $210. The **Sioux Lodge Apartments** have studios for $266 per person on the same package; a 1-bedroom with loft goes for $311 double occupancy.

Combination 7-night, 6-day ski packages are a great way to ski both sides of the Tetons. Start with 3 nights, 3 days at Teewinot Lodge and one ski lesson in Targhee; including a video critique and wine and cheese party. Move on to the **Sojourner Lodge** in Teton Village for 4 nights and 3 days. Cost, excluding ground transportation, is $331 per person, double occupancy. Call *Grand Targhee Ski Resort,* 307–353–2304, 800–443–8146, or 800–443–0637 in Wyoming, for reservations and information.

Lodging is also found in Driggs. Moderately priced ski packages are available at the Best Western, 426 N. Main St., Driggs, ID 83422; 800–528–1234; in western states, 800–252–2363, or 208–354–2363.

Inexpensive ($18–$35 per night) Driggs lodging is found at the **Pines Motel,** 105 S. Main St.; 208–354–2774; **Teton Peaks Motel,** 285 N. Main St., 208–354–8131 or 307–353–8176; and **Village Inn,** 88 N. Main St., 208–354–8121.

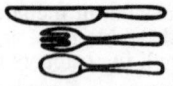

RESTAURANTS. At the base of Grand Targhee and in the Teton Valley, restaurants lean toward the *Inexpensive* and *Moderate* categories, ranging from $7 to $16 for a dinner for one. In the moderate category, **Targhee Steak House** is a full-service restaurant serving 3 meals—$16 tops for a steak dinner; also chef's specials nightly. **Martin's Sleigh Ride Yurt Dinner** is a must for visitors—a sleigh ride followed by a dinner in a tent. Reservations necessary; call the resort at 353–2304. The **Knockwurst Stand** on the lodge deck is open for lunch, which includes beer and wine. In the *Inexpensive* category are **The Pioneer Cafeteria** at the base, open during ski hours, and the **Mexican Snack Bar,** open 11:30 A.M. to 7:30 P.M.

In Teton Valley, there are two Oriental restaurants with fixed price menus which are considered *Expensive.* **Lost Horizons,** 353–8226, on the Wyoming side of the state line, is at the bottom of the road leading to Grand Targhee. Dining is an evening's experience; shoes are taken off at the door, drinks are served downstairs while diners go upstairs for a 10-course meal and a fabulous view of the Tetons through enormous windows. Fixed menu costs $25 per person.

More recently on the scene is the **Pepper Mill,** 354–2962, in Driggs; also Oriental, fixed menu and fixed price of $18 per person.

Moderate restaurants include the **Naughty Pine** (American), 787–2276; and **Victor Steak Bank** (American, some seafood), 787–2277.

Inexpensive includes **Macho's,** 354–9981, for Mexican; **The Tree,** 354–2293, for burgers and pizza; **O'Rouke's,** 354–8115, for sandwiches and pizza; the **Right Stuff,** 354–2768, for yogurt and Belgian waffles.

HOW TO GET AROUND. In Grand Targhee, it is strictly "shanks' mare." All facilities are within 50 yards of the lifts, so you can sleep late and still be the first on the lift. By staying in Driggs, the curvy, narrow 12-mile road must be negotiated twice a day—good enough reason for staying at the resort.

SEASONAL EVENTS. Each **December** the *Junior Olympics* hold qualifications; in **January** the *Idaho Area VII Special Olympics* are scheduled; **March** sees the *Pro-Am* race.

 OTHER SPORTS AND ACTIVITIES. Special complimentary après-ski activities are planned at Grand Targhee. On Monday, there is a wine and cheese party; Tuesdays and Thursdays, ski movies; Wednesdays, family casino night; Fridays, **sleighrides. Day trips** are available to Yellowstone National Park, 90 miles north; Teton National Park, 50 miles east; National Elk Refuge, 50 miles east in Jackson; and **cross-country** trips surrounding Grand Targhee. For longer ski tours and backcountry trips, contact *Teton Mountain Touring,* Box 514, Driggs ID 83422; 208–354–2768. Day trips, a 6-day **expedition** to Yellowstone's meadows and geysers, and a 15-day journey on Alaska's Mt. McKinley are offered, as well as backcountry avalanche courses and Telemark ski camp. Rentals available. There is also **ice fishing** and **ice skating;** call for information.

Scenic **glider rides** are available year-round from the Driggs Airport; 208–354–8131. Valley flight, $35; over Grand Targhee, $55; Grand Teton overflight, $75. Scenic flights in a 1–3 passenger plane is $60 an hour; a 206 Turbo carrying 1–5 passengers is $140 an hour.

 **DAY-CARE FACILITIES.** Babysitting is available for $2 per hour per child. It is free with a package stay of 3 nights or longer. The *Small Fry* ski school offers classes for children 5–7 years of age; 1-hour group lesson, $7; nursery lunch and two ski lessons, $22. With the *Kids are Free* program, the above is free except for lunch.

 **NIGHTLIFE.** The resort nightly specials are about as far as the nightlife goes. To really whoop it up, head for the *Trap Bar* and lounge in the Targhee Lodge; nightly entertainment; 353–2304.

JACKSON HOLE SKI RESORT

P.O. Box 290
Teton Village WY 83025
Tel: 307–733–2292

Snow Report: 307–733–2291
Area Vertical: 4,139 ft.
Number of Trails: 58 on 2,500 acres
Lifts: 1 tram (63 passengers), 1 triple chairlift, and 5 double chairs
Snowmaking: on 2 percent of terrain
Season: early December–early April

Jackson Hole is actually a valley 5–15 miles wide and 50 miles long, running north to south from the southern tip of Yellowstone National Park to Hoback Junction. It was named for fur trapper Davey Jackson; *hole* is a variation of a French word meaning valley. Jackson Hole also refers to the ski resort on Rendezvous Mountain. The town is Jackson —not Jackson Hole.

The Gros Ventre (pronounced *gro-vont*) Range juts up from the valley floor in dramatic, sudden thrusts. No foothills, no gentle approach—just big impressive mountains. The name means "big belly" in French and is the name of an Indian tribe that lived in the area. The bigness of the Grand Teton Mountains, part of the Gros Ventre, scares a lot of skiers. The ski area's former "tame the big one" publicity didn't dispel the notoriety of the tough terrain and vast mountain.

Make no mistake: It **is** a big mountain. The 4,139-ft. vertical drop is the highest in the U.S. Experts are in Nirvana attacking Rendezvous Bowl, served by the 63-passenger tram, the couloirs and chutes, bowls, cliffs, the Hogbacks, and 100 miles of trails. Guides are available to take strong skiers to "secret" powder spots and into the backcountry when conditions permit. The Jackson Hole powder is legendary.

But those with less expertise can head for Eagle's Rest, Lower Werner, and Teewinot; intermediates have 22 miles of groomed trails on Après Vous Mountain. Included in the Master Plan are 15 additional chairlifts in the existing permit area. Presently outside the ski-area boundary is the mostly intermediate terrain of Rock Springs Bowl, and there are plans to put lifts there as well.

Practical Information for Jackson Hole

HOW TO GET THERE. By air. Jackson is served by *Frontier* from Denver, *Western Airlines* from Salt Lake City. In the 1985–86 season *Southwest Airlines* initiated service into Jackson Hole every Saturday from Houston's Hobby Airport. At press time, American Airlines was scheduled to start daily service from Chicago and Dallas during 14 weeks of the 1986–87 ski season. Charters are also scheduled during ski season from major U.S. and Canadian cities. Call *Jackson Hole Central Reservations* at 800–443–6931 for the latest transportation schedule and reservations. The airport is 22 miles from Teton Village, the base area of Jackson Hole Ski Area, and 11 miles from the town of Jackson.

By car. Jackson Hole is 550 miles from Denver. Take I–25N to I–80W, to US 191, to US 89. From Salt Lake City, follow I–80 to Rte. 189, then to Rte. 89. From Idaho Falls, 100 miles to the west, take US 26 to Rtes. 31 and then 22.

TELEPHONES. The area code for all of Wyoming is 307.

ACCOMMODATIONS. Teton Village, at the base of Jackson Hole Ski Area, has several inns, a condo-style hotel, and a youth hostel. For the diehard skiers, the hostel is the place to be—a bed to fall into at the end of a hard ski day without a lot of late-night activity.

Condos, guest ranches, and resorts are found between Teton Village and the town of Jackson. In Jackson itself, there are numerous motels, coupled with down-home cowboy nightlife.

For lodging reservations, contact *Jackson Hole Central Reservations*, P.O. Box 510, Teton Village WY 83025; call 733–4005, 800–443–6931, or, in Wyoming, 800–442–3900. To reserve condominiums, call 733–7945 or 733–4610 and ask for the condo complex.

While accommodations quote nightly rates, Jackson Hole is just too far to travel to stay for just a day or two. A 7-night/6-day lift package is the common purchase. Prices given in the following are for the package.

Expensive

Alpenhof. P.O. Box 288, Teton Village WY 83025; 733–3242. The closest to the lifts; heated outdoor pool, hot tubs, saunas, massage by appointment, game room, laundry facilities; $425.50 per person, double occupancy.

The Inn at Jackson Hole. P.O. Box 328, in Teton Village; 733–2311 or 733–3657. A full-service hotel with heated outdoor pool and Jacuzzi; $345 per person, double occupancy. One-bedroom condos in the Teton Village Inn complex range $370–$488 per person, double occupancy. Spacious houses are available in the complex for $1,075 for 7 nights.

The Spring Creek Ranch. P.O. Box 3154, Jackson WY 83001; 2 miles from Jackson, 10 miles from Jackson Hole; 733–8833 or 800–443–6139. This resort on top of East Gros Ventre Butte is highly rated by AAA; there are condominiums, inn rooms, conference center. Package rates per person are $362 at the inn and $415 for a 1-bedroom condo.

Moderate

Crystal Springs Inn. P.O. Box 250, Teton Village; 733–4423. Only 100 ft. from the Aerial Tram; $306 per person, double occupancy, for the 7-night, 6-day package.

The Jackson Hole Racquet Club. Star Route, Box 362A, Jackson; 733–3990. A complete, year-round condominium resort complex. Guests have use of the athletic club with sauna, Jacuzzi, steam room, jogging track, lap pool, Nautilus, cross-country on the new Arnold Palmer championship golf course. A 1-bedroom condo or a 1-bedroom with loft goes for $355–$385 per person for a 7-night package. A house at the Racquet Club rents for $700 for 7 nights. The club is located between the ski area and town.

Sojourner Inn. P.O. Box 348, Teton Village; 773–2311 or 733–3657. A European-style lodge with pool, sauna, Jacuzzi, game room; $285.50 per person, double occupancy.

Americana Snow King Resort. P.O. Box SKI, Jackson; 733–5200. Packages for $255 per person, double occupancy and use of its very own Snow King Mountain.

The Antler Motel. P.O. Box 575, Jackson; 733–2535. Room packages for $247.

Wort Hotel. P.O. Box 89, Jackson; 733–2190. A half-block from the elk antler arches, is a highly rated hotel; rooms for $327.50.

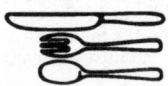 **RESTAURANTS.** There are 6 restaurants in Teton Village, including 2 on-mountain. The atmosphere in the village is a combination of Austria and the Wild West. In Jackson, where there are numerous eateries, it is pure Wild West. Restaurant categories are: *Expensive,* $15–$20; *Moderate,* $8–$15; *Inexpensive,* less than $8. These prices are for one meal for one person, exclusive of drinks or tip. Those in the expensive and moderate categories accept major credit cards.

Expensive

The Garden Room. In the Alpenhof; 731–3462. Wyoming's highest-rated restaurant; features veal, seafood, wild game, and delicious pastries. Serves 3 meals.

The Heritage Room. At the Inn at Jackson Hole; 733–1211. Steaks, lamb, fowl dishes are specialties; superb service.

Steigler's Restaurant. At the Jackson Hole Racquet Club; 733–1071. Features Austrian specialties, topped off with apple strudel and Williams pear brandy.

Moderate

The Mangy Moose (733–4913) in Teton Village is a must. Everyone eats or drinks here at least once during a visit. Menu includes crab legs, barbecued ribs, salad bar. Dinner only.

La Fondue. In the Sojourner Inn; 733–3657. An intimate restaurant featuring cheese, beef, and chocolate fondues; reservations suggested.

The Steak House. Also in the Sojourner Inn; 733–3657. Supposedly has the best prime rib in the area.

Dinner sleigh rides begin at the Tram building and go up Après Vous Mountain to a heated log cabin for a steak dinner. For reservations for the 2-hour dinner, call 733–6657.

In Jackson, the **Blue Lion,** 733–3912, is informal, featuring Continental cuisine and a full-service bar. The **Cadillac Grille,** 733–3279, on the west side of the town square, serves Mexican, Italian, and Chinese dishes in a 1940s Art Deco atmosphere. **Lame Duck,** 733–4311, 8 blocks east of the town square, has a wide variety of Szechuan, sushi, and sashimi—even American dishes and take-out service.

Inexpensive

At the slopes, **Valley Station Cafeteria** in the Tram building, no phone, features daily specials, good spaghetti dinners, all you can eat for $7.95. **The Village Store,** 733–4733, has breakfast and lunch as well as après-ski deli service. **Bear Claw Cafe,** 733–8715, serves breakfast, lunch, and après-ski buffalo burgers, soup, chili, and snack items. **Rocky Mountain Oyster,** downstairs from the Mangy Moose, 733–5525, has burgers, sandwiches, and skiers' specials for under $5.

On the way to Jackson on Village Road, the **Calico Pizza Parlor,** 733–2460, features delivery service to Teton Village and the Aspens.

In Jackson, **La Chispa Mexican Cafe,** downstairs from the Cowboy Bar, features standard and new Mexican dishes. **New York City Sub Shop,** 733–4414, serves Big Apple-style sandwiches and Philly cheese steaks.

 **HOW TO GET AROUND.** Amenities and facilities are spread out in the 12 miles between the ski area and the town of Jackson. The local **bus** system is called *START* and runs daily between Teton Village, the Racquet Club, and town from 7 A.M. to 12 midnight. There is a $1 charge to ride the bus; books of 10 tickets may be purchased for $5 at the customer service center in Teton Village, Jackson Hole Racquet Club, or the Wort Hotel in Jackson. **Rental car** agencies in Jackson are *Avis,* 733–3422; and *National,* 733–4132. *Budget,* 733–2206; *Dollar,* 733–9226; *Hertz,* 733–2272;

 **SEASONAL EVENTS.** The now-famous *Powder 8 Championships* are the highlight each **February.** Held in Cody Bowl on Rendezvous Mountain, expert powder skiers swirl down the mountain to form the most perfect set of figure-eights for the judges. In **March,** the *National Para-ski Championships* are held. Parachutists try to steer to a landing point on the mountain and hit a disc only a few inches in diameter; points for this are combined with points in a ski race to determine the winner.

Then there is the annual *Pole-Paddle-Paddle* competition in **April.** Only for the hardiest, it starts off with a timed race down Rendezvous Mountain, followed by a 10-km nordic leg, a 20-mile bicycle run, and finally a 9-mile kayak paddle in the icy spring waters.

 OTHER SPORTS AND ACTIVITIES. Skiing is the primary draw, of course. The *Ski the Big One* program awards pins for those who ski 100,000 or 150,000 vertical ft. in any one week, or 300,000, 500,000 or 1 million vertical ft. in a lifetime at Jackson Hole. Contact the *Marketing Department,* 733–2292, for details. The *Ski Week* instructional programs provide people with the same instructor for a week of maximum learning. Five half-day and full-day packages are available, with video tape evaluation. Also *Mountain Experience* classes, NASTAR races, alpine guides, and ski-racing camps. Contact *Ski School* director Pepi Stiegler, 733–2292.

There are four **nordic touring** centers, each with lodging: *Jackson Hole Karhu Center* at Teton Village; *Spring Creek Ranch; Togwotee Mountain Touring Center,* 45 miles north of Jackson; and *Teton Mountain Touring* at Grand Targhee, an hour's ride on the other side of Teton Pass. **Cross-country** skiing goes through Grand Teton National Park, Yellowstone National Park, and Bridger-Teton and Targhee National forests. Rental equipment is available, as are lessons, videos, clinics, and ski tours. Call 800–443–6931 for information on all the touring centers.

There is **snowmobiling** in Yellowstone, Granite Hot Springs (the water is 100° F), Grand Teton, and Togwotee Pass (snowmobile maps available at the Jackson Chamber of Commerce); **sleigh rides** of 45 minutes into the largest remaining elk herd in the U.S. at the National Elk Refuge; **helicopter skiing** or a snow-coach ride into Yellowstone National Park—have lunch, see the geysers and the elk and bison foraging in the steam. Pick up a free copy of *The Village Focus* for the latest in activities, events, and schedules.

 **CHILDREN'S ACTIVITIES.** The *Ski School* features the SKIWEE program for children 4–12 years old. This is a special child-centered teaching approach with games and ski instruction. Call the ski school at 733–2292 or *Central Reservations,* 800–443–6931. For children under 5 there are special lessons at *Pooh Corner,* the day-care facility in the hostel; call 733–4005.

 **NIGHTLIFE.** It all starts at the *Mangy Moose* in Teton Village—good view, good entertainment, and noisy crowd. A little more sedate is *Dietrich's Bar and Lounge* in the Alpenhof; cozy, ski movies, drink specials. *Wingback Lounge* at the Inn is comfy, too. *Stockman's Lounge* in the Sojourner Inn features ski movies, free hors d'oeuvres, drink specials.

For later-night activity, Jackson is the place and Cowboy is the bar. The *Million Dollar Cowboy Bar* is rowdy and rough, where you can shoot a game of pool; live entertainment to 2 A.M. The *Silver Dollar Bar* and the *Rancher* complete the "Bermuda Triangle" of popular Western bars. The *Shady Lake Saloon* in Americana Snow King Resort features live entertainment; ladies night Monday with free champagne. Or just walk down Jackson's wooden sidewalks, push open a swinging door, and find your own saloon. In Wilson, rub elbows with the cowboys at the *Stagecoach.*

EASTERN
CANADA

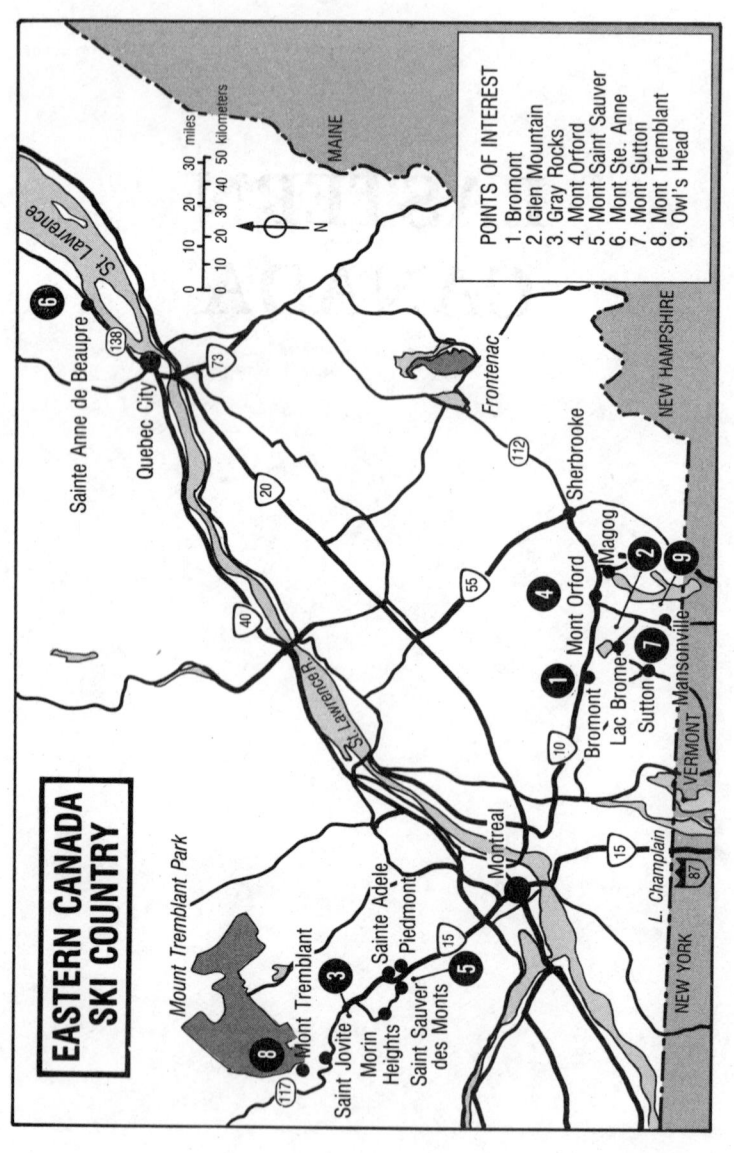

EASTERN CANADA SKI COUNTRY

POINTS OF INTEREST

1. Bromont
2. Glen Mountain
3. Gray Rocks
4. Mont Orford
5. Mont Saint Sauver
6. Mont Ste. Anne
7. Mont Sutton
8. Mont Tremblant
9. Owl's Head

miles

0   10   20   30
0   10   20   30   40   50 kilometers

N

MAINE

St. Lawrence

Sainte Anne de Beaupre

Quebec City

138

73

20

40

Mount Tremblant Park

Mont Tremblant

Saint Jovite

Morin Heights

Sainte Adele

Piedmont

Saint Sauver des Monts

15

Montreal

15

NEW YORK

L. Champlain

87

VERMONT

Frontenac

Sherbrooke

112

Magog

Mont Orford

55

Lac Brome

Bromont

10

Sutton

Mansonville

NEW HAMPSHIRE

EASTERN CANADA

Quebec

by
GUY THIBEADEAU

The words of French-Canadian poet Gilles Vigneault are most befitting to winter in Quebec. Says Vigneault: "Mon pays ce n'est pas un pays, c'est l'hiver!" (My country is not a country, it's winter!)

Quebec is a land of winter and while the summers are warm and pleasant the winters are long and snowy. It is the capital of skiing in Canada. While it does not have the vertical elevation and the scope of Western Canadian resorts, it has more ski areas per capita and more ski facilities than most other provinces or states in North America.

There are more than 100 alpine areas and about twice as many cross-country centers catering to everyone's needs. From the lofty, unexplored peaks in the Gaspésie to the impeccably groomed ski highways of Mont Tremblant, from small historical villages where the locals don't ski but are experts at hospitality to modern twentieth century cities, skiing in Quebec runs as deep as the snow that covers its mountains. It's a celebration of winter done with a zest and *joie de vivre* that makes a skiing vacation in Quebec something very special. It's called "Skiing à la Francaise" and its unique flavor has kept winter visitors coming back year after year.

Of the 6.5 million inhabitants of Quebec there are more than 800,000 alpine skiers and 1.6 million cross-country skiers. Skiing here, more than in any other province of Canada, is a way of life.

Quebec boasts seven distinct ski regions:

The Laurentians, north of Montreal with 26 alpine and as many cross-country areas.

The Eastern Townships, southeast of Montreal and north of the U.S. border with 10 alpine areas and half a dozen good cross-country centers.

The Quebec City region with eight alpine centers.

The Outaouais, north of the national capital Ottawa with 8 areas.

Charlevoix, a developing region northeast of Quebec City with two alpine areas and plenty of off-trail skiing.

Lanaudière, northeast of Montreal with seven areas running parallel to the Laurentians.

The Gaspésie, in the Gaspé Peninsula at the mouth of the mighty St. Lawrence River with nine alpine areas.

For North Americans, a ski vacation in Quebec is the closest thing to a European holiday. And while Quebec areas are no match for the Alps, life in Quebec combines the comforts and standards of North America with the charm and cosmopolitan atmosphere of the old world. French is the official language of Quebec but you'll have no trouble being understood in English except in a few remote villages east of Quebec City on the North Shore.

Quebec has a preponderence of great eateries. Deluxe restaurants abound in Quebec City, Montreal, and surrounding regions. In North America the only other cities to rival Montreal for its food are New York and San Francisco; in Canada it has no match. The best onion soup this side of Paris and local specialties such as French-Canadian *tourtière* and *ragout* all the way to the more common chicken barbecue are sure to tempt and please all tastes.

Montreal is the economic hub of the province. With a population of more than 2.5 million, it is the most cosmopolitain of Canadian cities. Being one of Canada's first cities, its architecture was strongly influenced by the French and the British.

Some of Montreal's landmarks are Mont Royal, the mountain in the heart of the city. Several lookouts will give you a scenic, bird's-eye view of the city from various angles. Mont Royal also has a 7.5-kilometer cross-country trail beautifully maintained by the city. From it are scenic views of downtown Montreal; you can almost touch the highrises.

Quebec City is the second largest city in Quebec. Its population of 650,000 is mostly French. The Upper Town overlooks the St. Lawrence River and is mostly residential. The Lower Town harbors industrial and commercial facilities.

Of particular interest is Old Quebec with its cobblestone streets and protected garrison, a well preserved testimony of the colony days. Fine restaurants, bars, and bistros provide visitors to Quebec with an even more genuine taste of French Quebec.

Lately the exchange rate for Americans traveling to Quebec has been extremely favorable, and with skiing rates in the province already lower than than in the U.S., a treasure of bargains awaits the budget conscious traveler.

Since 1983 the tourism branch of the Quebec Government has been strongly supportive of skiing, encouraging and subsidizing the necessary infrastucture to make skiing in Quebec competitive with the rest of eastern North America.

Modern facilities are second to none. Quadruple and detachable quadruple chairs are sprouting up every year at the more popular resorts to whisk a maximum number of skiers to various mountain tops, assuring more time on the slopes. Detachable quads are revolutionizing uphill technology. The difference between a fixed triple and a detachable quad is more than one more skier on the chair. It is almost as revolutionary as was the change from the rope-tow to the T-bar. The detachable quad allows you to board the chair when it is moving very slowly. You board as easily as you sit on a park bench. When the chair clamps onto the main cable, the chair accelerates to a speed more than double that of a fixed chair. Hence more comfort, more capacity, more safety, and less time waiting at the lift line.

Despite dependable winters, all of Quebec's major resorts have snow-making covering from 50 to 100 percent of their skiing terrain. The popularity of skiing in Quebec and the relatively high level of proficiency of Quebec skiers has made snowmaking as necessary as lifts to prevent sharp-edged carved turns from braking through to the ground.

Quebec's leading destination resorts are principally Mont Ste Anne near Quebec City, Mont Tremblant, and Gray Rocks in the Laurentians north of Montreal; the Eastern Townships centers are Mont Sutton, Mont Orford, and Bromont.

If skiing continues to develop successfully more areas now on the drawing board are likely to become reality. Le Massif at Petite Riviere St Francois could become a giant in the same league as Killington, Vermont. Vertical in excess of 2,000 feet, it is serviced by 14 lifts. In addition, Mont Ste Anne has expansion plans which could increase the mountain's capacity by 40–50 percent.

Skiing in Quebec has long been discovered by its residents. Skiing à la Francaise is fast becoming a contender in the North American ski market and a destination unlike anywhere else on this continent.

From mid-November to mid-April Tourism Quebec operates the Quebec Ski Lines where you can obtain up-to-the-minute snow conditions for all of Quebec's major ski resorts. Call 800–363–3624 from the eastern U.S., Ontario, and the Maritimes.

Further travel information can be obtained by calling Tourism Quebec at 800–443–7000 from the U.S., and 800–361–6490 from Ontario and the Maritimes.

The Laurentians

While skiing as a sport originated in Norway in the late 1800s, it was via the Laurentian Mountains north of Montreal that skiing made its foray into the North American continent.

Early in 1879 a Norwegian who had recently immigrated to Montreal appeared on skis. For Montrealers, who were most familiar with snowshoes in those days, skis were seen as a variation of the snowshoes and were in fact named "Norwegian snowshoes." At 9 feet long, 6 inches wide, with a toe-strap and a foot board, they made curious-looking snowshoes.

While skiing had made an early appearance in Montreal, it was only in the early 1900s that it began to develop as a sport. In 1904 the Montreal Ski Club was formed with 50 members. In 1909 skiing was part of the Montreal Winter Carnival. But it was after World War I that skiing finally took off. By 1920 the Montreal Ski Club Annual described skiing as "the king of winter sports in Montreal."

From the 1920s to the 1940s, ski trains took skiers north. Trails were opened for cross-country skiing by another Norwegian immigrant, Herman Smith-Johannsen, nicknamed "Jackrabbit" for his quickness and agility on skis. Johannsen is known as the "father of Laurentian skiing." He more than anyone else promoted skiing by blazing trails, organizing competitions, and coaching. At age 102 Johannsen was still skiing; at 110 still promoting skiing.

In 1932 Alex Foster installed the first mechanical ski tow in North America. The first T-bar in the Laurentians was installed at Gray Rocks in 1934. In 1938, Mont Tremblant inaugurated the first chairlift in Canada.

Skiing has since become the region's leading industry. There are now more than 25 alpine skiing areas with over 100 lifts, including the most modern in lift technology, quadruple detachable chairs. Every year snowmaking capacity is increased at the major resorts. All major areas now have at least 50 percent of their skiing terrain covered with machine-made snow.

More enchantment came to the high country with night skiing. Late afternoon and night skiing is as popular as day skiing in the Laurentians, particularly in the St Sauveur – Ste Adele region where seven of the ten areas which offer night skiing are found. What pleasure for the avid skier for whom ski days are always too short! And what a sight for those who just enjoy sitting in a comfortable lounge with a view of the brightly lit hills.

Cross-country is also very popular in the Laurentians with hundreds of kilometers of trails linking villages such as St Agathe, Val David, Val

Morin, Ste Adele, Ste Marguerite, Morin Heights, and St Sauveur. Within meters of every lodge and hotel there is a trail which permits you to link up with the main network. The Laurentians are a wonderland for the cross-country skier.

The Laurentian Mountains are blessed with abundant snow and good snow retention. Boosted a little with snowmaking, the season extends from mid-November to mid-April.

You will find professional ski schools at all major resorts. All full-time instructors are members of the Canadian Ski Instructor's Alliance.

There is lodging for every taste and budget in the Laurentians—from resort hotels, inns, and motels to condominiums, chalets, and youth hostels. From all-inclusive ski week packages to weekday and weekend specials, Laurentian hospitality is available everywhere at affordable prices.

Eating in the Laurentians is legendary as it is throughout most of Quebec. And nighttime activities are as diversified as the skiing itself.

Getting around in the Laurentians is simple enough. The toll-free Laurentian Autoroute 15, paralleled by Hwy. 117, are the backbone of the region with towns and villages strewn along the way from St Jerome, the gateway to the Laurentians, to Ste Jovite, the end of the run for alpine skiers. Nowadays the Laurentians are the playground of Montrealers. Numerous lakes coupled with skiing in winter have made the region the most popular four-season cottage country for thousands of residents of southwestern Quebec. And because of the region's proximity to Montreal—less than one hour's drive—more and more are making the Laurentians their permanent residence.

Colonized in great proportion by the Catholic Church and Curé Labelle who promoted the extension of the railway north of St Jerome in the late 1800s, the region has long since lost its frontier character. With the advent of the railway came growth to the region and development of tourism. From the 1930s to the early '50s the famous Laurentian Ski Trains shuttled thousands of skiers every weekend to ski the hills of St Sauveur, Morin Heights, Ste Marguerite and Ste Adele.

The construction of the autoroute in the mid 1950s opened the region to automobile traffic and marked the end of the ski train era. Efforts to revive the ski trains in the 1970s during the gas shortage failed. Skiers were too spoiled by the luxury of driving directly to the hills.

The Laurentians are home to more than 26 alpine areas between St Jerome and Mont Tremblant. There are hundreds of miles of cross-country ski trails linking every village and hotel. The greatest concentration of skiing is between St Sauveur and Ste Agathe. Of that 25-mile stretch of Hwy. 117 or Autoroute 15, there is a choice of some 20 alpine areas and probably 500 miles of cross-country skiing. A map of Laurentian cross-country trails is produced and distributed by Le Comptoir Kanuk, 390 Principale in St Sauveur; 514–227–3939.

What is most exciting is that this haven of winter sports and vacation wonderland is located less than an hour's drive from Montreal.

GRAY ROCKS INN

P.O. Box 1000, St-Jovite
QE, J0T 2H0
Tel: 514–861–0187 or
     819–425–2771

Snow Report: 819–425–2771
Area Vertical: 190 meters
     (620 ft.)
Number of Trails: 18
Lifts: 3 double chairs, 2
     T-bars
Snowmaking: 85 percent of trails
Season: mid-November–early May

In terms of statistics, this mountain is a shrimp compared to the giants with whom it competes for skiers every year. But in terms of its success, it rates with the best.

This is where the season begins for most skiers around Montreal and it has consistently been the first area in Quebec to open with good conditions year after year.

Snowmaking and grooming are an art here and excellence in snow conditions is the number one priority. And for good reason: with a relatively small vertical the area must offer distinctively and consistently better skiing conditions to succeed.

Snowmaking begins at Gray Rocks in early November and runs unabated until early March. Neither storm, wind, nor extreme cold will stop the snow factory at this area. The snow guns shut down only when temperatures rise above freezing. Snow is built up 10–15 feet thick in spots most vulnerable to the spring sun. Snow reserves are built up near lift terminals to be transported as needed as the season stretches into late April and May. One year there were leaves on the trees and flies on your neck and skiers were still schussing.

The mountain's 18 runs on three different exposures offer a very pleasant skiing experience. And while trail length is limited there is something for everyone, from beginner to advanced. The west side pitches, "Devil's Dip" and "Bon Voyage," will make you realize that skiing at Gray Rocks is not only for beginners. Three double chairs and two T-bars service the area, which was challenging enough in the 50s to produce Canada's first international ski star, Lucille Wheeler, who in 1958 won gold medals in giant slalom and downhill at the FIS Games in Bad Gastein, Austria.

But Gray Rock's reputation is built on more than just great skiing. In 1951 Gray Rocks packaged a week of skiing, including lessons and accommodations, for the Ski Club of Washington, DC. The Ski Week was invented. From that point on the area has been filled to capacity from mid-November to mid-April with skiers and would-be skiers whose main purpose is to learn to ski or improve their technique while having fun doing it.

The Snow Eagle Ski School built by Real Charette has no equal in the East. At full capacity there are 50 certified Canadian ski instructors dishing out the "bend zee knees" to over 500 guests. The ski school and its instructors are fully integrated into the ski week activities in much the same way as the G.O. (activities director) at a Club Med. In fact the ski vacation concept at Gray Rocks is an all-inclusive one where the package covers most expenses, save for bar bills.

It is also on the modest slopes of Gray Rocks that the modern North American skiing technique evolved. In the mid 1940s an Austrian immigrant named Luggi Foeger escaped Nazi-occupied Austria, settled at Gray Rocks, and began to teach the Alrberg skiing technique which he had learned in St Anton from its creator, Hannes Schneider.

This family-operated area was developed somewhat accidentally at the turn of the century when an American by the name of George Wheeler built a sawmill which led to a profitable construction business. Enchanted by the beauty of the area, many of Wheeler's friends came up to visit while enjoying the good hunting and fishing in the region. In 1906 the Wheelers built the inn which still today forms an integral part of the much extended complex.

Guests of Gray Rocks are treated to nothing but the best. Meals feature extensive *table d'hôte* menus of French and French-Canadian cuisine for gourmets and gourmands alike. Skiing is usually enough for most to work out the extra meal calories but for those who need more exercise, a complete fitness center including a lap-pool, sauna, whirlpool, and the best exercise machines.

Located within sight of famous Mont Tremblant, Gray Rocks lures skiers who wish to test their newly acquired skiing skills before taking on longer, more demanding slopes.

Although skiing is what has made Gray Rocks world famous, the inn is busy year-round. Situated on the shores of Lac Ouimet, the beautifully flowered property covers more than 2,000 acres, including a scenic 18-hole golf course, 22 Har Tru tennis courts, and a tennis school which is associated with the Van der Meer Tennis University and is building a reputation to match the ski school.

Practical Information for Gray Rocks

HOW TO GET THERE. Montreal is the gateway to the Laurentians and to Gray Rocks. Located 120 km (about 80 miles) north of Montreal, it is easily accessible via Laurentian Autoroute 15, a toll-free expressway which is linked to all of Montreal's major highways. Follow the autoroute to the end, where it merges with Hwy. 117. Follow signs to Mont Tremblant and you will arrive at Gray Rocks.

Montreal's two major airports are Dorval, for North American traffic, and Mirabel, for international destinations. The latter is most conveniently located 20 minutes north of Montreal at the gateway to the Laurentians. *People Express* and *Presidential Airlines* operate discount flights into Mirabel from various U.S. airports. Flying into Mirabel is preferable if you are not planning to visit Montreal. Most U.S. flights land at Dorval.

TELEPHONES. The area code for Gray Rocks is 819 and for Montreal it is 514.

ACCOMMODATIONS. Gray Rocks is the complete resort and vacationers stay at the *Gray Rocks Inn* or at adjacent *Le Chateau,* a smaller but equally attractive lodge on the lake less than a mile from the inn. Both are on the American Plan, which includes lodging, meals, and much of the recreation. The inn is the center of all activity for ski and tennis weeks and is the larger of the two. The chateau's dining room and lounge are smaller and more intimate offering a nice change of pace. Daily rates average $95 per person during the season, and weakly rates average $600 per person. Weekend rates are also available.

RESTAURANTS. Because of the all-inclusive nature of a Gray Rocks vacation, all meals are taken at the hotel. The menu is different every day and about the only complaint ever voiced is that there is too much to eat! Nonetheless, if you wish to sample local restaurants in the region there are a number of excellent ones at adjacent Mont Tremblant. (See *Mont Tremblant* section for suggestions.)

HOW TO GET AROUND. Everything is quite centrally located around the inn and you are always within walking distance of all facilities. However there are free **shuttle vans** to take you and your equipment to any point on the property should you need assistance or be unable to walk. This van is in regular service between the chateau and the inn, a distance of less than a mile.

SEASONAL EVENTS. *Canadian Ski-Laser Yachting Championships* are usually held on the first or second weekend in May. This unique event combines alpine skiing on the slopes of Gray Rocks one day with a Laser class sailing regatta on adjacent Lac Ouimet the next. The combination of snow on the slopes and sailboats on the lake make for quite a spectacular sight. On that weekend the golf course and tennis courts are often open with skiers purchasing a day lift ticket entitled to use all facilities that are open.

Every **summer** the *Butch Staples Tennis School* at Gray Rocks teams up with the world famous tennis school, *Van der Meer Tennis University,* for special, intensive week-long sessions. Information on dates and programs are available by writing or phoning Gray Rocks.

OTHER SPORTS AND ACTIVITIES. **Cross-country skiing** is quite plentiful around Gray Rocks. The area maintains 18 km of track-set trails on its golf course and from there you can tie in with the 90-km Ste Jovite–Mont Tremblant Ski Club network. Nearby Domaine St Bernard, which is run by monks, also offers a fine network in a most scenic environment.

Gray Rocks has a fully equipped *Fitness Center* which includes a lap **pool, whirlpools, sauna,** a dance **aerobics** room with regular classes, and a fully equipped **gym** with Nautilus, Global Gym, and Nordic Track equipment, and rowing machines, ergometers, and Monarch stationary bicycles. In addition, Gray Rocks offers fitness tests and computerized nutrition analyses.

Sleigh rides, movies, and a complete and diversified fare of indoor activities and entertainment are organized in conjunction with **ski weeks.**

Ski weeks at Gray Rocks usually have an optional ski day at Mont Tremblant. Another area worth visiting in the region is Mont Blanc in St Faustin on Hwy. 117. St Faustin is the first village south of Ste Jovite and you will pass Mont Blanc on the left side of the highway as you drive up. With a vertical rise of 300 meters, it is the second highest peak in the Laurentians. Two chairs, a triple and a double, and 3 T-bars service 23 runs, 12 of which have snowmaking. After Mont Tremblant this area offers the most challenging slopes in the Laurentians.

NIGHTLIFE. You need not look very far for night life at Gray Rocks. Live music and nightly entertainment make it the place where outsiders come for a good time. The *Thirsty Eagle Bar* is the focal point of the region's après-ski life. Here, you're as likely to meet someone from Florida up for the annual ski trip as you are to meet a ski instructor from one of the neighboring lodges. The bar has two main live periods: after skiing between 4 and 6 P.M. and in the evening from 8 P.M. on. There are also discos at the *Villa Bellevue Hotel,* just a mile up the road from Gray Rocks and at the base of Mont Tremblant. (See *Mont Tremblant* section.)

MONT ST-SAUVEUR

P.O. Box 910,
St. Sauveur-des-Monts
QE J0R 1R0
Tel: 514–227–2616

Snow Report: 514–227–2616
Area Vertical: 700 ft.
Number of Trails: 22 on 100 acres
Lifts: 1 quadruple chair, 1 triple
*   chair, 3 double chairs,*
*   1 T-bar, 1 Pony lift*
Snowmaking: 70 percent
Night skiing: 50% of the
*   trails*
Season: mid-November–mid-April

Back in 1934 an American named Fred Pabst, son of the Milwaukee brewer, installed the first permanent ski lift on the slopes of St-Sauveur, and for a time Hill 70 was one of the most famous ski hills in eastern Canada.

As the area grew in popularity, a group of businessmen joined Victor Nymark in 1945 to create UPHILL Ltd. Four years later, in 1949, they imported from Austria the first T-bar to be installed in North America and St-Sauveur-des-Monts became the cradle of skiing in eastern Canada. That first T-bar on Hill 70 was soon followed by tows on Hills 67–72, which are to this day the main ones at the area.

Through the 1940s and 1950s St-Sauveur was the focal point of skiing in the lower Laurentians. It had the steepest and longest hills and was the sight of club races almost every weekend.

It was in the early 1970s that St-Sauveur entered skiing's modern era. New ownership turned Uphill Ltd. into Mont St-Sauveur which was to become a solid company setting new standards for the ski industry in eastern Canada.

Nowadays the 700-foot vertical of Mont St-Sauveur with its 450 acres has been totally retrofitted. Slopes have been widened and recut, old lifts repositioned and brand new ones installed to handle the many skiers who make this the most popular area in the Laurentians. Among the area's 7 lifts, a quadruple detachable chairlift assures both a rapid ascent and a good capacity. A modern snowmaking system covers 70 percent of the skiing terrain and a fleet of the most sophisticated grooming machines guarantees the best possible conditions.

While Mont St-Sauveur was not the first to offer night skiing, it was the first to make it the big deal that it now is. From "candlelight" skiing on one or two runs in 1973, the area now offers night skiing on 16 of the area's 22 runs backed up by over 1.1 million watts of lighting power.

In elevation several neighboring areas approach Mont St-Sauveur's vertical but the length of the runs is not what draws crowds to the area. Mont St-Sauveur is the the place to be as well as the place to be seen. The first area in Quebec to pay attention to details and to market its skiing through activities and promotions, it has attracted skiing's leaders. The crowds have followed. If a star is going to be seen skiing anywhere, it's likely to be at St-Sauveur. If a picture of a bikini-clad skiing beauty is to make the front page of the Montreal papers announcing the arrival of spring skiing, it is likely to have been shot at Mont St-Sauveur.

The new base lodge built in 1978 is a combination stage and jewel box. It is the focal point of all activities at the area which occasionally can make for some congestion. But services are built with crowds in mind and even on the busiest day you can eat, rent your skis, and purchase your ticket without waiting too long.

There's always something happening at Mont St-Sauveur and that's what makes the area as popular as it is with Montreal skiers.

Practical Information for Mont St-Sauveur

HOW TO GET THERE. By car. Montreal is the gateway to the Laurentians and to Mont St-Sauveur. Located 60 km (about 40 miles) north of Montreal, it is easily accessible via Laurentian Autoroute 15, Take Exit 60 of the Laurentian autoroute and follow signs to Mont St-Sauveur.

By air. Montreal's two major airports are Dorval for North American traffic and Mirabel for international destinations. The latter is most conveniently located 20 minutes south of St-Sauveur at the gateway to the Laurentians. *People Express* and *Presidential Airlines* operate discount flights into Mirabel from various U.S. airports. Flying into Mirabel is preferable if you are not planning to visit Montreal.

TELEPHONES. The area code for the Mont St-Sauveur region of Quebec is 514.

 **ACCOMMODATIONS.** *Village Mont St-Sauveur,* slopeside condominiums, are available through Mont St-Sauveur, P.O. Box 910, St Sauveur-des-Monts QE, J0R 1R0; 227–1616. These beautifully-appointed ski-in, ski-out condos are furnished with sleeping accommodations for up to 6 people. Attractive 2–5-day packages are available, including lift tickets, accommodations, and the option of lessons and rentals.

The above condos are in the *Expensive* category, $65 and above, based on double occupancy. Other categories in this listing are: *Moderate,* $45–$65; and *Inexpensive,* less than $45.

Auberge St. Denis. *Expensive.* 21 St. Denis; 227–4766. Located in the heart of the Village, this charming French-Canadian lodge offers French cuisine, quality lodging and breakfast in bed.

L'Auberge De la Vallee. *Moderate.* 520 Principale; 227–5998. Dining room, bar, ski week packages.

Motel Jolibourg. *Moderate.* 60 Principale; 227–4651. Motel with panoramic view; rooms with fireplaces. Rates include Continental breakfast.

Motel Des Pentes. *Moderate.* P.O. Box 789; 227–5351. In the village, this motel is located within 5 minutes of the area on Hwy. 364 which runs through the village. Most units have kitchenettes. Chalets with 2–3–5 rooms are also available on a weekly basis.

Motel le 60. *Moderate.* 600 Chemin des Frenes; 227–4880. You can't miss it. Located at exit 60 of the Laurentian autoroute, the exit for St-Sauveur-des-Monts. Rooms with fireplaces and kitchenettes; packages available.

Pension du Cap. *Inexpensive.* 270 Chemin Constantineau, 227–3424 or 227–3878. Low-cost, clean bed and breakfast with good atmosphere and pleasantly located on the Simon River. Less than 10 minutes from ski areas.

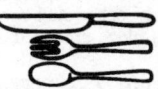 **RESTAURANTS.** If there is something St-Sauveur is famous for, other than skiing, it is the quality and diversity of its dining establishments. Whatever your taste or budget you'll find numerous places to suit your desire. Restaurants are listed in order of price category. *Expensive:* $18 and up; *Moderate:* $10–$18; *Inexpensive:* less than $10. These prices are for one meal, excluding drinks, tips, and taxes. Abbreviations for credit cards are: A, American Express; D, Diners Club; M, MasterCard; and V, Visa.

Expensive

Chez Roberto. 149 Principale; 227–6005. Italian nouvelle cuisine—light, healthy, and good. Attractive 1-room restaurant, owner-operated. Owner's wife is an opera singer. Expect a lively time. M, V.

La Gascogne. 358 Principale; 227–5171. Fine French cuisine and excellent rack of lamb. All major credit cards.

Gibby's. 414 Principale; 227–2623. Excellent steaks and seafood served in style. Dining room has 3 fireplaces. Meal portions are large and most orders come with appetizers. Reservations recommended, particularly weekends and holidays. Dinners only. All major credit cards.

Da Tulio's. 389 Principale; 227–4313. Italian haute cuisine, considered the best in the region. Always a busy place; reservations recommended. Dinners only. All major credit cards.

Moderate

Le Jardin des Oliviers. 239 Principale; 227–2110. Exceptionally fine French-Provencale cuisine served with a personal touch. Lunch and dinner; 7 days a week. A, M, V.

Le Kindli. 22 Lafleur North; 227–2229. Swiss with some French cuisine featuring raclette, fondues, steaks, veal, and brochettes. Closed Tuesdays. A, M, V.

Restaurant l'Ailloli. 140 Principale; 227–3383. On any good day there's a party going on in this Italian restaurant. Specializes in wood oven pizzas. Bring your own wine, available in Quebec at local convenience stores called *depanneurs.* Evenings only. M, V.

La Vieille Ferme. 967 Principale; 227–3083. Typical old-time French-Canadian farm house serving steaks and seafood and featuring roast beef dinner Sunday evenings. All major credit cards.

Moderate–Inexpensive

Le Chalet Grec. 138 Principale; 227–6612. Greek specialties; bring your own wine.

Le Jacar. 86 de la Gare; 227–2442. Say *bon jour* to owner Jacques, and he will personally make sure you're satisfied.

Le Jardin Lee. 163 Principale; 227–2828. Not French, but fine Chinese food.

Inexpensive

Restaurant la Boheme. 251 rue Principale; 227–6644. One of the village's most popular eateries. Small and intimate, it serves an unusual selection of fine food and wine. In addition to steaks, veal, and brochettes, it serves fine couscous and paella. No reservations. Eat early if you don't like waiting in line. M, V.

Restaurant Charlie. 61 de la Gare; 227–6001. Italian cuisine featuring wood oven pizzas and spaghetti buffet. Attractive decor. Reservations not necessary. A, M, V.

Giorgio's. Highway 364 and Laurentian Autoroute; 227–3151. Italian and rock-bottom ("How can you do it, Giorgio?") prices—and good too.

HOW TO GET AROUND. It is best to have a **car** at your disposal, since there is no public transportation within St-Sauveur. However, **taxi** service is available through *Taxi des Pays d'en Haut,* 229–3535 or 229–3150.

 **SEASONAL EVENTS.** *Mid-Summer Madness* takes place every **August.** It's a ski race on crushed ice terminating in the area pool. Points are given for speed and style. While there are few regularly scheduled major events at Mont St-Sauveur, some activity of interest takes place almost daily.

 OTHER SPORTS AND ACTIVITIES. Cross-country skiing is a popular activity in the St-Sauveur Valley with trails starting on the outskirts of the village. Some enjoyable trails begin from the *Chalet Pauline Vanier* (Community Center) off de l'Eglise and behind the Parish of St-Sauveur Town Hall. A more organized trail network is located in adjacent Morin Heights, 6 km north of St-Sauveur via either Hwy. 364 or Chemin de l'Eglise. The *Centre de Ski de Fond Morin Heights* (Morin Heights Cross-country Center) offers a wide variety of track-set trails for all abilities. Call 226–2417 for information.

Piedmont Golf Course (514–227–2562) in nearby Piedmont also offers a good selection of trails for all skiing abilities and even maintains some trails especially for ski-skating. To get there take Principale east toward Mont Olympia, cross Hwy. 117, and within a mile you'll be there.

Skating is also available on rinks adjacent to village schools.

Shopping is rounded up in two main areas: Rue Principale (Main St.) and Les Galeries des Monts, a shopping center which includes a liquor store, located off Hwy. 364. Stores in both areas are open 7 days a week.

 **NIGHTLIFE.** Après-ski activity around St-Sauveur revolves around a few key bars. *Les Vieilles Portes,* 185 Principale; 227–2662. "Operated for skiers by skiers" is their slogan, a good cozy bar where the locals meet regularly after skiing in a friendly atmosphere. Specials offered on different nights, such as free spaghetti Monday nights.

Common's Bar, on Lac Echo Rd. in Morin Heights; 226–2211. Features live, rock 'n' roll bands every weekend.

Nuits Blanches Bar, 762 Principale; 227–5419. Just what its name implies, a late night, late action bar frequented more by the "beautiful people" than the hard-core skiers who are normally tucked in when this place starts to shake.

La Louisianne - Bourbon Street, Located on Hwy. 117 between Piedmont and Ste Adele, this is the most active bar in the region drawing from all neighboring villages. Loud rock 'n' roll music, and plenty of dancing.

Bar Resto-Polo, 307 Principale; 227–2430. A good late night spot often featuring live entertainment.

Le Jacar, restaurant described above, turns into a bar and meeting place after 10:30 P.M. Live entertainment on weekends. Small, lavishly decorated place with friendly atmosphere.

OTHER SKI AREAS IN THE
ST-SAUVEUR VALLEY

While Mont St-Sauveur is the leading area of the lower Laurentians, the St-Sauveur Valley with neighboring Ste Adele and Morin Heights are home to another nine major areas which can offer the vacationing skier plenty of variety. All are within a 10–15-minute drive,

Avila (227–2603) is located in Piedmont at the easternmost end of Mont St-Sauveur. In fact, one of its trails comes within a few feet of a St-Sauveur trail making it possible to interconnect both areas. With a vertical of 185 meters and 9 snowmaking runs, it has 1 double chair, and 3 T-bars. Night skiing is available every night.

Mont Habitant (227–2637) is a good family area located on the same range as Mont St-Sauveur but at the western end. Its 170-meter vertical drop includes 7 well-groomed snowmaking runs serviced by 1 double chair and 3 T-bars. Night skiing every night on all trails.

Ski Morin Heights (226–1333) is in Morin Heights, a small municipality due north of St-Sauveur on Hwy. 364. This area opened in 1981 and has been growing steadily in popularity. At 214 meters of vertical with 21 trails serviced by 4 triple chairs, 1 double and 1 T-bar and 100 percent snowmaking, it is, with Mont St-Sauveur, one of the best areas in the region. Situated in a bowl, all trails converge around an attractive, comfortable base lodge and a spacious multilevel sun deck. There is night skiing every night of the week. Day-care facilities are also available on the premises.

Mont Olympia (227–3523) is in Piedmont, just east of St-Sauveur. A fine beginners' area with 13 wide, well-groomed slopes, snowmaking, and night skiing. It is serviced by 1 triple chair and 4 T-bars, and has a vertical of 174 meters.

Mont Gabriel (229–3547), located off Hwy. 117 between Piedmont and Ste Adele, is one of the first ski areas built in the Laurentians. With a 192-meter vertical drop and 19 runs on 4 different mountain sides, it offers a variety of slopes for all categories of skiers. Two of the best bump runs in the region are Tamarack and O'Connell. The area has snowmaking and night skiing 7 nights a week on both north and south faces. Lifts include 1 quadruple chair, 1 triple, 1 double, and 8 T-bars.

The Chantecler (229–3555) in Ste Adele has been recently renovated, refitted, recut, and redone. Built around a 200-room resort hotel—a very attractive mini-chateau—it should appeal to the ski week vacationer looking for a full-service hotel right on the mountain. The area has skiing on 4 mountains although skiers gather around the hotel's Mountain No. 1, where 5 gentle beginners' slopes allow for both day and night skiing, and on Mountain No 4, where 9 more trails offer a wider variety of slope difficulty for all abilities. Mountain No. 2 is basically a teaching mountain with very gentle slopes. The 195-meter vertical is serviced by 2 quadruple chairs, 1 triple, 2 doubles, and 2 poma lifts.

On a busy weekend to get away from it all you might retreat to the following smaller areas where children outnumber adults. **Mont Christie** (514–226–2412) in St-Sauveur north of the main village on Hwy. 364; **Bellevue Ski Hill** (514–226–2003) in the center of Morin Heights on Hwy. 364 north of St-Sauveur; and **Hills 40 and 80** (514–229–2921) in Ste Adele, just off Highway 117.

Paralleled by the Laurentian Autoroute, Hwy. 117 is the backbone of the Laurentian region. Off it there are many quaint and interesting villages to visit such as Mont-Rolland, Val Morin, Val-David, and municipalities of Ste Adele and Ste Agathe.

MONT TREMBLANT

Mont Tremblant QE J0T 1Z0
Tel: 819-425-8711

Snow Report: 514-861-1925
Area Vertical: 2,131 ft.
Number of Trails: 40 on 300
   acres
Lifts: 1 quadruple chair, 2
   triple chairs, 4 double chairs,
   1 T-bar, 2 poma lifts
Snowmaking: 45 percent
Season: end of November–early
   April

The legend of Mont Tremblant is as mighty as the mountain itself. Among the earliest settlers in the region were Algonquin Indians who sought refuge from the warring Iroquois tribe on the shores of Lac Tremblant. It was one of these old Indian legends that gave the mountain its name, Mont Tremblant, "the trembling mountain." The Indians called it Manitou-Ewitchi-Saga, the Mountain of the Dread Manitou. Manitou was the Indian god of the wilderness who, in his wrath, caused the great mountain to tremble "with tempest and falling rock" when he was aroused by the infringement of man on the sanctity of the wilds and the animals inhabiting it.

In more recent times earth tremors have been recorded emanating from the immediate region of the "trembling mountain."

The historical legend of Mont Tremblant in no way surpasses the skiing legend of Tremblant. Mont Tremblant was developed by Philadelphia millionaire Joseph Ryan, who first explored the mountain in 1932 with American newsman and travelogue producer, Lowell Thomas and another American, Harry Wheeler, owner of neighboring Lac Ouimet Club (now Gray Rocks). Together they planned the resort that would become, during World War II, a favorite of North American skiers as much for its skiing as for its gourmet food and French ambience. In 1939 The resort opened with a single chair, the second in North America; the first was erected at Sun Valley, Idaho, a year earlier in 1938.

Over the years the area has evolved into a fine destination resort with all the amenities necessary to attract vacationing skiers from all over. Sitting majestically at the end of the Laurentian Autoroute, yet only 90 minutes from Montreal, Mont Tremblant is the highest peak in the Laurentians. From its summit it commands a spectacular panorama of lakes, mountains, valleys, and forests. It also provides the highest skiable vertical in the province of Quebec, over 2,100 feet.

In the early days Tremblant was known for its narrow, difficult, twisting trails that started at the top in a forest of dwarfed frozen spruce trees. The frozen trees are still there but few of the original trails can be found. In the 1970s and early 1980s a major retrofit saw both the lift and trail networks upgraded and modernized. Many of the narrow, twisting chutes have been recut to favor faster, longer turns. As a result, intermediate and advanced skiers can often enjoy the same trails while skiing them somewhat differently.

Mont Tremblant is like two mountains atop each other. And before skiing it you must be prepared to deal with what locals consider almost four mountains: the upper north and south sides and the lower north and south sides, each providing skiing for all abilities.

Long known for its difficult skiing, Mont Tremblant has gone a long way to overcome its reputation in order to please the beginning skier. The North Side slopes, Sissy Schuss and Fuddle Duddle, are among the best teaching slopes the areas have for the novice skier. On the south side the Nansen runs top-to-bottom—over 3 miles—and is both an excellent beginners' run and a fun cruiser to get you to the south side base at day's end.

Intermediate and cruising trails are wide at Tremblant and tend to draw both the intermediate and advanced skier. Given a touch of fresh powder, there are no better runs than Beauchemin and Lower Duncan on the north side, and on the south side are Beauvallon and McCullough.

Expert skiing is found mostly on the upper mountain sections although the area's two toughest mogul trails, Expo and the Flying Mile, are on the lower sections of the north and south sides, respectively.

The area's lift system is basically made up of chairs: doubles, triples, and one quad, each one servicing the upper or lower section of the area. A gondola that would span the full length of the south side has been on the master plan for years.

Mont Tremblant, being the highest summit in the Laurentians, also is often exposed to some tough weather and you should come prepared with your warmest gear. A common fact of life in the high mountains: you never know till you get there what awaits you at the top!

The distinctive French Canadian atmosphere of the base village makes it unique in all of North America. English is of course spoken well but often with a heavy accent which adds to the flavor.

With an advanced snowmaking system covering 45 percent of the areas, Mont Tremblant now guarantees vacationing skiers good skiing on the key trails at the area.

Practical Information for Mont Tremblant

HOW TO GET THERE. Montreal is the gateway city to the Laurentians and Mont Tremblant. From Montreal by *car* take Laurentian Autoroute 15 to Ste Jovite. From there you'll see the mountain in the distance on your right, and the road is clearly marked. The *Voyageur Bus Line* also serves the Mont Tremblant region daily. For rates and schedule call 514–842–2281. The main Montreal bus terminal is downtown at 505 de Maisonneuve East. Voyageur also operates special day trips to the area.

TELEPHONES. The area code for Mont Tremblant is 819, and for Montreal it is 514.

ACCOMMODATIONS. *Mont Tremblant Reservations* is a central reservations center for hotels, chalets, and condominiums in the area. It represents 10 major hotels and 40 different private chalets and condominiums. For information, contact Mont Tremblant Reservations, P.O. Box 240, Mont Tremblant QE, J0T 1Z0; 819–425–8681.

Rates are per person, based on double occupancy, modified American Plan in Canadian dollars: Categories, determined by price, are: *Expensive,* $75 and up; *Moderate,* $45–$75; *Inexpensive* less, than $45. The mailing address for all is the same—Mont Tremblant QE, J0T 1Z0.

Mont Tremblant Lodge. *Expensive.* 425–8711; 514–861–6165 in Montreal, or 800–567–6761 from Quebec, Ontario, and the U.S. Part of the Mont Tremblant complex, this is the only slopeside accommodation. Four hundred rooms are available in your choice of French-Canadian chalets or condos. The lodge offers various package options.

Cuttle's Tremblant Club. *Moderate to Expensive.* 425-2731. A relaxed smaller lodge in the complex with accommodations in either rooms in the main lodge or adjacent condominium units. Two- and 5-day ski week packages including lessons with the hotel's own ski school. Overlooking Lake Tremblant, Cuttle's is renowned for its gourmet dining and cozy atmosphere; less than 3 miles from the mountain.

Hotel-Motel Villa Bellevue. *Moderate.* 425-2734 or 800-567-6763 from Quebec, Ontario, and the Maritimes. Located 3 miles from Mont Tremblant's south side, Villa Bellevue is one of the oldest inns of the region operating since the early 1920s. It offers 88 rooms in either hotel or motel units, or chalets. It is owned and has been operated by the Dubois family, a prominent and very sports active family in the region for three generations. Development director Luc Dubois coached the Canadian alpine ski team from 1971 to 1976 and during the year as many as 10 family members take part in making guests feel at home. Winter packages are 2 and 5 nights, MAP. Villa Bellevue operates its own ski school and free transportation to and from the mountain. Cross-country ski weeks are also offered.

Mandir Pinoteau. *Moderate.* 425-2795; 416-889-7531 in Toronto; 800-343-6768 in the U.S.; 800-322-5601 in Massachusetts. Overlooking Lake Tremblant, this rustic place has *the* view of Mont Tremblant, straight up the Flying Mile to the top of the mountain. You can chose accommodations in the inn *Le Manoir,* chalets, or condos. Packages include full ski weeks with the hotel's own ski school and transportation to and from the mountain only 5 minutes away.

Chateau Beauvallon. *Inexpensive.* 425-7275. Owned and operated by Judy and Alex Riddell, long-time skiers of Mont Tremblant, this is a ski lodge as it was meant to be. Originally an annex of Mont Tremblant Lodge, the 15-room chateau has maintained its original French-Canadian charm. Bar, dining room, and a cozy fireplace make it a place for those who prefer a more intimate atmosphere. Cash or personal checks. No cards.

Other accommodations in the region, all in the *Moderate–Inexpensive* range, include the following.

Auberge Sauvignon. 425-2658. Features one of the best tables in the region.

Chalet des Chutes. 425-2738. Motels and chalets less than a mile from the slopes.

Motel Mountain View. 425-3425. Few minutes drive from Mont Tremblant; 44 units.

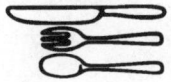 **RESTAURANTS.** Good food—French and French-Canadian cuisine—has been a drawing card for the area since its beginnings. Ski-week lodges generally offer excellent *table d'hote* fares with 4 or 5 choices daily and usually a once-a-week special buffet dinner. The area also offers a good selection of restaurants for all tastes Restaurant categories are: *Expensive,* $20 and up; *Moderate,* $10–$20; *Inexpensive,* less than $10. These prices are for one meal, exclusive of drinks, tips, and tax. Abbreviations for credit cars are A, American Express; M, MasterCard; V, Visa.

Auberge Sauvignon. *Expensive.* Mont Tremblant Village; 425-2658. Features steaks and seafood and is known as one of the finest eateries in the region. Reservations recommended. All major cards accepted.

Cafe de la Gare. *Moderate.* Located in Mont Tremblant Village; 425-3343. Serves hearty French-Canadian fare and excellent breakfast. V only.

Restaurant O Wok. *Moderate.* 878 Ouimet, St Jovite; 425-8442, does not serve Irish-Chinese cuisine as its name implies. If you are in the mood for excellent Chinese food O Wok is the only choice in the area. Typical Chinese decor. A, M, V.

Antipastos. *Inexpensive.* 444 St-Georges, St Jovite; 425-7580. Just off the main street is the region's best version of Italian cuisine. Pizza fresh from a brick oven is the specialty although the pasta dishes deserve special mention. M, V.

St Hubert Bar-B-Q. *Inexpensive.* 330 Ouimet, St Jovite; 425-2721. A must stop for out-of-province visitors not accustomed to the typically Quebecois barbecued chicken in special sauce. The restaurant is part of a chain with branches in other Canadian provinces as well as some states, including Florida. Good for the family. A, M, V.

HOW TO GET AROUND. Most lodges operate their own learn-to-ski weeks and their own ski school. As a result all have **shuttle** transportation to and from the mountain. Most accommodations serving Mont Tremblant are within 5 miles of the area and so are restaurants. **Car rental** is also available from *Location Jean Gagné*, 425–2767. Reserve well in advance because they have few cars. Getting around to other lodges, restaurants, or to go shopping in St Jovite is best done by **taxi**. Contact *Taxi Mont Tremblant,* 425–2153; *Taxi Central,* 425–5795; or *Taxi St Jovite,* 425–2153. The *Voyageur Bus* from Montreal to Mont Tremblant stops at several lodges and it is possible to hop a ride with them to St Jovite for less than a taxi. This is done only when space is available. Inquire with your lodge or hotel.

SEASONAL EVENTS. Standard races are open to all every Sunday. The *Easter Bonnet Parade* takes place on that holiday. *Annual Shovel and Tap-Q* race is on the last day of the season. This race features area employees, mainly liftees, who at days' end usually come back down sitting on their shovel or on a ski-bob-like home-made single-ski device called a "tap-Q," roughly translated: "bum-bruiser!"

OTHER SPORTS AND ACTIVITIES. **Cross-country** skiing is very popular in the area with two particularly interesting trail networks. *Mont Tremblant Provincial Park* offers free skiing on 77 km or 16 trails for all abilities. It is located near the north side base of the alpine ski area. From the south side base take the Devil's River Rd. to the north side. From there follow signs to Parc du Mont Tremblant. The St Jovite–Mont Tremblant trail network runs from St Jovite to Mont Tremblant and passes by most lodges and hotels. Trails are packed and track set by the *Club de Ski de Fond St Jovite-Mont Tremblant,* 425–5278, and access is free. Inquire at your lodge for closest starting point. **Telemark** programs are also available from *SkiTour in St Jovite;* 425–5278.

DAY-CARE FACILITIES. Located at the south side base next to the beginners' poma lift is the Mont Tremblant nursery and day care facility, *Les Tout P'tits,* where children 3 years and over can be left for several hours or a complete day. Children are taken outdoors to play in the snow—weather permitting—and children who can ski are taken on the adjacent poma-slope. Cost is $2.50 an hour per child. Lunch is available for $3 and a nap or quiet-time is encouraged after lunch. Further information at Mont Tremblant Lodge front desk, 425–8711.

NIGHTLIFE. Most lodges and hotels have bars where you can relax and kick up your feet by the fire after a hard day on the slopes or cross-country skiing. Many feature after-dinner entertainment by either a solo musician or a live band. At **slopeside,** *Mont Tremblant Express* is a train-shaped disco located in the Mont Tremblant Lodge featuring disco dancing from 9 P.M. to 3 A.M.

After skiing a favorite spot is the *Octogone* in the Chalet des Voyageurs at the bottom of the south side. Disco music videos on a giant screen all day and night except for supper hour from 6 to 9 P.M. A more relaxed place to kick up your heels after skiing is the *Catalogne Bar* located in the Mont Tremblant Lodge. Free appetizers from 4 to 7 P.M., giant screen TV for sporting events, and after 9 P.M. a musician provides live music. Call 425–8711 for any of the above.

The *Thirsty Eagle Bar* (425–2771) is in the main lodge at *Gray Rocks,* 4 miles from Mont Tremblant. This is one of the most popular of local bars and since Gray Rocks always packs a full house of about 450 to 500 guests, the place rocks and rolls to a live band from 3 P.M. to 3 A.M. with a break for dinner between 6 and 9 P.M.

La Musicale (425–2734) is the disco at Villa Bellevue, 3 miles from the mountain at Lac Ouimet, next to Gray Rocks. Live band 6 days a week and disco music daily.

If blending in with the locals is a higher priority for you try *Le Coin* at Hotel Mont Tremblant in Mont Tremblant Village; 425–3232. DJ-type disco operating every night from 10 P.M. to 3 A.M.

For a little more classical entertainment, *Manoir Pinoteau* (425–2795), just off Lake Tremblant, offers some live jazz Friday–Sunday evenings in its *Opera Jazz Bar*. They also have a concert piano standing by should Liberace decide to try his luck at a ski week. You can also hear local folk singer *chansonniers* in Pinoteau's *Le Petit Bar* upstairs.

Eastern Townships

Southeast of Montreal sits a region with a special heritage and some of the best skiing in Quebec. The Eastern Townships region is sandwiched between the St. Lawrence Valley and the U.S. border and that is what gives the region its cultural duality.

The region was settled jointly by French-speaking farmers and English United Empire Loyalists who came from the U.S. after the American Revolution. Today the Townships, as they are called, are a patchwork of distinctive French and English towns and villages.

Reading a map of Quebec, you might think you're in heaven with so many towns named after saints. But obviously the Eastern Townships were differently influenced. Names such as Abercorn, Knowlton, Mansonville, Eastman, and Ayer's Cliff underline an early English settlement. To this day you're likely to hear mostly English spoken in the streets and shops of Knowlton and Mansonville. On the other hand English and French are spoken equally by residents of Sherbrooke, Sutton, and Cowansville, while Bromont and Magog are more distinctively French. Although more international in scope, ski areas near those communities reflect the region's cultural heritage.

Though all areas are bilingual, the flavor at Mont Orford and Bromont is distinctly French, at Owl's Head and Glen Mountain it is English, with Sutton providing a more equal mix of French and English.

Compared to the Laurentians, skiing is a relatively new activity in the region. While there was skiing in the 1940s at Mont Orford, it was only in the early 1960s that skiing started to develop commercially with the opening of Mont Sutton with 7 trails on a 1,000-foot vertical drop served by a double chair and a T-bar. From that point the region was to develop to become one of the most important skiing regions of the province.

The topography of the Townships has its own peculiarities: 1,300-foot to 1,800-foot peaks that to stand alone are separated by wide valleys. This has an affect on local weather, which often produces large quantities of snow on the mountains while the towns and villages often receive much less. And that suits almost everyone.

Southeast from Montreal the region branches off Autoroute 10. The flatness of the St. Lawrence Valley extends to the foothills of the Townships region, which actually begins at Granby. Until that point there is little sign of any of the great skiing that lies ahead. But at a point shortly past Granby the peaks become visible and for awhile all five mountains can be seen at once—Bromont, Sutton, Glen, and Owl's Head lining up on the right, Mont Orford standing dead ahead in the distance. Each area is located within a 25-mile radius of Knowlton, the center point of the region, with the furthest distance about 40 miles from Sutton to Mont Orford.

In the 1960s an interchangeable ski lift ticket was created by Ski East, the marketing arm of the region. Today skiers purchasing ski week packages can ski at all four Ski East centers—Bromont, Sutton, Owl's Head, and Mont Orford. At one time Jay Peak, VT, which is just across the border from Owl's Head, was also part of the arrangement, but is no more. Jay Peak nonetheless is almost part of the Eastern Townships and considered by most Montrealers as a Montreal ski area. It is also an added skiing opportunity for someone vacationing in the Townships.

Unlike the Laurentians, which are purely a vacation and weekend chalet region, the Eastern Townships have more of a permanent population. There are farms from the minute you cross the St. Lawrence River at Montreal to the time you approach the ski areas. A few miles from the ski areas you'll begin seeing sparsely scattered chalets with condos developing more and more near the slopes. There are few large hotels and resorts but charming inns abound in the region.

While the Big Four Ski East areas are the most attractive for ski vacationers, two other areas of interest can provide an alternate on a busy weekend. Glen Mountain, located just southeast of Knowlton, is a good family area with 17 runs on a 1,050-foot vertical serviced by 5 lifts including a double chair. Skiing is on natural snow but the lack of heavy skier traffic makes skiing on the heaven-sent more often pleasant than not.

Located just minutes east of Granby is Mont Shefford, another low traffic, natural snow area with a 750-foot vertical and 12 runs served by 3 T-bars.

Alpine skiing has been the main star of the Eastern Townships' winter program but in the past decade four of the provinces best cross-country centers have been developed in the immediate vicinity of the major alpine areas. Sutton-en-Haut is near Sutton, Farmer's Rest between Sutton and Glen Mountain, Parc de la Yamaska is just East of Granby, and Mont Orford Park is at the foot of Mont Orford. These centers offer another option to skiing in the East and the versatile skier should pack skinny skis as well when heading for the Eastern Townships on a skiing vacation.

Contrary to other regions, the Eastern Townships of Quebec are still country. And that's part of the unique charm of the region.

BROMONT SKI CENTER

P.O. Box 29 Bromont QE J0E 1L0
Tel: 514–534–2200, 800–363–8920
  toll free from Montreal and
  area code 514

Snow Report: 514–534–2200
Area Vertical: 1,300 ft. (355 meters)
Number of Trails: 31
Lifts: 1 detachable quad chair,
  3 doubles, 2 T-bars, 1 Pony lift
Snowmaking: 18 trails
Season: late-November–mid-April

Developed in the early 1960s, Bromont has the highest vertical drop of any area close to Montreal: 1,300 feet. It is also one of the finest skiing mountains in the province for its size. The ratio of length of run per vertical foot of elevation is one of the best and could be compared to a smaller Mt. Mansfield at Stowe.

Bromont has come of age in the early 1980s, when newly appointed general manager Robert Desourdy, then 28 years old, literally launched the area into orbit. With all the natural elements in place to make the area successful—a good mountain and the proximity to a major market (Montreal with a population of 2.5 million)—the area was not, however, in the best possible snowbelt. Snowmaking became the first priority for Desourdy, who was quick to realize that "without the raw material—snow—you can't run a successful ski area."

Snowmaking now covers 18 of Bromont's 31 trails. This represents 82 percent of the skiing acreage and it won't be long until all trails are covered with machine-made snow.

Night skiing at Bromont is almost as popular as day skiing. You can purchase a night skiing ticket as early as 3 P.M., and on weekends you can go skiing until midnight. At one time night skiing at Bromont had been extended until 2 A.M., but that proved to be a little much. Not to say that it didn't work: in 1981 an all-night ski promotion called "La Grande Nuit Blanche" (the great white night) almost turned disastrously successful. Over 6,000 skiers managed to get to the area while another 4,000 had to be turned away. While management was somewhat embarrassed, at least 10,000 skiers knew that Bromont had installed lights for night skiing.

Bromont is just that kind of area: a happening place. And when they do something they do it big or they do it crazy. For example, don't be too frazzled if you're asked the right of way by a bed on skis. That'll be the day they have the annual Ski Bed Race. Every year local media members are teamed up with the various departments at Bromont (ski patrol, marketing, administration, etc.) for one of the whackiest off-the-wall events of the winter in the Eastern Townships. The race is run under a different theme every year and the sleds—beds—are lavishly decorated to fit the theme.

Bromont also hosted with much success and praise the 1986 Ski World Cup Finals and plans to make the area a regular venue of the annual White Circus.

In 1986 the area acquired a quadruple detachable chair lift which does wonders keeping lift lines moving at this very popular resort. Three more double chairs, two on Mont Brome, the larger mountain, and one on Mont Soleil, provide enough uphill capacity to handle all but the busiest spring weekends.

From the top of the mountain on a clear day you can see Montreal. Beginners will delight in the 2½-mile Brome trail, a wide, gentle, and scenic run which winds its way around the mountain. Even a more advanced skier will find it a perfect warm-up run. It is also lit for night skiing.

Intermediate skiers as well as experts will delight in one of the area's best cruisers—the Knowlton, a medium-wide steady pitch which has the quality of making you ski well.

An equally beautiful run for the more aggressive skier shoots from the top of the quad chair. The Waterloo is for advanced skiers and runs in a straight line with three or four good pitches along the way to wake you up. The Waterloo and Knowlton runs are exceptionally fine runs which would rate high on a list of top runs in the province.

One of Bromont's main qualities, however, is the desire to please its skiers. Arriving at the area, you get the feeling of being welcome; signs immediately say so! "Welcome to Bromont" written in a bubbly, fun style. There are few constraints at Bromont. Few signs saying "No poles," "No box lunches," "No checks," "No Fun!" Everything is planned to work. For example lift ticket prices vary with the hour of the day. You can chose from as many as 10 different price options depending on when you arrive and how long you wish to stay.

Bromont is the first ski area in Quebec to have become a four-season resort offering in the summertime golf, swimming, alpine and water slides, chairlift rides and picnics to the summit, conditioning and mountain bike trails, and a number of other activities.

Anyone visiting Bromont for any period of time will certainly succumb to the desire to try the "Super Glissade"—the Super Slide, on the golf course just before entering the alpine parking lot. For a small daily fee you can rent a jumbo inner-tube and tackle the 350-foot slope with reckless abandon. Try it at the end of your ski week however; Bromont's skiing is better than its tubing!

Bromont's proximity to Montreal, makes a trip to the Canadian metropolis a short hour's drive on the toll-free Eastern Townships Autoroute 10. It takes you over the Champlain Bridge and right into Montreal's busy downtown. While your ski vacation may be a break from it all if you've never visited the Paris of North America, dinner and an evening out in Montreal would certainly be a cultural plus to add to your stay in Quebec.

Practical Information for Bromont

HOW TO GET THERE. Montreal is the gateway to the Eastern Townships and Bromont for travelers arriving **by air** or traveling in from the west. Montreal's Dorval Airport is conveniently located on the Island of Montreal and is the most convenient of the city's two airports for travelers going to the Eastern Townships. Dorval Airport is also the main gateway for flights originating within North America. Only a few bargain rate airlines such as *People Express* and *Presidential Airways* operate service into Mirabel, Montreal's International Airport located north of Montreal at the foot of the Laurentian Mountains. Both Dorval and Mirabel offer a full slate of car rental companies including the big four: *Avis,* 800–331–1212; *Budget,* 800–527–0700; *Hertz,* 800–654–3131; and *Tilden,* the Canadian affiliate of *National,* 800–328–4567.

If you are particularly well-heeled, you can fly in with your private jet or prop plane. The *Aeroport Regional des Cantons de l'Est,* better known as Bromont Airport, is located only 6 km from the ski area. Full services, including UNICOM Radio, customs, regular and jet fuel, and maintainance are available between 6 A.M. and 9 P.M. as well as other hours by request. The 6,000-ft. runway is equipped for night landings, is accessible around the clock, 12 months a year and can handle aircrafts the size of a Challenger by *Canadair;* 534–2325.

By Car. From Montreal by automobile take Champlain Bridge across the St. Lawrence River. You will be heading east on Autoroute 10. At Exit 78 you have arrived; the mountain is right in front of you.

Coming from the U.S., there are various routes depending on your point of origin. From New York State and points west of Lake Champlain your best route is I–87 to Montreal, then Autoroute 10. From Connecticut, Massachusetts, Maine, New Hampshire, or Vermont, take I–91 which connects with Quebec Hwy. 33 and with Autoroute 10 at Magog, the easternmost point of the autoroute. From there, head west toward Montreal and take exit 78.

By bus. Regular daily bus service is also available from Montreal's Voyageur Terminal located at the intersection of Berri and DeMaisonneuve sts. Schedules may vary with time of year. For rates and schedules, call 842–2281.

TELEPHONES. The area code for Montreal and Bromont is 514.

ACCOMMODATIONS. Lodging prices in the Bromont area average about the same as at Mont Sutton, although there isn't as wide a selection. Rates are based on double occupancy. Categories, determined by price, are: *Expensive,* $50 and up; *Moderate,* $30–$50; *Inexpensive,* less than $30.

Auberge Bromont. *Moderate to Expensive.* P.O. Box 29; 534–2200. The main lodge locally; it is the best and the nearest to the area, less than a mile from the slopes. Located on the golf course adjacent to the mountain, this 55-room inn provides a peaceful get-away for both ski weekers and convention goers.

La Petite Auberge. *Inexpensive.* 360 Boulevard Pierre Laporte; 534–2707. The only other good lodging place, about 15 minutes from the ski center. It is small, however, with only 6 rooms, all with shower. The dining room features fine French cuisine, living-room type bar.

Outside the immediate Bromont region, the most convenient town is Granby, 12 miles east of the ski area. There you will find plenty of accommodations in the form of motels and hotels including **Le Castel de l'Estrie,** 378–9071; **Motel le Granbyen,** 378–8406; and Motel du Lac, 372–5930.

Travel a little farther for a little more distinguished lodging in the central part of the Eastern Townships. About 20 minutes away from the mountain you'll find Auberge Lac Brome in Foster, 243–5755 (see Mont Sutton section) and Auberge du Fenil in Eastman, 297–3367, ideally located for you to take full benefit of the interchangeability of your Ski East lift ticket which lets you ski at Bromont, Sutton, Mont Orford, or Owl's Head.

RESTAURANTS. While the immediate Bromont area offers a limited number of eateries, within a half-hour drive of the area can be found something to suit every taste, from Continental cuisine to nouvelle cuisine Quebecoise. In the sampling listed here, price classifications are based on the cost of an average dinner for one person, beverages and tip not included. *Expensive:* $15–$25; *Moderate:* $10–$15. All accept major credit cards.

Cote Jardin. *Moderate to Expensive.* In the resort's main lodge, Auberge Bromont; 534–5200. Among its many specialties are mussels prepared 16 different ways.

Le Castel de Brome. *Moderate.* 117 Boulevard Bromont; 534–3620. Specializes in fine Italian cuisine, including fetuccini Alfredo, mussels in a cream sauce, and seafood a l'Italienne.

La Maison de Chez Nous. *Moderate.* 847 Mountain Ave., in nearby Granby; 372–2991. Homey atmosphere; from 5 to 11 P.M. daily, except Mondays, it specializes in all-you-can-eat frogs legs and nouvelle cuisine Quebecoise, featuring duck, pheasant, rabbit, and other seasonal game dishes.

Viking Dining Room. *Moderate.* In Auberge Lac Brome, Hwy. 243, Foster, about a 20-minute drive; 243–5755. Features Scandinavian and French cuisine, including a local favorite, Lake Brome duck.

HOW TO GET AROUND. Bromont is a mountain on its own and it is strongly recommended that you use a **car** to get around. The Auberge Bromont is the nearest to the area, about one mile from the slopes. Getting to the village of Bromont and to the larger center of Granby requires wheels. **Car rental** companies are in Granby: *Hertz,* 378–8404; *Avis,* 378–9057; *Tilden,* 375–2818, and *Budget,* 378–4636. **Taxi** service is also available from *Taxi Bromont,* 534–3200.

OTHER SPORTS AND ACTIVITIES. Cross-country skiing is next after alpine skiing at Bromont, and if you're bunked in at the Auberge Bromont you can simply step out the front door onto the **cross-country** trails which begin on the golf course and extend beyond into the forest for 16 km of track-set skiing. A full service ski shop is available at the first tee.

NIGHTLIFE. Luckily Bromont's base lodge disco, *La Debarque,* 534–2200, is a humming place since there isn't much else around. However, you'll be kept on your toes with a good and steady turnover of people 7 days a week from 3 P.M. to the small hours of the night. Bars are people and La Debarque is sure to provide plenty of possibilities for encounters.

MONT ORFORD

P.O. Box 248
Magog QE J1X 3W8
Tel: 819-843-6548

Snow Report: 819-843-6548
Area Vertical: 1,640 ft.
(520 meters)
Number of Trails: 30
Lifts: 1 triple chair, 3
double chairs, 3 T-Bars,
1 Pony lift
Snowmaking: 12 trails
Season: late November–mid-
April

It is the oldest ski center in the Eastern Townships and yet in many ways the newest.

While they skied by snowcat in the 1930s and the first lift on Orford was erected in 1939, Mont Orford ski center would not be recognized by anyone who hadn't skied there since the mid 1970s.

The '70s were difficult times for the fourth largest mountain in the province. Ownership and management uncertainty made it a no-growth sleeping giant. But the 80s have seen the giant awakening and at mid-decade the area was enjoying its greatest boom ever. Skiers are rediscovering the *new* Orford and as a visitor you'll certainly be pleased with the current version.

Mont Orford is the lone peak in the region, thus affording from the top a magnificent view from all sides. The best view is unquestionably to the south—shooting down majestic Lake Memphremagog stretching 30 miles from Magog to Newport in Vermont. Conversely, in a drive to the area from Montreal or from the U.S. border, the icy white summit of Orford appears and disappears for miles around as you make your way through the scenic Townships hills.

The base installations at Orford are neatly nestled at the bottom of the bowl-shaped skiing facilities. One of the best base set-ups any ski area could ever hope for. Everything converges towards a practical and attractive pavillion and that makes it most convenient for rendezvous, pit stops, and the like.

The color of skiing changes from peak to peak. Orford is the main mountain with the most vertical, the most runs, the most lifts, and the most snowmaking. It has the most black trails—the most difficult. As ski areas are modernized, many trails in the East lose some difficulty when they are widened. But not at Orford. The main mountain has enough pitch that even the widening process has not killed the kick. And one trail is so steep and twisty that no one has yet dared climb it with an axe. It's the Contour, a trail you must avoid if you're a Floridian who's been convinced to take a learn-to-ski week. Modern teaching techniques cannot yet transform a beach bum into a mountain goat overnight.

Another good test for the advanced skier is the Maxi, which runs wide and mean right under the triple chair. It is unquestionably the area's best mogul run. Because of its width it is also safe enough for a good intermediate to handle. It provides that extra challenge we all need occasionally to improve our skiing skills. And if you feel real hot one of those days, try the Super just to the left of the Maxi under the summit double chair. It's usually difficult to ski at even the best of times.

Orford, as the main mountain is called, also has more gentle terrain. Intermediates will love the *Trois Ruisseaux,* a trail which, in the old days, crossed three creeks—hence its name—and was one of the toughest on the mountain. This is one trail which lost some punch as it was widened, straightened, and re-routed, but it has provided intermediate and advanced skiers with the area's most popular cruiser. If you're into long, carved turns, you'll also enjoy the Grande Coulee, a run which begins like a cross-country trail but eventually opens up into a good steady pitch.

The Tele-7 is a 4-km road which runs top-to-bottom on Orford, providing the beginner with the longest novice run on the mountain.

Mont Giroux is the smallest of the three peaks at Orford and it packs an odd assortment of trails. While most are easy, teaching slopes, there is this trail called *La 45.* The number refers to the slope's pitch, which may be slightly overstated but who cares? Ski it and you can claim you skied a 45° slope. Ski it and you'll probably believe it.

Mont Alfred Desrochers is the third and newest development at the area. It is named after a famous French Canadian poet who in the 1930s found much of his inspiration "in the shadow of Orford." Serviced by one double chair, it is the domain of the intermediate skier and an excellent shelter for anyone on those windy, cold days. Slopes are relatively narrow with the occasional dip forcing you to drive those knees a little more and carve that turn.

Because of Mont Orford's isolation, the very top of the mountain is often cold and windswept so no matter what time of year you should always come prepared with warm clothes.

Expansion plans are under way to increase snowmaking, develop the east side of Mont Giroux, and build a 30-unit ski-in, ski-out hotel.

Mont Orford's proximity to the town of Magog (5 miles) and to the popular summer attraction that is Lake Memphremagog gives it the best access to lodging and good restaurants of any ski resort in the Eastern Townships.

Practical Information for Mont Orford

HOW TO GET THERE. By air. Montreal is the gateway to the Eastern Townships and Mont Orford for travelers arriving by commercial airline or traveling in from the West. Montreal's Dorval Airport is conveniently located on the Island of Montreal and is the most convenient of the city's two airports for travelers going to the Eastern Townships. Dorval Airport is also the main gateway for flights originating within North America.

Only a few bargain rate airlines such as *People Express* and *Presidential Airways* operate service into Mirabel, Montreal's international airport, located north of Montreal at the foot of the Laurentian Mountains. Both Dorval and Mirabel offer a full slate of car rental companies, including *Avis,* 800–331–1212; *Budget,* 800–527–0700; *Hertz,* 800–654–3131; and *Tilden,* 800–328–4567. The Sherbrooke Airport, located approximately 30 miles from Magog, has a 5,000 ft. × 150 ft. runway and can accommodate any type of private aircraft, prop or jet. Flight services are available 24 hours a day; 819–832–2560.

From Montreal by **automobile** take the Champlain Bridge across the St. Lawrence River. You will be heading east on Autoroute 10 to Exit 115, a straight and easy 80-mile drive. At this point you're on the east shoulder of Mont Orford. Exit 115 takes you right to the mountain's base installations.

Coming from the U.S. by car, there are various routes depending on your point of origin. Any connection to I–91 will have you connecting with Quebec Hwy. 55 north and from there to Autoroute 10 west. Once on the autoroute at Magog, look for Exits 118 or 115, either one of which will take you to the mountain.

Regular daily **bus** service is also available from Montreal's *Voyageur Terminal* located at the intersection of Berri and DeMaisonneuve streets. Schedules may vary with time of year. For rates and schedules call 514–842–2281.

TELEPHONES. The area code for the Mont Orford region is 819, and for Montreal it is 514.

ACCOMMODATIONS. There is lodging for more than 4,000 people in the region and the *Mont Orford Reservation Bureau* can arrange your reservations or make suggestions. You can reach them by writing to Mont Orford Reservation Bureau, P.O. Box 248, Magog QE J1X 3W8; or calling 843–4200.

There are no *Expensive* ($65 and above) accommodations in the area although some suites at some of the *Moderate* ($40–$65) auberges can be considered relatively expensive. *Inexpensive* is less than $40.

Auberge Cheribourg. *Moderate to Expensive.* P.O. Box 336; 843–3313 or 800–567–6132 from Quebec, Ontario, and the Maritimes. One of the closest to the ski area, located on the mountain road—Cherry River Rd.—about 2 miles from the area. It offers 50 hotel rooms including 17 suites with fireplaces and 85 fully-equipped condos. The auberge features a highly rated dining room, a disco—*La Cerise* (the Cherry)—and a piano bar. Both the hotel and the surrounding condos have brightly colored orange metal roofs which make the place quite distinctive. In addition, the establishment is adjacent to Orford Provincial Park Cross-Country Center which features 42 km of meticulously maintained trails for all abilities. You can ski from the hotel to the park.

Auberge Estriemont. *Moderate to Expensive.* 44 Avenue de l'Auberge, Canton d'Orford QE J1X 3W7; 843–1616 or 800–567–3402 from Quebec, Ontario, and the Maritimes. A new complex which somewhat resembles the Cheribourg. It has 46 suite-type rooms, each equipped with a fireplace; 50 chalets with fireplace, fully equipped kitchen, dishwasher, color TV, are also available. Estriemont is also one of the few local hotels to offer a fitness center which includes squash and raquetball courts, weight room, sauna, and hot tub. There is also a 2-km cross-country trail right on the premises. The hotel has free mini-bus transport to and from the alpine or cross-country area.

O'Berge du Village. *Moderate to Expensive.* 261 Merry South, Magog; 843–6566 or 800–567–6089 from Quebec. Features fully-equipped condos, including fireplace and balcony overlooking Lake Memphremagog. Located about 10 minutes from Mont Orford, it also has saunas, whirlpool, and squash courts.

Auberge de l'Etoile. *Moderate.* 1133 Principale West, Magog; 843–6521. Has 26 motel-type rooms offering superior accommodations. All modern rooms have a view of Lake Memphremagog and cable color TV. There is also an excellent dining room featuring French cuisine.

Auberge Hatley. *Moderate.* P.O. 330 N. Hatley QE J0B 2C0; 842–2451. A romantic old country inn built in 1903, it has 22 rooms, some with fireplace and Jacuzzi and all furnished with old Quebec antiques. The dining room is rated Four Forks, the highest ranking of the Quebec Ministry of Tourism. It shares the same 100 km network of cross country trails with Auberge Ripplecove, and is about 20 minutes from Mont Orford.

Auberge Orford. *Moderate.* 20 Merry South, Magog; 843–9361. A friendly inn with 12 spacious and comfortable rooms with private bath. The dining room, complete with fireplace and antique furniture, features regional specialty Italian cuisine. Every meal at the Auberge is said to be an experience in fine dining. There is also a good after-ski bar *CLub Le Ski.*

Auberge Ripplecove. *Moderate.* P.O. Box 246, Ayer's Cliff QE J0B 1C0; 838–4296. On Lake Massawippi, equidistant from Mont Orford and the Vermont border, it offers a choice of 11 charming rooms furnished with antiques or 7 chalets and suites of 1, 2, or 3 bedrooms, many with fireplaces. The dining room boasts a gold medal at the Quebec Culinary Competition and is reputed for the excellence of its French menu. There are 100 km of cross-country skiing from the front door, sleigh rides, lighted skating rink, game rooms, ice fishing on the lake.

Hovey Manor. *Moderate.* P.O. Box 60, North Hatley QE J0B 2C0; 842–2421. Formerly a private estate modeled on the Virginia home of George Washington, Hovey Manor is alive with antiques and offers a refined, modern cuisine. Most of the 36 bedrooms face Lake Massawippi; many with fireplaces, 4-poster beds and whirlpool baths. Hovey Manor is located 20 minutes from Mont Orford.

Econ Auberge. *Inexpensive.* 100 Chemin de la Montagne, Cherry River QE J1X 3W3; 843–8887. Lodge located on the mountain road a little over a mile from the mountain; 42 rooms each equipped with kitchenette make it an affordable choice for a family. There is also transportation to and from the mountain available for a small fee.

RESTAURANTS. The Mont Orford-Magog region offers an excellent selection of restaurants, and within a 10-mile radius of the area, probably the best selection in the Eastern Townships. Restaurants are categorized on the basis of a full-course dinner for one, excluding drinks, tax, and tip: *Expensive*, $20 and more; *Moderate*, $10–$20; *Inexpensive*, less than $10. Credit card abbreviations are: A, American Express; M, MasterCard; E, En Route; and V, Visa.

Moderate–Expensive

Auberge Cheribourg. On the mountain road about 2 miles from the area; 843–3313. Offers excellent French cuisine, with all major credit cards accepted.

Auberge Estrimont. 44 avenue de l'Auberge; 843–1616, Offers traditional French cuisine prepared by chef Guy, a native of the Auvergnes region of France. *Table d'hôte* is the main attraction with a selection of four main dishes nightly. Pianist every night in the dining room. Reservations suggested on weekends. All major credit cards.

Chez Jean-Pierre. 112 rue Principale West, Magog; 843–8166. Features fine cuisine with a French touch. The *table d'hôte* menu is the main drawing card here offering appetizer, soup, and main course. Several dishes are *flambee* at your table including desserts like *crepes Suzette*. Decor is warm and classic with white and pink tablecloths and lots of brass. Reservations on weekends. A, E, V.

Le Melezes. In Eastman, 14 km northwest of Magog on Rte. 1; 297–3163. Fine cuisine, including rack of lamb cooked over maple embers. Service is usually *table d'hôte* which includes exceptionally fine home-made desserts such as chocolate cheesecake and homemade ice cream. Les Melezes also bakes its own bread. M, V.

Also found in this category are **Auberge de l'Etoile,** 1133 Principale West (843–6521), for fine French cuisine and **Le Moulin a Poivre** (843–4337), for fine Belgian cuisine.

Inexpensive–Moderate

Au Vieux Poele. Located on Rte. 2 (the mountain road) at the intersection of Autoroute 10, at exit 118; 843–6442. Specialties include different types of fondues—onion, mushroom, regular—and a good selection of brochettes. M, V.

La Bonne Bouffe. 233 Principale, Eastman; 514–297–2420. A small, intimate restaurant featuring fine French cuisine. Reservations are recommended since there are only 8 tables with a seating capacity of 30 people. House specialties include home-smoked trout, homemade pheasant paté, seafood platter *au gratin* and pepper steak, of which the owners are particularly proud. A, E, M,V.

Les Trois Marmittes, 475 Principale, Magog; 843–4448. A family restaurant you should keep high on your list if your family includes teenage boys with bottomless appetites. On Wednesdays, Fridays, and Saturdays it's all you can eat from a roast beef and salad bar, while on Thursdays you can indulge in your favorite Italian dishes—all you can eat Italian and salad bar. *Table d'hôte* specials are also included every night. A, M, V.

OTHER SPORTS AND ACTIVITIES. The other major sporting activity in the area is **cross-country skiing.** Mont Orford Provincial Park (843–6233) is located on the mountain road about 1 mile before arriving at the alpine area. It is the finest cross-country skiing facility in all of the Eastern Townships and features 42 km of well-groomed, double-tracked trails for all abilities. Skiing is free weekdays, while on weekends there is a small parking fee. A waxing room, warming huts, cafeteria, and ski patrol complete the center's offerings to the cross-country skier.

Skating is also available on Lake Memphremagog. A lighted skating oval is open whenever conditions permit through the winter months. Operated by the Magog Chamber of Commerce at no fee. Access to the skating area is by Hwy. 112 right across from Auberge de l'Etoile.

Snowmobiling. On the backside of Mont Orford sits the town of Valcourt, known as the birthplace of the **snowmobile.** This is the site of the Bombardier plant, 1 de la Montagne St., makers of Ski-Doo, the first snowmobiles produced for mass consumption. Here you can visit the plant and see how snowmobiles are produced. For guided tour information and reservations call 514–532–2211, ext. 226. While in Valcourt you must visit the J. Armand Bombardier Museum, 1000 J.A. Bombardier St. (514–532–2258), where you will discover that snowmobiles are almost as old as the automobile. Admission is free and the museum is open daily 1–4 P.M. You can also rent a snowmobile in the area from the Centre de la Motoneige de Valcour Inc., 9058 rue de la Montagne, 514–532–2262.

Ice Fishing. Every winter as soon as the ice is thick enough on Lake Memphremagog a village of wood-heated cabins is erected about 2,000 ft. off the north shore of the lake. Dress warmly and let yourself be taken to your rented cabin from which you can fish for trout, perch, bass, and pike. For information and reservations, call 843–8550 or 843–4322.

NIGHTLIFE. *La Grosse Pomme*—The Big Apple—270 Principale West, Magog (843–7205), is an entertainment complex of sorts with a cinema-bar featuring either two full-length movies, the Much Music Network, or sports on the giant screen. Disco with two dance floors, free admission, and free popcorn. You can also eat there between 11:30 A.M. and 9 P.M.–*bonne bouffe, pas cher* (good grub, cheap!), all in a bistro atmosphere. Clientele is generally 20–30 years of age.

La Lanterne, 70 du Lac, Magog (843–7205), is a popular spot since it is a multipurpose apres-ski bar, restaurant, and disco. Technically you could crawl into La Lanterne after the lifts close and leave there after the last call and all your needs would be taken care of. Clientele generally 25–45 years of age. The place is open Thursdays–Sundays only.

Chez Rene, 66 Meadow, Sherbrooke (565–8744), is a well-established disco-cruising bar. It can accommodate about 350 people, has a large dance floor with wood, brass, and neon decor. If you don't like the music or need a break, try the game room where you can unwind at the soccer table, the video games, or the pinball machines. General clientele 20–35 years of age.

Chez Josephine in Sherbrooke at the Le Baron Motel, 3200 King West; (567–3941) offers live bands in its cabaret every night except Sundays. There is no cover charge. Also worth visiting are *La Cerise* (The Cherry) at the Cheribourg Hotel on the mountain road (see Accommodations) and *Le Coup de Foudre,* 380 King W., Sherbrooke (567–5713), a recently opened bar, restaurant, and disco which appeals to the 25-and-over crowd.

Culture. During the winter months the University of *Sherbrooke Cultural Center* offers a variety of quality entertainment including plays, jazz, and ballet. For information call 821–7744.

MONT SUTTON

P.O. Box 280, Sutton QE J0E 2K0
Tel: 514–538–2338, 866–5156

Snow Report: 514–866–7718, 866–7639
Area vertical: 1500 ft. (460 meters)
Number of trails: 31
Lifts: 1 detachable quad, 5 double chairs, one T-bar, one Poma
Snowmaking: 60 percent of terrain
Season: late November–mid April

The first commercial area in the Townships, Sutton was developed in 1960 by the Boulanger family, who still run it today. Until recently the popularity of Sutton was based strictly on skiing—very good skiing. When you skied at Sutton, you skied there for the slopes, the vertical, the snow. A sort of Alta of Eastern Canada.

The variety of trails at Sutton is unparalleled in the East. There are 31 distinctive runs cut on the 1,500-foot vertical, but the number of ways down is practically unlimited. What makes this possible is Sutton's *Sous-bois,* the French word for glades. About 40 percent of Sutton's skiable acreage is made up of glades and that's what has made Sutton so popular with skiers from all over the Northeast.

Sutton is one of the East's busiest ski areas. Arrive early in the morning for the most convenient parking spot. From the parking lot you see little of Sutton's skiing.

The mountain is essentially divided into three sections. The main access to skiing is from the newly installed quadruple detachable chair which takes skiers to the main staging area, Top of Two. This refers to the lift number. There you'll also find a 120-seat chalet with sun-deck where you can enjoy the scenic view, the sun, and special mid-mountain *Quebecois* lunches.

From this mid-mountain plateau skiers can go three ways. Back down underneath and around the quad chair known as No. 2 area. This section provides mostly intermediate terrain. The lift-line run Sutton-ik is the toughest in the No. 2 area, a wide, intermediate trail. No. 2 can also offer you your first *sous-bois* test on a gentle intermediate glade known as *Sous-bois 2* and particularly enjoyable with a few inches of fresh powder.

Heading west from the mid-station, you head down toward beginner country also referred to as No. 1. Two double chairs serve another 10 trails for beginners and low intermediates.

Heading east and down from the mid-station, skiers enter Sutton's most advanced and exciting terrain served by the Nos. 4 and 5 double chairs and a poma lift. These lifts add another 500 vertical feet of skiing on mostly advanced terrain. And while there are easy ways down from this area, it is frequented mostly by the better skiers who can take advantage of superb glades and wild skiing to be found among the coniferous and twisted deciduous trees dwarfed by the altitude.

From the Top of Four you can catch a glimpse of Roundtop, the highest point on Sutton's range located just behind chair No. 4's summit terminal. With a top elevation of 968 meters (almost 3,200 feet) it is the focus of future development plans for the area.

Firm believers in natural snow, Sutton has succumbed to a few bad snow years and embarked on a major snowmaking program which has now weatherproofed 60 percent of the area. And since 1985 a program of lift and grooming equipment improvement has been underway to round off the area where skiing has in the past been everything.

There is no better testimonial for Sutton's quality of skiing than the faithfulness of its clientele: *Les gens de Sutton* (the Sutton Crowd). They are distinctively Sutton. It is a regular occurrence to meet skiers who have been there since the opening in 1960. To lure away the more than 2,000 season's pass holders is as difficult as getting a cat to do tricks. Much of this following is due to the fact that since 1960 Sutton has been developed and operated by a single owner, largely responsible for creating the very special atmosphere which has made Sutton one of the province's most successful ski centers.

Practical Information for Mont Sutton

 **HOW TO GET THERE.** Montreal is the gateway to the Eastern Townships and Sutton for travelers arriving **by air** or traveling in from the West. Montreal's Dorval Airport is conveniently located on the Island of Montreal and is the most convenient of the city's two airports for travelers going to the Eastern Townships. Dorval Airport is also the main gateway for flights originating within North America. Only a few bargain rate airlines such as *People*

Express and *Presidential Airways* operate service into Mirabel, Montreal's International Airport located north of Montreal at the foot of the Laurentian Mountains.

Both Dorval and Mirabel offer a full slate of car rental companies including the big four: *Avis*, 800–331–1212; *Budget*, 800–527–0700; *Hertz*, 800–654–3131; and *Tilden*, the Canadian affiliate of *National*, 800–328–4567.

From Montreal **by automobile** take Champlain Bridge across the St. Lawrence River. You will be heading east on Autoroute 10. At exit 68 take Hwy. 139 south to Sutton. Soon the northern edge of the Appalachian mountain range will appear before your eyes. Past Cowansville the road slaloms through magnificent vistas: you're almost there.

From the U.S., there are various routes depending on your point of origin. From New York and points west of Lake Champlain your best route is to travel to Montreal on I–87 which connects at Montreal's Champlain Bridge with Eastern Townships Autoroute 10. From Connecticut, Massachusetts, Maine, New Hampshire, or Vermont, take I–91 which connects with Eastern Townships Autoroute 10 at Magog, the easternmost point of the autoroute. From there head west toward Montreal and take exit 68.

Regular daily **bus** service is also available from Montreal's Voyageur Terminal located at the intersection of Berri and DeMaisonneuve streets. Schedules may vary with time of year. For rates and schedules, call 842–2281.

TELEPHONES: The area code for this section of Quebec is 514.

 **ACCOMMODATIONS.** Reservations and information on available accommodations can be obtained by contacting the Sutton Tourist Association, Sutton QE, J0E 2K0; 538–2538 or 538–2646. Condominiums, both slopeside and away from the mountain, offer a wide variety of choices in prices, depending on the size of the units and the packages. A studio condo, for instance, can start at $450 for 7 nights, while other units may cost $150 a night but can accommodate up to 6 people. In this listing, costs are estimated on what one person will pay per day. *Expensive:* $60 and up; *Moderate:* $30–$60; *Inexpensive:* less than $30.

AT THE SLOPES

Village Archimede. *Inexpensive to Moderate.* P.O. Box 600; 538–3440 or 538–3213. Sutton's slopeside condominium complex looks like it was conceived somewhere in outer space. Residence/hotel fully equipped; 40 units within walking distance of the lifts, 8 with full bathroom, 32 with shower only. Color TV in rooms; fireplace and/or sauna in some units; breakfast and dinner available at La Paimpolaise with a supplement.

La Paimpolaise. *Inexpensive.* P.O. Box 548; 538–3213. Located just below Sutton's chair No. 1. A small inn with plenty of atmosphere, it has 28 rooms with 2 double beds and one suite. All rooms with full bath and color TV. Because of its location, La Paimpolaise is also a very popular après-ski bar and has genuine French cuisine. Five-night package includes breakfast and dinner with wine.

IN THE AREA

Loft Acres. *Moderate to Expensive.* Hwy. 139, West Brome, J0E 2P0; 263–3294. Although it is located farther from the hills, this modern condo-hotel complex is sure to delight the most discriminating traveler. Located on an old farm the inn combines the ambience of a country inn with the comforts of more modern facilities. Sauna and hot tub, game room, bar, dining room, and 25 miles of cross-country skiing on a 200-acre farm. Accommodations in the inn are inexpensive while condos are moderate to expensive.

Auberge Lac Brome. *Moderate.* 400 Lakeside Rd., Foster, J0E 1R0; 243–5755. Located on the shores of Lake Brome in the heart of the Ski East region, Auberge Lac Brome is one of the region's finest country inns. From there you can use your Ski East interchangeable ticket to the maximum. All of the Ski East centers are no farther than 25 miles. Closest is Glen Mt., only 5 miles away. Scandinavian and French influence ensure fine dining in the Viking Dining

Room. Cross-country skiing on property. Indoor tennis and racquet club nearby.

Auberge De Sutton. *Moderate.* Rte. 139, about 6 miles from the mountain. P.O. Box 340, Sutton, J0E 2K0; 538–2324. Pleasant accommodation with good family atmosphere.

Hotel Horizon. *Inexpensive.* Mountain Rd., Sutton, J0E 2K0; 538–3212. Hotel-motel with spacious, modern rooms; has heated indoor swimming pool. Located about 1 mile from the alpine ski area, the Horizon can also offer cross-country skiing at adjacent Sutton-en-Haut center which has 40 km of well-groomed trails.

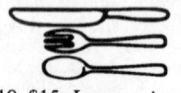 **RESTAURANTS.** The Sutton area has a number of excellent restaurants with a wide variety of menus, from French cuisine to Canadian standard. In this selection, *Expensive* is considered between $15 and $25; *Moderate,* $10–$15; *Inexpensive,* less than $10. These prices are for the average cost of a full-course meal for one person, excluding drinks, tip, and tax. Abbreviations for credit cards are A, American Express; M, MasterCard; V, Visa.

Auberge A La Fontaine. *Moderate to Expensive.* 30 Principale, Sutton; 538–3045. Located in a 150-year-old house with a renovated glassed-in section. Split-level dining room with lots of plants and an interesting French menu; open 7 days a week. AE, M, V.

Santiago. *Moderate to Expensive.* 29 Principale, Sutton; 538–2660. Features Franco-Spanish cuisine. Owners Jacques and Paule Conessa have a background that reflects what they serve. Locally raised fresh lamb and veal prepared "a la francaise" with Spanish style seafood and paella occasionally spiced with a touch of North African zest. Jacques is Spanish but was raised in Cuba, and Paule is half Swiss–half French and spent a good part of her life in Algeria. V.

Auberge Glen Sutton. *Moderate.* Glen Sutton; 538–2000. Mexican cuisine with excellent tacos, enchiladas, nachos, and burritos in a most unlikely spot, right behind Mont Sutton, equidistant from Owl's Head and Jay Peak and right on the Canada–U.S. border. It's the only Mexican restaurant in the region and well worth a 15-minute drive. M, V.

L'Auberge Le Refuge. *Moderate.* 33 Maple St., Sutton; 538–3802. Frenchman Patrice Falluel makes special crepes with seafood, snails, mushrooms provencale, scampi flambe au Ricard, and a chicken and pork brochette served with fruit. Open 7 days a week. AE, M, V.

Cafe Mocador. *Moderate.* 17 Principale, Sutton; 538–2426. French cuisine cooked by a Belgian chef. Full lunches and dinners, 7 days a week. Ask about their fine cuisine section for extra delicate dining; daily specials. A, M, V.

The Loft. *Moderate.* Hwy. 139 south, 5 miles from Sutton; 263–3294. Can't be beat for barbecued spare ribs, beef on a spit, and steaks. The focal point of the dining room is an open barbecue where you can see your order being prepared. Every day owners Rob and Dorothee Newcombe cook 100 lbs. of short hip of beef on an open pit outside for roast beef aficionados. AE, M, V.

Camille's. *Inexpensive.* In Hotel Camille on Principale St., Sutton; 538–2456. Family oriented and offers a standard Canadian fare of chicken, pizzas, brochettes, steaks, and sandwiches. M, V.

 **HOW TO GET AROUND.** The village of Sutton is 4 miles from the mountain. Most accommodations are either in the village or along mountain road. Many lodges have their own **shuttle vans** to take skiers to and from the mountain. In addition, the colorful *Sutton Shuttle* insures regular transportation from the village and the various inns and lodges to the mountain daily. Inquire at your lodge for schedule.

 OTHER SPORTS AND ACTIVITIES. The Sutton area offers some excellent **cross-country skiing** facilities. Less than a mile before reaching the alpine area on the mountain road is *Pistes D & M* (538–2271) also known as Sutton-en-Haut. The area offers 40 km of double-tracked trails through scenic forests running off the west shoulder of the alpine area. There are two warming huts and a waxing room, and the owners, Daniel Depelteau and Serge Menard, will do almost anything to make your visit enjoyable. Hit them on a klyster day and they will apply and remove the mucky stuff for you. Their philosophy is that klyster works wonders *under* your skis but is deadly on your hands and clothes. Since they don't mind getting their hands dirty you can better enjoy their good skiing.

An equally excellent facility is *The Farmer's Rest* located in Knowlton on the Mont Echo Rd.; 243–6843. There you'll find 50 km of track-set trails offering 10 different one-way runs for beginner and advanced skiers alike. A good base chalet with solid down-home cooking, a waxing room and a well-stocked ski and rental shop and two heated huts make it one of the favorite touring centers in the region.

The *Sutton Curling Club* (538–3225) is located at the corner of Pleasant and Academy in the village. It has two rinks and is open most nights and some afternoons.

The *Cowansville Cultural Center* (263–4311) and *Sports Pavilion* (263–4020) are located in the region's main town, Cowansville, which has a population of 12,000. They are at the Municipal Educational Complex , corner of Hwys. 139 and 104. The center has a 25-m indoor **swimming pool**, a large gym for **volleyball, basketball, badminton,** and **indoor running.** The adjacent Sports Pavilion has a **skating rink** which is open to free skating on weekends.

CHILD-CARE SERVICES. Right at the ski area on the upper level of the base pavilion is *La Garderie de Tante Lucille,* founded when the area opened in 1960 by Lucille Boulanger, wife of the late prime mover of the area, Real Boulanger. Since loyalty is one of the trademarks of the Sutton skier, many having been season's pass holders since 1960, many of the young adults now patronizing Sutton spent many a diaper day there, raised, so to speak, by Tante Lucille. Open 7 days a week from 9 A.M. to 4 P.M., La Garderie takes children 2 to 6 years old. You can check your child in by the hour, the half day, or the full day at rates comparable to regular babysitting. For information or reservations, call the main lodge at 538–2338 or 866–7639.

NIGHTLIFE. *La Pimpolaise* just at the entrance to Mont Sutton ski area (538–3213) is a favorite après-ski spot along with the disco at *Hotel Horizon* (538–3212), 1 mile from the ski area on the mountain road where the action really steps up in the evening; DJ-operated disco with dancing. *The Loft* on Hwy. 139 (243–5755) has a couple of popular bars. At the Club Bar you can relax at the fireplace listening to a folksinger Wednesday, Friday, and Saturday nights. Downstairs the disco offers continuous DJ-operated dance music to help you work out those muscles unaffected by skiing. Another popular spot is *Bri's Disco,* 418 Maple St., Sutton (538–2845), where you can shake off a few extra calories after dining at their excellent steak house.

OTHER EASTERN TOWNSHIP SKI AREAS

Your ski vacation in the Eastern Townships includes an interchangeable lift ticket valid at Bromont, Sutton, Mont Orford, and Owl's Head.

GLEN MOUNTAIN. P.O. Box 248, Lac Brome QE J0E 1V0; 514–243–6142.

Located off Hwy. 243, Glen Mountain is the family area of the Eastern Townships region, but with a 1,060-foot vertical it would be the envy of many other regions.

Somewhat belittled by the larger Eastern Townships centers, it is not a member of the Ski East group and therefore not on the interchangeable ticket.

The area has 11 trails offering all skiing conditions with some interesting terrain. As it should, steep trails are on the upper mountain with beginners' terrain at the bottom.

The area has one double chair and three T-bars but no snowmaking. However, skier traffic is very light most of the time and for that reason trails hold up reasonably well on natural snow alone.

OWL'S HEAD. Mansonville QE J0E 1X0; 819–292–5592 or Montreal direct 514–878–1453.

Although Owl's Head lacks nearby accommodations, this ski area is nonetheless worth experiencing on your interchangeable Ski East lift ticket. With a 1,770-foot rise, Owl's Head has the third highest vertical in Quebec. It has 6 double chairs and 19 trails.

Access to Owl's Head is not easy. Eleven km out of Mansonville on roller coaster roads is what keeps the area less busy than most other Township centers. Eastern Township's Hwy. 243 takes you to Mansonville and from there to Owl's Head.

It is more of a folksy area where the owner sometimes hands you the chair and the staff will answer the business line with a simple but friendly "hello" which can often make you wonder if you dialed a wrong number.

The area is located at the southwestern extremity of Lake Memphremagog right alongside the Canada–U.S. border. The original section of the mountain, developed in 1965–66, is on a fairly steep eastern exposure, giving one a clear day one of skiing's most spectacular views, along scenic Lake Memphremagog.

Many trails off the main peak have a difficulty level comparable to the Mont Tremblant of the early 1970s. Narrow trails snake their way down mostly advanced intermediate and expert terrain. Rough, steep liftlines, often barely covered, offer more "macho" skiing per acre than most other Townships areas.

The newer section, which includes the Lake Chair and two others, is more contemporary in design with wider, gentler trails serving the less experienced skier.

Snowmaking covers about 80 percent of the skiing terrain and the area was the recipient of the 1985 Award of Excellence for the best improvement in ski conditions that year. The award was given by The MRG Ski Network, Quebec's most important ski and snow reporting organization.

Quebec City Region

Along with Salt Lake City, Utah, Quebec City rates as one of North America's two largest ski towns.

Indeed, all skiing in the Quebec City region is within 30–45 minutes of the city center. When Mont Ste Anne opened in 1965, it was felt that the 30-mile drive would spell doom for the new resort.

Skiing in Quebec City started in the 1930s at Lac Beauport, just 15 minutes north of the city, and that's where all Quebecers learned to ski. Two ski areas, Mont St Castin-les-Neiges and Le Relais are now well established on the perimeter of the popular lake which has over the years been one of the main year-round playgrounds for Quebec residents.

Just 20 minutes north of Quebec City and only about 5 minutes past Lac Beauport lies Quebec's mid-range ski area, Stoneham, a 1,250-foot vertical, 15 run, aggressively developed mountain which can offer Mont Ste Anne its only competition.

So well within an hour's drive Quebecers have a choice of family skiing at Lac Beauport; big mountain, resort skiing at Mont Ste Anne; or a happy compromise at Stoneham.

But more important than the proximity of skiing in Quebec is the flavor of the 350-year-old town which was founded in 1608 by Samuel de Champlain. It is unquestionably a jewel of North America, the cradle of French civilization in the New World, and the only true French city of its size on the continent—Montreal being much more cosmopolitan.

While English is spoken here in most key areas when necessary, French more than any other language and more than in any other city is dominant. Ninety-six percent of the half-million people speak French. There is no second language in Quebec and that's what makes Quebec different from the rest of the continent. And while the province is French speaking generally, nowhere is the flavor felt more intensely than in Quebec City. Quebecers even have their own accent.

The focal point of Quebec is the Old Town dating back to the seventeenth century and the only walled city north of Mexico. Dominated by the Chateau Frontenac, a castle-like hotel built in 1892 by the Canadian Pacific Railway and still owned by the hotel arm of the company, CP Hotels, the Old Town is a treasury of history, with cobblestone streets, fine restaurants, guest houses, museums, and other attractions.

For many people, Quebec City is winter. This is one major city where snow has always been a fact of life and the population has learned to deal with it. It is indeed through the winter months that Quebec's *joie de vivre* reaches its climax as the city hosts its annual Winter Carnival. For 10 days each February the city—particularly the Old Town—becomes a sort of snowy Disneyland and all Quebecers are children again. Parades trumpet through the streets and some brave souls from all over North America show up for the annual International Canoe Race across the icy, 2-mile wide St. Lawrence River, facing up to 6-knot tidal currents, while thousands watch in awe from the cold shoreline.

Skiing in the Quebec City region offers the visitor the choice of either staying "in town" and enjoying the excitement of a moderate sized city to the fullest or staying at the areas with the option of an easy 15- to 45-minute drive to Quebec City for more excitement as desired. The choice is yours to make and to enjoy.

MONT STE ANNE

P.O. Box 400 Beaupre QE G0A 1E0
Tel: 418–827–4561

Snow Report: Quebec City, 418–827–4579
Montreal, 514–861–6670
Toronto, 416–482–1796
Area Vertical: 2,050 ft.
(625 m)
Number of Trails: 35
Lifts: 14, 1 gondola, 2
quadruple chairs, 1
triple chair, 3 double chairs, 3
T-bars, 3 Poma lifts,
1 pony lift
Snowmaking: 85 percent of area
(25 of 30 trails)
Season: mid-November–early May

Ste Anne de Beaupre, just 25 miles (40 km) east of Quebec City, has long been the "miracle capital" of North America, but over the past 25 years a new industry has been bringing more "manna" to the region: skiing.

With a 2,050-foot vertical drop, Mont Ste Anne is the largest skiable mountain in eastern Canada and the second most popular ski area in the country, just behind the Whistler-Blackcomb complex in British Columbia in terms of skier-days.

Ste Anne is somewhat of a late bloomer in terms of large, destination ski resorts in Quebec. Although it has been in operation since 1965 and skiing on the mountain without lifts goes back to the mid-40s, it is only since 1982 that it has started drawing more international attention.

While it has hosted several World Cup events since 1969, the area survived for 18 years with natural snow, abundant enough, particularly on the north slopes. But the snow drought that rocked Eastern ski areas in the early 1980s was to be the turning point for Mont Ste Anne. While Ste Anne cured the sick and the injured, she unfortunately could not make it snow on the mountain. The area quickly realized the problem and a high-tech snowmaking system was installed to cover 82 percent of the mountain, now extended to 85 percent.

With 35 trails on three facings, eastern Canada's only gondola lift, 6 chairlifts, including one detachable quad, and 7 other lifts, Mont Ste Anne is the showcase of Quebec skiing.

Like Whiteface in upstate New York, Mont Ste Anne is government owned and operated. It is felt by many a regular Ste Anne skier that if the government would be as good at minding the provincial coffers as it has been at operating the ski area Quebecers would be the fat cats of North America.

True, the area was long subsidized by the people, but it is now on its own feet. And while it certainly is not as lean as private areas in staff, with the government involved some benefits run down to the skier.

Prices, for example, are not the highest in the province despite the area being the biggest and the best. Signage and safety precautions are unparalleled in the province. Trails are seldom open prematurely and are often closed by midday if conditions deteriorate. Snow reports are dependable, which is a rare occurrence.

Grooming is also tops in the province in terms of large areas. Every night groomers tackle the mountain, leveling, resurfacing, and packing as many as 25 of the 35 runs. And while snowmaking is still a fairly recent art for Quebec's largest, it has already proven its will to produce and skills to make good snow. In the past season the area closed in early May with south side trails still skiable in late April.

Mont Ste Anne is an oddly shaped mountain. It has the shape of a sleeping bear; flat-topped, a stand-alone mountain wider than it is high and skiable on 300 degrees. On approach the area does not appear to have over 2,000 ft. of vertical. But as you stare attentively at the two straight chutes on the left of the gondola line and see that those tiny black specks are skiers grinding their way down, you suddenly become a little more respectful of the mountain's size.

But while your attention keeps drifting back to those monster tracks —they're not quite as mean as they look—there's more good cruising terrain for all abilities at Ste Anne than straight gut-wrenching drops. In fact the area's extensive grooming and snowmaking has opened up just about all trails to a good intermediate.

Mont Ste Anne is easy enough to get around and to understand. On the south side everything left of the gondola is most difficult terrain with trails becoming easier and longer the farther right you go. But stay alert while exploring the region as two mean traps await the unwary: a section of *dolce vita* turns into "unlucky" 13 and blue 4 into black 4 also known as "The Wall." Both are easily avoided but "The Wall" in particular could be a little distressing if it's been awhile since your last parachute jump.

Intermediate skiers as well as those who like good cruising will find their best pickings on the north and west sides each with just over 1,000 ft. of vertical. The latter for good intermediate skiers and up is, however, a bit short on uphill capacity serviced only by a T-bar. But it holds good future potential for expert skiers.

Beginner and novice country is mostly on the lower south and the upper right side shoulder of the mountain which is well serviced by two comfortable quadruple chairs, one of which is detachable, the latest in lift technology.

In the morning advanced skiers race to the south-side triple chair that services all of the south side's advanced runs. For openers trails 1 *(La Crete)* and 1–B *(L'Espoir)* when they have been freshly groomed are ideal warm-up runs. Although rated black, they are wide and usually kept smooth. If not groomed, however, look to something blue. The top of 1–B offers a breathtaking view of the surroundings, west to Quebec City and east down the wide and mighty St. Lawrence River to Ile-aux-Coudres, where fresh water turns to salt.

By the time you ski both those runs, each about a mile long, you'll probably have made enough turns to tackle your next challenge—2–A or 2–B, the area's toughest snowmaking serviced trails. Identical twins, the area differentiates them with grooming. And that separates the grown-ups from the kids. One is a rodeo trail with moguls that sometimes reach the size of a Volkswagen Beetle; the other, a steep but smooth drop which offers a tempting challenge to the strong intermediate skier and the challenge to ski it nonstop top-to-bottom for a good, strong expert.

Underneath the gondola lift is *La Gondoleuse,* another tough expert run made even tougher by the fact that it does not have snowmaking, which will remind you of what skiing was like "in the old days"!

For obvious reasons the north side staring out at Quebec's wilderness is often colder but also more powdery. So when the shell begins to pop up on the south, head for the north and you'll often be surprised at the quality of the snow awaiting you.

Night skiing is the latest addition to Mont Ste Anne's south side. In its first phase two trails are lit, including the 2-mile-long Pichard and a combination of two others to provide advanced and intermediate skiers their chance to ski under the lights.

Whatever your skiing ability you'll find a lot of what you like at Mont Ste Anne.

And quite important in the successful operation of any ski area is a staff which has been there for a long time, knows the mountain and how to deal with it and knows what skiers, regulars and visitors want from their mountain.

Since 1960 Mont Ste Anne has had only two area managers. The mountain manager—in charge of grooming operations—has been there since 1968; the ski school director, John Barclay, since 1969, and many other support staff there since opening day.

And chances are you'll look forward to returning time and time again.

Practical Information for Mont Ste Anne

HOW TO GET THERE. Quebec City is, of course, the gateway city to the Mont Ste Anne region. **By air.** Both *Air Canada* and *Quebecair* fly into Quebec's Loretteville Airport several times a day connecting with Montreal International and from there to the rest of the world. Major car rental companies are on site at the airport and you can reserve a car from wherever you are through *Avis* (800–331–1212), *Budget* (800–527–0700), *Hertz* (800–654–3131), or *Tilden,* which is the Canadian agency for *National* (800–328–4567). Transfer from the airport otherwise by taxi or by bus, stopping at the major hotels.

By car. From points west of Quebec you must first reach Montreal. From there take either Hwy. 20 to Quebec on the south shore of the St. Lawrence or Hwy. 40 on the north shore. From the U.S., both I–87 and I–89 will take you to Montreal. Coming from eastern New England on I–91, you can avoid Montreal by taking Hwy. 55 toward Sherbrooke and Drummondville and from there onto Hwy. 20 toward Quebec City.

From Quebec City, arriving from either the north or south shores, take *Autoroute de la Capitale*—the continuation of Hwy. 40 toward Beaupre. This autoroute bypasses Quebec City slightly to the north and will take you right to Beaupre. From there follow the signs to the area.

From the city center you'll easily find Autoroute 440 which connects with Hwy. 40 and eventually reaches Beaupre.

The 25-mile drive to Beaupre from Quebec City is mostly on a four-lane undivided highway which passes several villages along the way. Traffic is fast, particularly on weekends. Beware of unmarked police patrols and don't get your first heart attack between L'Ange-Gardien and Chateau Richer where overhead sensor lights on the highway begin flashing when you exceed the speed limit of 90 km/h (about 55 mph).

TELEPHONES. The area code for Mont Ste Anne and the city of Quebec is 418.

ACCOMMODATIONS. As stated elsewhere, you have the choice of either staying in Quebec City and driving the 25 miles daily to Mont Ste Anne or staying in the vicinity of the mountain. Of course, being the tourist attraction that it is, Quebec City has a wealth of accommodations of all types and for every purse. Listed here is but a selection. If you're going to stay in Quebec—as many skiers do—you'll be wise staying in or near the Old Town for its accessibility to the mountain. Otherwise, Mont Ste Anne should be your operating base.

Hotel rates listed here are per person, based on double occupancy. Categories, determined by price, are: *Expensive,* $50 and up; *Moderate,* $40–$50; *Inexpensive,* $25–$40. Most accept major credit cards. Those that do not are so indicated.

MONT STE ANNE AND VICINITY

Moderate to Expensive

Chalets Mont Ste Anne. P.O. Box 288; 827–3944, or 800–463–4395 in eastern Canada. Condominium rental complex nearest to the mountain. Offers completely furnished units with 2–5 bedrooms. All units have cable TV, fireplace, and kitchen; some have hot tub or sauna.

Le Chateau Mont Ste Anne. 500 Blvd. Beau-Pre; 827–5211 or 800–463–4467 in eastern Canada. Located next to the chalets. Its 258 luxurious rooms are very large and have kitchenettes. Ski week and weekend packages available. An urban accommodation slopeside with piano bar, disco, and good après-ski action.

Moderate

Chalets Hobec. 300 rue Dupont; 827–3767. At the foot of Mont Ste Anne, only 2 km from the lifts. Two-storied, 2-bedroom chalets sleeping a maximum of 6 people; all units have fireplace, cable TV, large living room, and complete kitchen. No credit cards accepted, deposit by check, balance by certified check or cash.

Chalets Montmorency. 1770 Royale, St Fereol-les-Neiges, G0A 3R0; 826–2238. Less than 1 km from the lifts. Swiss-type chalets owned by Mont Ste Anne Ski School Director John Barclay, and his wife Gisele, it offers luxurious, clean, and spacious 1–3 bedroom apartments, all with fireplace, complete kitchen, dishwasher, and bathroom. Motel units with or without kitchenettes are also available. Rec room, sauna, and free shuttle to the lifts. Located near bakery, restaurants, a grocery store, and right across from an access trail to the 175 km Parc du Mont Ste Anne cross-country network. Prepayment by check.

Le Refuge du Lac. St Fereol-les-Neiges, G0A 3R0; 826–2363. Located about 4 miles east of the mountain at the main entrance to Mont Ste Anne Park ski center. Its claims to fame is having been host to Ingemar Stenmark during World Cup events; a cozy and warm environment and excellent cuisine. Accommodation is available in either the lodge or in one of 14 chalets with full amenities and maid service. This is an attractive place not only to stay at but to visit, after skiing or for a delightful meal.

Moderate to Inexpensive

Auberge Ste Anne. 9341 Blvd. Ste Anne, Ste Anne de Beaupre QE G0A 3C0; 827–4988. A 5-minute drive from the lifts and one of the best in a strip of auberges and motels on the Quebec–Ste Anne highway. Owners are friendly and accommodating, the food good, the hospitality warm, the bar lively, and accommodations clean and reasonable. Your choice of a room in the lodge or a convenient motel unit with full bathroom.

Others in the inexpensive category include **Motel Orleans,** 2941 Blvd. Ste Anne, Beauport, G1E 3J2, 661–6916; **Hotel Regent,** 1006 Blvd. Ste Anne, Beauport, G1E 3M3, 667–1633 or 800–463–5291 from eastern Canada; **Auberge La Saisonniere,** 1930 Blvd. Les Neiges, St Fereol-les-Neiges, G0A 3R0, 826–2540; **Refuge du Faubourg,** 1910 Blvd. Les Neiges, St Fereol-les-Neiges, G0A 3R0, 826–2869.

QUEBEC CITY

Of course, being the tourist attraction that it is, Quebec City has a wealth of accommodations of all types and for every purse. We won't attempt to list them all. If you're going to stay in Quebec—as many skiers do—you'll be wise staying in or near the Old Town. Otherwise Mont Ste Anne being only 30 minutes away should be your operating base.

Expensive

Le Chateau Frontenac. 1 rue des Carrieres, G1R 4P5; 687–2814. The provincial capital's most famous landmark. This 520-room hotel built in 1892 occupies the city's most strategic piece of real estate, on a point high atop Cap Diamand with a commanding view down the majestic St. Lawrence River toward Ile d'Orleans and Mont Ste Anne, the south shore, the historic Plains of Abraham, and the Old Town. Wherever they put you, you'll have something interesting to look at. Ski packages including lift ticket at Mont Ste Anne available for 2 nights double occupancy. If you don't stay there, drop in.

Loews le Concorde. 1225 Place Montcalm (corner Grande Allee), G1R 4W6; 647–2222, 800–463–5256 from eastern Canada, or 800–223–0888 from eastern U.S. One of Quebec's most modern and luxurious hotels. Bordering the Plains of Abraham, the 424-room hotel offers cross-country skiing at your doorstep or alpine skiing at any of the Quebec region's ski areas including Mont Ste Anne. The area is ideally located in the heart of Grande Allee's best discos and restaurants.

Hilton Quebec. 3 Place Quebec, G1K 7M9; 647–2411. Part of the international chain and located right behind the National Assembly, Quebec's government house, and within yards of the famous *Palais de Glace* (Ice Castle), built every year for the annual Winter Carnival in February. SkiHilton packages include transportation to Mont Ste Anne and lift ticket.

Moderate

Auberge des Gouverneurs. 690 East Blvd. St. Cyrille G1K 7M9; 647–1717, 800–463–2820 from eastern Canada, or 800–654–2000 from eastern U.S. Similar to the Hilton next door, but somewhat less expensive. Ski packages available. Daily rate includes lift ticket to Mont Ste Anne.

Holiday Inn Quebec City. 395 rue de la Couronne, G1K 6Z7; 647–2611, 800–465–4329 from Canada. Needs little introduction. 232 rooms include lift ticket.

Hotel-Motel le Voyageur. 2250 Blvd. Ste Anne, G1J 1Y2; 661–7701 or 800–463–5568 from Eastern Canada. Somewhat of a compromise between staying in town or at the area. Located on the outskirts of Quebec City on the road to Mont Ste Anne, it has 64 rooms with lift ticket and breakfast included. Indoor pool.

Inexpensive

Centre International de Sejour de Quebec. 19 rue St. Ursule, G1R 4E1; 694–0755. Offers 40 rooms with breakfast and lift ticket included.

Hotel Clarendon. 57 Ste Anne, G1K 7M9; 692–2480. In the heart of the Old Town; offers packages to Mont Ste Anne.

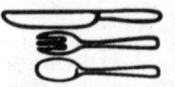 **RESTAURANTS.** There are three main areas around Mont Ste Anne in which to dine—in the adjacent village of St Fereol-les-Neiges, in Beaupre where the mountain road joins the main highway, and at Ste Anne de Beaupre, about 4 miles from the mountain. Restaurants are listed in order of price category. *Expensive:* $25 and up; *Moderate:* $13–$25; *Inexpensive:* less than $13. Credit card abbreviations are: A, American Express; M, MasterCard; V, Visa.

Moderate to Expensive

Auberge le Refuge du Lac. At the entrance to Parc Mont Ste Anne cross-country center, about 5 miles from the alpine base; 826–2363. Has always been an excellent choice for those who enjoy fine French and Canadian cuisine served in a relaxed, French-Canadian atmosphere. Excellent breakfasts, too. A, M, V.

Auberge la Saisonniere. 1930 Blvd. des Neiges in St Fereol; 826–2540. Features French nouvelle cuisine and some of the best food available in the region. Three *table d'hôte* choices are offered every night, including such delights as frogs legs, rabbit, and filet of pork in raspberry vinegar. There is also an 8-course gastronomical table offered and once a month the auberge prepares a *Gastronomie des Neiges* table featuring specialties from European ski countries such as Switzerland, Austria, Germany, Italy, and France. Reservations recommended on weekends. M, V.

Chateau Mont Ste Anne. At the gondola lift base; 827–5211. Has three restaurants worth mentioning. *Le St Moritz* is the hotel's deluxe dining room offering a refined and select menu, including chateaubriand, seafood, rack of lamb, etc., and can be rated expensive. More moderately priced are *La Grive des Bois* facing the ski slopes and the more intimate, *Le Soleil Levant,* which essentially have the same menu including house special pizzas, Italian dishes, fish, and seafood as well as hot and cold sandwiches and special children's menus.

Chez Albert. 1805 Blvd. des Neiges in St Fereol; 826–2184. Conveniently located just across the bridge on the left leaving the ski area—the one with the red roof. Features mostly Italian dishes including delicious open-hearth pizzas, the specialty of the house. The restaurant also serves meats, salads, and other pastas. A, M, V.

Chez Colette. 2190 Avenue Royale; 826–2944. One of the favorites with visitors to the region. Colette herself will be your hostess in this intimate (room for about 50), family-operated French-Canadian establishment. French onion soup *au gratin,* Caesar salads, beef strogonoff, bouillabaise, and several *table d'hôte* specials make up the enticing and diversified menu. Reservations recommended. M, V.

Restaurant Baker. 8790 Royale in Chateau Richer, just east of Ste Anne de Beaupre, 824–4478 or 4852. A must dining experience for anyone visiting Mont Ste Anne. The lovely nineteenth-century homestead converted into a cozy inn by Alvin Baker in 1935 is the region's finest eating establishment. Here you'll be offered anything from the most traditional of Quebec fare, Granny's pea soup, Aunt Gilberte's ragout of pig's feet and meatballs, Lac St Jean meat pie with beef, pork, veal, and potatoes, to more classical French-European dishes such as scallops on homemade puff pastry, onion soup *au gratin,* filet mignon with black peppercorns and salmon with sorrel. Reservations recommended. A, M, V.

Moderate

Aux Tourelles. 5 de la Visitation corner Blvd. Ste Anne, about ½ mile from the junction of the mountain road; 827–3603, A restaurant-bar, good place for a drink after skiing or for a good meal served in a bistro type of environment. From spaghetti and pizzas to fish, seafood, and meat dishes. A, M, V.

Inexpensive

Le Petrin. A bakery located on Avenue Royale just across Chalets Montmorency in St Fereol; 826–3490. Great for breakfast. While they specialize in homemade breads and delicious pastries—try the elephant ears—in the morning they do serve a hearty breakfast made up of eggs, thick ham, Quebec beans, and thick slices of toast with coffee served from an antique coffee pot brewing on a wood stove. The jolly, plump owner is a delightful host, a fine tribute to the carbohydrates he lovingly conjures up in the back room.

Restaurant les Neiges. 3069 Avenue Royale; 826–2741. The local diner-type restaurant in the region. Good for a fast lunch or breakfast specialties include pizzas, cheese fondues, steaks, and barbecued chicken as well as the standard fare of hot and cold sandwiches, hot dogs, burgers, and fries. Another house specialty is delivery. M, V.

Restaurant Roma. 9450 Blvd. Ste Anne (827–3681), and **Le Marie Antoinette** (827–3446) at the Carrefour, both in Ste Anne de Beaupre. Family restaurants where there's something for everyone from spaghetti and pizzas to burgers, sandwiches, chicken, and grilled cheeses for your 3-year-old. Le Marie Antoinette is somewhat similar to Howard Johnson's; standard white bread restaurants. Major credit cards.

Roulotte Bolduc. 10668 Blvd. Ste Anne Beaupre; 827–3226. For some typical Quebec greasies or a late night burger the region's best. The best *frites* (french fries) around will accompany your steamie with *choux* (chopped cabbage),

burger, or submarine. French fries, Quebec's national roadside dish also comes
a la poutine—only in Quebec—served with cheese curds and a brown sauce. If
you've survived Austrian schnapps, this will be a snap! Cash only.

HOW TO GET AROUND. Accommodations around
Mont Ste Anne are widely scattered and there is no real
base village, although the 258-room Chateau Mont Ste
Anne and adjacent condominiums do provide some ski-
in, ski-out facilities. Less than 1 km away from the mountain's south base is the
village of St Fereol-les-Neiges where there is some accommodation which generally requires your own, or rented, car. The village of Ste Anne de Beaupre is
less than 5 miles away from the mountain and has several motels. You'll be best
served with your own transportation although a few motels can give you a free
ride to the mountain. **Taxi** service is available from **Taxi Ste Anne,** 827–2330,
and Taxi Tremblay, 827–4514.

Many visitors to Mont Ste Anne stay in Quebec City since it is only 25 miles
away. Although car transportation is the best solution, a very efficient **Skibus**
service takes skiers from many points in the city to the region's ski centers (Mont
Ste Anne, Stoneham, and Lac Beauport) every morning and returns them again
in late afternoon. The Skibus has an extended route through the city but stops
at the following hotels: Holiday Inn St Roch, Quebec Hilton, Auberge des
Gouverneurs, Loew's Concorde, Chateau Frontenac, and Hotel/Motel des Lau-
rentides. For further information on service to Mont Ste Anne, call 529–0616;
for Lac Beauport and Stoneham, 627–2511.

A complete information packet on getting around in the Quebec City region
can be obtained by contacting the Quebec City Region Tourism and Convention
Bureau, 60 rue d'Auteuil, QE G1R 4C4; 692–2471.

For auto rental contact the following:

Avis. Airport, 872–2861; 225 East Blvd., Charest, 523–0041.

Hertz. Airport and Ste Foy, 871–1571; 44 du Palais, 694–1224.

Budget. Airport and Ste Foy, 872–9885; Cote du Palais, 692–3660; Place
Quebec, 529–0966.

Holiday. Ste Foy, 656–1411; 1779 de la Canardiere, 667–0129.

Rent-A-Wreck. 265 W. Blvd. Hamel, Vanier, 683–2333.

Tilden. Airport and Ste Foy, 871–1224; 295 rue St. Paul, 694–1727; Sillery,
687–3322; and 5115 Blvd. Hamel, 872–5655.

SEASONAL EVENTS. Quebec Carnival. For 10 days
in early **February** each year Quebec City becomes the
capital of winter fun as the internationally famous Quebec Winter Carnival, led by *Bonhomme Carnaval,* opens
its doors to the world. Fantastic ice sculptures and castles pop up everywhere,
parades trumpet through the streets, parties and balls are hosted by various
groups and hotels, and everywhere the people of Quebec City celebrate winter
with much gusto. Further information and the annual program of the Quebec
Winter Carnaval can be obtained either from the Quebec City Region Tourism
Bureau (692–2471) of by calling Tourism Quebec toll free, 800–361–6490 from
eastern Canada, or 800–443–7000 from the U.S.

**OTHER SPORTS AND ACTIVITIES. Cross-country
skiing** is very big in the region and one need look no
further than *Parc du Mont Ste Anne* (827–4561), in St
Fereol-les-Neiges, 5 miles east of the alpine area, to find
some of the best developed and maintained facilities in eastern Canada: 175 km
(109 miles) of double-track trails for all abilities are maintained and patrolled
throughout the winter with free access Monday through Friday and a $3.50
parking charge on weekends.

The trail network has been host to a number of prestigious events over the
years, including several Canadian championships, and was also the back-up site
for the 1980 Lake Placid Olympics. A restaurant, waxing facilities, and warming
huts on the trails are open daily.

Other cross-country centers in the region include *Lac Beauport,* 15 minutes
due north of the city; *Centre l'Eperon,* 506 Tour du Lac (849–2778), with 19
trails totaling 120 km and *Le Saisonnier,* 78 Chemin Brule (849–2821), with an
equal number of trails and km.

Should you be staying in Quebec City, the Plains of Abraham which run along Cap Diamand from the Chateau Frontenac to the borough of Sillery also offer several km of easily accessible trails for urban skiing. You can access the trail network from any entry point to the parc from Grande Allee.

OTHER ALPINE AREAS in the region include **Stoneham,** 1420 Avenue Hibou, Stoneham, (848–2411), only 20 minutes due north of Quebec City, just past Lac Beauport. The area has a respectable 1,250-ft. vertical and 18 runs serviced by 8 lifts, including 2 modern quadruple chairs. Snowmaking ensures good conditions on most trails and **night skiing** on 6 trails will give you a breathtaking view of the Quebec City lights in the near distance.

You can also enjoy night skiing at the two Lac Beauport centers, *Le Relais* (849–3073) and *Mont St Castin-Les-Neiges* (849–6776), both located on the lake road only 15 minutes north of the city via Hwy. 175.

Hockey is Canada's national sport and should you be in Quebec City while the home team Nordiques play their archrivals the Montreal Canadiens, do try to get tickets. You'll witness a confrontation that often goes beyond the sport itself and possibly gain some insight on the French-Canadian way of thinking which makes Quebec so different in the North American context. For ticket information call the Colisee, 691–7211.

NIGHTLIFE. Luckily Mont Ste Anne is a good, tough, ski mountain and if the skiing doesn't tire you out then the midwinter cold and the wind certainly will. Good skiing and good eating more than boogie are the trademarks of the region, so if your main objective is to party then you'll be best served in Quebec City where discotheques and bars abound. Nonetheless there are a few nearby spots worth noting.

On the **mountain** *Chateau Mont Ste Anne* on the south side base of the area is the main focus of après-ski and nightlife in the area witnessed by the parking problems every night. The après-ski crowd gathers from 4 to 8 P.M. in the *Piano Bar,* where live entertainment keeps the energy level high and free appetizers keep your appetite down. The day's competition or other mountain activity is usually showed on a giant screen video. For more intimate situations the small *Cumulus Bar* just across from the Piano Bar is quieter and appropriate for more meaningful discussion. Later on, from about 9 P.M., the focus turns to *Le Crepuscule* (dusk) disco where you can spend your last daily bit of energy until 3 A.M., if it takes that long. All bars are part of the Chateau Mont Ste Anne hotel, 500 Blvd. Beau-Pre (827–5211), and accept all major credit cards.

Aux Tourelles is a restaurant-bar in Beaupre (827–3603) discussed above in the *Restaurant* section. After 9 P.M. it turns into more of a bar than a restaurant, a good drinking place, bistro style where conversation is the main currency.

In **Quebec City** the selection of discos, bars, and watering holes runs long and wide, of course.

Like everywhere else the focus of night life in larger towns has a way of shifting from area to area. Quebec is no exception and the hot spots these days are along the Grande Allee near the Old Town and the government buildings. Between the Armory and the Loews Le Concorde Hotel you'll find three of the current top bars and disco: *Brandy, Vogue,* and *Dagobert,* with *Le Cabaret* at the Concorde Hotel said to be the top spot on the street. For a slightly younger crowd try the *Drugstore Livernois,* corner La Fabrique and St-Jean near City Hall. For a more mature atmosphere head to Ste Foy and Bogart's, 2590 Blvd. Laurier, between the two large shopping centers, Place Ste Foy and Place Laurier.

WESTERN
CANADA

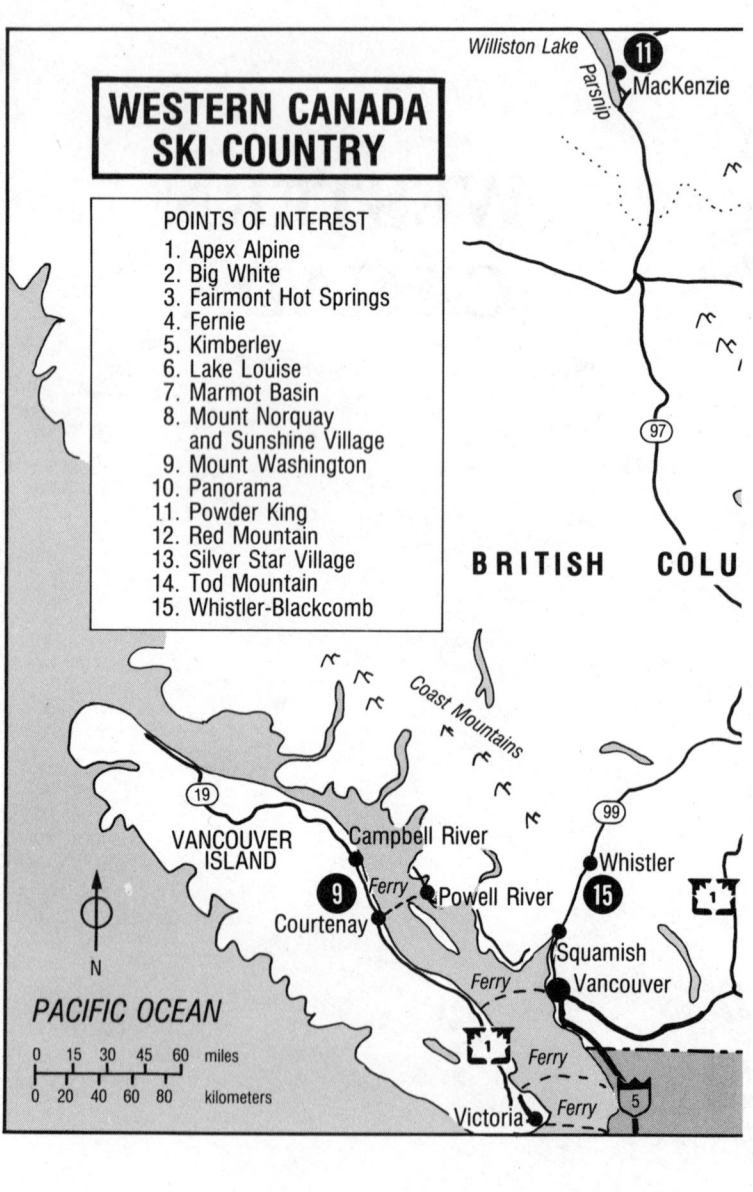

WESTERN CANADA SKI COUNTRY

POINTS OF INTEREST
1. Apex Alpine
2. Big White
3. Fairmont Hot Springs
4. Fernie
5. Kimberley
6. Lake Louise
7. Marmot Basin
8. Mount Norquay
   and Sunshine Village
9. Mount Washington
10. Panorama
11. Powder King
12. Red Mountain
13. Silver Star Village
14. Tod Mountain
15. Whistler-Blackcomb

Williston Lake

Parsnip

MacKenzie

97

BRITISH COLU

Coast Mountains

19

VANCOUVER
ISLAND

Campbell River

99

Whistler

N

Courtenay

Ferry

Powell River

15

Squamish
Vancouver

Ferry

PACIFIC OCEAN

| 0 | 15 | 30 | 45 | 60 | miles |

| 0 | 20 | 40 | 60 | 80 | kilometers |

Ferry

1

Ferry

5

Victoria

Ferry

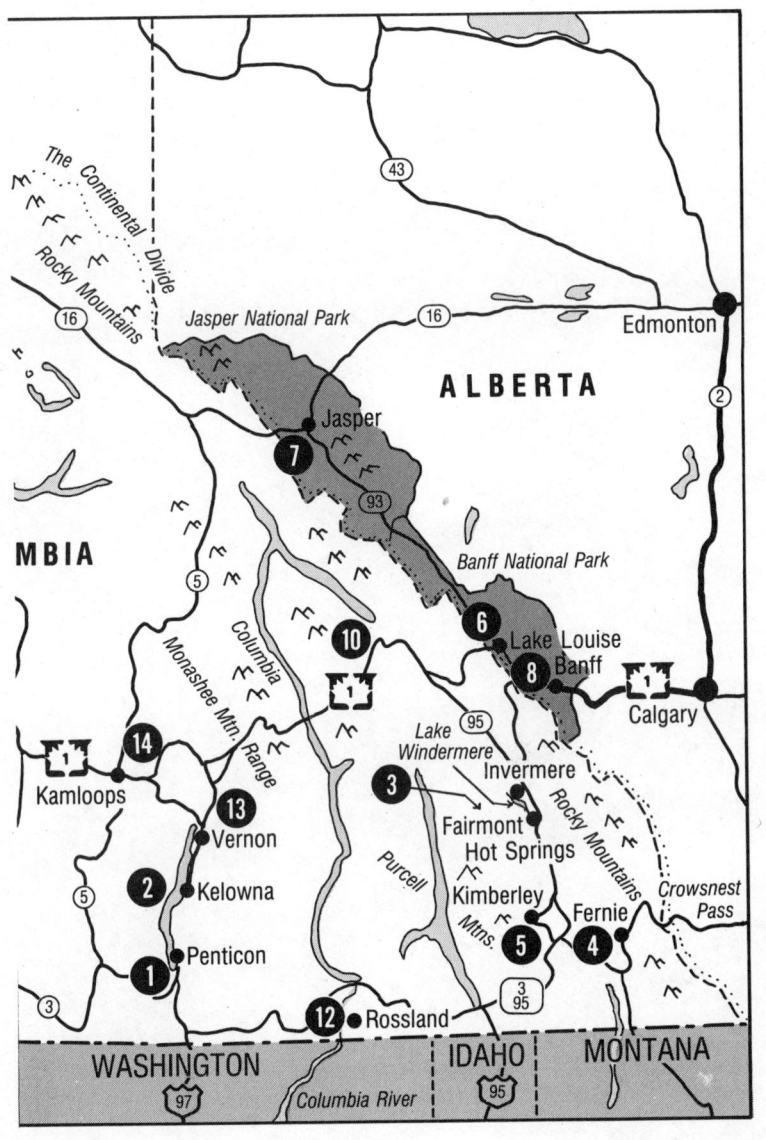

The Continental Divide

Rocky Mountains

43

16

Jasper National Park

16

Edmonton

ALBERTA

2

Jasper

⑦

93

Banff National Park

MBIA

5

⑩

1

6

Lake Louise

⑧

Banff

1

Calgary

Monashee Mtn. Range

Columbia

95

Lake
Windermere

Invermere

Rocky Mountains

⑭

Kamloops

1

3

Fairmont
Hot Springs

⑬

Vernon

Purcell

Kimberley

Crowsnest
Pass

⑤

Fernie

②

Kelowna

Mtns

④

5

⑤

①

Penticon

3
95

⑫

Rossland

3

WASHINGTON

IDAHO

MONTANA

97

Columbia River

95

WESTERN CANADA

by
DON BILODEAU

A regular ski columnist for the Montreal Gazette, *Don Bilodeau has contributed ski instruction features in the* Ski Canada *magazine as well as other publications. He is currently on the staff of the Lake Louise Ski Resort in Alberta.*

The Canadian West is considered to have some of the best skiing in the world. A combination of abundant snow, spectacular scenery, and natural undeveloped countryside give this vast region a sense of the last ski frontier.

Skiing takes place in two provinces: Alberta and British Columbia. Both are very different, yet both share the legend of Canada's western skiing. Most of Alberta is prairie land. Although there are plenty of cattle, horses, and oil wells, the western edge of the province borders on mountainous British Columbia and includes the Rocky Mountain range. Much of this range is preserved as part of the Banff and Jasper National parks where four major ski resorts are found.

The Rocky Mountains stretch 320 km north and south along the Continental Divide. It's some of the most awesome scenery in the world, for majestic peaks and huge glaciers dominate the view. There are hundreds of miles of uncrowded slopes and plenty of deep, dry powder.

Next door in British Columbia, one will discover an unlimited choice for skiing, ranging from super destination resorts to smaller inexpensive ski centers. British Columbia can be considered God's gift to skiers. Most of the province's land surface is mountain or valley.

It's difficult to imagine just how vast this mountainous province is. It spreads over an area larger than Washington, Oregon, and California combined. A European can measure it as larger than Italy, France, Austria, and Switzerland all put together.

Each resort has its own character. Some are more extensively developed than others, so the choice is yours: go adventurous or go deluxe. There are less than 2.5 million people in British Columbia, so expect sparsely crowded slopes. The overall climate is generally mild with abundant snowfall.

Throughout the Canadian West, you'll find comfortable accommodations and a variety of dining spots. Most are at prices that won't take a big chunk out of your wallet. The region is accessible through three major gateways: Vancouver, BC, and Calgary and Edmonton, AL. All are serviced by most major airlines from most North American cities.

Most skiers who discover super natural British Columbia or Alberta's Majestic Mountains, return more then once. There's too much to discover in only one visit.

Alberta

BANFF–LAKE LOUISE RESORTS

The town of Banff and the village of Lake Louise are located in Banff National Park, only a short drive west of Calgary International Airport. This first class tri-resort area is famous for its spectacular scenery and wide variety of skiing terrain. Norquay, Sunshine Village, and Lake Louise ski areas are located here.

The town of Banff is nestled at the junction of the valleys of the Bow and Spray rivers at an altitude of 4,538 feet. With a wide variety of hotels and restaurants, there is something for every taste and budget.

Banff was named after Banffshire, Scotland, the birthplace in 1883 of Lord Strathcona, then the president of the Canadian Pacific Railroad. The town has evolved from a CPR settlement called Siding 29, which serviced the railroad men, mines, and local trappers. By 1888 the area's hot springs and the 10 square miles around it had been made a natural reserve and several merchants had already established themselves on the main street, now called Banff Avenue. All the other streets in Banff are named for animals found in the park.

It wasn't until the early 1920s that skiing began to take place in the Banff-Lake Louise region. Hardy ski-tourers explored the backcountry and soon discovered the potential for expanded ski activities. In February 1934, Sunshine Village Ski Area hosted its first ski-week vacation for 10 paying guests from Vancouver. The ski cabin was a former CPR log building and the ski runs were entirely dependent upon the skier's climbing ability.

Lake Louise is spectacular country. You'll find Canada's largest ski area and across the valley one of the most beautiful lakes in the world situated at the base of Victoria Glacier. Back in 1882 an adventurer named Tom Wilson was guided up to the lake by a local Indian and was awestruck by its beauty. Word spread and in 1890 a chalet for climbers and visitors was built. It later burned down and was replaced by a CPR hotel in 1924, later named Chateau Lake Louise.

Skiing in the Lake Louise region began in the 1920s and '30s with the building of Skoki Lodge in the backcountry behind Lake Louise Ski Area. Another lodge, called Mount Temple Chalet, was built in 1937 on the route to Skoki. Located 8 km from Lake Louise Station, it became the site of the first mechanical lift in the area. By 1967 it had grown into a major destination along with Sunshine Village, 60 km down the valley.

Norquay is the smallest of the three ski areas and is conveniently situated overlooking the town of Banff. First developed in 1948 with the installation of the first single chairlift in western Canada, this ski area is noted for its super-steep terrain and pleasant view of the Bow Valley.

There's plenty of novice and intermediate skiing available also. In 1960 the single chair was changed into a double, and since 1965 additional lifts and facilities have been installed, including scary-looking nordic jumps at the left side of the main slopes.

Nordic skiing is equally spectacular in the Lake Louise region. Ski on 61 km of groomed trails in the immediate area or ski to the famous rustic Skoki Lodge 11 km from Temple Lodge.

LAKE LOUISE SKI AREA

Box 5
Lake Louise AL T0L 1E0
Tel: 403–522–3555

Snow Report: 403–244–6665
Area Vertical: 3,250 ft.
Number of Trails: 83+ on 3,000 acres
Skiing Terrain: 25 percent novice, 45 percent intermedi-ate, 30 percent expert
Lifts: 2 triple, 4 double, 1 T-bar, 1 poma, 1 rope tow
Snowmaking: two-thirds of front face
Season: mid-November–May

Lake Louise is the largest ski area in Canada with the most skiable terrain. It has three faces: the front face, Larch area, and the back bowls. It takes several days to truly discover its variety of trails. There's plenty for every level of ability. Green or novice runs are available off every lift except the Summit Platter.

The scenery is spectacular and often considered one of the most majestic panoramas in the world. The long runs are great for cruising. Eagle Meadow and Juniper are the most popular intermediate trails on the front face while Saddleback, also intermediate, offers breathtaking scenery above treeline in the back bowls. Lynx, at Larch area, and Outer Limits down to Men's Downhill are favorites for the experts. On a clear day, the Summit Platter, which serves the front face and back bowls, is a popular place.

Three main lodges—Whiskeyjack at the base, Whitehorn halfway up the front face, and Temple, on the other side at Larch area—offer skier services such as ski school and ski shop items. Rentals at $14 per day for full equipment are available located at Whiskeyjack. The Friends of Louise, a volunteer free guide service is available daily from the base of the front face at 10 A.M. and 1 P.M.

MOUNT NORQUAY

Box 1258
Banff AL T0L 0C0
Tel: 403–762–4421

Snow Report: 403–253–3383
Area Vertical: 1,300 ft.
Number of Trails: 17 on 130 acres
Skiing Terrain: 35 percent novice, 15 percent intermediate, 50 percent expert
Lifts: 2 double chairs, 2 T-bars, 1 platter, 1 rope tow
Snowmaking: over 25 percent of slope
Season: mid-November–early April

This is Banff's most convenient ski area, overlooking the Bow Valley and only a 10-minute drive from town. Although known for its challenging advanced terrain, there are pleasant novice and intermediate trails. In fact, its beginner–novice trails are some of the region's best to learn on.

Experts will choose the famous North American run off the upper chair. It's as steep and challenging as they come.

The view at the 7,000-foot elevation off the upper chair is spectacular, overlooking the town of Banff at the base of Mount Rundle across the valley.

Ski rentals and ski school lessons are available at the base day lodge, along with the ski shop goods in an adjacent building.

There is night skiing under the lights 4–9 P.M. each Wednesday, Thursday, Friday, and Saturday.

SUNSHINE VILLAGE

Box 1510
Banff AL T0L 1C0
Tel: 403–762–4000

Snow Report: 403–355–SNOW
Area Vertical: 3,514 ft. from gondola base
Number of Trails: 75 on 780 acres
Skiing Terrain: 20 percent novice, 60 percent intermediate, 20 percent expert
Lifts: 1 gondola, 1 triple, 5 double, 3 T-bars, 2 rope tows
Snowmaking: Not required
Season: mid-November–early June

Sunshine is known for its abundance of fluffy powder and its cozy atmosphere high up in alpine meadows. The 14,084-ft. long gondola ride up to the actual ski area is spectacular in itself. Once you arrive at the village, it's just a quick chair lift ride up to terrain varying from expert to novice.

Experts will enjoy the Tee-pee Town area which has steep chutes and big bumps. The majority of Sunshine's trails are intermediate. Brewster's Trail, off the Great Divide chair, is a favorite. You actually ride up the chair into the Province of British Columbia and ski back down into Alberta. Novices find runs off Strawberry lift a good place to learn and develop skills.

Rental equipment is available at the gondola base. The ski shop is found in the main day lodge up at the area as is the repair shop.

Sunshine boasts the longest ski season in Canada, running from November to early June. You'll find hundreds of sun worshipers each spring doing more tanning than skiing.

Nordic services are available with 20 km of track set trails in high alpine meadows. The nordic office is located adjacent to the upper gondola station.

Practical Information for Banff–Lake Louise

HOW TO GET THERE. Banff is located 128 km west of Calgary, on Trans-Canada Hwy. 1. Lake Louise is an additional 61 km northwest of Banff on Hwy. 1. **By air.** Calgary, Edmonton, and Vancouver International airports are the gateways to the region. There are direct and connecting flights from all major North American cities. Calgary International Airport serves major airlines, including *CP Air, Air Canada, United, American, PWA,* and *Western Airlines.*

By bus. Shuttle "Airporter" service is available once daily from the airport to Banff; phone 250–5734. *Greyhound Bus Lines* service is also available for Calgary–Banff–Lake Louise three times daily; phone 762–2286.

By car. Calgary–Banff–Lake Louise is an enjoyable and easy drive on Hwy. 1. From Vancouver eastward, it's a scenic 12-hour drive. For rental cars at Calgary Airport, phone *Avis,* 489–4710; *Budget,* 250–0760; *Hertz;* 426–7500; or Tilden, 489–1335.

TELEPHONES. The area code for all of Alberta is 403, and for British Columbia it is 604.

ACCOMMODATIONS. Banff has a wide variety of establishments. In the Lake Louise area you'll find a choice of 6 fine hotels and lodges. Sunshine has its own hotel right at the slopes. Based on double occupancy rates are: *Expensive,* $80–$120; *Moderate,* $45–$70; and *Inexpensive,* below $45. Most have saunas and whirlpools. Phone central reservations, 762–4561, or write Ski Banff–Lake Louise, Banff AL T0L 1C0. The region also offers a unique guiding and instruction program each Monday through Thursday.

BANFF

Expensive

Banff Park Lodge. 222 Lynx St.; 762–4433. With 210 rooms and pool, sauna, restaurant, TV.

Banff Springs Hotel. Spray Avenue, P.O. Box 960; 762–2211. Largest (and most famous) hotel in Banff with 557 rooms and many shops and amenities.

Inns of Banff Park. 600 Banff Ave.; 762–4581. Deluxe accommodation with many amenities.

Sunshine Village. 762–3381. These 89 rooms are situated at the base of the slopes in a self-contained hotel.

Moderate

Aspen Lodge. 503 Banff Ave.; 762–4418 Has 53 rooms, some with kitchens.

Banff Rocky Mountain Resort. Banff Ave. N.; 762–5531. Has 132 rooms condo-style and all facilities including pool, fireplaces.

Charlton's Cedar Court. 513 Banff Ave.; 762–4485. Has 63 rooms, outdoor heated pool,kitchenettes.

Douglas Fir Resort. Tunnel Mtn. Road; 762–5591. 133 rooms overlooking Banff.

Ptarmigan Inn. Box 1840, Banff; 762–2207. Has 130 rooms.

Rimrock Inn. Sulfur Mtn. Rd.; 762–3356. A 100-room hotel near the hot springs overlooking Banff.

Voyager Inn. 555 Banff Ave.; 762–3301. Has 88 rooms and many amenities.

Inexpensive

Alpine Motel. 521 Banff Ave.; 762–2332. Has 22 rooms and some with kitchens and fireplaces.

King Edward Hotel. 137 Banff Ave.; 762–2251. Has 56 rooms in the center of Banff.

Mt. Royal Hotel. 138 Banff Ave.; 762–3331. 95 rooms, also in the center of Banff.

Traveller's Inn. 401 Banff Ave. 762–4401. Has 90 rooms.

LAKE LOUISE

Chateau Lake Louise. *Expensive.* Box 96; 522–3511. Has 375 rooms located on the lake 5 minutes from the slopes. Many amenities.

Deer Lodge. *Moderate.* Box 100; 522–3747. Has 98 rooms near the Chateau Lake Louise and 5 minutes from the ski slopes.

Lake Louise Inn. *Moderate.* Box 209; 522–3791. Located in the valley floor near Hwy. 1, a few minutes from the ski slopes. Has a lounge, pool, 186 rooms and many amenities.

Post Hotel. *Inexpensive.* Box 69; 522–3989. Has 38 rooms and a famous Swiss dining room.

West Louise Lodge. *Inexpensive.* Box 5; 604–343–6311. Has 44 rooms located 20 km west on Hwy. 1, just across the British Columbia border. Owned and operated by Lake Louise Ski Area.

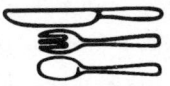 **RESTAURANTS.** Slopeside at the ski mountains, you'll find a variety of eating places and cafeteria services. At **Lake Louise,** three main lodges—*Whiskeyjack* at the base; *Whitehorn,* halfway up the front face, and *Temple,* on the other side of the mountain at the Larch area—offer cafeteria food. Whiskeyjack also has a dining room. At **Norquay,** the base *day lodge* has a cafeteria featuring great chili. At **Sunshine Village,** the 600-seat base *lodge dining room* features daily buffets as well as cafeteria and deli service.

In Banff, there's a great choice for varied tastes and budgets. The selection of restaurants listed here is arranged by price category. Restaurant categories are: *Expensive,* $15–$28; *Moderate,* $8–$15; *Inexpensive,* less than $8. These prices are for a meal for one person, exclusive of drinks or tip. All restaurants in this listing accept Visa and MasterCard unless otherwise noted.

Expensive

Giorgio's La Casa. 219 Banff Ave.; 762–5116. Sample the authentic cuisine of northern Italy: pasta, fish, meats. Excellent service. By reservation only. L, D.

Le Beaujolais. Corner of Buffalo St. and Banff Ave.; 762–2712. This is great Continental dining specializing in French cuisine and tableside service and elegant decor. One of the most prestigious dining rooms in Canada. Reservations necessary. D.

Post Hotel Dining Room. Lake Louise Village; 522–3989 Warm country hospitality. Specializes in European dishes. Reserve for dinner. B, L, D.

The Rob Roy Dining Room. Banff Springs Hotel, Spray Ave.; 762–2211. Fine dining featuring Alberta beef and seafood. By reservation. L, D.

Moderate

Balkan Restaurant. 120 Banff Ave.; 762–3454. Authentic Greek specialties. L, D.

Bumpers, The Beef House. 603 Banff Ave.; 762–2622. Popular family restaurant specializing in Alberta beef, barbecued ribs, and salad bar. D only.

Caboose. Located at the Banff railway depot; 762–3622. With interesting railroad history decor, Alaska king crab and charcoal-broiled steaks are the specialties. D only.

Cafe Louise. In Deer Lodge, Lake Louise; 522–3747. Serves braised chicken, salmon, Alberta beef. B, L, D.

Eagle Nest Dining Room. In Rimrock Inn on Sulfur Mtn. Road; 762–3356. Offers spectacular view of Bow Valley and a balanced menu of beef, fish, veal, and poultry. B, L, D. Reservations required for dinner.

Giorgio's La Pasta. 219 Banff Ave.; 762–5114. Features homemade pasta dishes. L, D.

Guido's. 116 Banff Ave.; 762–4002. Features Italian specialties and fine desserts. L, D.

Heritage Restaurant. In the Lake Louise Inn; 522–3791. Family dining with great burgers and a fine dinner menu including filet mignon. B, L, D. Dinner reservations welcome.

Joshua's. 204 Caribou St.; 762–2833. Has European specialties in addition to fish and beef plates. Turn-of-the-century atmosphere. L, D.

Magpie and Stump. 203 Caribou St.; 762–2014. With old west atmosphere, authentic Mexican dishes are a specialty. D only; nightly entertainment.

Melissa's Missteak. 217 Lynx St.; 762–5511. Rustic log building constructed in 1928 offers pleasant atmosphere. Has great muffins, homemade soups, and deep dish pizzas among other novel choices. B, L, D.

Paris Restaurant. 114 Banff Ave.; 762–3554. Serves veal, seafood, steaks, and pasta. L, D.

Reflections. At Inns of Banff Park Hotel, 600 Banff Ave.; 762–4581. Serves fine Alberta beef, seafood, and poultry. Reservations appreciated. B, L, D.

Ticino. 205 Wolf St.; 762–3848. You'll find fine Swiss-Italian dishes, cheese fondues, and steaks. D only. Reservations recommended.

Victoria Dining Room. Chateau Lake Louise; 522–3511. Popular buffet breakfasts and lunches. A la carte dinner menu. Evenings by reservation.

West Louise Lodge. On Hwy. 1, 11 km west of Lake Louise; 604–343–6486. Homemade soups, beef, and poultry. B, L, D.

The Yard. 206 Wolf St.; 762–5678. Has reputation for generous portions of Tex-Mex food. B, L, D.

Inexpensive

A & W. 100 Caribou St.; 762–2562. Specializes in A & W root beer and burgers. Open 7 A.M. to 11 P.M.

Dick Turpin's Pub. At Chateau Lake Louise; 762–3511. Offers pizza, salads, and sandwiches.

Harvey's Swiss Chalet. 304 Caribou St.; 762–4951. Charbroiled burgers, hot dogs, and broiled chicken. B, L, D.

Phil's Restaurant. 109 Spray Ave.; 762–3655. Serves pancakes, waffles, burgers, and steaks; open 7 A.M.–10 P.M.

Smitty's. 227 Banff Ave.; 762–2533. Family prices on Canadian dishes; open 6:30 A.M.–10 P.M.

HOW TO GET AROUND. Bus shuttles are available daily from Banff to each ski area. Contact *Brewster Transportation* at 762–2241 and *PWT* at 762–4558 or ask your hotel desk for specific shuttle times. In Lake Louise, a shuttle bus service runs each half hour from all hotels to Lake Louise Ski Area. **Car rentals** are available in Banff: *Avis,* 762–3222, or *Hertz,* 762–2027 or 522–3511 at Lake Louise. For **taxi** service in Banff only, phone *Banff Taxi,* 762–4444; *Mountain Taxi,* 762–3351; or *Legion Taxi,* 762–3353.

SEASONAL EVENTS. At **Lake Louise** there's the annual *Labatt's Downhill Dash,* a recreational downhill team race in **January**. The Banff *Winter Festival* takes place each **February** with a parade down Banff Ave., torchlight demonstration on Mount Norquay, sporting events, ice sculpture contest, costume party, and snow queen contest. The *Summit Cup* at Lake Louise in **March** and the *Ken Read Invitational* in **April** are popular races for locals and ex-national team members, respectively. An annual mogul skiing contest takes place in late April.

At **Sunshine** there's a special Telemark weekend in early **February** and a recreational team downhill race called the "Over the Divide" in March. May 25 is the *Slush Cup* where skiers race through an icy water puddle.

At **Norquay** each March there's the annual *Skiing Veterans Fun Race.*

OTHER SPORTS AND ACTIVITIES. There's an **indoor water slide** at Douglas Fir Resort on Tunnel Mountain Road; 762–5591. **Sleigh rides** and **dog sledding** rides are available daily at Chateau Lake Louise; 522–3511. Many of the larger hotels have **swimming pools,** saunas, and Jacuzzis. The **skating rink** at the steps of Chateau Lake Louise, (522–3511), is probably one of the most beautiful spots in the world to skate. The *Recreation Center* in Banff provides public ice time and the ice can be rented for private groups. Phone 762–4454 to reserve. **Curling** is popular in Banff; also at the Recreation Center.

The *Upper Hot Springs Pool* is open year round on Mountain Ave. The average temperature is 38°C (100°F) and it costs only $1.25. Phone 762–4454.

CHILDREN'S ACTIVITIES. All three ski areas provide children's programs. At **Lake Louise** (552–3555) in *Chocolate Moose Playpark,* a nursery, is available for children under 3 at $3.50 per hour by reservation. Daycare for children 3–6 years is $2.50 per hour. A *Kinder-Ski* program for children 3–6 years is available with indoor/outdoor play and ski instruction daily at $18 for a full day. *Kid's Ski* for 8–12 years is $19 per day with instruction. Lunch is a $3 option.

At **Sunshine,** 762–4000, the day-care accepts children 19 months to 12 years at $2.50 per hour. The *Kinder-Day* program runs daily for $23 including lunch and ski rental for 3–6-year-olds. The *Kids' Day Program* is advanced instruction for those 6–12 years old for $23 per day.

At **Norquay**, 764–4421, there is babysitting at $2 per hour. Kids under 8 years ski for free at each area.

 **NIGHTLIFE.** There's a good choice of après-ski activities after dark in Banff. *The Works* nightclub at the Banff Springs Hotel is popular for disco dancing. For top-40 live rock and recorded disco go to *Silver City,* 110 Banff Ave. For more hot dancing go to *Mr. C's* on Banff Ave. or to the *View Point Lounge* for easy listening music at the Rimrock Inn. The *Magpie and Stump* on Caribou St. has live entertainment, often in the form of folk music.

Other popular bars include *Melissa's* on Lynx St., the *Royal Express* in the Mont Royal Hotel, and the *Chimney Corner* up at Sunshine Village. In Lake Louise, go to *Dick Turpin's Pub* in Chateau Lake Louise or *Charlie II's* at Lake Louise Inn for casual disco atmosphere. Most other hotels have cozy lounges for drinks and quiet relaxation.

MARMOT BASIN SKI AREA

Box 1300
Jasper AL T0E 1E0
Tel: 403–852–3816

Snow Report: 403–488–5909
Area Vertical: 2,290 ft.
Number of Trails: 31 on 565 acres
Skiing Terrain: 35 percent novice, 35 percent intermediate, 30 percent expert
Lifts: 1 triple chair, 3 double chairs, 2 T-bars
Snowmaking: Yes
Season: early December–early May

Located 3 hours north of Banff via the Icefields Parkway, which is considered to be one of the world's most scenic and spectacular highways, Jasper is both a summer and winter destination playground. A man named Jasper Hawes opened up a boarding house here about 160 years ago to accommodate local trappers, explorers, traders, and mountain men. The railway was also just being developed. In 1846 he opened the Jasper House Hotel at the center of the fast-growing town that ultimately took his name.

It wasn't until the late 1920s when a fellow named Joe Weiss explored the east face of Marmot Basin discovering ideal skiing slopes and conditions, that the area was opened for skiing. The first trail was blazed in the '30s, ending by the present upper chalet location. A road to the area was constructed from 1940 to 1945. In 1963 Parks Canada proposed an expansion of the ski area, resulting in the construction the following year of the upper yellow T-bar, new trails, and the rustic upper chalet.

Marmot Basin has since become a favorite ski destination for Albertans and an expanding U.S. market. Jasper has comfortable accommodations and Marmot's skiing is great for the whole family. The park's untouched beauty is in every direction.

Only 22 km from the town of Jasper, the Marmot Basin ski slopes offer a broad range of terrain for all ability levels. The highest elevation is 8,517 feet, and there is a 158-inch annual snowfall. Lines are uncommon, so there's a lot of ski time from the top of the 6 lifts. The view of the Rockies is great. Lift tickets are $21 for adults and $13 for children 12 years old and younger. New trails have been cut recently in the lower area of the ski mountain and the upper trails have been expanded. The grooming is good. There are two main chalets, each with licensed cafeteria and deck. Rentals and lessons are available at the lower chalet.

Practical Information for Marmot Basin

 **HOW TO GET THERE.** Marmot Basin is located 371 km west of Edmonton and 450 northwest of Calgary. **By air.** Edmonton International Airport services major airlines, with connections from most North American cities. Contact *Air Canada, Canadian Pacific Air,* or *Pacific Western Airlines,* among others. Auto rentals available in Jasper are *Avis,* 852–3970; *Hertz,* 852–3798; and *Tilden,* 852–3978. In Edmonton: *Avis,* 955–7596; *Hertz,* 955–8500; and *Tilden,* 955–7232.

By car. Jasper is about a 4½-hour drive from Edmonton, along windy, scenic Hwy. 16.

By bus. *Greyhound Bus Lines* provides daily service between Edmonton, Jasper, and Vancouver. Phone 421–4211 for information and schedules.

By train. *Via Rail* has service between Edmonton and Jasper three days a week. Phone 800–665–8630 for information and schedules.

TELEPHONES. The area code for Jasper and all of Alberta is 403.

 **ACCOMMODATIONS.** Practically all accommodations at Marmot Basin can be arranged through *A Marmot Experience,* Box 1300, Jasper AL T0E 1E0; 852–4242. There's a wide selection of hotels and lodges, many with such amenities as saunas, whirlpools, and indoor swimming pools. Hotel rates are based on double occupancy. Categories, determined by price, are: *Expensive,* $60–$80; *Moderate,* $45–$60; *Inexpensive,* less than $45.

Expensive

Chateau Jasper. 96 Giekie St.; 852–5644. Very comfortable rooms, pool, dining room. Kitchenettes available.

Lobstick Lodge. 88 Giekie St.; 852–4431. Has 139 rooms, many with kitchenettes; indoor pool; dining services.

Marmot Lodge. 94 Connaught Dr.; 852–4471. Features swimming pool, kitchenettes, and fireplaces.

Moderate

Andrew Motor Lodge. 200 Connaught Dr.; 852–3394. Standard motor lodge with phones, TV, and restaurant.

Sawridge Hotel. 82 Connaught Dr.; 852–5111. Has 154 rooms, with pool and sauna.

Inexpensive

Astoria Motor Inn. 404 Connaught Dr.; 852–3351. In a convenient location, with pub and restaurant.

Athabasca Hotel. 25 Patricia St.; 852–3386. Has 60 rooms for all budgets; dining room and pub with satellite TV.

Diamond Motel. 424 Connaught Dr.; 852–3143. Some rooms with kitchenettes; dining room, TV, and sauna.

Mt. Robson Motor Inn. 215 Connaught Dr.; 852–3327. Some kitchenettes, dining room, TV.

Whistlers Motor Hotel. 34 Miette St.; 852–3361. 40 rooms with phones, TV; dining room.

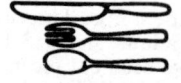 **RESTAURANTS.** There's a pleasant mix of eating places in Jasper, and most of them have reasonable prices. *Expensive:* $20 and up; *Moderate:* $10–$20; *Inexpensive:* less than $10. Prices are based on the average cost of a meal for one person, excluding drinks and tip. All but the inexpensive restaurants listed accept major credit cards, and no reservations are needed.

Moderate to Expensive

Amethyst Dining Room. 200 Connaught Dr.; 852–3394. Located in Andrew Motor Lodge, you'll find dishes ranging from fruit and cheese platter to British Columbia salmon and prime Alberta beef.

Marmot Dining Room. In Marmot Lodge, 94 Connaught Dr.; 852–4544. Has Continental cuisine with original pasta dishes and homemade desserts.

Walter's Dining Room. In Sawridge Hotel 82 Connaught Dr.; 852–5111. A distinctive a la carte menu featuring seafood and Alberta. beef.

Tokyo Tom's Place. On Giekie St. behind Marmot Lodge; 852–3780. Features complete sushi bar and intimate booths for eating fine Japanese dishes. D only.

Inexpensive

A & W. 624 Connaught Dr.; 852–4930. Home of the Papa burger, Teen burger, and A & W root beer. Fast service.

Jasper Pizza Place. 402 Connaught Dr.; 852–3225. Offers pizza, burgers, sandwiches, and barbecued chicken.

Papa George's. 404 Connaught Dr.; 852–4972. A family-oriented restaurant with traditional Canadian favorites. Rustic decor.

HOW TO GET AROUND. A ski **shuttle bus** departs from Jasper daily at 8:15 A.M. and 10 A.M. and returns at 4:15 P.M. For **taxi** service around town, phone *Jasper Taxi,* 852–3146. Car rentals are available through *Avis,* 852–3970 in Jasper and 955–7596 in Edmonton; *Hertz,* 852–3793 in Jasper and 955–8500 in Edmonton; and Tilden, 852–3978 in Jasper and 955–7232 in Edmonton.

SEASONAL EVENTS. The main event is *Labatt's St. Patricks Recreational Downhill* in **March.** About 40 teams made up of at least one woman and one person over 35 years old compete in a race down the mountain. The big prizes are drawn and the atmosphere is friendly competition and socializing.

OTHER SPORTS AND ACTIVITIES. In Jasper there's **skating** and other sports activities nearby. Try **dogsledding** with professional guides; phone 852–3078 to reserve. **Ice fishing** is available at Talbot Lake close by and on other local rivers. Licenses are available at Parks Canada office, 500 Connaught Dr.

Most larger hotels have indoor **swimming pools, saunas,** and **whirlpools.** The *Jasper Activity Center,* 393 Pyramid Ave. (852–3381) has a public **skating rink, curling rink, racquetball** courts, and exercise room. *Hoppy's Bowling* and *Billiard* is at 625 Patricia St.

CHILDREN'S ACTIVITIES. Babysitting services are offered through *Activity Center* on Pyramid Ave., 852–4666, for children 2–5 years old, by reservation only. Ski lessons are available at Lower Ski Chalet. The *Kid's Camp* runs daily 10 A.M.–noon with instruction for $10 per child or $20 with lunch for the full day.

NIGHTLIFE. At *Astoria Bar,* 404 Connaught Dr., you'll find a dance floor and imported beer. The *Night Club* in Athabasca Hotel on Patricia St. features top-40 music. More dancing can be found at *Champs* in the Sawridge Hotel. Most hotels have quiet lounges for relaxation. Go to *Marmot Lounge* in Marmot Lodge; *Whistle Stop Lounge* in Whistlers Motor Hotel; *Le Bonhomme Lounge* in Chateau Jasper. (See *Accommodations* above.)

British Columbia

APEX ALPINE SKI AREA

Box 448
Penticton BC V2A 6G9
Tel: 604–493–3606

Area Vertical: 2,000 ft.
Number of Trails: 36
Skiing Terrain: 12 percent
*   novice, 50 percent intermedi-*
*   ate, 38 percent expert*
Lifts: 1 triple chair, 1
*   double chair, 1 T-bar, 1 poma*
Snowmaking: limited
Season: November–mid-April

Situated 30 km west of Penticton in the mild Okanagan Valley of British Columbia, Apex Alpine is a rapidly developing ski center with lots of powder and challenging runs. Recent expansion included the installation of a new triple chairlift increasing the lift service to 2,000 vertical ft., the highest of the ski resorts in the Okanagan Mountain range.

Apex Alpine was first developed in 1961 following regional intentions to develop a provincial park in the area. In prior years, a miner named C.L. Aikins had mining rights to the present ski area site and decided to give them up as long as his cabin would be made available for use by the local Penticton Boy Scouts. In 1960 plans for a road were realized along the Shatford Creek to Beaconsfield Mountain where the Apex Alpine slopes were cut. Mt. Apex is actually close by but the name seemed suitable and marketable, hence Apex Alpine. The first double chair was installed in 1971.

Apex claims to be British Columbia's sunniest resort. Somehow it still gets plenty of snow—up to 200 cm (80 in.) a year.

Services at the mountain include condo-style accommodations, restaurants, and lounges, a grocery store, and recreational facilities. It's a family resort with plenty of kids' programs and services.

With a typically mild Okanagan climate, Apex represents a pleasant destination vacation at a full-service resort. Although much of the guests come from nearby Vancouver or Calgary, it is accessible from all North American locations.

Apex Alpine is powder snow under warm, sunny skies. It has a good variety of trails suitable for the whole family. Since 50 percent of the runs are intermediate, it's also a nice cruising mountain. Runs like Juniper, Spruce Hollow, and Okanagan give you good value from any ski equipment. The Pet and the Bowls runs treat any expert to fine open meadows, usually with lots of powder.

Its six lifts get you back to the top quickly and without lines. Lift passes cost $19 per person and $5 for the novice lift only.

The Ski School is certified by the Canadian Ski Instructors' Alliance with group lessons at $12 per person. Private lessons cost $25. Ski rentals are located at base area. Full equipment is $14 per day and $9 for juniors.

Restaurants, lounges, the grocery store, accommodations, and laundry facilities are located at the lower base area.

Mountain Magic Tours are available each day at 10 A.M. and 1 P.M. free of charge. There's a lot of "little extras" that make Apex Alpine more than just a good ski mountain. Other things like Sunday orientation evenings, farewell banquets, and a helpful guest services program.

Practical Information for Apex Alpine

 **HOW TO GET THERE.** Apex Alpine is located in the Okanagan mountain range, 30 km from Penticton, BC, and some 490 km from Vancouver.

By air. There are regularly scheduled flights from Vancouver, Calgary, Edmonton, and Toronto via *Pacific Western Airlines* into Kelowna Airport, some 60 km to the north. *Rime Air* flies in via Lethbridge, AL, and Vancouver, and *CP Holidays* from Vancouver.

By bus. *Greyhound Bus Lines,* 860–3835, services Penticton from all western Canadian cities. From Vancouver or Calgary it is about 7–10 hours travel time.

By car. From Vancouver, take Hwy. 1 east, then Rte. 97 south to Penticton. Follow signs to the ski area; the trip takes about 7 hours. An alternate southern route is to leave Hwy. 1 at Hope and follow Rte. 3 east to Rte. 97. This trip takes about 6 hours. From Calgary, it is about a 9-hour drive along Hwy. 1 and Rte. 97. Major car rental agencies at Kelowna Airport include *Budget,* 860–2464 or 800–527–0700 in the U.S., *Hertz,* 860–7808 or 800–654–3131 in the U.S.; and *Tilden (National* in the U.S.) 860–6000 or 800–328–4567 in the U.S.

TELEPHONES. The area code for all of British Columbia is 604.

 **ACCOMMODATIONS.** On-mountain lodging will handle up to 450 people and there's plenty more rooms available in Penticton 30 km away. There's an impressive new 1-, 2-, and 3-bedroom condominium complex with kitchens and fireplaces at the base of the slopes. For reservations contact *Apex Alpine,* Box 448, Penticton BC V2A 6G9; 493–3606. Video or TV rentals are available. Hot tubs compliment the comfortable lodging and evening relaxation. Apex Ski Week packages start at $199 and include 5 nights, 5 lifts, hot tubs and welcome party. Two-day packages go from $55 to $97, depending on season. The 4-day package begins at $119. In Penticton at the **Delta Lakeside Hotel,** 102 LakeShore Rd. (493–8220) ski packages range from $41 for one day to $187 for 5 days (double occupancy) with lift tickets and lesson discount.

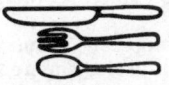 **RESTAURANTS.** Two restaurants, two lounges, and one cafeteria are situated at the ski village. The atmosphere is geared toward socializing with the help of organized theme nights and barbecues. Most major credit cards are accepted. Prices at all these restaurants range from $3 to $8 for entrees.

Murphy's Bar and Grill, (292–8668), a full service restaurant at the base of the slopes, is open 8 A.M. to 10:30 P.M. The **Gun Barrel** (292–8515), near the upper parking lot, has a casual atmosphere and a good selection of home-style food. The building also has a saloon and happens to be an Apex Alpine historical landmark. You ski right to the front door.

In Penticton, go to **Granny Bogners** (493–2911) for fine dining and European dishes. Pasta dishes and reasonable prices can be found at the **Rossi Pasta Bar;** 492–7717.

HOW TO GET AROUND. A **bus** runs up to Apex from Penticton each day at 9 A.M., returning at 4 P.M., and a limousine service is also available. Contact Apex Alpine (493–3606) for more information. For **cabs** phone *Courtesy Taxi* at 492–7778 or *Peach City Taxi* at 492–4111.

SEASONAL EVENTS. Among many events at Apex, the *Mad Dash for Cache Coors Combined Relay* is one of the most popular. There's also the *Mission Hill Vineyard's Winter Triathlon,* a combo of cross-country skiing, downhill, and an 8-km run. The *Labatt's Annual Veteran's Race* is a modified giant slalom for older skiers. The Shoot-the-Chute is Apex's zaniest event where some "crazy Canucks" race straight down the expert chute trail above the upper lodge.

OTHER SPORTS AND ACTIVITIES. Reservations for horse-drawn **sleigh rides** for groups or individuals can be made through the front desk (493–3606). The **ice skating** rink is located adjacent to the day lodge. **Broomball** games for all take place regularly. **Hot tubs** are popular after a day's skiing.

CHILDREN'S ACTIVITIES. The *Apex Alpine Day-Care* takes children from infants to age 6. It is open 9 A.M. to 4 P.M. Cost is $12 per day or $3 per hour on drop-in basis. *Kindercare* for ages 2–8 years is a full indoor/outdoor activity program operating from 9 A.M. to 9 P.M. Cost is $16 per day or $3 per hour night-time drop-in (6:30–9 P.M.). For reservations, contact the ski area reception desk, 493–3606.

NIGHTLIFE. Practically all of the après-ski activity at Apex Alpine centers around the bars at the lodges or the restaurants listed above.

BIG WHITE SKI RESORT LTD.

#226 1889 Springfield Rd.
Kelowna BC V1Y 5V5
Tel: 604–765–3101

Snow Report: 604–763–4400, 604–763–5500
Area Vertical: 1,850 feet
Number of Trails: 39 on 385 acres
Skiable Terrain: 37 percent novice, 42 percent intermediate, 21 percent expert
Lifts: 3 triple chairs, 1 double chair, 2 T-bars
Season: mid-November–mid-April

Located in the magnificent Monashee Mountain range, it's the highest ski resort in the Okanagan region. Known for its acres of deep, fluffy powder and mild temperatures, Big White is a self-contained ski village that caters to everyone.

The Doug Merlyn family began Big White's development about 17 years ago. It has since grown into an impressive facility sleeping up to 2,400 people in its varied accommodations.

As you drive into the village, probably the first impression will be of the snow banks along the narrow roads. They're massive and completely cover all road signs or anything 10 ft. or shorter. Big White is without a doubt "snow country."

One of the most enticing qualities of Big White is the "ski-to-your-door" aspect. From every condominium, chalet, or hotel on the mountainside, you need only walk outside, slip on your skis, and head for the slopes.

The city of Kelowna is 50 minutes (55 km) away and features a great variety of shopping and additional accommodations. This pleasant city, the main business center of the beautiful Okanagan Valley, is famous for its warm climate, lakes, vineyards, and summer fruit stands.

At Big White, the theme is "Ski a Village on a Mountain" and discover plenty of variety in accommodation and dining. The nightlife is good—it has to be when it is secluded up in the mountains. With an average snowfall of 300 inches (750 cms) and its great variety of slopes, Big White is the kind of place that makes you want to extend your vacation.

With 79 percent of its skiable terrain rated novice or intermediate, Big White is a great family ski resort. However, the expert terrain can challenge even the most experienced skier. Lots of snow and good grooming makes even the timid adventurer feel good on the skis. The longest run is a respectable 3 miles, and there's plenty of open and tree-line bowl skiing. Six lifts and 39 runs cover the mountain's 1,850-foot vertical and offer plenty of variety during week-long vacations.

Excellent equipment rental and ski school services are available for all ability levels. One-day full equipment rental is $13, and $9 for youths. A 1½-hour group lesson costs $14. Lift passes are priced at $20 per day, or $80 for 5 days at low season. Holiday packages are available for any number of days, and include a choice of options such as lifts, lessons, meals, and accommodations.

Skiing Big White is a pleasant experience, since mild weather and soft snow prevails. Cruising runs such as Poofter's Puff and Easy Out appeal to the slow and easy skiers, while Cliff and Dragon's Tongue keep the experts challenged during each ski turn.

Practical Information for Big White

HOW TO GET THERE. Big White is situated 55 km east of Kelowna and 512 km from Vancouver on Rte. 33 in Central British Columbia. **By air.** There are regularly scheduled flights into Kelowna Airport from Vancouver, Calgary, Edmonton, and Toronto via *Pacific Western Airlines; Time Air* via Lethbridge, Alberta, and Vancouver; and *CP Holidays* from Vancouver. Pre-booked transfers are available for individuals or groups from Kelowna to Big White Village.

By bus. *Greyhound Bus Lines* (860–3835) services Kelowna from all western Canadian cities. From Vancouver or Calgary it is approximately 7–10 hours travel time.

By car. From Vancouver, take Trans-Canada Hwy. 1 east, then south on Hwys. 97A and 97. The trip takes about 6 hours. Alternatively, take Hwy. 1 to Hwy. 3 east, and then north on Hwy. 97 to Kelowna; a scenic 7-hour drive. Calgary is 666 km east; take Hwy. 1, then Hwy. 97 south (about 8 hours). Seattle is 8 hours away and Spokane is only 6 hours. Major rental car agencies at Kelowna airport include *Budget,* 860–2464, or 800–527–0700 in the U.S.; *Hertz,* 860–7808, or 800–654–3131 in the U.S.; and *Tilden* (*National* in the U.S.), 860–6000, or 800–328–4567 in the U.S.

TELEPHONES. The area code for all of British Columbia is 604.

ACCOMMODATIONS. Phone *Central Reservation,* 861–1511 or 800–663–4151 in British Columbia and Alberta; or write *Big White Holidays,* 217–1889 Springfield Rd., Kelowna BC V1Y 5V5. Seven condominium complexes and a few chalets provide 2,400 beds all within walking or skiing distance of the slopes. Unit styles are hotel rooms, studios, and 1–3-bedroom suites with fully equipped kitchens. Most have fireplaces and underground or covered parking. Amenities include saunas, hot tubs, racquetball courts, swimming pools, and laundry facilities. Accommodations are available for any number of days with a good choice of packages that can include lifts, lessons, and meals. A variety of dining rooms and lounges are within convenient walking distance. The Village Center also features a Mountain Mart (groceries), gift shop, day-care, and shuttle bus system to main ski area day lodge.

All accommodations at Big White could be considered in the *Inexpensive-Moderate* price range. A hotel-style room for 2 persons, for instance, may cost $44, while a 2-bedroom for 4 people goes for $122, and 4-bedroom suite accommodating 8 persons goes for $175. A 2-person kitchenette and bedroom costs $55, and a studio $61. Each lodging place offers various combinations and each can be reached at the above listed Central Reservation address or phone number.

Listed below are the Big White Village lodges. A variety of motels and hotels is also available in Kelowna proper, but because of the distance, practically all skiers prefer to stay at the slopeside accommodations.

Das Hofgrauhaus. Features large 1- and 2-bedroom condominium units with kitchenettes, dining room, balcony, fireplace, and TV. This complex also has racquetball, indoor pool, hot tub, and sauna.

Greystone Inn. Offers sauna, outdoor hot tub, satellite TV, and laundry. Most rooms have fireplace and balcony.

The Monashee. Closest to the ski day lodge, has large 1- to 3-bedroom units with large common area. Most rooms with fireplace and balcony.

The Ponderosa. Features large family condo units ranging from studio to 4 bedrooms. Each unit has full kitchen, satellite TV, and laundry.

Ptarmigan Inn. Situated close to center of village and activities. Offers sauna, dip pools, satellite TV, laundry, fireplaces, and balconies.

Tamarack Inn. Cozy surroundings in center of village; has sauna, laundry, satellite TV, fireplaces, and balconies.

Whitefoot Lodge. All the amenities, including gift shop, food mart, rental shop, ski school, lift ticket outlet, sauna, laundry, pools, and satellite TV; some units with fireplaces and balconies.

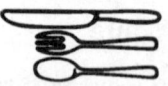

RESTAURANTS. This small mountain village features four restaurants and a deli, all in the *Moderate-Inexpensive* price range ($5-$12 for entrees), and all accepting major credit cards. **Jimmy's Deli** has a wide selection of thick sandwiches and other deli-type foods. **McGrew's** is a favorite for breakfasts and lunches. **The Red Onion** serves three meals daily. **Snow Shoe Sam's** serves only dinners, with reservations welcome; 765-1416. **Whisky Jack** offers fine dishes at lunch and dinner; 765-0855.

HOW TO GET AROUND. All facilities and services at Big White are within walking distance. A **shuttle bus,** however, makes 3-5 daily trips between the village and Kelowna, depending on the season. Contact the base lodge for schedules and information; 765-3101.

SEASONAL EVENTS. The *Team Supreme Race,* a recreational giant slalom, takes place every **March.** It's mainly for local media and restaurant people. In **April,** The *Ski to Sea* race entertains everyone. Designed as a relay, one team member skis downhill to a cross-country *skier,* who meets a *cyclist,* who rides down the road to Kelowna to a *runner,* who goes to a *canoist,* who then paddles to the city park in Kelowna.

OTHER SPORTS AND ACTIVITIES. Alpine skiing is the main activity, but not the only one up in these mountains. There are 25 km of **cross-country** trails accessible from the village and designed for all abilities. For information, call the main lodge, 265-3101.

Swimming and **racquetball** offer a nice change of pace and an opportunity to develop other muscles than those used in skiing. For court reservations, call 765-7578.

FAIRMONT HOT SPRINGS

Box 10
Fairmont Hot Springs BC V0B 1L0
Tel: 604–345–6311
Telex: 041–45108
Reservations Tel: 604–345–6311

Snow Report: 604–345–6311
Area Vertical: 1,000 ft. (300 meters)
Number of Trails: 10 on 60
*   acres (night skiing available)*
Lifts: 1 platter, 1 triple chair
Snowmaking: 70 percent of
*   acreage (5 trails)*
Season: mid-December–end of
*   March*

This family-owned luxury resort is nestled on the western slopes of the British Columbia Rockies overlooking the beautiful Columbia River Valley and Lake Windermere. Fairmont was homesteaded back in 1887, then grew into a rest stop for the valley stage coaches. Around the turn of the century a wealthy visiting Englishman named W. H. Holland was so impressed by the quality of the mineral hot pools and the region's natural beauty he settled in with his family to operate a resort ranch. Later, in 1956, some local businessmen, including Lloyd and Earl Wilder, purchased the resort. The Wilder brothers soon bought out the other partners and began the development toward today's grand resort.

Lloyd Wilder purchased his brother's share in 1965 and quickly stepped up expansion to include a ski area, an 18-hole, par-70 cham-pionship golf course, time-share villas, and improved mineral hot pool facilities. In 1985 access to Fairmont increased significantly with the building of a new 1,500-foot airstrip capable of handling Dash 7 class airplanes via connections from major airports.

Fairmont continues to grow and improve as a fabulous ski-and-swim family resort. Although their famous hot pools remain the main attrac-tion, the moderate-sized ski area offers a pleasant experience for any level skier seeking a unique ski vacation.

Although famous for its combination of sports activities, the Fair-mont Ski Area offers an enjoyable experience to any skier. Its respect-able 1,000-foot vertical offers challenge on its 10 runs ranging from 2,000 to 6,000 feet in length. There's a great view of the Columbia River Valley and the Parcell Mountains beyond. The slopes sit at the base of majestic Rocky Mountain cliffs and peaks. Night skiing is available.

There are superb on-mountain facilities, including a large day-lodge and deck. There's a cafeteria and lounge with fireplace. Lifts cost $15 for a full day and $10 for a half-day. Rental equipment costs $13 per day for a full set, and children's equipment costs $11.

The Ski School plays an active role in the ski packages. A pleasant mix of skiing, instruction, and social activities, such as a western barbe-cue and a fun race, enhance the snow vacation. Use of hot pools is also included as well as optional ski day at nearby Panorama or Kimberly ski areas.

Practical Information for Fairmont Hot Springs

HOW TO GET THERE. Fairmont Hot Springs is located in the Columbia River Valley on Hwy. 93 near Invermere, between Cranbrook and Golden, BC. Calgary, AL, is 270 km east and Cranbrook, a much smaller city, is 110 km to the south.

By air. Major airlines fly into Calgary International Airport with connections to Cranbrook via *Pacific Western Airlines*. From the west, Vancouver is another gateway to the region, with *Pacific Western* connections to Cranbrook. Car rentals available in Calgary include *Avis,* 489–4710, or 800–331–1212 in U.S.; *Budget,* 489–4371, or 800–527–0700 in U.S.; and *Tilden,* 489–1335, or 800–328 –4567 in U.S. Rentals available in Cranbrook are *Hertz,* 800–268–1311, or 800–654–3131 in U.S.; and *Tilden,* 344–5914.

By bus. *Greyhound Bus Lines* services are available from Calgary,Cranbrook, and Vancouver. For information on schedules and fares, phone 403–762–2236.

By car. It takes approximately 3 hours to drive to Fairmont Hot Springs from Calgary, and 1½ hours from Cranbrook. From Calgary, take Hwy. 1 west, then Hwy. 93 south. From Cranbrook, drive north on Hwy. 93–95 to the resort. Vancouver is a 10–hour drive on scenic Hwy. 1 northward and eastward, then south on Hwy. 95 from Golden.

TELEPHONES. The area code for all of British Columbia is 604, and for Alberta it is 403.

ACCOMMODATIONS. Fairmont has 700 pillows at the resort. For reservations at any of the lodgings contact Box 10, Fairmont Hot Springs, BC B0B 1L0; phone 345–6311; 403–264–0746 in Calgary; or 800–663–4979 in other parts of British Columbia, Alberta, or Saskatchewan.

Deluxe hotel accommodations are available in the **Fairmont Lodge** or the resort's new condominiums. Recent renovations to the lodge feature 140 rooms with full hotel services and access to its own mineral pool. There is a full-service dining room, a residents' lounge, and a selection of conference rooms for large or small groups. Prices per person, based on double occupancy, range from $55 to $84, depending on the season.

Lofts cost $80–$117 for a minimum of 4 people. Interval ownership is also available for **deluxe villas.**

A variety of packages, ranging from 3 to 5 days, is also available at the lodge, with special rates for children. Some packages offer ski instructions as well as passes for Fairmont and 3 other ski areas—Fernie, Kimberly, and Panorama.

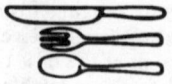

RESTAURANTS. The **Fairmont Lodge Restaurant** has fine dining and reasonable prices. Entres range from $7.95 to about $20. The town of Invermere is 25 km away and includes several restaurants and bars as well as daytime shopping. (See section on Panorama for more information on Invermere).

HOW TO GET AROUND. For recreational vehicles, there are 30 year-round RV sites located near the main lodge and hot pools. A free **ski bus** service is available for guests to the ski slopes.

SEASONAL EVENTS. The *Fairmont Annual Snow Golf* event takes place each year in late **January** or early **February.**

 **OTHER SPORTS AND ACTIVITIES.** This is where Fairmont shines. There are more than enough things to do for the active guest. **Racquetball** and squash are available in the new recreational complex, the *Fairmont Sports Center,* which has a regular indoor **swimming pool,** saunas, Jacuzzi, and a gym. **Aerobic** classes are also scheduled.

No one can resist the 930 square meters of steaming hot mineral water in natural, odorless **hot pools.** Open year-round, the water temperatures vary between 34° and 45° C. There are small indoor soaking pools as well as a giant outdoor heated swimming pool, which is also open in winter. Soaking in the hot pools at the base of the Rockies surrounded by snow is an exhilarating experience. Pools are open 8 A.M. to 10 P.M. daily.

If you're lucky and visiting in early spring, the valley's warm climate enables the 18-hole **golf** course to open early. Ski in the morning and golf in the afternoon. **Snowmobiling** and **fishing** are also offered nearby. For any activity, contact the resort's main office, 345–6311.

 **DAY-CARE FACILITIES.** *Ski Chalet* baby-sitting services are available upon request. Phone 604–345–6311 for reservations. Baby-sitters are on duty 10 A.M.–4 P.M. daily for children 2–6 years old, at $2 per hour for 1 child, $1 per extra child. Ski lessons are available for children aged 3–12 years. Skiing is free for kids under 8 years old. It's easy to keep track of kids on the slopes because of the easy terrain.

NIGHTLIFE. The *Devil's Outlet Lounge* features nightly live entertainment for those with leftover energy. The town of Invermere, 25 km away, has several bars. (See section on Panorama.)

FERNIE SNOW VALLEY

P.O. Box 788
Fernie BC V0B 1M0
Tel: 604-423-9221

*Snow Report: 604–423–9921,
403–246–2736
Area Vertical: 2,100 ft.
Number of Trails: 34
Skiing Terrain: 25 percent
novice, 40 percent intermediate, 35 percent expert
Lifts: 1 triple chair, 1
double chair, 3 T-bars
Snowmaking: for patching only
Season: mid-November–late
April*

Situated in the Crowsnest Pass area only a few minutes from the town of Fernie and a 3½-hour drive southwest of Calgary, Fernie Snow Valley is a paradise for skiers who want powder.

With over 600 cm of snow annually, this quaint ski resort is considered (by *Ski Canada Magazine*) one of the best ski values in North America. The recent addition of the new Boomerang Triple Chair lift has increased that value and the skiing terrain by 30 percent.

The community of Fernie was founded in the nineteenth century as a coal mining center. The lumber industry also contributed to its growth, and Fernie now has 7,500 or so people. In the winter, it becomes a real ski town nestled beneath the high peaks of Trinity Mountain, which is often called the Three Sisters because of its distinct triple-peak formation. The late Edwardian-style red brick buildings add to the town's charm with an awesome view of the ski area's peaks and bowls above.

Fernie Snow Valley has developed rapidly into a unique destination, including new accommodations within walking distance of the slopes.

In 1989, it will host the ninth annual British Columbia Winter Games. More then 2,000 amateur athletes will participate.

Fernie credits its abundance of snow to a local legend named Griz, a century-old man of the mountains who hibernates in rock caves during the summers. He appears each fall ready to make more and more powder. He's worth visiting.

Fernie Snow Valley is famous for its snow and upper-bowl skiing. Its 2,100-foot vertical stretches out into a combination of wide bowls, ridges, and rolling tree runs, making it an interesting ski center for any level of skier.

The novice will enjoy the Meadow run off the Deer T-bar, while the intermediate skier can test his skills off the mile-long Guy Chair on runs such as Lizard. The experts frolic in the deep stuff up in the Lizard or Cedar bowls or on Boomerang Ridge.

Fernie's longest run is about 5 km and its newest triple chair, called Boomerang, has been long awaited. This 1,300-meter chair opens up great skiing terrain which was previously accessible only by long traverses in and out of the area. This is where the mountain's deeper and drier snow is found. Adult lift tickets cost $18.

There is a CSIA-certified ski school open to teach both beginners and powder-hounds. Group 1½-hour lessons run $15 per person; private lessons are $25. The rental shop offers complete equipment rentals for $12 per day. The day lodge facility answers all your skiing needs with licensed cafeteria, ski shop, and other facilities.

Practical Information for Fernie

HOW TO GET THERE. Fernie is 320 km from Calgary, and 60 km from Cranbrook, BC. **By air.** Fly to Calgary International or Vancouver airports via most major airlines such as *Air Canada, Canadian Pacific Air, United,* or *Western.* Connections can be made at either airport to *Pacific Western Airlines* to the Kimberly/Cranbrook Airport, but it's probably cheaper to drive from Calgary. For rental cars at Calgary, phone *Avis,* 403–250–0770, or *Budget* 403–250–0760.

By bus. *Greyhound Bus Lines,* 403–265–9111, makes two trips to Fernie daily from Calgary.

By car. It takes 3½–4 hours to drive from Calgary, south on Hwy. 2, then west on Hwy. 3 to Fernie and the ski area. From Cranbrook, the trip is about 1½ hours east on Hwy. 3. The trip from Vancouver takes 10–11 hours, driving east on Hwy. 1, which connects with Hwy. 3 at Hope BC. From Spokane WA, 189 km away, drive north on Rte. 2 through the tip of Idaho onto Hwy. 3.

TELEPHONES. The area code for all of British Columbia is 604, and for Alberta it is 403.

ACCOMMODATIONS. At the ski resort itself the new 36-unit **Griz Inn,** 423–9221, enables visitors to ski to their doors. Suites are self-contained condominiums with complete kitchens, microwave ovens, and dishwashers. Other facilities include Jacuzzi, sauna, game room, and dining room. Prices, considered *Expensive* in these parts, range from $57 per person, double occupancy, for a 1-bedroom unit to $128 for a 3-bedroom loft. Ski week packages are also available for 5 nights and include lift passes, lessons, and social activities.

Listed here are some accommodations in the town of Fernie, just a few miles away. Categories, determined by price, are *Moderate,* $30–$50; and *Inexpensive,* less than $30.

Cedar Lodge. *Moderate.* P.O. Box 1477; 423–4622. Has 48 rooms, with cable TV, swimming pool, whirlpool, and sauna.

Park Place Lodge. *Moderate.* P.O. Box 2199; 423–6871. 47 well-appointed rooms, swimming pool, sauna, and lounge.

Anco Motel. *Inexpensive.* P.O. Box 1230; 423–4492. Features whirlpool, sauna, satellite TV.

Inn Towner Motel. *Inexpensive.* 601 Second Ave.; 423–6308. Has 14 rooms with color TV, and some with kitchenettes.

Snow Valley Motel. *Inexpensive.* 423–4421. Pleasant facility with 21 units and cable TV.

Three Sisters Motel. *Inexpensive.* P.O. Box 280; 423–4492. Has a whirlpool and sauna for 38 comfortable units; 14 units have kitchens.

RESTAURANTS. As in the case of accommodations, the pocketbook can be spared either at the ski resort itself or in the small town of Fernie. For an *Expensive* meal in this area, expect to pay $9–$14; *Moderate,* $5–$9; *Inexpensive,* less than $5. Reservations are not required at any of the places listed, and all but the inexpensive places accept major credit cards.

Grizzly's Restaurant and Bar. *Expensive.* At the resort's Griz Inn on the slopes; 432–9221. Fine dining offers a wide choice of entrees; Continental cuisine.

Olde Elevator Steak House. *Expensive.* 291 First Ave., Fernie; 423–7115. Steaks done the way you like them.

Alpine Restaurant. *Moderate.* Hwy. 3, Fernie; 423–3211. Both Swiss and Chinese specialties.

Coal Valley Steak and Pancake House. *Moderate.* Hwy. 3, Fernie; 423–3118. Like the name says, steaks and pancakes.

Cravings Cafe. *Moderate.* 602 Second Ave., Fernie; 423–4815. Wholesome homemade food, served family style.

Libby's. *Inexpensive.* Hwy. 3; Fernie; 423–7444. Pizza and lasagna.

HOW TO GET AROUND. It's best to have your own (or rented) **car** at this resort, but it will mostly stay put once you get here. There's **taxi** service available in the town of Fernie; call *Kootenay Taxi,* 423–4514.

SEASONAL EVENTS. Enjoy *Griz Days* in late **January.** In recognition of the legendary "Griz," Fernie's powdermaker, the townspeople hold a week-long festival, including sporting events, competitions, and parades. *Powder 8* championships take place in **March** when teams attempt to make perfect figure eights in the powder. The *OKEE DOKEE Downhill* is a recreational downhill race in late March. The *Powder-Peddle-Paddle* is a fun-filled relay race each **April.**

OTHER SPORTS AND ACTIVITIES. As noted, Fernie is a small town and **skiing** is the biggest activity. For relaxing the muscles, there's a **hot tub** at the ski center. In the village, the Cedar Lodge, 423–2622, and Park Place Lodge, 423–6871, both have **swimming pools,** and most other in-town hotels have **saunas.**

CHILDREN'S ACTIVITIES. Babysitting services are available upon reservation at the resort; 423–9221. The Nursery Ski School operates 7 days per week for toddlers 3–5 years old from 10 A.M. to 3 P.M. Cost is $20 per day and includes indoor play and outdoor skiing and instruction. Children under 6 ski free.

NIGHTLIFE. There's good entertainment here for a small town. *Papa John's* at the corner of Second Ave. and 3rd St., 423–3343, is a popular pub with dancing and a big screenTV. *J.P.'s Place,* 691 First Ave. (423–6444), is where all the sports people meet. The *Sundown Nite Club* at 892 Sixth Ave. (423–7223) has lots of rock and roll for those looking for dancing. For a more sedate evening at the movies, there's the *Vogue Theater* at 321 Second Ave. (423–6665).

KIMBERLEY SKI RESORT

P.O. Box 40
Kimberley BC V1A 2S5
Tel: 604–427–4881

Snow Report: 604–427–4861
Area Vertical: 2,300 ft.
Number of Trails: 32 over 322
    skiable acres
Skiing Terrain: 15 percent
    novice, 60 percent intermedi-
    ate, 25 percent expert
Lifts: 1 double, 1 triple, 1
    T-Bar, 2 pony
Snowmaking: 10 percent of
    terrain
Season: December–mid April

The small alpine city of Kimberley is situated in British Columbia's Purcell Mountains. Across the broad valley below is a great view of the Rockies. As the site of one of the world's largest underground lead and zinc mines, Kimberley is also a year-round resort offering many events and sports activities.

Kimberley was transformed into a "Bavarian" city in 1972 as part of a major downtown beautification plan. Kimberley is actually a mix of Austrian, Swiss, and English Tudor styles. The Bavarian theme is appropriate to its alpine setting with its very own community ski area above the valley.

The Platzl, meaning "people's place," represents the two main commercial streets lined with Bavarian-style store fronts and home to the world's largest cuckoo clock. It's Kimberley's focal point, only minutes from the ski slopes. The Bavarian alpine architecture in this beautiful mountain setting, with cross-country and downhill facilities within city limits, evokes the feeling of a European ski village. These skiing facilities were built by volunteer labor in the 1950s as recreation for the local mine workers. The development of recreation was crucial to the Cominco Mines to retain miners in the region.

At first, ski-jumping was the big sport right downtown. The *Kimberley Ski Club* then decided to build a ski hill 2 miles from the present site that required an overnight touring trek to get there. Finally, with Cominco's approval, the present ski area site was developed. A T-bar was installed in 1964 to begin today's well-developed ski and accommodation resort.

Overlooking the Bavarian city of the Rockies, the Kimberley Ski Resort stretches to the top of North Star Mountain. You'll find an impressive 2,300-foot vertical with runs stretching out in 32 directions. The weather is typically mild for this part of British Columbia. The snow is abundant and easy to slice into with your skis.

The three major lifts service a mostly intermediate mountain for good cruising. Expert terrain represents 25 percent and novice is 15 percent of the total skiable area. The highest elevation is 6,500 ft. offering a pleasant view of the Kootenay River Valley lined with the Rockies to the east. Lift tickets are $19 per day on weekends and $18 per day during midweek.

There's great night skiing, too. The Main, North America's largest illuminated run, is a unique ski experience with the lights of Kimberley town and the mountain village twinkling below. It presents yet another choice of activities for vacation evenings.

Complete ski rental packages cost $12 per day. The 5-day rental package costs $50. There's a well-qualified ski school offering $14 group lessons and private lessons for $25. There's also a unique free guide service provided by local volunteers familiar with all the runs as well as local history and folklore.

Practical Information for Kimberley

HOW TO GET THERE. Kimberley is 30 miles north of Cranbrook BC, on Hwy. 95A, and 70 miles from the U.S. border near the Montana and Idaho state line. **By air.** Fly to Calgary International or Vancouver airports via most major airlines such as *Air Canada, Canadian Pacific Air, United,* or *Western.* Connections can be made at either airport to *Pacific Western Airlines,* which flies into Kimberley/Cranbrook Airport. Car rentals are available there from *Avis,* 489–4710, or 800–331–1212 in the U.S.; *Budget,* 489–4371 or 800–527–0700 in the U.S.; or *Tilden,* 489–1335.

By bus. *Greyhound Bus Lines* serves Kimberley from most major western cities of Canada and the U.S. From Calgary, the bus ride is about 5 hours; 403–265–9111.

By car. Driving distance from Vancouver is 870 km, east on Hwy. 1, which connects with Hwy. 3 at Hope BC, and onto 95A at Cranbrook. From Spokane WA, drive north on Rte. 2 through the tip of Idaho onto Hwy. 3. From any direction, it's a very scenic drive through various mountain ranges.

TELEPHONES. The area code for all of British Columbia is 604, and for Alberta it is 403.

ACCOMMODATIONS. The resort has condominium and chalet lodgings for 1,400 guests within walking distance of the ski lifts. Most lodgings have saunas, hot tubs, and recreation centers. Furthermore, all feature affordable prices. Reservations for on-mountain accommodations can be made either through *Kimberley Ski Resort,* P.O. Box 40, Kimberley BC V1A 2S5; (427–4881) or by calling the number for each individual listing. Although most skiers prefer to stay at slopeside accommodations, a selection of hotels and motels is available in the city of Kimberley just a few minutes (7 km) away.

Hotel rates are per person, based on double occupancy. *Moderate:* $30–$40; *Inexpensive:* less than $30.

ON-MOUNTAIN

Inn West/Kirkwood Inn. *Moderate.* 427–7616. Condominium units of 1–2 bedrooms, each with fireplace, kitchen, and balcony. Two-day packages include lift privileges and breakfast. Five-day packages also available. Children under 9 years stay free.

Mountain Edge Resort Inn. *Moderate.* 427–5381. The newest accommodation on the slopes with 42 1-bedroom condos with living room, kitchen, fireplace, balcony, satellite TV, and protected parking. Three-day packages available.

Purcell Condo Hotel. *Moderate.* 427–5385. Units of 1, 2, and 3 bedrooms, with kitchens, wood-burning stoves, and balconies. Two- and 5-day packages available, with breakfast and lift tickets.

Rocky Mountain Condo Hotel. *Moderate;* 427–5385. A short walk to the ski slopes. Amenities include breakfast with a 2-day package.

Silver Birch Chalets. *Moderate;* 427–5385. Located at eastern end of Kimberley Village; three chalets are available as are 2-day packages with breakfast and ski lifts.

KIMBERLEY

Rhinecastle Inn. *Moderate.* 300 Wallington Ave.; 427–2266. Just 5 minutes from the lifts; 41 well-appointed rooms, satellite TV and disco; 2-day package available.

Kimbrook Inn. *Inexpensive.* 2665 Warren Ave.; 427–4855. Offers 33 rooms with satellite TV, direct dial phones, dining room, and cocktail lounge.

CAMPING. The **Happy Hans Campgrounds** is located 2 km from Kimberley on Rte. 95A on the way to the ski resort; 427–3666. There are some 130 fully-serviced wooded sites available for RVs. Fees are $10 for full service, including water and electrical hookups.

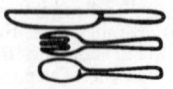

RESTAURANTS. On the mountain, there is a selection of eating places, from seated dining in the North Star Center, with burgers, club sandwiches, homemade soups, and full-course dinners, to cafeteria services in the main lodge. In Kimberley, there is a wider selection. The price categories are based on the cost of a 3-course dinner for one person; beverages and tip not included. *Expensive:* $13–$20; *Moderate:* $7–$13; *Inexpensive:* less than $7. All the dining places at the resort are in the *Inexpensive–Moderate* range. Listed below is a selection of restaurants in Kimberley. All except the inexpensive places take MasterCard and Visa.

Expensive

Gasthaus Am Platzl. 240 Spokane St.; 426–4851. Specializes in fine German dining. Lunch and dinner served; reservations suggested for dinner.

Moderate

Aikmans Restaurant. 175 Deer Park Rd.; 427–3626. Family dining. Canadian dishes, breakfast, lunch, and dinner.

Alpenrose. 136 Wallinger Ave.; 427–7461. Family dining for breakfast, lunch, and dinner.

Kimberley City Bakery. 287 Spokane St.; 427–2131. Swiss bakery, tea room, and sidewalk cafe. Lunches and takeout service.

Kimbrook Inn. 2665 Warren Ave.; 427–4855. Serves breakfast, lunch, and dinner. Canadian dishes.

La Casa Amigos. 290 Spokane St.; 427–3739. Breakfast and lunches only. Features Mexican dishes. Takeout available.

Inexpensive

BJ's Breakfast. 340 Mark St.; 427–7618. Specializes in breakfasts, as name implies. Homemade food.

Dixie Lee Chicken and Seafood. 490 Wallinger Ave.; 427–7814. Lunches and dinner.

Hunter's Haus of Burgers. 385 Wallinger Ave.; 427–7224. Lunches and dinner. Fast food and soft ice cream.

Marg's Kitchen. 324 Archibald St.; 427–3412. Breakfast, lunch, dinner, and takeouts.

The Station. 350 Ross St.; 427–2766. Serves lunch and dinner family style in Kimberley's original CP Railroad station.

HOW TO GET AROUND. There's a complimentary **shuttle** service between Kimberley Village and downtown Kimberley each half hour on weekends. During the week, **taxi** service is available from *L & K Taxi Company,* 427–4442, at $4 for the 7-mile trip. If you wish to venture farther afield, it's best to have a **car.**

SEASONAL EVENTS. February brings disabled skiers from across the country for the *Disabled Skiers Challenge.* On the second weekend of February, the *Winterfest* kicks off with a beerfest. The *Rocky Mountain Super Giant Slalom* is scheduled for the beginning of **March.** *Winter Carnival* takes place the end of March. The spectacular *Bavarian Iron Legs* competition is in early **April.** Mid-April brings in the *Spring Slash.* You'll see crazy skiers in the true spring spirit attempting to ski through a pond of ice-cold snow-melt water at the base.

OTHER SPORTS AND ACTIVITIES. The lineup of slopeside activities include **indoor tennis, hot tubs, saunas** and 26 km of groomed **cross-country ski** trails. For information and reservations, contact the ski area, 427–4881. In the town of Kimberley, **curling** is available at the *Kimberley Curling Club,* 427–2591, and **bowling** is at *Head Pins Bowling,* 427–7514.

CHILDREN'S ACTIVITIES. This is a new program at Kimberley. Day-care for children 2–6 years old is available daily. Cost is $5 per hour and includes indoor and outdoor activities. Although no formal lessons are available, kids are grouped together in lessons as much as possible. For information and reservations, contact the lodge office, 427–4881.

NIGHTLIFE. There are three hot spots in Kimberley. In the North Star Center at the ski hill, the *Disco Cabaret* (427–4881) has live entertainment and dancing. In town, visit the *Kimbrook Inn,* 2665 Warren St. (427–4855), a disco and lounge. The Rhine Castle Disco Cabaret, at 300 Wallinger (427–2266), is another dance spot. Most hotels have quiet lounges for pleasant relaxation.

MOUNT WASHINGTON SKI RESORT LTD.

Box 217
Campbell River BC V9W 5B1
Tel: 604–338–1386

Snow Report: 604–338–1515
Area Vertical: 1,600 ft.
Number of Trails: 24 on 112
*   skiable acres*
Skiing Terrain: 30 percent
*   novice, 40 percent intermedi-*
*   ate, 30 percent expert*
Lifts: 2 triple chairs, 2
*   double chairs, 1 handletow*
Snowmaking: none
Season: mid-November–end of
*   April*

To ski Mount Washington is to ski an island in the Pacific. With a yearly average snowfall of 1,200 cm (472 inches), this relatively new ski area is attracting more and more attention.

Located on Vancouver Island in the Comox Valley, this fairly remote ski center offers a unique experience and the opportunity to get away from it all.

The slopes are varied from steep to easy. There are complete services at the base, including a mountain village with modern 1- and 2-bedroom units. Down in the Comox Valley and the town of Courtenay, you'll find plenty of other shopping and entertainment services.

The area was originally settled for the mining and lumber industries. Mount Washington Ski Area was begun in 1979 with the installation of two double chairlifts. Two businessmen from Campbell River foresaw the potential of the island resort and it hasn't stopped growing since.

Just 31 km (19 miles) from the town of Comox, Mount Washington boasts scenic grandeur with ideal terrain for all levels of skiers. The highest elevation is 1,576 m (5,168 ft.) above sea level, with an average annual snowfall of 1,200 cm (472 inches). Beginners can conveniently reach the handletow just 50 m from the rental shop.

Lift tickets are $18 for an adult full day, $12 half day, $10 for children 6–12 and $8 half day. Seniors over 65 can purchase a full day pass for $10. Children 6 and under ski for free.

Maintained nordic trails and wilderness skiing are also available at this resort.

Alpine rentals, cross-country rentals, and a certified CSIA ski school are located at the base of the mountain.

Adventure ski weeks are popular at Mount Washington. With the ski pros as your hosts, the program includes a Sunday evening greeting presentation and a Friday farewell dinner party. Also included in addition to accommodations are lifts, movies, evening entertainment in the lounge, and one other meal.

Practical Information for Mount Washington

HOW TO GET THERE. Mount Washington is located 31 km west of Courtenay BC, 250 km from Victoria, and 135 km from Vancouver. **By air.** Daily flights run via Dash 7 planes from Vancouver to Comox. *Pacific Western Airlines* (684–6161) has two flights daily into Comox Airport on Vancouver Island. All connections to most North American cities can be made at Vancouver International Airport;

By bus. *Conmac Tours* buses go directly to Mount Washington resort daily from Sydney and Tuesdays, Thursdays, Saturdays, and Sundays from Victoria. *Pacific Coach Lines* provides bus service twice daily between Victoria and Courtenay. *Hilo Transportation* provides transport from Comox to Mount Washington. For information on any of these lines, call 656–3102.

By car. Auto rentals are available at the Comox Airport from *Budget,* 338–7717; and *Tilden,* 339–6331.

By ferry. Every 2 hours, from 7 A.M. to 9 P.M., the *BC Ferries* serve the Island between Vancouver and Nanaimo. Phone 669–1211.

TELEPHONES. The area code for all of British Columbia is 604.

ACCOMMODATIONS. For lodgings at the mountain, contact *Mount Washington Central Reservations,* 2040 Cliffe Ave., Courtenay BC, V9N 2L3; 338–1386. Fully-equipped 1–2-bedroom condominiums are available. In Courtenay there is a variety of hotels, lodges, inns, and motels. Hotel prices are based on double occupancy. Categories are: *Expensive,* $50–$80; *Moderate,* $35–$50; *Inexpensive,* less than $35. The mountain condo units fall in the moderate range. Listed below is a selection of accommodations in Courtenay.

Westerly Hotel. *Expensive.* 1590 Cliffe Ave.; 338–7741. Features pool, sauna, Jacuzzi, lounge, restaurant, satellite TV, ski rentals.

Arbutus TraveLodge. *Moderate.* 275 Eighth St.; 334–3121. Features sauna, lounge, restaurant, and satellite TV.

Best Western/The Pointe. *Moderate.* Island Hwy. RR 1; 338–5456. Has kitchenettes, pool, sauna, Jacuzzi, lounge, restaurant, and ski rentals.

Collingwood Inn. *Moderate.* 1675 Cliffe Ave.; 338–1464. Cozy place with kitchenettes, lounge, restaurant, ski rentals, and laundromat.

Pacific Village. *Moderate.* Island Hwy. RR 1; 338–1464. Chalets with kitchenettes available; restaurant on property.

Port Augusta Motel. *Moderate.* 2082 Comox Ave.; 339–2277. Rooms with kitchenettes; pool, sauna, restaurant, laundromat.

Sleepy Hollow Motel. *Moderate.* 1190 Cliffe Ave.; 334–4476. Has kitchenettes, pool, sauna, and Jacuzzi.

Washington Inn. *Moderate.* 1001 Ryan Rd.; 338–5441. Features pool, sauna, Jacuzzi, lounge, restaurant, satellite TV, and ski rentals.

Anco Slumber Lodge. *Inexpensive.* 1885 Cliffe Ave.; 334–2451. Basic accommodations with kitchenettes, satellite TV.

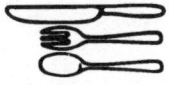

RESTAURANTS. The Comox Valley has several eating spots popular with skiers. *Expensive* prices range from $14 to $19; *Moderate,* $8–$13; *Inexpensive,* under $8. All major credit cards are accepted unless otherwise noted.

Cafeteria food is available in the Alpine Daylodge, breakfast and lunches. Moderately priced meals are served in the lodge's dining room. Reservations are welcome. Phone 338–1386.

La Cremaillere. *Expensive.* 975 Comox Ave.; 338–8131. French cuisine in a mansion on the banks of the Courtenay River. By reservation.

The Gaff Rig Restaurant. *Expensive.* 1984 Buenavista Ave.; 339–7181. Fine European specialties, steaks, and seafood. Reservations required for dinner.

The Old House Restaurant. *Moderate.* 100 17th St.; 338–5406. Seafood and wild game.

The Pewter Room. *Moderate.* 498 North Island Hwy.; 334–4401. European atmosphere.

Bino's Restaurant. *Inexpensive.* 2601 South Island Hwy.; 334–3931. Canadian dishes.

Columbo Steak House. *Inexpensive.* 1450 Ryan Rd.; 338–1488. Steaks and seafood.

HOW TO GET AROUND. Once in the Comox Valley, the two options for traveling up to the mountain are driving your own—or rented—**car** or availing yourself of the convenient **shuttle bus** service between the mountain and Courtenay. For information and schedules, call the lodge office, 338–1386. For **car rentals** at Courtenay, contact *Budget,* 338–7717, or *Hertz,* 800–286–1311.

SEASONAL EVENTS. In **January** the *Toyota Giant Slalom* takes place. In **March,** the *Canadian Armed Forces Championship* is held. These are recreational fun races with light competition. Also in March is the *Mount Washington Annual Cross-Country Marathon* and the *Canadian Masters Alpine Series.* The *Spring Fest* takes place every **April** and features a beer garden, a breakfast barbecue, and a fun costume race.

OTHER SPORTS AND ACTIVITIES. In Courtenay, there are 4 **golf** courses and 13 public **tennis** courts that sometimes open in early April. With a choice of 8 **fitness centers, tanning salons,** and **aerobics classes,** you're bound to leave healthier than you came. Phone 338–1386.

Other facilities in the Comox Valley include large indoor **pools,** whirlpools, and saunas at Best Western Hotel (338–5456) and Westerly Hotel (338–7741).

CHILDREN'S ACTIVITIES. The *Mount Washington Ski School* divides the *Kid's Brigade* into three programs. For 3–7-year-olds, there are full days of skiing, building snowmen, and tobogganing, and the charge is $7–$8 a day. For 8–15-year-olds there are ski lessons, which cost $12 for 1½ hours, $50 for 5 lessons, and $90 for 10 lessons.

Evening activities are scheduled daily for children 6–12 years of age. From 4 P.M. to 6 P.M. supervision is offered for the kids while the parents relax in the lounge. Formal activities, 7–10 P.M., include games, crafts, and movies. All evening programs are free of charge. Contact the Ski School for details, 338–1386.

NIGHTLIFE. The lounge at the *Alpine Daylodge* features après-ski and dancing each evening until 11. In Courtenay the *Courtenay House,* 334–4401, features Doc's Cabaret. The *Leeward Pub,* 339–5400, on Anderson Rd. has homemade country cooking for snacks. The *Soft Cabaret,* 339–4022, features live bands. The *Whistle Stop,* 334–4500, on Mansfield St. is another relaxing neighborhood pub.

PANORAMA RESORT

Box 7000
Invermere BC V0A 1K0
Tel: 604–342–6941

Snow Report: 403–246–2736
Area Vertical: 3,800 ft.
Trails: 26 on 260 acres of
  skiable terrain
Lifts: 1 triple chair,
  2 double chairs, 2 T-bars,
  1 poma
Snowmaking: 60 percent of
  acreage (10 trails)
Season: December–mid-April

Panaroma has come a long way in the past 5 years. Once just a small community ski center on a winding dirt road used by miners on their way to nearby silver claims like Paradise Mines, this full-service resort has grown into a year-round luxury destination. Activities are abundant in any season and the accommodations can't be beat for convenience and comfort. Panorama calls itself "Canada's Alpine Family Resort."

By hosting the 1985 men's World Cup downhill race, it has established its ski slopes as world class. The skiing is exciting for any level and the scenery of the Purcell Mountains, including huge, jagged Mount Nelson, is spectacular.

Located only 20 minutes from the town of Invermere on Lake Windermere, it's the climax of a scenic drive up Toby Creek Rd. All services are within walking distance, so if you're driving just park your auto underground and enjoy your vacation. Choose from 350 comfortable hotel rooms, condos, or suites just a few steps from the slopes.

With a combination of impressive ski services including heli-skiing and the varied après-ski activities, there's never a dull moment. The mild weather typical of the region is an extra treat.

The very impressive 3,800-foot vertical splits up into 26 well-designed runs served by 7 lifts. The state-of-the-art snowmaking system assures you of an extra snow base. Panorama boasts the highest-serviced vertical in the Rockies complemented by great fall-line trails without uneven side slopes common to many ski areas.

A recently-installed champagne T-bar at the top of the mountain takes you to the top of ski runs up to 5.5 km long. It's an ideal family ski area with 82 percent of the runs rated as novice and intermediate, leaving 18 percent for expert runs as a challenge to any ski adventurer. Lift tickets cost $19 a day, $12 for juniors, and are free for 8-year-olds and under.

One thing that makes Panorama even more unique is its heli-skiing package that offers an easy-paced program with an on-hill prep course, heli-skiing in Purcell Mountains with the instructor and guide, and a hearty lunch. Intermediates are welcome. Cost is $110 per person. This is an extraordinary opportunity to try powder heli-skiing a bit at a time.

Panorama's (CSIA) qualified ski school will enhance your vacation with group, private, and multi-day lesson packages. The popular Ski Week program features video, 6 hours of group lessons, fun race, and social activities. Price is $65 per person. Other packages without lessons are the weekender from $67 for skiing and accommodations and the 5-day, 5-night package from $170, based on 4-person occupancy.

Enjoy cross-country skiing on 20 km of groomed trails. Equipment rentals and lessons are available.

Practical Information for Panorama

HOW TO GET THERE. Panorama is 120 km from Cranbrook and 297 km from Calgary. **By air.** *Pacific Western Airlines,* 489–4393, flies to Cranbrook from Vancouver and Calgary. There are three flights daily Mondays–Fridays from either city. The weekend service has fewer flights. All connections to other airlines can be made in Vancouver and Calgary.

By bus. Originating from Cranbrook, Calgary, and Vancouver, *Greyhound Bus Lines,* 344–6172, stops in Invermere daily. Panorama has its own private pickup to take guests to and from the depot. Roundtrip from Cranbrook costs $11.35; from Calgary, $9; from Vancouver, $55.

By train. The *Via Rail,* 800–665–8630, passenger train stops in Golden; bus connections leave daily from Golden and Invermere.

By car. The routes are well maintained, paved, and easy to follow. Traveling from Calgary, follow Hwy. 1 to Hwy. 93 south. Hwy. 93 is a 2½-hour scenic drive to Invermere. From Vancouver, take Hwy. 1 to Golden and Hwy. 95 south to Invermere. This route takes approximately 10 hours. **Car rentals** in Calgary: *Avis,* 403–250–0763; *Budget,* 403–250–0760; *Hertz,* 403–250–0746; *Tilden,* 403–250–0770. In Cranbrook: *Avis,* 604–489–4710; *Budget,* 604–489–4371; *Hertz,* 604–426–7500; *Tilden,* 604–489–1335. In the U.S.: *Avis,* 800–331–1212; *Budget,* 800–527–0900; *Hertz,* 800–634–3131.

TELEPHONES. The area code for all of British Columbia is 604.

ACCOMMODATIONS. A central reservation office at Panorama handles all the lodging, which is conveniently located at the base of the resort. Contact *Central Reservations,* Panorama Resort, Box 7000, Invermere BC V0A 1K0; 342–6941.

All rates can be considered *Moderate,* with prices for rooms for 1–4 persons ranging from $42 to $72 in value season and $70–$99 for high skiing season. Studios cost $98–$139, depending on season, and lofts with 2 bedrooms accommodating 5–7 persons, $202–$243 in ski season.

Horsethief Lodge. This facility consists of 195 comfortable 1-, 2-, and 3-bedroom condominiums with fireplaces, full kitchens, and balconies or patios. Some units have lofts. Underground parking, outdoor hot tubs, and saunas are all featured.

Toby Creek Lodge. There are 60 studio, 1-, and 2-bedroom condominiums, all of them spacious and some with lofts. Each offers a fireplace and full kitchen, balcony, or patio. In addition, Toby Creek has 24 hotel rooms with underground parking. The hot tubs are outdoor as well as indoor with sauna.

Pine Inn. This newly expanded establishment offers 102 varied rooms. Some have lofts and balconies. There are also executive suites, convention facilities, exercise room, and hot tub.

Vacation Villa Condominiums. This is a variety of luxurious "interval ownership" condos complete with quality furnishings and full kitchens. Available for purchase; phone Vacation Villa office, 343–6941, ext. 363.

RESTAURANTS. At the base of the mountain, you'll find two fine restaurants and five lounges and bars which also serve food. All can be contacted through the resort's main phone, 342–6941, and all accept major credit cards. No reservations are needed. In this area, consider an *Expensive* meal for one person to cost $10–$16; *Moderate,* $6–$10; and *Inexpensive,* less than $6.

Paradise Dining Room and Lounge. *Expensive.* In Toby Creek Lodge. Fine cuisine served by a lovely stone fireplace in the lounge or by candlelight in the dining room.

Starbird Dining Room and Lounge. *Moderate.* In Pine Inn Serves three meals from a location overlooking the ski hill.

Glacier Deck. *Inexpensive.* In Pine Inn. Outdoor service includes snacks and drinks.

Glacier Pub. *Inexpensive.* In Pine Inn. Standard pub fare, but gets hopping in the evenings.

Inn at the Beginning. *Inexpensive.* In day lodge at base of the lifts. Cafeteria-style service and drinks.

Strathcona Patio. *Inexpensive.* Located above Horsethief Lodge reception area. Full-service and self-service outdoor barbecues for private use and groups.

Strathcona Pub. *Inexpensive.* English-style atmosphere, down to the ales and dart games.

If the skier ventures to Invermere, 32 km away, some delightful dining facilities can be found. In the *Expensive* range are the *Black Forest,* 342–9417, which provides authentic Bavarian atmosphere and decor, and *Strands Restaurant,* 342–6344, a charming older village home setting with superb cuisine for dinners only. On the *Moderate* side are the *Greenery,* 342–9246, for standard fare, and *Lakeside Inn,* 342–6711, which specializes in fish and chips.

HOW TO GET AROUND. Once you arrive at Panorama wheels won't be needed, for all services and ski lifts are within walking distance of accommodations. However, if you wish to travel to, say, Invermere, a **car** is necessary.

SEASONAL EVENTS. Each **February** Panorama hosts the *Women's Ski, Fitness, and Health Week* designed for women only. It includes lessons, fitness classes, manicure, pedicure, massage, and more. The *Strand Cup* takes place in mid-February as a crazy costume team race with restaurant employees from around the valley. The *Citizen Downhill* is the race of the season for recreational racers 30 years and older.

OTHER SPORTS AND ACTIVITIES. Horseback rides are available through *Hopeful Creek Stables,* situated right at the resort. A nice relaxing ride through the Purcell Mountains on a crisp winter day is a unique and enjoyable experience. The **skating** rink invites you to try another alternative to skiing. Skate at day or at night under the lights. Lively games of **broomball** are common among guests. If you've never had a professional **massage,** here's your chance to ease those well-used muscles. A registered massage therapist is always on call. Another way to relax is by visiting nearby **hot pools** only 40 minutes away at *Radium Hot Springs* with temperatures of 27–41° C; open year-round. For information on these and other activities, contact the main office, 342–6941.

CHILDREN'S ACTIVITIES. The *Kiddies Korral Child Care* service is provided for $3 per hour with snack, or $17 for the day with lunch. The services require an 18-month minimum age; however, babysitters can usually be arranged for younger ones. All skiing programs, which are set up for 3–5 year-olds, 6–9 year-olds, and 10 years and up, are priced $27 per day with lunch and snacks, or $17 for a half-day without lunch.

Teens will enjoy the *Activities Center and Arcade.* Children 8 and under ski free; juniors (9–14) ski for $12.00 per day, $9.00 for afternoons.

NIGHTLIFE. Skiers at Panorama tend to spend their evenings at the resort, for the restaurants and pubs listed above offer pleasant après-ski activities. The *Glacier Pub* is of particular interest, since it features dancing either to live music or a "DJ extraordinaire." Otherwise, skiers spend the evening relaxing by a fireplace or playing darts or shuffleboard.

POWDER KING SKI VILLAGE

P.O. Box 2405
MacKenzie BC V0J 2C0
Tel: 604–750–4414

Snow Report: 604–750–4414
Area Vertical: 2,017 ft.
Number of Trails: 14 on 145
acres
Lifts: 1 triple, 2 T-bars, 1
handletow
Snowmaking: none
Season: November 15–April 30

Powder King was named Azu Mountain prior to its recent facelift. It is situated in big-time lumber and sawmill country midway between Dawson Creek and Prince George BC. Although the alpine mountain resort is only some 15 years old, skiers have been ski touring its flanks long before lifts were installed, attracted by the abundance of powder snow.

It's a fairly remote area where once the only real action was Tumbler Ridge Mining. Nowadays, Powder King even has its own on-site accommodations at the base of its slopes with a tavern, disco, and large video screen. This is a unique resort in a unique part of the country.

The base facilities provide a casual atmosphere with a licensed cafeteria and tavern. There is a rental shop to outfit you in *Salomon Equipment.* Full equipment rental is $12 per day. The retail gift shop offers accessories and souvenirs. Lessons are available through a CSIA-certified ski school. One-hour group lessons cost $10 per person.

The view is of the majestic Northern Rocky Mountain Range and their snowcapped peaks. And yes, there's plenty of snow. With an average annual snowfall of 495 inches, the Powder King name is indeed suitable. While experts frolic in the powder, groomed runs please both intermediate and novice skiers. The longest run is 8,690 feet stretching out the mountain's respectable 2100-foot vertical. Not bad for a $19 lift ticket. Cost for children is $10; free for those 7 years and younger.

Seven of the 15 runs are easy cruising intermediate. The expert runs keep even the best working at each turn. Many of the runs are named after Beatles' songs—novice runs such as "Strawberry Fields," "Penny Lane," and "Ob-La-Di, Ob-La-Da." Try the intermediate "Let It Be" or "No. 9".

Powder King combines great scenery and plenty of powder in northern British Columbia.

Practical Information for Powder King

HOW TO GET THERE. Powder King is located 421 km north of Prince George BC along John Hart River Highway (Hwy. 97). **By air.** *Canadian Pacific Air,* 266–1241, and *Pacific Western Airlines,* 684–6161, fly into Prince George from Vancouver, where connections are made from Canadian and American major airlines. A car can be rented at Prince George Airport from *Tilden,* 963–7474.

By bus. *Greyhound Bus Lines* has transportation to and from Powder King at Azu Village, near the base of the slopes. For information and schedules from Prince George, call 564–5454.

By car. From Vancouver, take Hwy. 1 east and north, connecting with Hwy. 97 near Ashcroft into Prince George, which is 787 km from Vancouver. Continue northward on Hwy. 97 for 203 km to Dawson Creek and 203 km eastward to Powder King.

TELEPHONES. The area code for all of British Columbia is 604.

 **ACCOMMODATIONS.** Since Powder King is so remote, most visitors prefer to stay at the self-contained ski resort. Powder King recently built a 50-room modular complex at the base of the lift to complement its **Village Beds Resort Hotel.** For reservations at either, contact Powder King Resort, Box 2405, MacKenzie BC; 750–4414. Rates are considered *inexpensive,* starting at $28 per person, double occupancy, on weekdays and $34 on weekends. Packages for multi-day or groups are also available. Children 12 years old and under are free, if staying with parents in their room.

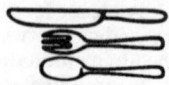 **RESTAURANTS.** Because of its seclusion, the Powder King Resort offers only one dining area. It seems sufficient, however, to suit the demand. Prices are very reasonable for full meals, as low as $5–$6 per plate. They serve good steak. The base facilities include the newly renovated **Azu Mountain Cafe** and a bar. Both services offer a lovely view and friendly staff.

 **SEASONAL EVENTS.** Powder King has an exciting lineup of activities that kick off with a *Challenge Santa Race* and *New Year's Eve Bash.* Every Sunday the *Pine Pass Ski Club* fun race is open to all abilities and ages. Every Wednesday is *Ladies Day.* **February** hosts a summer bash and boogie and a *Family Day.* The annual *Powder 8* contest is featured in February as well. Other events include triple slaloms, costume classics, Easter egg hunts, celebrity sweeps, and a suitcase race.

 **CHILDREN'S ACTIVITIES.** The resort's *Pups' Playroom* program offers daily babysitting for children 2 years old and up. Reservations are encouraged at the main office, 750–4414. For children old enough to ski, the program provides lessons and equipment as well as fun-in-the-snow. The age limit is 7 years. For older children, there are a number of green runs served by the resort's platter lift. Penny Lane is a run that is easy to get to off the base's triple chair.

RED MOUNTAIN SKI AREA

Box 939
Rossland BC V0G 1Y0
Tel: 604-362-7384

Snow Report: 604–362–5500
Area Vertical: 2,800 ft.
Number of Trails: 26 over 600
    skiable acres
Skiing Terrain: 10 percent
    novice, 40 percent intermediate, 50 percent expert
Lifts: 1 triple chair, 2
    double chairs, 1 T-bar
Snowmaking: none
Season: November 15–April 15

Red Mountain is known for its powder snow and challenging slopes. Located only 3 km from the heritage village of Rossland, "Big" Red is a low-profile world-class ski area waiting to be discovered.

The town of Rossland was settled in 1896 at one of the richest gold strikes in Canadian history. The hard-rock miners who flocked here were captivated by the region's ski terrain. Scandinavian ski champions set world records here in downhill, cross-country, and jumping half a century before modern ski lifts were installed.

The Rossland Ski Club, which developed skiing in the area, was founded in 1898 by a fellow named Olaus Jildness. As a means of keeping the miners around a little longer, skiing became a major recreational activity. A blend of Portuguese, Polish, Italian, and other nationalities matured into a down-to-earth community with some of the best "unknown" skiing in North America.

Alpine skiing began at Red Mountain with the installation of a single chair lift in 1947; since then, development has expanded skiing terrain to two mountains. Granite is the largest and most recently developed and Red Mountain is as steep as they come. Lodging is located at the mountain and few minutes away in Rossland.

Red is an out-of-the-way paradise. It's in south-central British Columbia's Monashee Mountains, a short distance from the U.S. border.

As home of a very successful racing development program and Olympic gold medalist Nancy Green, Red Mountain is a pleasant destination for any level of skier.

Skiing Red Mountain means lots of snow, bargain prices, and small crowds. The two mountains called Red and Granite offer three distinct slopes with 26 runs and plenty of tree skiing. It's a skier's mountain.

Red Mountain is serviced by a high-capacity double chair and a T-bar. Its 1,420 vertical feet offers some of the most challenging skiing as well as wide-open intermediate and novice trails. A majority of these trails are lit for night skiing.

The adjacent Granite Mountain is a big-shouldered, two-faced hulk with 2,800 vertical feet of varied skiing. The longest run is 7 km, winding around the numerous meadows, glades, and powder fields. The Paradise side of this mountain is 1,200 vertical feet with a triple chair servicing mostly intermediate skiing in tree-lined, protected, rolling alpine meadows.

Cruising runs like Southern Comfort and Southern Belle are a treat on the Paradise side. Buffalo Ridge and Papoose Bowl take skiers down the other side of Granite into a void of bowls and bumps or in the direction of cruising runs like Mountain Chief. Ninety percent of Red Mountain Ski Area is intermediate or expert, which is a perfect match for the deep snow.

The Red Mountain Ski Shop located at the area provides equipment rentals or purchases. There's a cafeteria and a licensed lounge as well at the base.

Cross-country skiing is available by taking Granite lift to skiable terrain. Over 20 km of well-maintained trails are located nearby.

Practical Information for Red Mountain

HOW TO GET THERE. Red Mountain is on Hwy. 38 in south-central British Columbia, about 630 km east of Vancouver and 210 km north of Spokane WA.

By air. Daily flights from Vancouver on *Pacific Western Airlines,* 684–6161, or from Calgary on *Time Air,* 800–661–1484 in British Columbia, to Castlegar 30 minutes away. The airport has a shuttle to Trail, where you can taxi the last 8 km. Some hotels have pick-up service. Calgary and Vancouver are served by major airlines from most Canadian and U.S. cities. Flying into Spokane is a good alternative for U.S. visitors.

By bus. *Empire Lines,* 509–624–4116, provides daily service from Spokane at 8 A.M. and 5:20 P.M. *Coach Charters,* 509–624–4116, also has service. *Greyhound,* 604–368–5733, buses come through Rossland daily from Calgary or Vancouver regions.

By car. Driving time along Hwy. 38 is 8 hours from Calgary or Vancouver. **Car rentals** are available at Castlegar Airport from *Budget;* 604–363–5733).

TELEPHONES. The area code for all of British Columbia is 604. For Spokane it is 509.

ACCOMMODATIONS. A good variety of lodgings is available, including moderately priced motels (many with kitchen facilities), cabins, chalets, European-style inns, and modern full-service hotels. For central reservations call 362–7700 or write Box 939, Rossland BC, V0G 1Y0. Based on double occupancy, *Expensive* accommodations are $40–$60; *Moderate,* $30–$40; and *Inexpensive,* below $30.

ON-MOUNTAIN

Ram's Head Inn. *Expensive.* Box 636; 362–9577. Has telephones, sauna, and licensed facilities.

Red Mountain Resort Motel. *Moderate.* Box 816; 362–9000. Has cabins and approximately 30 rooms.

Red Shutter Inn. *Moderate.* Red Mountain Rd.; 362–5131. This is a quaint 8-room inn within walking distance of the mountain.

ROSSLAND

Uplander Hotel. *Moderate.* 1919 Columbia Ave.; 362–7375. Telephones, television, kitchenettes, sauna/whirlpool, and licensed facilities.

Rossland Motel. *Inexpensive.* Cascade St.; 362–7218. Has 20 comfortable rooms with telephones.

Scotsman Motel. *Inexpensive.* Box 1527; 263–7364. Has 35 rooms with telephone. Kitchenettes available.

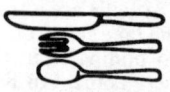

RESTAURANTS. Skiers at Red Mountain generally take their meals in the hotel or inn at which they are staying. The resort, however, sees to it that skiers don't go hungry. In the base lodge, 362–7384, the **Rafter Lounge and Cafeteria** provides breakfasts and lunches. In town, **moderate** ($8–$13) homemade dinners are served at the **Red Mountain Resort Hotel** as well as in the **Louis Blue Room** and the **Powder Keg** Pub, both in the Uplander Hotel. (See *Accommodations* for phone numbers.) Nearby on Columbia Ave., the **Sunshine Cafe,** 362–7630, serves *inexpensive* ($8 and under) breakfasts, lunches, and dinners.

HOW TO GET AROUND. A **car** is a necessity at this small resort. The only **shuttle** transportation available is to and from the mountain from the Uplander Hotel on special request; 362–7375. For **taxi** service, contact *Rossland Taxi,* 362–7600.

OTHER SPORTS AND ACTIVITIES. Besides **night skiing,** 362–7384, from 4 to 10 P.M. daily and **cross-country** skiing, 362–9611, there's **ice skating** at the *Rossland Civic Arena,* 362–5344. Other events include regularly scheduled amateur races, which take place periodically here, and the regularly held Adult Racing League's competitions each Saturday evening.

CHILDREN'S ACTIVITIES. Daycare for children 3–8 years old is located at the base of the mountain. Hours are 10 A.M. to 3:30 P.M. Cost is $2.50 per child for the first hour and $2 for each additional hour. Contact ski school office, 362–7384.

NIGHTLIFE. Après-ski activities traditionally begin in the base lodge at the *Rafter Lounge and Cafeteria.* In town, it's generally a laid-back atmosphere at lounges or bars in the hotels. The *Powder Keg Pub,* however, in the Uplander Hotel, does swing a bit with dance music.

SILVER STAR MOUNTAIN

P.O. Box 7000
Vernon BC V1T 8X5
Tel: 604–542–0224

*Snow Report: 604–542–1745,
604–860–7827
Area Vertical: 1,600 ft.
Number of Trails: 35 on 300
acres
Skiing Terrain: 30 percent
novice, 55 percent intermediate,
15 percent expert
Lifts: 3 doubles, 3 T-Bars,
1 Poma
Snowmaking: None
Season: mid-November–late
April*

This Okanagan Mountain resort prides itself on its excellent snow conditions and its recent dramatic improvements in base facilities. When it comes to convenience and powder, Silver Star has got it all.

Named for a local turn-of-the-century silver mine, Silver Star presents old-fashioned quality and affordability.

The new on-mountain development is built in the tradition of the 1890s gaslight theme, including three hotels, a saloon, chapel, ski shop, and other facilities. It has come a long way since its first primitive poma back in 1959, which, although slow moving, opened up the silky smooth powder.

It's typical Okanagan feather-light snow that draws the still surprisingly small crowds. Short lift lines are another benefit.

Situated high on a southern plateau above the city of Vernon, 22 km down in the valley, the snow blankets Silver Star early in November and stays late, making a long, reliable season. The climate is ideal with lots of sunshine and an average winter temperature of -5° C. The Silver Star management even offers a money-back guarantee on their snow!

Silver Star, although predominately an intermediate mountain, offers challenges to even experts. The 7 lifts are accessible from each hotel with just a "click" into the skis. Silver Star is a self-contained village nestled in a snowbelt.

The resort's seven lifts make the 1,600-foot vertical drop feel bigger. You can choose from 35 well-groomed trails on moderately rolling slopes up to 2 miles in length. Steep verticals such as the Chute and Suicide are ideal for high performance skiing. The intermediate runs are great cruisers.

Silver Star receives lots of snow, making conditions soft-paced or powder most of the time. Anybody can make "hero turns" at this resort. The average annual snowfall is 508 cm (200 inches).

The ski school is good and specializes in ski week lessons at $60 for 10 hours of instruction, $50 for those 12 and under. Rental equipment is available. The special instruction ski weeks offer something extra in après-ski activities such as wine and cheese reception, equipment workshops, movies, sleigh rides, and more.

Night skiing is a real bonus at Silver Star. If you haven't had enough during the day, go make some turns under the lights. Skiing at night feels different and is enjoyable.

The 500-seat Town Hall serves as the day lodge (evenings too) with full cafeteria services, snack bar, and playroom. The après-ski life is plentiful in the saloon, pubs, or the Wine Cellar.

All in all, Silver Star is a mix of good alpine skiing complemented by super facilities, all located in their unique village. The overall experience is as good as the snow.

Silver Star also features very well developed nordic trails. Deep snow on well-groomed tracks make for great gliding November through April. A wide variety of trails are suited for all levels of nordic skiers ranging from short loops to all-day treks into the nearby Provincial Park. Night cross-country skiing is also available on a 4-km loop.

Practical Information for Silver Star

HOW TO GET THERE. Located in the mild Okanagen Valley region of British Columbia, Silver Star is relatively easy to reach It's a scenic 22 km east of Vernon. **By air.** *Pacific Western Airlines* (763–6620) provides daily flights to Kelowna Airport from Calgary and Vancouver, which are both served by airlines from most major North American cities. *Time Air,* 800–552–8007, flies in via Lethbridge AL and Vancouver. Ground transportation to the mountain via airport bus is available at the airport.

By bus. *Greyhound Bus Lines,* 860–3835, provides transportation from both Vancouver and Calgary. The 6-hour ride from Vancouver costs $28.75, and the 9-hour ride from Calgary costs $47.80. Greyhound also provides service from Prince George BC and Edmonton AL.

By car. Silver Star is approached from both Calgary and Vancouver via Hwy. 1, from which Hwy. 97 leads into Vernon. From Seattle, US 5 leads directly into Vancouver, but, weather permitting, many miles can be lopped off the trip by turning off US 5 onto Rte. 542 at Bellingham, WA, then onto Rte. 9 north connecting with Hwy. 1 at Abbotsford BC. **Car rentals** are available at the Kelowna/Vernon Airport from *Budget,* 860–2464, in the U.S. 800–527–0700, or in Canada, 800–268–8900; *Hertz,* 860–7808, in the U.S. 800–654–3131, or in Canada 800–268–1311; *Tilden,* 860–2464.

TELEPHONES. The area code for all of British Columbia is 604.

ACCOMMODATIONS. With the resort offering 6 choices, most skiers stay at lodgings at the base. To make reservations, contact the *Silver Star Mountain Resorts,* P.O. Box 7000, Vernon BC, V1T 8X5; phone 542–0224 or 800–663–4431 in western Canada; Ski Can at 800–268–8880 in eastern Canada; Ski Pak at 800–562–2262 in Washington. Lodging rates are based on double occupancy. *Expensive:* $80 and up; *Moderate:* $45–$80; *Inexpensive: $20–$45.*

SILVER STAR

Putnam Station. *Moderate to Expensive.* 542–0224. Offers ski-week packages of 5 days and 5 nights as well as ski-weekend packages of 2 days. All the amenities of a resort hotel.

Kickwillie Inn. *Moderate.* 542–4548. Has a great view of the mountains, with 7 suites featuring full-size kitchens. Private entries, outside lockers, and some lofts for additional sleeping space. Permits sleeping bags for more economical stay.

Silverlode Inn. *Moderate;* 549–5105. Introduces a new flavor to the resort with 20 traditional European-style rooms, dining room, and lounge. The inn's home country Swiss cuisine is a delight. Package rates also available.

Vance Creek Hotel. *Moderate;* 542–2459. Located in the heart of the village, it offers 22 inn-style rooms and 8 fully contained suites; complete dining and lounge facilities, plus the Okanagan Valley Cellars with an array of local cheeses. Package rates also available.

Prospector Hotel. *Inexpensive to Moderate;* 542–4838. In center of the village, it features budget prices for 50 rooms with twin beds and shared washroom facilities.

The Bunkhouse Inn. *Inexpensive;* 542–5880. An alternative to conventional lodging, offers low-cost bed and breakfast accommodations.

VERNON

Village Green Inn. *Moderate to Expensive.* 4801 27th St.; 542–3321. Has 140 well-appointed rooms and suites; indoor swimming pool, Jacuzzi, sauna, and game rooms.

Sandman Motor Inn. *Moderate.* 4201 Third St.; 545–4325. Features color TV, sauna, whirlpool, and swimming pool.

Vernon Lodge Hotel. *Moderate.* 3914 Third St.; 545–3385. Neat place with color TV, sauna, whirlpool, swimming pool.

 **RESTAURANTS.** A visitor to this resort would be hard-pressed to spend more than $16 for a full-course dinner, exclusive of beverage and tips. *Expensive:* $9–$16; *Moderate: $5–$9; Inexpensive:* less than $5. All of the dining facilities in the compact Silver Star Mountain Village serve moderately priced meals, including the dining rooms at Prospector Hotel, Putnam Station, Silverlode Inn, and Vance Creek Hotel. Prospector Hotel features Mexican specialties, and Silverlode Inn has Swiss-style cuisine. All serve breakfast, lunch, and dinner, and all accept major credit cards. Phone 542–0224 for all. The lodgings also feature inexpensive cafeteria-style meals as well as coffee shops.

Two *Expensive* restaurants are located in lodges in Vernon: **Hy's Restaurant** at the Village Green Inn, 4801 27th St. (542–5321), and the dining room at **Vernon Lodge,** 3914 Third St. (545–3385). Both serve lunch and dinner; reservations recommended for dinner.

HOW TO GET AROUND. Everything is within walking—or skiing—distance in this tiny mountain village, but to travel to Vernon or other nearby towns, it is necessary to have a car.

 SEASONAL EVENTS. Recreational downhill racing is popular in western Canada and this is where it all started with the *Over-The-Hill Downhill* every second weekend in **February.** Forty teams or so each with 4 racers including one female and one person over 35 compete for the best combined time. The competition became secondary to the excitement of the event itself.

During the second weekend in **April,** the *Funner Daze* event takes place. It's a costume fun day with barbecue, race events, prizes, and decoration themes at each store, hotel, and restaurant.

 **CHILDREN'S ACTIVITIES.** A program called *Kids Country* coordinates all youngsters' activities at the resort's main offices; call 542–0334. Babysitting services are available through reservations. For tots there's a playroom complete with expert child-care. The *Stardusters* program combines ski instruction and playroom activities for children 3–8 years old. The ski slopes are wide and suitable for children. Special après-ski activities for kids include games, movies, and poolside fun.

 **NIGHTLIFE.** With a seating of 200, the *Vance Creek Saloon* in the mountain village provides live entertainment guaranteed to fill the dance floor. For a quieter, more intimate atmosphere, the *Okanagan Wine Cellar,* also in the village, offers rustic warmth by the fireplace. Each Mountain Village hotel features charming lounges with relaxing atmospheres. Even the *Bunkhouse* has its own 60-seat pub lounge. All are within walking (or skiing) distance of each other; 542–0224.

TOD MOUNTAIN SKI AREA

P.O. Box 869
Kamloops BC V2C 5M8

Snow Report: 604–578–7151
Area Vertical: 3,100 ft.

Tel: 604–578–7222, Ski Kamloops
     604–374–3377

*Number of Trails: 33 over 330
     acres*
*Skiing Terrain: 25 percent
     novice, 35 percent intermedi-
     ate, 40 percent expert*
*Lifts: 1 triple chair, 2
     double chairs, 2 platter lifts,
     and 1 handle-tow*
Snowmaking: none
*Season: Beginning of December–
     mid-April*

Practical Information for Tod Mountain

 **ACCOMMODATIONS.** Tod Mountain is a skier's para-
dise for the budget-minded. The resort recently made
available European-style bed and breakfast accommodations at the mountain. For reservations or information,
contact the Tod Mountain Ski Area. These facilities are *inexpensive,* or about
$15 per person per night.

For those preferring to travel the 53 km, the town of Kamloops has several
popular hotels and motels normally used by skiers. Many offer "Ski Kamloops"
packages that include room and amenities such as whirlpools and saunas. All
the following are in the *Inexpensive* to *Moderate* range, $22–$50 per person,
double occupancy.

The Dome Motor Inn. 555 W. Columbia St.; 374–0358. With 89 rooms, most
overlook city of Kamloops. This is a comfortable choice with satellite TV,
sauna, whirlpool, and auto winter plug-ins.

Hospitality Inn. 500 W. Columbia St.; 374–4164. Features a nice view,
satellite TV, and a restaurant.

Panorama Inn. 610 W. Columbia St.; 374–1515. Has 90 units with nice view
at modest prices. Features sauna and whirlpool.

The Place Inn. 1875 Hwy. 5; 374–5911. Has an indoor pool, Jacuzzi, sauna,
pub, and dining room.

The Plaza Motor Hotel. 405 Victoria St.; 372–7121. Features large rooms,
TV, telephone, and private parking.

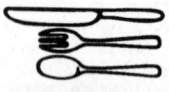 **RESTAURANTS.** There's a nice little variety of restau-
rants in Kamloops, most of them located in the afore-
mentioned inns and motor hotels. Prices are in the
Moderate range, $10–$20, which is the price of a meal
for one person, excluding drinks, tax, and tip. Try the glass-domed dining room
of the Dome Motor Inn for some native Kamloops trout or British Columbia
salmon. Also on the menu: lobster tails, steak, veal and poultry dishes.

Other restaurants in the town are:

Champs Elysee. 9–177 Tranquille, Riverside Plaza; 376–3311 or 3431. Enjoy
French cuisine and seafood with a riverfront view.

Chapter's Viewpoint. 610 W. Columbia St.; 374–3224. Some Mexican dishes
and a great salad bar accompany a Canadian menu.

Clock Tower. 1315 Summit, Tudor Village Mall; 372–2166. Mostly European menu, including sauerbraten and wiener schnitzel.

Town Crier. 265 Victoria St.; 374–1775. English pub-style setting, with roast
beef and Yorkshire pudding a favorite choice.

 **HOW TO GET AROUND.** Tod Mountain **shuttle bus**
departs from most Kamloops shopping malls and major
hotels (Dome and Plaza) daily up to Tod Mountain for
$8 per person. Contact the ski area, 578–7222, or your
hotel for specific information. For taxi transportation, phone *Yellow Cab,* 374–
3333, or *Kami Cabi,* 374–5151.

 **SEASONAL EVENTS.** Late **January** starts up the racing series with *Yukon Jack* and *Uniglobe Cable 10* for a giant slalom and triple slalom. The famed *Penguin Challenge* is a fun-filled weekend in **February.** It's a top-to-bottom race centered around the annual *Tod Celebration.* In **March,** the *Royal Canadian Mounted Police* trials for *World Police Skiing Championships* and the *Interior Keg Cup* take place.

 OTHER SPORTS AND ACTIVITIES. The base lodge's *Ski School,* 578–7222, offers certified instructions at $12 for groups and $20 for private lessons. Equipment rentals cost $13 per day and $55 per week.

For **nordic skiing** and **ice-fishing,** contact *Lac Le Jeune Ski and Sports Ranch* at 374–2604. Public **skating** takes place at the *Memorial Arena* (374–4824). For **racquetball** reservations, phone *The Court Yard* at 554–4291. There are movie theaters in town and saunas or whirlpools can be found at most of the hotels.

DAY-CARE FACILITIES. Babysitting service is available for $5 per day. Contact main lodge, 578–7222. Ski lessons are also offered, but not specifically for kids.

 **NIGHTLIFE.** Après-ski happens at the *Piano Bar Lounge* and nonstop dancing is at *Rothschild's Night Club* both at the Dome Motor Inn on Columbia St. Or try the *Dukes Cabaret* featuring live country-rock bands; the *Victoria Street Lounge* for a quiet atmosphere; and the *Plaza Pub* with satellite TV on big screen, all located at the Plaza Motor Hotel.

WHISTLER SKI MOUNTAIN

Box 67
Whistler BC V0N 1B0
Tel: 604–932–3434

Snow Report: 604–687–6761
Area Vertical: 4,280 ft.
Number of Trails: 60+ on 800+
    acres
Skiing Terrain: 28 percent
    novice, 50 percent intermediate, 22 percent expert
Lifts: 1 gondola, 3 triple
    chairs, 7 double chairs, 2
    T-bars, 1 poma, and 2 others
Snowmaking: none
Season: November–May

BLACKCOMB SKI AREA

Box 98
Whistler BC V0N 1B0
Tel: 604–932–3141

Snow Report: 604–932–4211
Area Vertical: 5,280 ft.
Number of Trails: 47 on 1,100
    acres
Skiing Terrain: 20 percent
    novice, 55 percent intermediate, 25 percent expert
Lifts: 5 triple chairs, 1
    double chair, 1 T-bar
Snowmaking: none
Season: November–May

Just 120 km northeast of Vancouver is the town of Whistler; a four-season international resort. Located at the base of Whistler and Blackcomb mountains, Whistler Village is a unique European-style center featuring luxurious condominiums, gourmet restaurants, many shops, and an exciting nightlife. The lifts sit side-by-side reaching out of the village and joining the two giant ski slopes and their 86 marked and groomed runs. Until recently, Whistler Mountain boasted the highest vertical drop in North America at 4,280 feet. Now Blackcomb, with the addition of its High Alpine T-bar, tripled its *own* ski terrain and raised its vertical to an incredible 5,280 feet. Small wonder that they call it the "mile-high mountain."

Whistler-Blackcomb is a complete resort only 2 hours from Vancouver International Airport. It's an exciting blend of convenience and snowy adventure. Its scientifically designed runs enhance the skiing experience even more.

The Whistler-Blackcomb ski center has a reputation for snow—lots of it. An incredible 1,140 cm (450 in.) falls annually. The east of edging skis into this soft, thick pack makes even the novice look good.

The village is a first class resort with emphasis on quality. It has been called a "flowing" village because of its pedestrian orientation, light and shadowing, and view corridors. The architectural style maintains harmony with its natural environment, including the two flanking ski areas.

Whistler Ski Mountain was first opened in 1965 when Garibaldi Lifts Ltd. spent $1 million on 4 lifts and 8 runs. It quickly gained fame as the highest vertical mountain in North America.

A $6-million expansion in 1978 added three new lifts serving the north side and connecting it to the proposed new Whistler Village.

The 1985–86 fare-lift costing $750,000 improved the ski center even more. Whistler has become more than just a "skier's mountain." It's now a modern, internationally rated ski area with lots of terrain for any level of skier.

Blackcomb is a new resort. Completed in the winter of 1980, this $16-million project enhanced the Whistler ski destination by more than doubling the skiable terrain in the area. Built directly adjacent to Whistler Mountain, Blackcomb's skiing offers ideal rolling trails for some very exciting cruising enjoyed by any level of skier.

Owned jointly by the Federal Business Development Bank and Aspen Ski Corporation, Blackcomb is now known as the "Mile High Mountain" with the opening of the new High Alpine T-bar. This has opened up high alpine terrain much like the skiing offered in Europe.

Blackcomb has some of the continent's most technically modern facilities. Three main lodges—one at the base, one slopeside, and one near the top service customers effectively.

Whistler is still called "Skier's Mountain" or "Big Old Softie." It's been a favorite of diehard skiers for many years.

The top opens up into a wide choice of open bowls and exciting trails. Many keen skiers traverse across the upper snowfields in search of fresher powder routes. Mogul fields like "Chunky's Choice" seem to go on forever and challenge any steel-legged expert. Nicely groomed intermediate runs such as "Porcupine" and "Franz's Run" are old-time favorites for many loyalists. This giant mountain also has novice runs like "Fantastic" and "Foxy Hollow."

In addition to the Whistler Village services, you'll find eating facilities in the Round House at the top and at the gondola base. Choose from Mexican food, custom sandwiches, and quality cafeteria food.

Blackcomb Mountain represents super-long fall-line runs with an abundance of snow. Beginning at the top, the vast bowls above tree line served by the new High Alpine T-bar provide skiers with steep chutes or wide-open intermediate terrain. This newly ski accessible terrain is named "Seventh Heaven" and adds 22 runs.

These trails feed down into the other well designed slopes like Jersey Cream and Cougar's Milk. Most of the upper mountain below the bowls is well-groomed intermediate terrain with popular trails like

"Springboard" and "Cruiser." Some of the expert runs like "Cat Skinner" and "Gear Jammer" test even the best of skiing skills. Novice runs on the lower double chair are easy to get to.

The Mountain Snow Hosts offer directions, general information, and free guided tours. They are found at the Skier Service Centers in the Carleton (lower) and Rendezvous lodges and the Summit restaurant. On-mountain picnics are also available for small groups served up by the Snow Hosts.

Full retail, rental, and ski repair services are available in the Carleton and Rendezvous lodges. Good cafeteria food is offered in the Rendezvous and the Summit Restaurant.

Although the quality of grooming makes the skiing that much easier, the Blackcomb Ski School can help you ski even better. Group and private lessons are available daily.

Practical Information for Whistler–Blackcomb

 **HOW TO GET THERE. Driving** into Whistler–Blackcomb is an adventure in itself. Hwy. 99 north from Vancouver, called the "Sea-to-Sky Highway," takes you on a dazzling 120-km ride along fjord-like Howe Sound along the west coast of British Columbia. It's breathtaking scenery on a clear day. The drive from Vancouver takes about 1½ hours. From Seattle, it's a 4½ drive along I-5, which leads into Hwy. 99 at Vancouver.

By air. Fly to Vancouver International Airport via most major airlines including *Air Canada,* 688–5515; *CP Air,* 266–1241; *United,* 683–7111; *Wardair,* 669–3355; *Lufthansa,* and *P.W.A.,* 684–6161. Connections with most other major airlines is through Seattle, a half-hour flight away.

Car rentals are available at Vancouver airport. Phone *Avis,* 604–273–4577; *Budget,* 604–278–3994; *Hertz,* 604–278–3051; or *Tilden;* 604–273–3121.

By Bus. *Maverick Coach Lines,* 604–255–1171, runs daily service from the main depot on Dunsmuir St. in Vancouver with transfers available from *Greyhound Bus Lines* servicing most Canadian cities. There are 3 departures daily to Whistler. *Perimeter Transportation,* 604–273–0071, offers service directly from the airport to Whistler.

By train. *British Columbia Rail* has a weekend ski train from North Vancouver. Phone 984–5213 for rates and schedule information.

TELEPHONES. The area code for all of British Columbia is 604.

 **ACCOMMODATIONS.** Whistler-Blackcomb has over 1,100 rooms ranging from luxury condos to hotels and pensions. There are amenities of every kind: saunas, Jacuzzis, lounges and bars, conference center, shops, liquor store, pharmacy, and even a bank. Price ranges are: *Expensive,* $110 and up per night; *Moderate,* $75–$110; *Inexpensive,* $50–$75, based on double occupancy. For central reservations phone 932–4222, or write *Whistler Resort Association,* Box 1400, Whistler BC, VON 1BO. All hotels are located in the village or very close by in the valley.

Expensive

Blackcomb Lodge. 932–4155. Has 72 studios, some with lofts; saunas, Jacuzzi, fireplaces.

Delta Mountain Inn. 800–268–1133. A large 161-unit hotel. Sauna, Jacuzzi, fireplaces, and kitchenettes.

Mountainside Lodge. 932–4511. Has 89 studio rooms, sauna, Jacuzzi, fireplaces, and kitchenettes.

Moderate

Carleton Lodge. 932–4183. Has 31 units, 1–2 bedrooms with lofts, Jacuzzi, fireplaces, and kitchenettes.

Crystal Lodge. 932–4700. Has 46 units, hotel rooms to large studios, sauna, Jacuzzi, and fireplaces.

The Fireplace Inn. 932–3200. Has 45 hotel rooms, saunas, fireplaces, and kitchenettes.

Highland Lodge. 932–5525. Has 55 hotel and studio units with sauna, Jacuzzi and kitchens.

Nancy Green's Lodge. 932–2221. Has 90 new units with Jacuzzi.

Tantalus Lodge. 932–4146. Has 76 units as 1 bedroom studios or 4 person 2 bedroom studios with sauna, Jacuzzi, fireplaces and kitchenettes.

Whistler Creek Lodge. 932–4111. Has 43 units, 2-person studios or studios with lofts. Sauna, Jacuzzi, fireplaces, and kitchenettes.

Whistler Village Inn. 932–4004. Has 88 hotel and studio units with saunas, Jacuzzi, fireplaces, and kitchenettes.

Inexpensive

Chalet Luise Pension. 932–4187. A small cozy place with only 4 hotel units, sauna, and fireplace.

Fitzsimmons Creek. 932–3338. Has 45 hotel rooms, saunas, fireplaces, and kitchenettes.

The Vale Inn. 932–3805. Has 62 hotel and studio units, fireplaces, and kitchenettes.

Whistler Resort and Club. 932–5756. Has 42 hotel and studio units, saunas, Jacuzzi, fireplaces, and kitchenettes.

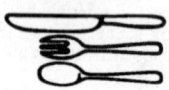 **RESTAURANTS.** Whistler restaurants cater to a variety of tastes. You'll find steaks served in wood-finished rooms, classic European cuisine in elegant surroundings, charbroiled burgers and pizza. *Expensive* entrees run from $15 to $24; *Moderate,* $8–$15; *Inexpensive,* $7 and under. All restaurants accept major credit cards unless otherwise noted, and all are in the village with no specific street address. Reserve at each unless specified.

Expensive

The Sundial. 932–5858. Dinners only. Canadian cuisine.

Sushi Village: 932–3330. Japanese dishes; lunch and dinner.

Twigs. In Delta Hotel; 932–1982. Canadian cuisine; breakfast, lunch, and dinner.

Umberto's. 932–4442. Deluxe, Italian dishes; dinners only.

Moderate

Araxis. 932–4540. Salmon specialties; breakfast, lunch, and dinner.

Chez Joel. 932–2112. French dishes for lunch and dinner.

Citta Bistro. 932–4177. Great sandwiches and original dishes; lunch and dinner.

Isabel's. 932–6611. General Canadian menu; lunch and dinner.

Nasty Jack's. 932–3531. Great snacks and quick service; lunch and dinner. Credit cards not accepted. No reservations.

Original Restaurante. 932–6408. Wholesome Italian meals; lunch and dinner.

Inexpensive

Keg and Cleaver. 932–4511. Great salad bar; caters to groups. No reservations; lunch and dinner.

Peter's Underground. 932–4811. Great sandwiches. Breakfast, lunch and dinner. No reservations.

 **HOW TO GET AROUND.** There's a **shuttle bus** between the Whistler gondola, a few miles around the mountain, and the village several times daily beginning at 7:30 A.M. For schedules, call 932–3928. For those who insist on having wheels, *Avis Car Rentals,* 932–4870, is found in the village.

SEASONAL EVENTS. Recreational race camps are held throughout the season, and a *Women Only Program* takes place in **January** and **February.** The Whistler Super *"G" Top to Bottom Team* race is an exciting annual event each January.

In **February** there's the *Whistler Powder 8* contest, followed by the *McConkey Cup* in **March.** In March Whistler has hosted *World Cup downhill* races and in **April** *World Cup speed skiing* takes place.

OTHER SPORTS AND ACTIVITIES. In Whistler Village you'll find **ice-skating,** on Whistler Lake and hot-tubs in most hotels. **Snowmobiling** (932–4086), and **sleigh rides** at *Bryson Stables* (932–5850), are also available. An indoor **swimming pool** is located in *Blackcomb Lodge* (932–4155). Go to *Whistler Body Works* for a workout or massage; 932–4001.

Cross-country ski on groomed trails in *Lost Lake Park* near the village. User fee is $2 per day; phone 932–3327 for information. Free cross-country is available on other trails close by.

For exciting **heli-skiing** nearby, phone *Whistler Heli-Skiing,* 932–4105. Prices run $195 per person for 10,000–12,000 vertical feet.

Ski **rentals** and C.S.I.A.-certified ski school lessons are available at the base. The Never-Ever ski package is a great deal and includes lift ticket, full equipment rental, and 2-hour lessons, all for $15. **Nordic skiing** is also available. Phone 932–6436.

HINTS TO THE HANDICAPPED. Whistler's program for the handicapped has been curtailed in recent seasons. The resort's racing department, however, still conducts coaching clinics for the disabled and hearing- and sight-impaired. For details contact the main office at 932–3434, and ask for the racing department.

CHILDREN'S ACTIVITIES. At **Whistler,** the *7-Eleven Wee Patrol Day-Care Center* is located at the gondola base and operates 8 A.M.–5:30 P.M. daily. Lunch vouchers are available. Full-day costs $20. The *Ski Scamps Program* for kids 2½–12 years is a supervision and ski instruction program with morning and afternoon lessons and playtime. Open 9 A.M. to 3:30 P.M. daily; costs $24 per day including lift ticket. Lunch vouchers are available. Phone 932–3434 to arrange participation in any of these programs.

At **Blackcomb,** the *Kid's Kamp* has as many as 25 instructors supervising and teaching kids to ski. *Kinder Kamp* is for those 3–6 years old and the *Black Busters* handles the 7–12 year category. Contact the main office, 932–4211.

NIGHTLIFE. There's an active nightlife in Whistler. For dancing and live bands go to the *Longhorn Pub, Club 10 Disco,* or *Stumps.* Dancing also takes place in *The Umberto Cabaret* and *Shooters.* Other favorite spots for skiers are *The Brass Rail, Tapley's Pub, Brandy's Lounge,* and *Stoney's,* where you'll find a mix of relaxing atmospheres and upbeat music. All are within walking distance in the village.

INDEX

Map pages are in **boldface**.